STATISTICAL METHODS IN MEDICAL RESEARCH

STATISTICAL METHODS IN MEDICAL RESEARCH

P. ARMITAGE

Professor of Medical Statistics,
London School of Hygiene and
Tropical Medicine,
University of London

BLACKWELL SCIENTIFIC PUBLICATIONS

OXFORD LONDON EDINBURGH

BOSTON MELBOURNE

Editorial offices:
Osney Mead, Oxford, OX2 0EL
8 John Street, London, WC1N 2ES
9 Forrest Road, Edinburgh, EH1 2QH
52 Beacon Street, Boston, Mass., USA
214 Berkeley Street, Carlton
Victoria 3053, Australia

First published 1971
Reprinted 1973, 1974, 1977, 1980

Italian edition 1975

ISBN 0 632 05430 1

Distributed in the U.S.A. and Canada
by Halsted Press, a division of
John Wiley & Sons, Inc., New York

Printed in Great Britain by
Whitstable Litho Ltd., Whitstable, Kent
and bound by
Kemp Hall Bindery, Oxford.

TO J.O.IRWIN

Mentor and Friend

CONTENTS

PREFACE

There are many short introductory books on medical statistics, providing clear and simple expositions of basic statistical techniques and describing some of the problems which beset the statistician practising his art in medical applications. Some of these are listed on page 476. I have for many years felt the need for a more ambitious book, gathering together the majority of statistical techniques which are at all frequently used in medical research, yet written primarily for the non-mathematician. Many medical research workers have expressed a similar need. There are, of course, very many books on general applied statistics, assuming various levels of mathematical knowledge. Several of these are as useful for medical research workers as for those working in other subjects. I hope, though, that the present book, which is explicitly directed towards medical applications, will have two special assets. First, the use of examples almost entirely selected from medical research projects will, I think, help the reader to understand the underlying conceptual points. Second, the choice of statistical topics reflects the extent of their usage in medical research. Several topics, such as vital statistical methods, epidemiological techniques and biological assay, would not normally be included in a general book on applied statistics, but find a natural place here.

The book is intended to be useful both for the medical research worker with very little mathematical expertise, and for the professional statistician interested in medical applications of his subject. The emphasis throughout is on the general concepts underlying statistical techniques, the purposes for which they are designed, and the form of calculations required for them. Proofs are regarded as of secondary importance and are usually omitted or (when they involve relatively simple mathematics) are relegated to small type. The reader scanning the pages of the book will observe many mathematical formulae. These are necessary to provide a succinct definition of the computations required and the relationships between various methods. They rarely involve other than very simple algebraic manipulations, and the symbolism (such as the use of the summation sign) can be mastered quite easily. Calculus is used very occasionally for explanations which would otherwise be difficult, but the reader unfamiliar with calculus will not find the continuity broken by these references. Some conceptual steps, such as those involved in sampling theory and significance tests, are perhaps more difficult than the algebra, and for this reason I have developed the arguments at a rather deliberate rate. Readers who are already familiar with these basic concepts will be able to skip much of the early part of the book and make immediate use of the later material. In my view, research workers in quantitative medicine—and this term nowadays covers a large proportion of medical research—will increasingly be called upon to use standard statistical methods for the analysis of their data. Statisticians are in too short supply to act as collaborators in more than a fraction of all statistically-oriented studies. This book may help research workers to extend the range of statistical methods which they can confidently apply without recourse to expert advice.

The statisticians engaged in medical work or interested in medical applications will, I hope, find many points of interest in this review of the subject. In particular, the book may provide a useful framework for teaching courses for students trained in medical or biological sciences. Much of the exposition and many of the examples are based on material used in statistics courses for postgraduate students at the London School of Hygiene and Tropical Medicine, which have been offered in various forms over a period of more than thirty years. The book as a whole is more extensive than would be required for a single course, but the statistics teacher would have little difficulty in making appropriate selections for particular groups of students. It may be of interest to note here the sections of the book which correspond roughly to three successive parts of the statistics course currently given at the London School of Hygiene and Tropical Medicine. Each lecture, of one hour's duration, is followed by a practical session of one and a half to two hours.

Course 1, Basic Statistics (12 lectures): 1.1 to 1.6; 2.1 to 2.7; 3.1 to 3.3, and 3.5; 4.1 to 4.4 and 4.6 to 4.8 (large-sample methods only); 5.1 to 5.3; 7.4 and 7.5.

Course 2, Statistics in Experimentation (12 lectures): 4.3 and 4.6 (t distribution); topics in Chapter 13; 5.4; 6.1, 6.4 and 6.5; 7.1 and 7.2; 8.1; topics in 8.2 and in Chapter 9.

Course 3, Survey Analysis (18 lectures): 6.2 and 6.3; topics in 9.4 and 9.5; 10.1; topics in Chapter 11, in 12.5 and 12.6, and in Chapter 14; 16.1 to 16.3.

For much of the material included in the book, both illustrative and general, I owe thanks to present and past colleagues in the Department of Medical Statistics and Epidemiology. Any attempt to define this indebtedness would be incomplete, but I must mention the foundations laid by Dr J.O.Irwin, under whose guidance I first undertook teaching and research in medical statistics. Several of the numerical examples have been used in lectures or practical classes for many years, and some are now of doubtful provenance. I have not, therefore, attempted systematically to give attributions for all quoted data, and must apologize to any authors who find their own data put to unsuspected purposes in these pages.

In preparing the book for the press I have again had much help from colleagues. In particular, Miss M.Richards typed most of the manuscript and Miss M.Chandler helped with various stages of checking and cross-referencing.

P. Armitage

CHAPTER 1
THE SCOPE OF STATISTICS

1.1 GENERAL

In one sense medical statistics are merely numerical statements about medical matters: how many people die from a certain cause each year, how many hospital beds are available in a certain area, how much money is spent on a certain medical service. Such facts are clearly of administrative importance. To plan the maternity bed service for a community we need to know how many women in that community give birth to a child in a given period, and how many of these should be cared for in hospitals or maternity homes. Numerical facts also supply the basis for a great deal of medical research; examples will be found throughout this book. It is no purpose of the book to list or even to summarize numerical information of this sort. Such facts may be found in official publications of national or international health departments, in the published reports of research investigations and in textbooks and monographs on medical subjects. The book is concerned with the general rather than the particular, with methodology rather than with factual information, with the general principles of statistical investigations rather than with the results of particular studies.

Statistics may be defined as the discipline concerned with the treatment of numerical data derived from groups of individuals. These individuals will often be people—for instance, those suffering from a certain disease or those living in a certain area. They may be animals or other organisms. They may be different administrative units, as when we measure the case-fatality rate in each of a number of hospitals. They may be merely different occasions on which a particular measurement has been made.

Why should we be interested in the numerical properties of groups of people or objects? Sometimes, for administrative reasons like those mentioned earlier, statistical facts are needed: these may be contained in official publications; they may be derivable from established systems of data collection such as cancer registries or systems for the notification of congenital malformations; they may, however, require specially designed statistical investigations.

This book is concerned particularly with the use of statistics in medical *research*, and here—in contrast to its administrative uses—the case for statistics is not free from controversy. The argument is occasionally heard that statistical information contributes little or nothing to the progress of medicine, because the physician is concerned at any one time with the treatment of a single patient, and every patient differs in important respects from every other patient. An eminent psychiatrist wrote, in a recent letter to the *Lancet*, 'One must go on repeating the fact that if, in the past thirty years, one had ever paid very much attention to statistics, especially when they were not supported by clinical bedside findings, treatment progress in psychiatry in this country would not have got very far.' Two points may be made at this stage. First, the variability of disease is an argument for statistical information, not against it. If the bedside physician finds that on one occasion a patient with migraine feels better after drinking plum juice, it does not follow, from this single observation, that plum juice is a useful therapy for migraine. The doctor needs statistical information showing, for example, whether in a group of patients improvement is reported more frequently after the administration of plum juice than after the use of some alternative treatment. Secondly, the 'bedside findings' referred to in the quotation above are likely to be essentially statistical comparisons derived from a lifetime of clinical practice. The argument, then, is whether such information should be stored in a rather informal way in the physician's mind or whether it should be collected and reported in a systematic way. Very few doctors acquire, by personal experience, factual information over the whole range of medicine, and it is partly by the collection, analysis and reporting of statistical information that a common body of knowledge is built and solidified.

The difficulty of arguing from a single instance is equally apparent in studies of the aetiology of disease. The fact that a particular person was alive and well at the age of 95, and that he smoked 50 cigarettes a day and drank heavily, would not convince one that such habits are conducive to good health and longevity. Individuals vary greatly in their susceptibility to disease. Many abstemious non-smokers die young. To study these questions one should look at the morbidity and mortality experience of groups of people with different habits; that is, one should do a statistical study.

The first chapter in this book is concerned mainly with some of the basic tools for collecting and presenting numerical data, a part of the subject usually called *descriptive statistics.*

The statistician needs to go beyond this descriptive task, in two important respects. First, he may be able to improve the quality of the information by careful planning of the data collection. Secondly, the methods of *statistical inference* provide a largely objective means of drawing conclusions from the data about the issues under research. Both these developments, of planning and inference, owe much to the work of R. A. (later Sir Ronald) Fisher (1890–1962), whose influence is apparent throughout modern statistical practice.

Almost all the techniques described in this book can be used in a wide variety of branches of medical research, and indeed frequently in the non-medical sciences also. To set the scene it may be useful to mention four quite different investigations in which statistical methods played an essential part.

(a) Smith *et al.* (1962) described a study of antibody titres after vaccination against yellow fever. The investigators had records of blood samples from a hundred or so vaccinated subjects, and wanted to know whether the level of antibody production depended on the level before vaccination; whether it depended on the presence of antibodies against certain other viruses related to yellow fever; whether the antibody level against the other viruses was also affected; and so on. The investigation of all these possible associations was clearly a substantial task. Moreover, the determination of antibody level from each blood sample required an animal experiment in which groups of animals were inoculated with mixtures of serum and varying dilutions of virus, the results of which had to be interpreted statistically.

(b) Brinkley and Haybittle (1959) reported the follow-up results for various methods of treating breast cancer, from records in the radiotherapy centre of a large hospital. A comparison of particular interest was that of simple and radical mastectomy. For women of clinical stage II (non-advanced local growth, with axillary lymph-node involvement), 72 per cent of those treated by simple mastectomy were free of symptoms two years after treatment, as against 50 per cent of those treated by radical mastectomy. Superficially this comparison favours simple mastectomy, but a number of questions were raised by the authors. Were the numbers large enough to enable the investigators to regard this as an established difference? If so, could it have been due to some selective bias in the way the two treatments were allotted to patients? If the comparison could have been biased, how should a better investigation be planned? In a later paper (1966) the same authors report the results of a controlled clinical trial, in which the difference between the results from these two treatments is much less striking.

(c) In the United States deaths from motor vehicle accidents amount to about 50,000 each year. One question that arises is the importance of mechanical failures as distinct from human errors. In some states all vehicles must be inspected regularly and it would be interesting to know whether the motor vehicle accident mortality is lower in these states than in those which do not require inspection. Buxbaum and Colton (1966) examined this question and found that there was indeed a difference. For example for white men aged 45–54 years, the annual rate was 37·4 per 100,000 in the states without inspection, and 23·4 per 100,000 in those with inspection. It might be argued, though, that this difference was due not to inspection but to some other distinction between the states; perhaps they were concentrated in different parts of the United States, or perhaps they differed markedly in social and economic characteristics. The authors proceeded to investigate various possibilities of this sort, but found that the difference could not be explained by any of the factors they examined.

(d) A final example of the use of statistical arguments is the epidemiological study of Speizer *et al.* (1968) into the recent increase in mortality from asthma. These authors examined time trends in the number of deaths attributed to asthma, in the death rate from asthma for various countries, and in the death rates for people of particular ages. Marked increases were observed in England and Wales between 1960 and 1965, particularly at ages 10–14 years. Smaller increases took place in other countries. Sometimes when trends like this are observed they are due to changes in diagnostic criteria or in ways of classifying causes of death which lead to compensatory reductions in deaths from other causes. In this instance no such reductions could be found, and it therefore appeared that the increase was real. The authors now examined morbidity data which provided no evidence of an increase in the prevalence of asthma. It seemed, therefore, that the disease was not becoming more common, yet more people were dying from it. In a search for possible causes of this increased fatality risk, the authors examined various environmental hazards and methods of treatment. The only change which seemed relevant was the increased use during this period of the pressurized inhalant containing isoprenaline. The authors did not *prove* that the inhalant was the responsible agent, but they provided a hypothesis, supported by strong circumstantial evidence, which could be put to the test in subsequent studies.

We now consider some basic methods of presenting statistical data.

1.2 DIAGRAMS

One of the principal methods of displaying statistical information is the use of diagrams. Trends and contrasts are often more readily apprehended, and perhaps retained longer in the memory, by casual observation of a well-proportioned diagram than by scrutiny of the corresponding numerical data presented in tabular form. Diagrams must, however, be simple. If too much information is presented in one diagram it becomes too difficult to unravel and the reader is unlikely even to make the effort. Furthermore, details will usually be lost when data are shown in diagrammatic form. For any critical analysis of the data, therefore, reference must be made to the relevant numerical quantities.

Statistical diagrams serve two main purposes. The first is the presentation of statistical information in articles and other reports, when it may be felt that the reader will appreciate a simple, evocative display. Official statistics of trade, finance and medical and demographic data are often illustrated by diagrams in newspaper articles and in annual reports of government departments. The powerful impact of diagrams makes them also a potential means of misrepresentation by the unscrupulous. The reader should pay little attention to a diagram unless the definition of the quantities represented, and the scales on which they are shown, are all clearly explained. In research papers it is inadvisable to present basic data solely in diagrams because of the loss of detail referred to above. The use of diagrams should here be restricted to the emphasis of important points, the detailed evidence being presented separately in tabular form.

The second main use is as a private aid to statistical analysis. The statistician will often have recourse to diagrams to gain insight into the structure of the data, and to check assumptions which might be made in an analysis. This informal use of diagrams will often reveal new aspects of the data, or suggest hypotheses which may be further investigated.

For a detailed description of statistical diagrams reference should be made to Huff (1954), who gives many examples of deliberate misrepresentation. Various types of diagrams are discussed at appropriate points in this book. It will suffice here to mention a few of the main uses to which statistical diagrams are put, illustrating these from official publications.

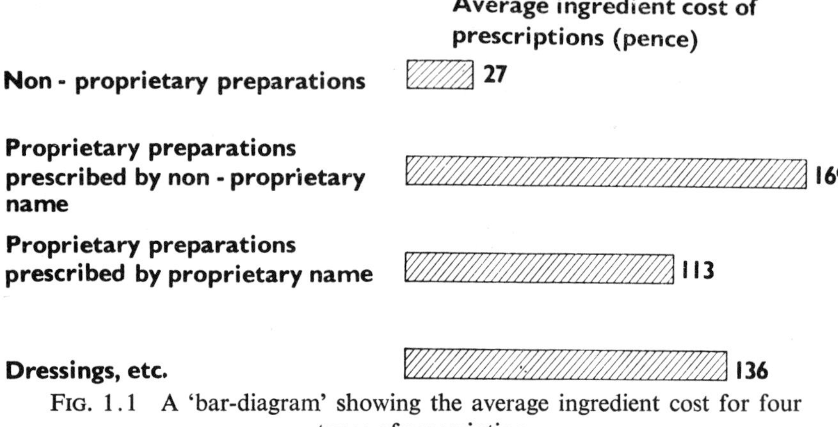

FIG. 1.1 A 'bar-diagram' showing the average ingredient cost for four types of prescription.

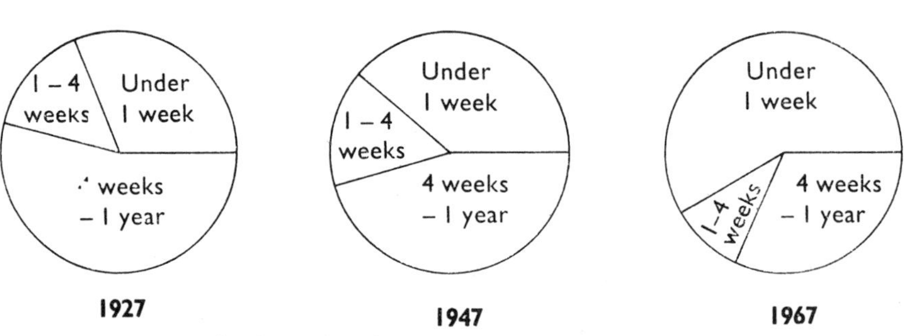

FIG. 1.2 A 'pie-chart' showing for three different years the proportions of infant deaths in England and Wales which occur in different parts of the first year of life. The amount for each category is proportional to the angle subtended at the centre of the circle and hence to the area of the sector.

(1) To compare two or more numbers. The comparison is often by bars of different lengths (Fig. 1.1), but another common method is to use rows of repeated symbols; for example, the populations of different countries may be depicted by rows of 'men', each 'man' representing 1,000,000 people. Care should be taken not to use symbols of the same shape but different sizes because of ambiguity in interpretation; for example, if exports of different countries are represented by money bags of different sizes the reader is uncertain whether the numerical quantities are represented by the linear or the areal dimensions of the bags.

(2) To express the distribution of individual objects or measurements into different categories. The frequency distribution of different values of a numerical measurement is usually depicted by a histogram, a method discussed more fully in section 1.4. (See Figs. 1.7–1.9). The distribution of individuals into non-numerical categories can be shown as a bar-diagram as in (1), the length of each bar representing the number of observations (or *frequency*) in each category. If the frequencies are expressed as percentages, totalling 100 per cent, a convenient device is the pie-chart (Fig. 1.2).

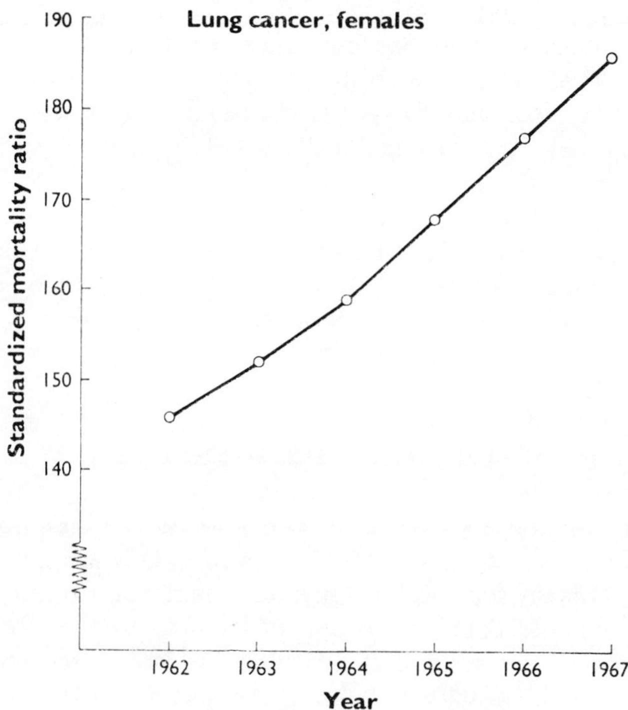

FIG. 1.3 A 'line diagram' showing the increase during six successive years of the standardized mortality ratio for lung cancer amongst females in England and Wales.

(3) To express the change in some quantity over a period of time. The natural method here is a graph in which points, representing the values of the quantity at successive times, are joined by a series of straight line segments (Fig. 1.3). If the time intervals are very short the graph will become a smooth curve. If the variation in the measurement

is over a small range centred some distance from zero it will be undesirable to start the scale (usually shown vertically) at zero for this will leave too much of the diagram completely blank. A non-zero origin should be indicated by a zig-zag mark breaking the lower end of the scale, to attract the reader's attention (Fig. 1.3). A slight trend can, of course, be made to appear much more dramatic than it really is by the judicious choice of a non-zero origin, and it is unfortunately only too easy for the unscrupulous practitioner to support a chosen interpretation of a time trend by a careful choice of origin. A sudden change of scale over part of the range of variation is even more misleading and should almost always be avoided. Special scales based on logarithmic and other transformations are discussed in Chapter 11.

(4) To express the relationship between two measurements, in a situation where they occur in pairs. The usual device is the scatter diagram (Fig. 5.1), which is described in detail in Chapter 5 and will not be discussed further here. Time-trends, discussed in (3), are of course a particular form of relationship, but called for special comment because the data often consist of one measurement at each point of time (these times being often equally spaced). In general, data on relationships are not restricted in this way and the continuous graph is not generally appropriate.

1.3 DATA PROCESSING

Much of this book is concerned with arithmetic procedures for the analysis of numerical data and with the principles which underlie these methods. In many statistical investigations, particularly those involving large quantities of data, the analysis of the data gives rise to administrative, clerical or mechanical difficulties, which collectively may be referred to as the problems of *data processing*, and it is convenient to discuss these before describing the more technical aspects of statistical practice.

We may distinguish first between the problems of preparing the data in a form suitable for computation, and the mechanical problems of getting the computations done. In laboratory experimentation the problems of data preparation are usually slight. In the first place laboratory experiments commonly give rise to relatively few observations, so the difficulties of handling vast quantities of data are not normally present. Secondly, in controlled laboratory experimentation there is usually little doubt which are the relevant measurements, and it should be part of the purpose of the plan of the experiment to ensure that these measurements in fact become available. The preparation of the data will, therefore, often consist of little more than the copying down from laboratory work-books of the relevant data, in a format convenient for the subsequent calculations. Some rather more technical problems of the editing of data, including the question of whether to omit aberrant readings, are discussed in Chapter 11.

Data preparation is, by contrast, a problem of serious proportions in many large-scale investigations on the 'human' scale. In large-scale therapeutic and prophylactic trials, in prognostic investigations, in studies in epidemiology and social medicine and in many other fields, a large number of people may be included as subjects, and very many observations may be made on each subject. Furthermore, much of the information may be difficult to obtain in unambiguous form and the precise definition of the variables may require careful thought.

In most investigations of this type it will be necessary to collect the information on specially designed record forms or questionnaires. The design of forms and questionnaires is considered in some detail by Hogben and Cross (1960). The following points may be noted briefly here.

(1) There is a temptation to attempt to collect more information than is clearly required, in case it turns out to be useful in either the present or some future study. While there is obviously a case for this course of action, it carries serious disadvantages. The collection of data costs money, and although the cost of collecting extra information from an individual who is in any case providing some information may be relatively low, it must always be considered. The most serious disadvantage, though, is that the collection of marginally useful information may detract from the value of the essential data. The interviewer faced with 50 items for each subject may take appreciably less care than if only 20 items were required. If there is a serious risk of non-cooperation of the subject, as perhaps in postal surveys using questionnaires which are self-administered, the length of a questionnaire may be a strong disincentive and the list of items must be severely pruned.

(2) Care should be taken over the wording of questions to ensure that their interpretation is unambiguous and in keeping with the purpose of the investigation. Whenever possible the various categories of response which are of interest should be enumerated on the form. This helps to prevent meaningless or ambiguous replies and saves time in the later

classification of results. For example,

Tick the statement below that best describes your working status:

1 ☐ I am a housewife and have in addition a paid job outside the home.
2 ☐ I am a housewife and have no paid job outside the home.
3 ☐ I have a job (tick here even if you are temporarily unemployed).
4 ☐ I am retired due to disability (specify cause)

....

5 ☐ I am retired for other reasons.
6 ☐ I am not working for other reasons.

Similarly, if the answer to a question is a numerical quantity which may be recorded with varying degrees of precision it may be useful to specify the units required (for example weight in pounds rather than to the nearest stone) or a number of groups into which the measurement should be placed. For example,

How many years have you lived in this town?

1 ☐ Less than 5	**4** ☐ 20–29
2 ☐ 5–9	**5** ☐ 30–39
3 ☐ 10–19	**6** ☐ 40 or more

The first step in the analysis of data recorded on this type of form or questionnaire is usually the formation of tables showing how many observations of some type (usually individual people) fall into various categories on one question, or various combinations of categories on two or more questions. For example, Table 1.1, page 12 taken from the Perinatal Mortality Survey report by Butler and Bonham (1963), shows that the proportion of mothers for whom certain informaton about blood groups is available varies considerably with the type of antenatal care received.

It would be possible to form tables of this sort by manual sorting and counting of the original records, but if there were many observations or if many tables had to be produced the labour would obviously be immense. The approach most usually adopted for some time past has been the use of punch-card machinery. A standard 80-column card is shown in Fig. 1.4.

In each column of the card there are 12 positions at which holes may be punched. The 10 lowest holes are numbered 0–9 and the two upper holes, which are used for special purposes, have various designations, one of which is X and Y. There are various ways in which information from a form or questionnaire can be represented on a card. In the simplest method the reply to each question is represented by one or

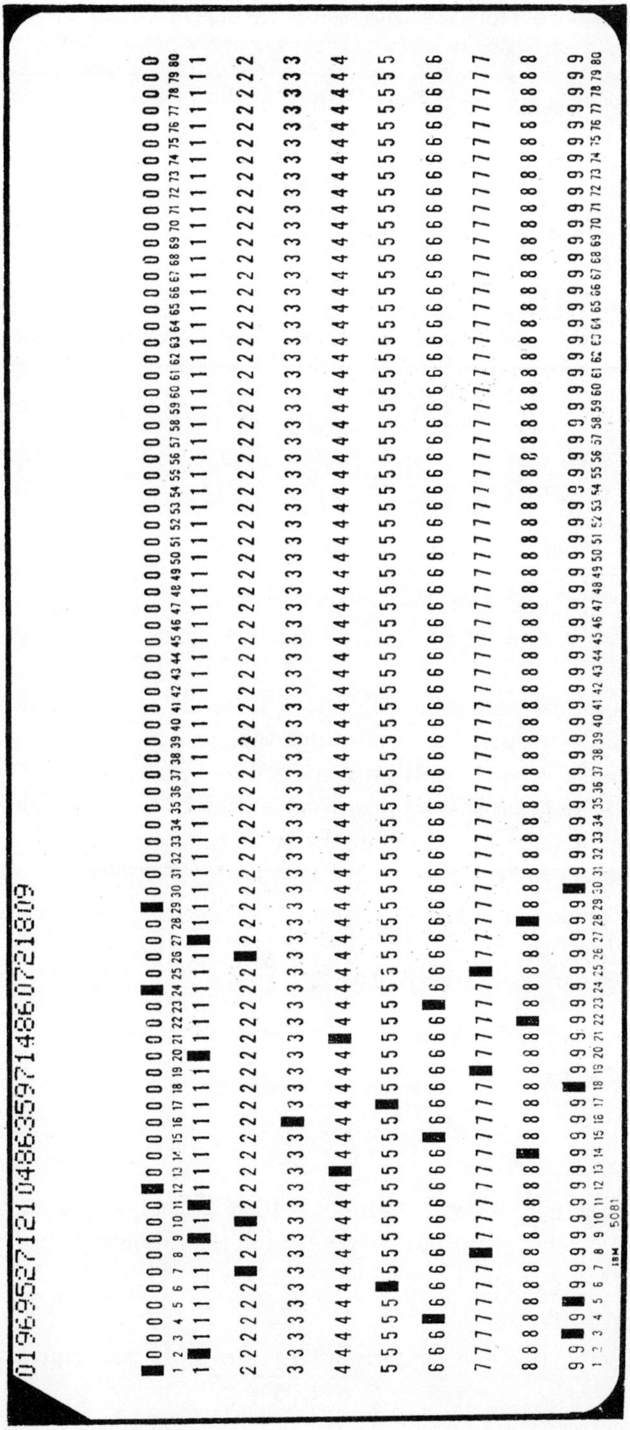

FIG. 1.4 An 80-column punch card, with the first 30 columns punched and 'interpreted' at the top of the card. The two upper positions are not marked on this card.

TABLE 1.1 Distribution of mothers according to grade of prenatal care and whether Rh-blood group was tested or known (From Butler and Bonham, 1963).

Grade of prenatal care		Tested for this pregnancy	Not known but previous record	Not tested and no previous record	No information	Total
Hospital only	Number	3133	248	25	30	3436
	Per cent	*91·2*	*7·2*	*0·7*	*0·9*	*100·0*
Hospital in part	Number	4072	708	82	44	4906
	Per cent	*83·0*	*14·4*	*1·7*	*0·9*	*100·0*
Clinic only or in part	Number	2453	675	160	13	3301
	Per cent	*74·3*	*20·4*	*4·8*	*0·4*	*99·9*
General practitioner only	Number	1150	488	227	30	1895
	Per cent	*60·7*	*25·8*	*12·0*	*1·6*	*100·1*
G.P. and midwife	Number	1638	1110	412	17	3177
	Per cent	*51·6*	*34·9*	*13·0*	*0·5*	*100·0*
Remainder	Number	160	50	25	45	280
	Per cent	*57·1*	*17·9*	*8·9*	*16·1*	*100·0*
Total	Number	12606	3279	931	179	16995
	Per cent	*74·2*	*19·3*	*5·5*	*1·0*	*100·0*

more specific columns and each column is punched in one and only one position. This means that non-numerical information must be 'coded' so that each possible reply corresponds to a number from 0 to 9 or perhaps one of the two special positions X and Y. For example, the coding for three adjacent questions might be as follows:

		7
Marital Status	Single	□ **1**
	Married	□ **2**
	Widowed/Divorced/Separated	□ **3**
		8
Race	White	□ **1**
	Negro	□ **2**
	Other	□ **3**
		9 10
Age (years)		□ □

This information would occupy columns 7–10 of a card. For a married Negro aged 37 the columns would be punched in the following positions.

Column	7	8	9	10
Position	2	2	3	7

'Overpunching', i.e. the use of more than one hole per column, is occasionally useful if it is important to get more than twelve possible replies on to one column and is used particularly for the transmission of alphabetic characters. In some systems non-significant zeros must be punched (i.e., if three digits were allowed for a variable like diastolic blood pressure a reading of 88 mm would be recorded as 088), whereas other systems allow the operator not to punch a column in which a non-significant zero would appear.

Clearly, the card-punch operator must know which code number to punch for any particular column. Two different approaches are possible. The information may be transferred from the original record to a 'transfer sheet' which will show, for each column of each card, precisely which hole is to be punched. This may conveniently be a large sheet of paper in which the horizontal rows represent the different individuals and the vertical columns represent the columns on the card. Alternatively, the coding may be shown clearly on the basic record form so that the punching may be done direct from this form and the need for an intermediate transfer sheet is removed. If sufficient care is given to the design of the record form this second method is preferable, as it removes a potential source of copying errors. An example of a well-designed form of this type is shown in Fig. 1.5. Several questions on this form, like 6(a), (b) and (c) are pre-coded; others like 6(d) need to be coded by a clerical worker before punching.

The basic operations of sorting and counting the cards according to the numbers punched in certain columns are usually performed on 'sorter' or 'counter-sorter' machines. These and other machines can be used for certain simple arithmetic operations and facilities for printing results are often available. Basically, however, conventional punch-card machinery is designed for sorting and counting. A full description of punch-cards is given in the U.N. and F.A.O. handbooks (1959, 1962).

We have now reached the second broad topic of this section, the mechanical methods of computation. Punch-card machinery is appropriate for simple counting operations on large quantities of data. For more general use in statistical analysis the basic tool is the calculating machine. The most convenient form is the electric automatic desk machine, which permits automatic multiplication and division; an additional feature which is particularly useful in statistical work is the automatic calculation and accumulation of squares of numbers. A more recent development is the electronic desk calculator.

The user of a calculating machine often finds it difficult to know how much rounding-off is permissible in the data and in the intermediate

Rev Q(W3)

THIS IS A MEDICAL RESEARCH SURVEY UNDERTAKEN BY THE UNIVERSITY OF LONDON
ALL INFORMATION WILL BE TREATED AS STRICTLY CONFIDENTIAL AND WILL NOT BE REVEALED TO YOUR DEPARTMENT

HEALTH SURVEY

Conducted by the London School of Hygiene and Guy's Hospital

Please answer **all** the questions in this health record, and bring it with you when you come to the medical examination.

If you cannot give an exact answer, give the best estimate you can. Write a tick (√) in the appropriate boxes.

FULL NAME (Block Letters) Mr. .... (6)
(Surname)
....
(Others)

ADDRESS (No. and Street)..
(Town) ....
(Postal District/County) .... (7)

1. (*a*) **In what ministry/department do you work?**
.... (8–9)
(*b*) **In what building do you work?**
.... (10-11)

2. **Do you wish a report of the examination to be sent to your general practitioner?**
We shall notify you directly if we find anything seriously wrong otherwise a record of our findings will be sent only to your general practitioner.
1. ☐ Yes 2. ☐ No 12
If "Yes", please state:—
Doctor's Name ....
Address (No. and Street)..
(Town) ....
(Postal District/County) ....

3. **What is your Civil Service Grade?** (Please state precisely within the appropriate group or give your departmental equivalent)
Administrative..
Executive..
Clerical..
Professional Scientific and Technical ....
Other.. (13–14)

4. **What is your date of birth?**
Day of Month .... Month .... Year 15–16

5. **Are you:-**
1. ☐ Married? 3. ☐ Single?
2. ☐ Widowed? 4. ☐ Other? 17

6. (*a*) **Do you smoke cigarettes now?**
1. ☐ Yes
2. ☐ No (If "No", go to question 7) 18
(*b*) **Do you inhale?**
1. ☐ Yes 2. ☐ No 19
(*c*) **What kind of cigarettes do you smoke . . .**
1. ☐ Manufactured, with filters?
2. ☐ Manufactured, without filters?
3. ☐ Hand-rolled? 20
(*d*) **What brand do you usually smoke?** (Please state precisely)
.... (21-22)
(*e*) **How many manufactured cigarettes do you usually smoke per day?** [Number per day] (23–4)
(*f*) **About how many ounces of tobacco do you use per week for rolling your own cigarettes?** [Oz. per week] (23–4)
(*g*) **What is the most that you ever smoked regularly for as long as a year?** [Cigarettes per day] 25–6
and/or
If you roll your own cigarettes [Oz. per week] 25-6
(*h*) **How old were you when you began to smoke cigarettes?** [Age] 27–8

7. (*a*) **If you do not smoke cigarettes now, did you ever smoke them?**
1. ☐ Yes 2. ☐ No, never 29
(*b*) **If you used to smoke, what is the most you ever smoked regularly for as long as a year?** [Number per day] 30–1
(*c*) **Did you inhale?**
1. ☐ Yes 2. ☐ No 32
(*d*) **How old were you when you began to smoke cigarettes?** [Age] 33–4
(*e*) **When did you stop smoking cigarettes?** (Give year) [Year] 35–6
(*f*) **What brand did you usually smoke?** (Please state precisely)
.... (37-8)
(*g*) **Why did you stop?**
.... (39)

FOR USE OF MEDICAL TEAM ONLY

1.01	1.02	1.03	1.04	1.05	1.06	1.07	1.08	1.09	1.10	1.11	1.12	1.13	1.14	1.15	1.16	1.17	1.18	1.19	1.20	1.21	1.22	1.23	1.24	1.25

1.26	1.27	1.28	1.29	1.30	1.31	1.32	1.33	1.34	1.35	1.36	1.37	1.38	1.39

PLEASE BRING THIS WITH YOU WHEN YOU COME FOR THE TESTS

Fig. 1.5 A record form to be filled in by the subject before attendance for medical tests.

or final steps of the computations. Some guidance will be derived from the examples in this book, but the following general points may be noted.

(1) Different values of any one measurement should normally be expressed to the same degree of precision. If a series of children's heights are generally given to the nearest inch, but a few are expressed to the nearest $\frac{1}{4}$ inch, this extra precision will be wasted in any calculations done on the series as a whole. All the measurements should therefore be rounded to the nearest inch for convenience of calculation.

(2) A useful rule in rounding mid-point values (such as a height of 127·5 cm when rounding to whole numbers) is to round to the nearest even number. Thus 127·5 would be rounded to 128. This rule prevents a slight bias which would otherwise occur if the figures were always rounded up or always rounded down.

(3) It may occasionally be justifiable to quote the results of calculations to a little more accuracy than the original data. For example, if a large series of heights are measured to the nearest centimetre the mean may sometimes be quoted to one decimal point. The reason for this is that, as we shall see, the effect of the rounding errors is reduced by the process of averaging.

(4) If any quantity calculated during an intermediate stage of the calculations is quoted to, say, n significant digits, the result of any multiplication or division of this quantity will be valid to, at the most, n digits. The significant digits are those from the first non-zero digit to the last meaningful digit, irrespective of the position of the decimal point. Thus, 1·002, 10·02, 100,200 (if this number is expressed to the nearest 100) all have 4 significant digits. Cumulative inaccuracy arises with successive operations of multiplication or division.

(5) The result of an addition or subtraction is valid to at most the number of decimal digits of the least accurate figure. Thus the result of adding 101 (accurate to the nearest integer) and 4·39 (accurate to two decimal points) is 105 (to the nearest integer). The last digit may be in error by one unit; for example, the exact figure corresponding to 101 may have been 101·42, in which case the result of the addition now should have been 105·81, or 106 to the nearest integer. These considerations are particularly important in subtraction. Very frequently in statistical calculations one number is subtracted from another of very similar size. The result of the subtraction may then be accurate to many fewer significant digits than either of the original numbers. For example, $3212{\cdot}78 - 3208{\cdot}44 = 4{\cdot}34$; three digits have been lost by the subtraction. For this reason it is essential in some of the early parts of

a computation to keep more significant digits than will be required in the final result.

A final general point about desk calculation is the importance of keeping a tidy lay-out on paper, with adequate labelling and vertical and horizontal alignment of figures and without undue crowding. Paper ruled in two directions at intervals of about ¼ inch is often found convenient.

Most of the calculations described in this book can be readily carried out on a calculating machine, and any student or practitioner of statistics will find the use of such a machine almost essential. However, there is now an increasing realization of the value of the electronic computer for statistical calculations. A computer will perform arithmetic and logical operations at extraordinarily high speeds, but is useless until provided with a program containing instructions for these operations. For most of the calculations described in this book it will be much quicker for the operator to work with a desk calculating machine than to write a computer program *ab initio*, prepare the data for the computer and arrange for the execution of the work on the computer. However, many forms of statistical analysis are of standard types which may be used repeatedly for different sets of data. It may therefore be well worth while to write a program initially for any such analyses; once the program becomes available it may then be economical to use it for subsequent sets of data. The writing of computer programs has become very much easier since the introduction of programming languages like FORTRAN, ALGOL and various autocodes. These languages permit the instructions for a computation to be written in a form which is rather like a mixture of ordinary language and algebraic symbolism. Most modern computers can accept programs written in one or more of these languages, so that programs written for one machine may sometimes be used on other machines with only slight modification. The statistician may well find that a program for a particular type of analysis has been written by someone else and is available for general use. If the reader has access to a computer installation he should enquire about the availability of statistical programs.

The data and the program must be fed into the computer by whatever means are required by the particular machine. Two methods of input are widely used. One is the 80-column punch-card described earlier. The other is punched paper tape. In this second method (Fig. 1.6) holes may be punched in a certain number of positions (usually 5, 7 or 8) in a row across the tape, each numerical or alphabetic character

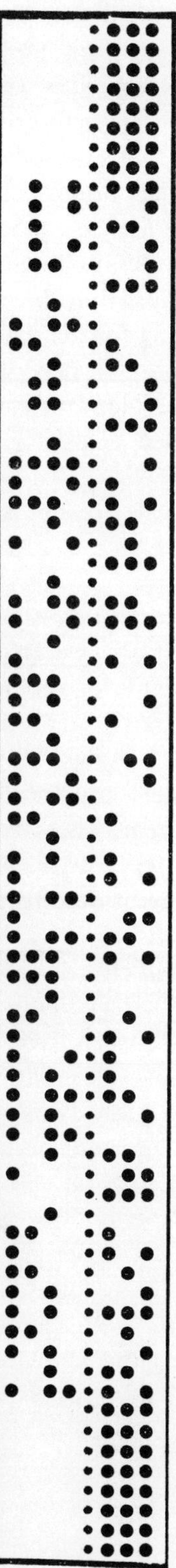

FIG. 1.6 A section of 7-hole paper tape.

being represented by holes in certain combinations of positions in one row. It is essential that data and programs be punched, either on card or tape, in precisely the form specified by the program or by the general system of operation of the computer in question. This remark is particularly relevant to the analysis of large-scale questionnaire and survey data of the type described earlier. Computers are used increasingly as an alternative to conventional punch-card machinery for the tabulation of such data. The investigator contemplating the use of one of the various general survey programs for this purpose must study the specification of the program before arranging for the data to be punched on cards or tape. If at all possible this should be done at an early stage in the planning of the investigation, before the design and wording of the questionnaire are finally decided.

1.4 SUMMARIZING NUMERICAL DATA

The raw material of all statistical investigations consists of individual observations, and these almost always have to be summarized in some way before any use can be made of them. For the remainder of this chapter we shall consider the basic methods of summarizing data—the methods of *descriptive statistics*. As we have seen, the aim of statistical methods goes beyond the mere presentation of data to include the drawing of inferences from them. These two aspects—description and inference—cannot entirely be separated. We cannot discuss the descriptive tools without some consideration of the purpose for which they are needed. So, in the next few sections, we shall occasionally have to anticipate questions of inference which will be discussed in more detail later in the book.

It is useful to distinguish between two types of observation, *qualitative* and *quantitative*. Qualitative observations are those which are not characterized by a numerical quantity. Typical examples are sex, hair colour, death or survival in a certain period of time, and nationality. The problem of summarizing qualitative data is relatively simple. The main task is to count the numbers of observations in various categories or combinations of categories, and perhaps to express them as proportions or percentages of appropriate totals. These counts are often called *frequencies*, and the proportions or percentages of totals are called *relative frequencies*. Examples are shown in Tables 1.1 and 1.2. If relative frequencies in certain sub-groups are shown, it is useful to add them to give 1·00, or 100 per cent, so that the reader can immediately see which total frequencies have been subdivided. (Slight discrepancies in these totals, due to rounding the relative frequencies or percentages, may be ignored.)

TABLE 1.2 Result of sputum examination three months after operation in group of patients treated with streptomycin and control group treated without streptomycin.

	Streptomycin		Control	
	Frequency	Per cent	Frequency	Per cent
Smear negative, culture negative	141	*45·0*	117	*41·8*
Smear negative, not cultured	90	*28·8*	67	*23·9*
Smear or culture positive	82	*26·2*	96	*34·3*
Total with known sputum result	313	*100·0*	280	*100·0*
Results not known	12		17	
Total	325		297	

A particularly important type of qualitative observation is that in which a certain characteristic is either present or absent, so that observations fall into one of two categories. Examples are sex, and survival or death. Such data are variously called *quantal*, *all-or-none* or *binary*.

The problems of summarizing quantitative data, in which the individual observations are numerical quantities, are much more complex, and the remainder of this chapter will be devoted almost entirely to them. Any class of measurement on which individual observations are made is called a *variable* or *variate*. For instance, in one problem the variable might be a particular measure of respiratory function in schoolboys, in another it might be the number of bacteria found in samples of water. In most problems many variables are involved. In a study of the natural history of a certain disease, for example, observations are likely to be made, for each patient, on a number of variables measuring the clinical state of the patient at various times throughout the illness, and also on certain variables, such as age, not directly relating to the patient's health.

It is useful to subdivide quantitative observations into *discrete* and *continuous* measurements. Discrete measurements are those for which the possible values are quite distinct and separated. They will usually be either (a) counts, which must be positive whole numbers; or (b) some sort of artificial grading, such as an assessment of the healing of a bone as shown by an x-ray picture, which might be arbitrarily scored from 0 $\frac{1}{2}$, 1, . . ., up to 5.

Continuous measurements are those which can assume a continuous, uninterrupted range of values. Examples are height, weight, age, and blood pressure. Continuous measurements may have an upper or a lower limit. For instance, a man cannot have a height below zero. There is presumably some upper limit, and also some lower limit above zero, but it would be difficult to say what they are. The distinction between discrete and continuous variables is not always clear, because all continuous measurements are in practice rounded off; for instance, a series of heights might all be recorded to the nearest $\frac{1}{2}$ inch and so be strictly discrete. This ambiguity rarely matters, since the same statistical methods can often be safely applied to both continuous and discrete measurements, particularly if the scale used for the latter is fairly finely subdivided. On the other hand, there are some special methods applicable to counts, which as we have seen must be positive whole numbers.

A useful first step in summarizing a fairly large collection of quantitative data is the formation of a *frequency distribution*. This is a table showing the number of observations, or frequency, at different values or within certain ranges of values of the variable. For a discrete variable the frequency may be tabulated at each value of the variable, as in Table 1.3. Alternatively, if there is a wide range of possible values, it will be convenient to form suitable groups by subdivision of the range

TABLE 1.3 Frequency distribution of number of males in sibships of eight children.

Number of males	Frequency (number of sibships)
0	161
1	1,152
2	3,951
3	7,603
4	10,263
5	8,498
6	4,948
7	1,655
8	264
	38,495

TABLE 1.4 Frequency distribution of number of lesions caused by smallpox virus in egg membranes.

Number of lesions	Frequency (number of membranes)
0–	1
10–	6
20–	14
30–	14
40–	17
50–	8
60–	9
70–	3
80–	6
90–	1
100–	0
110–119	1
	80

into *grouping intervals*. An example is shown in Table 1.4. (In this example the reader should note the distinction between two types of count—the variable, which is the number of lesions on an individual chorio-allantoic membrane, and the frequency, which is the number of membranes on which the variable falls within a specified range.) With continuous measurements one *must* form grouping intervals (Table 1.5).

The advantages in presenting numerical data in the form of a frequency distribution rather than a long list of individual observations are

TABLE 1.5 Frequency distribution of age for 1,357 male patients with lung cancer.

Age	Frequency (number of patients)
25–	17
35–	116
45–	493
55–	545
65–74	186
	1,357

too obvious to need stressing. On the other hand, if there are only a few observations a frequency distribution will be of little value since the number of readings falling into each group will be too small to permit any meaningful pattern to emerge.

We now consider in more detail the practical task of forming a frequency distribution. If the variable is to be grouped a decision will have to be taken about the end-points of the groups. For convenience these should be chosen, as far as possible, to be 'round' numbers. For distributions of age, for example, it is customary to use multiples of 5 or 10 as the boundaries of the groups. Care should be taken in deciding in which group to place an observation falling on one of the group boundaries, and the decision must be made clear to the reader. Usually such an observation is placed in the group of which the observation is the lower limt. For example, in Table 1.4 a count of 20 lesions would be placed in the group 20—, which includes all counts between 20 and 29, and this convention is indicated by the notation used for the groups.

How many groups should there be? No clear-cut rule can be given. To provide a useful, concise indication of the nature of the distribution less than 5 groups will usually be too few, more than 20 will usually be too many. Again, if too large a number of groups is chosen, the investigator may find that many of the groups contain frequencies which are too small to provide any regularity in the shape of the distribution. For a given size of grouping interval this difficulty will become more acute as the total number of observations is reduced, and the choice of grouping interval may, therefore, depend on this number. If in doubt, the grouping interval may be chosen smaller than that to be finally used, and groups may be amalgamated in the most appropriate way after the distribution has been formed.

The count should be made by going systematically through the list of measurements and making a mark in the appropriate group. This process, called *tallying*, is illustrated in Table 1.6. It is convenient to form groups of 5 marks to facilitate counting. The whole process should be repeated as a check. The alternative method of taking each group in turn, and counting the observations falling into that group, is not to be recommended, as it requires the scanning of the list of observations once for each group (or more than once if a check is required), and thus encourages mistakes.

Frequency distributions can be illustrated visually by means of *histograms*. Here the values of the variable are by convention represented on the horizontal scale, and the vertical scale represents the frequency

TABLE 1.6 The formation of a frequency distribution by tallying.

Counts of trypanosomes in the tail blood of a rat, each count being from a different cell of a haemocytometer.

4	6	2	2	2	1	3	5	1	2	2	3	2	4	1	1
5	3	2	6	4	3	3	1	2	6	7	3	5	5	2	2
5	5	6	2	5	1	3	1	9	1	1	2	2	4	1	1
4	4	4	6	1	2	2	1	2	1	0	3	3	4	3	1
4	2	6	2	3	3	7	4	2	6	1	5	2	2	1	9
3	4	4	1	4	6	4	2	5	4	5	4	5	5	6	2
3	1	0	1	5	5	2	2	6	1	3	1	1	1	5	3
1	0	1	5	3	3	6	8	2	0	1	3	6	2	3	5

Steps in the formation of a frequency distribution

Count	First tally mark	First five tally marks (reading along first row)	Final tally	Frequency
0			IIII	4
1			𝍸 𝍸 𝍸 𝍸 𝍸 II	27
2		III	𝍸 𝍸 𝍸 𝍸 𝍸 II	27
3			𝍸 𝍸 𝍸 𝍸	20
4	I	I	𝍸 𝍸 𝍸 I	16
5			𝍸 𝍸 𝍸 II	17
6		I	𝍸 𝍸 II	12
7			II	2
8			I	1
9			II	2
				128

at each value or in each group. If the variable is discrete and ungrouped (Table 1.3 and Fig. 1.7) the frequencies may be represented by vertical lines. The more general method, which must be applied if the variable is grouped, is to draw rectangles based on the different groups (Figs. 1.8, 1.9). It may happen that the grouping intervals are not of constant length. In Table 1.4, for example, suppose we decided to pool the groups 60–, 70– and 80–. The total frequency in these groups is 18, but it would clearly be misleading to represent this frequency by a rectangle on a base extending from 60 to 90 and with a height of 18. The correct

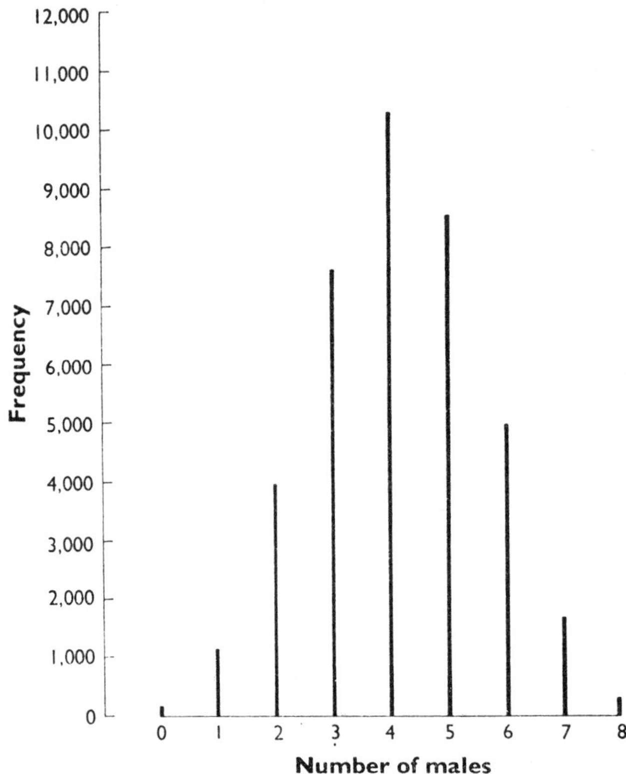

FIG. 1.7 Histogram representing the frequency distribution for an ungrouped discrete variable (Table 1.3).

procedure would be to make the height of the rectangle 6, the average frequency in the three groups (as indicated by the dotted line in Fig. 1.8). One way of interpreting this rule is to say that the height of the rectangle in a histogram is the frequency per standard grouping of the variable; (in this example the standard grouping is 10 lesions). Another way is to say that the frequency for a group is proportional to the *area* rather than the height of the rectangle; (in this example the area of any of the original rectangles, or of the composite rectangle formed by the dotted line, is 10 times the frequency for the group). If there is no variation in length of grouping interval, areas are of course proportional to heights and frequencies are represented by either heights or areas.

The frequency in a distribution or in a histogram is often expressed not as an absolute count but as a relative frequency, i.e. as a proportion or percentage of the total frequency. If the standard grouping of the variable in terms of which the frequencies are expressed is a single unit,

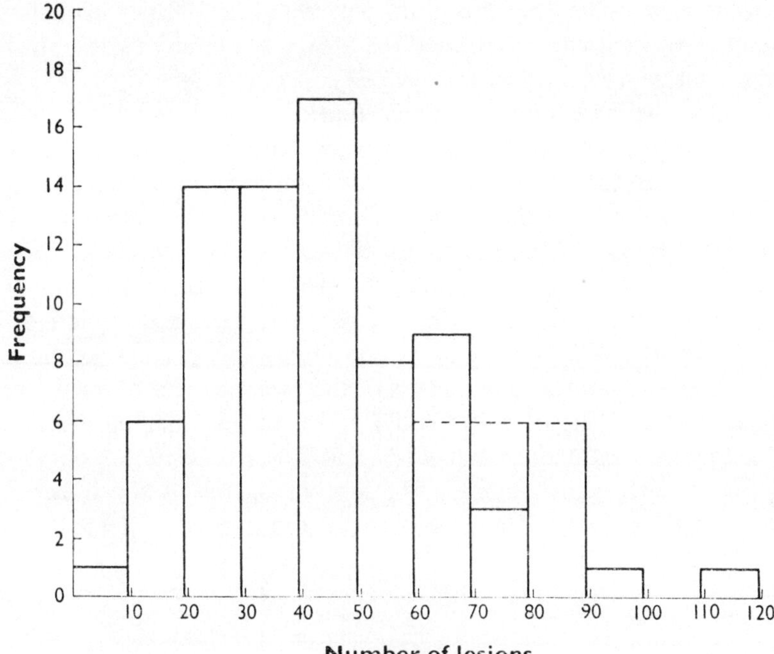

FIG. 1.8 Histogram representing the frequency distribution for a grouped discrete variable (Table 1.4).

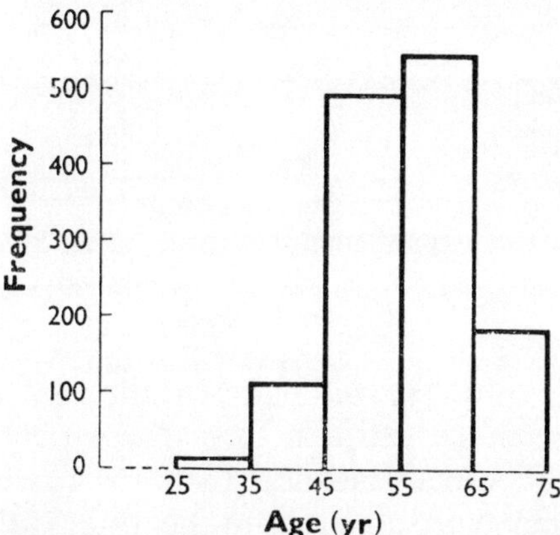

FIG. 1.9 Histogram representing the frequency distribution for a continuous variable (Table 1.5). Note that the variable shown here is exact age. The age at the last birthday is a discrete variable and would be represented by groups displaced half a year to the left from those shown here.

the total area under the histogram will be 1 (or 100 per cent if percentage frequencies are used), and the area between any two points will be the relative frequency in this range.

Suppose we had a frequency distribution of heights of 100 men, in 1 inch groups. The relative frequencies would be rather irregular, especially near the extremes of the distribution, owing to the small frequencies in some of the groups. If the number of observations were increased to, say, 1,000, the trend of the frequencies would become smoother and we might then reduce the grouping interval to $\frac{1}{2}$ inch, still making the vertical scale in the histogram represent the relative frequency per inch. We could imagine continuing this process indefinitely, if there were no limit to the fineness of the measurement of length or to the number of observations we could make. In this imaginary situation the histogram would approach closer and closer to a smooth curve, the *frequency curve*, which can be thought of as an idealized form of histogram (Fig. 1.10). The area between the ordinates erected at any

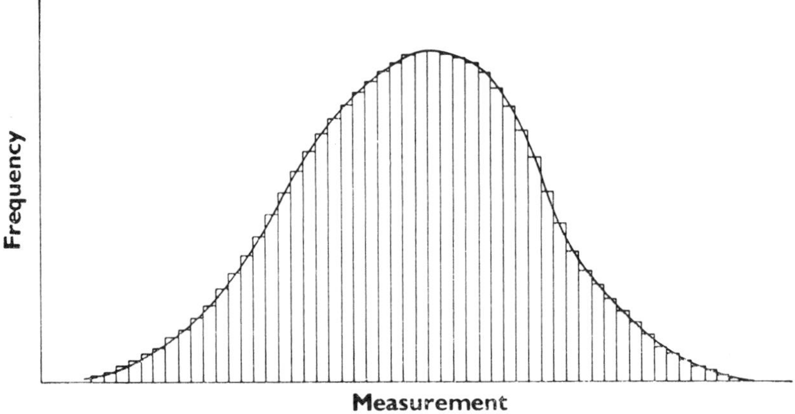

FIG. 1.10 Histogram representing the frequency distribution for a very large number of measurements finely subdivided, with an approximating frequency curve.

two values of the variable will represent the relative frequency of observations between these two points. These frequency curves are useful as models on which statistical theory is based, and should be regarded as idealized approximations to the histograms which might be obtained in practice with a large number of observations on a variable which can be measured extremely accurately.

We now consider various features which may characterize frequency distributions. Any value of the variable at which the frequency curve reaches a peak is called a *mode*. Most frequency distributions encountered in practice have one peak and are described as *unimodal*. For example, the distribution in Table 1.3 has a mode at 4 males, and that in Table 1.4 at 40–49 lesions. Usually, as in these two examples, the curve is 'bell-shaped'; that is, the mode occurs somewhere between the two extremes of the distribution. These extreme portions, where the frequency becomes low, are called *tails*. Some unimodal distributions have the mode at one end of the range. For instance, if the emission of γ-particles by some radioactive material is being studied, the frequency distribution of the time interval between successive emissions is shaped like a letter *J* (or rather its mirror image), with a mode at zero. Similarly, if we take families with 4 children and record the numbers of families in which there have been 0, 1, 2, 3 or 4 cases of poliomyelitis, we shall find a very pronounced mode at zero.

Some distributions will appear to have more than one mode owing to the inevitable random fluctuations of small numbers. In Table 1.4, for example, the observed frequencies show subsidiary modes at 60–69, 80–89 and 110–119, although we should be inclined to pay no great attention to these. Occasionally, even with very large numbers of observations, distributions with more than one mode are found. There has been a great deal of discussion as to whether the distribution of casual blood pressure in a large population free from known circulatory diseases is *bimodal*, i.e. has two modes, because the presence of a second mode at blood pressures higher than the principal mode might indicate that a substantial proportion of the population suffered from essential hypertension.

Another characteristic of some interest is the symmetry or lack of symmetry of the distribution. An asymmetric distribution is called *skew*. The distribution in Table 1.3 and Fig. 1.7 is fairly symmetric about the mode. That in Table 1.4 and Fig. 1.8, in which the upper tail is longer than the lower, would be called *positively* skew. The distribution in Table 1.5 and Fig. 1.9 has a slight negative skewness.

Two other characteristics of distributions are of such importance that separate sections will be devoted to them. They are the general location of the distribution on the scale of the variable, and the degree of variation of the observations about the centre of the distribution. Indeed, measures of location and variation are of such general importance that we shall discuss them first without reference to frequency distributions.

1.5 MEANS AND OTHER MEASURES OF LOCATION

It is often important to give, in a single figure, some indication of the general level of a series of measurements. Such a figure may be called a *measure of location*, a *measure of central tendency*, a *mean* or an *average*. The most familiar of these measures is the *arithmetic* mean, and is customarily referred to as the 'average'. In statistics the term is often abbreviated to 'mean'.

The mean is the sum of the observations divided by the number of observations. It is awkward to have to express rules of calculation verbally in this way, and we shall therefore digress a little to discuss a convenient notation. A single algebraic symbol, like x or y, will often be used to denote a particular variable. For each variable there may be one or more observations. If there are n observations of variable x they will be denoted by

$$x_1, x_2, x_3, \ldots, x_{n-1}, x_n.$$

The various x's are not necessarily or even usually arranged in order of magnitude. They may be thought of as arranged in the order in which they were calculated or observed. It is often useful to refer to a typical member of the group in order to show some calculation which is to be performed on each member. This is done by introducing a 'dummy' suffix which will often be i or j. Thus, if x is the height of a schoolchild and $x_1, x_2, \ldots, x_n$ are n values of x, a typical value may be denoted by x_i.

The arithmetic mean of the x's will be denoted by $\bar{x}$ (spoken 'x bar'). Thus,

$$\bar{x} = \frac{x_1 + x_2 + \ldots + x_n}{n}.$$

The summation occurring in the numerator can be denoted by use of the *summation sign* $\sum$ (the capital Greek letter 'sigma'), which means 'the sum of'. The range of values taken by the dummy suffix is indicated above and below the summation sign. Thus,

$$\sum_{i=1}^{n} x_i = x_1 + x_2 + \ldots + x_n$$

and

$$\bar{x} = \frac{\sum_{i=1}^{n} x_i}{n}.$$

If, as in this instance, it is clear which values the dummy suffix assumes throughout the summation, the range of the summation, and even occasionally the dummy suffix, may be omitted. Thus,

$$\sum_{i=1}^{n} x_i \text{ may be abbreviated to } \sum x_i \text{ or to } \sum x.$$

Sometimes the capital letter S is used instead of $\sum$. It is important to realize that $\sum$ stands for an operation (that of obtaining the sum of quantities which follow), rather than a quantity itself.

Some simplification in the calculation of the mean may occasionally be achieved by the introduction of *working units*. Some simple examples are shown in Table 1.7. In (a), the x's are close to each other, relative

TABLE 1.7 The use of working units in the calculation of a mean.

(a)		(b)		(c)	
x	$u=x-100$	x	$u=x/1{,}000$	x	$u=(x-1{,}000)/10$
102	2	2,000	2	1,020	2
104	4	4,000	4	1,040	4
105	5	5,000	5	1,050	5
109	9	9,000	9	1,090	9
	20		20		20
$\bar{u}=20/4=5$		$\bar{u}=20/4=5$		$\bar{u}=20/4=5$	
$\bar{x}=100+\bar{u}=105$		$\bar{x}=1{,}000\bar{u}=5{,}000$		$\bar{x}=1{,}000+10\bar{u}=1{,}050$	

to their mean, and a convenient working unit is $u=x-100$, involving a change of origin. We find $\bar{u}=5$ and convert back by taking $\bar{x}=100+\bar{u}=105$. In (b) the factor of 1,000 is superfluous to the calculation. We therefore make a change of scale, taking as working unit $u=x/1{,}000$. We find $\bar{u}=5$ and convert back by the formula $\bar{x}=\bar{u}\times 1{,}000$. A change of both origin and scale is illustrated in (c).

Working units would be particularly useful if all calculations had to be done by hand. In practice, with a calculating machine it is often felt to be preferable to do rather more calculation than necessary to save writing down working units and perhaps introducing errors in doing so. Nevertheless, the principle underlying working units is important and the reader should make himself familiar with their use.

It is sometimes required to obtain the mean of a series of measurements which have already been formed into a frequency distribution, without having recourse to the original list. Indeed, if the number of observations is very large and computational aids are lacking, the preliminary formation of a distribution may be undertaken to save computational labour, although if a calculating machine is available it is usually preferable to work from the original observations.

If the distribution is expressed in terms of a grouping of the original variable, no further calculations will yield the exact value of the mean (except by a fluke). For the mean depends on the precise value of each observation, and these values are lost once a grouping system is adopted. The best we can hope to do, therefore, is to get an approximation to the mean. The calculations are illustrated in Table 1.8. Some definite value must be attached to the observations in each group, and the simplest rule is to suppose them all to be located at the mid-point of the group. In Table 1.8, therefore, we suppose there are 10 observations at age 25,

TABLE 1.8 Calculation of mean from frequency distribution.

Age x (yr)	Frequency f	Mid-point (yr)	Working unit, u	(a) fu
20–	10	25	−2	−20
30–	30	35	−1	−30
40–	30	45	0	0
50–	20	55	1	20
60–	10	65	2	20
	$n=100$			−10

$$\bar{u}=\frac{-10}{100}=-0{\cdot}1$$

$$\bar{x}=45+10(-0{\cdot}1)=44 \text{ yr.}$$

30 observations at age 35, and so on. To obtain the mean age we could form a sum by adding in 25 ten times, 35 thirty times, and so on, and finally dividing by 100. To simplify the arithmetic it is convenient to use working units. If, as in most cases, the groups are equally spaced, the working unit can change by 1 unit for each group. It is convenient to locate the working origin somewhere near the mode of the distribution, and in this case the group 40– was chosen. Column (a) shows the contribution made by each group to the sum of the working units. The

mean working unit is calculated as $-0{\cdot}1$. The relationship between age, x, and working unit, u, is

$$u=0{\cdot}1\,(x-45)$$

or

$$x=45+10u.$$

The calculated mean age is therefore

$$\begin{aligned}\bar{x}&=45+10\bar{u}\\&=45+10\,(-0{\cdot}1)\\&=45-1\\&=44 \text{ years.}\end{aligned}$$

The determination of the mid-point of each group requires a knowledge of the extent, if any, to which the original readings have been rounded off. In the above example the ages of individuals included in the group 20– would range from 20 years 0 days to 29 years 364 days, and the mid-point would be 25 years. If, on the other hand, the variable was length in metres, rounded off to the nearest half metre, the group would include lengths from 19·75 to 29·75 metres, and the mid-point would be 24·75 metres. If the original readings were integers, or were rounded off to the nearest integer, the midpoint would be 24·5. Age is an unusual variable in that by convention it is rounded downwards. In the example we assumed that an estimate of the mean 'true' age was required. In many calculations the rounded value (age last birthday) is used throughout. If this convention had been followed in the example, the mid-points would have been 24·5, 34·5, etc., and the calculated mean age last birthday would have been 43·5 years.

Another useful measure of location is the *median*. If the observations are arranged in increasing or decreasing order the median is the middle observation. If the number of observations, n, is odd, there will be a unique median—the $\frac{1}{2}(n+1)$th observation from either end in the ordered sequence. If n is even there is strictly no middle observation, but the median is defined by convention as the mean of the two middle observations—the $\frac{1}{2}n$th and the $(\frac{1}{2}n+1)$th from either end.

The median has several disadvantages in comparison with the mean.

(1) It takes no account of the precise magnitude of most of the observations, and is therefore in general less efficient than the mean because it wastes information.

(2) If two groups of observations are pooled the median of the combined group cannot be expressed in terms of the medians of the two component groups. This is not so with the mean. If groups containing

n_1 and n_2 observations have means of $\bar{x}_1$ and $\bar{x}_2$ respectively, the mean of the combined group is $(n_1\bar{x}_1 + n_2\bar{x}_2)/(n_1 + n_2)$.

(3) The median is much less amenable than the mean to mathematical treatment, and is not much used in the more elaborate statistical techniques.

For descriptive work, however, the median is occasionally useful. Consider the following series of durations (in days) of absence from work owing to sickness.

1, 1, 2, 2, 3, 3, 4, 4, 4, 4, 5, 6, 6, 6, 6, 7, 8, 10, 10, 38, 80.

From a purely descriptive point of view the mean might be said to be misleading. Owing to the highly skew nature of the distribution the mean of 10 days is not really typical of the series as a whole, and the median of 5 days might be a more useful index. Another point is that in skew distributions of this type the mean is very much influenced by the presence of isolated high values. The median is therefore more stable than the mean in the sense that it is likely to fluctuate less from one series of readings to another.

TABLE 1.9 Calculation of median from frequency distribution. (Same data as in Table 1.8).

Age x	Cumulative frequency less than x
30	10
40	40
50	70
60	90
70	100

$$\text{Median} = 40 + \left(\frac{10}{30} \times 10\right) = 43 \cdot 3 \text{ yr.}$$

The calculation of a median from a grouped frequency distribution is illustrated in Table 1.9. We require a value of age below which it is estimated that $\frac{1}{2}n$ (i.e. 50) observations lie. The second column shows, by accumulating the frequencies, how many observations fall below successive points of the grouping. Thus,

10 individuals have an age less than 30 years
40 individuals have an age less than 40 years
70 individuals have an age less than 50 years,

and so on. The median clearly lies between 40 and 50 years, and is estimated by linear interpolation as

$$40+\left(\frac{10}{30}\times 10\right)=43\cdot 3 \text{ years,}$$

very slightly lower than the mean of 44 years. The point to note about this calculation is that, because the form in which the data are presented preclude actual counting of observations but do refer to the number of observations below certain limits, the quantity $\frac{1}{2}n$ is used rather than $\frac{1}{2}(n+1)$.

The median and mean are equal if the series of observations is symmetrically distributed about their common value (as is nearly the case in Table 1.8). For a positively skew distribution (as in Table 1.4) the mean will be greater than the median, while if the distribution is negatively skew the median will be the greater.

A third measure of location, the mode, was introduced in section 1.4. It is not widely used in analytical statistics, mainly because of the ambiguity in its definition as the fluctuations of small frequencies are apt to produce spurious modes. An interesting empirical relationship, which seems to hold fairly closely for extensive series of observations following unimodal distributions, is:

$$\text{Mode}-\text{Median}=2(\text{Median}-\text{Mean}).$$

A useful mnemonic is that the three measures occur in alphabetic order (or in the reverse of alphabetical order), with one gap about twice the size of the other; the larger gap is between the two measures which would be the more widely separated in the dictionary. For a symmetric unimodal distribution all three measures are equal.

Finally, reference must be made to the *geometric mean*, which is used extensively in microbiological and serological research. Observations are sometimes expressed as *titres*, which are the dilutions of certain suspensions or reagents at which a specified phenomenon, like agglutination of red cells, first takes place. If repeated observations are made during the same investigation the possible values of a titre will usually be multiples of the same dilution factor: for example, 2, 4, 8, 16, etc., for two-fold dilutions. It is commonly found that a series of titres, obtained, for example, from different sera, are distributed with marked positive skewness on account of the increasingly wide intervals between possible values. Now, if a series of numbers increases by a constant multiplying factor, their logarithms must increase by a constant difference which is the logarithm of the multiplying factor. The series of titres 2, 4, 8, 16, etc., for example, have logarithms very nearly equal to 0·3, 0·6, 0·9, 1·2, etc., which increase successively by an increment of 0·3 (=log 2). It is often found, empirically, that the use of log titres rather than titres gives a series of observations which is more symmetrically distributed and for which, therefore, the use of the arithmetic mean is more appropriate. Denote the titre by x and the log titre by $u(=\log x)$. The arithmetic mean of u is, like the individual values of u, measured on a logarithmic scale, and to get back to the original scale of titres we take $\bar{x}_g = \text{antilog } \bar{u}$. This is called the geometric mean of x. It can never be greater than the arithmetic mean, and the two means will be equal only if all the x's are the same.

The geometric mean cannot be used if any of the original observations are negative, since a negative number has no logarithm. Its use with series of dilutions is particularly appropriate because of the underlying equally-spaced logarithmic series, but it may occasionally be used more generally whenever a series of positive readings shows a degree of positive skewness which is largely removed by taking logarithms. The conditions under which its use is appropriate are thus rather similar to those for which the median is often used, and indeed for this type of data the median and the geometric mean will often have similar values. As an example, consider the following set of antibody titres: 4, 8, 16, 16, 64. Their logarithms are 0·60, 0·90, 1·20, 1·20, 1·81, the mean logarithm is 1·142, and the geometric mean antilog 1·142 ≏ 13·9. By contrast, the arithmetic mean of the titres is 21·6 and the median is 16.

Another measure, the *harmonic mean*, which is much more rarely used, is described in section 11.3.

1.6 MEASURES OF VARIATION

When the mean value of a series of measurements has been obtained it is usually a matter of considerable interest to express the degree of variation or scatter around this mean. Are the readings all rather close to the mean or are some of them scattered widely in each direction? This question is important for purely descriptive reasons, as we shall emphasize below. It is important also since the measurement of variation plays a central part in the methods of statistical inference which are described in this book. To take a simple example, the reliability of the mean of 100 values of some variable depends on the extent to which the 100 readings differ among themselves; if they show little variation the mean value is more reliable, more precisely determined, than if the 100 readings vary widely. The role of variation in statistical inference will be clarified in later chapters of this book. At present we are concerned more with the descriptive aspects.

In works of reference it is common to find a single figure quoted for the value of some biological quantity and the reader may not always realize that the stated figure is some sort of average. In a text-book on nutrition, for example, we find the vitamin A content of 'Cheese—Cheddar-type' given as 2,000 international units per 100 grammes. Clearly, not all specimens of 'Cheese—Cheddar-type' contain precisely 2,000 i.u. per 100 g; how much variation, then, is there from one piece of cheese to another? To take another example from nutrition, the daily calorie requirement for a man of 25 years is given as 3,200. This requirement must vary from one person to another; how large is the variation?

There is unlikely to be a single answer to questions of this sort, because the amount of variation to be found in a series of measurements will usually depend on the circumstances in which they are made, and in particular on the way in which these circumstances change from one reading to another. Specimens of Cheddar cheese are likely to vary in their vitamin A content for a number of reasons: major differences in the place and method of manufacture; variation in composition from one specimen to another even within the same batch of manufacture; the age of the cheese, and so on. Variation in the recorded measurement may be partly due to measurement error; in the method of assay, for example, or because of observer errors. Similarly, if reference is made to the variation in systolic blood pressure it must be made clear what sort of comparison is envisaged. Are we considering differences between various types of individual (for example, groups defined by age or by clinical state); differences between individuals classified in the same group; variation from one occasion to another on the same individual; and are the instrument and the observer kept constant throughout the series?

We now consider some methods of measuring the variation or scatter of a series of continuous measurements.

This scatter is, of course, one of the features of the data which is elucidated by a frequency distribution. It is, however, convenient to use some single quantity to measure this feature of the data, firstly for economy of presentation, secondly because the statistical methods to be described later require such an index, and thirdly because the data may be too sparse to enable a distribution to be formed. We therefore require what is variously termed a measure of *variation, scatter, spread* or *dispersion.*

An obvious candidate is the *range*, which is defined as the difference between the maximum value and the minimum value. (Note that the range is a definite quantity, measured in the same units as the original observations; if the highest and lowest of a series of diastolic blood pressures are 95 and 65 mmHg, we may say not only (as in conversation) that the readings range from 65 to 95 mmHg, but that the range *is* 30 mmHg). There are three main difficulties about the use of the range as a measure of variation. The first is that the numerical value assumed by the range is determined by only two of the original observations. It is true that if we say that the minimum and maximum readings have the values 65 and 95, we are saying something about the other readings—that they are between these extremes—but apart from this their exact values have no effect on the range. In this example, the range would be 30 whether (a) all the other readings were concentrated between 75 and 80, or (b) they were spread rather evenly between 65 and 95. A desirable measure of the variation of the whole set of readings should be greater in case (b) than in case (a). Secondly, the interpretation of the range depends on the number of observations. If observations are selected serially from a large group (for example, by taking the blood pressures of one individual after another), the range cannot possibly decrease; it will increase whenever a new reading falls outside the interval between the two previous extremes. The interpretation of the range as a measure of variation of the group as a whole must therefore depend on a knowledge of the number of observations on which it is based. This is an undesirable feature; no such allowance is required, for instance, in the interpretation of a mean value as a measure of location. Thirdly, calculations based on extreme values are rather unreliable because big differences in these extremes are liable to occur between two similar investigations.

If the number of observations is not too small a modification may be introduced which avoids the use of the absolute extreme values. If the readings are arranged in ascending or descending order two values may be ascertained which cut off a small fraction of the observations at each end, just as the median breaks the distribution into two equal parts. The value below which $\frac{1}{4}$ of the ordered observations fall is called the *lower quartile*, that which is exceeded by $\frac{1}{4}$ of the observations is called the *upper quartile*, and the distance between them is called the *inter-quartile distance.* This is not subject to the second disadvantage of the range and is less subject to the other disadvantages. However, it is not a satisfactory measure of variation for small series of observations because of the impossibility of dividing the observations into exact quarters unless the number is divisible by 4.

An alternative approach is to make some use of all the deviations from the mean, $x_i - \bar{x}$. Clearly, the greater the scatter of the observations the greater will the magnitude of these deviations tend to be. It would be of no use to take the mean of the deviations $x_i - \bar{x}$, since some of these will be negative and some positive. In fact

$$\begin{aligned}\sum(x_i - \bar{x}) &= \sum x_i - \sum \bar{x} \\ &= \sum x_i - n\bar{x} \\ &= 0, \text{ since } \bar{x} = \sum x_i/n.\end{aligned}$$

Therefore the mean of the deviations $x_i - \bar{x}$ will always be zero. We could, however, take the mean of the deviations ignoring their sign, i.e. counting them all as positive. These quantities are called the absolute values of the deviations and are denoted by $|x_i - \bar{x}|$. Their mean, $\sum|x_i - \bar{x}|/n$, is called the *mean deviation.* This measure has the drawback of being difficult to handle mathematically, and we shall not consider it any further in this book.

Another way of getting over the difficulty caused by the positive and negative signs is to square them. The mean value of the squared deviations is called the *variance* and is a most important measure in statistics. Its formula is

$$\text{Variance} = \frac{\sum(x_i - \bar{x})^2}{n}. \qquad (1.1)$$

The numerator is often called the *sum of squares about the mean.* The variance is measured in the square of the units in which x is measured. For example, if x is height in cm, the variance will be measured in cm^2. This might seem not to matter, because these units are often used for the measurement of area. On the other hand, if x was a time measurement in seconds, it would be undesirable to have variation measured in square seconds. It is convenient, therefore, to have a measure of variation expressed in the original units of x, and this can be easily done by taking the square root of the variance. This quantity is known as the *standard deviation,* and its formula is

$$\text{Standard deviation} = \sqrt{\left(\frac{\sum(x_i - \bar{x})^2}{n}\right)}. \qquad (1.1a)$$

In practice, in calculating variances and standard deviations, the n in the denominator is almost always replaced by $n-1$. The reason for this is that in applying the methods of statistical inference developed later in this book it is useful to regard the collection of observations as being a *sample* drawn from a much larger group of possible readings. The large group is often called a *population*. When we calculate a variance or a standard deviation we may wish not merely to describe the variation in the sample with which we are dealing, but also to estimate as best we can the variation in the population from which the sample is supposed to have been drawn. In a certain respect (see section 3.4) a better estimate of the population variance is obtained by using a divisor $n-1$ instead of n. Thus, we shall almost always use the formula for the *estimated variance*:

$$\text{Estimated variance, } s^2 = \frac{\sum(x_i - \bar{x})^2}{n-1}, \tag{1.2}$$

and similarly,

$$\text{Estimated standard deviation, } s = \sqrt{\left(\frac{\sum(x_i - \bar{x})^2}{n-1}\right)}. \tag{1.2a}$$

Having established the convention we shall very often omit the word 'estimated' and refer to s^2 and s as 'variance' and 'standard deviation', respectively.

The modification of the divisor from n to $n-1$ is clearly not very important when n is large. It is more important for small values of n. Although the theoretical justification will be discussed more fully in section 3.4, two heuristic arguments may be used now, which may make the divisor $n-1$ appear more plausible. Firstly, consider the case when $n=1$; that is, there is a single observation. Formula (1.1) with a divisor n gives a variance $0/1=0$. Now, this is a reasonable expression of the complete absence of variation in the available observation: it cannot differ from itself. On the other hand, a single observation provides no information at all about the variation in the population from which it is drawn, and this fact is reflected in the calculation of the estimated variance, s^2, from (1.2), which becomes $0/0$, an indeterminate quantity.

Secondly, in the general case when n takes any value, we have already seen that $\sum(x_i - \bar{x}) = 0$. This means that if $n-1$ of these deviations $x_i - \bar{x}$ are chosen arbitrarily, the nth is automatically determined. (It is the sum of the $n-1$ chosen values of $x_i - \bar{x}$ with the sign changed.) In other words, only $n-1$ of the n deviations which are squared in the numerator of (1.1) or (1.2) are *independent*. The divisor $n-1$ in (1.2) may be regarded as the number of independent quantities amongst the sum of squared deviations in the numerator. The divisor $n-1$ is, in fact, a particular case of a far-reaching concept known as the *degrees of freedom* of an estimate of variance, which will be developed in section 3.4.

The direct calculation of the estimated variance is illustrated in Table 1.10.

TABLE 1.10 Calculation of estimated variance and standard deviation: direct formula.

x_i	$x_i-\bar{x}$	$(x_i-\bar{x})^2$
8	0	0
5	−3	9
4	−4	16
12	4	16
15	7	49
5	−3	9
7	−1	1
$\sum x_i=56$		$\sum(x_i-\bar{x})^2=100$

$n=7$

$\bar{x}=56/7=8$

$s^2=100/6=16\cdot67$

$s=\sqrt{16\cdot67}=4\cdot08$

In this particular example the calculation was fairly straightforward. In general, two features of the method are likely to cause trouble. Errors can easily arise in the subtraction of the mean from each reading. Further, if the mean is not a 'round' number, as it was in this example, it will need to be rounded off. The deviations $x_i-\bar{x}$ will then need to be written with several significant digits and doubt will arise as to whether an adequate number of significant digits was retained for $\bar{x}$. These difficulties have led to the almost universal adoption of an alternative method of calculating the sum of squares about the mean, $\sum(x_i-\bar{x})^2$. It is based on the following algebraic identity:

$$\begin{aligned}\sum(x_i-\bar{x})^2 &= \sum(x_i^2-2x_i\bar{x}+\bar{x}^2)\\ &= \sum x_i^2-2\bar{x}\sum x_i+n\bar{x}^2\end{aligned}$$

$$=\sum x_i^2-2\frac{(\sum x_i)^2}{n}+\frac{(\sum x_i)^2}{n}$$

$$=\sum x_i^2-\frac{(\sum x_i)^2}{n}. \tag{1.3}$$

This is called the short-cut formula for the sum of squares about the mean. The derivation of (1.3) uses the fact that $\sum x_i = n\bar{x}$. Using this relation in the second term of (1.3), the following alternative forms are obtained:

$$\sum(x_i-\bar{x})^2=\sum x_i^2-n\bar{x}^2 \tag{1.3a}$$

$$=\sum x_i^2-\bar{x}(\sum x_i). \tag{1.3b}$$

In general (1.3) is the most useful of these formulae. On multiplying (1.3) by n, a further variant is obtained:

$$\sum(x_i-\bar{x})^2=\frac{n\sum x_i^2-(\sum x_i)^2}{n}, \tag{1.3c}$$

which is sometimes found more useful for desk computation.

The important point about (1.3) and its variants is that the computation is performed without the need to calculate individual deviations from the mean, $x_i-\bar{x}$. The sum of squares of the original observations, x_i, is corrected by subtraction of a quantity dependent only on the mean (or, equivalently, the total) of the x_i. This second term is therefore often called the *correction term*, and the whole expression a *corrected* sum of squares.

The previous example is re-worked in Table 1.11. The result $\sum(x_i-\bar{x})^2=100$ is again obtained, and the subsequent calculations follow as in Table 1.10.

The short-cut formula avoids the need to square individual deviations with many significant digits, but involves the squares of the x_i which may be large numbers. This rarely causes trouble if a calculating machine is available, although care must be taken to carry sufficient digits in the correction term to give the required number of digits in the difference between the two terms. (For example, if $\sum x_i^2=2025$ and $(\sum x_i)^2/n=2019{\cdot}3825$, the retention of all these decimals will give $\sum(x_i-\bar{x})^2=5{\cdot}6175$; if the correction term had been rounded off to the nearest whole number it would have given $\sum(x_i-\bar{x})^2=6$—an accuracy of only 1 significant digit.) Simplification may sometimes be achieved by the use of working units, as in section 1.5. Table 1.12 gives examples

TABLE 1.11 Calculation of estimated variance and standard deviation: short-cut formula (same data as in Table 1.10).

x_i	x_i^2
8	64
5	25
4	16
12	144
15	225
5	25
7	49
56	548

$$\sum(x_i-\bar{x})^2 = \sum x_i^2 - (\sum x_i)^2/n$$
$$= 548 - 56^2/7$$
$$= 548 - 448$$
$$= 100$$

Subsequent steps as in Table 1.10

TABLE 1.12 Use of working units in calculation of standard deviation.

x_i	(a) $u_i = x_i - 500$	x_i	(b) $u_i = x_i/100$	x_i	(c) $u_i = 100(x_i - 1)$
508	8	800	8	1·08	8
505	5	500	5	1·05	5
504	4	400	4	1·04	4
512	12	1,200	12	1·12	12
515	15	1,500	15	1·15	15
505	5	500	5	1·05	5
507	7	700	7	1·07	7
s_u (from Table 1.10)	4·08		4·08		4·08
s_x	4·08	$(=100s_u)$	408	$(=0{\cdot}01s_u)$	0·0408

of three series of observations all of which conveniently reduce to working units, u, taking the same numerical values as the x's in Table 1.10. The purpose of the working units should be clear in each case. The important point is that the standard deviation, being defined by (1·2a) in terms of deviations from the mean, is unaffected by a change of origin as in (a), since this leaves the deviations from the mean unaffected. On the other hand, if the working units involve a change of scale, as in (b) and (c), the standard deviation is affected in the same ratio. Thus, in (c), $x=1+0{\cdot}01u$, and the standard deviation of x is 0·01 times the standard deviation of u.

If the observations are presented in the form of a frequency distribution, the standard deviation may be obtained by a method analogous to that used for the mean. If the original variable is grouped, only an approximate estimate of the standard deviation may be obtained. The calculations are illustrated in Table 1.13, which shows the same data as

TABLE 1.13 Calculation of standard deviation from frequency distribution (same data as in Table 1.8).

Age x	Frequency f	(1) Working unit, u	(2) fu	$fu^2=(1)\times(2)$
20–	10	−2	−20	40
30–	30	−1	−30	30
40–	30	0	0	0
50–	20	1	20	20
60–	10	2	20	40
	$n=100$		$\sum u=-10$	$\sum u^2=130$
				$(\sum u)^2/n=\ \ 1$
				$\sum(u-\bar{u})^2=129$

$$s_u^2=129/99=1{\cdot}303$$
$$s_u=\sqrt{1{\cdot}303}=1{\cdot}141$$
$$\text{Standard deviation of } x=10\times 1{\cdot}141 = 11{\cdot}41 \text{ yr.}$$

Note that $\sum u$ denotes the sum of u over all $n(=100)$ observations. It is calculated as $\sum fu$, where the summation now refers to the 5 groups. Similarly $\sum u^2$ over all observations is calculated as $\sum fu^2$ over the 5 groups.

in the corresponding calculations for the mean (Table 1.8). The standard deviation of the working unit, u, is calculated to be 1·141. The standard deviation of x is therefore 10 (1·141)=11·41 years.

The assumption that all the values of x within a group can safely be replaced by the mid-point of the interval, although reasonable for the calculation of the mean, is slightly suspect for the calculation of the standard deviation, for the following reason. When the distribution is unimodal, as in Table 1.10, the observations within each group will tend to be pulled towards the middle of the distribution instead of being distributed evenly throughout the interval. That is, the mean values of the observations in the intervals 20–, 30– are likely to be rather greater than 25 and 35; those in the intervals 50–, 60– rather less than 55 and 65, respectively. These biases will tend to even out in the calculation of the mean age, and may safely be ignored. The calculated standard deviation will, however, tend to be exaggerated. An appropriate correction for this effect, called *Sheppard's correction*, is to subtract $\frac{1}{12}h^2$ from the calculated variance, h being the size of the grouping interval. (If the grouping interval is not constant an average value may be used.) In the present example, the corrected variance of u would be

$$1{\cdot}303 - \tfrac{1}{12}(1^2) = 1{\cdot}220$$

giving

$$\mathrm{SD}(u) = 1{\cdot}104$$
$$\mathrm{SD}(x) = 11{\cdot}04 \text{ years.}$$

The correction is thus rather small unless the grouping is rather crude, and for this reason is often ignored.

The standard deviation of a set of measurements is expressed in the same units as the measurements and hence in the same units as the mean. It is occasionally useful to describe the variability by expressing the standard deviation as a proportion, or a percentage, of the mean. The resulting measure, called the *coefficient of variation*, is thus a dimensionless quantity—a pure number. In symbols,

$$\mathrm{CV}(x) = \frac{s}{\bar{x}} \times 100\%. \qquad (1.4)$$

The coefficient of variation is most useful as a descriptive tool in situations in which a change in the conditions under which measurements are made alters the standard deviation in the same proportion as it alters the mean. The coefficient of variation then remains unchanged and is a useful single measure of variability. It is mentioned again in a more substantial context in section 3.6.

CHAPTER 2
PROBABILITY

2.1 THE MEANING OF PROBABILITY

A clinical trial shows that 50 patients receiving treatment A for a certain disease fare better, on the average, than 50 similar patients receiving treatment B. Is it safe to assume that treatment A is really better than treatment B for this condition? Should the investigator use A rather than B for future patients? These are questions typical of those arising from any statistical investigation. The first is one of inference: what conclusions can reasonably be drawn from this investigation? The second question is one of decision: what is the rational choice of future treatment, taking into account the information provided by the trial and the known or unknown consequences of using an inferior treatment? The point to be emphasized here is that the answers to both questions, and indeed those to almost all questions asked about statistical data, are in some degree couched in uncertainty. There may be a very strong suggestion indeed that A is better than B, but can we be entirely sure that the patients receiving B were not more severely affected than those on A and that this variability between the patients was not a sufficient reason for their different responses to treatment? This possibility may, in any particular instance, seem unlikely, but it can rarely, if ever, be completely ruled out. The questions that have to be asked, therefore, must receive an answer phrased in terms of uncertainty. If the uncertainty is low, the conclusion will be firm, the decision will be safe. If the uncertainty is high the investigation must be regarded as inconclusive. It is thus important to consider the measurement of uncertainty, and the appropriate tool for this purpose is the *theory of probability*. Initially the approach will be rather formal; later chapters are concerned with the application of probability theory to statistical problems of various types.

If a coin is tossed a very large number of times, and the result of each toss written down, the results may be something like the following

(*H* standing for heads and *T* for tails):

TTHTHHTHTTTHTHHTHHHHTTH . . .

Such a sequence will be called a *random sequence* or *random series*, each place in the sequence will be called a *trial*, and each result will often be called an *event* or *outcome*. A random sequence is characterized by a complete lack of pattern or of predictability. The chance of finding *H* at any one stage is just the same as at any other stage, and is quite uninfluenced by the outcomes of the previous tosses. (Contrary to some people's intuition, the chance of getting a head would be neither raised nor lowered by a knowledge that there had just occurred a run of, say, 6 tails.)

In such a sequence it will be found that as the sequence gets larger and larger the proportion of trials resulting in a particular outcome becomes less and less variable and settles down closer to some limiting value. This long-run proportion is called the *probability* of the particular outcome. Fig. 2.1 shows the proportion of heads after various numbers of tosses, in an actual experiment. Clearly the proportion is settling down close to $\frac{1}{2}$, and it would be reasonable to say that the probability of a head is about $\frac{1}{2}$. Considerations of symmetry would of course have

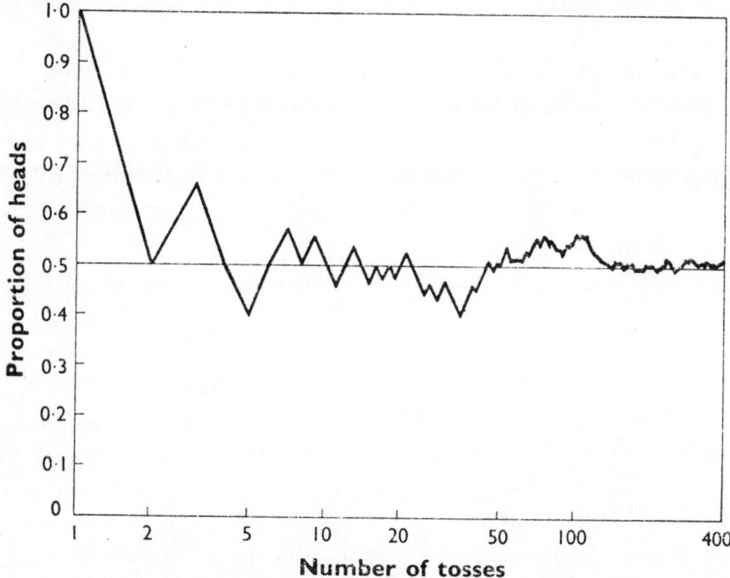

FIG. 2.1 Proportion of heads in a sequence of tosses of a coin with a logarithmic scale for the number of tosses. (Reprinted from Cramér, 1946, by permission of the author and publishers.)

led us to this conclusion before seeing the experimental results. The slight differences between the indentations on the two sides of a coin, possible variations in density, and even some minor imbalance in the tossing method, might make the probability very slightly different from $\frac{1}{2}$, but we should be unlikely ever to do a tossing experiment sufficiently long to distinguish between a probability of 0·5 and one of, say, 0·5001.

The reader will observe that this definition of probability is rather heuristic. We can never observe a sequence of trials and say unambiguously 'This is a random sequence'; we observe only a finite portion of the sequence and there may be underlying patterns in the outcomes which cannot readily be discerned. Nor can we observe a sequence and state precisely the probability of a certain outcome; the probability is a long-run property and again an insufficient portion of the sequence is observed. Nevertheless, there are many phenomena which apparently behave in this way, and the concept of a random sequence should be regarded as an idealistic concept which apparently describes these phenomena very faithfully indeed. Here are some other examples of empirical 'random' sequences.

(a) The throws of a die (commonly, but incorrectly, called a 'dice'); this is a cube, the sides of which are inscribed with the numbers 1 to 6. If the die is well made the probability of each outcome will be very close to $\frac{1}{6}$.

(b) The sex of successive live births occurring in a large human population. The probability of a male is known to vary from population to population (for example, it depends on the stillbirth rate) but it is usually a little over $\frac{1}{2}$. In England and Wales it is currently about 0·515; the probability of a female birth is correspondingly about $1-0{\cdot}515=0{\cdot}485$.

(c) A sequence of births, each classified as normal or as one of a specified number of congenital malformations or combinations thereof. Thus, the probability that an infant (live or stillborn) suffers from spina bifida is about 0·0024.

A consequence of this definition of probability is that it is measured by a number between 0 and 1. If an event never occurs in any of the trials in a random sequence, its probability is zero. If it occurs in every trial, its probability is unity.

A further consequence is that probability is not defined for sequences in which the succession of events follows a manifestly non-random pattern. If a machine were invented which tossed heads and tails in strict alternation (H, T, H, T, H, T, . . . etc.), the long-run proportions of heads and tails would both be $\frac{1}{2}$, but it would be incorrect to say that the probabilities of these events were $\frac{1}{2}$. The sequence is non-random because the behaviour of the odd-numbered trials is different from that of the even-numbered trials. It would be better to think of the series as a mixture of two separate series: the odd-numbered trials in which the probability of H is 1, and the even-numbered trials in which this probability is 0.

This concept of probability provides a measure of uncertainty for certain types of phenomena which do occur in nature. There is a fairly high degree of certainty that any one future birth will not exhibit spina bifida because the probability for that event is low. There is considerable uncertainty about the sex of a future birth because the probabilities of both outcomes are about $\frac{1}{2}$. The definition is, however, much more restrictive than might be wished. What is the probability that smoking is a contributory cause of lung cancer? This question uses the word 'probability' in a perfectly natural conversational way. It does not, however, accord with our technical definition, for it is impossible to think of a random sequence of trials, in some of which smoking is a contributory cause of lung cancer and in some of which it is not.

It will appear in due course that the so-called 'frequency' definition of probability, which has been put forward above, can be used as the basis of statistical inference, and often some rewording of the question can shed some light on the plausibility of hypotheses such as 'Smoking is a contributory cause of lung cancer'. However, many theoretical statisticians, probabilists and logicians advocate a much wider interpretation of the concept of probability than is permitted in the frequency definition outlined above. On this broader view, one should interpret probability as a measure of one's degree of belief in a proposition, and direct statements about the probability that a certain scientific hypothesis is true are quite in order. We return to this point of view in section 2.9, but until that section is reached we shall restrict our attention to the frequency definition.

2.2 PROBABILITY CALCULATIONS

The main purpose of allotting numerical values to probabilities is to allow calculations to be performed on these numbers. The two basic operations which concern us here are *addition* and *multiplication*, and we consider first the addition of probabilities.

Consider a random sequence of trials with more than one possible outcome for each trial. In a series of throws of a die, for example, we might ask for the probability of *either* a 1 *or* a 3 being thrown. The answer is fairly clear. If the die is perfectly formed, the probability of a 1 is $\frac{1}{6}$, and the probability of a 3 is $\frac{1}{6}$. That is, a 1 will appear in $\frac{1}{6}$ of trials in the long run, and a 3 will appear in the same proportion of a long series of trials. In no trial will a 1 *and* a 3 appear together. Therefore the compound event 'either a 1 or a 3' will occur in $\frac{1}{6}+\frac{1}{6}$, or $\frac{1}{3}$, of the trials in the long run. The probabilities for the two separate events have been added together.

Note the importance of the observation that a 1 and a 3 cannot both occur together; they are, in other words, *mutually exclusive*. Without this condition the simple form of the addition rule could not be valid. For example, if a doctor's name is chosen haphazardly from the British Medical Register, the probability that the doctor is male is about 0·8. The probability that the doctor qualified at an English medical school is about 0·6. What is the probability that the doctor either is male or qualified in England, or both? If the two separate probabilities are added the result is $0{\cdot}8+0{\cdot}6=1{\cdot}4$, clearly a wrong answer since probabilities cannot be greater than 1. The trouble is that the probability of the double event—male *and* qualified in England—has been counted twice, once as part of the probability of being male and once as part of the probability of being qualified in England. To obtain the right answer, the probability of the double event must be subtracted. Thus, denoting the two events by A and B, we have the more general form of the *addition rule*.

Probability of A or B or both = (Probability of A) + (Probability of B) − (Probability of A and B).

It will be convenient to write this as

$$\mathrm{P}(A \text{ or } B \text{ or both}) = \mathrm{P}(A) + \mathrm{P}(B) - \mathrm{P}(A \text{ and } B). \qquad (2.1)$$

In this particular example the probability of the double event has not been given, but it must clearly be greater than 0·4, to ensure that the right side of the equation (2.1) is less than 1.

If the two events are mutually exclusive, the last term on the right of (2.1) is zero, and we have the *simple form of the addition rule*:

$$\mathrm{P}(A \text{ or } B) = \mathrm{P}(A) + \mathrm{P}(B).$$

Suppose now that two random sequences of trials are proceeding simultaneously; for example, at each stage a coin may be tossed and a die thrown. What is the probability of a particular combination of results, for example a head (H) on the coin and a 5 on the die? The result is given by the *multiplication rule*:

$$\mathrm{P}(H \text{ and } 5) = \mathrm{P}(H) \times \mathrm{P}(5, \text{ given } H). \tag{2.2}$$

That is, the long-run proportion of pairs of trials in which both H and 5 occur is equal to the long-run proportion of trials in which H occurs on the coin, multiplied by the long-run proportion *of those trials* which occur with 5 on the die.

In this particular example, there would be no reason to suppose that the probability of 5 on the die was in the least affected by whether or not H occurred on the coin. In other words,

$$\mathrm{P}(5, \text{ given } H) = \mathrm{P}(5).$$

The two events are now said to be *independent*, and we have the *simple form of the multiplication rule*:

$$\begin{aligned}\mathrm{P}(H \text{ and } 5) &= \mathrm{P}(H) \times \mathrm{P}(5)\\ &= \tfrac{1}{2} \times \tfrac{1}{6}\\ &= \tfrac{1}{12}.\end{aligned}$$

Effectively, in this example, there are 12 combinations which occur equally often in the long run: $H1, H2, \ldots, H6, T1, T2, \ldots, T6$.

In general, pairs of events need not be independent, and the general form of the multiplication rule (2.2) must be used. In the earlier example we referred to the probability of a doctor being male and having qualified in England. If these events were independent, we could calculate this as

$$0{\cdot}8 \times 0{\cdot}6 = 0{\cdot}48,$$

and, denoting the events by A and B, (2.1) would give

$$\begin{aligned}\mathrm{P}(A \text{ or } B \text{ or both}) &= 0{\cdot}80 + 0{\cdot}60 - 0{\cdot}48\\ &= 0{\cdot}92.\end{aligned}$$

These events may not be independent, however, since some medical schools are more likely to accept women than others. The correct value for $\mathrm{P}(A \text{ and } B)$ could only be ascertained by direct investigation.

As another example of the lack of independence, suppose that in a certain large community 30 per cent of individuals have blue eyes. Then

$$\mathrm{P}(\text{blue right eye}) = 0{\cdot}3$$

and

$$\text{P(blue left eye)} = 0{\cdot}3.$$

P(blue right eye and blue left eye) is *not* given by

$$\text{P(blue right eye)} \times \text{P(blue left eye)} = 0{\cdot}09.$$

It is obtained by the general formula (2.2) as

$$\begin{aligned}\text{P(blue right eye)} \times \text{P(blue left eye, given blue right eye)}\\ = 0{\cdot}3 \times 1{\cdot}0\\ = 0{\cdot}3.\end{aligned}$$

Addition and multiplication may be combined in the same calculation. In the double sequence with a coin and a die, what is the probability of getting either heads and 2 *or* tails and 4? Each of these combinations has probability $\frac{1}{12}$ (by the multiplication rule for independent events). Each combination is a possible outcome in the double sequence and the outcomes are mutually exclusive. The two probabilities of $\frac{1}{12}$ may therefore be added to give a final probability of $\frac{1}{6}$ that either one or the other combination occurs.

As a slightly more complicated example, consider the sex composition of families of four children. As an approximation, let us assume that the proportion of males at birth is 0·51, that all the children in the families may be considered as independent random selections from a sequence in which the probability of a boy is 0·51, and that the question relates to all live-born infants so that differential survival does not concern us. The question is, what are the probabilities that a family of four contains no boys, one boy, two boys, three boys and four boys?

The probability that there will be no boys is the probability that each of the four children will be a girl. The probability that the first child is a girl is $1-0{\cdot}51=0{\cdot}49$. By successive applications of the multiplication rule for independent events, the probability that the first two are girls is $(0{\cdot}49)^2$; the probability that the first three are girls is $(0{\cdot}49)^3$; and the probability that all four are girls is $(0{\cdot}49)^4=0{\cdot}0576$. About 1 in 17 of all families of four will consist of four girls. Write this

$$\text{P}(GGGG) = 0{\cdot}0576.$$

A family with one boy and three girls might arise in any of the following ways: *BGGG*, *GBGG*, *GGBG*, *GGGB*, according to which of the four children is the boy. Each of these ways has a probability of $(0{\cdot}49)^3(0{\cdot}51)=0{\cdot}0600$. The total probability of one boy is therefore, by the addition rule,

$$0{\cdot}0600+0{\cdot}0600+0{\cdot}0600+0{\cdot}0600$$
$$=4(0{\cdot}0600)=0{\cdot}2400.$$

A family with two boys and two girls might arise in any of the following ways: *BBGG, BGBG, BGGB, GBBG, GBGB, GGBB.* Each of these has a probability of $(0{\cdot}49)^2(0{\cdot}51)^2$, and the total probability of two boys is

$$6(0{\cdot}49)^2(0{\cdot}51)^2=0{\cdot}3747.$$

Similarly for the other family composition types. The complete results are shown in Table 2.1.

TABLE 2.1 Calculation of probabilities of families with various sex composition.

Composition Boys	Girls	Probability
0	4	$(0{\cdot}49)^4=0{\cdot}0576$
1	3	$4(0{\cdot}49)^3(0{\cdot}51)=0{\cdot}2400$
2	2	$6(0{\cdot}49)^2(0{\cdot}51)^2=0{\cdot}3747$
3	1	$4(0{\cdot}49)(0{\cdot}51)^3=0{\cdot}2600$
4	0	$(0{\cdot}51)^4=0{\cdot}0677$
		1·0000

Note that the five probabilities total to 1, as they should since this total is the probability that one or other of the five family composition types arises (these being mutually exclusive). Since these five types exhaust all the possibilities, the total probability must be unity. If one examined the records of a very large number of families experiencing four live births, would the proportions of the five types be close to the values shown in the last column? Rather close, perhaps, but it would not be surprising to find some slight but systematic discrepancies because the formal assumptions underlying our argument may not be strictly correct. For one thing, the probability of a male birth may vary slightly from family to family (as pointed out in section 2.1). More importantly, families which start in an unbalanced way, with several births of the same sex, are more likely to be continued than those which are better balanced. The first two births in families which are continued to the third stage will then not be representative of all two-birth families.

A similar bias may exist in the progression from two births to three. The extent of these biases would be expected to differ from one community to another, and this seems to be borne out by actual data, some of which agree more closely than others with the theoretical probabilities.

2.3 PROBABILITY DISTRIBUTIONS

Table 2.1 provides our first example of a *probability distribution*. That is, it shows how the total probability, equal to 1, is distributed among the different types of family. A variable, the different values of which follow a probability distribution, is known as a *random variable*. In Table 2.1 the number of boys in a family is a random variable. So is the number of girls.

If the random variable can be associated with different points on a scale the probability distribution can be represented visually by a histogram, just as for frequency distributions. We shall consider first some examples of ungrouped discrete random variables. Here the vertical scale of the histogram measures the probability for each value of the random variable, and each probability is represented by a vertical line.

Example 2.1

In repeated tosses of an unbiased coin, the outcome is a random variable with two values, H and T. Each value has a probability $\frac{1}{2}$. The distribution is shown in Fig. 2.2, where the two outcomes, H and T, are allotted to arbitrary points on the horizontal axis.

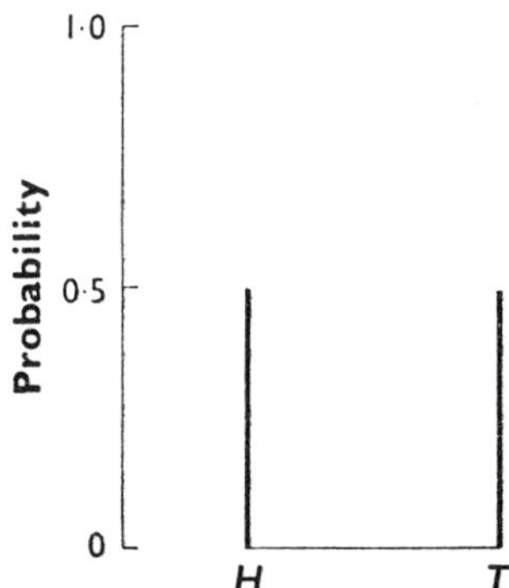

FIG. 2.2 Probability distribution for random variable with two values; the results of tossing a coin with equal probabilities of heads and tails.

Example 2.2

In a genetic experiment we may cross two heterozygotes with genotypes *Aa*; (that is, at a particular gene locus, each parent has one gene of type *A* and one of type *a*). The progeny will be homozygotes (*aa* or *AA*) or heterozygotes (*Aa*), with the probabilities shown below.

Genotype	No. of *A* genes in genotype	Probability
aa	0	$\frac{1}{4}$
Aa	1	$\frac{1}{2}$
AA	2	$\frac{1}{4}$
		1

The three genotypes may be allotted to points on a scale by using as a random variable the number of *A* genes in the description of the genotype. This random variable takes the values 0, 1 and 2, and the probability distribution is depicted in Fig. 2.3.

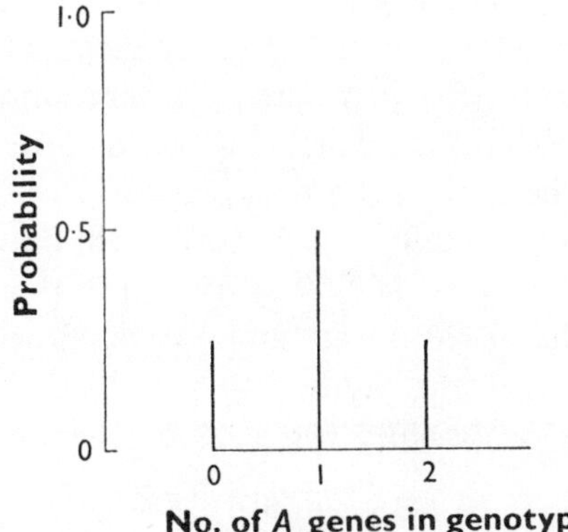

FIG. 2.3 Probability distribution for random variable with three values; the number of *A* genes in the genotype of progeny of an $Aa \times Aa$ cross.

Example 2.3

A third example is provided by the characterization of families of four children by the number of boys. The probabilities, in the particular numerical case considered in section 2.2, are given in Table 2.1, and they are depicted in Fig. 2.4.

When the random variable is continuous it is of little use to refer to the probabilities of particular values of the variable, because these probabilities are in general zero. For example, the probability that the

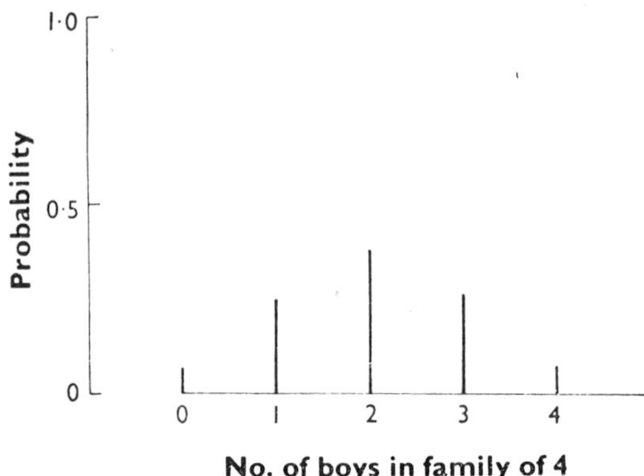

FIG. 2.4 Probability distribution of number of boys in family of 4 children if male births occur independently with probability 0·51 (Table 2.1).

exact height of a male adult is 70 in. is zero, because in the virtually infinite population of exact heights of adult males a negligible proportion will be exactly 70 in. If, however, we consider a small interval centred at 70 in., say $70-h$ to $70+h$, where h is very small, there will be a small non-zero probability associated with this interval. Furthermore, the probability will be very nearly proportional to h. Thus, the probability of a height between 69·98 and 70·02 in. will be very nearly double the probability for the interval 69·99 to 70·01. It is therefore a reasonable representation of the situation to suppose that there is a *probability density* characteristic of the value 70 in., which can be denoted by $f(70)$, such that the probability for a small interval $70-h$ to $70+h$ is very close to

$$2hf(70).$$

The probability distribution for a continuous random variable, x, can therefore be depicted by a graph of the probability density $f(x)$ against x, as in Fig. 2.5. This is, in fact, the frequency curve discussed in section 1.4. The reader familiar with the calculus will recognize $f(x)$ as the derivative with respect to x of the probability $F(x)$ that the random variable assumes a value less than or equal to x. $F(x)$ is called the *distribution function* and is represented by the area underneath the curve in Fig. 2.5 from the left end of the distribution (which may be at minus infinity) up to the value x. The distribution function corresponding to the density function of Fig. 2.5 is shown in Fig. 2.6. Note that the height of the density function is proportional to the slope of the distribution function; in the present example both these quantities are zero at

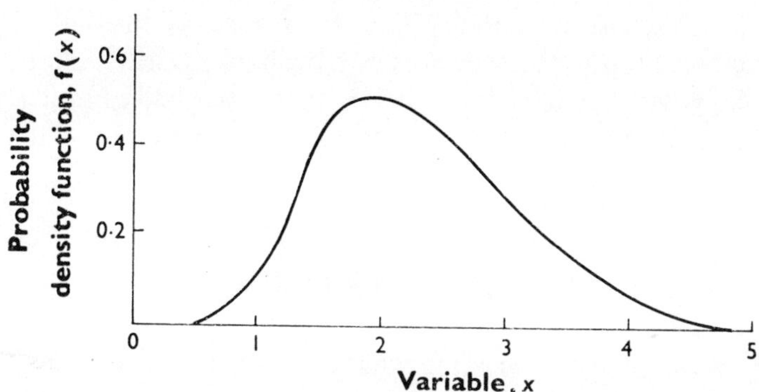

FIG. 2.5 Probability density function for a continuous random variable.

the lower and upper extremes of the variables and attain a maximum at an intermediate point.

The shape of a probability distribution may be characterized by the features already used for frequency distributions. In particular, we may be concerned with the number and position of the modes, the values of the random variable at which the probability, or (for con-

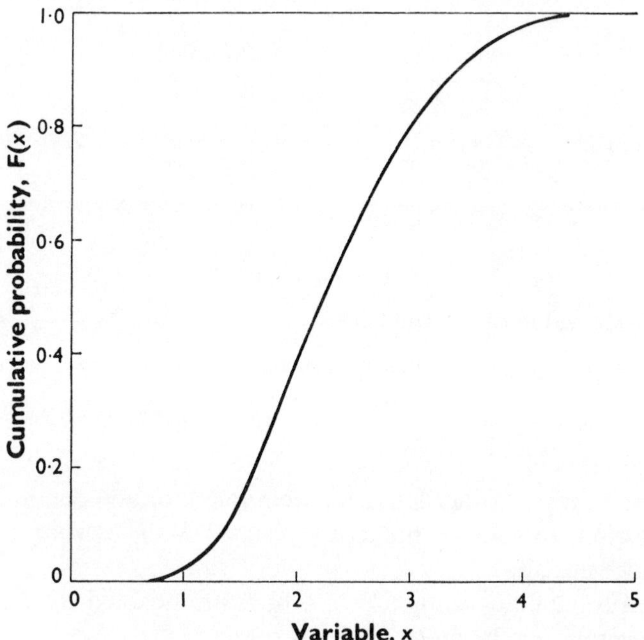

FIG. 2.6 Distribution function corresponding to the density function shown in Fig. 2.5.

tinuous variables) the probability density, reaches a maximum. We may be interested too in the skewness of a probability distribution.

By analogy with sections 1.5 and 1.6 we are particularly interested in the mean and standard deviation of a random variable, and these concepts are discussed in the next section.

2.4 EXPECTATION

There is some difficulty in deciding what is meant by the phrase 'mean of a random variable'. The mean has been defined earlier only for a finite number, n, of observations. With a probability distribution such as that in Table 2.1 the number of observations must be thought of as infinite. How, then, is the mean to be calculated?

Suppose n is very large: so large that the relative frequencies of the different values of a discrete random variable like that in Table 2.1 can be taken to be very nearly equal to the probabilities. If they were exactly equal to the probabilities, the frequency distribution of the number of boys would be as follows:

x No. of boys	Frequency
0	$0{\cdot}0576n$
1	$0{\cdot}2400n$
2	$0{\cdot}3747n$
3	$0{\cdot}2600n$
4	$0{\cdot}0677n$
	n

The mean value of x would be

$$\frac{(0\times 0{\cdot}0576n)+(1\times 0{\cdot}2400n)+(2\times 0{\cdot}3747n)+(3\times 0{\cdot}2600n)+(4\times 0{\cdot}0677n)}{n}.$$

The factor n may be cancelled from the numerator and denominator of the expression, to give the numerical result 2·04. The arbitrary sample size, n, does not appear.

If the probabilities of 0, 1, . . ., 4 boys are denoted by P_0, P_1, . . ., P_4, the formula for the mean is clearly

$$(0\times P_0)+(1\times P_1)+(2\times P_2)+(3\times P_3)+(4\times P_4).$$

In general, if x is a discrete random variable taking values $x_0, x_1, x_2, \ldots$ with probabilities $P_0, P_1, P_2, \ldots$, the mean value of x is calculated as

$$\sum_i x_i P_i. \tag{2.3}$$

The mean value of a random variable, calculated in this way, is often called the *expected value*, *mathematical expectation*, or simply the *expectation* of x, and the operation involved (multiplying each value of x by its probability, and then adding) is denoted by $E(x)$. The expectation of a random variable is often allotted a Greek symbol like μ (lower case Greek letter 'mu'), to distinguish it from a mean value calculated from a finite number of observations (denoted usually by symbols such as $\bar{x}$ or $\bar{y}$).

As a second example, consider the probability distribution of x, the number of A genes in the genotypes shown in Example 2.2. Here,

$$\begin{aligned} E(x) &= (0 \times 0{\cdot}25) + (1 \times 0{\cdot}50) + (2 \times 0{\cdot}25) \\ &= 1. \end{aligned}$$

If x follows a continuous distribution the formula given above for $E(x)$ cannot be used. However, one could consider a discrete distribution in which possible values of x differed by a small interval $2h$. To any value X_0 we could allot the probability given by the continuous distribution for values of x between $X_0 - h$ and $X_0 + h$ (which, as we have seen, will be close to $2hf(x)$ if h is small enough). The expectation of x in this discrete distribution can be calculated by our general rule. As the interval h gets smaller and smaller, the discrete distribution will approach more and more closely the continuous distribution, and in general the expectation will approach a quantity which formally is given by the expression

$$\mu = \int_{-\infty}^{\infty} xf(x)\, dx.$$

This provides a definition of the expectation of x for a continuous distribution.

The *variance* of a random variable is defined as

$$E(x - \mu)^2;$$

that is, as the expectation of the squared difference from the mean. This is an obvious development from the previous formula $\sum (x_i - \bar{x})^2/n$ for the variance of a finite number, n, of observations, since this quantity is the mean value of the squared difference from the sample mean, $\bar{x}$.

The distinction between the divisor of n and that of $n-1$ becomes of no importance when we are dealing with probability distributions since n is effectively infinite.

The variance of a random variable is customarily given the symbol σ^2 (σ being the lower case Greek letter 'sigma'). The standard deviation is again defined as σ, the square root of the variance.

By analogy with the short-cut formula for the sample variance (section 1.6), we shall find it convenient to use the following relationship:

$$\sigma^2 = \text{E}(x^2) - \mu^2.$$

The proof* is as follows:

$$\begin{aligned}\sigma^2 &= \text{E}(x-\mu)^2 \\ &= \text{E}(x^2 - 2x\mu + \mu^2) \\ &= \text{E}(x^2) - 2\mu\,\text{E}(x) + \mu^2 \\ &= \text{E}(x^2) - 2\mu^2 + \mu^2 \\ &= \text{E}(x^2) - \mu^2. \qquad (2.4)\end{aligned}$$

The two formulae for the variance may be illustrated by the distribution in Example 2.2, for which we have already obtained $\mu = 1$. With the direct formula, we proceed as follows:

x	P	$x-\mu$	$(x-\mu)^2$
0	0·25	−1	1
1	0·50	0	0
2	0·25	1	1

$$\begin{aligned}\sigma^2 &= \text{E}(x-\mu)^2 \\ &= (1\times 0{\cdot}25) + (0\times 0{\cdot}50) + (1\times 0{\cdot}25) \\ &= 0{\cdot}5.\end{aligned}$$

With the short-cut formula,

x	P	x^2
0	0·25	0
1	0·50	1
2	0·25	4

* Note that in this proof we make use of some properties of the expectation which are intuitively acceptable, but which we shall not attempt to prove rigorously: (a) in going from the second to the third line, the expectation of a sum (or difference) of two random variables is the sum (or difference) of their expectations; (b) in treating the middle term on the third line, the expectation of a constant times a random variable is equal to the constant times the expectation.

$$
\begin{aligned}
E(x^2) &= (0\times 0{\cdot}25)+(1\times 0{\cdot}50)+(4\times 0{\cdot}25)\\
&= 1{\cdot}5;\\
\sigma^2 &= E(x^2)-\mu^2\\
&= 1{\cdot}5-1^2\\
&= 0{\cdot}5, \text{ as before.}
\end{aligned}
$$

2.5 THE BINOMIAL DISTRIBUTION

We have already met a particular case of this form of distribution in the example of section 2.2 on the sex-distribution in families of four.

In general, suppose we have a random sequence in which the outcome of each individual trial is of one of two types, A or B, these outcomes occurring with probabilities π and $1-\pi$, respectively. (The symbol π, the lower case Greek letter 'pi', is used merely as a convenient Greek letter and has no connection at all with the mathematical constant $\pi = 3{\cdot}14159\ldots$). In the previous example, A and B were boys and girls, and π was $0{\cdot}51$.

Consider now a group of n observations from this random sequence (in the example $n=4$). It will be convenient to refer to each such group as a 'sample' of n observations. What is the probability distribution of the number of A's in the sample? This number we shall call r, and clearly r must be one of the numbers 0, 1, 2, . . ., $n-1$, n. Define also $p=r/n$, the *proportion* of A's in the sample, and $q=(n-r)/n=1-p$, the proportion of B's.

As in the example, we argue that the probability of r A's and $n-r$ B's is

$$\pi^r(1-\pi)^{n-r}$$

multiplied by the number of ways in which one can choose r out of the n sample members to receive a label 'A'. This multiplying factor is called a *binomial coefficient*. In the example the binomial coefficients were worked out by simple enumeration, but clearly this could be tedious with large values of n and r. The binomial coefficient is usually denoted by

$$\binom{n}{r} \quad \text{(referred to in speaking as '}n\text{ binomial }r\text{')}$$

or

$$^{n}C_{r}.$$

Tables of binomial coefficients are provided in most books of mathematical tables. For moderate values of n and r they can be calculated directly from the formula

$$\binom{n}{r}=\frac{n(n-1)(n-2)\ldots(n-r+1)}{1.2.3.\ldots.r} \tag{2.5}$$

(where the single dots are multiplication signs and the rows mean that all the intervening integers are used). The quantity $1.2.3\ldots r$ is called 'factorial r' or 'r factorial' and is usually written $r!$ Since the expression $n(n-1)\ldots(n-r+1)$, which occurs in the numerator of $\binom{n}{r}$ can be written as $\frac{n!}{(n-r)!}$, it follows that

$$\binom{n}{r}=\frac{n!}{r!\,(n-r)!}. \tag{2.6}$$

This formula involves unnecessarily heavy multiplication, but it draws attention to the symmetry of the binomial coefficients:

$$\binom{n}{r}=\binom{n}{n-r}. \tag{2.7}$$

This is, indeed, obvious from the definition. Any selection of r objects out of n is automatically a selection of the $n-r$ objects which remain.

If we put $r=0$ in (2.5), both the numerator and the denominator are meaningless. Putting $r=n$ would give

$$\binom{n}{n}=\frac{n!}{n!}=1,$$

and it would accord with the symmetry result to put

$$\binom{n}{0}=1. \tag{2.8}$$

This is clearly the correct result, since there is precisely one way of selecting 0 objects out of n to be labelled as A's: namely to select all the n objects to be labelled as B's. Note that (2.8) accords with (2.6) if we agree to call $0!=1$; this is merely a convention since $0!$ is strictly not covered by our previous definition of the factorial, but it provides a useful extension of the definition which is used generally in mathematics.

The binomial coefficients required in the example of section 2.2

could have been obtained from (2.5) as follows:

$$\binom{4}{0}=1$$

$$\binom{4}{1}=\frac{4}{1}=4$$

$$\binom{4}{2}=\frac{4.3}{1.2}=6$$

$$\binom{4}{3}=\frac{4.3.2}{1.2.3}=4$$

$$\binom{4}{4}=\frac{4.3.2.1}{1.2.3.4}=1.$$

A useful way to obtain binomial coefficients for small values of n, without any multiplication, is by means of Pascal's triangle:

n	
	1
1	1 1
2	1 2 1
3	1 3 3 1
4	1 4 6 4 1
5	1 5 10 10 5 1
etc.	etc.

In this triangle of numbers, which can be extended downwards indefinitely, each entry is obtained as the sum of the two adjacent numbers on the line above. Thus, in the fifth row (for $n=4$),

$$4=1+3, \quad 6=3+3, \quad \text{etc.}$$

Along each row are the binomial coefficients

$$\binom{n}{0}, \binom{n}{1}, \quad \ldots \text{ up to } \binom{n}{n-1}, \binom{n}{n}.$$

The probability that the sample of n individuals contains r A's and $n-r$ B's, then, is

$$\binom{n}{r} \pi^r(1-\pi)^{n-r}. \qquad (2.9)$$

If this expression is evaluated for each value of r from 0 to n, the sum of these $n+1$ values will represent the probability of obtaining 0 A's *or* 1 A *or* 2 A's etc. up to n A's. These are the only possible results from the whole sequence and they are mutually exclusive; the sum of the probabilities is, therefore, 1. That this is so follows algebraically from the classical binomial theorem, for

$$\begin{aligned}\binom{n}{0}\pi^0(1-\pi)^n+\binom{n}{1}\pi^1(1-\pi)^{n-1}+\ldots+\binom{n}{n}\pi^n(1-\pi)^0 &= \{\pi+(1-\pi)\}^n \\ &= 1^n \\ &= 1.\end{aligned}$$

This result was verified in the particular example of Table 2.1.

The expectation and variance of r can now be obtained by applying the general formulae (2.3) and (2.4) to the probability distribution (2.9) and using standard algebraic results on the summation of series. We shall defer a proof until we can apply some general results given in Chapter 3, and merely give the results here:

$$E(r)=n\pi \tag{2.10}$$

and

$$\text{var}(r)=n\pi(1-\pi). \tag{2.11}$$

The formula for the expectation is intuitively acceptable. The mean number of A's is equal to the number of observations multiplied by the probability that an individual result is an A. The expectation of the number of boys out of four, in our previous example, was shown in section 2.4 to be 2·04. We now see that this result could have been obtained from (2.10):

$$E(r)=4\times 0{\cdot}51=2{\cdot}04.$$

The formula (2.11) for the variance is less obvious. For a given value of n, var(r) reaches a maximum value when $\pi=1-\pi=\frac{1}{2}$ (when var(r)$=\frac{1}{4}n$), and falls off markedly as π approaches 0 or 1. If π is very small the factor $1-\pi$ in (2.11) is very close to 1, and var(r) becomes very close to $n\pi$, the value of E(r).

We shall often be interested in the probability distribution of p, the *proportion* of A's in the sample. Now $p=r\times(1/n)$, and the multiplying factor $1/n$ is constant from one sample to another. It follows that

$$E(p)=E(r)\times(1/n)=\pi \tag{2.12}$$

and

$$\text{var}(p)=\text{var}(r)\times(1/n)^2=\frac{\pi(1-\pi)}{n}. \tag{2.13}$$

The square in the multiplying factor for the variance arises because the units in which the variance is measured are the squares of the units of the random variable.

It will sometimes be convenient to refer to the standard deviations of r or of p. These are the square roots of the corresponding variances:

$$\mathrm{SD}(r) = \sqrt{\{n\pi(1-\pi)\}} \quad \text{and} \quad \mathrm{SD}(p) = \sqrt{\left\{\frac{\pi(1-\pi)}{n}\right\}}.$$

Some further properties of the binomial distribution are given in section 3.3. A brief table of the probabilities for various values of π and n is in Pearson and Hartley (1966; Table 37). Fuller tables for $n \leqslant 25$ are given by Owen (1962; Table 9.5); for $n < 50$ by National Bureau of Standards (1950); and for $50 \leqslant n \leqslant 100$ by Romig (1947).

Example 2.4

In an investigation of the extent to which doctors agree in the recording of physical signs, n doctors each record the presence or absence of a certain physical sign on each of k subjects. How might one measure the extent of agreement?

If the doctors agreed completely they would unanimously record the sign as present in certain patients and absent in others. The number of positive findings for each subject, r, would, therefore, be either 0 or n. If, on the other hand, the doctors disagreed considerably about each subject, the values of r obtained for different subjects would be more nearly equal. It would be surprising if they were exactly equal, because even if the doctors showed no skill at all, guessing entirely at random, there would be some purely random variation in r from one subject to another. A reasonable measure of observer agreement, then, would be the standard deviation of r. If the observers guessed at random, with a probability π of a positive finding for any patient, the standard deviation of r, over a large series of subjects, would be $\sqrt{\{n\pi(1-\pi)\}}$. In practice we should not know π, but it might be reasonable to estimate this by p, the observed proportion of positive findings in the whole series of nk observations. The maximum value of SD(r) will occur when each value of r is 0 or n, and may be shown to be about $n\sqrt{\{p(1-p)\}}$, as compared with the binomial value $\sqrt{\{np(1-p)\}}$.

In an investigation of agreement in the recording of respiratory signs, with $k=20$ and $n=9$, three signs showed about the same value of p:

	p	SD(r)	$\sqrt{\{np(1-p)\}}$	$n\sqrt{\{p(1-p)\}}$
Tachypnoea	0·156	2·27	1·09	3·27
Dyspnoea	0·150	2·05	1·07	3·22
Clubbing	0·156	3·15	1·09	3·27

Tachypnoea and dyspnoea gave a standard deviation about mid-way between the 'chance' value and the maximum value. The standard deviation for clubbing, in contrast, was very near the maximum value possible for the observed value of p. The limited experience of this investigation suggests that the recording of clubbing produces better agreement among the observers than that of either of the other two signs.

TABLE 2.2 Distribution of number of dominant genes at five loci, in crosses between parents heterozygous for each factor and those homozygous recessive for each (Lancaster, 1965).

Number of dominant genes	Number of offspring Observed	Expected
0	17	17·2
1	81	86·1
2	152	172·2
3	180	172·2
4	104	86·1
5	17	17·2
	551	551·0

Example 2.5

Table 2.2 is given by Lancaster (1965) from data published by Roberts *et al.* (1939). These authors observed 551 crosses between rats, with one parent heterozygous for each of five factors and the other parent homozygous recessive for each. The distribution is that of the number of dominant genes, out of five, for each offspring. The theoretical distribution is the binomial with $n=5$ and $\pi=\frac{1}{2}$, and the 'expected' frequencies, obtained by multiplying the binomial probabilities by 551, are shown in the table. The agreement between observed and expected frequencies is satisfactory.

The binomial distribution is characterized by the parameters* π and n. Fig. 2.7 illustrates the shape of the distribution for various combinations of π and n. Note that for a particular value of n, the distribution

* Variables which partly or wholly characterize a probability distribution are known as *parameters*.

is symmetrical for $\pi = \frac{1}{2}$ and asymmetrical for $\pi < \frac{1}{2}$ or $\pi > \frac{1}{2}$; and that for a particular value of π the asymmetry decreases as n increases.

Statistical methods based on the binomial distribution are described in detail in sections 4.4, 4.7, 4.8, and 7.4.

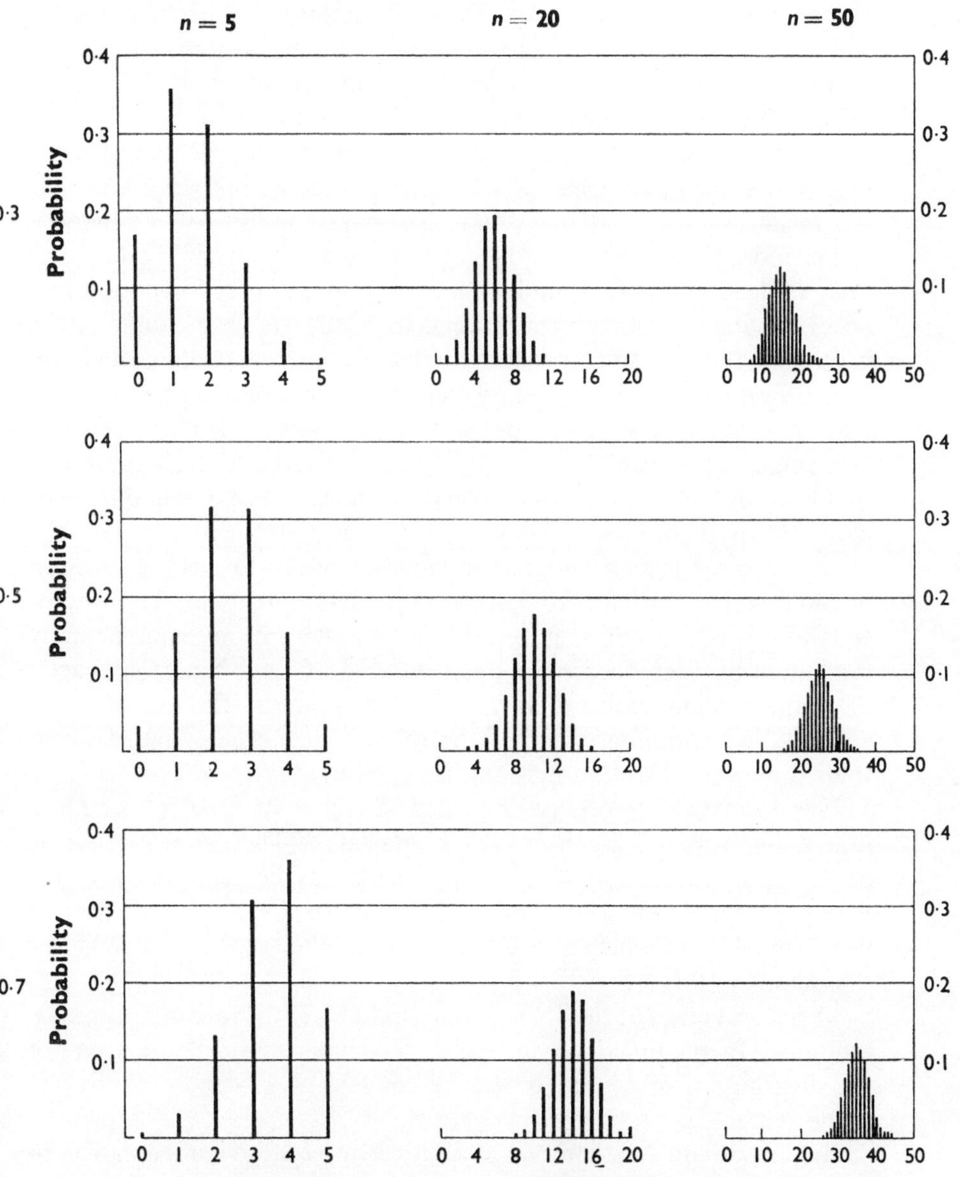

FIG. 2.7 Binomial distribution for various values of π and n. The horizontal scale in each diagram shows values of r.

2.6 THE POISSON DISTRIBUTION

This distribution is named after S.D.Poisson, a French mathematician (1781–1840). It is sometimes useful as a limiting form of the binomial, but it is important also in its own right as a distribution arising when events of some sort occur randomly in time, or when small particles are distributed randomly in space.

We shall consider first random events in time. Suppose that a certain type of event occurs repeatedly, with an average rate of λ per unit time but in an entirely random fashion. To make the idea of randomness rather more precise we can postulate that in any very small interval of time of length h (say 1 milli-second) the probability that an event occurs is approximately proportional to h, say λh. (For example, if h is doubled the very small probability that the interval contains an event is also doubled.) The probability that the interval contains more than one event is supposed to be proportionately smaller and smaller as h gets smaller, and can therefore be ignored. Furthermore, we suppose that what happens in any small interval is independent of what happens in any other small interval which does not overlap the first.

A very good instance of this probability model is that of the emission of radio-active particles from some radio-active material. The rate of emission, λ, will be constant, but the particles will be emitted in a purely random way, each successive small interval of time being on exactly the same footing, rather than in a regular pattern. The model is the analogy, in continuous time, of the random sequence of independent trials discussed in section 2.1, and is called the *Poisson process*.

Suppose that we observe repeated stretches of time, of length T time units, from a Poisson process with a rate λ. The number of events occurring in an interval of length T, which may be denoted by x, will vary from one interval to another. In fact, it is a random variable the possible values of which are 0, 1, 2, . . . etc. What is the probability of a particular value x?

A natural guess at the value of x would be λT, the rate of occurrence multiplied by the time interval. We shall see later that λT is the mean of the distribution of x, and it will be convenient to denote λT by the single symbol μ.

Let us split any one interval of length T into a large number n of sub-intervals each of length T/n (Fig. 2.8). Then, if n is sufficiently large, the number of events in the sub-interval will almost always be 0, will occasionally be 1, and will hardly ever be more than 1. The situation is therefore almost exactly the same as a sequence of n binomial trials (a trial being the observation of a sub-interval), in each of which there is a probability $\lambda(T/n)=\mu/n$ of there being an event, and $1-\mu/n$ of there

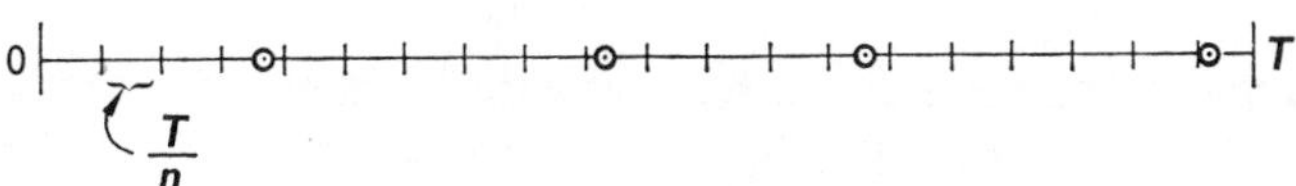

FIG. 2.8 The occurrence of events in a Poisson process, with the time scale subdivided into small intervals.

being no event. The probability that the whole series of n trials provides exactly x events is, in this approximation, given by the binomial distribution:

$$\frac{n(n-1)\ldots(n-x+1)}{x!}\left(\frac{\mu}{n}\right)^x\left(1-\frac{\mu}{n}\right)^{n-x}. \qquad (2.14)$$

Now, this binomial approximation will get better and better as n increases. What happens to (2.14) as n increases indefinitely? We can replace

$$n(n-1)\ldots(n-x+1)$$

by n^x since x will be negligible in comparison with n. Similarly we can replace $(1-\mu/n)^{n-x}$ by $(1-\mu/n)^n$ since $(1-\mu/n)^x$ will approach 1 as n increases. It is a standard mathematical result that as n increases indefinitely, $(1-\mu/n)^n$ approaches $e^{-\mu}$, where e is the base of natural (or Napierian) logarithms ($e=2{\cdot}718\ldots$).

Finally, then, in the limit as n increase indefinitely, the probability of x events approaches

$$P_x=\frac{n^x}{x!}\left(\frac{\mu}{n}\right)^x e^{-\mu}=\frac{\mu^x e^{-\mu}}{x!}. \qquad (2.15)$$

The expression (2.15) defines the Poisson probability distribution. The random variable x takes the values 0, 1, 2, ... with the successive probabilities obtained by putting these values of x in (2.15). Thus,

$$P_0=e^{-\mu}$$

$$P_1=\mu e^{-\mu}$$

$$P_2=\tfrac{1}{2}\,\mu^2 e^{-\mu}, \text{ etc.}$$

Note that, for $x=0$, we replace $x!$ in (2.15) by the value 1, as was found to be appropriate for the binomial distribution. To verify that the sum of the probabilities is 1,

$$P_0+P_1+P_2+\ldots=e^{-\mu}(1+\mu+\tfrac{1}{2}\mu^2+\ldots)$$
$$=e^{-\mu}\times e^{\mu}$$
$$=1,$$

the replacement of the infinite series on the right hand side by e^{μ} being a standard mathematical result.

Before proceeding to further consideration of the properties of the Poisson distribution, we may note that a similar derivation may be applied to the situation in which particles are randomly distributed in space. If the space is one-dimensional (for instance the length of a cotton

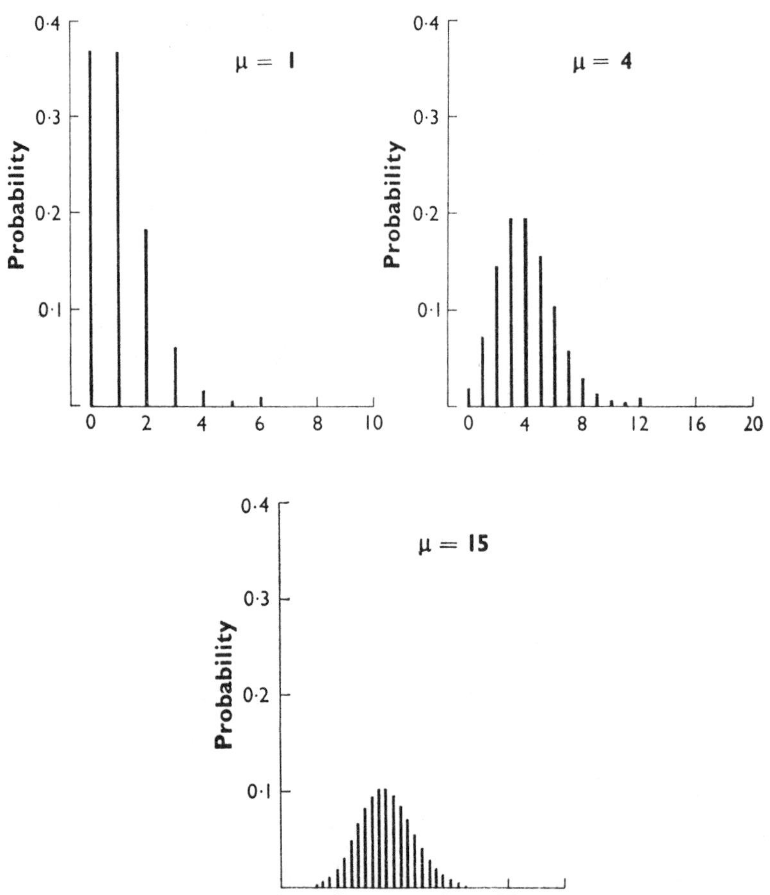

FIG. 2.9 Poisson distribution for various values of μ. The horizontal scale in each diagram shows values of x.

thread along which flaws may occur with constant probability at all points) the analogy is immediate. With two-dimensional space (for instance a microscopic slide over which bacteria are distributed at random with perfect mixing technique) the total area of size A may be divided into a large number n of sub-divisions each of area A/n; the argument then carries through with A replacing T. Similarly, with three-dimensional space (bacteria well-mixed in a fluid suspension), the total volume V is divided into n small volumes of size V/n. In all these situations the model envisages particles distributed at random with density λ per unit length [area or volume]. The number of particles found in a length [area or volume] of size $l[A$ or $V]$ will follow the Poisson distribution (2.15) where the parameter $\mu = \lambda l[\lambda A$ or $\lambda V]$.

The shapes of the distribution for $\mu = 1$, 4 and 15 are shown in Fig. 2.9. Note that for $\mu = 1$ the distribution is very skew, for $\mu = 4$ the skewness is much less and for $\mu = 15$ it is almost absent.

The distribution (2.15) is determined entirely by the one parameter μ. It follows that all the features of the distribution in which one might be interested are functions only of μ. In particular the mean and variance must be functions of μ. The mean is

$$\begin{aligned}
\mathrm{E}(x) &= \sum_{x=0}^{\infty} x P_x \\
&= \sum_{x=0}^{\infty} \frac{x\mu^x e^{-\mu}}{x!} \\
&= \sum_{x=1}^{\infty} \frac{\mu^x e^{-\mu}}{(x-1)!} \quad \text{since} \quad \frac{x}{x!} = \frac{1}{(x-1)!}
\end{aligned}$$

and the term in the summation corresponding to $x = 0$ is zero.

$$\begin{aligned}
\mathrm{E}(x) &= \mu \sum_{x=1}^{\infty} \frac{\mu^{x-1} e^{-\mu}}{(x-1)!} \\
&= \mu \sum_{i=0}^{\infty} \frac{\mu^i e^{-\mu}}{i!}, \quad \text{putting} \quad i = x-1 \\
&= \mu,
\end{aligned}$$

since the summation contains all the terms of the Poisson distribution which sum to 1.

To find the variance, which by the short-cut formula is $\mathrm{E}(x^2) - \mu^2$, we first find $E\{x(x-1)\}=E(x^2)-E(x)$.

$$\begin{aligned} E\{x(x-1)\} &= \sum_{x=0}^{\infty} x(x-1)P_x \\ &= \mu^2 \sum_{x=2}^{\infty} \frac{\mu^{x-2}e^{-\mu}}{(x-2)!} \\ &= \mu^2 \end{aligned}$$

by the same sort of argument as before. Thus,

$$E(x^2)-E(x)=\mu^2,$$

$$\begin{aligned} E(x^2) &= \mu^2+E(x) \\ &= \mu^2+\mu \end{aligned}$$

and

$$\begin{aligned} \text{var}(x)=E(x^2)-\mu^2 &= (\mu^2+\mu)-\mu^2 \\ &= \mu. \end{aligned} \tag{2.16}$$

Thus, the variance of x, like the mean, is equal to μ. The standard deviation is therefore $\sqrt{\mu}$.

Much use is made of the Poisson distribution in bacteriology. To estimate the density of live organisms in a suspension the bacteriologist may dilute the suspension by a factor of, say, 10^{-5}, take samples of, say, 1 cm^3 in a pipette and drop the contents of the pipette on to a plate containing a nutrient medium on which the bacteria grow. After some time each organism dropped on to the plate will have formed a colony and these colonies can be counted. If the original suspension was well-mixed, the volumes sampled are accurately determined and the medium is uniformly adequate to sustain growth, the number of colonies in a large series of plates could be expected to follow a Poisson distribution. The mean colony count per plate, $\bar{x}$, is an estimate of the mean number of bacteria per 10^{-5} cm^3 of the original suspension, and a knowledge of the theoretical properties of the Poisson distribution permits one to measure the precision of this estimate (see sections 4.9, 7.7).

Similarly for total counts of live and dead organisms, repeated samples of constant volume may be examined under the microscope and the organisms counted directly.

Example 2.6

As an example, Table 2.3 shows a distribution observed during a count of the root nodule bacteria (*Rhizobium trifolii*) in a Petroff-Hausser counting chamber. The 'expected' frequencies are obtained by calculating the mean

TABLE 2.3 Distribution of counts of root nodule bacterium (*Rhizobium trifolii*) in a Petroff-Hausser counting chamber. (Data from Wilson and Kullman, 1931).

Number of bacteria per square	Number of squares Observed	Expected
0	34	32·8
1	68	82·1
2	112	102·6
3	94	85·5
4	55	53·4
5	21	26·7
6	12	11·1
7–	4	5·7
	400	399·9

number of organisms per square, $\bar{x}$, from the frequency distribution (giving $\bar{x}=2{\cdot}50$) and calculating the probabilities P_x of the Poisson distribution with μ replaced by $\bar{x}$. The expected frequencies are then given by $400P_x$. The observed and expected frequencies agree quite well. This organism normally produces gum and therefore clumps readily. Under these circumstances one would not expect a Poisson distribution, but the data in Table 2.3 were collected to show the effectiveness of a method of overcoming the clumping.

In the derivation of the Poisson distribution use was made of the fact that the binomial distribution with a large n and small π is an approximation to the Poisson with mean $\mu=n\pi$.

Conversely, when the correct distribution is a binomial with large n and small π, one can approximate this by a Poisson with mean $n\pi$. For example, the number of deaths from a certain disease, in a large population of n individuals subject to a probability of death π, is really binomially distributed but may be taken as approximately a Poisson variable with mean $\mu=n\pi$. Note that the standard deviation on the binomial assumption is $\sqrt{\{n\pi(1-\pi)\}}$, whereas the Poisson standard deviation is $\sqrt{(n\pi)}$. When π is very small these two expressions are almost equal. Table 2.4 shows the probabilities for the Poisson distribution with $\mu=5$, and those for various binomial distributions with $n\pi=5$. The similarity between the binomial and the Poisson improves with increases in n (and corresponding decreases in π).

TABLE 2.4 Binomial and Poisson distributions with $\mu = 5$.

π	0·5	0·10	0·05	Poisson
n	10	50	100	
r				
0	0·0010	0·0052	0·0059	0·0067
1	0·0098	0·0286	0·0312	0·0337
2	0·0439	0·0779	0·0812	0·0842
3	0·1172	0·1386	0·1396	0·1404
4	0·2051	0·1809	0·1781	0·1755
5	0·2461	0·1849	0·1800	0·1755
6	0·2051	0·1541	0·1500	0·1462
7	0·1172	0·1076	0·1060	0·1044
8	0·0439	0·0643	0·0649	0·0653
9	0·0098	0·0333	0·0349	0·0363
10	0·0010	0·0152	0·0167	0·0181
>10	0	0·0094	0·0115	0·0137
	1·0000	1·0000	1·0000	1·0000

Probabilities for the Poisson distribution are tabulated in Tables 7 and 39 of Pearson and Hartley (1966).

2.7 THE NORMAL (OR GAUSSIAN) DISTRIBUTION

The binomial and Poisson distributions both relate to a discrete random variable. The most important continuous probability distribution is the *Gaussian* (C.F.Gauss, 1777–1855, German mathematician), or as it is frequently called, the *normal* distribution. Figs. 2.10 and 2.11 show two frequency distributions, of height and of blood pressure, which are similar in shape. They are both approximately symmetrical about the middle and exhibit a shape rather like a bell, with a pronounced peak in the middle and a gradual falling-off of the frequency in the two tails. The observed frequencies have been approximated by a smooth curve which is in each case the probability density of a normal distribution.

Frequency distributions resembling the normal probability distribution in shape are often observed, but this form should not be taken as the norm, as the name 'normal' might lead one to suppose. Many

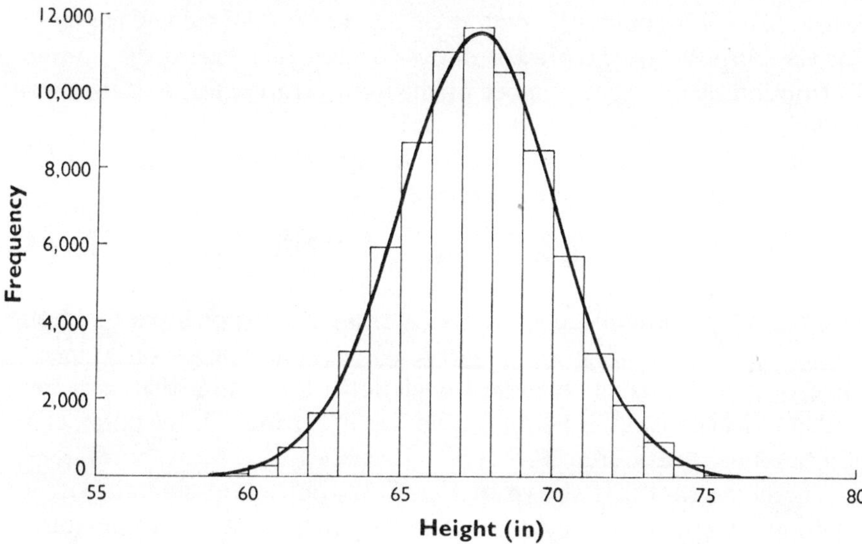

FIG. 2.10 A distribution of heights of young adult males, with an approximating normal distribution (Martin, 1949, Table 17 (Grade 1)).

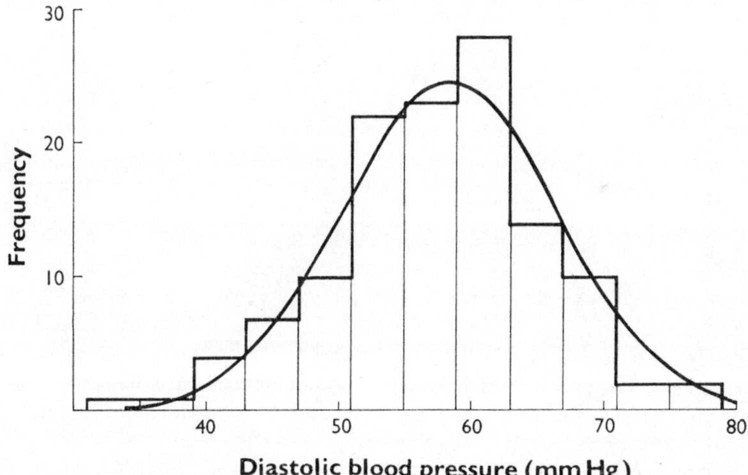

FIG. 2.11 A distribution of diastolic blood pressures of schoolboys with an approximating normal distribution (Rose, 1962, Table 1).

observed distributions are undeniably far from 'normal' in shape, yet cannot be said to be abnormal in the ordinary sense of the word. The importance of the normal distribution lies not so much in any claim to represent a wide range of observed frequency distributions, but in the central place it occupies in sampling theory, as we shall see in Chapter 3. For the purposes of the present discussion we shall regard the normal distribution as one of a number of theoretical forms for a continuous random variable, and proceed to describe some of its properties.

The probability density, $f(x)$, of a normally distributed random variable, x, is given by the expression

$$f(x)=\frac{1}{\sigma\sqrt{(2\pi)}}\exp\left\{-\frac{(x-\mu)^2}{2\sigma^2}\right\}, \tag{2.17}$$

where $\exp\{z\}$ is a convenient way of writing the exponential function e^z (e being the base of natural logarithms), μ is the expectation or mean value of x and σ is the standard deviation of x. (Note that π is the mathematical constant 3·14159 . . ., not, as in section 2·5, the parameter of a binomial distribution.)

The curve (2.17) is shown in Fig. 2.12, on the horizontal axis of which are marked the positions of the mean μ, and the values of x

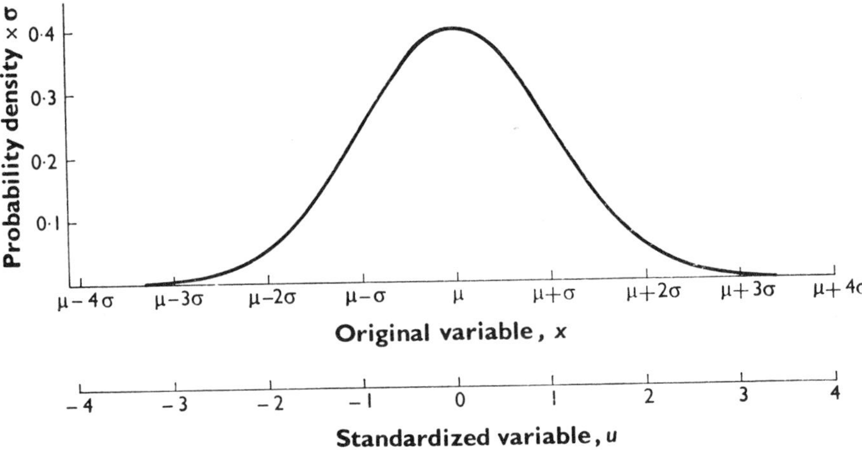

FIG. 2.12 The probability density function of a normal distribution showing the scales of the original variable and the standardized variable.

which differ from μ by $\pm\sigma$, $\pm 2\sigma$ and $\pm 3\sigma$. The symmetry of the distribution about μ may be inferred from (2.17), since changing the sign but not the magnitude of $x-\mu$ leaves $f(x)$ unchanged.

Fig. 2.12 shows that a relatively small proportion of the area under the curve lies outside the pair of values $x=\mu+2\sigma$ and $x=\mu-2\sigma$. The area under the curve between two values of x represents the probability that the random variable x takes values within this range (see section 2.3). In fact the probability that x lies within $\mu\pm 2\sigma$ is very nearly 0·95, and the probability that x lies outside this range is, correspondingly, 0·05.

It is important for the statistician to be able to find the area under any part of a normal distribution. Now, the density function (2.17) depends on two parameters, μ and σ. It might be thought, therefore, that any relevant probabilities would have to be worked out separately for every pair of values of μ and σ. Fortunately this is not so. In the previous paragraph we made a statement about the probabilities inside and outside the range $\mu \pm 2\sigma$, without any assumption about the particular values taken by μ and σ. In fact the probabilities depend on an expression of the departure of x from μ as a multiple of σ. For example, the points marked on the axis of Fig. 2.12 are characterized by the multiples ± 1, ± 2 and ± 3, as shown on the lower scale. The probabilities under various parts of any normal distribution can therefore be expressed in terms of the *standardized deviate*

$$u = \frac{x - \mu}{\sigma}.$$

A few important results are given in Table 2.5. More detailed results are given in the appendix table A1.

TABLE 2.5 Some probabilities associated with the normal distribution.

Standardized deviate	Probability of greater deviation	
	In either direction	In one direction
$u = (x - \mu)/\sigma$		
0·0	1·000	0·500
1·0	0·317	0·159
2·0	0·046	0·023
3·0	0·0027	0·0013
1·645	0·10	0·05
1·960	0·05	0·025
2·576	0·01	0·005

The use of tables of the normal distribution may be illustrated by the next example.

Example 2.7

The heights of a large population of men are found to follow closely a normal distribution with a mean of 67·5 in. and a standard deviation of 2·5 in. We shall use Table A1 to find the proportions of the population corresponding to various ranges of height.

(a) *Above* 70·5 *in.* If $x=70·5$, the standardized deviate $u=(70·5-67·5)/2·5=1·20$. The required proportion is the probability that u exceeds 1·20, which is found from Table A1 to be 0·115.

(b) *Below* 67·0 *in.* $u=(67·0-67·5)/2·5=-0·20$. The probability that u falls below $-0·20$ is the same as that of exceeding $+0·20$, namely 0·421.

(c) *Below* 72·0 *in.* $u=(72·0-67·5)/2·5=1·80$. The probability that u falls below 1·80 is one minus the probability of exceeding 1·80, namely $1-0·036=0·964$.

(d) *Between* 65·0 *and* 68·0 *in.* For $x=65·0$, $u=-1·0$; for $x=68·0$, $u=0·2$. The probability that u falls between $-1·0$ and 0·2 is one minus the probability of (i) falling below $-1·0$ or (ii) exceeding 0·2, namely

$$1-(0·159+0·421)=1-0·580=0·420.$$

The normal distribution is often useful as an approximation to the binomial and Poisson distributions. The binomial distribution for any particular value of π approaches the shape of a normal distribution as the other parameter n increases indefinitely; the approach to normality is more rapid for values of π near $\frac{1}{2}$ than for values near 0 or 1, since all binomial distributions with $\pi=\frac{1}{2}$ have the advantage of symmetry. Thus, provided n is large enough a binomial variable r (in the notation of section 2.5) may be regarded as approximately normally distributed with mean $n\pi$ and standard deviation $\sqrt{\{n\pi(1-\pi)\}}$.

The Poisson distribution with mean μ approaches normality as μ increases indefinitely. A Poisson variable x may, therefore, be regarded as approximately normal with mean μ and standard deviation $\sqrt{\mu}$.

If tables of the normal distribution are to be used to provide approximations to the binomial and Poisson distributions, account must be taken of the fact that these two distributions are discrete whereas the normal distribution is continuous. It is useful to introduce what is known as a *continuity correction*, whereby the exact probability for, say, the binomial variable r (taking integral values) is approximated by the probability of a normal variable between $r-\frac{1}{2}$ and $r+\frac{1}{2}$. Thus, the probability that a binomial variable took values greater than, or equal to, r would be approximated by the normal tail area beyond a standardized normal deviate

$$u=\frac{|r-n\pi|-\frac{1}{2}}{\sqrt{\{n\pi(1-\pi)\}}},$$

(the vertical lines indicating that the 'absolute value', or the numerical value ignoring the sign, is to be used.)

Tables 2.6 and 2.7 illustrate the normal approximations to some probabilities for binomial and Poisson variables.

TABLE 2.6 Examples of the approximation to the binomial distribution by the normal distribution with continuity correction.

		Mean	Standard deviation	Values	Exact	Normal approximation with continuity correction	
π	n	$n\pi$	$\sqrt{\{n\pi(1-\pi)\}}$	of r	probability	u	Probability
0·5	10	5	1·581	⩽2 ⩾8	*0·0547* *0·0547*	1·581	*0·0579*
0·1	50	5	2·121	⩽2 ⩾8	*0·1117* *0·1221*	1·179	*0·1192*
0·5	40	20	3·162	⩽14 ⩾26	*0·0403* *0·0403*	1·739	*0·0410*
0·2	100	20	4·000	⩽14 ⩾26	*0·0804* *0·0875*	1·375	*0·0846*

TABLE 2.7 Examples of the approximation to the Poisson distribution by the normal distribution with continuity correction.

Mean	Standard deviation	Values	Exact	Normal approximation with continuity correction	
μ	$\sqrt{\mu}$	of x	probability	$u=\dfrac{\lvert x-\mu\rvert-\frac{1}{2}}{\sqrt{\mu}}$	Probability
5	2·236	0	*0·0067*	2·013	*0·0221*
		⩽2	*0·1246*	1·118	*0·1318*
		⩾8	*0·1334*	1·118	*0·1318*
		⩾10	*0·0318*	2·013	*0·0221*
20	4·472	⩽10	*0·0108*	2·124	*0·0168*
		⩽15	*0·1565*	1·006	*0·1572*
		⩾25	*0·1568*	1·006	*0·1572*
		⩾30	*0·0218*	2·124	*0·0168*
100	10·000	⩽80	*0·0226*	1·950	*0·0256*
		⩽90	*0·1714*	0·950	*0·1711*
		⩾110	*0·1706*	0·950	*0·1711*
		⩾120	*0·0282*	1·950	*0·0256*

2.8 BAYES'S THEOREM

It was pointed out in section 2.1 that the frequency definition of probability does not normally permit one to allot a numerical value to the probability that a certain proposition or hypothesis is true. There are, however, some situations in which the relevant alternative hypotheses can be thought of as presenting themselves in a random sequence so that numerical probabilities can be associated with them. For instance, a doctor in charge of a clinic may be interested in the hypothesis: 'This patient has disease *A*.' By regarding this patient as a random member of a large collection of patients presenting themselves at the clinic he may be able to associate with the hypothesis a certain probability, namely the long-run proportion of patients with disease *A*. This may be regarded as a *prior probability*, since it can be ascertained (or at least estimated roughly) from retrospective observations. Suppose the doctor now makes certain new observations, after which he again considers the probability of the hypothesis: 'This patient has disease *A*.' The new value may be called a *posterior probability* because it refers to the situation after the new observations have been made. Intuitively one would expect the posterior probability to exceed the prior probability if the new observations were particularly common on the hypothesis in question and relatively uncommon on any alternative hypothesis. Conversely, the posterior probability would be expected to be less than the prior probability if the observations were not often observed in disease *A* but were common in other situations.

Consider a simple example in which there are only three possible diseases (*A*, *B* and *C*), with prior probabilities π_A, π_B and π_C (with $\pi_A+\pi_B+\pi_C=1$). Suppose that the doctor's observations fall conveniently into one of four categories 1, 2, 3, 4, and that the probability distributions of the various outcomes for each disease are as follows:

Disease	Outcome				
	1	2	3	4	Total
A	l_{A1}	l_{A2}	l_{A3}	l_{A4}	1
B	l_{B1}	l_{B2}	l_{B3}	l_{B4}	1
C	l_{C1}	l_{C2}	l_{C3}	l_{C4}	1

Suppose the doctor observes outcome 2. The total probability of this outcome is

$$\pi_A l_{A2}+\pi_B l_{B2}+\pi_C l_{C2}.$$

The three terms in this expression are in fact the probability of disease A and outcome 2, disease B and outcome 2, disease C and outcome 2. Once the doctor has observed outcome 2, therefore, the posterior probabilities of A, B and C are

$$\frac{\pi_A l_{A2}}{\pi_A l_{A2}+\pi_B l_{B2}+\pi_C l_{C2}},\quad \frac{\pi_B l_{B2}}{\pi_A l_{A2}+\pi_B l_{B2}+\pi_C l_{C2}},\quad \frac{\pi_C l_{C2}}{\pi_A l_{A2}+\pi_B l_{B2}+\pi_C l_{C2}}.$$

The prior probabilities have been multiplied by factors proportional to l_{A2}, l_{B2}, and l_{C2}. Although these three quantities are straightforward probabilities they do not form part of the same distribution, being entries in a column rather than a row of the table above. Probabilities of a particular outcome on different hypotheses are often called *likelihoods* of these hypotheses.

This is an example of the use of Bayes's theorem (named after an English clergyman, Thomas Bayes, 1702–1761). More generally, if the hypothesis H_i has a prior probability π_i, and the outcome j has a probability l_{ij} when H_i is true, the posterior probability of H_i after outcome j has been observed is

$$\frac{\pi_i l_{ij}}{\sum_i \pi_i l_{ij}}. \tag{2.18}$$

In some examples, the outcomes will be continuous random variables, in which case the l_{ij}'s will be probability densities rather than probabilities. The hypothesis H_i may form a continuous set (for example H_i may specify that the mean μ of a normal distribution is equal to i, which can therefore take any negative or positive value); in this case the summation in the denominator of (2.18) must be replaced by an integral. But Bayes's theorem always takes the same basic form: prior probabilities are converted to posterior probabilities by multiplication in proportion to likelihoods.

The example provides an indication of the way in which Bayes's theorem may be used as an aid to diagnosis. In practice there are severe problems in estimating the prior probabilities appropriate for the population of patients under treatment; for example, the distribution of diseases observed in a particular centre is likely to vary with time. The determination of the likelihoods will involve extensive and carefully planned surveys and the definition of the outcome categories may be difficult.

One of the earliest applications of Bayes's theorem to medical diagnosis was that of Warner *et al.* (1961). They examined data from a large number of patients with congenital heart disease. For each of 33 different diagnoses they estimated the prior probability, π_i, and the probabilities l_{ij} of various combinations of symptoms. Altogether 50 symptoms, signs and other variables were measured on each individual. Even if all these had been dichotomies there would have been 2^{50} possible values of j, and it would clearly be impossible to get reliable estimates of all the l_{ij}. Warner *et al.* overcome this problem by making an assumption which has often been made by later workers in this field, namely that the symptoms and other variables are statistically independent. The probability of any particular combination of symptoms, j, can then be obtained by multiplying together the separate probabilities of each. In this study firm diagnoses for certain patients could be made by intensive investigation and these were compared with the diagnoses given by Bayes's theorem and also with those made by experienced cardiologists using the same information. Bayes's theorem seems to emerge well from the comparison. Nevertheless the assumption of independence of symptoms is potentially dangerous and should not be made without careful thought. For a more detailed discussion see Bailey (1967, chapter 11).

2.9 SUBJECTIVE PROBABILITY

The use of Bayes's theorem described in section 2.8 is restricted to situations in which the hypothesis can be regarded as having prior and posterior probabilities in the usual sense of long-run frequencies. It would be attractive if one could allot probabilities to hypotheses like the following: 'The use of tetanus antitoxin in cases of clinical tetanus reduces the fatality of the disease by more than 20 per cent', for which no frequency interpretation is possible.

Suppose we interpret the probability of a hypothesis as a measure of our degree of belief in its truth. A probability of zero would correspond to complete disbelief, a value of one representing complete certainty. Such numerical values could now be manipulated by Bayes's theorem, measures of prior belief being modified in the light of observations on random variables by multiplication by likelihoods, resulting in measures of posterior belief. Some writers (Jeffreys, 1961; Good 1950; Savage, 1954; Lindley, 1965) have advocated this method as the basis of statistical inference, and the so-called Bayesian approach is at present very influential.

The main problem is how to determine prior probabilities in situations in which frequency interpretations are meaningless. One approach is to accept arbitrary 'indifference' rules for distributing probability amongst the alternative hypotheses when one is in a state of ignorance about their relative plausibilities. Another approach is to ask oneself what odds one would be prepared to accept for a bet on the truth or falsehood of a particular proposition. If the acceptable odds were judged to be 4 to 1 against, the proposition could be regarded as having a probability of $\frac{1}{5}$ or 0·2.

The main body of statistical methods described in this book was built on the basis of a frequency view of probability, and we shall adhere mainly to this approach. Methods based on subjective (that is, non-frequency) probabilities are at present in a developmental stage, but it appears that those based on suitable indifference rules (Lindley, 1965) often correspond precisely to the more traditional methods, when appropriate changes of wording are made. We shall indicate many of these points of correspondence (for example in section 4.11), and draw attention to some points at which conflicts arise.

CHAPTER 3
SAMPLING

3.1 POPULATION AND SAMPLE

Statistics as a subject is very much concerned with the properties of large collections of individual items. Such large collections are usually called *populations*. The word 'population' is commonly used in conversation to refer to a large collection of human beings or other living organisms. The statistician refers also to collections of inanimate objects, such as birth certificates or parishes. He will also often refer to a population of observations; for example, the population of heights of adult males resident in England at a certain moment, or the population of outcomes (death or survival) for all patients suffering from a particular illness during some period.

To study the properties of some populations we often have recourse to a *sample* drawn from that population. This is a sub-group of the individuals in the population, usually proportionately few in number, selected so as to be, to some degree, representative of the population. In most situations the sample will not be fully representative. Something is lost by the process of sampling. Any one sample is likely to differ in some respect from any other sample which might have been chosen and there will be some risk in taking any sample as representing the population. However, much may be gained by having to make relatively few observations. If a national census is conducted by interviewing, say, only 1 in 100 rather than the whole of the population, it may be possible to devote more resources to training the interviewers who will be fewer in number, and thereby to obtain more accurate records.

The most familiar example of a sampling enquiry is perhaps the public opinion poll, in which a very small proportion of the populaton is interviewed for some specific purpose. Examples of sampling enquiries in medicine are (1) the United States National Health Survey, in which over 2,000 people are interviewed each week to provide a continuous picture of the nation's health; (2) the British Hospital

In-patient Enquiry, in which records are collected about 10 per cent of all discharges from hospital; and (3) a scheme whereby a sample of all prescriptions issued by doctors in the British National Health Service is examined to give information about the prescribing habits of doctors.

Techniques for the design of sample surveys are discussed in section 6.2. In the present section we are concerned with only the simplest sort of sampling procedure, *random sampling*, and in the remainder of the present chapter we shall consider the consequences of following this procedure in various circumstances.

The first step is usually to define the *sampling frame*, which is essentially a list or form of identification of the individuals in the population to be sampled. For example, if the aim is to sample adults resident in England, one useful way is to define the sampling frame as the individuals listed in the current electoral registers (lists of people entitled to vote at elections). If the intention is to sample small areas of a country, the sampling frame may be defined by marking a map into appropriate subdivisions by a grid. Once the individuals to be sampled have been defined they can be numbered, and the problem will now be to decide which numbers to select for the sample.

How is the sample to be chosen? If some characteristics of the population are known, perhaps as a result of previous surveys, it is sometimes suggested that the sample should be chosen by *purposive selection*, whereby certain features of the sample are made to agree exactly or almost exactly with those of the population. For example, in sampling for market research or opinion polls, some organizations use *quota sampling*, a method by which each interviewer is given instructions about certain characteristics (such as age, sex and social status of the individuals to be selected), the proportions in various sub-groups being chosen to agree with the corresponding proportions in the population. The difficulty with this method is that serious discrepancies between the sample and the population may arise in respect of characteristics which have not been taken into account. There is nothing in the sampling procedure to give any general confidence about the representativeness of the sample.

In general it is preferable to use some form of random sampling. In *simple random sampling*, every possible sample of a given size from the population has an equal probability of being chosen. A particular sample may, purely by chance, happen to be dissimilar from the population in some serious respect, but the theory of probability enables us to calculate how large these discrepancies are likely to be. Much of statistical analysis is concerned with the estimation of the likely magnitude of these *sampling errors*, and in this chapter we consider some of the most important results.

To draw a simple random sample from a population we could imagine some physical method of randomization. For instance, if 10 people were to be selected at random from a population of 100, a card could be produced for each member of the population, the cards thoroughly shuffled, and 10 cards selected. Such a method would be tedious, particularly with larger population sizes, and it is convenient to make use of tables of *random sampling numbers*, which effectively give the results of very extensive random selections made in the past by various reliable methods. A set of random numbers is given in Table A6, and instructions on the use of the table will be found on page 474.

3.2 THE SAMPLING ERROR OF A MEAN

Suppose that x is a quantitative random variable with mean μ and variance σ^2, and that $\bar{x}$ is the mean of a random sample of n values of x. For example x may be the systolic blood pressure of men aged 30–34 employed in a certain industrial occupation, and $\bar{x}$ the mean of a random sample of n men from this very large population. We may think of $\bar{x}$ as itself a random variable, for each sample will have its own value of $\bar{x}$, and if the random sampling procedure is repeated indefinitely the values of $\bar{x}$ can be regarded as following a probability distribution (Fig. 3.1). The nature of this distribution of $\bar{x}$ is of considerable importance, for it determines how much uncertainty is conferred upon $\bar{x}$ by the very process of sampling.

Two features of the variability of $\bar{x}$ seem intuitively clear. First, it must depend on σ: the more variable is the blood pressure in the industrial population, the more variable will be the means of different samples of size n. Secondly, the variability of $\bar{x}$ must depend on n: the larger the size of each random sample the closer together the values of $\bar{x}$ will be expected to lie.

Mathematical theory provides three basic results concerning the distribution of $\bar{x}$, which are of great importance in applied statistics. The first two results are proved at the end of this section, but a proof of the third result is beyond the scope of this book:

(1) $\mathrm{E}(\bar{x}) = \mu$. That is, the mean of the distribution of the sample mean is the same as the mean of the individual measurements.

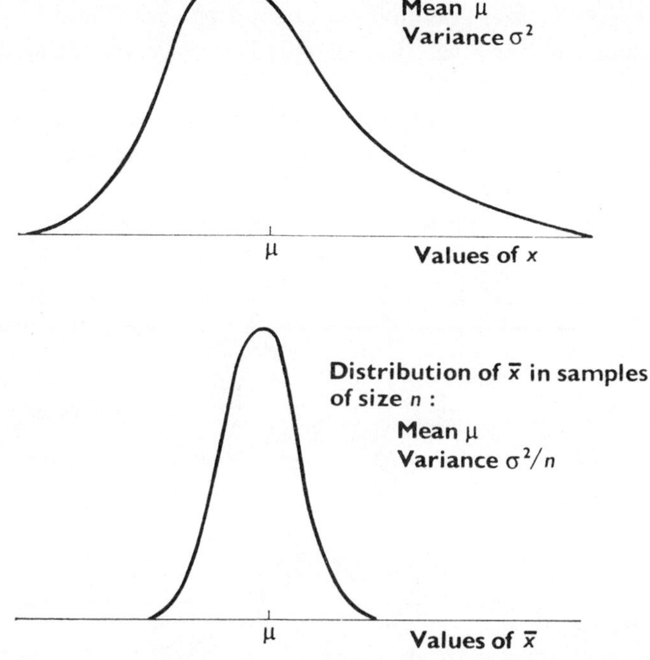

FIG. 3.1 The distribution of a random variable and the sampling distribution of means in random samples of size n.

(2) $\text{var}(\bar{x}) = \sigma^2/n$. The variance of the sample mean is equal to the variance of the individual measurements divided by the sample size. This provides a formal expression of the intuitive feeling, mentioned above, that the variability of $\bar{x}$ should depend on both σ and n; the precise way in which this dependence acts would perhaps not have been easy to guess. The standard deviation of $\bar{x}$ is

$$\sqrt{\left(\frac{\sigma^2}{n}\right)} = \frac{\sigma}{\sqrt{n}}. \tag{3.1}$$

This quantity is often called the *standard error* of the mean, and written $\text{SE}(\bar{x})$. It is quite convenient to use this nomenclature as it helps to avoid confusion between the standard deviation of x and the standard deviation of $\bar{x}$, but it should be remembered that a standard error is not really a new concept: it is merely the standard deviation of some statistic calculated from a sample (in this case, the mean) in an indefinitely long series of repeated samplings.

(3) If the distribution of x is normal, so will be the distribution of $\bar{x}$.

Much more importantly, even if the distribution of x is not normal, that of $\bar{x}$ will become closer and closer to the normal distribution with mean μ and variance σ^2/n as n gets larger. This is a consequence of a mathematical result known as the *Central Limit Theorem*, and it accounts for the central importance of the normal distribution in statistics.

The normal distribution is strictly only the limiting form of the

TABLE 3.1 Distribution of means of 2,000 samples of 5 random numbers.

Mean, $\bar{x}$	Frequency
0·4–	1
0·8–	4
1·2–	11
1·6–	22
2·0–	43
2·4–	88
2·8–	104
3·2–	178
3·6–	196
4·0–	210
4·4–	272
4·8–	200
5·2–	193
5·6–	154
6·0–	129
6·4–	92
6·8–	52
7·2–	30
7·6–	13
8·0–	7
8·4–	1
	2,000

sampling distribution of $\bar{x}$ as n increases to infinity, but it provides a remarkably good approximation to the sampling distribution even when n is small and the distribution of x is far from normal. Table 3.1 shows the results of taking random samples of 5 digits from tables of random numbers. These tables may be thought of as forming a probability distribution for a discrete random variable x, taking the values 0, 1, 2, . . ., 9 with equal probabilities of 0·1. This is clearly far from normal in shape. The mean and variance may be found by the methods of section 2.4.

$$\mu = \mathrm{E}(x) = 0{\cdot}1\ (1+2+\ \ldots\ +9) = 4{\cdot}5$$

$$\begin{aligned}\sigma^2 &= \mathrm{E}(x^2) - \mu^2\\ &= 0{\cdot}1\ (1^2+2^2+\ldots+9^2) - (4{\cdot}5)^2\\ &= 8{\cdot}25\end{aligned}$$

$$\sigma = \sqrt{8{\cdot}25} = 2{\cdot}87$$

$$\mathrm{SE}(\bar{x}) = \sqrt{(8{\cdot}25/5)} = \sqrt{1{\cdot}65} = 1{\cdot}28.$$

2,000 samples of size 5 were taken (actually, by generating the random numbers on a computer rather than reading from printed tables), the mean $\bar{x}$ was calculated for each sample, and the 2,000 values of $\bar{x}$ formed into the frequency distribution shown in Table 3.1. The distribution can be seen to be similar in shape to the normal distribution. The closeness of the approximation may be seen from Fig. 3.2, which shows the histogram corresponding to Table 3.1, together with a curve the height of which is proportional to the density of a normal distribution with mean 4.5 and standard deviation 1.28.

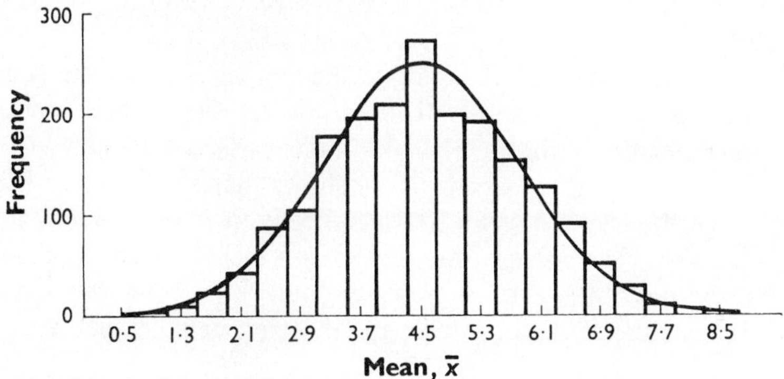

FIG. 3.2 The distribution of means from 2,000 samples of 5 random digits (Table 3.1), with the approximating normal distribution.

The theory outlined above applies strictly to random sampling from an infinite population or for successive independent observations on a random variable. Suppose a sample of size n has to be taken from a population of finite size N. Sampling is usually *without replacement*, which means that if an individual member of the population is selected as one member of a sample it cannot again be chosen in that sample. The expectation of $\bar{x}$ is still equal to μ, the population mean. The formula

(3.1) must however be modified by a 'finite population correction', to become

$$\mathrm{SE}(\bar{x}) = \frac{\sigma}{\sqrt{n}} \sqrt{(1-f)}, \tag{3.2}$$

where $f = n/N$, the *sampling fraction*. In (3.2), σ is defined as the standard deviation of x in the population, using a divisor $N-1$. Thus

$$\mu = \frac{\sum_{i=1}^{N} x_i}{N}$$

and

$$\sigma^2 = \frac{\sum_{i=1}^{N} (x_i - \mu)^2}{N-1}.$$

The effect of the finite population correction, $1-f$, is to reduce the sampling variance substantially as f approaches 1, i.e. as the sample size approaches the population size. Clearly, when $n = N$, there is only one possible random sample, consisting of all the members of the population, and for this sample $\bar{x} = \mu$.

The sampling error of the sample median has no simple general expression. In random samples from a normal distribution however, the standard error of the median for large n is approximately $1{\cdot}253\ \sigma/\sqrt{n}$. The fact that this exceeds $\sigma/\sqrt{n}$ shows that the median is more variable than the sample mean (or, technically, it is less *efficient* as an estimator of μ). This comparison depends on the assumption of normality for the distribution of x, however, and for certain other distributional forms the median provides the more efficient estimator.

Proofs of results (1) and (2)

(1) $\mathrm{E}(\bar{x}) = \mu$.

Denote the individual observations in the sample by $x_1, x_2, \ldots, x_n$. Then

$$\bar{x} = (x_1 + x_2 + \ldots + x_n)/n$$
$$= (1/n)x_1 + (1/n)x_2 + \ldots + (1/n)x_n.$$

Using the intuitive steps referred to in the footnote on page 58,

$$\mathrm{E}(\bar{x}) = (1/n)\mathrm{E}(x_1) + (1/n)\mathrm{E}(x_2) + \ldots + (1/n)\mathrm{E}(x_n).$$

But

$$E(x_1)=E(x_2)=\ldots=E(x_n)=\mu, \text{ and so}$$
$$E(\bar{x})=(1/n)\mu+(1/n)\mu+\ldots+(1/n)\mu$$
$$=\mu,$$

since there are n identical terms to be added.

(2) $\text{var}(\bar{x})=\sigma^2/n$.

$$\text{var}(\bar{x})=E(\bar{x}-\mu)^2$$
$$=E\left(\frac{x_1+x_2+\ldots+x_n}{n}-\mu\right)^2$$
$$=E\left\{\frac{(x_1-\mu)+(x_2-\mu)+\ldots+(x_n-\mu)}{n}\right\}^2$$
$$=(1/n^2)E\{(x_1-\mu)^2+(x_2-\mu)^2+\ldots+2(x_1-\mu)(x_2-\mu)+\ldots\},$$

where the curly bracket includes all squared terms like $(x_i-\mu)^2$ and twice each product of terms like $(x_i-\mu)(x_j-\mu)$. The expectation of each term $(x_i-\mu)^2$ is σ^2. The expectation of each term $(x_i-\mu)(x_j-\mu)$ is zero since, for any value of x_i, x_j independently ranges over all possible values so that $E(x_j-\mu)=0$. Hence

$$\text{var}(\bar{x})=(1/n^2)(\sigma^2+\sigma^2+\ldots\text{ (to } n \text{ terms) }\ldots+0)$$
$$=(1/n^2)(n\sigma^2)$$
$$=\sigma^2/n.$$

3.3 THE SAMPLING ERROR OF A PROPORTION

This has already been fully discussed in section 2.5. If individuals in an infinitely large population are classified into two types A and B, with probabilities π and $1-\pi$, the number r of individuals of type A in a random sample of size n follows a binomial distribution. We shall now apply the results of section 3.2 to prove the formulae previously given for the mean and variance of r.

Suppose we define a quantitative variable x, which takes the value 1 for each A individual and 0 for each B. We may think of x as a score attached to each member of the population. The point of doing this is that, in a sample of n consisting of r A's and $n-r$ B's,

$$\sum x=(r\times 1)+\{(n-r)\times 0\}$$
$$=r$$

and

$$\bar{x}=r/n, =p \text{ in the notation of section 2.5.}$$

The sample proportion p, may, therefore be identified with the sample mean of x, and to study the sampling variation of p we can apply the general results established in the last section. We shall need to know the population mean and standard deviation of x. From first principles these are

$$\begin{aligned} E(x) &= (\pi \times 1) + \{(1-\pi) \times 0\} \\ &= \pi \end{aligned} \tag{3.3}$$

and

$$\begin{aligned} \text{var}(x) &= E(x^2) - \{E(x)\}^2 \\ &= (\pi \times 1^2) + ((1-\pi) \times 0^2) - \pi^2 \\ &= \pi(1-\pi). \end{aligned}$$

From (3.1),

$$\text{var}(\bar{x}) = \frac{\pi(1-\pi)}{n}. \tag{3.4}$$

Writing (3.3) and (3.4) in terms of p rather than $\bar{x}$, we have

$$E(p) = \pi \quad \text{and} \quad \text{var}(p) = \frac{\pi(1-\pi)}{n},$$

as in (2.12) and (2.13). Since $r = np$,

$$E(r) = n\pi \quad \text{and} \quad \text{var}(r) = n\pi(1-\pi),$$

as in (2.10) and (2.11).

One more result may be taken from section 3.2. As n approaches infinity, the distribution of $\bar{x}$ (that is, of p) approaches the normal distribution with the corresponding mean and variance. The increasing symmetry has already been noted in section 2.5.

3.4 THE SAMPLING ERROR OF A VARIANCE

Suppose that a quantitative random variable x follows a distribution with mean μ and variance σ^2. In a sample of size n, the estimated variance is

$$s^2 = \frac{\sum(x_i - \bar{x})^2}{n-1}.$$

In repeated random sampling from the distribution, s^2 will vary from one sample to another; it will itself be a random variable. We now consider the nature of the variation in s^2.

The expectation of s^2 can be derived as follows:

$$\begin{aligned}E(s^2) &= \frac{1}{n-1} E[\sum(x_i-\bar{x})^2] \\ &= \frac{1}{n-1} E[\sum\{(x_i-\mu)-(\bar{x}-\mu)\}^2] \\ &= \frac{1}{n-1} E[\sum(x_i-\mu)^2 - 2\sum(x_i-\mu)(\bar{x}-\mu)+\sum(\bar{x}-\mu)^2] \\ &= \frac{1}{n-1} E[\sum(x_i-\mu)^2 - n(\bar{x}-\mu)^2],\end{aligned}$$

since

$$\sum(x_i-\mu)(\bar{x}-\mu) = \sum(\bar{x}-\mu)^2 = n(\bar{x}-\mu)^2.$$

Now, $E(x_i-\mu)^2 = \sigma^2$ by definition, and $E(\bar{x}-\mu)^2 = \text{var}(\bar{x}) = \sigma^2/n$. Hence

$$\begin{aligned}E(s^2) &= \frac{1}{n-1}\left\{n\sigma^2 - n\left(\frac{\sigma^2}{n}\right)\right\}, \\ &= \frac{1}{n-1}(n-1)\sigma^2 \\ &= \sigma^2. \end{aligned} \qquad (3.5)$$

Another way of stating the result (3.5) is that s^2 is an *unbiased* estimator of σ^2. It is this property which makes s^2, with its divisor of $n-1$, a satisfactory estimator of the population variance: the statistic (1.1), with a divisor of n, has an expectation $(n-1)\sigma^2/n$, which is less than σ^2. Note that $E(s)$ is *not* equal to σ; it is in fact less than σ. The reason for paying so much attention to $E(s^2)$ rather than $E(s)$ will appear in chapters 7 and 8.

What else can be said about the sampling distribution of s^2? Let us, for the moment, tighten our requirements about the distribution of x by assuming that it is strictly normal. In this particular instance, the distribution of s^2 is closely related to one of a family of distributions called the χ^2-distributions ('chi-square' or 'chi-squared'), which are of very great importance in statistical work, and it will be useful to introduce these distributions by a short discussion before returning to the distribution of s^2 which is the main concern of this section.

Denote by X_1 the standardized deviate corresponding to the variable x. That is, $X_1=(x-\mu)/\sigma$. X_1^2 is a random variable, whose value must be non-negative. The distribution of X_1^2 is called the *χ^2 distribution on one degree of*

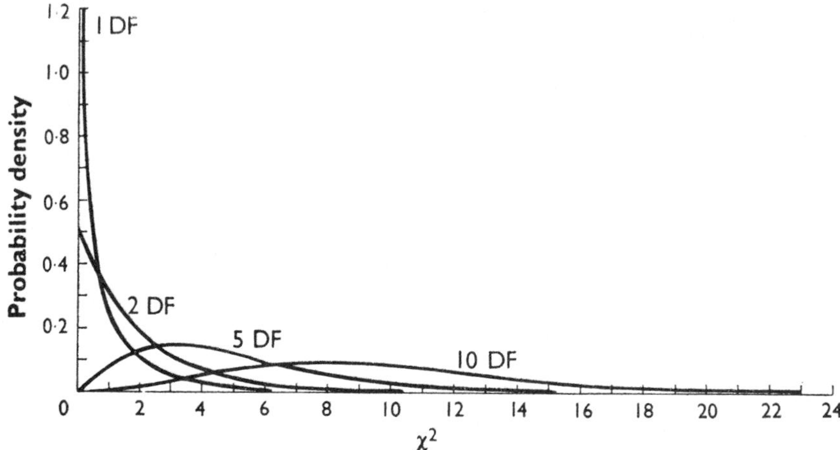

FIG. 3.3 Probability density functions for χ^2 distributions with various numbers of degrees of freedom.

freedom (1 DF), and is often called the $\chi^2_{(1)}$ distribution. It is depicted as the first curve in Fig. 3.3. The *percentiles* of the χ^2 distribution (i.e. the values of the variable which are exceeded with specified probabilities) are tabulated along the first line of Table A2. Two points may be noted at this stage:

(a) $E(X_1^2)=E(x-\mu)^2/\sigma^2=\sigma^2/\sigma^2=1$. The mean value of the distribution is 1.

(b) The percentiles may be obtained from those of the normal distribution. From Table A1 we know, for instance, that there is a probability 0·05 that $(x-\mu)/\sigma$ exceeds $+1{\cdot}960$ or falls below $-1{\cdot}960$. Whenever either of these events happens, $(x-\mu)^2/\sigma^2$ exceeds $(1{\cdot}960)^2=3{\cdot}84$. Thus, the 0·05 level of the $\chi^2_{(1)}$ distribution is 3·84. A similar relationship holds for all the other percentiles.

Now let x_1 and x_2 be two independent observations on x, and define

$$X_2^2=\frac{(x_1-\mu)^2}{\sigma^2}+\frac{(x_2-\mu)^2}{\sigma^2}.$$

X_2^2 follows what is known as the χ^2 *distribution on two degrees of freedom* ($\chi^2_{(2)}$). The variable X_2^2, like X_1^2, is necessarily non-negative. Its distribution is shown as the second curve in Fig. 3.3, and is tabulated along the second line of Table A2. Note that X_2^2 is the sum of two independent observations on X_1^2. Hence

$$E(X_2^2)=2E(X_1^2)=2.$$

Similarly, in a sample of n independent observations x_i, define

$$X_n^2=\sum_{i=1}^{n}\frac{(x_i-\mu)^2}{\sigma^2}=\frac{\Sigma(x_i-\mu)^2}{\sigma^2}. \qquad (3.6)$$

This follows the χ^2 *distribution on n degrees of freedom* ($\chi^2_{(n)}$), and $E(X^2_n)=n$.

Fig. 3.3 and Table A2 show that as the degrees of freedom increase, the χ^2 distribution becomes more and more symmetric. Indeed, since it is the sum of n independent $\chi^2_{(1)}$ variables, the central limit theorem (which applies to sums as well as to means) shows that $\chi^2_{(n)}$ tends to normality as n increases. The variance of the $\chi^2_{(n)}$ distribution is $2n$.

The result (3.6) enables us to find the distribution of the sum of squared deviations about the population mean μ. In the formula for s^2, we use the sum of squares about the sample mean $\bar{x}$, and it can be shown that

$$\sum(x_i-\bar{x})^2 \leq \sum(x_i-\mu)^2.$$

In fact, $\sum(x_i-\bar{x})^2/\sigma^2$ follows the $\chi^2_{(n-1)}$ distribution. The fact that differences are taken from the sample mean rather than the population mean is compensated for by the subtraction of 1 from the degrees of freedom. Now

$$s^2=\frac{\sum(x_i-\bar{x})^2}{n-1}=\frac{\sigma^2}{n-1}\frac{\sum(x_i-\bar{x})^2}{\sigma^2}$$

$$=\frac{\sigma^2}{n-1}\chi^2_{(n-1)}.$$

That is, s^2 behaves as $\sigma^2/(n-1)$ times a $\chi^2_{(n-1)}$ variable. It follows that

$$E(s^2)=\frac{\sigma^2}{n-1}E(\chi^2_{(n-1)})=\frac{\sigma^2}{n-1}(n-1)=\sigma^2,$$

as we proved directly at (3.5), and

$$\text{var}(s^2)=\frac{\sigma^4}{(n-1)^2}\text{var}(\chi^2_{(n-1)})=\frac{\sigma^4}{(n-1)^2}2(n-1)$$

$$=\frac{2\sigma^4}{(n-1)}. \tag{3.7}$$

The formula (3.7) for var(s^2) is true only for samples from a normal distribution; indeed, the whole sampling theory for s^2 is more sensitive to non-normality than that for the mean.

Fig. 3.4 shows the histogram formed by the 2,000 values of s^2 in the samples of 5 random numbers referred to in section 3.2, together with the approximating curve given by the $\chi^2_{(4)}$ distribution which would have been a good fit if the original distribution had been normal. There is an obvious systematic discrepancy between the actual results and the

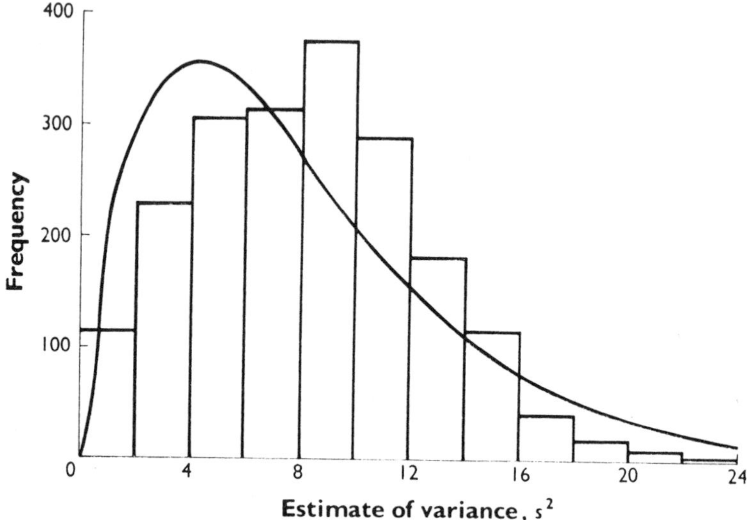

FIG. 3.4 The distribution of estimates of variance from 2,000 samples of 5 random digits with the theoretical distribution (based on χ^2 on 4 degrees of freedom) appropriate for normal samples.

normal theory, in striking contrast to the good agreement found with the distribution of means.

3.5 THE SAMPLING ERROR OF A DIFFERENCE

Many statistical investigations lead to a consideration of a difference between two quantities—the difference between the mean weight gain in two groups of animals receiving different diets, for example; or the difference between the proportions of 10-year-old children in two different areas who show a certain serum antibody level.

We shall therefore be much concerned with the sampling error to be attached to the difference between two quantities, such as means or proportions calculated from two independently drawn random samples. It will be useful to consider a rather general situation first, and to consider cases of particular interest later. Suppose, then, that we have two random variables y_1 and y_2, that y_1 is distributed with mean m_1 and variance v_1, and y_2 with mean m_2 and variance v_2. We take an observation at random on y_1 and an *independent* random observation on y_2. What can be said about the distribution of $y_1 - y_2$ in an indefinite series of repetitions of this procedure?

$$\mathrm{E}(y_1-y_2)=\mathrm{E}(y_1)-\mathrm{E}(y_2)=m_1-m_2. \tag{3.8}$$

$$\begin{aligned}\mathrm{var}(y_1-y_2)&=\mathrm{E}\{(y_1-y_2)-(m_1-m_2)\}^2\\&=\mathrm{E}\{(y_1-m_1)-(y_2-m_2)\}^2\\&=\mathrm{E}\{(y_1-m_1)^2-2\mathrm{E}(y_1-m_1)(y_2-m_2)+\mathrm{E}(y_2-m_2)^2\}\\&=v_1+v_2,\end{aligned} \tag{3.9}$$

the middle term on the previous line being zero, because for any given value of y_1, $\mathrm{E}(y_2-m_2)=0$, and consequently when y_1 is allowed to vary $\mathrm{E}(y_1-m_1)(y_2-m_2)$ is also zero. This term could *not* be equated to zero if y_1 and y_2 were not drawn independently.

We now apply the general results (3.8) and (3.9) to the particular case in which $y_1=\bar{x}_1$, the mean of a random sample of size n_1 from a population with mean μ, and variance σ_1^2; and $y_2=\bar{x}_2$, the mean of an independent random sample of size n_2 from a population with mean μ_2 and variance σ_2^2. Here, from the results of section 3.2,

$$m_1=\mu_1 \quad \text{and} \quad v_1=\sigma_1^2/n_1;$$

$$m_2=\mu_2 \quad \text{and} \quad v_2=\sigma_2^2/n_2.$$

Therefore, from (3.8) and (3.9),

$$\left.\begin{aligned}&\mathrm{E}(\bar{x}_1-\bar{x}_2)=\mu_1-\mu_2\\ \text{and}\quad&\\&\mathrm{var}(\bar{x}_1-\bar{x}_2)=\frac{\sigma_1^2}{n_1}+\frac{\sigma_2^2}{n_2}.\end{aligned}\right\} \tag{3.10}$$

Similarly, suppose $y_1=p_1$, the proportion of individuals showing some characteristic in a random sample of size n_1 from a population in which this characteristic occurs with probability π_1; and $y_2=p_2$, the proportion in an independent sample of size n_2 from a population with parameter π_2. Then, from section 3.3,

$$m_1=\pi_1 \quad \text{and} \quad v_1=\pi_1(1-\pi_1)/n_1;$$

$$m_2=\pi_2 \quad \text{and} \quad v_2=\pi_2(1-\pi_2)/n_2.$$

From (3.8) and (3.9),

$$\left.\begin{aligned}&\mathrm{E}(p_1-p_2)=\pi_1-\pi_2\\ \text{and}\quad&\\&\mathrm{var}(p_1-p_2)=\frac{\pi_1(1-\pi_1)}{n_1}+\frac{\pi_2(1-\pi_2)}{n_2}.\end{aligned}\right\} \tag{3.11}$$

The results (3.10) and (3.11) are of great importance in the statistical methods to be described in the next chapter. It is important here to emphasize the condition of independence. If the two samples are not independent, for example because of some constraint in the design of the investigation, the expectation formulae in (3.10) and (3.11) will still hold, but the variance formulae will be invalid.

We might consider using the general formula for a comparison of two estimates of variance. Indeed, with the same notation as was used above for the comparison of means, suppose the sample estimated variances are s_1^2 and s_2^2. Then, applying the results of section 3.4,

$$\left.\begin{aligned} \mathrm{E}(s_1^2 - s_2^2) &= \sigma_1^2 - \sigma_2^2 \\ \text{and} \qquad \mathrm{var}(s_1^2 - s_2^2) &= \frac{2\sigma_1^4}{n_1 - 1} + \frac{2\sigma_2^4}{n_2 - 1}. \end{aligned}\right\} \tag{3.12}$$

In practice these results are not often used, because it is more convenient to compare two estimated variances by taking their ratio rather than their difference.

We defer a discussion of the sampling error of variance ratios until section 4.10.

3.6 SOME OTHER VARIANCE FORMULAE

In section 3.5 we derived a general formula for the variance of a difference between two random variables, and applied it to two different sampling problems. It is convenient to mention here one or two other useful formulae for the variances of various functions of independent random variables.

LINEAR FUNCTION

Suppose $x_1, x_2, \ldots, x_k$ are independent random variables, and

$$y = a_1x_1 + a_2x_2 + \ldots + a_kx_k,$$

the a's being constants. Then,

$$\mathrm{var}(y) = a_1^2\,\mathrm{var}(x_1) + a_2^2\,\mathrm{var}(x_2) + \ldots + a_k^2\,\mathrm{var}(x_k). \tag{3.13}$$

The result (3.9) is a particular case of (3.13) when $k=2$, $a_1=1$ and $a_2=-1$.

The independence condition is important. If the x's are not independent, there must be added to the right-hand side of (3.13) a series of terms like

$$2a_i a_j \operatorname{covar}(x_i, x_j), \tag{3.14}$$

where 'covar' stands for the *covariance* of x_i and x_j, which is defined by

$$\operatorname{covar}(x_i, x_j) = \mathrm{E}\{(x_i - \mathrm{E}(x_i))(x_j - \mathrm{E}(x_j))\}.$$

The covariance is the expectation of the product of deviations of two random variables from their means. When the variables are independent, the covariance is zero (see the proof of (3.9)). When all k variables are independent, all the covariance terms vanish and we are left with (3.13).

RATIO

Let $y = x_1/x_2$, where again x_1 and x_2 are independent. No general formula can be given for the variance of y. Indeed, it may be infinite. However, if x_2 has a small coefficient of variation, the distribution of y will be rather similar to a distribution with a variance given by the following formula:

$$\operatorname{var}(y) = \frac{\operatorname{var}(x_1)}{\{\mathrm{E}(x_2)\}^2} + \frac{\{\mathrm{E}(x_1)\}^2}{\{\mathrm{E}(x_2)\}^4} \operatorname{var}(x_2). \tag{3.15}$$

Note that if x_2 has no variability at all, (3.15) reduces to

$$\operatorname{var}(y) = \frac{\operatorname{var}(x_1)}{{x_2}^2},$$

which is an exact result when x_2 is a constant.

GENERAL FUNCTION

Suppose we know the mean and variance of the random variable x. Can we calculate the mean and variance of any general function of x such as $3x^3$ or $\sqrt{(\log x)}$? There is no simple general formula, but again a useful approximation is available when the coefficient of variation of x is small. We have to assume some knowledge of calculus at this point. Denote the function of x by y. Then

$$\operatorname{var}(y) \simeq \left(\frac{dy}{dx}\right)^2_{x=\mathrm{E}(x)} \operatorname{var}(x), \tag{3.16}$$

the symbol $\simeq$ standing for 'approximately equal to'. In (3.16), dy/dx is the differential coefficient (or derivative) of y with respect to x, evaluated at the mean value of x.

If y is a function of two variables, x_1 and x_2,

$$\text{var}(y) \simeq \left(\frac{\partial y}{\partial x_1}\right)^2 \text{var}(x_1) + 2\left(\frac{\partial y}{\partial x_1}\right)\left(\frac{\partial y}{\partial x_2}\right) \text{covar}(x_1, x_2) + \left(\frac{\partial y}{\partial x_2}\right)^2 \text{var}(x_2), \tag{3.17}$$

where $\partial y/\partial x_1$ and $\partial y/\partial x_2$ are the *partial* derivatives of y with respect to x_1 and x_2, and these are again evaluated at the mean values. The reader with some knowledge of calculus will be able to derive (3.9) as a particular case of (3.17) when $\text{covar}(x_1, x_2) = 0$. An obvious extension of (3.17) to k variables gives (3.13) as a special case.

CHAPTER 4
STATISTICAL INFERENCE

4.1 GENERAL

The argument in Chapter 3 has been essentially from the population to the sample. Given the distribution of a variable in a population we obtained results about the distributions of various statistics (a *statistic* being any quantity calculated from sample observations). These results are of direct interest in the planning of sampling enquiries, as they enable the investigator to estimate the precision attainable with a sample of a given size, and hence help him to decide how large a sample should be taken. This question will be discussed again in section 6.5.

We have not yet, however, come to grips with another problem which interests the investigator. When the sample has been taken, what sort of inferences can be drawn about the population, on the basis of the sample? The argument here must be in the opposite direction to that previously used. We do not know the characteristics of the population. We have taken one random sample and wish to use our knowledge of sampling theory to make whatever inference can be made about the population. One fundamental difficulty usually arises. The expressions of sampling variation given by the various formulae for standard errors or variances in the last chapter usually involve some parameters of the population. For instance the standard error of the sample mean is $\sigma/\sqrt{n}$. If we are attempting to make an inference about a normal distribution on the basis of one random sample, we shall know the sample size, n, but not the population standard deviation, σ. We cannot, therefore, calculate the standard error exactly. A similar point arises in other situations, and the discussion of methods to overcome the difficulty will be a constant theme in this chapter.

We shall continue to suppose that the data at our disposal form a random sample from some population. In some sampling enquiries this is known to be true by virtue of the design of the investigation. In other studies a more complex form of sampling may have been used; consideration of some more complex designs is deferred until Chapter 6. A more serious conceptual difficulty is that in many statistical investigations there is no formal process of sampling from a well-defined population. For instance the prevalence of a certain disease may be calculated for all the inhabitants of a village and compared with that for another village. A clinical trial may be conducted in a clinic, with the participation of all the patients seen at the clinic during a given period. A doctor may report the mean duration of symptoms amongst a consecutive series of 50 patients with a certain form of illness. Individual readings vary haphazardly whether they form a random sample or whether they are collected in a less formal way, and it will often be desirable to assess the effect which this basic variability has on any statistical calculations which are performed. How can this be done if there is no infinite population and no strictly random sample?

It can be done by arguing that the observations are subject to random, unsystematic variation which makes them appear very much like observations on random variables. The population formed by the whole distribution is not a real, well-defined entity, but it may be helpful to think of it as a hypothetical population which would be generated if an indefinitely large number of observations, showing the same sort of random variation as those at our disposal, could be made. This concept seems satisfactory when the observations vary in a patternless way. We are putting forward a 'model', or conceptual framework, for the random variation, and propose to make whatever statements we can about the relevant features of this model, just as we wish to make statements about the relevant features of a population in a strict sampling situation. Sometimes, of course, the supposition that the data behave like a random sample is blatantly unrealistic. There may, for instance, be a systematic tendency for the earliest observations to be greater in magnitude than those made later. Such trends, and other systematic features, can be allowed for by increasing the complexity of the model. When such modifications have been made, there will still remain some degree of apparently random variation, the underlying probability distribution of which is a legitimate object of study.

In section 6.4 we shall discuss comparative experiments in which experimental units are allocated at random to various groups which are to receive different treatments. It will be of considerable importance to compare two or more groups of observations made on units receiving different treatments, and to assess the extent to which such contrasts are affected by random variation. In most experiments the whole collection of units is not selected by strictly random sampling; the clinical trial mentioned earlier provides an example. Nevertheless, because of random allocation the differences between groups behave like differences between random samples—from the same population if all treatments are alike, from different populations if the treatments differ in their effects. The sampling theory of differences is therefore directly relevant.

4.2 SIGNIFICANCE TESTS ON A SAMPLE MEAN

One of the most important techniques of statistical inference is the *significance test*. Suppose a series of observations is selected randomly from a population. We might be interested in a certain hypothesis (called the '*null*' *hypothesis*) which specifies values for the parameters of the population. The question then arises: do the observations in the sample throw any light on the plausibility of the hypothesis? Some samples will be, in some sense, reasonably typical of those which might be expected by sampling theory if the null hypothesis were true. Other samples will have certain features which would be unlikely to arise if the null hypothesis were true; if such a sample were observed it would give reason for suspecting that the null hypothesis was untrue.

The significance test is a rule for deciding whether any particular sample is in the 'likely' or 'unlikely' class, or more usefully for assessing the strength of the conflict between what is found in the sample and what is predicted by the null hypothesis. The test to be used in any situation will depend on what alternatives to the null hypothesis are contemplated. If the null hypothesis specifies the mean and standard deviation of a normal distribution as μ_0 and σ_0, a significance test which is particularly designed to detect departures of the population mean from μ_0 could reasonably be based on an examination of the sample mean, $\bar{x}$. A test designed to detect departures of the standard deviation from σ_0 should be based on some measure of variation in the sample, such as the sample standard deviation, s.

Let us consider in some detail the problem of testing this null hypothesis (which we shall denote by H_0) that the parameters of a normal distribution are $\mu=\mu_0$ and $\sigma=\sigma_0$, using the mean, $\bar{x}$, of a random sample of size n.

If H_0 is true, we know from section 3.2 that the probability is only

0·05 that $\bar{x}$ falls outside the interval $\mu_0 - 1{\cdot}96\ \sigma_0/\sqrt{n}$ to $\mu_0 + 1{\cdot}96\ \sigma_0/\sqrt{n}$. For a value of $\bar{x}$ outside this range, the standardized normal deviate

$$u = \frac{\bar{x} - \mu_0}{\sigma_0/\sqrt{n}} \tag{4.1}$$

would be less than $-1{\cdot}96$ or greater than 1·96. Such a value of $\bar{x}$ could be regarded as sufficiently far from μ_0 to cast doubt on the null hypothesis. Certainly, H_0 *might* be true, but if so an unusually large deviation would have arisen—one of a class that would arise by chance only once in twenty times. On the other hand such a value of $\bar{x}$ would be quite likely to occur if μ had some value other than μ_0, closer, in fact, to the observed $\bar{x}$. The particular critical values adopted here for u, $\pm 1{\cdot}96$, correspond to the quite arbitrary probability level of 0·05. If u is numerically greater than 1·96 the difference between μ_0 and $\bar{x}$ is said to be *significant at the* 5 *per cent level.* Similarly, an even more extreme difference yielding a value of u numerically greater than 2·58, is *significant at the* 1 *per cent level.*

The 5 per cent level, and to a lesser extent the 1 per cent level, have become widely accepted as convenient yardsticks for assessing the significance of departures from a null hypothesis. This is unfortunate in a way, because there should be no rigid distinction between a departure which is just beyond the 5 per cent significance level and one which just fails to reach it. It is perhaps preferable to avoid the dichotomy—'significant' or 'not significant'—by attempting to measure *how* significant the departure is. In the present example we might enquire how far into the tails of the expected sampling distribution the observed value of $\bar{x}$ falls. A convenient way of measuring this tendency is to measure the probability, P, of obtaining, if the null hypothesis were true, a value of $\bar{x}$ as extreme as, or more extreme than, the value observed. If $\bar{x}$ is just significant at the 5 per cent level, $u = \pm 1{\cdot}96$ and $P = 0{\cdot}05$ (the probability being that in *both* tails of the distribution). If $\bar{x}$ is beyond the 5 per cent significance level, $u > 1{\cdot}96$ or $< -1{\cdot}96$ and $P < 0{\cdot}05$. If $\bar{x}$ is not significant at the 5 per cent level, $P > 0{\cdot}05$ (see Fig. 4.1). If the observed value of u were, say, 2·20, one could either give the exact value of P as 0·028 (from Table A1), or, by comparison with the percentage points of the normal distribution, write $0{\cdot}02 < P < 0{\cdot}05$.

Although a 'significant' departure provides some degree of evidence against a null hypothesis, it is important to realise that a 'non-significant' departure does not provide positive evidence *in favour* of that hypo-

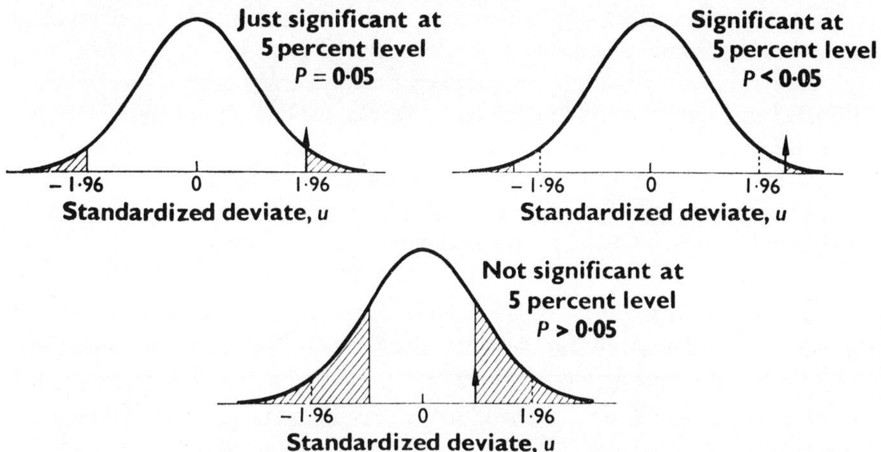

FIG. 4.1 Significance tests at the 5 per cent level based on a standardized normal deviate. The observed deviate is marked by an arrow.

thesis. The situation is rather that we have failed to find strong evidence against the null hypothesis. To draw an analogy with a court of law, the null hypothesis is rather like a presumption of the innocence of an accused person. A significant result is then like a verdict of guilty, but a non-significant result is more like the Scottish verdict of 'not proven' than the English verdict of 'not guilty'.

Example 4.1

A large number of patients with cancer at a particular site, and of a particular clinical stage, are found to have a mean survival time from diagnosis of 38·3 months with a standard deviation of 43·3 months. One hundred patients are treated by a new technique and their mean survival time is 46·9 months. Is this apparent increase in mean survival explicable as a random fluctuation?

We test the null hypothesis that the 100 recent results are effectively a random sample from a population with mean $\mu_0 = 38{\cdot}3$ and standard deviation $\sigma_0 = 43{\cdot}3$. Note that this distribution must be extremely skew, since a deviation of even one standard deviation below the mean gives a negative value $(38{\cdot}3 - 43{\cdot}3 = -5{\cdot}0)$, and no survival times can be negative. However, 100 is a reasonably large sample size, and it would be safe to use the normal theory for the distribution of the sample mean. Putting $n = 100$ and $\bar{x} = 46{\cdot}9$, we have a standardized normal deviate

$$\frac{46{\cdot}9 - 38{\cdot}3}{(43{\cdot}3/\sqrt{100})} = \frac{8{\cdot}6}{4{\cdot}33} = 2{\cdot}0.$$

This value just exceeds the 5 per cent value of 1·96, and the difference is therefore just significant at the 5 per cent level ($P<0{\cdot}05$).

This significant difference suggests that the increase in mean survival time is rather unlikely to be due to chance. It would not be safe to assume that the new treatment has improved survival, since certain characteristics of the patients may have changed since the earlier data were collected; for example, the disease may be diagnosed earlier. All we can say is that the difference is not very likely to be a chance phenomenon.

The significance test we have considered above is *two-sided*, in the sense that sufficiently large departures of $\bar{x}$ from μ_0, in either direction, will be judged significant. If, for some reason, we decided that we were interested in possible departures of μ from μ_0 only in one particular direction, say in excess of μ_0, it would be reasonable to count as significant only those values of $\bar{x}$ which differed sufficiently from μ_0 in that direction. Such a test is called *one-sided*. For a one-sided test at, say, the 5 per cent level, sensitive to positive deviations from the null hypothesis, a standardized normal deviate u would be significant if it exceeded $+1{\cdot}64$, since this is the value exceeded in one direction with probability 0·05.

The critical value for a one-sided test at level P is therefore the same as that for a two-sided test at level $2P$. In a sense the distinction is semantic. On the other hand there is often a temptation to use one-sided tests rather than two-sided tests because the probability level is lower, and therefore the apparent significance is greater. A decision to use a one-sided test should *never* be made after looking at the data and observing the direction of the departure. Before the data are examined one should decide to use a one-sided test only if it is quite certain that departures in one particular direction will always be ascribed to chance, and therefore regarded as non-significant however large they are. This situation rarely arises in practice, and it will be safe to assume that significance tests should almost always be two-sided. We shall make this assumption in this book unless otherwise stated.

THE t DISTRIBUTION

Suppose now that we wish to test a null hypothesis which specifies the mean value of a normal distribution ($\mu=\mu_0$) but does not specify the variance σ^2, and that we have no evidence about σ^2 besides that contained in our sample. The procedure outlined above cannot be followed because the standard error of the mean, $\sigma/\sqrt{n}$, cannot be calculated. It seems reasonable to replace σ by the estimated standard deviation in the sample, s, giving a standardized deviate

$$t=\frac{\bar{x}-\mu_0}{s/\sqrt{n}} \tag{4.2}$$

instead of the normal deviate u given by (4.1). The statistic t would be expected to follow a sampling distribution close to that of u (i.e. close to a standard normal distribution with mean 0 and variance 1) when n is large, because then s will be a good approximation to σ. When n is small, s may differ considerably from σ, purely by chance, and this will cause t to have substantially greater random variability than u.

In fact, t follows what is known as the *t distribution on $n-1$ degrees of freedom*. The t distributions form a family, distinguished (rather like the χ^2 distributions) by an index, the 'degrees of freedom', which in the present application is one less than the sample size. As the degrees of freedom increase the t distribution tends towards the standard normal distribution (Fig. 4.2). Appendix Table A3 shows the percentiles of t, i.e. the values exceeded with specified probabilities, for different values of the degrees of freedom, ν. For $\nu=\infty$, the tabulated values agree with those of the standard normal distribution. The 5 per cent point, which always exceeds the normal value of 1·960, is nevertheless close to 2·0 for all except quite small values of ν.

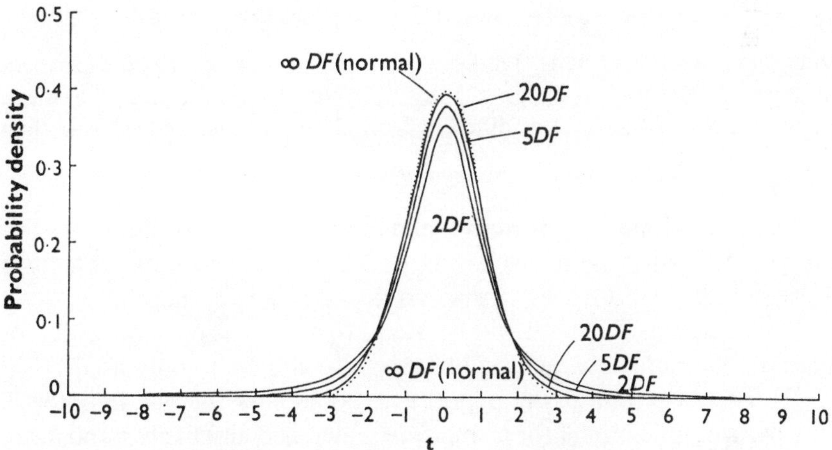

FIG. 4.2 Probability density function for t distributions on 2, 5, 20 and infinite degrees of freedom; the latter is the standard normal distribution.

Example 4.2

The following data are the uterine weights (in mgm) of each of 20 rats drawn at random from a large stock. Is it likely that the mean weight for the whole stock could be 24 mgm, a value observed in some previous work?

9	18	21	26
14	18	22	27
15	19	22	29
15	19	24	30
16	20	24	32

Here $n=20$, $\sum x=420$ and $\bar{x}=420/20=21{\cdot}0$. For t, we need the estimated standard error of the mean, $s/\sqrt{n}$, which it is convenient to calculate as $\sqrt{(s^2/n)}$, to avoid taking two separate square roots. From the usual short-cut formula,

$$\sum(x-\bar{x})^2=\sum x^2-(\sum x)^2/n$$
$$=9{,}484-8{,}820$$
$$=664,$$
$$s^2=664/19=34{\cdot}947$$
$$s^2/n=34{\cdot}947/20=1{\cdot}7474$$
$$\sqrt{(s^2/n)}=1{\cdot}3219$$

and

$$t=\frac{21{\cdot}0-24{\cdot}0}{1{\cdot}3219}=-2{\cdot}27.$$

The degrees of freedom are $\nu=20-1=19$, and Table A3 shows the relevant percentage points as

P	0·05	0·02
t	2·093	2·539

Thus, the observed value is significant at between 2 per cent and 5 per cent ($0{\cdot}02<P<0{\cdot}05$), and there is a rather strong suggestion that the mean uterine weight of the stock is different from 24 mgm (and, indeed, *less* than this value).

The t distribution is strictly valid only if the distribution of x is normal. Nevertheless, it is reasonably 'robust' in the sense that it is approximately valid for quite marked departures from normality.

In closing this section it will be useful to comment on some different types of situations in which significance tests are commonly used:

(1) To test a simplifying hypothesis. Sometimes the null hypothesis provides a simple model for a situation which is really likely to be more complex than the model admits. For example, if a certain quantity is varying in time, the null hypothesis might specify that the mean rate

of increase is zero. Even though this is not likely to be exactly true, it may be useful to be able to ignore a time trend in any inferences made from the data, and one might be prepared to do this if there is no strong evidence against the null hypothesis. Similarly, in studying the relationship between two variables, as in Chapter 5, it will often be useful to assume for simplicity that a trend is linear (i.e. follows a straight line) if there is no evidence to the contrary, even though common sense tells us that the true trend is highly unlikely to be precisely linear.

(2) To test a null hypothesis which may be approximately true. In a clinical trial to test a new drug against a placebo, it may be that the drug will either be very nearly inert or will have a marked effect. The null hypothesis that the drug is completely inert (and therefore has exactly the same effect as a placebo) is then a close approximation to a possible state of affairs.

(3) To test the direction of a difference from a critical value. Suppose we are interested in whether a certain parameter, θ, has a value greater or less than some value θ_0. We could test the null hypothesis that θ is precisely θ_0. It may be quite clear that this will not be true. Nevertheless we give ourselves the opportunity to assert in which direction the difference lies. If the null hypothesis is significantly contradicted we shall have good evidence either that $\theta > \theta_0$ or that $\theta < \theta_0$.

4.3 INTERVAL ESTIMATION OF A MEAN

With the same assumptions as in the last section, that $\bar{x}$ is the mean of a random sample of size n, we may wish to draw inferences about the population mean, μ, without concentrating on a single possible value μ_0. In a rough sense, μ is more likely to be near $\bar{x}$ than very far from $\bar{x}$. Can this idea be made more precise by asserting something about the probability that μ lies within a given interval around $\bar{x}$?

As in section 4.2 we consider first the situation in which the population standard deviation, σ, is known; later we consider what to do when σ is unknown.

KNOWN σ

Suppose the distribution of x is normal. From the general sampling theory (section 3.2), the probability is 0·95 that $\bar{x} - \mu$ lies between

$-1{\cdot}96\sigma/\sqrt{n}$ and $+1{\cdot}96\sigma/\sqrt{n}$; i.e. that

$$-1{\cdot}96\sigma/\sqrt{n} < \bar{x} - \mu < 1{\cdot}96\sigma/\sqrt{n}. \tag{4.3}$$

Rearrangement of the left part of (4.3), namely $-1{\cdot}96\sigma/\sqrt{n} < \bar{x} - \mu$, gives $\mu < \bar{x} + 1{\cdot}96\sigma/\sqrt{n}$; similarly the right part gives $\bar{x} - 1{\cdot}96\sigma/\sqrt{n} < \mu$. Therefore (4.3) is equivalent to the statement that

$$\bar{x} - 1{\cdot}96\sigma/\sqrt{n} < \mu < \bar{x} + 1{\cdot}96\sigma/\sqrt{n}. \tag{4.4}$$

The statement (4.4), which as we have seen, is true with probability 0·95, asserts that μ lies in a certain interval called the 95 *per cent confidence interval*. The ends of this interval, which are called the 95 *per cent confidence limits*, are symmetrical about $\bar{x}$ and (since σ and n are known) can be calculated from the sample data. The confidence interval provides a formal expression of the uncertainty which must be attached to $\bar{x}$ on account of sampling errors alone.

Two slightly different ways of interpreting (4.4) may be useful:

(1) The values of μ inside the confidence interval are precisely those which would not be significantly contradicted by a two-sided test at the 5 per cent level, because for any such value of μ, the standardized

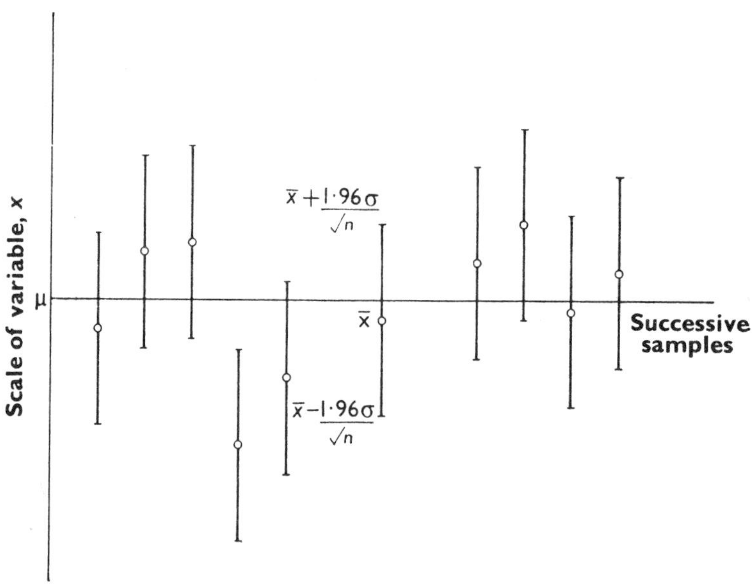

FIG. 4.3 Confidence limits (95 per cent) for the mean of a normal distribution with known standard deviation, from a series of random samples of size n.

normal deviate $(\bar{x}-\mu)/(\sigma/\sqrt{n})$ lies between $-1{\cdot}96$ and $+1{\cdot}96$. Values of μ outside the interval, on the other hand, would all be contradicted by a test at the 5 per cent level.

(2) We have said that (4.4) is true with probability 0·95, that is, 19 times out of 20 in the long run. This is not quite the same thing as saying that μ has a probability of 0·95 of being within the limits, because μ is not a random variable. In any particular case μ either is or is not in the interval. What we are doing is to imagine a series of repeated random samples from a population with a fixed value of μ (Fig. 4.3). In the long run, 95 per cent of the confidence intervals will include μ: the confidence statement (4.4) will then be true. Five per cent of the time $\bar{x}$ will be more than 1·96 standard errors away from μ (as in the fourth sample in Fig. 4.3) and the interval will not include μ: the confidence statement is then untrue. If, in any particular problem we calculate a confidence interval, we may happen to be unlucky in that this may be one of the 5 per cent of cases in which (4.4) is untrue; but we are applying a procedure which will work 95 per cent of the time. For a somewhat different approach, see section 4.11.

The assumption of normality is not crucial if n is reasonably large, because of the near-normality of the distribution of $\bar{x}$ in samples from almost any population.

For a higher degree of confidence than 95 per cent we may use some other percentile of the normal distribution. The 99 per cent limits, for instance, are

$$\bar{x} \pm 2{\cdot}58\sigma/\sqrt{n}.$$

The probability that μ is contained in the interval is called the *confidence coefficient*. In general, the $1-2\alpha$ confidence limits are

$$\bar{x} \pm u_{2\alpha}\sigma/\sqrt{n},$$

where $u_{2\alpha}$ is the standardized normal deviate exceeded (in either direction) with probability 2α.

Example 4.1, continued from section 4.2

In this example, the 95 per cent confidence limits are

$$46{\cdot}9 \pm (1{\cdot}96)(4{\cdot}33)$$
$$= 38{\cdot}4 \quad \text{and} \quad 55{\cdot}4.$$

The fact that this interval just excludes the possible value 38·3 which was tested previously, corresponds to the fact that this value was just contradicted by a significance test at the 5 per cent level.

UNKNOWN σ

The argument proceeds as before, but using the t distribution instead of the normal distribution. If

$$t = \frac{\bar{x} - \mu}{s/\sqrt{n}},$$

the probability is 0·95 that t lies between $\pm t_{\nu, 0.05}$, the tabulated 5 per cent point of the t distribution on $\nu = n - 1$ degrees of freedom. A little rearrangement gives an equivalent statement: the probability is 0·95 that

$$\bar{x} - t_{\nu, 0.05}(s/\sqrt{n}) < \mu < \bar{x} + t_{\nu, 0.05}(s/\sqrt{n}). \quad (4.5)$$

This is the 95 per cent confidence interval. It differs from (4.4) in the replacement of the percentage point of the normal distribution by that of the t distribution, which as we have seen is a somewhat larger number. The necessity to estimate the standard error from the sample has led to an interval based on a somewhat larger multiple of the standard error.

As in significance tests, normality of the distribution of x is necessary for the strict validity of (4.5), but moderate departures from normality will have little effect on the validity.

Example 4.2, continued from section 4.2

In this problem, $\nu = 19$, and $t_{19, 0{\cdot}05} = 2{\cdot}093$. The 95 per cent confidence limits for μ are, therefore,

$$21{\cdot}00 \pm (2{\cdot}093)(1{\cdot}3219)$$
$$= 18{\cdot}23 \quad \text{and} \quad 23{\cdot}77.$$

The exclusion of the value 24 corresponds to the significant result of testing this value at the 5 per cent level. The 99 per cent limits are

$$21{\cdot}00 \pm (2{\cdot}861)(1{\cdot}3219)$$
$$= 17{\cdot}22 \quad \text{and} \quad 24{\cdot}78,$$

now including 24, since this value for μ was not significantly contradicted at the 1 per cent level.

The limits calculated here are sometimes called *fiducial limits,* this being the term used by R.A.Fisher in his approach to the problem of interval estimation. Fisher's approach was more akin to interpretation (1) rather than (2), the latter being particularly stressed by J.Neyman, who was responsible for the concept of confidence limits. In most situations, fiducial and confidence limits are (as here) numerically the same, and the interpretation is a matter of choice. In a few situations minor differences arise, a circumstance which has given rise to some controversy.

4.4 INFERENCES FROM PROPORTIONS

Consider now the binomial situation discussed in sections 2.5 and 3.3. Individuals drawn at random from a large population have a probability π of being of type A. In a random sample of n individuals, a proportion $p(=r/n)$ are of type A. What can be said about π?

Suppose first that we wish to test a null hypothesis specifying that π is equal to some value π_0. On this hypothesis, the number of type A individuals, r, found in repeated random samples of size n would follow a binomial distribution. To express the departure of any observed value, r, from its expected value, $n\pi_0$, we could state the extent to which r falls into either of the tails of its sampling distribution. As in section 4.2 this extent could be measured by calculating the probability in the tail area. The situation is a little different here because of the discreteness of the distribution of r. Do we calculate the probability of obtaining a larger deviation than that observed, $r-n\pi_0$, or the probability of a deviation at least as great? Since we are saying something about the degree of surprise elicited by a certain observed result, it seems reasonable to include the probability of this result in the summation. Thus, if $r>n\pi_0$ and the probabilities in the binomial distribution with parameters π_0 and n are $P_0, P_1, \ldots, P_n$, the P-value for a one-sided test will be

$$P_+=P_r+P_{r+1}+\ldots+P_n.$$

For a two-sided test we could add the probabilities of deviations at least as large as that observed, in the other direction. The P-value for the other tail is

$$P_-=P_{r'}+P_{r'-1}+\ldots+P_0,$$

where r' is equal to $2n\pi_0-r$ if this is an integer, and the highest integer less than this quantity otherwise. The P-value for the two-sided test is then $P=P_-+P_+$.

For example, if $r=8$, $n=10$ and $\pi_0=\frac{1}{2}$,

$$P_+=P_8+P_9+P_{10}$$

and

$$P_- = P_2 + P_1 + P_0.$$

If $r = 17$, $n = 20$ and $\pi_0 = \frac{1}{3}$,

$$P_+ = P_{17} + P_{18} + P_{19} + P_{20}$$

$$P_- = 0.$$

If $r = 15$, $n = 20$ and $\pi_0 = 0{\cdot}42$,

$$P_+ = P_{15} + P_{16} + P_{17} + P_{18} + P_{19} + P_{20}$$

$$P_- = P_1 + P_0.$$

An alternative, and perhaps preferable, approach is to obtain the two-sided P value by doubling the one-sided value (see p. 137).

Considerable simplification is achieved by approximating to the binomial distribution by the normal (section 2.7). On the null hypothesis

$$\frac{r - n\pi_0}{\sqrt{\{n\pi_0(1 - \pi_0)\}}}$$

is approximately a standardized normal deviate. Using the continuity correction, the tail area required in the significance test is approximated by the area beyond a standardized normal deviate

$$u = \frac{|r - n\pi_0| - \frac{1}{2}}{\sqrt{\{n\pi_0(1 - \pi_0)\}}}, \tag{4.6}$$

and the result will be significant at, say, the 5 per cent level if this probability is less than 0·05.

Example 4.3

In a clinical trial to compare the effectiveness of two analgesic drugs, X and Y, each of 100 patients receives X for a period of one week and Y for another week, the order of administration being determined randomly. Each patient then states a preference for one of the two drugs. Sixty-five patients prefer X and 35 prefer Y. Is this strong evidence for the view that, in the long run, more patients prefer X than Y?

Test the null hypothesis that the preferences form a random series in which the probability of an X preference is $\frac{1}{2}$. This would be true if X and Y were equally effective in all respects affecting the patients' judgments. The standard error of r is

$$\sqrt{\{100 \times \tfrac{1}{2} \times \tfrac{1}{2}\}} = \sqrt{25} = 5.$$

The observed deviation, $r - n\pi_0$, is

$$65 - 50 = 15.$$

With continuity correction, the standardized normal deviate is $(15-\frac{1}{2})/5=2{\cdot}90$. Without continuity correction, the value would have been $15/5=3{\cdot}00$, a rather trivial difference. In this case the continuity correction could have been ignored. The normal tail area for $u=2{\cdot}90$ is 0·0037; the departure from the null hypothesis is highly significant, and the evidence in favour of X is strong. The exact value of P, from the binomial distribution, is 0·0035, very close to the normal approximation.

The 95 per cent confidence limits for π are the two values, π_L and π_U, for which the observed value of r is just significant on a one-sided

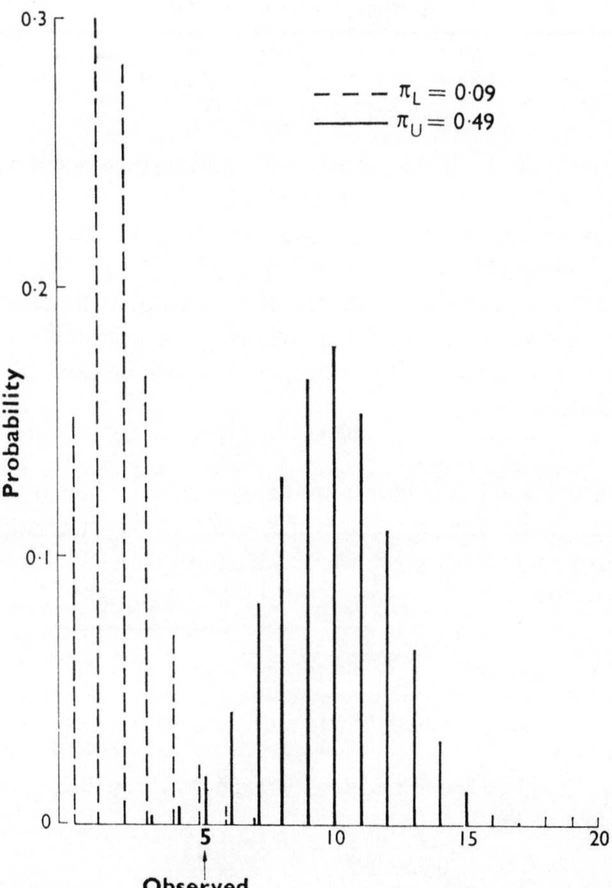

FIG. 4.4 Binomial distributions illustrating the 95 per cent confidence limits for the parameter π based on a sample with 5 individuals of a certain type out of 20. For $\pi=\pi_L=0{\cdot}09$ the probability of 5 or more is 0·025; for $\pi=\pi_U=0{\cdot}49$ the probability of 5 or less is 0·025.

test at the $2\frac{1}{2}$ per cent level (Fig. 4.4). These values may be obtained fairly readily from tables of the binomial distribution, and are tabulated by Mainland *et al.* (1956) and in the Documenta Geigy Scientific Tables. They may be obtained also from Fisher and Yates (1963), Table VIII1.

The normal approximation may be used in a number of ways:

(1) The tail areas could be estimated from (4.6). Thus, for 95 per cent confidence limits, approximations to π_L and π_U are given by the formulae

$$\frac{r-n\pi_L-\frac{1}{2}}{\sqrt{\{n\pi_L(1-\pi_L)\}}}=1{\cdot}96$$

and

$$\frac{r-n\pi_U+\frac{1}{2}}{\sqrt{\{n\pi_U(1-\pi_U)\}}}=-1{\cdot}96.$$

(2) In method (1), if n is large, the continuity correction of $\frac{1}{2}$ may be omitted. Methods (1) and (2) both involve the solution of a quadratic equation for each of π_L and π_U. A further simplification is as follows:

(3) Replace $\pi_L(1-\pi_L)$ and $\pi_U(1-\pi_U)$ by $p(1-p)$. This is not too drastic a step, as $p(1-p)$ changes rather slowly with changes in p, particularly for values of p near $\frac{1}{2}$. Ignoring the continuity correction, as in (2), we have the most frequently used approximation to the 95 per cent confidence limits:

$$p\pm 1{\cdot}96\sqrt{(pq/n)},$$

where, as usual, $q=1-p$. The simplification here is due to the replacement of the standard error of p, which involves the unknown value π, by the approximate form $\sqrt{(pq/n)}$, which can be calculated entirely from known quantities.

Example 4.3, continued

With $n=100$, $p=0{\cdot}65$, the exact 95 per cent confidence limits are found to be 0·548 and 0·743.

Method (1) will be found to give 0·548 and 0·741, method (2) gives 0·552 and 0·736, and method (3) gives

$$0{\cdot}65\pm 1{\cdot}96\sqrt{\left\{\frac{(0{\cdot}65)(0{\cdot}35)}{100}\right\}}$$

$$=0{\cdot}65\pm(1{\cdot}96)(0{\cdot}0477)$$

$$=0{\cdot}557 \quad \text{and} \quad 0{\cdot}743.$$

In this example method (3) is quite adequate.

Example 4.4

As a contrasting example with small numbers, suppose $n=20$ and $p=0{\cdot}25$. The exact 95 per cent confidence limits are 0·087 and 0·491; see Fig. 4.4.

Method (1) gives 0·096 and 0·494, method (2) gives 0·112 and 0·469, method (3) gives 0·060 and 0·440. Method (3) is clearly less appropriate here than in Example 4.3. In general method (3) should be avoided if either np or $n(1-p)$ are small (say less than 10).

The exact confidence limits for the binomial parameter are conservative in the sense that the probability of including the true value is *at least* as great as the nominal confidence coefficient. This fact arises from the debatable decision to include the observed value in the calculation of tail-area probabilities. The same tends to be true of the approximate limits using the continuity correction. The limits obtained by methods (2) and (3), however, which ignore the continuity correction, will tend to have a probability of inclusion nearer to the nominal value. This suggests that the neglect of the continuity correction is not a serious matter, and may, indeed, be an advantage.

4.5 INFERENCES FROM VARIANCES

For normally distributed variables the methods follow immediately from the results of section 3.4.

Suppose s^2 is the usual estimate of variance in a random sample of size n from a normal distribution with variance σ^2; the population mean need not be specified. For a test of the null hypothesis that $\sigma^2=\sigma_0^2$, calculate

$$X^2=\frac{(n-1)s^2}{\sigma_0^2}, \quad \text{or equivalently} \quad \frac{\sum(x-\bar{x})^2}{\sigma_0^2}, \tag{4.7}$$

and refer this to the $\chi^2_{(n-1)}$ distribution. For a two-sided test at a significance level α, the critical values for X^2 will be those corresponding to tabulated probabilities of $1-\frac{1}{2}\alpha$ and $\frac{1}{2}\alpha$. For a two-sided 5 per cent level, for example, the entries under the headings 0·975 and 0·025 must be used. We may denote these by $\chi^2_{n-1,\,0.975}$ and $\chi^2_{n-1,\,0.025}$.

For confidence limits for σ^2 we can argue that the probability is, say, 0·95 that

$$\chi^2_{n-1,\,0.975}<\frac{\sum(x-\bar{x})^2}{\sigma^2}<\chi^2_{n-1,\,0.025}$$

and hence that

$$\frac{\sum(x-\bar{x})^2}{\chi^2_{n-1,\,0.025}} < \sigma^2 < \frac{\sum(x-\bar{x})^2}{\chi^2_{n-1,\,0.975}}.$$

These are the required confidence limits.

As pointed out in section 3.4, the sampling theory for s^2 is particularly sensitive to non-normality, and the results in the present section should be interpreted cautiously if serious departures from normality are present.

4.6 COMPARISON OF TWO MEANS

The sampling error of the difference between two means has been considered in section 3.5, where the importance of the independence or non-independence of the two samples was stressed. We shall accordingly distinguish between two situations: the paired case, in which the two samples are of equal size and the individual members of one sample are paired with particular members of the other sample; and the unpaired case, in which the samples are quite independent.

PAIRED CASE

Suppose we have two samples of size n:

$$x_{11}, x_{12}, \ldots, x_{1i}, \ldots, x_{1n}$$

drawn at random from a normal distribution with mean μ_1 and variance σ_1^2, and

$$x_{21}, x_{22}, \ldots, x_{2i}, \ldots, x_{2n}$$

drawn at random from a normal distribution with mean μ_2 and variance σ_2^2. If there is some sense in which x_{1i} is paired with x_{2i}, it will usually be true that high values of x_{1i} tend to be associated with high values of x_{2i}, and low with low. For example, x_{1i} and x_{2i} might be blood pressure readings on the ith individual in a group of n, on each of two occasions. Some individuals would tend to give high values on both occasions, and some would tend to give low values. In such situations,

$$\mathrm{E}(x_{1i}-x_{2i}) = \mu_1 - \mu_2,$$

but $\mathrm{var}(x_{1i}-x_{2i})$ is (by application of (3.13) and (3.14)) less than the value $\sigma_1^2+\sigma_2^2$ which would be appropriate for independent observations. Now, $\bar{x}_1-\bar{x}_2$, the difference between the two means, is the mean of the n individual differences $x_{1i}-x_{2i}$, and these differences are independent of each other. The sampling error of $\bar{x}_1-\bar{x}_2$ can therefore be obtained by applying the methods of section 4.3 to the n individual differences. This automatically ensures that, whatever the nature of the relationship between the paired readings, the appropriate sampling error is calculated.

Example 4.5

In a small clinical trial to assess the value of a new tranquillizer on psychoneurotic patients, each patient was given a week's treatment with the drug and a week's treatment with a placebo, the order in which the two sets of treatments were given being determined at random. At the end of each week the patient had to complete a questionnaire, on the basis of which he was given an 'anxiety score' (with possible values from 0 to 30), high scores corresponding to states of anxiety. The results are shown in Table 4.1.

TABLE 4.1 Anxiety scores recorded for ten patients receiving a new drug and a placebo in random order.

Patient	Anxiety score Drug	Placebo	Difference d_i (Drug-placebo)
1	19	22	−3
2	11	18	−7
3	14	17	−3
4	17	19	−2
5	23	22	1
6	11	12	−1
7	15	14	1
8	19	11	8
9	11	19	−8
10	8	7	1
			−13

The last column of Table 4.1 shows the difference, d_i, between the anxiety score for the ith subject on the drug and on the placebo. A t test on the 10 values of d_i gives

$$\Sigma d_i = -13$$
$$\Sigma d_i^2 = 203$$
$$\Sigma(d_i - \bar{d})^2 = 186{\cdot}1.$$

Whence

$$\bar{d} = -1{\cdot}30$$
$$s^2 = 186{\cdot}1/9 = 20{\cdot}68$$
$$\surd(s^2/n) = \surd(20{\cdot}68/10) = \surd 2{\cdot}068 = 1{\cdot}438$$

and, to test the null hypothesis that $E(d_i) = 0$,

$$t = \frac{-1{\cdot}30}{1{\cdot}438} = -0{\cdot}90 \text{ on 9 DF.}$$

The difference is clearly not significant.

Ninety-five per cent confidence limits for the mean difference are

$$-1{\cdot}30 \pm (2{\cdot}262)(1{\cdot}438)$$
$$= -4{\cdot}55 \quad \text{and} \quad 1{\cdot}95.$$

In Table 4.1, some subjects, like numbers 6 and 10, tend to give consistently low scores, whereas others, like numbers 1 and 5, score highly on both treatments. These systematic differences between subjects are irrelevant to the comparison between treatments, and it is therefore appropriate that the method of differencing removes their effect. If the means of two samples of independent readings, each of size n, are to be compared it would still be possible to arrange the series in random order, form pairs from corresponding members of the two series and apply the t distribution to the set of n differences. There are, however, various objections to this proposal:

(1) It would not work with unequal samples.

(2) The ordering could be done in a large number of ways, and the results are therefore highly arbitrary.

(3) The analysis would neglect information of value, for the differences between readings in the same sample, which were irrelevant in the paired case, are now quite relevant as an expression of random variation.

UNPAIRED CASE

Suppose $x_{11}, x_{12}, \ldots, x_{1n_1}$ are drawn at random from a distribution with mean μ_1 and variance σ_1^2, and $x_{21}, x_{22}, \ldots, x_{2n_2}$ from a distribution with mean μ_2 and variance σ_2^2. Let $\bar{x}_1$ and $\bar{x}_2$ be the sample means. If the two samples are independent, we have, from (3.8) and (3.9),

$$\left.\begin{aligned} E(\bar{x}_1-\bar{x}_2)&=\mu_1-\mu_2 \\ \text{and}\qquad & \\ \operatorname{var}(\bar{x}_1-\bar{x}_2)&=\frac{\sigma_1^2}{n_1}+\frac{\sigma_2^2}{n_2}. \end{aligned}\right\} \tag{4.8}$$

If the distributions of the x's are normal, and σ_1^2 and σ_2^2 are known, (4.8) can be used immediately for inferences about $\mu_1-\mu_2$. To test the null hypothesis that $\mu_1=\mu_2$, the standardized normal deviate

$$u=\frac{\bar{x}_1-\bar{x}_2}{\sqrt{\left(\frac{\sigma_1^2}{n_1}+\frac{\sigma_2^2}{n_2}\right)}}$$

is used. For confidence limits for $\mu_1-\mu_2$, the appropriate multiple of the standard error (i.e. of the denominator of u) is measured on either side of $\bar{x}_1-\bar{x}_2$.

The normality of the x's is not a serious restriction if the sample sizes are not too small, because $\bar{x}_1-\bar{x}_2$, like $\bar{x}_1$ and $\bar{x}_2$ separately, will be almost normally distributed. The lack of knowledge of σ_1^2 and σ_2^2 is more serious. These variances have to be estimated in some way, and we shall distinguish between two situations, in the first of which σ_1^2 and σ_2^2 are assumed to be equal and a common estimate is used for both parameters, and in the second of which no such assumption is made.

(a) *Equal variances: the two-sample t test*

There are many instances in which it is reasonable to assume $\sigma_1^2=\sigma_2^2$.

(i) In testing a null hypothesis that the two samples are from distributions with the same mean *and variance*. For example, if the two samples are observations made on patients treated with a possibly active drug and on other patients treated with a pharmacologically inert placebo, the null hypothesis might specify that the drug was completely inert. In that case equality of variances is as much a part of the null hypothesis as equality of means, although we want a test based on $\bar{x}_1-\bar{x}_2$ so that we can hope to detect drugs which particularly affect the mean value of x.

(ii) It may be known from general experience that the sort of changes which distinguish sample 1 from sample 2 may affect the mean but are not likely to affect the variance appreciably. The sample estimates of variance, s_1^2 and s_2^2, may differ considerably, but in these situations we should, on general grounds, be prepared to regard most of the difference as due to sampling fluctuations in s_1^2 and s_2^2 rather than to a corresponding difference in σ_1^2 and σ_2^2.

If σ_1^2 and σ_2^2 are equal, their common value may be denoted by σ^2 without a suffix. How should σ^2 be estimated? From the first sample we have the estimator

$$s_1^2 = \frac{\sum_1 (x-\bar{x}_1)^2}{n_1 - 1},$$

the suffix 1 after $\sum$ denoting a summation over the first sample. From the second sample, similarly, σ^2 is estimated by

$$s_2^2 = \frac{\sum_2 (x-\bar{x}_2)^2}{n_2 - 1}.$$

A common estimate could be got by a straightforward mean of s_1^2 and s_2^2, but it is better to take a weighted mean, giving more weight to the estimate from the larger sample. It can be shown to be appropriate to take

$$s^2 = \frac{(n_1-1)\,s_1^2 + (n_2-1)\,s_2^2}{(n_1-1)+(n_2-1)}$$

$$= \frac{\sum_1 (x-\bar{x}_1)^2 + \sum_2 (x-\bar{x}_2)^2}{n_1+n_2-2}.$$

This step enables us to use the t distribution on n_1+n_2-2 degrees of freedom, as an exact solution to the problem if the x's are exactly normally distributed and as an approximate solution if the distribution of the x's is not grossly non-normal.

The standard error of $\bar{x}_1 - \bar{x}_2$ is now estimated by

$$\mathrm{SE}(\bar{x}_1 - \bar{x}_2) = \sqrt{\left\{ s^2 \left(\frac{1}{n_1} + \frac{1}{n_2} \right) \right\}}.$$

To test the null hypothesis that $\mu_1 = \mu_2$, we take

$$t = \frac{\bar{x}_1 - \bar{x}_2}{\mathrm{SE}(\bar{x}_1 - \bar{x}_2)}$$

as following the t distribution on n_1+n_2-2 DF.

Confidence limits are given by

$$\bar{x}_1 - \bar{x}_2 \pm t_{\nu,\,0.05}\,\mathrm{SE}(\bar{x}_1 - \bar{x}_2)$$

with $\nu = n_1+n_2-2$.

Example 4.6

Two groups of female rats were placed on diets with high and low protein content, and the gain in weight between the 28th and 84th days of age was measured for each rat. The results are given in Table 4.2.

TABLE 4.2 Gain in weight (g) between 28th and 84th days of age of rats receiving diets with high and low protein content.

	High protein	Low protein
	134	70
	146	118
	104	101
	119	85
	124	107
	161	132
	107	94
	83	
	113	
	129	
	97	
	123	
Total	1,440	707

The calculations proceed as follows

$$\Sigma_1 x = 1440 \qquad \Sigma_2 x = 707$$

$$n_1 = 12 \qquad n_2 = 7$$

$$\bar{x}_1 = 120{\cdot}0 \qquad \bar{x}_2 = 101{\cdot}0$$

$$\Sigma_1 x^2 = 177832 \qquad \Sigma_2 x^2 = 73959$$

$$(\Sigma_1 x)^2/n_1 = 172800{\cdot}00 \qquad (\Sigma_2 x)^2/n_2 = 71407{\cdot}00$$

$$\Sigma_1(x-\bar{x}_1)^2 = 5032{\cdot}00 \qquad \Sigma_2(x-\bar{x}_2)^2 = 2552{\cdot}00$$

$$s^2 = \frac{5032+2552}{17} = 446{\cdot}12$$

$$\begin{aligned}\mathrm{SE}(\bar{x}_1-\bar{x}_2) &= \sqrt{\{(446{\cdot}12)(\tfrac{1}{12}+\tfrac{1}{7})\}}\\ &= \sqrt{\{(446{\cdot}12)(0{\cdot}22619)\}}\\ &= \sqrt{100{\cdot}9}\\ &= 10{\cdot}04.\end{aligned}$$

To test the null hypothesis that $\mu_1 = \mu_2$,

$$t = \frac{120\cdot0 - 101\cdot0}{10\cdot04} = \frac{19\cdot0}{10\cdot04} = 1\cdot89 \text{ on 17 DF } (0\cdot05 < P < 0\cdot10).$$

The difference is not quite significant at the 5 per cent level, and would provide merely suggestive evidence for a dietary effect.

Ninety-five per cent confidence limits for $\mu_1 - \mu_2$ are

$$\begin{aligned} &19\cdot0 \pm (2\cdot110)(10\cdot04) \\ &= 19\cdot0 \pm 21\cdot2 \\ &= -2\cdot2 \quad \text{and} \quad 40\cdot2. \end{aligned}$$

The range of likely values for $\mu_1 - \mu_2$ is large. If the experimenter feels dissatisfied with this range of uncertainty, his easiest remedy is to repeat the experiment with more observations. Higher values of n_1 and n_2 will tend to decrease the standard error of $\bar{x}_1 - \bar{x}_2$ and hence increase the precision of the comparison.

(b) *Unequal variances*

In other situations it may be either clear that the variances differ considerably or prudent to assume that they may do so. One possible approach, in the first case, is to work with a transformed scale of measurement (Chapter 11). If the means, as well as the variances, differ, it may be possible to find a transformed scale, such as the logarithm of the original measurement, on which the means differ but the variances are similar. On the other hand, if the original means are not too different it will usually be difficult to find a transformation which substantially reduces the disparity between the variances.

In these situations the main defect in the methods based on the t distribution is the use of a pooled estimate of variance. It is better to estimate the standard error of the difference between the two means as

$$\text{SE}(\bar{x}_1 - \bar{x}_2) = \sqrt{\left\{\frac{s_1^2}{n_1} + \frac{s_2^2}{n_2}\right\}}.$$

A significance test of the null hypothesis may be based on the statistic

$$d = \frac{\bar{x}_1 - \bar{x}_2}{\sqrt{\left\{\frac{s_1^2}{n_1} + \frac{s_2^2}{n_2}\right\}}},$$

which is approximately a standardized normal deviate if n_1 and n_2 are reasonably large. Similarly, approximate confidence limits are given by

$$\bar{x}_1 - \bar{x}_2 \pm u_{2\alpha}\,\mathrm{SE}(\bar{x}_1 - \bar{x}_2),$$

where $u_{2\alpha}$ is the appropriate standardized normal deviate corresponding to the two-sided probability 2α.

However, this method is no more exact for finite values of n_1 and n_2 than would be the use of the normal approximation to the t distribution in the case of equal variances. The appropriate analogue of the t distribution is both more complex than the t distribution and more contentious. One solution, due to B.L.Welch, is to use a distribution for d (tabulated, for example, in Pearson and Hartley (1966) Table 11). The critical value for any particular probability level depends on s_1^2/s_2^2, n_1 and n_2. Another solution, similarly dependent on s_1^2/s_2^2, n_1 and n_2, is that of W.V.Behrens, tabulated as Table VI in Fisher and Yates (1963). The distinction between these two approaches is due to different approaches to the logic of statistical inference. Underlying Welch's test is an interpretation of probability levels, either in significance tests or confidence intervals, as long-term frequencies in repeated samples from the same populations. The Behrens test was advocated by R.A. Fisher as an example of the use of fiducial inference, and it arises also from the Bayesian approach (section 4.11).

Example 4.7

A suspension of virus particles is prepared at two dilutions. If the experimental techniques are perfect, preparation B should have 10 times as high a concentration of virus particles as preparation A. Equal volumes from each suspension are inoculated onto the chorioallantoic membrane of chick embryos. After an appropriate incubation period the membranes are removed and the number of pocks on each membrane is counted. The numbers are as follows:

Preparation	A	B
Counts	0	10
	0	13
	1	13
	1	14
	1	19
	1	20
	2	21
	2	26
	3	29

Are these results consistent with the hypothesis that, in a large enough series of counts, the mean for preparation B will be 10 times that for preparation A? If the counts on B are divided by 10 and denoted by x_2, the counts on A being denoted by x_1, an equivalent question is whether the means of x_1 and x_2 differ significantly.

Preparation	A	B
Counts	x_1	x_2
	0	1·0
	0	1·3
	1	1·3
	1	1·4
	1	1·9
	1	2·0
	2	2·1
	2	2·6
	3	2·9

$n_1=9$ $\qquad n_2=9$

$\bar{x}_1=1·2222$ $\qquad \bar{x}_2=1·8333$

$s_1^2=0·9444$ $\qquad s_2^2=0·4100$

The estimates of variance are perhaps not sufficiently different here to cause great disquiet, but it is known from experience with this type of data that estimates of variance of pock counts, standardized for dilution as we did for x_2, tend to decrease as the original counts increase. The excess of $s_1{}^2$ over $s_2{}^2$ is therefore probably not due to sampling error. We have

$$d=\frac{1·2222-1·8333}{\sqrt{\left\{\frac{0·9444}{9}+\frac{0·4100}{9}\right\}}}=\frac{-0·6111}{0·3879}=-1·58.$$

Note that when, as here, $n_1=n_2$, d turns out to have exactly the same numerical value as t, because the expression inside the square root can be written either as

$$\frac{s_1^2}{n}+\frac{s_2^2}{n} \quad \text{or as} \quad \tfrac{1}{2}(s_1^2+s_2^2)\left(\frac{1}{n}+\frac{1}{n}\right).$$

However, we shall proceed with Welch's test for d. The tables are tabulated in terms of

$$\frac{s_1^2/n_1}{(s_1^2/n_1)+(s_2^2/n_2)}=\frac{0·1049}{0·1504}=0·697,$$

which is near to the tabulated value of 0·7. In the column headed 0·7, and for degrees of freedom $\nu_1=8$ $(=9-1)$ and $\nu_2=8$, the 10 per cent point is shown as 1·76. The observed value of $-1·58$ is numerically less than the tabulated value, and we conclude that the difference is not significant at the 10 per cent level.

The next example illustrates the use of paired and unpaired t tests to answer different questions about the same data.

Example 4.8

In a clinical trial of a new drug for the treatment of enuresis each of 29 patients was given the drug for a period of 14 days and a placebo for a separate period of 14 days, the order of administration being chosen randomly for each patient. Table 4.3 shows the number of dry nights experienced during each treatment period.

TABLE 4.3 Number of dry nights out of 14 nights experienced by patients with enuresis treated by drug and placebo.

Serial number	(1) Drug	(2) Placebo	(3) Difference (1)−(2)	Serial number	(4) Placebo	(5) Drug	(6) Difference (5)−(4)
1	8	5	3	2	12	11	−1
3	14	10	4	5	6	8	2
4	8	0	8	8	13	9	−4
6	9	7	2	10	8	8	0
7	11	6	5	12	8	9	1
9	3	5	−2	14	4	8	4
11	6	0	6	15	8	14	6
13	0	0	0	17	2	4	2
16	13	12	1	20	8	13	5
18	10	2	8	23	9	7	−2
19	7	5	2	26	7	10	3
21	13	13	0	29	7	6	−1
22	8	10	−2				
24	7	7	0				
25	9	0	9				
27	10	6	4				
28	2	2	0				

A test for the relative effectiveness of drug and placebo is obtained from the complete series of 29 paired observations. The t test on the 29 differences in columns (3) and (6) gives

$$\bar{d}=2{\cdot}172$$

$$s^2=11{\cdot}005$$

$$\mathrm{SE}(\bar{d})=\sqrt{(11{\cdot}005/29)}=0{\cdot}616$$

$$t=\bar{d}/\mathrm{SE}(\bar{d})=3{\cdot}53 \text{ on 28 DF } (P<0{\cdot}01). \qquad (4.9)$$

To see whether the order of administration has any effect, we can compare the mean, $\bar{d}_1$, of the 17 differences in column (3) for patients receiving the the drug first, with $\bar{d}_2$, the mean of the 12 differences in column (6) for patients receiving the placebo first. The two-sample (or unpaired) t test for this comparison gives

$$\bar{d}_1 = 2{\cdot}824 \qquad \bar{d}_2 = 1{\cdot}250$$

$$s_0^2 = 10{\cdot}767$$

$$\text{SE}(\bar{d}_1 - \bar{d}_2) = \sqrt{\{(10{\cdot}767)(\tfrac{1}{17} + \tfrac{1}{12})\}} = 1{\cdot}237$$

$$t = (\bar{d}_1 - \bar{d}_2)/\text{SE}(\bar{d}_1 - \bar{d}_2) = 1{\cdot}27 \text{ on 27 DF } (0{\cdot}2 < P < 0{\cdot}3).$$

There is thus no strong evidence of any effect of order of administration.

However, this result suggests another test for the relative effect of drug and placebo. The paired t test on all 29 patients, while perfectly valid, ignored the evidence about the effect of order. Rather more patients received the drug before the placebo than the reverse; if anything, the order (D, P) favours the drug rather more than the order (P, D). The drug is therefore shown to slightly better advantage than if the numbers had been exactly equal. If there had been equal numbers receiving each of the two orders of administration the estimated mean difference would have been

$$\bar{d}_0 = \tfrac{1}{2}(\bar{d}_1 + \bar{d}_2) = 2{\cdot}037$$

$$\text{SE}(d_0) = \tfrac{1}{2}\sqrt{s_0^2(\tfrac{1}{17} + \tfrac{1}{12})} = 0{\cdot}619$$

and

$$t = \bar{d}_0/\text{SE}(\bar{d}_0) = 3{\cdot}29 \text{ on 27 DF } (P < 0{\cdot}01).$$

The result is very similar to that given by the one-sample t test at (4.9). If the order effect had been greater we should have expected a more noticeable change in the value of t after taking it into account. Not only would the estimated mean difference have been affected more, but the residual variation would have been more markedly reduced.

4.7 COMPARISON OF TWO PROPORTIONS

As in the comparison of two means, considered in the last section, we can distinguish between two situations according to whether individual members of the two samples are or are not paired.

PAIRED CASE

Suppose there are N observations in each sample, forming therefore N pairs of observations. Denoting the samples by 1 and 2, and describing each individual as A or not A, there are clearly four types of pairs:

Type	Sample 1	Sample 2	Number of pairs
1	A	A	k
2	A	not A	r
3	not A	A	s
4	not A	not A	m

If the numbers of pairs of the four types are as shown above, another way of exhibiting the same results is in the form of a two-way table:

		Sample 2: A	Sample 2: not A	
Sample 1	A	k	r	$k+r$
	not A	s	m	$s+m$
		$k+s$	$r+m$	N

The proportions of A-individuals in the two samples are $(k+r)/N$ in sample 1 and $(k+s)/N$ in sample 2. We are interested in the difference between the two proportions, which is clearly $(r-s)/N$.

Consider first a significance test. The null hypothesis is that the expectation of $(r-s)/N$ is zero, or in other words that the expectations of r and s are equal. This can conveniently be done by restricting our attention to the $r+s$ pairs in which the two members are of different types. Denote $r+s$ by n. On the null hypothesis, given n disparate or 'untied' pairs, the number of pairs of type 2 (or, indeed, of type 3) would follow a binomial distribution with a parameter equal to $\frac{1}{2}$. The test therefore follows precisely the methods of section 4.4. A large sample test is obtained by regarding

$$u=\frac{r-\frac{1}{2}n}{\frac{1}{2}\sqrt{n}} \tag{4.10}$$

as a standardized normal deviate. A continuity correction may be aplied by reducing the absolute value of $r-\frac{1}{2}n$ by $\frac{1}{2}$. This test is sometimes known as McNemar's test.

Approximate confidence limits for the difference between the two proportions are given by taking its standard error to be $\sqrt{(r+s)}/N$, and using the usual normal theory.

Example 4.9

Fifty specimens of sputum are each cultured on two different media, A and B, the object being to compare the ability of the two media to detect tubercle

TABLE 4.4 Distribution of 50 specimens of sputum according to results of culture on two media.

Type	Medium A	Medium B	Number of sputa
1	+	+	20
2	+	−	12
3	−	+	2
4	−	−	16
			50

Alternative layout

		Medium B +	Medium B −	Total
Medium A	+	20	12	32
	−	2	16	18
Total		22	28	50

bacilli. The results are shown in Table 4.4. The null hypothesis that the media are equally effective is tested by the standardized normal deviate

$$u=\frac{12-(\frac{1}{2})(14)}{\frac{1}{2}\sqrt{14}}=\frac{5}{1\cdot871}=2\cdot67\ (P<0\cdot01).$$

There is very little doubt that A is more effective than B. The continuity correction would reduce the normal deviate to $4\cdot5/1\cdot871=2\cdot41$, still a significant result.

Ninety-five per cent confidence limits for the difference between the proportions of positive sputum on the two media are given by

$$\frac{(12-2)}{50}\pm\frac{1\cdot96\sqrt{14}}{50}$$

$$=0\cdot20\pm0\cdot15$$

$$=0\cdot05 \text{ and } 0\cdot35.$$

It should be noted that although the significance test is based entirely on the two frequencies r and s, the estimated difference between the proportions of positives, and its standard error, depend also on N. That is, evidence as to the existence of a difference is provided solely by the untied pairs; an assessment of the *magnitude* of that difference must allude to the remainder of the data.

UNPAIRED CASE

Suppose there are two populations in which the probabilities that an individual shows characteristic A are π_1 and π_2. A random sample of size n_1 from the first population has r_1 members showing the characteristic (and a proportion $p_1=r_1/n_1$), while the corresponding values for an independent sample from the second population are n_2, r_2, and $p_2=r_2/n_2$. From (3.8) and (3.9),

$$E(p_1-p_2)=\pi_1-\pi_2$$

and

$$\mathrm{var}(p_1-p_2)=\frac{\pi_1(1-\pi_1)}{n_1}+\frac{\pi_2(1-\pi_2)}{n_2}.$$

For confidence limits, π_1 and π_2 are unknown and may be replaced by p_1 and p_2, respectively, to give

$$\mathrm{var}(p_1-p_2)=\frac{p_1q_1}{n_1}+\frac{p_2q_2}{n_2}, \tag{4.11}$$

where

$$q_1=1-p_1 \quad \text{and} \quad q_2=1-p_2.$$

Approximate limits then follow by applying the usual normal theory.

Suppose we wish to test the null hypothesis that $\pi_1=\pi_2$. Call the common value π. Then p_1 and p_2 are both estimates of π, and there is little point in estimating π (as in (4.11)) by two different quantities in two different places in the expression. If the null hypothesis is true both samples are from effectively the same population, and the best estimate of π will be obtained by pooling the two samples, to give

$$p=\frac{r_1+r_2}{n_1+n_2}.$$

This pooled estimate is now substituted for both π_1 and π_2 to give

$$\mathrm{var}(p_1-p_2)=pq\left(\frac{1}{n_1}+\frac{1}{n_2}\right),$$

writing as usual $q=1-p$. The null hypothesis is thus tested approximately by taking

$$u = \frac{p_1 - p_2}{\sqrt{\left\{pq\left(\frac{1}{n_1} + \frac{1}{n_2}\right)\right\}}}$$

as a standardized normal deviate.

Example 4.10

In a clinical trial to assess the value of a new method of treatment (A) in comparison with the old method (B), patients were divided at random into two groups. Of 257 patients treated by method A, 41 died; of 244 patients treated by method B, 64 died. Thus, $p_1 = 41/257 = 0{\cdot}1595$ and $p_2 = 64/244 = 0{\cdot}2623$.

The difference between the two fatality rates is estimated as $0{\cdot}1595 - 0{\cdot}2623 = -0{\cdot}1028$. For 95 per cent confidence limits we take

$$\begin{aligned} \text{var}(p_1 - p_2) &= \frac{(0{\cdot}1595)(0{\cdot}8405)}{257} + \frac{(0{\cdot}2623)(0{\cdot}7377)}{244} \\ &= 0{\cdot}0005216 + 0{\cdot}0007930 \\ &= 0{\cdot}0013146 \end{aligned}$$

and

$$\text{SE}(p_1 - p_2) = \sqrt{0{\cdot}0013146} = 0{\cdot}0363.$$

Thus 95 per cent confidence limits are

$$-0{\cdot}1028 \pm (1{\cdot}96)(0{\cdot}0363) = -0{\cdot}0317 \quad \text{and} \quad -0{\cdot}1739,$$

the minus sign merely serving to indicate in which direction the difference lies.

For the significance test, we form the pooled proportion

$$p = 105/501 = 0{\cdot}2096$$

and estimate $\text{SE}(p_1 - p_2)$ as

$$\begin{aligned} &\sqrt{\{(0{\cdot}2096)(0{\cdot}7904)(\tfrac{1}{257} + \tfrac{1}{244})\}} \\ &= 0{\cdot}0364. \end{aligned}$$

Thus, the normal deviate is

$$\frac{-0{\cdot}1028}{0{\cdot}0364} = -2{\cdot}82 \ (P < 0{\cdot}01).$$

There is strong evidence of a difference in fatality rates, in favour of A.

Note that, in Example 4.10, the use of p changed the standard error only marginally, from 0·0363 to 0·0364. In fact, there is likely to be an appreciable change only when n_1 and n_2 are very unequal and when p_1 and p_2 differ substantially. In other circumstances, either standard error formula may be regarded as a good approximation to the other, and used accordingly.

4.8 FOURFOLD TABLES AND χ^2 TESTS

An alternative way of displaying the data of Example 4.10 is shown in Table 4.5. This is often called a *fourfold* or 2×2 *contingency table.* The total frequency, 501 in this example, is shown in the lower right corner of the table. This total frequency or *grand total* is split into two

TABLE 4.5 Fourfold table showing results of a clinical trial.

	Outcome		
Treatment	Death	Survival	Total
A	41	216	257
B	64	180	244
Total	105	396	501

different dichotomies represented by the two 'horizontal' rows of the table and the two 'vertical' columns. In this example the rows represent the two treatments and the columns represent the two outcomes of treatment. There are thus $2 \times 2 = 4$ combinations of row and column categories, and the corresponding frequencies occupy the four *inner cells* in the body of the table. The total frequencies for the two row categories and those for the two columns are shown at the right and at the foot, and are called *marginal totals.*

We have already used a 2×2 table (Table 4.4) to display the results needed for a comparison of proportions in paired samples, but the purpose was a little different from the present approach which is concerned solely with the *unpaired* case.

We are concerned, in Table 4.5, with possible differences between the fatality rates for the two treatments. Given the marginal totals in Table 4.5 we can easily calculate what numbers would have had to be observed in the body of the table to make the fatality rates for *A* and *B* exactly equal. In the top left cell, for example, this *expected* number is

$$\frac{105 \times 257}{501} = 53{\cdot}862,$$

since the overall fatality rate is 105/501 and there are 257 individuals treated with A. Similar expected numbers can be obtained for each of the four inner cells, and are shown in Table 4.6 (where the observed and expected numbers are distinguished by the letters O and E). The

TABLE 4.6 Expected frequencies and contributions to X^2 for data in Table 4.5.

Treatment		Outcome: Death	Outcome: Survival	Total
	O	41	216	257
	E	*53·862*	*203·138*	*257*
A	$O-E$	−12·862	12·862	0
	$(O-E)^2$	165·431	165·431	
	$(O-E)^2/E$	3·071	0·814	
	O	64	180	244
	E	*51·138*	*192·862*	*244*
B	$O-E$	12·862	−12·862	0
	$(O-E)^2$	165·431	165·431	
	$(O-E)^2/E$	3·235	0·858	
Total	O	105	396	501
	E	*105*	*396*	
	$O-E$	0	0	

expected numbers are not integers and have been rounded off to 3 decimals. Clearly one could not possibly observe 53·862 individuals in a particular cell. These expected numbers should be thought of as expectations or mean values over a large number of possible tables with the same marginal totals as those observed, when the null hypothesis is true.

Note that the values of E sum, over both rows and columns, to the observed marginal totals. It follows that the *discrepancies*, measured by the differences $O-E$, add to zero along rows and columns; in other words, the four discrepancies are numerically the same (12·862 in this example), two being positive and two negative.

In a rough sense, the greater the discrepancies, the more evidence we have against the null hypothesis. It would therefore seem reasonable to base a significance test somehow on these discrepancies. It also seems reasonable to take account of the absolute size of the frequencies: a discrepancy of 5 is much more important if $E=5$ than if $E=100$.

It turns out to be appropriate to calculate the following index:

$$X^2=\sum\frac{(O-E)^2}{E}, \tag{4.12}$$

the summation being over the four inner cells of the table. The contributions to X^2 from the four cells are shown in Table 4.6. The total is

$$\begin{aligned} X^2 &= 3{\cdot}071+0{\cdot}814+3{\cdot}235+0{\cdot}858 \\ &= 7{\cdot}978. \end{aligned}$$

On the null hypothesis, X^2 follows the $\chi^2_{(1)}$ distribution (see section 3.4), the approximation improving as the expected numbers get larger. Reference to Table A2 shows that the observed value of 7·978 is beyond the 0·01 point of the $\chi^2_{(1)}$ distribution, and the difference between the two fatality rates is therefore significant at the 1 per cent level.

We have already observed that the $\chi^2_{(1)}$ distribution is the distribution of the square of a standardized normal deviate. In section 4.7, we derived a standardized normal deviate by calculating the standard error of the difference between the two proportions, obtaining the numerical value 2·82. Squaring 2·82 gives 7·95, which agrees with X^2 apart from rounding errors. In fact, it can be shown algebraically that the X^2 index is always the same as the square of the normal deviate given by the first method. The probability levels given by the two tests are therefore always in agreement, just as in this example both tests gave $P<0{\cdot}01$.

The X^2 index is often denoted by χ^2, although it seems slightly preferable to reserve the latter for the theoretical distribution, denoting the calculated value by X^2.

There are various alternative formulae for X^2, of which we may note one. Denote the entries in the table as follows:

		Column		
		1	2	
Row	1	a	b	r_1
	2	c	d	r_2
		s_1	s_2	N

Then

$$X^2 = \frac{(ad-bc)^2 N}{r_1 r_2 s_1 s_2}. \tag{4.13}$$

The repeated product in the numerator of this formula makes the version rather less suited for the use of a desk calculator unless it has provision for repeated divisions.

We have, then, two entirely equivalent significance tests. Which the user chooses to use is to some extent a matter of taste and convenience. However there are two points to be made. First, the standard error method, as we have seen, not only yields a significance test but also leads naturally into the calculation of confidence intervals. In general, a statistical analysis which provides merely a significance test and fails to estimate the magnitude of the relevant contrast with some allowance for sampling error must be judged inadequate. This, then, is a strong argument for calculating differences and standard errors, and basing the test on these values rather than on the X^2 index. The main counter-argument is that, as we shall see in Chapter 7, the X^2 method can be generalized to contingency tables with more than two rows and columns.

It is important to remember that the X^2 index can only be calculated from 2×2 tables in which the entries are frequencies. A common error is to use it for a table in which the entries are mean values of a certain variable; this practice is completely erroneous.

Both the standard error and the χ^2 tests are based on approximations which are valid particularly when the frequencies are high. In general two methods of improvement are widely used: the application of a continuity correction and the calculation of exact probabilities.

CONTINUITY CORRECTION FOR FOURFOLD TABLES

This method was described by F.Yates and is often called *Yates's correction.* The $\chi^2_{(1)}$ distribution has been used as an approximation to the distribution of X^2 on the null hypothesis and subject to fixed marginal totals. Under the latter constraint only a finite number of tables are possible. For the marginal totals of Table 4.5, for example, all the possible tables can be generated by increasing or decreasing one of the entries by one unit at a time, until either that entry or some other reaches zero. (A fuller discussion follows later in this section.) The position therefore is rather like that discussed in section 2.7 where a discrete distribution (the binomial) was approximated by a continuous distribution (the normal). In the present case it would be reasonable to base the significance test on the probability of the observed table or one showing a more extreme departure from the null hypothesis. An improvement in the estimation of this probability is achieved by reducing the absolute value of the discrepancy, $O-E$, by $\frac{1}{2}$ before calculating X^2. In Example 4.10, Table 4.6, this would mean taking $|O-E|$ to be 12·362 instead of 12·862, and the corrected value of X^2, denoted by X_c^2, is 7·369, somewhat less than the uncorrected value but still highly significant.

The continuity correction has a relatively greater effect when the expected frequencies are small than when they are large, but it is probably wise practice to apply it for almost all χ^2 tests for 2×2 tables. One exception to this suggestion is when a number of X^2 values are being combined, a problem discussed in section 12.3.

The continuity-corrected version of (4.13) is

$$X_c^2=\frac{(|ad-bc|-\frac{1}{2}N)^2N}{r_1r_2s_1s_2}. \tag{4.14}$$

If the continuity correction is applied in the χ^2 test, it should logically be applied in the standard error test. The procedure there is to calculate p_1-p_2 after the frequencies have been moved half a unit nearer their expected values, the standard error remaining unchanged. Thus, in Example 4.10, we should have $p_{1(c)}=41{\cdot}5/257=0{\cdot}1615$, $p_{2(c)}=63{\cdot}5/244=0{\cdot}2602$, giving $u_{(c)}=-0{\cdot}0987/0{\cdot}0364=-2{\cdot}71$. Since $(-2{\cdot}71)^2=7{\cdot}34$, the result agrees with that for X_c^2 apart from rounding errors.

THE EXACT TEST FOR FOURFOLD TABLES

Even with the continuity correction there will be some doubt about the adequacy of the χ^2 approximation when the frequencies are particularly small. An exact test was suggested almost simultaneously in the mid-1930s by R.A.Fisher, J.O.Irwin and F.Yates. It consists in calculating the exact probabilities in the distribution described in the previous subsection. The probability of a table with frequencies

a	b	r_1
c	d	r_2
s_1	s_2	N

is given by the formula

$$\frac{r_1!\, r_2!\, s_1!\, s_2!}{N!\, a!\, b!\, c!\, d!}. \tag{4.15}$$

Given any observed table, the probabilities of all tables with the same marginal totals can be calculated, and the *P*-value for the significance test calculated by summation. Example 4.11 illustrates the calculations and some of the difficulties of interpretation which may arise.

Example 4.11

The data in Table 4.7, due to M.Hellman, are discussed by Yates (1934a).

TABLE 4.7 Data on malocclusion of teeth in infants (Yates, 1934a).

	Infants with normal teeth	Infants with malocclusion	Total
Breast-fed	4	16	20
Bottle-fed	1	21	22
Total	5	37	42

There are six possible tables with the same marginal totals as those observed, since neither *a* nor *c* (in the notation given above) can fall below 0 or exceed 5, the smallest marginal total in the table. The cell frequencies in each of these tables are shown in Table 4.8.

TABLE 4.8 Cell frequencies in tables with same marginal totals as those in Table 4.7.

0	20	20	1	19	20	2	18	20
5	17	22	4	18	22	3	19	22
5	37	42	5	37	42	5	37	42
3	17	20	4	16	20	5	15	20
2	20	22	1	21	22	0	22	22
5	37	42	5	37	42	5	37	42

The probability that $a=0$ is, from (4.15),

$$P_0=\frac{20!\,22!\,5!\,37!}{42!\,0!\,20!\,5!\,17!}=0{\cdot}03096.$$

Tables of log factorials (Fisher and Yates, Table XXX) are often useful for this calculation. The probabilities for $a=1, 2, \ldots, 5$ can be obtained by successive multiplying factors. Thus,

$$P_1=\frac{5\times 20}{1\times 18}\times P_0$$

$$P_2=\frac{4\times 19}{2\times 19}\times P_1, \text{ etc.}$$

The results are:

a	Probability
0	0·0310
1	0·1720
2	0·3440
3	0·3096
4	0·1253
5	0·0182
	1·0001

The observed table has a probability of 0·1253. To assess its significance we could measure the extent to which it falls into the tail of the distribution by calculating the probability of that table or of one more extreme. For a one-sided test the procedure clearly gives

$$P=0{\cdot}1253+0{\cdot}0182=0{\cdot}1435.$$

The result is not significant at even the 10 per cent level.

For a two-sided test the other tail of the distribution must be taken into account, and here some ambiguity arises. Many authors advocate that the one-tailed P-value should be doubled. In the present example, the one-tailed test gave $P=0{\cdot}1435$ and the two-tailed test would give $P=0{\cdot}2870$. An alternative approach is to calculate P as the total probability of tables, in either tail, which are at least as extreme as that observed in the sense of having a probability at least as small. In the present example we should have

$$P=0{\cdot}1253+0{\cdot}0182+0{\cdot}0310=0{\cdot}1745.$$

The first procedure is probably to be preferred on the grounds that a significant result is interpreted as strong evidence for a difference *in the observed direction*, and there is some merit in controlling the chance probability of such a result to no more than half the two-sided significance level. The tables of Finney *et al.* (1963) enable one-sided tests at various significance levels to be made without computation provided the frequencies are not too great.

The results of applying the exact test in this example may be compared with those obtained by the χ^2 test with Yates's correction. We find $X^2=2{\cdot}39$ ($P=0{\cdot}12$) without correction and $X_c^2=1{\cdot}14$ ($P=0{\cdot}29$) with correction. The probability level of 0·29 for X_c^2 agrees well with the two-sided value 0·29 from the exact test.

Cochran (1954) recommends the use of the exact test, in preference to the χ^2 test with continuity correction, (i) if $N<20$, or (ii) if $20<N<40$ and the smallest expected value is less than 5.

4.9 COMPARISON OF TWO COUNTS

Suppose that x_1 is a count, say, of the number of events occurring during a certain period or the number of small objects observed in a certain region, which can be assumed to follow a Poisson distribution with mean μ_1 (section 2.6). Similarly let x_2 be a count independently following a Poisson distribution with mean μ_2. How might we test the null hypothesis that $\mu_1=\mu_2$?

One approach would be to use the fact that the variance of x_1-x_2 is $\mu_1+\mu_2$ (by virtue of (2.16) and (3.9)). The best estimate of $\mu_1+\mu_2$ on the basis of the available information is x_1+x_2. On the null hypothesis $E(x_1-x_2)=\mu_1-\mu_2=0$, and x_1-x_2 can be taken to be approximately normally distributed unless μ_1 and μ_2 are very small. Hence,

$$u=\frac{x_1-x_2}{\sqrt{(x_1+x_2)}} \qquad (4.16)$$

can be taken as approximately a standardized normal deviate.

A second approach has already been indicated in the test for the comparison of proportions in paired samples (section 4.7). Of the total frequency x_1+x_2, a portion x_1 is observed in the first sample. Writing $n=x_1+x_2$ and $r=x_1$ in (4.10) we have

$$u=\frac{x_1-\frac{1}{2}(x_1+x_2)}{\frac{1}{2}\sqrt{(x_1+x_2)}}=\frac{x_1-x_2}{\sqrt{(x_1+x_2)}}$$

as in (4.16). The two approaches thus lead to exactly the same test procedure.

A third approach uses a rather different application of the χ^2 test from that described for the 2×2 table in section 4.8. Corresponding to each observed frequency we can consider the expected frequency, on the null hypothesis, to be $\frac{1}{2}(x_1+x_2)$:

Observed	x_1	x_2
Expected	$\frac{1}{2}(x_1+x_2)$	$\frac{1}{2}(x_1+x_2)$

Applying the usual formula (4.12) for a χ^2 statistic, we have

$$X^2=\frac{\{x_1-\frac{1}{2}(x_1+x_2)\}^2}{\frac{1}{2}(x_1+x_2)}+\frac{\{x_2-\frac{1}{2}(x_1+x_2)\}^2}{\frac{1}{2}(x_1+x_2)}$$

$$=\frac{(x_1-x_2)^2}{x_1+x_2}. \tag{4.17}$$

From a general result described in section 12.7 X^2 follows the $\chi^2_{(1)}$ distribution, which we already know to be the distribution of the square of a standardized normal deviate. It is therefore not surprising that X^2 given by (4.17) is precisely the square of u given by (4.16). The third approach is thus equivalent to the other two, and forms a particularly useful method of computation since no square root is involved in (4.17). This is one of the few statistical calculations that really *can* be done in one's head.

Consider now an estimation problem. What can be said about the ratio μ_1/μ_2? The second approach described above can be generalized, when the null hypothesis is not necessarily true, by saying that $x_1/(x_1+x_2)$ follows a binomial distribution with parameters x_1+x_2 (the n of section 2.5) and $\mu_1/(\mu_1+\mu_2)$ (the π of section 2.5). The methods of section 4.4 thus provide confidence limits for $\pi=\mu_1/(\mu_1+\mu_2)$, and hence for μ_1/μ_2 which is merely $\pi/(1-\pi)$.

Example 4.12

Equal volumes of two bacterial cultures are spread on nutrient media and after incubation the numbers of colonies growing on the two plates are 13 and 31. We require confidence limits for the ratio of concentrations of the two cultures.

The estimated ratio is 13/31=0·4194. From the Geigy tables a binomial sample with 13 successes out of 44 provides the following 95 per cent confidence limits for π: 0·1676 and 0·4520. Calculating $\pi/(1-\pi)$ for each of these limits gives the following 95 per cent confidence limits for μ_1/μ_2:

$$0{\cdot}1676/0{\cdot}8324=0{\cdot}2013$$

and

$$0{\cdot}4520/0{\cdot}5480=0{\cdot}8248.$$

The normal approximations described in section 4.4 can of course be used when the frequencies are not too small.

Example 4.13

Just as the distribution of a proportion, when n is large and π is small, is well approximated by assuming that the number of successes, r, follows a Poisson distribution, so a comparison of two proportions under these conditions can be effected by the methods of this section. Suppose, for example, that in a group of 1,000 men observed during a particular year, 20 incurred a certain disease, whereas in a second group of 500 men, four cases occurred. Is there a significant difference between these proportions? This question could be answered by the methods of section 4.7. As an approximation we could compare the observed proportion of deaths falling into group 2, $p=4/24$, with the theoretical proportion $\pi=500/1500=0{\cdot}3333$. The equivalent χ^2 test would run as follows:

	Group 1	Group 2	Total
Observed cases	20	4	24
Expected cases	$\frac{1000\times 24}{1500}=16$	$\frac{500\times 24}{1500}=8$	24

With continuity correction

$$\begin{aligned} X_c^2 &= (3\tfrac{1}{2})^2/16+(3\tfrac{1}{2})^2/8 \\ &= 0{\cdot}766+1{\cdot}531 \\ &= 2{\cdot}30\ (0{\cdot}1<P<0{\cdot}25). \end{aligned}$$

The difference is not significant.

If the full analysis for the 2×2 table is written out it will become clear that this abbreviated analysis differs from the full version in omitting the contributions to X^2 from the non-affected individuals. Since these are much more numerous than the cases, their contributions to X^2 have large denominators and are therefore negligible in comparison with the terms used above. This makes it clear that the short method described here must be used only when the proportions concerned are very small.

4.10 COMPARISON OF TWO VARIANCES

Suppose that two independent samples provide observations on a variable x, the first sample of n_1 observations giving an estimated variance s_1^2, and the second sample of n_2 observations giving an estimated variance s_2^2. If each sample is from a normal distribution the two estimates of variance can be compared approximately by the use of formula (3.12). The population variances σ_1^2 and σ_2^2 are unknown. For confidence limits σ_1^4 and σ_2^4 can be replaced in (3.12) by the sample estimates s_1^4 and s_2^4. For a significance test of the null hypothesis it would be preferable to replace each by s^4, where s^2 is the usual pooled estimate of variance:

$$s^2 = \frac{(n_1 - 1)\, s_1^2 + (n_2 - 1)\, s_2^2}{n_1 + n_2 - 2}.$$

However, as pointed out in section 3.5, the standard error of the *difference* between two estimates of variance is not commonly used, mainly because the normal approximation to the distribution of $s_1^2 - s_2^2$ is poor except in very large samples.

A more useful approach is to consider the *ratio* of the two variance estimates,

$$F = s_1^2/s_2^2.$$

If the null hypothesis is true, the distribution of F, in repeated pairs of samples of size n_1 and n_2 from normal distributions, is known exactly. It depends on n_1 and n_2 (or, equivalently, on the degrees of freedom, $\nu_1 = n_1 - 1$ and $\nu_2 = n_2 - 1$) but not on the common population variance σ^2. A tabulation of the F distributions as complete as that provided in Table A2 for the χ^2 distributions is impracticable because of the dependence on both ν_1 and ν_2. The standard books of tables (Fisher and Yates, 1963; Pearson and Hartley, 1966) provide a table of critical levels for F at each of a number of significance levels. An abbreviated version is shown in Table A4.

For particular values of ν_1 and ν_2, F can clearly assume values on either side of 1, and significant departures from the null hypothesis may be marked either by very small or by very large values of F. The tabulated critical values are, however, all greater than 1 and refer only to the upper tail of the F distribution. This is not a serious restriction because the labelling of the two samples by the numbers 1 and 2 is arbitrary and a mere reversal of the labels will convert a ratio less than 1 into a value greater than 1.

To use Table A4 we denote by s_1^2 the *larger* of the two variance estimates; ν_1 is the corresponding number of degrees of freedom (which, of course, is not necessarily the larger of ν_1 and ν_2). For a two-sided test care should be taken to set P in Table A4 equal to half the two-sided significance level. For a two-sided test at the 5 per cent level, for instance, the entries for $P = 0{\cdot}025$ are used.

The tables of the F distribution may be used to provide confidence limits for σ_1^2/σ_2^2. If the null hypothesis is not true, the ratio

$$F' = \frac{s_1^2/\sigma_1^2}{s_2^2/\sigma_2^2}$$

follows the F distribution on ν_1 and ν_2 degrees of freedom; (on the null hypothesis $\sigma_1^2 = \sigma_2^2$ and $F' = F$). We no longer require $s_1^2 > s_2^2$. Denote by F_{α,ν_1,ν_2} the tabulated critical value of F for ν_1 and ν_2 degrees of freedom and a one-sided significance level α; and by F_{α,ν_2,ν_1} the corresponding entry with ν_1 and ν_2 interchanged. Then the probability is α that

$$F' > F_{\alpha,\nu_1,\nu_2}$$

i.e. that

$$F > F_{\alpha,\nu_1,\nu_2}(\sigma_1^2/\sigma_2^2);$$

and also α that

$$1/F' > F_{\alpha,\nu_2,\nu_1}$$

i.e. that

$$F < (1/F_{\alpha,\nu_2,\nu_1})\,(\sigma_1^2/\sigma_2^2).$$

Consequently, the probability is $1 - 2\alpha$ that

$$(1/F_{\alpha,\nu_2,\nu_1})(\sigma_1^2/\sigma_2^2) < F < F_{\alpha,\nu_1,\nu_2}(\sigma_1^2/\sigma_2^2)$$

or that

$$F/F_{\alpha,\nu_1,\nu_2} < \sigma_1^2/\sigma_2^2 < F.F_{\alpha,\nu_2,\nu_1}.$$

For a 95 per cent confidence interval, therefore, the observed value of F must be divided by the tabulated value $F_{0.025,\nu_1,\nu_2}$ and multiplied by the value $F_{0.025,\nu_2,\nu_1}$.

Example 4.14

Two different microscopic methods, A and B, are available for the measurement of very small dimensions. Repeated observations on the same standard object give estimates of variance as follows:

Method	A	B
Number of observations	$n_1 = 10$	$n_2 = 20$
Estimated variance (microns²)	$s_1^2 = 1{\cdot}232$	$s_2^2 = 0{\cdot}304$

For a significance test we calculate

$$F = s_1^2/s_2^2 = 4{\cdot}05.$$

The tabulated value for $\nu_1 = 9$ and $\nu_2 = 19$ for $P = 0{\cdot}025$ is 2·88 and for $P = 0{\cdot}005$ is 4·04. (Interpolation in Table A4 is needed.) The observed ratio is thus just significant at the two-sided 1 per cent level.

For 95 per cent confidence limits we need the tabulated values

$$F_{0\cdot025,9,19}=2\cdot88 \quad \text{and} \quad F_{0\cdot025,19,9}=3\cdot69$$

(interpolating in the table where necessary). The confidence limits for the ratio of population variances, σ_1^2/σ_2^2, are therefore

$$\frac{4\cdot05}{2\cdot88}=1\cdot24 \quad \text{and} \quad (4\cdot05)(3\cdot69)=14\cdot9.$$

Two connections may be noted between the F distributions and other distributions already met.

(i) When $\nu_1=1$, the F distribution is that of the square of a quantity following the t distribution on ν_2 DF. For example, for a one-sided significance level 0·05, the tabulated value of F for $\nu_1=1$, $\nu_2=10$ is 4·96; that for t on 10 DF is 2·228; $(2\cdot228)^2=4\cdot96$.

This relationship follows because a t statistic is essentially the ratio of a normal variable with zero mean to an independent estimate of its standard deviation. Squaring the numerator gives a χ^2 variable (equivalent to an estimate of variance on 1 DF), and squaring the denominator similarly gives an estimate of variance on the appropriate number of degrees of freedom.

(ii) When $\nu_2=\infty$, the F distribution is the same as that of a $\chi^2_{(\nu_1)}$ variable divided by ν_1. Thus, for $\nu_1=10$, $\nu_2=\infty$, the tabulated F for one-sided level 0·05 is 1·83; that for $\chi^2_{(10)}$ is 18·31; $18\cdot31/10=1\cdot83$.

The reason here is similar to that advanced above. An estimate of variance s_2^2 on $\nu_2=\infty$ DF must be exactly equal to the population variance σ^2. Thus, F may be written as $s_1^2/\sigma^2=\chi^2_{(\nu_1)}/\nu_1$ (see section 3.4).

The F test and the associated confidence limits provide an exact treatment of the comparison of two variances estimates from two independent *normal* samples. Unfortunately the methods are rather sensitive to the assumption of normality—much more so that in the corresponding cases of the t distribution to compare two means. This defect is called a lack of *robustness*.

The methods described in this section are appropriate only for the comparison of two *independent* estimates of variances. Sometimes this condition fails because the observations in the two samples are paired, as in the first situation considered in section 4.6. The appropriate method for this case makes use of a technique described in Chapter 5, and is therefore postponed until page 165.

4.11 LIKELIHOOD AND BAYESIAN METHODS

The statistical methods described earlier in this chapter have all been based on the frequency concept of probability. Reference is made to repeated random samples from the same population and the probabilities cited in significance tests or confidence limits indicate the relative frequency of certain outcomes ('significant' results, or the inclusion of a parameter value in a confidence interval) in a long series of such repetitions.

We referred in section 2.9 to another approach in which the numerical values allotted to probabilities do not necessarily relate to long-run frequencies, and in which an attempt is made to account for prior knowledge by quantitative measurement. Certainly any sensible use of statistical information must take some account of prior knowledge and of prior assessments about the plausibility of various hypotheses. In a card-guessing experiment to investigate extra-sensory perception, for example, a score in excess of chance expectation which was just significant at the 5 per cent level would be regarded by most people with some scepticism: many would prefer to think that the excess had arisen by chance (to say nothing of the possibility of experimental laxity) rather than by the intervention of telepathy or clairvoyance. On the other hand, in a clinical trial to compare an active drug with a placebo, a similarly significant result would be widely accepted as evidence for a drug effect in the observed direction because such findings are commonly made. The question is, though, whether such prior experience can usefully be incorporated in the quantitative assessment of the statistical data, or whether it should be used rather informally in conjunction with the statistical analysis.

It will be useful to discuss this controversy further in terms of a relatively simple example. Denote a normal distribution with mean μ and variance σ^2 by $N(\mu, \sigma^2)$. Suppose we make one observation on a random variable, x, which follows a distribution $N(\mu, 1)$ where μ is unknown. What can be said about μ on the basis of the single observation x? The methods of this chapter would lead us to base a significance test on the standardized normal deviate $x - \mu$, and to obtain confidence limits by taking standardized normal percentiles on either side of x (95 per cent limits being, for instance, $x \pm 1{\cdot}960$).

In discussing Bayes's theorem in section 2.8 we noted that the posterior probability of a particular hypothesis was expressed in terms of prior probabilities and likelihoods, the latter being the probabilities of obtaining the observed results on the various alternative hypotheses.

Since we are concerned in the present problem with continuous distributions we must consider probability densities rather than probabilities. The likelihoods of the various possible values of μ for a particular observed x are shown in Fig. 4.5. This curve, showing the *likelihood function*, is exactly the same shape as a normal distribution with mean

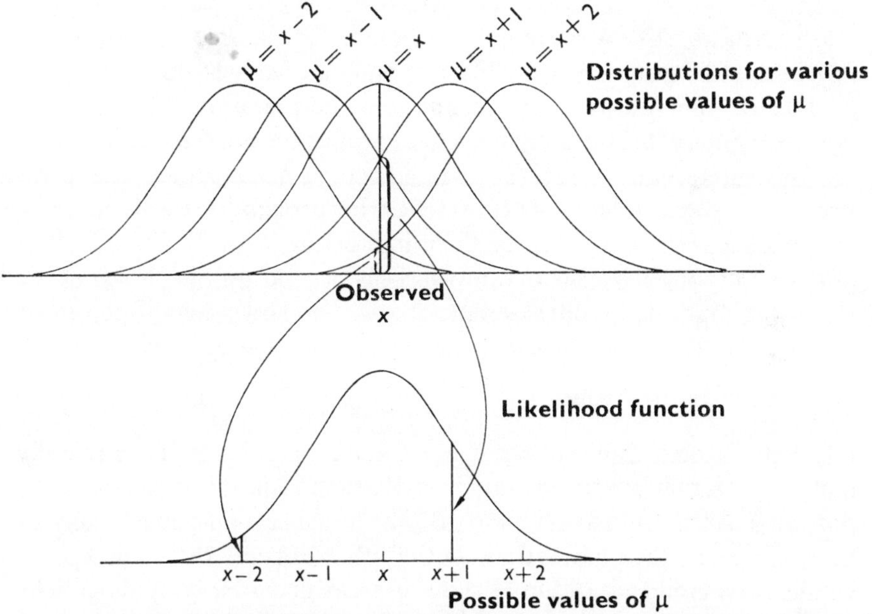

FIG. 4.5 The likelihood function for an observation x from a normal distribution with unit variance. The likelihood for a particular value of μ in the lower diagram is equal to the probability density of x in the distribution with mean μ in the upper diagram.

x and variance 1, but it should not be thought of as a probability distribution since the ordinate for each value represents a density from a *different* distribution.

If inferences about parameters are based on Bayes's theorem the only way in which the observed values of the random variables are used is by their appearance in the likelihood function. Moreover, quite apart from the use of prior probabilities, there are strong logical arguments in favour of basing inferences on the likelihood function. How might this be done? One reasonable proposal would be to take the value of the parameter with the highest likelihood to be the 'best' estimate of this parameter. This is the method of *maximum likelihood*, advocated and developed by R.A.Fisher, which is the most useful general method of statistical estimation. In our example the value of μ with the highest likelihood is (from Fig. 4.5) x, and we should say that x is the maximum likelihood estimate (or estimator) of μ.

Secondly, to express a range of likely values of μ around x, we could take all those values whose likelihood is not less than a certain fraction of the maximum likelihood. The width of the interval would depend on the critical ratio. A ratio of 0·146 would, for example, include values of μ within the range $x \pm 1{\cdot}960$, corresponding exactly to our 95 per cent confidence interval. With this change in interpretation, therefore, we are led to intervals of exactly the same form as the confidence intervals.

This interpretation makes no reference to prior probabilities. We know from Bayes's theorem (2.18) that prior probabilities are converted into posterior probabilities by their interaction with likelihoods. The posterior probability distribution will thus depend on the choice of the prior distribution. In our example it can be shown that if the prior distribution for μ is $N(0, \sigma_0^2)$, the posterior distribution after the observation of the value x is $N\left(\frac{x}{1+1/\sigma_0^2}, \frac{1}{1+1/\sigma_0^2}\right)$. Let us see how this depends on a choice of σ_0^2. If $\sigma_0^2=0$ this means that we are initially quite certain that $\mu=0$; not surprisingly, the mean and variance of the posterior distribution are similarly 0; our initial certainty has in no way been shaken by the observation. At the other extreme the value $\sigma_0^2=\infty$ would correspond to an initial state of great uncertainty about μ. The posterior distribution is then $N(x, 1)$. This is precisely the lower curve of Fig. 4.5 if we now interpret this curve not as a likelihood function but as a probability distribution. The interval $x \pm 1{\cdot}960$ could now be regarded as the interval which includes the central 95 per cent of the posterior distribution. Here, then, is yet another interpretation of the same numerical result.

The detailed application of Bayesian methods to standard statistical problems is developed in the two volumes by Lindley (1965). It turns out to be widely, but not universally, true that Bayesian methods can be made to correspond (with appropriate changes in interpretation) to the standard frequency methods when a suitable widely dispersed prior distribution is used to indicate a state of initial ignorance. It is interesting that the Bayesian solution to the problem of comparing two means when the variances are unequal (section 4.6) yields the Fisher-Behrens rather than the Welch test. One branch of statistics in which there are serious divergencies between the Bayesian and non-Bayesian approaches is that of sequential analysis, discussed in Chapter 15.

CHAPTER 5
REGRESSION AND CORRELATION

5.1 ASSOCIATION

In earlier chapters we have been concerned with the statistical analysis of observations on a single variable. In some problems data were divided into two groups, and the dichotomy could, admittedly, have been regarded as defining a second variable. These two-sample problems are, however, rather artificial examples of the relationship between two variables.

In this chapter we examine more generally the association between two quantitative variables. We shall concentrate on situations in which the general trend is linear; that is, as one variable changes the other variable follows *on the average* a trend which can be represented approximately by a straight line. More complex situations will be discussed in Chapters 9 and 10.

The basic graphical technique for the two-variable situation is the *scatter diagram*, and it is good practice to plot the data in this form before attempting any numerical analysis. An example is shown in Fig. 5.1. In general the data refer to a number of *individuals*, each of which provides observations on two variables. In the scatter diagram each variable is allotted one of the two co-ordinate axes, and each individual thus defines a point the co-ordinates of which are the observed values of the two variables. In Fig. 5.1 the individuals are towns and the two variables are the infant mortality rate and a certain index of overcrowding.

The scatter diagram gives a compact illustration of the distribution of each variable and of the relationship between the two variables. Further statistical analysis serves a number of purposes. It provides, first, numerical measures of some of the basic features of the relationship, rather as the mean and standard deviation provide concise measures of the most important features of the distribution of a single variable. Secondly, the investigator may wish to make a prediction of the value of one variable when the value of the other variable is known. It will normally be impossible to predict with complete certainty, but we may hope to say something about the mean value and the variability of the predicted variable. From Fig. 5.1, for instance, it appears roughly that a town with 0·6 persons per room was in 1961 likely to have an infant

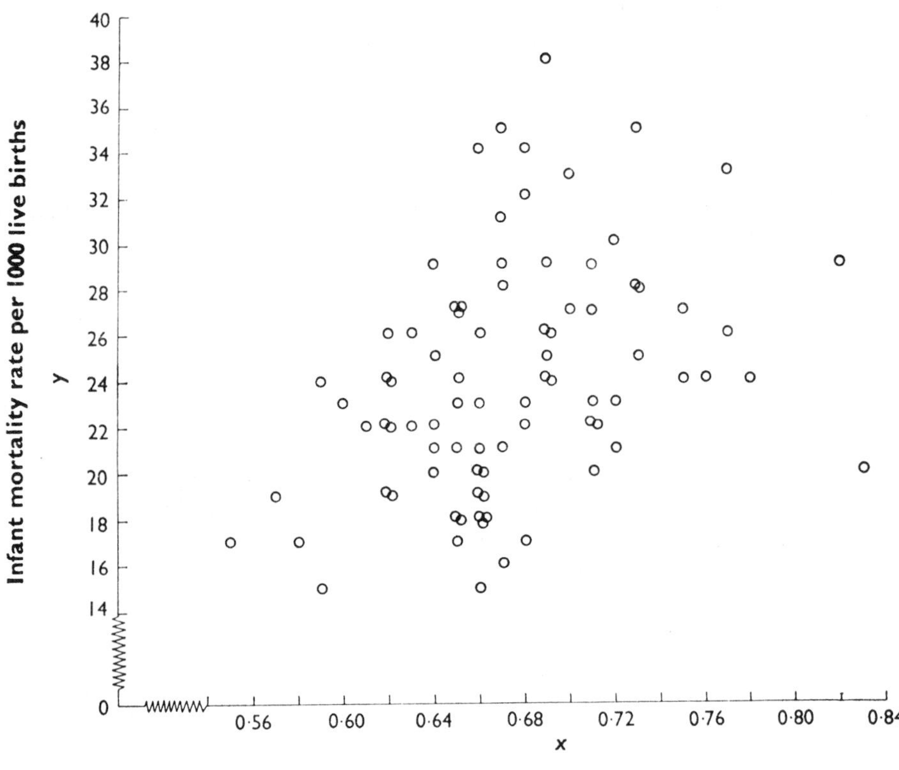

FIG. 5.1 Scatter diagram showing the mean number of persons per room and the infant mortality per 1,000 live births for the 83 county boroughs in England and Wales in 1961.

mortality rate of about 20 per 1,000 live births on average, with a likely range of about 14 to 26. A proper analysis might be expected to give more reliable figures than these rough guesses.

Thirdly, the investigator may wish to assess the significance of the direction of an apparent trend. From the data of Fig. 5.1, for instance, could it safely be asserted that infant mortality increases on the average as the overcrowding index increases, or could the apparent trend in this direction have arisen easily by chance?

Yet another aim may be to correct the measurements of one variable for the effect of another variable. In a study of the forced expiratory volume (FEV) of workers in the cadmium industry who had been exposed for more than a certain number of years to cadmium fumes, a comparison was made with the FEV of other workers who had not been exposed. The mean FEV of the first group was lower than that of the second. However, the men in the first group tended to be older than those in the second, and FEV tends to decrease with age. The question therefore arises whether the difference in mean FEV could be explained purely by the age difference. To answer this question the relationship between FEV and age must be studied in some detail. The method is described in section 9.5.

We must be careful to distinguish between *association* and *causation.* Two variables are associated if the distribution of one is affected by a knowledge of the value of the other. This does not mean that one variable *causes* the other. There is a strong association between the number of divorces made absolute in this country in each of the last 80 years or so and the amount of tobacco imported into the country (the 'individuals' in the scatter diagram here being the individual years). It does not follow either that tobacco is a serious cause of marital discontent, or that those whose marriages have broken down turn to tobacco for solace. Association does not imply causation.

A further distinction is between situations in which both variables can be thought of as random variables, the individuals being selected randomly, or at least without reference to the values of either variable; and situations in which the values of one variable are deliberately selected by the investigator. An example of the first situation would be a study of the relationship between the height and the blood pressure of schoolchildren, the individuals being restricted to one sex and one age group. Here the sample may not have been chosen strictly at random, but it can be thought of as roughly representative of a population of children of this age and sex from the same area and type of school. An example of the second situation would arise in a study of the growth of children between certain ages. The nature of the relationship between height and age, as illustrated by a scatter diagram, would depend very much on the age range chosen and the distribution of ages within this range. We return to this point in section 5.3.

5.2 LINEAR REGRESSION

Suppose that observations are made on variables x and y for each of a large number of individuals, and that we are interested in the way in which y changes on the average as x assumes different values. If it is appropriate to think of y as a random variable for any given value of x, we can enquire how the expectation of y changes with x. The probability distribution of y when x is known is referred to as a *conditional* distribution, and the conditional expectation is denoted by $\mathrm{E}(y \mid x)$. We make no assumption at this stage as to whether x is a random variable or not. In a study of heights and blood pressures of randomly chosen individuals both variables would be random; if x and y were respectively the age and height of children selected according to age only y would be random.

The conditional expectation, $\mathrm{E}(y \mid x)$, depends in general on x. It is called the *regression function* of y on x. If $\mathrm{E}(y \mid x)$ is drawn as a function of x it forms the *regression curve*. Two examples are shown in Fig. 5.2. The regression in Fig. 5.2(b) differs in two ways from that in Fig. 5.2(a). The curve in 5.2(b) is a straight line—the *regression line* of y on x. Secondly, the variation of y for fixed x is constant in 5.2(b), whereas in 5.2(a) the variation changes as x increases. The regression in (b) is called *homoscedastic*, that in (a) being *heteroscedastic*.

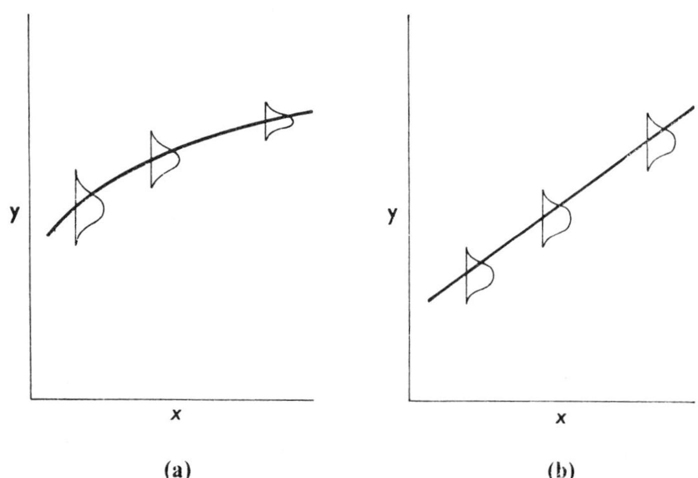

FIG. 5.2 Two regression curves of y on x: (a) non-linear and heteroscedastic; (b) linear and homoscedastic. The distributions shown are those of values of y at certain values of x.

The situation represented by Fig. 5.2(b) is important not only because of its simplicity, but also because regressions which are approximately linear and homoscedastic occur frequently in scientific work. In the present discussion we shall make one further simplifying assumption—that the distribution of y for given x is normal.

The model may, then, be described by saying that for a given x, y follows a normal distribution with mean

$$\mathrm{E}(y \mid x) = \alpha + \beta x$$

(the general equation of a straight line) and variance σ^2 (a constant). Any set of data consists of n pairs of observations, denoted by (x_1, y_1), $(x_2, y_2), \ldots, (x_n, y_n)$, each y_i being an independent observation from the distribution $N(\alpha + \beta x_i, \sigma^2)$. How can we estimate the parameters α, β and σ^2, which characterize the model?

Theoretical arguments* lead to the following rule: α and β are estimated by the '*least squares*' estimators, a and b, namely the quantities which minimize the *residual* sum of squares, $\sum(y_i - Y_i)^2$, where Y_i is given by the estimated regression equation

$$Y_i = a + bx_i. \tag{5.1}$$

This is intuitively an attractive proposal. The regression line is drawn through the n points on the scatter diagram so as to minimize the sum of squares of the distances, $y_i - Y_i$, of the points from the line, these distances being measured parallel to the y-axis (Fig. 5.3).

It can be shown by elementary calculus that a and b are given by the formulae

$$a = \bar{y} - b\bar{x}, \tag{5.2}$$

$$b = \frac{\sum(x_i - \bar{x})(y_i - \bar{y})}{\sum(x_i - \bar{x})^2}. \tag{5.3}$$

A proof without the use of calculus is as follows. Note first that for any n numbers $p_1, p_2, \ldots, p_n$, the quantity P which minimizes $\sum(p_i - P)^2$ is $P = \bar{p}$. To show this, note that, for any P,

$$\sum(p_i - P)^2 = \sum(p_i - \bar{p})^2 + n(\bar{p} - P)^2 \tag{5.4}$$

(as can be shown by expanding $(p_i - P)^2$ as $\{(p_i - \bar{p}) + (\bar{p} - P)\}^2$). The right side of (5.4) is a minimum when the second term is zero, i.e., when $P = \bar{p}$.

* The 'least squares' estimators of α and β are also maximum likelihood estimators (see section 4.11); furthermore, among all unbiased estimators they have the smallest standard errors.

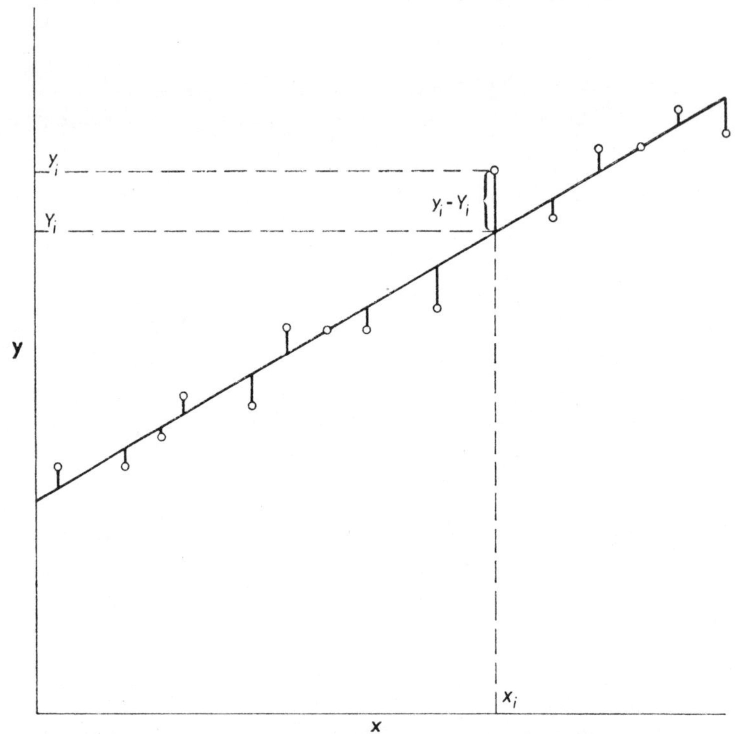

FIG. 5.3 A linear regression line fitted by least squares showing a typical deviation between an observed value y_i and the value Y_i given by the regression line.

Now consider $S=\Sigma(y_i-Y_i)^2=\Sigma(y_i-a-bx_i)^2$. For any value of b, the minimum S occurs when

$$a=\Sigma(y_i-bx_i)/n$$

(from the previous result with $p_i=y_i-bx_i$); that is,

$$a=\bar{y}-b\bar{x}$$

as in (5.2). The regression line can thus be written

$$\begin{aligned} Y_i &= a+bx_i \\ &= \bar{y}+b(x_i-\bar{x}), \end{aligned} \tag{5.5}$$

from which it follows that the line goes through the point $(\bar{x}, \bar{y})$.

We now have to find the value of b minimizing

$$\begin{aligned} S &= \Sigma\{y_i-\bar{y}-b(x_i-\bar{x})\}^2 \\ &= \Sigma(x-\bar{x})^2\left\{b-\frac{\Sigma(x-\bar{x})(y-\bar{y})}{\Sigma(x-\bar{x})^2}\right\}^2+\Sigma(y-\bar{y})^2-\frac{\{\Sigma(x-\bar{x})(y-\bar{y})\}^2}{\Sigma(x-\bar{x})^2} \end{aligned} \tag{5.6}$$

as may be seen by multiplying out the right side. (The suffix i has been dropped for convenience.) Now the second and third terms of (5.6) do not involve b. The first term is a sum of squares and cannot be negative; it is, however, zero when

$$b = \frac{\sum(x-\bar{x})(y-\bar{y})}{\sum(x-\bar{x})^2}$$

which is therefore the required value of b, as in (5.3).

Note that the minimum value of S is given by the last two terms of (5.6), namely

$$\sum(y-\bar{y})^2 - \frac{\{\sum(x-\bar{x})(y-\bar{y})\}^2}{\sum(x-\bar{x})^2}. \tag{5.7}$$

Finally, it can be shown that an unbiased estimator of σ^2 is

$$s_0^2 = \frac{\sum(y-Y)^2}{n-2} \tag{5.8}$$

the residual sum of squares, $\sum(y-Y)^2$ being obtainable from (5.7). The divisor $n-2$ is often referred to as the residual degrees of freedom, and s_0^2 as the *residual mean square*.

The quantities a and b are called the *regression coefficients*; the term is often used particularly for b, the slope of the regression line.

The expression in the numerator of (5.3) is the sum of products of deviations of x and y about their means. A short-cut formula analogous to (1.3) is useful for computational work. By an argument similar to that used to derive (1.3) we find

$$\begin{aligned}\sum(x_i-\bar{x})(y_i-\bar{y}) &= \sum(x_iy_i - x_i\bar{y} - \bar{x}y_i + \bar{x}\bar{y}) \\ &= \sum x_iy_i - \bar{y}\sum x_i - \bar{x}\sum y_i + n\bar{x}\bar{y} \\ &= \sum x_iy_i - \frac{2(\sum x_i)(\sum y_i)}{n} + \frac{(\sum x_i)(\sum y_i)}{n} \\ &= \sum x_iy_i - \frac{(\sum x_i)(\sum y_i)}{n}. \end{aligned} \tag{5.9}$$

Equivalent expressions are $\sum x_iy_i - \bar{x}\sum y_i$, $\sum x_iy_i - \bar{y}\sum x_i$ and $\sum x_iy_i - n\bar{x}\bar{y}$. Note that whereas a sum of squares about the mean must be positive or zero, a sum of products of deviations about the mean may be negative (in which case, from (5.3), b will also be negative).

Example 5.1

Table 5.1 gives the values for 32 babies of x, the birth weight, and y, the increase in weight between the 70th and 100th day of life expressed as a percentage of the birth weight. A scatter diagram is shown in Fig. 5.4 which suggests an association between the two variables in a negative direction. The trend seems reasonably linear.

TABLE 5.1 Birth weights of 32 babies and their increases in weight between 70 and 100 days after birth, expressed as percentages of birth weights.

x, Birth weight (oz)	y, Increase in weight, 70–100 days, as % of x
72	68
112	63
111	66
107	72
119	52
92	75
126	76
80	118
81	120
84	114
115	29
118	42
128	48
128	50
123	69
116	59
125	27
126	60
122	71
126	88
127	63
86	88
142	53
132	50
87	111
123	59
133	76
106	72
103	90
118	68
114	93
94	91

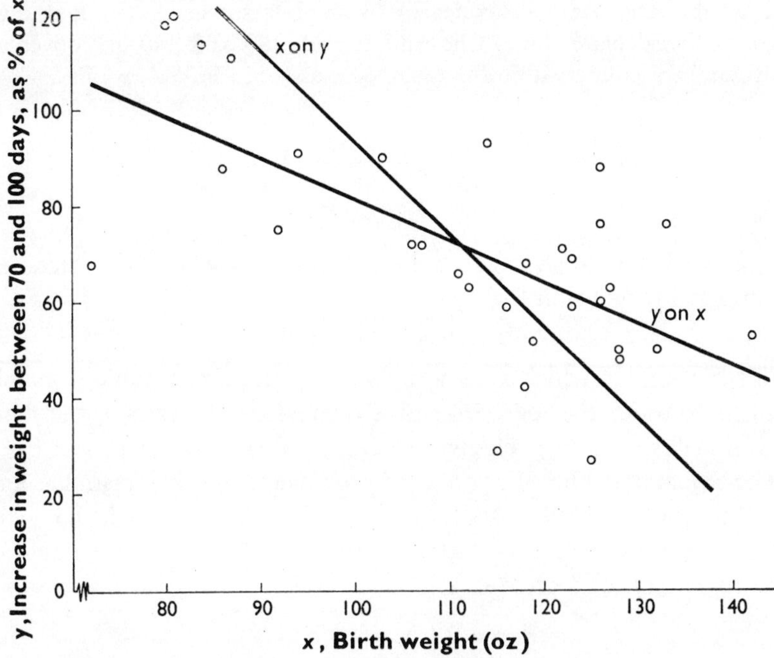

FIG. 5.4 Scatter diagram showing the birth weight, x, and the increase of weight between 70 and 100 days as a percentage of x, for 32 babies, with the two regression lines (Table 5.1).

From Table 5.1 we proceed as follows:

$$n=32 \qquad \sum x=3576 \qquad \sum y=2281$$

$$\bar{x}=3576/32 \qquad \bar{y}=2281/32$$

$$= 111{\cdot}75 \qquad = 71{\cdot}28$$

$\sum x^2=409880$	$\sum xy=246032$	$\sum y^2=179761$
$(\sum x)^2/n=399618{\cdot}00$	$(\sum x)(\sum y)/n=254901{\cdot}75$	$(\sum y)^2/n=162592{\cdot}53$
$\sum(x-\bar{x})^2=10262{\cdot}00$	$\sum(x-\bar{x})(y-\bar{y})=-8869{\cdot}75$	$\sum(y-\bar{y})^2=17168{\cdot}47$

To predict the weight increase from the birth weight the regression of y on x is needed.

$$b=-\frac{8869{\cdot}75}{10262{\cdot}00}$$

$$=-0{\cdot}8643.$$

The equation of the regression line is, from (5.5),

$$Y=71{\cdot}28-0{\cdot}8643(x-111{\cdot}75)$$

$$=167{\cdot}87-0{\cdot}8643\,x.$$

To draw the line, the coordinates of two points suffice, but it is a slight safeguard to calculate three. Choosing $x=80$, 100 and 140 as convenient round numbers falling within the range of x used in Fig. 5.4, we find

x	Y
80	98·73
100	81·44
140	46·87.

The regression line is now drawn through the three points with these coordinates and is shown in Fig. 5.4.

In situations in which x, as well as y, is a random variable it may be useful to consider the regression of x on y. This shows how the mean value of x, for a given y, changes with the value of y.

The regression line of x on y may be calculated by formulae analogous to those already used, with x and y interchanged. To avoid confusion between the two lines it will be useful to write the equation of the regression of y on x as

$$Y=\bar{y}+b_{y.x}(x-\bar{x}),$$

with $b_{y.x}$ given by (5.3). The regression equation of x on y is then

$$X=\bar{x}+b_{x.y}(y-\bar{y}),$$

with

$$b_{x.y}=\frac{\sum(x-\bar{x})(y-\bar{y})}{\sum(y-\bar{y})^2}.$$

That the two lines are in general different may be seen from Fig. 5.4. Both lines go through the point $(\bar{x}, \bar{y})$ which is therefore their point of intersection. In Example 5.1 we should probably be interested primarily in the regression of y on x, since it would be natural to study the way in which weight changes vary with birth weight and to investigate the distribution of weight changes for a particular value of birth weight, rather than to enquire about the distribution of birth weights for a given weight change (particularly as the latter is expressed in terms of birth weight). In some other circumstances both regressions may be of interest.

5.3 CORRELATION

When both x and y are random variables it may be useful to have a measure of the extent to which the relationship between the two variables approaches the extreme situation in which every point on the scatter diagram falls exactly on a straight line. Such an index is provided by the *correlation coefficient* defined by

$$r = \frac{\sum(x-\bar{x})(y-\bar{y})}{\sqrt{\{\sum(x-\bar{x})^2\sum(y-\bar{y})^2\}}}. \tag{5.10}$$

It can be shown that for any set of data r falls within the range -1

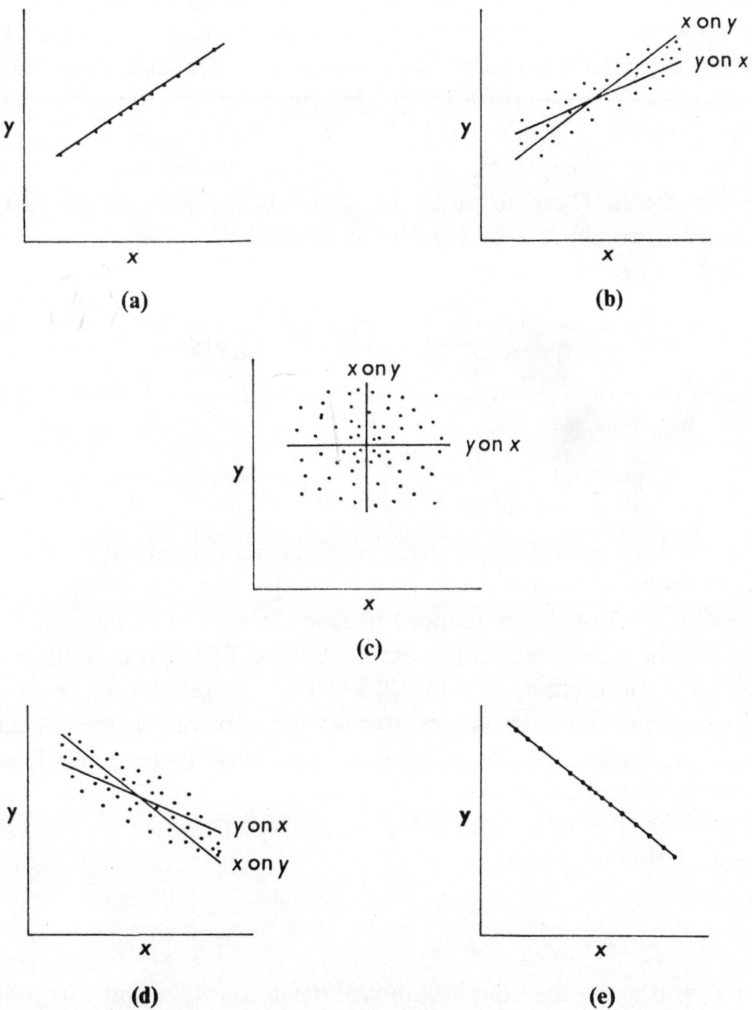

FIG. 5.5 Five scatter diagrams with regression lines illustrating different values of the correlation coefficient. In (a), $r=1$; (b) $0<r<1$; (c) $r=0$; (d) $-1<r<0$; (e) $r=-1$.

to $+1$. Fig. 5.5 shows five sets of data in which the variation in x and that in y remains approximately constant from one set to another. The marked differences between the five scatter diagrams are summarized by the values of r. Figs. 5.5(a) and (e) are examples of perfect correlation in which the value of y is *exactly* determined as a linear function of x. The points lie exactly on a straight line; if both variables increase together, as in (a), $r=+1$, while if one variable decreases as the other increases, as in (e), $r=-1$. In each of these cases the two regression lines coincide. Fig. 5.5(c) is a very different situation, in which $r=0$. The two regression coefficients $b_{y.x}$ and $b_{x.y}$ are also zero and the regression lines are perpendicular. Intermediate situations are shown in (b), where $0<r<1$, and (d), where $-1<r<0$. Here the two regression lines are set at an angle, but point in the same direction.

From the short-cut formulae for sums of squares and products an alternative formula for the correlation coefficient, more convenient for computation, is

$$r=\frac{\sum xy-(\sum x)(\sum y)/n}{\sqrt{[\{\sum x^2-(\sum x)^2/n\}\{\sum y^2-(\sum y)^2/n\}]}}. \tag{5.11}$$

From (5.7) the sum of squares of y about the regression line of y on x is

$$\sum(y-\bar{y})^2\left\{1-\frac{\{\sum(x-\bar{x})(y-\bar{y})\}^2}{\sum(x-\bar{x})^2\sum(y-\bar{y})^2}\right\}=\sum(y-\bar{y})^2.(1-r^2). \tag{5.12}$$

This provides a useful interpretation of the numerical value of r. The squared correlation coefficient is the fraction by which the sum of squares of one variable is reduced to give the sum of squares of deviations from its regression on the other variable. (The same result is true if x and y are interchanged in (5.12).) In Figs. 5.5(a) and (e), $r^2=1$, and (5.12) becomes zero. In (c), $r^2=0$ and the sum of squares of either variable is unaffected by regression on the other. In (b) and (d) some reductions take place since $0<r^2<1$.

Two other formulae are easily derived from those for the regression and correlation coefficients:

$$b_{y.x}=r\frac{s_y}{s_x} \quad \text{and} \quad b_{x.y}=r\frac{s_x}{s_y}, \tag{5.13}$$

where s_x and s_y are the sample standard deviations of x and y. It follows that

$$b_{y.x}\,b_{x.y}=r^2.$$

The correlation coefficient has played an important part in the history of statistical methods. It is now of considerably less value than the regression coefficients. If two variables are correlated it is usually much more useful to study the positions of one or both of the regression lines, which permit the prediction of one variable in terms of the other, than to summarize the degree of correlation in a single index.

The restriction of validity of the correlation coefficient to situations in which both variables are observed on a random selection of individuals is particularly important. If, from a large population of individuals, a selection is made by restricting the values of one variable, say x, to a limited range, the correlation coefficient will tend to decrease in absolute value. In the data of Fig. 5. 4, for instance, the correlation coefficients calculated on subsets of the data obtained by restricting the range of x-values are as follows:

	Range of x		Number of	Correlation
	Lower limit	Upper limit	observations	coefficient
All data:	70	150	32	−0·668
Subsets:	85	135	27	−0·565
	100	120	11	−0·578
	105	115	6	−0·325

The interpretation of the numerical value of a correlation coefficient calculated from data selected by values of one variable is thus very difficult.

5.4 SAMPLING ERRORS IN REGRESSION AND CORRELATION

In the regression model of section 5.2, suppose that repeated sets of data are generated, each with the same n values of x but with randomly varying values of y. The statistics $\bar{y}$, a and b will vary from one set of data to another. Their sampling variances are obtained as follows:

$$\mathrm{var}(\bar{y}) = \sigma^2/n, \tag{5.14}$$

by an argument similar to that used in section 3.2. Note that here σ^2 is the variance of y *for fixed* x, not (as in (3.1)) the overall variance of y.

$$\mathrm{var}(b) = \mathrm{var}\left\{\frac{\sum y(x-\bar{x})}{\sum(x-\bar{x})^2}\right\}$$

(using the fact that $\sum(x-\bar{x})(y-\bar{y}) = \sum(x-\bar{x})y$, the remaining terms vanishing),

$$=\frac{1}{\{\sum(x-\bar{x})^2\}^2}\sum(x-\bar{x})^2\text{var}(y)$$

$$=\frac{\sum(x-\bar{x})^2}{\{\sum(x-\bar{x})^2\}^2}\sigma^2$$

$$=\frac{\sigma^2}{\sum(x-\bar{x})^2}. \tag{5.15}$$

$$\text{var}(a)=\text{var}(\bar{y}-b\bar{x})$$

$$=\text{var}(\bar{y})+\bar{x}^2\text{var}(b)$$

(since it can be shown that b and $\bar{y}$ have zero covariance)

$$=\sigma^2\left\{\frac{1}{n}+\frac{\bar{x}^2}{\sum(x-\bar{x})^2}\right\}. \tag{5.16}$$

Formulae (5.14), (5.15) and (5.16) all involve the parameter σ^2. If inferences are to be made from one set of n pairs of observations on x and y, σ^2 will be unknown. It can, however, be estimated by the residual mean square, s_0^2 (5.8). Estimated variances are, therefore,

$$\text{var}(\bar{y})=s_0^2/n, \tag{5.17}$$

$$\text{var}(b)=s_0^2/\sum(x-\bar{x})^2 \tag{5.18}$$

and

$$\text{var}(a)=s_0^2\left\{\frac{1}{n}+\frac{\bar{x}^2}{\sum(x-\bar{x})^2}\right\}, \tag{5.19}$$

and hypotheses about $\bar{y}$, a or b can be tested using the t distribution on $n-2$ DF. For example, to test the null hypothesis that $\beta=0$, i.e., that in the whole population the mean value of y does not change with x, the statistic

$$t=\frac{b}{\text{SE}(b)} \tag{5.20}$$

can be referred to the t distribution on $n-2$ DF, SE(b) being the square root of (5.18). Similarly, confidence limits for β at, say, the 95 per cent level can be obtained as

$$b\pm t_{n-2,\,0.05}\text{SE}(b).$$

An important point about the t statistic (5.20) is seen by writing b as $b_{y.x}$ and using (5.3) and (5.10). We find

$$t=r\sqrt{\left\{\frac{n-2}{1-r^2}\right\}}. \tag{5.21}$$

$$\text{S.D.}=\frac{\sigma}{r}\sqrt{\frac{(1-r^2)n}{n-2}}$$

Since r is symmetric with respect to x and y, it follows that if, for any set of n paired observations we calculate the t statistics from $b_{y.x}$ and (by interchanging x and y in the formulae) from $b_{x.y}$, both values of t will be equal and both will be equal to (5.21). As far as concerns the significance test of zero regression and correlation, therefore, it is immaterial whether one tests $b_{y.x}$, $b_{x.y}$ or r. We must, however, remember that in some problems only one of the regressions may have a sensible interpretation and it will then be natural to express the test in terms of that regression.

Example 5.1, continued from section 5.2

The sum of squares of deviations of y from the regression line is, from (5.7),

$$\begin{aligned} &17168{\cdot}47-\frac{(-8869{\cdot}75)^2}{10262{\cdot}00} \\ &=17168{\cdot}47-7666{\cdot}39 \\ &=9502{\cdot}08. \end{aligned}$$

The residual mean square is, from (5·8),

$$\begin{aligned} s_0^2&=9502{\cdot}08/(32-2) \\ &=316{\cdot}74. \end{aligned}$$

From (5·18),

$$\begin{aligned} \text{var}(b)&=316{\cdot}74/10262{\cdot}00 \\ &=0{\cdot}030865 \\ \text{SE}(b)&=\sqrt{0{\cdot}030865} \\ &=0{\cdot}1757. \end{aligned}$$

From (5.20),

$$\begin{aligned} t&=-0{\cdot}8643/0{\cdot}1757 \\ &=-4{\cdot}92 \text{ on 30 DF } (P<0{\cdot}001). \end{aligned}$$

Alternatively, we could calculate the correlation coefficient

$$\begin{aligned} r&=\frac{-8869{\cdot}75}{\sqrt{\{(10262{\cdot}00)(17168{\cdot}47)\}}} \\ &=-\frac{8869{\cdot}75}{13273{\cdot}39} \\ &=-0{\cdot}668 \end{aligned}$$

and, from (5.21),

$$\begin{aligned} t&=-0{\cdot}668\sqrt{\left\{\frac{30}{0{\cdot}554}\right\}} \\ &=-4{\cdot}92 \text{ as before.} \end{aligned}$$

The sampling error of a correlation coefficient was introduced above in connection with a test of the null hypothesis that its population value is zero. This is the context in which the question usually arises. More rarely we may wish to give confidence limits for the population value in situations in which the individuals providing paired observations can be regarded as randomly drawn from some population. A need arises here to define the nature of the two-dimensional distribution of x and y. A convenient form is the *bivariate normal distribution*, a rough sketch of which is shown in Fig. 5.6. This is a generalization of the familiar univariate normal distribution in which the distribution of y for given x is normal with constant variance, the distribution of x for given y is also normal with constant variance, and both regressions are linear. In large samples from such a distribution the standard error of the correlation coefficient, r, is approximately $(1-r^2)/\sqrt{n}$, a result which enables approximate confidence limits to be calculated. More refined methods are available for small samples (Geigy tables; chapter on 'Statistical methods', section 19A).

The utility of these results is limited by the importance of the

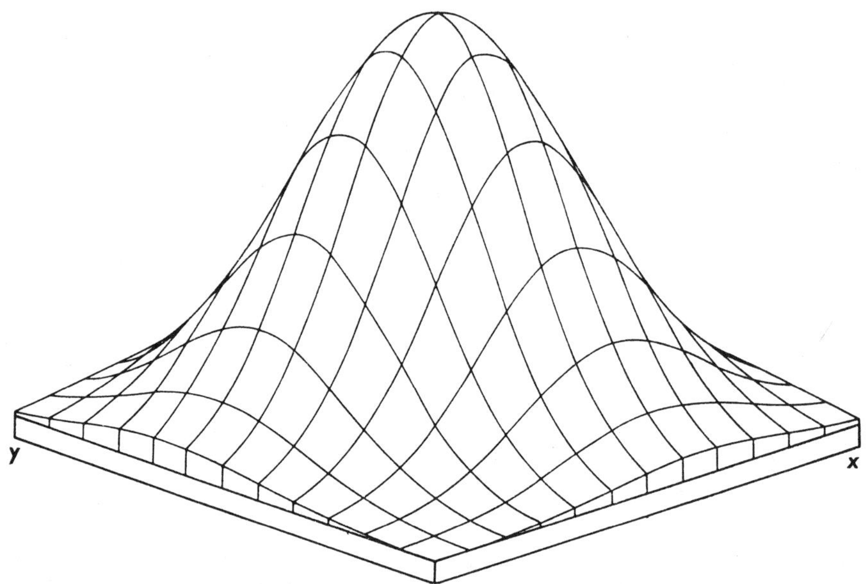

FIG. 5.6 A three-dimensional representation of a bivariate normal distribution, the vertical dimension representing probability density. (Reprinted from Yule and Kendall, 1950, by permission of the authors and publishers.)

assumption of bivariate normality, and also by the difficulty, referred to earlier, of interpreting the numerical value of a correlation coefficient.

ERRORS OF PREDICTION

The best estimate of the mean value of y at a given value of x, say x_0, is given by the regression equation

$$Y = a + bx_0 = \bar{y} + b(x_0 - \bar{x}). \tag{5.22}$$

The sampling variance of Y is

$$\begin{aligned}\text{var}(Y) &= \text{var}(\bar{y}) + (x_0 - \bar{x})^2 \text{var}(b)\\ &= \sigma^2\left\{\frac{1}{n} + \frac{(x_0 - \bar{x})^2}{\sum(x - \bar{x})^2}\right\},\end{aligned}$$

which may be estimated by

$$\text{var}(Y) = s_0^2\left\{\frac{1}{n} + \frac{(x_0 - \bar{x})^2}{\sum(x - \bar{x})^2}\right\}.$$

Again the t distribution on $n-2$ DF is required. For instance, 95 per cent confidence limits for the predicted mean are

$$Y \pm t_{n-2,\,0.05}\, s_0 \sqrt{\left\{\frac{1}{n} + \frac{(x_0 - \bar{x})^2}{\sum(x - \bar{x})^2}\right\}}. \tag{5.23}$$

In (5.23) the width of the confidence interval increases with $(x_0 - \bar{x})^2$, and is therefore a minimum when $x_0 = \bar{x}$. Fig. 5.7 shows the limits for various values of x_0 in Example 5.1. The reason for the increase in the width of the interval is that slight sampling errors in b will have a greater effect for values of x_0 distant from $\bar{x}$ than for those near $\bar{x}$. The regression line can be thought of as a rod which is free to move up and down (corresponding to the error in $\bar{y}$) and to pivot about a central point (corresponding to the error in b). Points near the ends of the rod will then be subject to greater oscillations than those near the centre.

A different prediction problem is that of estimating an individual value y_1 of y corresponding to a given x_0. The best single estimate is again the value given by the regression equation, but the limits of error are different from those in the previous case. Two slightly different problems can be distinguished.

(a) A single prediction is required. The appropriate limits are not strictly confidence limits because the quantity to be estimated is a value

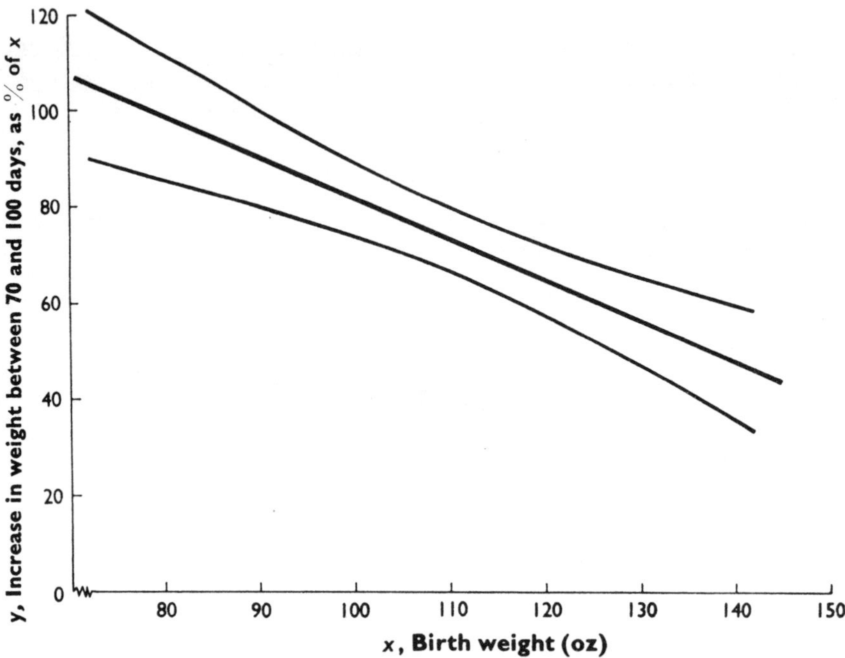

FIG. 5.7 Confidence limits (95 per cent) for the predicted mean value of y for specified values, x_0, of x (data as in Fig. 5.4).

taken by a random variable, not a parameter of a distribution. However, writing

$$y_1 = Y + \epsilon,$$

where ϵ is the deviation of y_1 from the predicted value Y, we have

$$\begin{aligned}\operatorname{var}(y_1) &= \operatorname{var}(Y) + \operatorname{var}(\epsilon)\\ &= \sigma^2\left\{1 + \frac{1}{n} + \frac{(x_0 - \bar{x})^2}{\sum(x-\bar{x})^2}\right\},\end{aligned}$$

and the limits

$$Y \pm t_{n-2,\,0.05}\, s_0 \sqrt{\left\{1 + \frac{1}{n} + \frac{(x_0 - \bar{x})^2}{\sum(x-\bar{x})^2}\right\}} \tag{5.24}$$

will include y_1 95 per cent of the time.

(b) The object may be to estimate limits within which a certain percentage (say 95 per cent) of the values of y lie when $x = x_0$. These limits are

$$\alpha + \beta x_0 \pm 1{\cdot}96\sigma$$

and are estimated by

$$a+bx_0 \pm 1{\cdot}96s_0 = Y \pm 1{\cdot}96s_0. \tag{5.25}$$

These limits are a fixed distance from the regression line and lie wholly within the limits (5.24). When n is very large $t_{n-2,\,0{\cdot}05}$ is close to 1·96, and the second and third terms inside the square root in (5.24) are very small; (5.24) and (5.25) are then almost the same.

Finally, it should be remembered that prediction from a regression formula may be subject to errors other than those of sampling. The linear model may be an inadequate description of the relationship between the two variables. A visual examination of the scatter diagram will provide a partial check, and analytic methods are described in section 9.2. Non-linearity may, of course, exist and remain unsuspected because the data at hand provide no indication of it. The danger of using the wrong model is particularly severe if an attempt is made to extrapolate beyond the range of values observed. In Fig. 5.1, for instance, it would be very dangerous to use the regression of y on x to predict the infant mortality in towns with an overcrowding index of 0 or 1·0.

COMPARISON OF VARIANCES IN TWO PAIRED SAMPLES

We now return to the comparison of two variances, treated in section 4.10 in the case of independent samples. Suppose the two samples are of equal size, n, and there is a natural relationship between a particular value x_{1i} of one sample and the corresponding member x_{2i} of the second sample. Define $X_i = x_{1i} + x_{2i}$ and $Y_i = x_{1i} - x_{2i}$, the sum and difference of paired observations. Thus, we have

Pair	Values of x_1	Values of x_2	Sum	Difference
1	x_{11}	x_{21}	X_1	Y_1
2	x_{12}	x_{22}	X_2	Y_2
.	.	.	.	.
.	.	.	.	.
.	.	.	.	.
n	x_{1n}	x_{2n}	X_n	Y_n

The covariance of X_i and Y_i is

$$\begin{aligned} \text{covar}(X_i,\ Y_i) &= \text{covar}(x_{1i}+x_{2i},\ x_{1i}-x_{2i}) \\ &= \text{var}(x_{1i}) - \text{var}(x_{2i}). \end{aligned} \tag{5.26}$$

since the term in covar(x_{1i}, x_{2i}) vanishes. Equation (5.26) can be interpreted in terms either of the population variances and covariance or of the sample values.

A test of the equality of var(x_{1i}) and var(x_{2i}) is, therefore, the same as a test of the hypothesis that the covariance of X_1 and Y_1 is zero, which means that the correlation coefficient also must be zero. (The numerator of (5.11) is a multiple of the sample covariance of the two variables.) The test of equality of variances may, therefore, be effected by any of the equivalent tests described above for the hypothesis of zero association between X_i and Y_i. This test is due to Pitman. Its adaptation for purposes of estimation is described by Snedecor and Cochran (1967; section 7.12).

CHAPTER 6
THE PLANNING OF STATISTICAL INVESTIGATIONS

6.1 GENERAL

Statistical investigations—those in which observations are made on groups of individuals—are made necessary by the presence of random variation. If all patients suffering from the common cold experienced well-defined symptoms for precisely seven days, it might be possible to demonstrate the merits of a purported drug for the alleviation of symptoms by administering it to one patient only. If the symptoms lasted only five days the reduction could safely be attributed to the new treatment. Similarly, if blood pressure were an exact function of age, varying neither from person to person nor between occasions on the same person, the blood pressure at age 55 could be determined by one observation only. Such studies would not be statistical in nature and would not call for statistical analysis. This situation, of course, does not hold. The duration of symptoms from the common cold varies from one attack to another; blood pressures vary both between individuals and between occasions. Comparisons of the effects of different medical treatments must therefore be made on groups of patients; studies of physiological norms require population surveys.

In the planning of a statistical study a number of administrative and technical problems are likely to arise. These will be characteristic of the particular field of research and cannot be discussed fully in the present general context. Two aspects of the planning will almost invariably be present and are of particular concern to the statistician. The investigator will wish the inferences from the study to be sufficiently precise; he will also wish the results to be relevant to the questions he is asking. Discussions of the statistical design of investigation are concerned especially with the general considerations which bear on these two objectives. Some of the questions which arise are (1) how to select the individuals on which observations are to be made, (2) how to decide on the numbers of observations falling into different groups, and (3) how to allocate observations between different possible categories of individuals, such as groups of animals receiving different treatments or groups of people living in different areas.

It is useful to make a conceptual distinction between two different types of statistical investigation, the *experiment* and the *survey*. Experimentation involves a planned interference with the natural course of events so that its effect can be observed. In a survey, on the other hand, the investigator is a more passive observer, interfering as little as possible with the phenomena he wishes to record. It is easy to think of extreme examples to illustrate this antithesis, but in practice the distinction is sometimes hard to draw. Consider, for instance, the following series of statistical studies.

(1) A survey of the types of motor vehicle passing a check-point during a certain period.

(2) A public opinion poll.

(3) A study of the respiratory function (as measured by various tests) of men working in a certain industry.

(4) Observations of the survival times of mice of three different strains after inoculation with the same dose of a toxic substance.

(5) A clinical trial to compare the merits of surgery and conservative treatment for patients with a certain condition, the subjects being allotted randomly to the two treatments.

Studies (1) to (3) are clearly surveys, although they involve an increasing amount of interference with nature. Study (5) is equally clearly an experiment. Study (4) occupies an equivocal position. In its statistical aspects it is conceptually a survey, since the object is to observe and compare certain characteristics of three strains of mice. It happens, though, that the characteristic of interest requires the most extreme form of interference—the death of the animal—and the non-statistical techniques involved are more akin to those of a laboratory experiment than to those required in most survey work.

In the next two sections we discuss some of the general principles of the planning of surveys and follow with a discussion of the principles of experimental design.

6.2 THE PLANNING OF SURVEYS: ESTIMATION OF POPULATION PARAMETERS

It is useful to distinguish between surveys designed to provide estimates of certain simple characteristics of populations and those designed to investigate associations between certain variables. Examples of the first type are surveys to estimate the prevalence of a certain illness in a population or the frequency distribution of medical consultations during a certain period. An example of the second type would be a study of the association between the use of a certain drug and the occurrence of a particular adverse effect. The distinction is by no means clear cut. In a population survey we may be interested also in associations; for example, that between the prevalence of an illness and a person's age. Conversely, in an association survey it would be quite reasonable to regard the association in question as a population parameter and to enquire how it varies from one population to another. Nevertheless, in population surveys the main emphasis is on the provision of reliable estimates of the features of a well defined population; in association surveys (to be considered further in section 6.3) the definition of the population is less important than the relationship between the variables.

Statistical interest in population surveys arises primarily when these are carried out by sampling methods. Some surveys are, of course, performed by complete enumeration; population censuses are familiar examples. The advantages of sampling lie in the economy of cost, manpower and time. Any of these factors may make complete enumeration out of the question. Furthermore, as noted in section 3.1, the smaller scale of sampling enquiry may permit more reliable observations to be made.

In section 3.1 the concept of a sampling frame was introduced and a case was made for some form of random sampling rather than a form of purposive selection such as quota sampling. Simple random sampling, in fact, has formed the model for all the basic results of sampling theory. Some alternative forms of random sampling must now be discussed.

SYSTEMATIC SAMPLING

When the units or individuals in the population are listed or otherwise ordered in a systematic fashion it may be convenient to arrange that the units chosen in any one sample occupy related positions in the sampling frame, the first unit being selected at random. For example, in drawing a sample of 1 in 50 of the entries in a card index, the first card may be selected by choosing a number at random from 1 to 50, after which every 50th card would be included. If the initial selection was 39 the selected cards would be those occupying positions 39, 89, 139, 189, . . . etc. This is called a *systematic sample*. Another example might arise in two-dimensional sampling. Suppose a health survey is to be conducted in geographical units determined by a rectangular grid. If, say, 1 in 25 units are to be selected the initial 'horizontal' and 'vertical' co-ordinates could be chosen at random, each from the numbers 1 to 5. If the initial random numbers were 5 and 3, the selected units would have the following positions (the first number being the 'vertical' position and the second the 'horizontal' position).

```
. . . (5, 3) . . . (5, 8) . . . (5, 13) . . .
        .            .            .
        .            .            .
        .            .            .
. . . (10, 3) . . . (10, 8) . . . (10, 13) . . .
        .            .            .
        .            .            .
        .            .            .
. . . (15, 3) . . . (15, 8) . . . (15, 13) . . .
        .            .            .
        .            .            .
        .            .            .
```

Systematic sampling is often at least as precise as random sampling. It is likely to be dangerous only if the ordering of the units in the sampling frame imposes a positive correlation between units whose distance apart is equal to the sampling interval. In the geographical example above, if there were a series of populated valleys running east to west at about five sampling units apart, the chosen units might almost all be rather heavily populated or almost all lightly populated. The sampling error of the method would therefore be unusually high. In general it will be difficult to estimate the sampling error from a single systematic sample unless it is assumed that such correlations do not exist and that the sample can therefore be regarded as effectively random. One useful device is to choose simultaneously several systematic samples by different choices of the starting point. A mean value or other relevant statistic could then be worked out separately for each systematic sample, and the sampling variance of the overall mean obtained by the usual formula in terms of the variance of the separate means.

STRATIFIED SAMPLING

In this method the population is divided into subgroups, or *strata*, each of which is sampled randomly with a known sample size. Suppose that we wish to estimate the mean value of a certain variable in the population and that strata are defined so that the mean varies considerably from one stratum to another. In simple random sampling the distribution of observations over the strata will vary from sample to sample, and this lack of control will contribute to the variability of the sample mean. By contrast, in repeated sampling with the *same* distribution over the strata this component of variability is irrelevant.

Strata may be defined qualitatively; for example, in a national health survey different regions of the country may be taken as strata. Or they may be defined in terms of one or more quantitative variables, for example as age-groups. The fraction of the stratum to be sampled may be constant or it may vary from stratum to stratum. The important points are that the distribution of both the population and the sample over the strata should be known and that the between-stratum variability should be as high as possible.

Suppose there are k strata and that in the ith stratum the population size is N_i, and the mean and variance of variable x are μ_i and σ_i^2. A random sample of size n_i is taken from the ith stratum; the sampling fraction n_i/N_i will be denoted by f_i. The sample mean and estimate of variance in the ith stratum are $\bar{x}_i$ and s_i^2. The total population size is

$$N = \sum_{i=1}^{k} N_i,$$

and the total sample size is

$$n = \sum_{i=1}^{k} n_i.$$

The mean value of x in the whole population is clearly

$$\mu = \frac{\sum N_i \mu_i}{N}.$$

The appropriate estimate of μ is

$$\hat{\mu}=\frac{\sum N_i\bar{x}_i}{N}, \tag{6.1}$$

which is easily seen to be unbiased. (Since $E(\bar{x}_i)=\mu_i$, $E(\hat{\mu})=\sum N_i\mu_i/N=\mu$.) The variance of $\hat{\mu}$ is

$$\begin{aligned}\operatorname{var}(\hat{\mu})&=\frac{1}{N^2}\sum N_i^2\operatorname{var}(\bar{x}_i)\\&=\frac{1}{N^2}\sum\frac{N_i^2\sigma_i^2}{n_i}(1-f_i)\end{aligned} \tag{6.2}$$

by (3.2), and this may be estimated from the sample as

$$\operatorname{var}(\hat{\mu})=\frac{1}{N^2}\sum\frac{N_i^2s_i^2}{n_i}(1-f_i). \tag{6.3}$$

If all the f_i are sufficiently small, the terms $(1-f_i)$ in (6.2) may be replaced by unity. In general (6.2) will be smaller than the variance of the mean of a random sample because the terms σ_i^2 measure only the variability *within* strata. Variability between the μ_i is irrelevant.

If n is fixed and the f_i are small, $\operatorname{var}(\hat{\mu})$ becomes a minimum if the n_i are chosen to be as nearly as possible proportional to $N_i\sigma_i$. Thus, if σ_i is constant from one stratum to another, the n_i should be chosen in proportion to N_i, i.e., the sampling fraction should be constant. Strata with relatively large σ_i have correspondingly increased sampling fractions. Usually, little will be known about the σ_i before the survey is carried out and the choice of a constant sampling fraction will be the most reasonable strategy.

If the survey is designed to estimate a proportion, π, the above formulae hold with $\bar{x}_i$ and μ_i replaced by p_i and π_i, the observed and true proportions in the ith stratum, $\sigma_i{}^2$ by $\pi_i(1-\pi_i)$ and s_i^2 by $n_ip_i(1-p_i)/(n_i-1)$.

Apart from the increased precision in the estimation of the population mean, stratification may be adopted to provide reasonably precise estimates of the means for each of the strata. This may lead to departures from the optimal allocation described above so that none of the sample sizes in the separate strata become too small.

Example 6.1

It is desired to estimate the prevalence of a certain condition (i.e., the proportion of affected individuals) in a population of 5,000 people by taking a sample of size 100. Suppose that the prevalence is known to be affected by age and that the population can be divided into three strata defined by age groups, with the following numbers of individuals (which have been made artificially simple for ease of presentation).

Stratum, i	Age (years)	N_i
1	0–14	1,200
2	15–44	2,200
3	45–	1,600
		5,000

Suppose that the true prevalences, π_i, in the different strata are as follows:

Stratum, i	π_i
1	0·02
2	0·08
3	0·15

It is easily verified that the overall prevalence, π $(=\Sigma N_i\pi_i/\Sigma N_i)$, is 0·088. A simple random sample of size $n=100$ would therefore give an estimate p with variance (0·088)(0·912)/100=0·000803.

For stratified sampling with optimal allocation the sample sizes in the strata should be chosen in proportion to $N_i\sqrt{\{\pi_i(1-\pi_i)\}}$. The values of this quantity in the three strata are 168, 597 and 571, which are in the proportions 0·126, 0·447 and 0·427 respectively. The optimal sample sizes are, therefore, $n_1=12$, $n_2=45$ and $n_3=43$, or numbers very close to these (there being a little doubt about the effect of rounding to the nearest integer). Let us call this *Allocation A*. This depends on the unknown π_i, and therefore could hardly be used in practice. If we knew very little about the likely variation in the π_i, we might choose the $n_i \propto N_i$, ignoring the effect of the changing standard deviation. This would give, for *Allocation B*, $n_1=24$, $n_2=44$ and $n_3=32$. Thirdly, we might have some idea that the prevalence (and therefore the standard deviation) increased with age, and therefore adjust the allocation rather arbitrarily to give, say, $n_1=20$, $n_2=40$ and $n_3=40$ (*Allocation C*).

The estimate $\hat{\pi}$ is, in each case, given by the formula equivalent to (6.1),

$$\hat{\pi}=\frac{\Sigma N_i p_i}{N},$$

where p_i is the estimated prevalence in the ith stratum. The variance of $\hat{\pi}$ is given by the equivalent of (6.2), in which we shall drop the terms f_i as being small:

$$\text{var}(\hat{\pi})=\frac{1}{N^2}\Sigma\frac{N_i^2\pi_i(1-\pi_i)}{n_i}.$$

The values of var($\hat{\pi}$) for the three allocations are as follows:

Allocation	var($\hat{\pi}$)
A	0·000714
B	0·000779
C	0·000739

As would be expected, the lowest variance is for *A* and the highest for *B*, the latter being only a little lower than the variance for a random sample.

This example illustrates the fact that the reduction in sampling variance by stratification, even with optimal allocation, is unlikely to be very striking unless the differences between strata in the μ_i value are much greater than the standard deviations σ_i. When the estimation is concerned with proportions (as in the example) this condition is unlikely to hold since the standard deviations $\sqrt{\{\pi_i(1-\pi_i)\}}$ are similar in magnitude to the π_i.

MULTI-STAGE SAMPLING

In this method the sampling frame is divided into a population of 'first-stage sampling units', of which a 'first-stage' sample is taken. This will usually be a simple random sample, but may be a systematic or stratified sample; it may also, as we shall see, be a random sample in which some first-stage units are allowed to have a higher probability of selection than others. Each first-stage unit thus selected is sub-divided into 'second-stage sampling units', which are sampled. The process can continue as long as is appropriate.

There are two main advantages of multi-stage sampling. First, it enables the resources to be concentrated in a limited number of portions of the whole sampling frame with a consequent reduction in cost. Secondly, it is convenient for situations in which a complete sampling frame is not available before the investigation starts. A list of first-stage units is required, but the second-stage units need be listed only within the first-stage units selected in the sample.

Consider as an example a health survey of men working in a certain industry. There would probably not exist a complete index of all men in the industry, but it would be easy to obtain a list of factories, which could be first-stage units. From each factory selected in the first-stage sample a list of men could be obtained, and a second-stage sample selected from this list. Apart from the advantage of having to make lists of men only within the factories selected at the first stage, this procedure would result in an appreciable saving in cost by enabling the investigation to be concentrated at selected factories instead of necessitating the examination of a sample of men all in different parts of the country.

The economy in cost and resources is unfortunately accompanied by a loss of precision as compared with simple random sampling. Suppose that in the example discussed above we take a sample of 20 factories and second-stage samples of 50 men in each of the 20 factories. If there is systematic variation between the factories, due perhaps to variation in health conditions in different parts of the country or to differing occupational hazards, this variation will be represented by a sample of only 20 first-stage units. A random sample of 1,000 men, on the other hand, would represent 1,000 random choices of first-stage units (some of which may, of course, be chosen more than once) and would consequently provide a better estimate of the national mean.

A useful device in two-stage sampling is called *self-weighting*. Each first-stage unit is given a probability of selection which is proportional to the number of second-stage units it contains. Second-stage samples are then chosen to have equal size. It follows that each second-stage unit in the whole population has an equal chance of being selected and the formulae needed for estimation are somewhat simplified.

Sometimes, in the final stage of sampling, complete enumeration of the available units is undertaken. In the industrial example, once a survey team has installed itself in a factory it may cost little extra to examine all the men in the factory; it may indeed be useful to avoid the embarrassment which might be caused by inviting some men but not others to participate.

OTHER CONSIDERATIONS

The planning, conduct and analysis of sample surveys give rise to many problems which cannot be discussed here. The books by Moser (1958) and Yates (1960) contain excellent discussions of the practical aspects of sampling. Applications to morbidity surveys and public health investigations are described briefly in a report by the World Health Organization (1966). The books by Cochran (1963) and Yates (1960) may be consulted for the main theoretical results.

The statistical theory of sample surveys is concerned largely with the measurement of sampling error. This emphasis may lead the investigator to overlook the importance of non-sampling errors. In a large survey the sampling errors may be so small that systematic non-sampling errors may be much the more important. Indeed, in a complete enumeration, such as a complete population census, sampling errors disappear altogether, but there may be very serious non-sampling errors.

Some non-sampling errors are non-systematic, causing no bias on the average. An example would be random inaccuracy in the reading of a test instrument. These errors merely contribute to the variability of the observation in question and therefore diminish the precision of the survey. Other errors are systematic, causing a bias in a mean value which does not decrease with increasing sample size: for example, in a health survey certain types of illness may be systematically under-reported.

One of the most important types of systematic error is that due to inadequate coverage of the sampling frame, either because of non-co-operation by the individual or because the investigator finds it difficult to make the correct observations. For example, in an interview survey some people may refuse to be interviewed and others may be hard to find or may have moved away from the supposed address or even have died. Individuals who are missed for any of these reasons are likely to be atypical of the population in various relevant respects. Every effort must therefore be made to include the chosen individuals in the enquiry, by persistent attempts to make the relevant observations on all the non-responders or by concentrating on a sub-sample of them so that the characteristics of the non-responders can at least be estimated.

Reference must finally be made to another important type of study, the *longitudinal survey*. Many investigations are concerned with the changes in certain measurements over a period of time: for example, the growth and development of children over a 10-year period, or the changes in blood pressure during pregnancy. It is desirable where possible to study each individual over the relevant period of time rather than to take different samples of individuals at different points of time. Some of the statistical problems are discussed by Tanner (1951).

6.3 SURVEYS TO INVESTIGATE ASSOCIATIONS

A question commonly asked in epidemiological investigations into the aetiology of disease is whether some manifestation of ill-health is associated with certain personal characteristics or habits, with particular aspects of the environment in which a person has lived, or with certain experiences which he has undergone. Examples of such questions are the following.

(a) Is the risk of death from lung cancer related to the degree of cigarette smoking, whether current or in previous years?

(b) Is the risk that a child dies from acute leukaemia related to whether or not the mother experienced irradiation during pregnancy?

(c) Is the risk of incurring a certain illness increased for individuals who were treated with a particular drug during a previous illness?

Sometimes questions like these can be answered by controlled experimentation in which the presumptive personal factor can be administered or withheld at the investigator's discretion; in example (c), for instance, it might be possible for the investigator to give the drug in question to some patients and not to others and to compare the outcomes. In such cases the questions are concerned with causative effects: 'Is this drug a partial *cause* of this illness?'. More often, however, the experimental approach is out of the question. The investigator must then be satisfied to observe whether there is an *association* between factor and disease and to take the risk which was emphasized in section 5.1 if he wishes to infer a causative link.

These questions, then, will usually be studied by surveys rather than by experiments. The precise population to be surveyed is not usually of primary interest here. One reason is that in epidemiological surveys it is usually administratively impossible to study a national or regional population, even on a sample basis. The investigator may, however, have facilities to study a particular occupational group or a population geographically related to a particular medical centre. Secondly, although the mean values or relative frequencies of the different variables may vary somewhat from one population to another, the magnitude and direction of the associations between variables are unlikely to vary greatly between, say, different occupational groups or different geographical populations.

There are two main designs for aetiological surveys—the *case-control* study and the *cohort* study. In a case-control study a group of individuals affected by the disease in question is compared with a control group of unaffected individuals. Information is obtained, usually in a retrospective way, about the frequency in each group of the various environmental or personal factors which might be associated with the disease. This type of survey is convenient in the study of rare conditions which would appear too seldom in a random population sample. By starting with a group of affected individuals one is effectively taking a much higher sampling fraction of the cases than of the controls. The method is appropriate also when the classification by disease is simple (particularly for a dichotomous classification into the presence or absence of a specific condition), but in which many possible aetiological factors have to be studied. A further advantage is that, by means of the retrospective enquiry, the relevant information can be obtained comparatively quickly.

In a cohort study a population of individuals, selected usually by geographical or occupational criteria rather than on medical grounds, is studied either by complete enumeration or by a representative sample. The population is classified by the factor or factors of interest and followed prospectively in time so that the rates of occurrence of various manifestations of disease can be observed and related to the classifications by aetiological factors. The prospective nature of the cohort study means that it will normally extend longer in time than the case-control study and is likely to be administratively more complex. The corresponding advantages are that many medical conditions can be studied simultaneously and that direct information is obtained about the health of each subject through an interval of time.

Case-control and cohort studies are often called respectively *retrospective* and *prospective* studies. These latter terms are usually appropriate, but the nomenclature may occasionally be misleading since a cohort study may be based entirely on retrospective records. For example, if medical records are available of workers in a certain factory for the past 30 years, a cohort study may relate to workers employed 30 years ago and be based on records of their health in the succeeding 30 years.

A central problem in a case-control study is the method by which the controls are chosen. Ideally, they should be on average similar to the cases in all respects except in the medical condition under study and in associated aetiological factors. Cases will often be selected from one or more hospitals and will then share the characteristics of the population using those hospitals, such as social and environmental conditions or ethnic features. It will usually be desirable to select the control group from the same area or areas, perhaps even from the same hospitals, but suffering from quite different illnesses unlikely to share the same aetiological factors. Further, the frequencies with which various factors are found will usually vary with age and sex. Comparisons between the case and control groups must, therefore, take account of any differences there may be in the age and sex distributions of the two groups. Such adjustments are commonly avoided by arranging that each affected individual is paired with a control individual who is deliberately chosen to be of the same age and sex and to share any other demographic features which may be thought to be similarly relevant.

The remarks made in section 6.2 about non-sampling errors, particularly those about non-response, are relevant also in aetiological surveys. Non-responses may be less important here for the reason adduced for the lack of emphasis on the particular population sampled. Nevertheless, they are always a potential danger and every attempt should be made to reduce them to as low a proportion as possible.

Example 6.2

Doll and Hill (1950) reported the results of a retrospective study of the aetiology of lung cancer. A group of 709 patients with carcinoma of the lung in 20 hospitals was compared with a control group of 709 patients without carcinoma of the lung and a third group of 637 patients with carcinoma of the stomach, colon or rectum. For each patient with lung cancer a control patient was selected from the same hospital, or the same sex and within the same five-year age group. Each patient in each group was interviewed by a social worker, all interviewers using the same questionnaire.

TABLE 6.1 Recent tobacco consumption of patients with carcinoma of the lung and control patients without carcinoma of the lung (Doll and Hill, 1950).

	Non-smoker	Daily consumption of cigarettes 1–	5–	15–	25–	50–	Total
Male							
Lung carcinoma	2	33	250	196	136	32	649
Control	27	55	293	190	71	13	649
Female							
Lung carcinoma	19	7	19	9	6	0	60
Control	32	12	10	6	0	0	60

The only substantial differences between the case and control groups was in their reported smoking habits. Some of the findings are summarized in Table 6.1. The difference in the proportion of non-smokers in the two groups is clearly significant, at any rate for males. (If a significance test for data of this form were required an appropriate method would be the test for the difference of two paired proportions, described in section 4.7.) The group of patients with other forms of cancer had similar smoking histories to those of the control group and differed markedly from the lung cancer group. The comparisons involving this third group are more complicated because the individual patients were not paired with members of the lung cancer or control groups and had a somewhat different age distribution. The possible effect of age had to be allowed for by methods of age standardization (see section 12.6).

This paper by Doll and Hill is an excellent illustration of the care which should be taken to avoid bias due to unsuspected differences between case and control groups or to different standards of data recording. This study, and many others like it, strongly suggest an association between smoking and the risk of incurring lung cancer. In such retrospective studies, however, there is room for arguments about the propriety of a particular choice of control group; little information is obtained about the time relationships involved, and nothing is known about the association between smoking and diseases other than those selected for study. Doll and Hill (1954, 1956, 1964) carried out a cohort study prospectively by sending questionnaires to all the 59,600 doctors in the United Kingdom in October, 1951. Adequate replies were received from 68·2 per cent of the population (34,445 men and 6,192 women). These doctors were followed for 10 years and notifications of deaths from various causes were obtained. Some results for male doctors are shown in Table 6.2. The groups defined by different smoking categories have different age distributions, and the death rates shown in the table have again been standardized for age (section 12.6). Cigarette smoking is again shown to be associated with a sharp increase in the death rate from lung cancer, and also shows a less marked association with the death rates from some other causes.

TABLE 6.2 Standardized annual death rates for three causes of death, related to smoking habits (Doll and Hill, 1964).

		Standardized death rate per 1,000						
			Cigarette smokers					
			Number of cigarettes smoked daily					
Cause of death	Number of deaths	Non-smokers	1–14	15–24	25–	Ex-smokers	Mixed smokers	Pipe or cigar smokers
Lung cancer	207	0·07	0·57	1·29	2·23	0·24	0·52	0·43
Chronic bronchitis	111	0·05	0·34	0·64	1·06	0·38	0·33	0·15
Coronary disease without hypertension	1,287	3·31	4·35	4·28	4·97	3·73	3·87	3·18

Doll and Hill's prospective study provides strong evidence that the association between smoking and lung cancer is causative. About one-third of the doctors who smoked stopped during the first 10 years of the follow-up period. The death rate from lung cancer (age-standardized) for the whole group of male doctors decreased during this period, in striking contrast with that of males in the whole country, and with those of other civilized communities, almost all of which increased during the period.

The measurement of the degree of association between the risk of disease and the presence of an aetiological factor is discussed in detail in section 16.2.

6.4 THE DESIGN OF EXPERIMENTS

We consider now the planning of experiments to compare the effects of various treatments on some type of experimental units. The treatment to be applied to any particular unit is to be decided by the investigator. Examples are the following:

(a) A comparison of the effects of inoculating animals with different doses of a chemical substance. The units here will be the animals.

(b) A prophylactic trial to compare the effectiveness for children of different vaccines against measles. Each child will receive one of the vaccines and may be regarded as the experimental unit.

(c) A comparison in one patient suffering recurrent attacks of a chronic disease of different methods of alleviating discomfort. The successive occasions on which attacks occur are now the units for which the choice of treatment is to be made.

(d) A study of the relative merits of different programmes of community health education. Each programme would be applied in a different area, and these areas would form the experimental units.

In all such examples a crucial question is how the treatments are to be allotted to the available units. One would clearly wish to avoid any serious disparity between the characteristics of units receiving different treatments. In example (b), for instance, it would be dangerous to give one vaccine to all the children in one school and another vaccine to all the children in a second school, for the exposure of the two groups of children to measles contacts might be quite different. It would then be difficult to decide whether a difference in the incidence of measles was due to different protective powers of the vaccines or to the different degrees of exposure to infection.

It would be possible to arrange that the groups of experimental units to which different treatments were to be applied were made alike in various relevant respects. For example, in (a), groups of animals with approximately the same mean weight could be formed; in (b) children from different schools and of different age groups could be represented equally in each treatment group. But however careful the investigator is to balance factors which seem important, he can never be sure that the treatment groups do not differ markedly in some factor which is also important but which has been ignored in the allocation.

The accepted solution to this dilemma is that advocated by Fisher in the 1920s and 1930s: the allocation should incorporate an element of *randomization*. In its simplest form this means that the choice of treatment for each unit should be made by an independent act of randomization such as the toss of a coin or the use of random number tables. This would lead to some uncertainty in the numbers of units finally allotted to each treatment, and if these are fixed in advance the groups may be formed by choosing random samples of the appropriate sizes from the total pool of experimental units. More detailed instructions in the use of random number tables are given on page 474.

In clinical trials the total number of patients is often not known in advance since many patients may become available for inclusion in the trial some time after it has started. The simplest method is then to allocate treatment by an independent random choice for each patient. A method by which the numbers allocated to different treatments are kept close together, called *restricted randomization*, is described on page 474.

Sometimes a form of *systematic allocation*, analogous to systematic sampling, is used as an alternative to random allocation. The units are arranged in a certain order and are then allotted systematically to the treatment groups. In a clinical trial with serial entry, for example, an allocation to two treatment groups might be carried out by strict alternation. This method has much the same advantages and disadvantages as systematic sampling. It is likely to be seriously misleading only if the initial ordering of the units presents some systematic variation of a cyclic type which happens to run in phase with the allocation cycle. In clinical trials this is perhaps unlikely to happen, although if the allocation is systematic and therefore known to the investigator responsible for forming the serial index of patients, he may be influenced by this knowledge in deciding the ordering and thereby create a bias. In general alternation and other forms of systematic allocation are best avoided in favour of strictly random methods.

A second important principle of experimental design is that of *replication*, the use of more than one experimental unit for each treatment. Various purposes are served by replication. First, an appropriate amount of replication ensures that the comparisons between treatments are sufficiently precise; the sampling error of the difference between two means, for instance, decreases as the amount of replication in each group increases. Secondly, the effect of sampling variation can be estimated only if there is an adequate degree of replication. In the comparison of the means of two groups, for instance, if both sample sizes were as low as 2 the degrees of freedom in the t test would only be 2 (section 4.6); the percentage points of t on 2 degrees of freedom are very high and the test therefore loses a great deal in effectiveness merely because of the inadequacy of the estimate of within-group variance. Thirdly, replication may be useful in enabling observations to be spread over a wide variety of experimental conditions. In the comparison of two surgical procedures, for instance, it might be useful to organize a co-operative trial in which the methods were compared in each of a number of hospitals, so that the effects of variations in medical and surgical practice and perhaps in the precise type of disease could be studied.

A third basic principle concerns the reduction in random variability between experimental units. The formula for the standard error of a mean, $\sigma/\sqrt{n}$, shows that the effect of random error can be reduced, either by increasing n (more replication) or by decreasing σ. This suggests that experimental units should be as homogeneous as possible in their response to treatment. However, too strenuous an effort to remove heterogeneity will tend to counteract the third reason given above for replication—the desire to cover a wide range of extraneous conditions. In a clinical trial, for example, it may be that a precise comparison could be effected by restricting the age, sex, clinical condition and other features of the patients, but these restrictions may make it too difficult to generalize from the results. A useful solution to this dilemma is to subdivide the units into relatively homogeneous sub-groups, called *blocks*. Treatments can then be allocated randomly within blocks so that each block provides a small experiment. The precision of the overall comparisons between treatments is then determined by the random variability *within* blocks rather than that between different blocks. This is called a *randomized block* design. More complex designs, allowing simultaneously for more than one source of extraneous variation, are discussed in Chapter 8. Other extensions dealt with in that chapter are designs for the simultaneous comparison of more than one set of treatments; those appropriate for situations similar to that of multi-stage sampling, in which some units are sub-divisions of others; and designs which allow in various ways for the natural restrictions imposed by the experimental material.

Brief references have been made to an important class of controlled experiments—the comparison on human beings of the effectiveness of therapeutic and prophylactic measures. Clinical and prophylactic trials, strictly controlled by random allocation, date from the mid-1940s. They give rise to ethical and administrative problems which are largely beyond the scope of this book. Reference may be made to Hill (1966, Chapter XX) and to Mainland (1960). Many of the pioneering collaborative trials organized by the Medical Research Council are reported in Hill (1962).

6.5 THE SIZE OF A STATISTICAL INVESTIGATION

One of the questions most commonly asked about the planning of a statistical study, and one of the most difficult to answer, is: how many observations should be made? Other things being equal, the greater the sample size or the larger the experiment, the more precise will be the estimates of the parameters and their differences. The difficulty lies in deciding what degree of precision to aim for. An increase in the size of a survey or of an experiment costs more money and takes more time. Sometimes a limit is imposed by financial resources or by the time available, and the investigator will wish to make as many observations as his resources permit, allowing in his budget for the time and cost of the processing and analysis of the data. In other situations there will be no obvious limit, and the investigator will have to balance the benefits of increased precision against the cost of increased data collection or experimentation. In some branches of technology the whole problem can be looked at from a purely economic point of view, but this will rarely be possible in medical research since the benefit of experimental or survey information is so difficult to measure financially.

In any review of these problems at the planning stage it is likely to be important to relate the sample size to a specified degree of precision. We shall consider the problem of comparing the means of two populations, μ_1 and μ_2, assuming that they have the same known standard deviation, σ, and that two equal random samples of size n are to be taken. If the standard deviations are known to be different the present results may be thought of as an approximation (taking σ to be the mean of the two values). If the comparison is of two proportions, π_1 and π_2, σ may be taken approximately to be the pooled value

$$\sqrt{[\tfrac{1}{2}\{\pi_1(1-\pi_1)+\pi_2(1-\pi_2)\}]}.$$

We now consider three ways in which the precision may be specified.

(a) *Given standard error.*

Suppose it is required that the standard error of the difference between the observed means, $\bar{x}_1-\bar{x}_2$, is less than ϵ; equivalently the width of the 95 per cent confidence intervals might be specified to be not wider than $\pm 2\epsilon$. This implies

$$\sigma\sqrt{(2/n)}<\epsilon$$

or

$$n>2\sigma^2/\epsilon^2. \tag{6.4}$$

If the requirement is that the standard error of the mean of *one* sample shall be less than ϵ, the corresponding inequality for n is

$$n>\sigma^2/\epsilon^2. \tag{6.5}$$

(b) *Given difference to be significant.*

We might require that if $\bar{x}_1-\bar{x}_2$ is greater in absolute value than some value d_0, then it shall be significant at some specified level (say at a two-sided 2α level). Denote by $u_{2\alpha}$ the standardized normal deviate exceeded (in either direction) with probability 2α; (for $2\alpha=0{\cdot}05$, $u_{2\alpha}=1{\cdot}96$). Then

$$d_0>u_{2\alpha}\sigma\sqrt{(2/n)}$$

or

$$n>2\left(\frac{u_{2\alpha}\sigma}{d_0}\right)^2. \tag{6.6}$$

(c) *Given power against specified difference.*

Criterion (b) is defined in terms of a given *observed* difference, $\bar{x}_1-\bar{x}_2$. The true difference, $\mu_1-\mu_2$, may be either less or greater than $\bar{x}_1-\bar{x}_2$, and it seems preferable to base the requirement on the value of $\mu_1-\mu_2$. It might be possible to specify a value of $\mu_1-\mu_2$, say δ_0, which one did not wish to overlook, in the sense that if $(\mu_1-\mu_2)>\delta_0$ one would like to get a significant result at, say, the two-sided 2α level. However, a significant difference cannot be guaranteed. Sampling fluctuations may lead to a value of $|\bar{x}_1-\bar{x}_2|$ much less than $|\mu_1-\mu_2|$ and not significantly different from zero. One might, however, ask that the probability of a significant difference at the stated level should be not less than some high value, $1-\beta$. This probability is called the *power* of the test.

To evaluate the required value of n, note that positive values of $\bar{x}_1-\bar{x}_2$ are significant at the stated level if

$$\bar{x}_1-\bar{x}_2>u_{2\alpha}\sigma\surd(2/n). \tag{6.7}$$

For a power $>1-\beta$, the right side of (6.7) must be below the point cutting off a one-sided probability of β when $\mu_1-\mu_2=\delta_0$. That is,

$$u_{2\alpha}\sigma\surd(2/n)<\delta_0-u_{2\beta}\sigma\surd(2/n),$$

whence

$$\delta_0>(u_{2\alpha}+u_{2\beta})\sigma\surd(2/n)$$

or

$$n>2\left\{\frac{(u_{2\alpha}+u_{2\beta})\sigma}{\delta_0}\right\}^2. \tag{6.8}$$

The distinction between (b) and (c) is important. For instance, if $2\alpha=0{\cdot}05$ and $1-\beta=0{\cdot}95$, $u_{2\alpha}=1{\cdot}96$ and $u_{2\beta}=1{\cdot}64$. If d_0 is put equal to δ_0, the values of n given by (6.8) and (6.6) are thus in the ratio $(1{\cdot}96+1{\cdot}64)^2:1{\cdot}96^2$ or $3{\cdot}4:1$.

For the comparison of two proportions, Mainland *et al.* (1956) provide a table for determining sample sizes by approach (c), using a more exact method than that given above. See also Kramer and Greenhouse (1959).

The formulae given above assume a knowledge of the standard deviation, σ. In practice σ will rarely be known in advance, although sometimes the investigator will be able to make use of an estimate of σ from previous data which he feels to be reasonably accurate. If no preliminary estimate of σ is available the comparison of two means will involve the t distribution. The approaches outlined above may be modified in two ways. The first way would be to recognize that the required values of n can be specified only in terms of the ratio of a critical interval (ϵ, d_0 or δ_0) to an estimated or true standard deviation (s or σ). For instance, in (a) we might specify the estimated standard error to be a certain multiple of s; in (b) d_0 might be specified as a certain multiple of s; in (c), the power might be specified against a given ratio of δ_0 to σ. In (b) and (c), because the test will use the t distribution rather than the normal, the required values of n will be rather greater than those given by (6.6) or (6.8), but the adjustments are unlikely to be important.

The specification of critical distances as multiples of an unknown standard deviation is not an attractive suggestion. An alternative approach would be to estimate σ by a relatively small pilot investigation and then to use this value in formulae (6.4) to (6.8), to provide an estimate of the total sample size, n. Again, some adjustment is called for because of the uncertainty introduced by estimating σ, but the effect will be small provided that the initial pilot sample is not too small.

The above discussion has assumed that the random variation measured by the standard deviation σ is that between the individual measurements in each sample. If the two groups are paired the random variation is correspondingly reduced. In terms of the methods of analysis of variance to be introduced in Chapter 7, σ is the 'residual' standard deviation.

Many investigations are concerned with more than one variable measured on the same individual. In a morbidity survey, for example, a wide range of symptoms, as well as the results of certain diagnostic tests, may be recorded for each person. Sample sizes deemed adequate for one purpose may, therefore, be inadequate for others. In many investigations the sample size chosen would be the largest of the separate requirements for the different variables; it would not matter too much that for some variables the sample size was unnecessarily high. In other investigations, by contrast, this may be undesirable, because either the cost or the trouble incurred by taking the extra observations is not negligible. A useful device in these circumstances is *multi-phase sampling*. In the first phase certain variables are observed on all the members of the initial sample. In the second phase a sub-sample of the original sample is then taken, either by simple random sampling or by one of the other methods described in section 6.2, and other variables are observed only on the members of the sub-sample. The process could clearly be extended to more than two phases.

Some population censuses have been effectively multi-phase samples in which the first phase is a 100 per cent sample to which some questions are put. In the second phase a sub-sample (say, 1 in 10 of the population) is asked certain additional questions. The justification here would be that complete enumeration is necessary for certain basic demographic data, but that for certain more specialized purposes (perhaps information about fertility or occupation) a 1 in 10 sample would provide estimates of adequate precision. Material savings in cost are achieved by restricting these latter questions to a relatively small sub-sample.

CHAPTER 7
COMPARISON OF SEVERAL GROUPS

7.1 ONE-WAY ANALYSIS OF VARIANCE

The body of techniques called the *analysis of variance* forms a powerful method of analysing the way in which the mean value of a variable is affected by classifications of the data of various sorts. This apparent paradox of nomenclature—that the techniques should be concerned with comparisons of means rather than variances—will be clarified when we come to study the method in detail.

We have already, in section 4.6, used the t distribution for the comparison of the means of two groups of data, distinguishing between the paired and unpaired cases. The *one-way analysis of variance*, the subject of the present section, is a generalization of the unpaired t test, appropriate for any number of groups. As we shall see, it is entirely equivalent to the unpaired t test when there are just two groups. The analogous extension of the paired t test will be described in section 8.1.

Some examples of a one-way classification of data into several groups are as follows:

(a) the reduction in blood sugar recorded for groups of rabbits given different doses of insulin;

(b) the value of a certain lung function test recorded for men of the same age group in a number of different occupational categories;

(c) the volumes of liquid taken up by an experimenter using various pipettes to measure a standard quantity, the repeated measurements on any one pipette being grouped together.

In each of these examples a similar question might be asked: What can be said about the variation in blood sugar reduction from one dose group to another, in lung function test from one occupational category to another, or in volume of liquid from one pipette to another? There are, however, important differences in the nature of the classification into groups in these three examples. In (a) the groups are defined by dose of insulin and fall into a natural order; in (b) the groups may not fall into a unique order, but some very reasonable classifications of the groups may be suggested—for instance, according to physical effort, intellectual demand, etc.; in (c) the groups of data almost certainly will fall into no natural order. In the present section we are concerned with situations in which no account is taken of any logical ordering of the groups, either because, as in (c), there is none, or because a consideration of ordering is deferred until a later stage of the analysis.

Suppose there are k groups of observations on a variable y, and that the ith group contains n_i observations. The numbering of the groups from 1 to k will be quite arbitrary, although if there is a simple ordering of the groups it will be natural to use this in the numbering. Further notation is as follows:

Group	1	2 ... i ... k	All groups combined
Number of observations	n_1	n_2 ... n_i ... n_k	$N=\sum_{i=1}^{k} n_i$
Mean of y	$\bar{y}_1$	$\bar{y}_2$ ... $\bar{y}_i$ ... $\bar{y}_k$	$\bar{y}=T/N$
Sum of y	T_1	T_2 ... T_i ... T_k	$T=\sum_{i=1}^{k} T_i$
Sum of y^2	S_1	S_2 ... S_i ... S_k	$S=\sum_{i=1}^{k} S_i$

Note that the entries N, T and S in the final column are the sums along the corresponding rows, but $\bar{y}$ is not the sum of the $\bar{y}_i$. ($\bar{y}$ will be the *mean* of the y_i if all the n_i are equal; otherwise $\bar{y}$ is the *weighted mean* of the $\bar{y}_i$, $\sum n_i\bar{y}_i/\sum n_i$). Let the observations within each group be numbered in some arbitrary way, and denote the jth observation in the ith group by y_{ij}.

When a summation is taken over all the N observations, each contributing once to the summation, we shall use the summation sign $\sum_{i,j}$. When the summation is taken over the k groups, each group contributing once, we shall use the sign $\sum_i$.

The deviation of any observation from the 'grand mean', $\bar{y}$, may be split into two parts, as follows:

$$y_{ij}-\bar{y}=(y_{ij}-\bar{y}_i)+(\bar{y}_i-\bar{y}). \tag{7.1}$$

The first term on the right of (7.1) is the deviation of y_{ij} from its 'group mean', $\bar{y}_i$, and the second term is the deviation of the group mean from the grand mean. We show below that when each of these terms is squared and summed over all N observations, a similar result holds:

$$\sum_{i,j}(y_{ij}-\bar{y})^2 = \sum_{i,j}(y_{ij}-\bar{y}_i)^2 + \sum_{i,j}(\bar{y}_i-\bar{y})^2. \tag{7.2}$$

This remarkable result means that the 'total' sum of squares about the mean of all N values of y can be partitioned into two parts: (i) the sum of squares of each reading about its own group mean; and (ii) the sum of squares of the deviations of each group mean about the grand mean (these being counted once for every observation). We shall write this result as

Total SSq = *Within groups* SSq + *Between groups* SSq,

'SSq' standing for 'sum of squares'.

Now, if there are very large differences between the group means, as compared with the within-group variation, the Between groups SSq is likely to be larger than the Within groups SSq. If, on the other hand, all the $\bar{y}_i$ are nearly equal and yet there is considerable variation within groups, the reverse is likely to be true. The relative sizes of the Between and Within groups SSq should, therefore, provide an opportunity to assess the variation between group means in comparison with that within groups.

To prove (7.2) we write

$$\begin{aligned}
\sum_{i,j}(y_{ij}-\bar{y})^2 &= \sum_{i,j}\{(y_{ij}-\bar{y}_i)+(\bar{y}_i-\bar{y})\}^2 \\
&= \sum_{i,j}(y_{ij}-\bar{y}_i)^2 + 2\sum_{i,j}(y_{ij}-\bar{y}_i)(\bar{y}_i-\bar{y}) + \sum_{i,j}(\bar{y}_i-\bar{y})^2 \\
&= \sum_{i,j}(y_{ij}-\bar{y}_i)^2 + 2\sum_{i} 0(\bar{y}_i-\bar{y}) + \sum_{i,j}(\bar{y}_i-\bar{y})^2 \\
&= \sum_{i,j}(y_{ij}-\bar{y}_i)^2 + \sum_{i,j}(\bar{y}_i-\bar{y})^2,
\end{aligned}$$

the transition from the second to the third line following because the middle summation can be done group by group, and for the ith group $\sum_j (y_{ij}-\bar{y}_i)=0$. The whole summation is therefore zero. Note that the Between groups SSq may be written

$$\sum_{i,j}(\bar{y}_i-\bar{y})^2 = \sum_i n_i(\bar{y}_i-\bar{y})^2,$$

since the contribution $(\bar{y}_i-\bar{y})^2$ is the same for all the n_i observations in the ith group.

The partitioning of the total sum of squares is most conveniently done by the use of computing formulae analogous to the short-cut formula (1.3) for the sum of squares about the mean of a single sample. These are obtained as follows.

Total SSq

$$\sum_{i,j} (y_{ij} - \bar{y})^2 = S - \frac{T^2}{N}, \tag{7.3}$$

by direct application of (1.3).

Within groups SSq

For the ith group,

$$\sum_{j} (y_{ij} - \bar{y}_i)^2 = S_i - \frac{T_i^2}{n_i}.$$

Summing over the k groups, therefore,

$$\begin{aligned}\sum_{i,j} (y_{ij} - \bar{y}_i)^2 &= \left(S_1 - \frac{T_1^2}{n_1}\right) + \ldots + \left(S_k - \frac{T_k^2}{n_k}\right) \\ &= \sum_i S_i - \sum_i (T_i^2/n_i) \\ &= S - \sum_i (T_i^2/n_i).\end{aligned} \tag{7.4}$$

Between groups SSq

By subtraction, from (7.2),

$$\begin{aligned}\sum_{i,j} (\bar{y}_i - \bar{y})^2 &= \text{Total SSq} - \text{Within groups SSq} \\ &= S - (T^2/N) - \{S - \sum_i (T_i^2/n_i)\} \\ &= \sum_i (T_i^2/n_i) - T^2/N.\end{aligned} \tag{7.5}$$

Note that, from (7.5), the Between groups SSq is expressible entirely in terms of the group totals, T_i, and the numbers in each group, n_i (and hence in terms of the $\bar{y}_i$ and n_i since $T_i = n_i\bar{y}_i$). This shows clearly that it represents variation between the group means and not in any way the variation within groups.

Summarizing these results, we have the following formulae for partitioning the total sum of squares:

$$\left.\begin{array}{ll} \text{Between groups} & \sum_i (T_i^2/n_i) - T^2/N \\ \text{Within groups} & S - \sum_i (T_i^2/n_i) \\ \hline \text{Total} & S - T^2/N \end{array}\right\} \tag{7.6}$$

Consider now the problem of testing for evidence of real differences between the groups. Suppose that the n_i observations in the ith group form a random sample from a population with mean μ_i and variance σ^2. As in the two-sample t test we assume for the moment that σ^2 is the same for all groups. To examine the evidence for differences between the μ_i we shall test the null hypothesis that the μ_i do not vary, being equal to some common unknown value μ. Three ways of estimating σ^2 suggest themselves as follows.

(i) From Total SSq. The whole collection of N observations may be regarded as a random sample of size N, and consequently

$$s_T^2 = \frac{\text{Total SSq}}{N-1}$$

is an unbiased estimate of σ^2.

(ii) From Within groups SSq. Separate unbiased estimates may be got from each group in turn:

$$\frac{S_1 - T_1^2/n_1}{n_1 - 1}, \frac{S_2 - T_2^2/n_2}{n_2 - 1}, \dots, \frac{S_k - T_k^2/n_k}{n_k - 1}.$$

A combined estimate based purely on variation within groups may be derived (by an extension of the procedure used in the two-sample t test) by adding the numerators and denominators of these ratios, to give the *Within groups mean square* (or MSq):

$$s_W^2 = \frac{\textit{Within groups}\text{ SSq}}{\sum_i (n_i - 1)} = \frac{\textit{Within groups}\text{ SSq}}{N-k}.$$

(iii) From Between groups SSq. Since both s_T^2 and s_W^2 are unbiased,

$$\text{E}(s_T^2) = \sigma^2;\ \text{hence E(Total SSq)} = (N-1)\sigma^2. \qquad (7.7)$$

$$\text{E}(s_W^2) = \sigma^2;\ \text{hence E(Within groups SSq)} = (N-k)\sigma^2. \qquad (7.8)$$

Subtracting (7.8) from (7.7),

$$\begin{aligned}\text{E(Between groups SSq)} &= (N-1)\sigma^2 - (N-k)\sigma^2 \\ &= (k-1)\sigma^2.\end{aligned}$$

Hence, a third unbiased estimate is given by the *Between groups mean square*:

$$s_B^2 = \frac{\textit{Between groups}\text{ SSq}}{k-1}.$$

The divisor $k-1$ is reasonable, being one less than the number of groups, just as the divisor for s_T^2 is one less than the number of observations.

These results hold if the null hypothesis is true. Suppose, however, that the μ_i are not all equal. The Within groups MSq is still an unbiased estimate of σ^2, since it is based purely on the variation within groups. The Between groups MSq, being based on the variation between group means, will tend to increase. In fact, in general, when the μ_i differ

$$E(s_B^2) = \sigma^2 + \frac{\sum_i n_i(\mu_i - \bar{\mu})^2}{k-1}, \tag{7.9}$$

where $\bar{\mu}$ is the weighted mean of the μ's, $\sum_i n_i\mu_i/n$. Some indication of whether the μ_i differ can therefore be obtained from a comparison of s_B^2 and s_W^2. On the null hypothesis these two mean squares estimate the same quantity and therefore should not usually be too different; if the null hypothesis is not true s_B^2 is, from (7.9), on average greater than σ^2 and will tend to be greater than s_W^2.

An appropriate test of the null hypothesis, therefore, may be based on the ratio s_B^2/s_W^2, which will be denoted by F. The distribution of F depends on the nature of the distributions of the y_{ij}'s about their mean $\bar{y}_i$. If the further assumption is made that these distributions are normal, it can be shown that s_B^2 and s_W^2 behave like two *independent* estimates of variance*, on $k-1$ and $N-k$ degrees of freedom, respectively. The relevant distribution, the F distribution, has been discussed in section 4.10. Departures from the null hypothesis will tend to give values of F greater than unity. A significance test for the null hypothesis should, therefore, count as significant only those values of F which are sufficiently large; that is, a one-sided test is required. As observed in section 4.10, the critical levels of F are tabulated in terms of single-tail probabilities, so the tabulated values (Table A4) apply directly to the present situation; (the single-tail form of tabulation in fact arose to serve the needs of the analysis of variance).

If $k=2$ the situation considered above is precisely that for which the unpaired (or two-sample) t test was introduced in section 4.6. The variance ratio, F, will have 1 and $N-2$ degrees of freedom and t will

* In fact, our previous applications of the t distribution depended for their validity on the fact that in samples of size N from a normal distribution the mean and estimate of variance are independently distributed. In the present group of k samples, therefore, all the separate within-group estimates (and hence the pooled estimate s_W^2) are independent of all the sample means $\bar{y}_i$ (and hence of the Between groups mean square s_B^2).

have n_1+n_2-2, i.e. $N-2$ degrees of freedom. The two solutions are, in fact, equivalent in the sense that (a) the value of F is equal to the square of the value of t; (b) the distribution of F on 1 and $N-2$ degrees of freedom is precisely the same as the distribution of the square of a variable following the t distribution on $N-2$ degrees of freedom. The former statement may be proved algebraically in a few lines. The second has already been noted in section 4.10.

If $k=2$ and $n_1=n_2=\frac{1}{2}N$ (i.e. there are two groups of equal size), a useful result is that the Between groups SSq (7.5) may be written in the alternative form

$$\frac{(T_1-T_2)^2}{N}. \tag{7.10}$$

If $k>2$ we may wish to examine the difference between a particular pair of means, chosen because the contrast between these particular groups is of logical interest. The standard error of the difference between two means, say $\bar{y}_g$ and $\bar{y}_h$, may be estimated by

$$\text{SE}(\bar{y}_g-\bar{y}_h)=\sqrt{\left\{s_W^2\left(\frac{1}{n_g}+\frac{1}{n_h}\right)\right\}}, \tag{7.11}$$

and the difference $\bar{y}_g-\bar{y}_h$ tested by referring

$$t=\frac{\bar{y}_g-\bar{y}_h}{\text{SE}(\bar{y}_g-\bar{y}_h)}$$

to the t distribution on $N-k$ degrees of freedom (since this is the number of DF associated with the estimate of variance s^2). Confidence limits for the difference in means may be set in the usual way, using tabulated percentiles of t on $N-k$ DF. The only function of the analysis of variance in this particular comparison has been to replace the estimate of variance on n_g+n_h-2 DF (which would be used in the two-sample t test) by the pooled within-groups mean square on $N-k$ DF. This may be a considerable advantage if n_g and n_h are small. It has been gained, however, by invoking an assumption that all the groups are subject to the same within-groups variance and if there is doubt about the near-validity of this assumption it will be safer to rely on the data from the two groups alone.

If there are no contrasts between groups which have an *a priori* claim on our attention, further scrutiny of the differences between means could be made to depend largely on the F test in the analysis of variance. If the variance ratio is not significant, or even suggestively large, there will be little point in examining differences between pairs of means. If F is significant there is reasonable evidence that real differences exist and are large enough to reveal themselves above the random variation. It then seems natural to see what can safely be said about the direction and magnitude of these differences. This topic will be taken up again in section 7.3.

Example 7.1

During each of four experiments on the use of carbon tetrachloride as a worm killer, ten rats were infested with larvae. Eight days later five rats were treated with carbon tetrachloride, the other five being kept as controls. After two more days the rats were killed and the number of adult worms counted.

TABLE 7.1 One-way analysis of variance: differences between four groups of rats in counts of adult worms.

	Experiment				All
	I	II	III	IV	groups
	279	378	172	381	
	338	275	335	346	
	334	412	335	340	
	198	265	282	471	
	303	286	250	318	
T_i	1,452	1,616	1,374	1,856	$T=$ 6,298
n_i	5	5	5	5	$N=$ 20
$\bar{y}_i$	290·4	323·2	274·8	371·2	
S_i	434,654	540,274	396,058	703,442	$S=$2,074,428
T_i^2/n_i	421,661	522,291	377,575	688,947	

Between groups SSq = 421,661 + ... + 688,947 − (6,298)²/20
= 2,010,474 − 1,983,240
= 27,234

Total SSq = 2,074,428 − 1,983,240
= 91,188

Within groups SSq = 91,188 − 27,234
= 63,954

Analysis of variance

	SSq	DF	MSq	VR
Between groups	27,234	3	9,078	2·27
Within groups	63,954	16	3,997	
Total	91,188	19		

It was thought useful to examine the significance of the differences between the means for the four control groups. If significant differences could be established they might be related to definable changes in experimental conditions, thus leading to a reduction of variation in future work. The results and the details of the calculations are shown in Table 7.1. The value of F is 2·27, and comparison with the F table for $\nu_1=3$ and $\nu_2=16$ shows the result to be non-significant at $P=0{\cdot}05$. (Actually $0{\cdot}1 < P < 0{\cdot}2$.)

The standard error of the difference between two means is $\sqrt{\{2(3997)/5\}}=40{\cdot}0$. Note that the difference between $\bar{y}_3$ and $\bar{y}_4$ is more than twice its standard error, but since the F value is not significant we should not pay much attention to this particular comparison unless it presents some prior interest (see also section 7.3).

Two important assumptions underlying the F test in the one-way analysis of variance are (a) the normality of the distribution of the y_{ij}'s about their mean μ_i, and (b) the equality of the variances in the various groups. The F test is not unduly sensitive to moderate departures from normality, but it will often be worth considering whether some form of transformation (Chapter 11) will improve matters. The assumption about equality of variances is more serious. It has already been suggested that for comparisons of two means, where there is doubt about the validity of a pooled within-group estimate of variance, it may be advisable to estimate the variance from the two groups alone. A transformation of the scale of measurement may bring about near-equality of variances. If it fails to do so an approximate test for differences of means may be obtained by calculating, for each group,

$$w_i=n_i/s_i^2,$$

where

$$s_i^2=(S_i-T_i^2/n_i)/(n_i-1).$$

The quantity w_i, called a *weight*, is the reciprocal of the estimated variance of the mean $\bar{y}_i$. Then calculate

$$G=\sum_i w_i\bar{y}_i^2-(\sum_i w_i\bar{y}_i)^2/\sum_i w_i. \tag{7.12}$$

On the null hypothesis G is distributed approximately as $\chi^2_{(k-1)}$, high values of G indicating excessive disparity between the $\bar{y}_i$'s. The approximation is increasingly inadequate for smaller values of the n_i (say, below about 10) and a refinement is given by James (1951) and Welch (1951). For an application of this approximate method in a comparison of sets of pock counts see Armitage (1957, p. 579).

7.2 COMPONENTS OF VARIANCE

In some studies which lead to a one-way analysis of variance the groups may be of no great interest individually, but may nevertheless represent an interesting source of variation. The result of a pipetting operation may, for example, vary from one pipette to another. A comparison between a particular pair of pipettes would be of little interest; furthermore, a test of the null hypothesis considered in the last section may be pointless because there may quite clearly be a systematic difference between instruments. A more relevant question here will be: how great is the variation between pipettes as compared with that of repeated readings on the same pipette?

A useful framework is to regard the k groups as being randomly selected from a population of such groups. This will not usually be strictly true, but it serves as an indication that the groups are of interest only as representing a certain type of variation. This framework is often called *Model II*, or the *Random Effects Model*, as distinct from *Model I*, or the *Fixed Effects Model*, considered in section 7.1.

Suppose, in the first instance, that each group contains the same

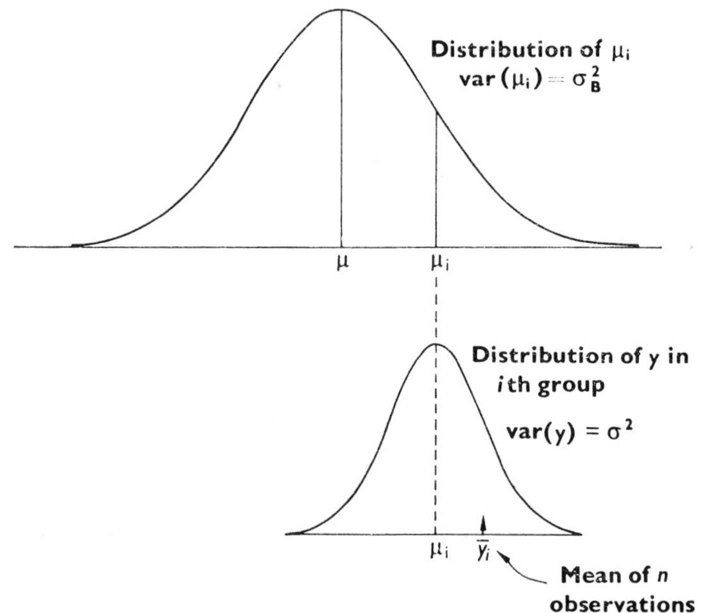

FIG. 7.1 Components of variance between and within groups, with normal distributions for each component of random variation.

number, n, of observations. (In the notation of section 7.1, all the n_i are equal to n.) Let μ_i be the 'true' mean for the ith group and suppose that in the population of groups μ_i is distributed with mean μ and variance σ_B^2. Readings within the ith group have mean μ_i and variance σ^2. The quantities σ^2 and σ_B^2 are called *components of variance* within and between groups respectively. The situation is illustrated in Fig. 7.1. The data at our disposal consist of a random sample of size n from each of k randomly selected groups.

Consider first the variance of a single group mean, $\bar{y}_i$. We have

$$\bar{y}_i - \mu = (\mu_i - \mu) + (\bar{y}_i - \mu_i),$$

and the two terms in brackets represent independent sources of variation —that of μ_i about μ and that of $\bar{y}_i$ about μ_i. Therefore

$$\begin{aligned} \text{var}(\bar{y}_i) &= \text{var}(\mu_i) + \text{var}(\bar{y}_i) \text{ given } \mu_i \\ &= \sigma_B^2 + (\sigma^2/n). \end{aligned} \tag{7.13}$$

Now, the analysis of variance will have the following structure:

	DF	MSq
Between groups	$k-1$	s_B^2
Within groups	$k(n-1)$	s_W^2
	$nk-1(=N-1)$	

The Between groups SSq is (with notation for T_i and T as in the last section),

$$\begin{aligned} &\frac{\sum T_i^2}{n} - \frac{T^2}{N} \\ &= n\{\sum \bar{y}_i^2 - (\sum \bar{y}_i)^2/k\}, \end{aligned}$$

summations running from $i=1$ to k. Thus the Between groups MSq, s_B^2,

$= n\{\sum \bar{y}_i^2 - (\sum \bar{y}_i)^2/k\}/(k-1)$

$= n$ times an unbiased estimate of $\text{var}(\bar{y}_i)$

$= n$ times an unbiased estimate of $\sigma_B^2 + (\sigma^2/n)$, from (7.13),

$=$ an unbiased estimate of $n\sigma_B^2 + \sigma^2$.

That is,

$$E(s_B^2) = \sigma^2 + n\sigma_B^2. \tag{7.14}$$

This important result is similar to (7.9), which is the analogous result for the situation in which the μ_i are fixed.

The Within groups MSq is (from section 7.1) an unbiased estimate of σ^2. The result (7.14) thus confirms the plausibility of the F test, for the null hypothesis is that $\sigma_B^2=0$ and in this case both mean squares are unbiased estimates of σ^2. If $\sigma_B^2>0$, s_B^2 will on average be greater than s_W^2, and F will tend to be greater than 1.

To estimate σ_B^2, note that

$$\begin{aligned} E(s_B^2-s_W^2) &= E(s_B^2)-E(s_W^2) \\ &= (\sigma^2+n\sigma_B^2)-\sigma^2 \\ &= n\sigma_B^2. \end{aligned}$$

Hence, an unbiased estimate of σ_B^2 is given by

$$\hat{\sigma}_B^2=\frac{s_B^2-s_W^2}{n}. \tag{7.15}$$

If $s_B^2<s_W^2$ (as will often be the case if σ_B^2 is zero or near zero), $\hat{\sigma}_B^2$ is negative. There is a case for replacing $\hat{\sigma}_B^2$ by 0 when this happens, but it should be noted that the unbiased property of (7.15) is then lost.

Example 7.2

Bacharach *et al.* (1940) carried out an experiment on 'diffusing factor', a substance which, when present in an inoculation into the skin of rabbits, spreads the blister caused by the inoculation. They gave inoculations of the same dose at six sites on the back of each of six animals. Their experimental design permitted a study of the influence of the particular site and the order of administration, but there was no evidence that these factors had any effect and we shall regard the data as forming a one-way classification: between and within animals. The variable analysed is the area of the blister (cm^2).

An analysis of variance was as follows:

	SSq	DF	MSq	VR
Between animals	12·8333	5	2·5667	4·39
Within animals	17·5266	30	0·5842	
	30·3599	35		

We have

$$\begin{aligned} \hat{\sigma}_B^2 &= (2{\cdot}5667-0{\cdot}5842)/6 \\ &= 0{\cdot}3304. \end{aligned}$$

The two components of variance are then estimated as follows, where each is expressed as a percentage of the total:

Between animals	$\hat{\sigma}_B^2$	0·3304	36%
Within animals	s_W^2	0·5842	64%
	$\hat{\sigma}_B^2+s_W^2$	0·9146	100%

The sum of the two components is the estimated variance of a single reading from a randomly chosen rabbit, and the analysis shows that of this total variance 36 per cent is estimated to be attributable to systematic differences between rabbits. (For further analysis of these data, see below; also Example 8·5.)

Confidence limits for σ^2 are obtained from the Within groups SSq by use of the χ^2 distribution, as in section 4.5. Confidence limits for σ_B^2 are rather more troublesome. An approximate solution is due to Moriguti (1954), and we use here notation given by Snedecor and Cochran (1967). For $100(1-\alpha)$ per cent confidence limits we need various entries in the F table corresponding to a tabulated one-sided level of $\frac{1}{2}\alpha$. Thus, for 95 per cent confidence limits we need entries corresponding to $P=0{\cdot}025$. Denoting the entry for degrees of freedom ν_1 and ν_2 as F_{ν_1,ν_2}, and putting $f_1=k-1$, $f_2=k(n-1)$, we need

$$F_1=F_{f_1,f_2}$$
$$F_2=F_{f_1,\infty}$$
$$F_3=F_{f_2,f_1}$$
$$F_4=F_{\infty,f_1}$$
$$F=\text{observed value, } s_B^2/s_W^2.$$

Then the upper limit for σ_B^2 is

$$\hat{\sigma}_{BU}^2=\left\{FF_4-1+\frac{(F_3-F_4)}{FF_3^2}\right\}\frac{s_W^2}{n} \qquad (7.16)$$

and the lower limit is

$$\hat{\sigma}_{BL}^2=\frac{(F-F_1)(F+F_1-F_2)}{FF_2}\frac{s_W^2}{n}. \qquad (7.17)$$

Note that the lower limit is zero if $F=F_1$, i.e. if F is just significant by the usual test. If $F<F_1$, the lower limit will be negative and in some instances the upper limit also may be negative. For a discussion of this apparent anomaly, see Scheffé (1959, section 7.2). The validity of these limits will depend rather heavily on the assumption of normality, particularly for the between-group variation.

Example 7.2 (continued)

Ninety-five per cent confidence limits for σ^2 are (from section 4.5)

$$\frac{17{\cdot}5266}{46{\cdot}98} \quad \text{and} \quad \frac{17{\cdot}5266}{16{\cdot}79}$$

i.e. 0·373 and 1·043,

the divisors being the appropriate percentiles of the $\chi^2_{(30)}$ distribution.

For confidence limits for σ^2_B we need the following tabulated values of F, writing $f_1=5, f_2=30$:

$$F_1=3{\cdot}03,\ F_2=2{\cdot}57,\ F_3=6{\cdot}23,\ F_4=6{\cdot}02,$$

and the observed F is 4.39. Thus, from (7.16) and (7.17),

$$\hat{\sigma}^2_{BU}=\left\{(4{\cdot}39)(6{\cdot}02)-1+\frac{(0{\cdot}21)}{(4{\cdot}39)(6{\cdot}23)^2}\right\}(0{\cdot}0974)=2{\cdot}54$$

and

$$\hat{\sigma}^2_{BL}=\frac{(4{\cdot}39-3{\cdot}03)(4{\cdot}39+3{\cdot}03-2{\cdot}57)(0{\cdot}0974)}{(4{\cdot}39)(2{\cdot}57)}=0{\cdot}057.$$

The wide ranges of error associated with these estimates makes it clear that the percentage contributions of 36 per cent and 64 per cent are very imprecise estimates indeed.

If the numbers of observations from the groups are unequal, with n_i from the ith group, (7.15) must be modified as follows:

$$\hat{\sigma}^2_B=\frac{s^2_B-s^2_W}{n_0}, \qquad (7.18)$$

where

$$n_0=\frac{1}{(k-1)}\left\{N-\frac{(\sum n_i^2)}{N}\right\}.$$

A further difficulty is that (7.18) is not necessarily the best way of estimating σ^2_B. The choice of method depends, however, on the unknown ratio of the variance components which are being estimated, and (7.18) will usually be a sensible method if the n_i are not too different. See Robertson (1962) and Kendall and Stuart, Vol. 3 (1966, section 36.26).

7.3 MULTIPLE COMPARISONS

We return now to the fixed effects model of section 7.1. In the analysis of data in this form it will usually be important not to rely solely on the analysis of variance table and its F test, but to examine the differences between groups more closely to see what patterns emerge. It is, in fact, good practice habitually to report the mean values $\bar{y}_i$ and their standard errors, calculated as $s_W/\sqrt{n_i}$, in terms of the Within groups mean square s_W^2 unless the assumption of constant variance is clearly inappropriate.

The standard error of the difference between two means is given by (7.11), and the t distribution may be used to provide a significance test or to assign confidence limits as indicated in section 7.1. If all the n_i are equal (to n, say), it is sometimes useful to calculate the *least significant difference* (LSD) at a certain significance level. For the 5 per cent level, for instance, this is

$$t_{f_2,\,0\cdot05}\, s_W \sqrt{(2/n)},$$

where $f_2 = k(n-1)$, the degrees of freedom within groups. Differences between pairs of means which are significant at this level can then be picked out by eye.

Sometimes interest is focussed on comparisons between the group means other than simple differences. These will usually be measurable by a *linear contrast* of the form

$$L = \sum \lambda_i \bar{y}_i, \tag{7.19}$$

where $\sum \lambda_i = 0$. From (3.13)

$$\text{var}(L) = \sum \lambda_i^2 \text{var}(\bar{y}_i),$$

and the standard error of L is thus estimated as

$$\text{SE}(L) = s_W \sqrt{(\sum \lambda_i^2 / n)}, \tag{7.20}$$

and the usual t test or confidence limits may be applied.

Some examples of linear contrasts are as follows.

(a) A contrast of one group with the mean of several other groups. One group may have a special identity, perhaps as a control group, and there may be some reason for pooling a set of q other groups (e.g. if related treatments were applied to these groups). The relevant comparison will then be

$$\bar{y}_c - \left(\sum_{i=1}^{q} \bar{y}_i \right) \Big/ q,$$

which when multiplied by q becomes

$$L_1 = q\bar{y}_c - \sum_{i=1}^{q} \bar{y}_i,$$

a particular case of (7.19) with $\lambda_c = q$, $\lambda_i = -1$ for all i in the set of q groups and $\lambda_i = 0$ otherwise. Note that $\sum \lambda_i = 0$.

(b) A linear regression coefficient. Suppose a set of q groups is associated with a variable x_i (for example, the dose of some substance).

It might be of interest to ask whether the regression of y on x is significant. Using the result quoted in the derivation of (5.15)

$$L_2 = \sum(x_i - \bar{x})\bar{y}_i,$$

which again is a particular case of (7.19) with $\lambda_i = x_i - \bar{x}$, and again $\sum\lambda_i = 0$.

(c) A difference between $\bar{y}_g$ and $\bar{y}_h$ is another case of (7.19) with $\lambda_g = 1$, $\lambda_h = -1$ and all other $\lambda_i = 0$.

Corresponding to any linear contrast, L, the t statistic, on $k(n-1)$ DF, is, from (7.20)

$$t = \frac{L}{\text{SE}(L)} = \frac{L}{s_W\sqrt{(\sum\lambda_i^2/n)}}.$$

As we have seen, the square of t follows the F distribution on 1 and $k(n-1)$ DF. Thus,

$$F = t^2 = \frac{L^2}{s_W^2\sum\lambda_i^2/n} = \frac{s_1^2}{s_W^2},$$

where $s_1^2 = L^2/\sum\lambda_i^2/n$. In fact, s_1^2 can be regarded as a MSq on 1 DF, derived from a SSq also equal to s_1^2, which can be shown to be part of the SSq between groups of the analysis of variance. The analysis thus takes the following form:

	SSq	DF	MSq	VR
Between groups				
Due to L	$L^2/(\sum\lambda_i^2/n)$	1	s_1^2	$F_1 = s_1^2/s_W^2$
Other contrasts	$\sum T_i^2/n_i - T^2/n - L^2/(\sum\lambda_i^2/n)$	$k-2$	s_R^2	$F_2 = s_R^2/s_W^2$
Within groups	$S - \sum T_i/n_i$	$k(n-1)$	s_W^2	
Total	$S - T^2/n$	$nk-1$		

Separate significance tests are now provided (a) by F_1 on 1 and $k(n-1)$ DF for the contrast L; as we have seen, this is equivalent to the t test for L; and (b) by F_2 on $k-2$ and $k(n-1)$ for differences between group means other than those measured by L.

Suppose there are two or more linear contrasts of interest:

$$L_1 = \sum\lambda_{1i}\bar{y}_i,\ L_2 = \sum\lambda_{2i}\bar{y}_i, \text{ etc.}$$

Can the single degrees of freedom for these contrasts all be incorporated in the same analysis of variance? They can, provided the L's are uncorrelated when the null hypothesis is true, and the condition for this is that for any two contrasts (L_p and L_q, say) the sum of products of the coefficients is zero:

$$\sum_{i=1}^{k} \lambda_{pi}\lambda_{qi} = 0.$$

In this case L_p and L_q are said to be *orthogonal.* If there are k' such orthogonal contrasts, the analysis of variance will run as follows:

	SSq	DF
Between groups		
Due to L_1	$L_1^2/(\sum\lambda_{1i}^2/n)$	1
Due to L_2	$L_2^2/\sum(\lambda_{2i}^2/n)$	1
⋮	⋮	⋮
Due to $L_{k'}$	$L_{k'}^2/(\sum\lambda_{k'i}^2/n)$	1
Other contrasts	$T_i^2/n-T^2/n-\sum_{j=1}^{k'} L_j^2/(\sum\lambda_{ji}^2/n)$	$k-k'-1$
Within groups	$S-\sum T_i^2/n$	$k(n-1)$
	$S-T^2/n$	$nk-1$

the undesignated summations running from $i=1$ to k.

The straightforward use of the t or F tests is appropriate for any differences between means or for more general linear contrasts which arise naturally out of the structure of the investigation. However, a difficulty must be recognized. If there are k groups, there are $\frac{1}{2}k(k-1)$ pairs of means which might conceivably be compared and there is no limit to the number of linear contrasts which might be formed. These comparisons are not all independent, but it is fairly clear that, even when the null hypothesis is true, in any set of data *some* of these contrasts are likely to be significant. A sufficiently assiduous search will reveal some remarkable contrasts which have arisen purely by chance. This may not matter if scrutiny is restricted to those comparisons which the data were designed to throw light on. If, on the other hand, the data are subjected to what is sometimes called a *dredging* procedure—a search for significant contrasts which would not have been thought of initially—there is a real danger that a number of comparisons will be reported as significant, but that they will almost all have arisen by chance.

A number of procedures have been devised to reduce the chance of this happening. They are referred to as methods of making *multiple comparisons* or *simultaneous inference*, and are described in detail by Miller (1966). We mention briefly two methods, one for differences between means and the other for more general linear contrasts.

The first method, based on the distribution of the *studentized range*, is due to Newman (1939) and Keuls (1952). Given a set of p means, each based on n observations, the studentized range, Q, is the range of the $\bar{y}_i$ divided by the estimated standard error. In an obvious notation,

$$Q = \frac{\bar{y}_{max} - \bar{y}_{min}}{s/\sqrt{n}}. \tag{7.21}$$

The distribution of Q, on the null hypothesis that all the μ_i are equal, has been studied and some upper 5 per cent and 1 per cent points are given in Table A5. They depend on the number of groups, p, and the within-groups degrees of freedom, f_2, and are written $Q_{p,\,0\cdot05}$ and $Q_{p,\,0\cdot01}$. The procedure is to rank the $\bar{y}_i$ in order of magnitude and to test the studentized range for all pairs of adjacent means (when it actually reduces to the usual t test), for all adjacent triads, all groups of four adjacent means, and so on. Two means are regarded as differing significantly only if *all* tests for sets of means including these two give a significant result. The procedure is most readily performed in the opposite order to that described, starting with all k, following by the two sets of $k-1$ adjacent means, and so on. The reason for this is that if at any stage a non-significant Q is found, that set of means need not be used for any further tests. The procedure will, for example, stop after the first stage if Q for all k means is non-significant.

The following example is taken from Miller's book (section 6.1). Five means, arranged in order, are 16·1, 17·0, 20·7, 21·1 and 26·5; $n=5$ and the standard error $s/\sqrt{5}=1\cdot2$. The values of $Q_{p,\,0\cdot05}$ for $p=2$, 3, 4 and 5 are, respectively, 3·0, 3·6, 4·0 and 4·2. Tests are done successively for $p=5$, 4, 3 and 2, and the results are as follows, where non-significant groupings are indicated by underlining.

A	*B*	*C*	*D*	*E*
16·1	17·0	20·7	21·1	26·5

The interpretation is that E differs from $A-D$, and that within the latter group A differs from C and D, with B occupying an ambiguous position.

In Example 7.1, where we noted that $\bar{y}_3$ and $\bar{y}_4$ differed by more than twice the standard error of the difference, Q calculated for all four groups is

$$(371\cdot2-274\cdot8)/\sqrt{(3997/5)}=96\cdot4/28\cdot3=3\cdot4,$$

and from Table A5 $Q_{4,\,0\cdot05}$ is 4·0, so the test shows no significant difference, as might have been expected in view of the non-significant F test.

The Newman-Keuls procedure has the property that, for a set of groups with equal μ_i, the probability of asserting a significant difference between any of them is at most equal to the chosen level (0·05 in the examples above).

If linear contrasts other than differences are being 'dredged', the infinite number of possible choices suggests that a very conservative procedure should be used; that is, one which indicates significance much less readily than the *t* test. A method proposed by Scheffé (1959) is as follows. A linear contrast, *L*, is declared significant at, say, the 5 per cent level if the absolute value of $L/\text{SE}(L)$ exceeds

$$\sqrt{\{(k-1)F_{0\cdot05}\}}, \qquad (7.22)$$

where $F_{0\cdot05}$ is the tabulated 5 per cent point of the *F* distribution with $\nu_1=k-1$ and $\nu_2=k(n-1)$. When $k=2$, this rule is equivalent to the use of the *t* test. For $k>2$ it is noticeably conservative in comparison with a *t* test, in that the numerical value of (7.22) may considerably exceed the 5 per cent level of *t* on $k(n-1)$ degrees of freedom. Scheffé's method has the property that, if the null hypothesis that all μ_i are equal is true, only in 5 per cent of cases will it be possible to find any linear contrast which is significant by this test. Any contrast significant by this test, even if discovered by an exhaustive process of data dredging, may therefore be regarded with a reasonable degree of confidence. In Example 7.1 the contrast between the means for experiments III and IV gives $L/\text{SE}(L)=(371\cdot2-274\cdot8)/40\cdot0=2\cdot41$; by Scheffé's test the 5 per cent value would be $\sqrt{\{3(3\cdot24)\}}=3.12$, and the observed contrast should not be regarded as significant.

It should again be emphasized that the Newman-Keuls and Scheffé procedures, and other multiple comparison methods, are deliberately conservative in order to reduce the probability of too many significant differences arising by chance in any one study. They are appropriate only when means are being compared in an exploratory way to see what might 'turn up'. When comparisons are made which flow naturally from the plan of the experiment or survey the usual *t* test is appropriate.

7.4 COMPARISON OF SEVERAL PROPORTIONS: THE 2 × k CONTINGENCY TABLE

In sections 4.7 and 4.8 the comparison of two proportions was considered from two points of view—the sampling error of the difference between the proportions and the χ^2 significance test applied to the 2×2 table. We saw that these two approaches led to equivalent significance tests of the null hypothesis.

Where more than two proportions are to be compared the calculation of standard errors between pairs of proportions raises points similar to those discussed in the last section: many comparisons are possible and an undue number of significant differences may arise by chance. However, an overall significance test, analogous to the F test in the analysis of variance, is provided by a straightforward extension of the χ^2 test.

Suppose there are k groups of observations and that in the ith group n_i individuals have been observed, of whom r_i show a certain characteristic (say, being 'positive'). The proportion of positives, r_i/n_i, is denoted by p_i. The data may be displayed as follows:

Group	1	2	...	i	...	k	All groups combined
Positive	r_1	r_2	...	r_i	...	r_k	R
Negative	n_1-r_1	n_2-r_2	...	n_i-r_i	...	n_k-r_k	$N-R$
Total	n_1	n_2	...	n_i	...	n_k	N
Proportion positive	p_1	p_2	...	p_i	...	p_k	$P=R/N$

The frequencies form a $2 \times k$ contingency table (there being 2 rows and k columns, excluding the marginal totals). The χ^2 test follows the same lines as for the 2×2 table (section 4.8). For each of the observed frequencies, O, an expected frequency is calculated by the formula

$$E=\frac{\text{Row total} \times \text{Column total}}{N}, \tag{7.23}$$

the quantity $(O-E)^2/E$ is calculated, and, finally

$$X^2=\sum\frac{(O-E)^2}{E} \tag{7.24}$$

the summation being over the $2k$ cells in the table.

On the null hypothesis that all k samples are drawn randomly from populations with the same proportion of positives, X^2 is distributed approximately as $\chi^2_{(k-1)}$, the approximation improving as the expected frequencies increase in size. An indication of the extent to which the $\chi^2_{(k-1)}$ distribution is valid for small frequencies is given in the next section. No continuity correction is required, because unless the observed frequencies are very small the number of tables which may be formed with the same marginal totals as those observed is very large, and the distribution of X^2 is consequently more nearly continuous than is the case for 2×2 tables.

An alternative formula for X^2 is of some value. The value of $O-E$ for an entry in the first row of the table (the positives for group i, for instance) is

$$r_i - Pn_i,$$

and this is easily seen to differ only in sign from the entry for the negatives for group i:

$$(n_i - r_i) - (1-P)n_i = -(r_i - Pn_i).$$

The contribution to X^2 from these two cells is, therefore,

$$(r_i - Pn_i)^2\left(\frac{1}{Pn_i} + \frac{1}{Qn_i}\right)$$

where $Q = 1 - P$. The expression in the second bracket simplifies to give the following expression for X^2:

$$X^2 = \frac{\sum n_i (p_i - P)^2}{PQ}, \tag{7.25}$$

the summation now being over the k groups. A little manipulation with the summation in (7.25) gives two equivalent expressions

$$X^2 = \frac{\sum n_i p_i^2 - NP^2}{PQ}$$

and

$$X^2 = \frac{\sum (r_i^2/n_i) - R^2/N}{PQ}. \tag{7.26}$$

The last two expressions are more convenient as computing formulae than (7.25).

The expression (7·25) provides an indication of the reason why X^2 follows the $\chi^2_{(k-1)}$ distribution. In the explanation of the $\chi^2_{(n)}$ distribution given in section 3.4, suppose the x_i's had different variances, σ_i^2. Then

$$X_n^2 = \sum_{i=1}^{n} \frac{(x-\mu_i)^2}{\sigma_i^2}$$

would be the sum of squares of n standardized normal deviates and would therefore follow the $\chi^2_{(n)}$ distribution. It can be shown that, if $\bar{x}$ is a *weighted* mean of the x_i, the weights being inversely proportional to the variances, i.e.

$$\bar{x} = \frac{\sum (x_i/\sigma_i^2)}{\sum (1/\sigma_i^2)}, \tag{7.27}$$

then

$$X^2 = \sum_{i=1}^{n} \frac{(x_i - \bar{x})^2}{\sigma_i^2} \tag{7.28}$$

follows the $\chi^2_{(n-1)}$ distribution.

Applying this result to the $2 \times k$ contingency table, we could estimate the variance of p_i on the null hypothesis by PQ/n_i. Replacing x_i by p_i and σ_i^2 by PQ/n_i in (7.27), we find $\bar{x}$ becomes

$$\frac{\Sigma(n_i p_i/PQ)}{\Sigma(n_i/PQ)} = \frac{\Sigma n_i p_i}{\Sigma n_i} = \frac{R}{N} = P$$

and (7.28) becomes

$$X^2 = \sum_{i=1}^{k} \frac{(p_i - P)^2}{(PQ/n_i)} = \frac{\Sigma n_i (p_i - P)^2}{PQ}$$

in agreement with (7.25). We have departed from (7.28) in two respects: the variation in p_i is binomial, not normal, and the true variance σ_i^2 has been replaced by the estimated variance PQ/n_i. Both these approximations decrease in importance as the expected frequencies increase in size.

Example 7.3

Table 7.2 shows the numbers of individuals in various age groups who were found in a survey to be positive and negative for *Schistosoma mansoni* eggs in the stool.

TABLE 7.2 Presence or absence of *S. mansoni* eggs in the stool.

Age (yrs)	0–	10–	20–	30–	40–	Total
Positive	14	16	14	7	6	57
Negative	87	33	66	34	11	231
	101	49	80	41	17	288

The expected number of positives for the age group 0– is

$$(57)(101)/288 = 19{\cdot}99.$$

The set of expected numbers for the ten cells in the table is

						Total
	19·99	9·70	15·83	8·11	3·36	57
	81·01	39·30	64·17	32·89	13·64	231
Total	101	49	80	41	17	288

The fact that the expected numbers add to the same marginal totals as those observed is a useful check.

The contribution to X^2 from the first cell is

$$(14-19{\cdot}99)^2/19{\cdot}99=1{\cdot}79,$$

and the set of contributions for the ten cells is

1·79	4·09	0·21	0·15	2·07
0·44	1·01	0·05	0·04	0·51

giving a total of

$$X^2=10{\cdot}36.$$

The degrees of freedom are $k-1=4$, for which the 5 per cent point is 9·49. The departures from the null hypothesis are thus significant at the 5 per cent level.

In this example the column classification is based on a continuous variable, age, and it would be natural to ask whether the proportions of positives exhibit any smooth trend with age. The estimated proportions, with their standard errors calculated as $\sqrt{(p_i q_i/n_i)}$, are

0·14	0·33	0·18	0·17	0·35,
±0·03	±0·07	±0·04	±0·06	±0·12

the last being based on particularly small numbers. No clear trend emerges. About half the contribution to X^2 comes from the second age group (10–19 years) and there is some suggestion that the proportion of positives in this group is higher than in the neighbouring age groups.

To illustrate the use of (7.26), call the numbers of positives r_i. Then (7.26) gives

$$X^2=(14^2/101+\ldots+6^2/17-57^2/288)/(0{\cdot}1979)(0{\cdot}8021),$$

where $P=57/288=0{\cdot}1979$. This gives

$$X^2=10{\cdot}37$$

as before, the discrepancy being due to rounding errors. Note that if the *negatives* rather than the positives had been denoted by r_i, each of the terms in the numerator of (7.26) would have been different, but the result would have been the same.

7.5 GENERAL CONTINGENCY TABLES

The form of table considered in the last section can be generalized by allowing more than two rows. Suppose that a total frequency, N, is subdivided by r row categories and c column categories. The null hypothesis, corresponding to that tested in the simpler situations, is that the probabilities of falling into the various columns are independent of the rows; or, equivalently, that the probabilities for the various rows are the same for each column.

The χ^2 test follows closely that applied in the simpler cases. For each cell in the body of the table an expected frequency, E, is calculated by (7.23) and the X^2 index obtained from (7·23) by summation over the rc cells. Various alternative formulae are available, but none is as simple as (7·25) or (7·26) and it is probably most convenient to remember the basic formula (7·24). On the null hypothesis, X^2 follows the $\chi^2_{(f)}$ distribution with $f=(r-1)(c-1)$. This number of degrees of freedom may be thought of as the number of arbitrary choices of the frequencies in the body of the table, with the constraint that they should add to the same margins as those observed and thus give the same values of E. (If the entries in $r-1$ rows and $c-1$ columns are arbitrarily specified, those in the first row and column are determined by the marginal totals.)

Again, the χ^2 distribution is an approximation, increasingly valid for large expected frequencies. A rough rule (Cochran, 1954) is that the approximation is safe provided that relatively few expected frequencies are less than 5 (say in 1 cell out of 5 or more, or 2 cells out of 10 or more), and that no expected frequency is less than 1. In tables with smaller expected frequencies the result of the significance test should be regarded with caution. If the result is not obviously either significant or non-significant, it may be wise to pool some of the rows and/or columns in which the small expected frequencies occur and recalculate X^2 (with, of course, a reduced number of degrees of freedom). See also the suggestions made by Cochran (1954, p. 420).

Example 7.4

Table 7.3 shows results obtained in a trial to compare the effects of PAS and streptomycin in the treatment of pulmonary tuberculosis. In each cell of the table are shown the observed frequencies, O, the expected frequencies, E, and the discrepancies, $O–E$. For example, for the first cell, $E=(99)(139)/273 =50·41$. Note that the values of $O–E$ add to zero along each row and down each column, a useful check on the arithmetic.

$$X^2=(5·59)^2/50·41+\ldots+(12·58)^2/22·42$$
$$=17·64.$$

The degrees of freedom for the χ^2 distribution are $(3-1)(3-1)=4$, and from Table A2 the 1 per cent point is 13·28. The relationship between treatment and

TABLE 7.3 Degrees of positivity of sputa from patients with pulmonary tuberculosis treated with PAS, streptomycin or a combination of both drugs (Medical Research Council, 1950).

Treatment	Sputum	Positive smear	Negative smear, positive culture	Negative smear, negative culture	Total
PAS	*O*	56	30	13	99
	E	*50·41*	*23·93*	*24·66*	
	O−E	5·59	6·07	−11·66	
Streptomycin		46	18	20	84
		42·77	*20·31*	*20·92*	
		3·23	−2·31	−0·92	
Streptomycin and PAS		37	18	35	90
		45·82	*21·76*	*22·42*	
		−8·82	−3·76	12·58	
Total		139	66	68	273

type of sputum is thus significant at the 1 per cent level. The magnitudes and signs of the discrepancies, *O–E*, show clearly that the main difference is between PAS (tending to give more positive results) and the combined treatment (more negative results).

7.6 COMPARISON OF SEVERAL VARIANCES

The one-way analysis of variance (section 7.1) is a generalization of the two-sample t test (section 4.6). Occasionally one requires a generalization of the F test (used, as in section 4.10, for the comparison of two variances) to the situation where more than two estimates of variance are to be compared. In a one-way analysis of variance, for example, the primary purpose is to compare means, but one might wish to test the significance of differences between variances, both for the intrinsic interest of this comparison and also because the analysis of variance involves an assumption that the group variances are equal.

Suppose there are k estimates of variance, s_i^2, having possibly different degrees of freedom, ν_i. (If the ith group contains n_i observations, $\nu_i = n_i - 1$). On the assumption that the observations are randomly selected from normal distributions, an approximate significance test due to Bartlett (1937) consists in calculating

$$\bar{s}^2 = \sum \nu_i s_i^2 / \sum \nu_i$$

$$M = 2{\cdot}3026\{(\sum \nu_i) \log \bar{s}^2 - \sum \nu_i \log s_i^2\}$$

and

$$C = 1 + \frac{1}{3(k-1)}\left\{\sum\left(\frac{1}{\nu_i}\right) - \frac{1}{\sum \nu_i}\right\}$$

and referring M/C to the $\chi^2_{(k-1)}$ distribution. C is likely to be near 1 and need be calculated only in marginal cases. Worked examples are given by Snedecor and Cochran (1967, section 10.21).

Bartlett's test is perhaps less useful than might be thought, for two reasons. First, like the F test it is rather sensitive to non-normality. Secondly, with samples of moderate size the true variances σ_i^2 have to differ very considerably before there is a reasonable chance of obtaining a significant test result. To put this point another way, even if M/C is non-significant, the estimated s_i^2 may differ substantially, and so may the true σ_i^2. If possible inequality in the σ_i^2 is important it may therefore be wise to assume it even if the test result is non-significant. In some situations moderate inequality in the σ_i^2 will not matter very much, so again the significance test is not very relevant.

7.7 COMPARISON OF SEVERAL COUNTS: THE POISSON HETEROGENEITY TEST

Suppose that k counts, denoted by $x_1, x_2, \ldots x_i, \ldots, x_k$, are available. It may be interesting to test whether they could reasonably have been drawn at random from Poisson distributions with the same (unknown) mean μ. In many microbiological experiments, as we saw in section 2.6, successive counts may be expected to follow a Poisson distribution if the experimental technique is perfect. With imperfect technical methods the counts will follow Poisson distributions with *different* means. In bacteriological counting, for example, the suspension may be inadequately mixed, so that clustering of the organisms occurs; the volumes of the suspension inoculated for the different counts may not be equal; the culture media may not invariably be able to sustain growth. In each of these circumstances heterogeneity of the expected counts is present and is likely to manifest itself by excessive variability of the observed counts. It seems reasonable, therefore, to base a test on the sum of squares about the mean of the x_i's. An appropriate test statistic is given by

$$X^2 = \frac{\sum(x-\bar{x})^2}{\bar{x}}, \tag{7.29}$$

which, on the null hypothesis of constant μ, is approximately distributed as $\chi^2_{(k-1)}$. The method is variously called the Poisson *heterogeneity* or *dispersion* test.

The formula (7.29) may be justified from two different points of view. First, it is closely related to the test statistic (4.7) used for testing the variance of a normal distribution. On the present null hypothesis the distribution is Poisson, which we know is similar to a normal distribution if μ is not too small; furthermore, $\sigma^2 = \mu$, which can best be estimated from the data by the sample mean $\bar{x}$. Replacing σ^2 by $\bar{x}$ in (4.7) gives (7.29). Secondly, we could argue that, given the total count $\sum x$, the frequency 'expected' at the ith count on the null hypothesis is $\sum x/k = \bar{x}$. Applying the usual formula for a χ^2 index, $\sum\{(O-E)^2/E\}$, immediately gives (7.29). In fact, just as the Poisson distribution can be regarded as a limiting form of the binomial for large n and small p, so the present test can be regarded as a limiting form of the χ^2 test for the $2 \times k$ table (section 7.4) when R/N is very small and all the n_i are equal; under these circumstances it is not difficult to see that (7.25) becomes equivalent to (7.29).

Example 7.5

The following data were given by 'Student' (1907), who first proposed the heterogeneity test.

Twenty counts of yeast cells in squares of a haemocytometer were as follows:

2	4	4	8
3	3	5	6
7	7	2	7
4	8	5	4
4	1	5	7

Here

$$k = 20$$
$$\sum x = 96$$
$$\bar{x} = 4{\cdot}8$$
$$\sum x^2 = 542$$
$$(\sum x)^2/k = 460{\cdot}8$$
$$\sum(x-\bar{x})^2 = 81{\cdot}2$$
$$X^2 = 81{\cdot}2/4{\cdot}8 = 16{\cdot}92 \text{ on 19 DF } (0{\cdot}5 < P < 0{\cdot}75).$$

There is no suggestion of variability in excess of that expected from the Poisson distribution.

In referring X^2 to the $\chi^2_{(k-1)}$ distribution we should normally do a one-sided test since heterogeneity tends to give *high* values of X^2. Occasionally, though, departures from the Poisson distribution will lead to reduced variability. In microbiological counting this might be caused by omission of counts differing widely from the average; Lancaster (1950) has shown that unskilled technicians counting blood cells (which under ideal circumstances provide another example of the Poisson theory) tend to omit extreme values or take repeat observations, presumably because they underestimate the extent of random variation. Other causes of reduced variability are an inability to record accurately high counts (for instance, because of overlapping of bacterial colonies), or physical interference between particles which prevents large numbers from settling close together. The latter phenomenon has been noted by Lancaster (1950) in red blood cell counting.

The use of the $\chi^2_{(k-1)}$ distribution in the heterogeneity test is an approximation, but is quite safe provided $\bar{x}$ is greater than about 5, and is safe even for much smaller values of $\bar{x}$ (as low as 2, say) provided k is not too small (>15, say). For very small values of $\bar{x}$ Fisher (1950, 1964) has shown how to obtain an exact test; the method is illustrated in Oldham (1968, section 5.15).

Finally, note that for $k=2$, (7.29) is equivalent to $(x_1-x_2)^2/(x_1+x_2)$, which was used as a $\chi^2_{(1)}$ variate in section 4.9.

CHAPTER 8
FURTHER ANALYSIS OF VARIANCE

8.1 TWO-WAY ANALYSIS OF VARIANCE: RANDOMIZED BLOCKS

In this chapter we consider various extensions of the analysis of variance. We shall be concerned throughout with studies in which changes in the mean value of some variable are of primary interest, but in which the data have a more complicated structure than the one-way classification into groups considered in sections 7.1 to 7.3.

The simplest extension is to data classified in two ways: by one set of categories which may be represented, say, as the rows of a table, and by another set forming the columns. This structure arises naturally in the 'randomized block' experimental design, where one classification defines the different treatments and the other consists of the blocks of experimental material. If there are r blocks and c treatments, each block containing c experimental units to which treatments are randomly allocated, there will be a total of $N=rc$ observations on any variable, simultaneously divided into r blocks with c observations in each and c treatment groups with r observations in each.

In other experimental situations both the rows and columns of the two-way table may represent forms of treatment. In a blood-clotting experiment, for instance, clotting times may be measured for each combination of r periods of storage of plasma and c concentrations of adrenalin mixed with the plasma. This is a simple example of a *factorial experiment*, to be discussed more generally in section 8.2. The distinction between this situation and the randomized block experiment is that in the latter the 'block' classification is introduced mainly to provide extra precision for treatment comparisons; differences between blocks are usually of no intrinsic interest.

Two-way classifications may arise also in non-experimental work, either by classifying in this way data already collected in a survey, or by arranging the data collection to fit a two-way classification.

We consider first the situation in which there is just one observation at each combination of a row and a column; for the ith row and jth column the observation is y_{ij}. To represent the possible effect of the row and column classifications on the mean value of y_{ij}, let us consider an 'additive model' by which

$$\mathrm{E}(y_{ij}) = \mu + \alpha_i + \beta_j, \tag{8.1}$$

where α_i and β_j are constants characterizing the rows and columns. By suitable choice of μ we can arrange that

$$\sum_{i=1}^{r} \alpha_i = 0 \quad \text{and} \quad \sum_{j=1}^{c} \beta_j = 0.$$

According to (8.1), the effect of being in one row rather than another is to change the mean value by adding or subtracting a constant quantity, irrespective of which column the observation is made in. Changing from one column to another has a similar additive or subtractive effect. Any observed value y_{ij} will in general vary randomly round its expectation given by (8.1). We suppose that

$$y_{ij} = \mathrm{E}(y_{ij}) + \epsilon_{ij}, \tag{8.2}$$

where the ϵ_{ij} are independently and normally distributed with a constant variance σ^2. These assumptions are, of course, not necessarily true, and we shall consider later ways of testing their truth and of overcoming difficulties due to departures from the model.

TABLE 8.1 Notation for two-way analysis of variance data.

		Column						
		1	2	... j	... c	Total	Mean (R_i/c)
	1	y_{11}	y_{12}	... y_{1j}	... y_{1c}	R_1	$\bar{y}_{1.}$
	2	y_{21}	y_{22}	... y_{2j}	... y_{2c}	R_2	$\bar{y}_{2.}$
	.	.	.	.	.	.	.
	.	.	.	.	.	.	.
	.	.	.	.	.	.	.
Row	i	y_{i1}	y_{i2}	... y_{ij}	... y_{ic}	R_i	$\bar{y}_{i.}$
	.	.	.	.	.	.	.
	.	.	.	.	.	.	.
	.	.	.	.	.	.	.
	r	y_{r1}	y_{r2}	... y_{rj}	... y_{rc}	R_r	$\bar{y}_{r.}$
Total		C_1	C_2	... C_j	... C_c	T	
Mean (C_j/r)		$\bar{y}_{.1}$	$\bar{y}_{.2}$	... $\bar{y}_{.j}$	... $\bar{y}_{.c}$		($\bar{y} = T/N$)

Denote the total and mean for the ith row by R_i and $\bar{y}_{i.}$, those for the jth column by C_j and $\bar{y}_{.j}$, and those for the whole group of $N = rc$ observations by T and $\bar{y}$ (see Table 8.1). As in the one-way analysis of variance, the total SSq, $\sum(y_{ij} - \bar{y})^2$, will be sub-divided into various parts. For any one of these deviations from the mean, $y_{ij} - \bar{y}$, the following is true:

$$y_{ij} - \bar{y} = (\bar{y}_{i.} - \bar{y}) + (\bar{y}_{.j} - \bar{y}) + (y_{ij} - \bar{y}_{i.} - \bar{y}_{.j} + \bar{y}). \qquad (8.3)$$

The three terms on the right-hand side reflect the fact that y_{ij} differs from $\bar{y}$ partly on account of a difference characteristic of the ith row, partly because of a difference characteristic of the jth column and partly by an amount which is not explicable by either row or column differences. If (8.3) is squared and summed over all N observations, we find (the suffixes i, j being implied below each summation sign):

$$\sum(y_{ij} - \bar{y})^2 = \sum(\bar{y}_{i.} - \bar{y})^2 + \sum(\bar{y}_{.j} - \bar{y})^2 + \sum(y_{ij} - \bar{y}_{i.} - \bar{y}_{.j} + \bar{y})^2. \qquad (8.4)$$

To show (8.4) we have to show that all the product terms which arise from squaring the right-hand side of (8.3) are zero. For example, $\sum(\bar{y}_{i.} - \bar{y})(y_{ij} - \bar{y}_{i.} - \bar{y}_{.j} + \bar{y}) = 0$. These results can be proved by fairly simple algebra.

The three terms on the right-hand side of (8.4) are called the Between rows SSq, the Between columns SSq and the Residual SSq. The first two are of exactly the same form as the Between groups SSq in the one-way analysis, and the usual short-cut method of calculation may be used:

$$\text{Between rows:} \qquad \sum(\bar{y}_{i.} - \bar{y})^2 = \sum_{i=1}^{r} R_i^2/c - T^2/N$$

$$\text{Between columns:} \quad \sum(\bar{y}_{.j} - \bar{y})^2 = \sum_{j=1}^{c} C_j^2/r - T^2/N.$$

The Total SSq is similarly calculated as:

$$\text{Total} = \sum(y_{ij} - \bar{y})^2 = \sum y_{ij}^2 - T^2/N,$$

and the Residual SSq may be obtained by subtraction:

$$\text{Residual SSq} = \text{Total SSq} - \text{Between rows SSq} - \text{Between columns SSq}. \qquad (8.5)$$

The analysis so far is purely a consequence of algebraic identities. The relationships given above are true irrespective of the validity of the model. We now complete the analysis of variance by some steps which depend for their validity on that of the model. First, the degrees of freedom are allotted as shown in Table 8.2. Those for rows and columns follow from the one-way analysis; if the only classification had been into rows, for example, the first line of Table 8.2 would have been shown as Between groups and the SSq shown in Table 8.2 as Between

TABLE 8.2 Two-way analysis of variance table.

	SSq	DF	MSq	VR
Between rows	$\sum_i R_i^2/c - T^2/N$	$r-1$	s_R^2	$F_R = s_R^2/s^2$
Between columns	$\sum_j C_j^2/r - T^2/N$	$c-1$	s_C^2	$F_C = s_C^2/s^2$
Residual	by subtraction	$(r-1)(c-1)$	s^2	
Total	$\sum_{i,j} y_{ij}^2 - T^2/N$	$rc-1$ $(=N-1)$		

columns and Residual would have added to form the Within groups SSq. With $r-1$ and $c-1$ as degrees of freedom for rows and columns, respectively, and $N-1$ for the Total SSq, the DF for Residual SSq follow by subtraction:

$$(rc-1)-(r-1)-(c-1)=rc-r-c+1=(r-1)(c-1).$$

The mean squares for rows, columns and residual are obtained in each case by the formula MSq=SSq/DF, and those for rows and columns may each be tested against the Residual MSq, s^2, as shown in Table 8.2. The test for rows, for instance, has the following justification. On the null hypothesis (which we shall call H_R) that all the row constants α_i in (8.1) are equal (and therefore equal to zero, since $\sum\alpha_i=0$), both s_R^2 and s^2 are unbiased estimates of σ^2. If H_R is not true, so that the α_i differ, s_R^2 has expectation greater than σ^2, whereas s^2 is still an unbiased estimate of σ^2. Hence F_R tends to be greater than 1, and sufficiently high values indicate a significant departure from H_R. This test is valid whatever values the β_j take, since adding a constant on to all the readings in a particular column has no effect on either s_R^2 or s_2.

Similarly, F_C provides a test for the null hypothesis, H_C, that all the $\beta_j=0$, irrespective of the values of the α_i.

If the additive model (8.1) is not true the Residual SSq will be inflated by discrepancies between $E(y_{ij})$ and the approximations given by the best fitting additive model, and the Residual MSq will thus be an unbiased estimate of a quantity greater than the random variance. How do we know whether this has happened? There are two main approaches, the first of which is to examine *residuals*. These are the individual expressions $y_{ij}-\bar{y}_{i.}-\bar{y}_{.j}+\bar{y}$. Their sum of squares was obtained, from (8.4), by subtraction, but it could have been obtained by direct evaluation of all the N residuals and by summing their squares. These residuals add to zero along each row and down each column, like the discrepancies between observed and expected frequencies in a contingency table (section 7.5), and (as for contingency tables) the number of DF, $(r-1)(c-1)$, is the number of values of residuals which may be independently chosen (the others being then automatically determined). Because of this lack of independence the residuals are not quite the same as the random error terms ϵ_{ij} of (8.2), but they have much the same distributional properties. In particular, they should not exhibit any striking patterns. Sometimes the residuals in certain parts of the two-way table seem to have predominantly the same sign: provided the ordering of the rows or columns has any meaning this will suggest that the row-effect constants are not the same for all columns. There may be a correlation between the size of the residual and the 'expected' value* $\bar{y}_{i.}+\bar{y}_{.j}-\bar{y}$: this will suggest that a change of scale would provide better agreement with the additive model.

A second approach is to provide replication of observations, and this is discussed in more detail after Example 8.1.

Example 8.1

Table 8.3 shows the results of a randomized block experiment to compare the effects on the clotting time of plasma of four different methods of treatment of the plasma. Samples of plasma from eight subjects (the 'blocks') were assigned in random order to the four treatments.

The correction term, T^2/N, denoted here by C.T., is needed for three items in the SSq column, and it is useful to calculate this at the outset. The analysis is straightforward, and the F tests show that differences between subjects and treatments are both highly significant. Differences between subjects do not interest us greatly as the main purpose of the experiment was to study differences between treatments. The standard error of the difference between two treatment means is $\sqrt{\{2(0{\cdot}6559)/8\}}=0{\cdot}405$. Clearly, treatments 1, 2 and 3 do not differ significantly among themselves, but treatment 4 gives a significantly higher mean clotting time than the others.

* This is the value expected on the basis of the average row and column effects, as may be seen from the equivalent expression $\bar{y}+(\bar{y}_{i.}-\bar{y})+(\bar{y}_{.j}-\bar{y})$.

TABLE 8·3 Clotting times (mins) of plasma from eight subjects, treated by four methods.

Subject	Treatment 1	2	3	4	Total	Mean
1	8·4	9·4	9·8	12·2	39·8	9·95
2	12·8	15·2	12·9	14·4	55·3	13·82
3	9·6	9·1	11·2	9·8	39·7	9·92
4	9·8	8·8	9·9	12·0	40·5	10·12
5	8·4	8·2	8·5	8·5	33·6	8·40
6	8·6	9·9	9·8	10·9	39·2	9·80
7	8·9	9·0	9·2	10·4	37·5	9·38
8	7·9	8·1	8·2	10·0	34·2	8·55
Total	74·4	77·7	79·5	88·2	319·8	
Mean	9·30	9·71	9·94	11·02		(9·99)

Correction term, C.T. $=(319\cdot 8)^2/32$ $=3{,}196\cdot 0013$

Between subjects SSq $=\{(39\cdot 8)^2+\ \dots\ +(34\cdot 2)^2\}/4-$ C.T. $=$ 78·9888

Between treatments SSq $=\{(74\cdot 4)^2+\ \dots\ +(88\cdot 2)^2\}/8-$ C.T. $=$ 13·0163

Total SSq $=(8\cdot 4)^2+\ \dots\ +(10\cdot 0)^2-$ C.T. $=$ 105·7788

Residual SSq $=105\cdot 7788-78\cdot 9888-13\cdot 0163$ $=$ 13·7737

Analysis of variance

	SSq	DF	MSq	VR	
Subjects	78·9888	7	11·2841	17·20	($P<0\cdot 005$)
Treatments	13·0163	3	4·3388	6·62	($P<0\cdot 005$)
Residual	13·7737	21	0·6559	1·00	
	105·7788	31			

For purposes of illustration the residuals are shown below:

Subject	Treatment 1	2	3	4	Total
1	−0·86	−0·27	−0·10	1·22	−0·01
2	−0·33	1·66	−0·87	−0·45	0·01
3	0·37	−0·54	1·33	−1·15	0·01
4	0·37	−1·04	−0·17	0·85	0·01
5	0·69	0·08	0·15	−0·93	−0·01
6	−0·51	0·38	0·05	0·07	−0·01
7	0·21	−0·10	−0·13	−0·01	−0·03
8	0·04	−0·17	−0·30	0·42	−0·01
Total	−0·02	0·00	−0·04	0·02	−0·04

The first entry, for example, is calculated from Table 8.3 as

$$8{\cdot}4-9{\cdot}95-9{\cdot}30+9{\cdot}99=-0{\cdot}86.$$

The sum of squares of the 32 residuals in the body of the table is 13·7744, in agreement with the value found by subtraction in Table 8.3 apart from rounding errors. (These errors account also for the fact that the residuals as shown do not add exactly to zero along the rows and columns.) No particular pattern emerges from the table of residuals, nor does the distribution appear to be grossly non-normal. There are 16 negative values and 16 positive values; the highest three in absolute value are positive (1·66, 1·33 and 1·22), which suggests mildly that the random error distribution may have slight positive skewness.

If the linear model (8.1) is wrong there is said to be an *interaction* between the row and column effects. In the absence of an interaction the expected differences between observations in different columns are the same for all rows (and the statement is true if we interchange the words 'columns' and 'rows'). If there is an interaction, the expected column differences vary from row to row (and, similarly, expected row differences vary from column to column). With one observation in each row/column cell the effect of an interaction is inextricably mixed with the residual variation. Suppose, however, that we have more than one observation per cell. The variation between observations *within the same cell* provides direct evidence about the random variance σ^2, and may therefore be used as a basis of comparison for the between-cell residual. This is illustrated in the next example.

Example 8.2

In Table 8.4 we show some hypothetical data related to the data of Table 8.3. There are 3 subjects and 3 treatments, and for each subject/treatment combination 3 replicate observations are made. The mean of each group of 3 replicates will be seen to agree with the value shown in Table 8.3 for the same subject and treatment. Under each group of replicates is shown the total T_{ij}, and the sum of squares, S_{ij} (as indicated for T_{11} and S_{11}).

The Subjects and Treatments SSq are obtained straightforwardly, using the divisor 9 for the sums of squares of row (or column) totals since there are 9 observations in each row (or column), and using a divisor 27 in the correction term. The Interaction SSq is obtained in a similar way to the Residual in Table 8.3, but using the totals T_{ij} as the basis of calculation. Thus

Interaction SSq =
SSq for differences between the 9 subject/treatment cells − Subjects SSq − Treatments SSq,

TABLE 8.4 Clotting time (mins) of plasma from three subjects, three methods of treatment and three replications for each subject-treatment combination

Subject		Treatment 2		Treatment 3		Treatment 4	Total	
6		9·8		9·9		11·3		
		10·1		9·5		10·7		
		9·8		10·0		10·7		
	T_{11}	29·7		29·4		32·7	R_1	91·8
	S_{11}	294·09		288·26		356·67		
7		9·2		9·1		10·3		
		8·6		9·1		10·7		
		9·2		9·4		10·2		
		27·0		27·6		31·2	R_2	85·8
		243·24		253·98		324·62		
8		8·4		8·6		9·8		
		7·9		8·0		10·1		
		8·0		8·0		10·1		
		24·3		24·6		30·0	R_3	78·9
		196·97		201·96		300·06		
Total	C_1	81·0	C_2	81·6	C_3	93·9	T 256·5	$\sum y^2$ 2,459·85

C.T. $= T^2/27$ = 2,436·75

Subjects SSq = {(91·8)^2 + ... + (78·9)^2}/9 − C.T. = 9·2600

Treatments SSq = {(81·0)^2 + ... + (93·9)^2}/9 − C.T. = 11·7800

Interaction SSq = {(29·7)^2 + ... + (30·0)^2}/3 − C.T. − Subj. SSq − Treat. SSq = 0·7400

Total SSq = (9·8)^2 + ... + (10·1)^2 − C.T. = 2,459·85 − C.T. = 23·1000

Residual SSq = Total − Subjects − Treatments − Interaction = 1·3200

Analysis of variance

	SSq	DF	MSq	VR	
Subjects	9·2600	2	4·6300	63·1	
Treatments	11·7800	2	5·8900	80·3	
Interaction	0·7400	4	0·1850	2·52	($P > 0·05$)
Residual	1·3200	18	0·0733	1·00	
	23·1000	26			

and the degrees of freedom are, correspondingly, $8-2-2=4$. The Total SSq is obtained in the usual way and the Residual SSq follows by subtraction. The Residual SSq could have been obtained directly as the sum over the 9 cells of the sum of squares about the mean of each triplet, i.e. as

$$(S_{11}-T_{11}^2/3)+(S_{12}-T_{12}^2/3)+\ldots+(S_{33}-T_{33}^2/3).$$

The F tests show the effects of subjects and treatments to be highly significant. The interaction term is not significant at the 5 per cent level, but the variance ratio is nevertheless rather high. It is due mainly to the mean value for subject 8 and treatment 4 being higher than expected.

The interpretation of significant interactions and the interpretation of the tests for the 'main effects' (subjects and treatments in Examples 8.1 and 8.2) when interactions are present will be discussed in the next section.

In Example 8.2 the number of replications at each row/column combination was constant. This is not a necessary requirement. The number of observations at the ith row and jth column, n_{ij}, may vary, but the method of analysis indicated in Example 8.2 is valid only if the n_{ij} are proportional to the total row and column frequencies; that is, denoting the latter by $n_{i.}$ and $n_{.j}$,

$$n_{ij}=\frac{n_{i.}n_{.j}}{N}. \tag{8.6}$$

In Example 8.2 all the $n_{i.}$ and $n_{.j}$ were equal to 9, N was 27, and $n_{ij}=81/27=3$, for all i and j. If (8.6) is not true an attempt to follow the standard method of analysis may lead to negative sums of squares for the interaction or residual, which is, of course, an impossible situation. Appropriate methods of analysis are described in section 8.7.

If, in a two-way classification without replication, $c=2$, the situation is the same as that for which the paired t test was used in section 4.6. There is a close analogy here with the relationship between the one-way analysis of variance and the two-sample t test noted in section 7.1. In the two-way case the F test provided by the analysis of variance is equivalent to the paired t test in that (a) F is numerically equal to t^2; (b) the F statistic has 1 and $r-1$ DF while t has $r-1$ DF, and as noted in section 4.10 the distributions of t^2 and F are identical. The Residual MSq in the analysis of variance is *half* the corresponding s^2 in the t test, since the latter is an estimate of the variance of the difference between two readings.

8.2 FACTORIAL DESIGNS

In section 8.1 an example was described of a design for a factorial experiment in which the variable to be analysed was blood clotting time and the effects of two factors were to be measured: r periods of storage and c concentrations of adrenalin. Observations were made at each combination of storage periods and adrenalin concentrations. There are two factors here, one at r *levels* and the other at c levels, and the design is called an $r \times c$ *factorial.*

This design contravenes what is sometimes regarded as a good principle of experimentation, namely that only one factor should be changed at a time. The advantages of factorial experimentation over the one-factor-at-a-time approach were pointed out by Fisher. If we make one observation at each of the rc combinations we can make comparisons of the mean effects of different periods of storage on the basis of c observations at each period. To get the same precision with a non-factorial design we should have to choose one particular concentration of adrenalin and make c observations for each storage period: rc in all. This would give us no information about the effect of varying the concentration of adrenalin. An experiment to throw light on this factor with the same precision as the factorial design would need a further rc observations, all with the same storage period. Twice as many observations as in the factorial design would therefore be needed. Moreover, the factorial design permits a comparison of the effect of one factor at different levels of the other: it permits the detection of an interaction between the two factors. This cannot be done without the factorial approach.

The two-factor design considered in section 8.1 can clearly be generalized to allow the simultaneous study of three or more factors. Strictly, the term 'factorial design' should be reserved for situations in which the factors are all controllable experimental treatments and in which all the combinations of levels are randomly allocated to the experimental units. The analysis is, however, essentially the same in the slightly different situation in which one or more of the factors represents a form of blocking—a source of known or suspected variation which can usefully be eliminated in comparing the real treatments. We shall therefore include this extended form of factorial design in the present discussion.

Notation becomes troublesome if we aim at complete generality, so we shall discuss in detail a three-factor design. The directions of generalization should be clear. Suppose there are three factors: A at I levels, B at J levels and C at K levels. As in section 8.1 we consider a linear model whereby the mean response at the ith level of A, the jth level of B and the kth level of C is

$$E(y_{ijk}) = \mu + \alpha_i + \beta_j + \gamma_k + (\alpha\beta)_{ij} + (\alpha\gamma)_{ik} + (\beta\gamma)_{jk} + (\alpha\beta\gamma)_{ijk}, \quad (8.7)$$

with $\sum_i \alpha_i = \ldots = \sum_i (\alpha\beta)_{ij} = \ldots = \sum_i (\alpha\beta\gamma)_{ijk} = 0$, etc.

Here the terms like $(\alpha\beta)_{ij}$ are to be read as single constants, the notation being chosen to indicate the interpretation of each term as an interaction between two or more factors. The constants α_i measure the effects of the different levels of factor A averaged over the various levels of the other factors; these are called the *main effects* of A. The constant $(\alpha\beta)_{ij}$ indicates the extent to which the mean response at level i of A and level j of B, averaged over all levels of C, is not determined purely by α_i and β_j, and it thus measures one aspect of the interaction of A and B. It is called a *first-order interaction term* or *two-factor interaction term*. Similarly, the constant $(\alpha\beta\gamma)_{ijk}$ indicates how the mean response at the triple combination of A, B and C is not determined purely by main effects and first-order interaction terms. It is called a *second-order* or *three-factor interaction term*.

To complete the model, suppose that y_{ijk} is distributed normally about $E(y_{ijk})$ with a constant residual variance σ^2.

TABLE 8.5 Structure of analysis of variance for three-factor design with replication.

	SSq	DF	MSq	VR(=MSq/s_R^2)
Main effects				
A	S_A	$I-1$	s_A^2	F_A
B	S_B	$J-1$	s_B^2	F_B
C	S_C	$K-1$	s_C^2	F_C
2-factor interaction				
AB	S_{AB}	$(I-1)(J-1)$	s_{AB}^2	F_{AB}
AC	S_{AC}	$(I-1)(K-1)$	s_{AC}^2	F_{AC}
BC	S_{BC}	$(J-1)(K-1)$	s_{BC}^2	F_{BC}
3-factor interaction				
ABC	S_{ABC}	$(I-1)(J-1)(K-1)$	s_{ABC}^2	F_{ABC}
Residual	S_R	$IJK(n-1)$	s_R^2	1
	S	$N-1$		

Suppose now that we make n observations at each combination of A, B and C. The total number of observations is $nIJK=N$, say. The structure of the analysis of variance is shown in Table 8.5. The DF for the main effects and two-factor interactions follow directly from the results for two-way analyses. That for the three-factor interaction is a natural extension. The residual DF are $IJK(n-1)$ because there are $n-1$ DF between replicates at each of the IJK factor combinations. The SSq terms are calculated as follows.

Main effects. As for a one-way analysis, remembering that the divisor for the squares of a group total is the total number of observations in that group. Thus, if the total for ith level of A is $T_{i..}$, and the grand total is T, the SSq for A is

$$\sum_i T_{i..}^2/nJK - T^2/N. \tag{8.8}$$

Two-factor interactions. Form a two-way table of totals, calculate the appropriate corrected sum of square between these totals and subtract the SSq for the two relevant main effects. For AB, for instance, suppose $T_{ij.}$ is the total for levels i of A and j of B. Then

$$S_{AB}=\left\{\sum_{i,j} T_{ij.}^2/nK - T^2/N\right\} - S_A - S_B. \tag{8.9}$$

Three-factor interaction. Form a three-way table of totals, calculate the appropriate corrected sum of squares and subtract the SSq for all relevant two-factor interactions and main effects. If T_{ijk} is the total for the three-factor combination at levels i, j, k of A, B, C respectively,

$$S_{ABC}=\left\{\sum_{i,j,k} T_{ijk}^2/n - T^2/N\right\}$$
$$- S_{AB} - S_{AC} - S_{BC} - S_A - S_B - S_C. \tag{8.10}$$

Total. As usual by $\sum_{i,j,k,r} y_{ijkr}^2 - T^2/N$, where the suffix r (from 1 to n) denotes one of the n replicate observations at each factor combination.

Residual. By subtraction. It could also have been obtained by adding, over all three-factor combinations, the sum of squares between replicates:

$$\sum_{i,j,k}\left\{\sum_{r=1}^{n} y_{ijkr}^2 - T_{ijk}^2/n\right\}. \tag{8.11}$$

This alternative formulation unfortunately does not provide an independent check on the arithmetic, as it follows immediately from the other expressions.

The MSq terms are obtained as usual from SSq/DF. Each of these divided by the residual MSq, s_R^2, provides an F test for the appropriate null hypothesis about the main effects or interactions. For example, F_A (tested on $I-1$ and $IJK(n-1)$ degrees of freedom) provides a test of the null hypothesis that all the α_i are zero; that is, that the mean responses at different levels of A, averaged over all levels of the other factors, are all equal. Some problems of interpretation of this rather complex set of tests are discussed at the end of this section.

Suppose $n=1$, so that there is no replication. The DF for the residual become zero, since $n-1=0$. So does the SSq, since all the contributions in curly brackets in (8.11) are zero, being sums of squares about the mean of a single observation. The 'residual' line therefore does not appear in the analysis. The position is exactly the same as in the two-way analysis with one observation per cell. The usual practice is to take the highest order interaction (in this case ABC) as the residual term, and to calculate F ratios using this MSq as the denominator. As in the two-way analysis, this will be satisfactory if the highest order interaction term in the *model* (in our case $(\alpha\beta\gamma)_{ijk}$) is zero or near zero. If this term is substantial the makeshift Residual MSq, s_{ABC}^2, will tend to be higher than σ^2 and the tests will be correspondingly insensitive.

Example 8.3

Table 8.6* shows the relative weights of right adrenals (expressed as a fraction of body weight, $\times 10^4$) in mice obtained by crossing parents of four strains. For each of the 16 combinations of parental strains, four mice (two of each sex) were used.

This is a three-factor design. The factors—mother's strain, father's strain and sex— are not, of course, experimental treatments imposed by random allocation. Nevertheless they represent potential sources of variation whose main effects and interactions may be studied. The DF are shown in the table. The SSq for main effects follow straightforwardly from the subtotals. That for mother's strain, for example, is

$$\{(19{\cdot}14)^2+\ldots+(19{\cdot}71)^2\}/16-\text{C.T.},$$

* The data were kindly provided by Drs. R.L.Collins and R.J.Meckler. In their paper 'Histology and weight of the mouse adrenal: a diallel genetic study', *J. Endocrin.*, **31**, 95–105, 1965, results from both adrenals are analysed.

TABLE 8.6 Relative weights of right adrenals in mice.

Mother's strain	Father's strain 1 ♀	1 ♂	2 ♀	2 ♂	3 ♀	3 ♂	4 ♀	4 ♂	Totals ♀	Totals ♂	Totals ♀+♂
1	0·93	0·69	1·76	0·67	1·46	0·88	1·45	0·95	12·57	6·57	19·14
	1·70	0·83	1·58	0·73	1·89	0·96	1·80	0·86			
2	1·42	0·50	1·85	0·72	2·14	1·00	1·94	0·63	15·25	6·08	21·33
	1·96	0·74	1·69	0·66	2·17	0·96	2·08	0·87			
3	2·22	0·86	1·96	1·04	1·62	0·82	1·51	0·82	15·32	6·69	22·01
	2·33	0·98	2·09	0·96	1·63	0·57	1·96	0·64			
4	1·25	0·56	1·56	1·08	1·88	1·00	1·85	0·43	13·39	6·32	19·71
	1·76	0·75	1·90	0·80	1·81	1·11	1·38	0·59			
Total	13·57	5·91	14·39	6·66	14·60	7·30	13·97	5·79	56·53	25·66	
	19·48		21·05		21·90		19·76				82·19

C.T. = 105·5499

Analysis of variance

	DF	SSq	MSq	VR
Mother's strain, M	3	0·3396	0·1132	2·87
Father's strain, F	3	0·2401	0·0800	2·03
Sex of animal, S	1	14·8900	14·8900	376·96**
MF	9	1·2988	0·1443	3·65**
MS	3	0·3945	0·1315	3·33*
FS	3	0·0245	0·0082	0·21
MFS	9	0·2612	0·0290	0·73
Residual	32	1·2647	0·0395	1·00
Total	63	18·7134		

** $P<0{\cdot}005$
* $0{\cdot}01<P<0{\cdot}05$

where the correction term, C.T., is $(82{\cdot}19)^2/64=105{\cdot}5499$. The two-factor interaction, MF, is obtained as

$$\{(4{\cdot}15)^2+\ldots+(4{\cdot}25)^2\}/4-\text{C.T.}-S_M-S_F,$$

where 4·15 is the sum of the four responses in the first cell (0·93 + 1·70 + 0·69 + 0·83), and S_M and S_F are the SSq for the two main effects. Similarly the three-factor interaction is obtained as

$$\{(2{\cdot}63)^2+(1{\cdot}52)^2+\ldots+(3{\cdot}23)^2+(1{\cdot}02)^2\}/2-\text{C.T.}$$
$$-S_M-S_F-S_S-S_{MF}-S_{MS}-S_{FS}.$$

Here the quantities 2·63, etc., are subtotals of pairs of responses (2·63=0·93+1·70). The Residual SSq may be obtained by subtraction once the Total SSq has been obtained. Alternatively, as a check it may be obtained from the *differences* between replicate observations:

$$\{(0{\cdot}93-1{\cdot}70)^2+\ldots+(0{\cdot}43-0{\cdot}59)^2\}/2=1{\cdot}2648,$$

the difference from the value obtained by subtraction being due to rounding error.

When, as in this example, one of the factors has only two levels the calculation of the main effect and the interactions involving this factor may be simplified by considering contrasts between the two levels of the factor. The differences between the totals for the two females and for the two males, at each parental cross, are as follows:

		Father's strain				
		1	2	3	4	Total
	1	1·11	1·94	1·51	1·44	6·00
Mother's	2	2·14	2·16	2·35	2·52	9·17
strain	3	2·71	2·05	1·86	2·01	8·63
	4	1·70	1·58	1·58	2·21	7·07
Total		7·66	7·73	7·30	8·18	30·87

The SSq for the main effect, S, is, from (7.10), given by $(30{\cdot}87)^2/64=14{\cdot}8900$ as before. The SSq for MS is

$$\{(6{\cdot}00)^2+\ldots+(7{\cdot}07)^2\}/16-14{\cdot}8900=0{\cdot}3944,$$

that for FS is

$$\{(7{\cdot}66)^2+\ldots+(8{\cdot}18)^2\}/16-14{\cdot}8900=0{\cdot}0244,$$

and the SSq for MFS is

$$\{(1{\cdot}11)^2+\ldots+(2{\cdot}21)^2\}/4-14{\cdot}8900-S_{MS}-S_{FS}=0{\cdot}2614.$$

These SSq agree with those in Table 8.6 apart from rounding errors. Note that the divisors for the various squares are, as usual, the number of basic observations contributing to the quantity squared although in each case these quantities are linear contrasts in which half the observations are multiplied by +1 and half by −1.

The F tests show the main effects M and F to be non-significant, although each F is greater than 1. The interaction MF is highly significant. The main effect of sex is highly significant, and also its interaction with M. To elucidate the strain effects it is useful to tabulate the sums of observations for the 16 crosses:

		Father's strain				
		1	2	3	4	Total
	1	4·15	4·74	5·19	5·06	19·14
Mother's	2	4·62	4·92	6·27	5·52	21·33
strain	3	6·39	6·05	4·64	4·93	22·01
	4	4·32	5·34	5·80	4·25	19·71
Total		19·48	21·05	21·90	19·76	82·19

Strains 2 and 3 give relatively high readings for both M and F, suggesting a systematic effect which has not achieved significance for either parent separately. The interaction is due partly to the high reading for ($M3$, $F1$).

Each of the 16 cell totals is the sum of four readings, and the difference between any two has a standard error $\sqrt{\{(2)(4)(0{\cdot}0395)\}}=0{\cdot}56$. For $M3$ the difference between $F1$ and $F3$ is significantly positive, whereas for each of the other maternal strains the $F1-F3$ difference is significant in a negative direction. A similar reversal is provided by the four entries for $M2$ and $M3$, $F2$ and $F3$.

The MS interaction may be studied from the previous table of sex contrasts. Each of the row totals has a standard error $\sqrt{\{16(0{\cdot}0395)\}}=0{\cdot}80$. Maternal strains 2 and 3 show significantly higher sex differences than $M1$, and $M2$ is significantly higher also than $M4$. The point may be seen from the right-hand margin of Table 8.6, where the high responses for $M2$ and $M3$ are shown strongly in the female offspring, but not in the males.

THE 2^p FACTORIAL DESIGN

An interaction term in the analysis of a factorial design will in general have many degrees of freedom, and will represent departures of various types from an additive model. The interpretation of a significant interaction may therefore require careful thought. If, however, all the factors are at two levels, each of the main effects and each of the interactions will have only 1 degree of freedom, and consequently represent linear contrasts which can be interpreted relatively simply. If there are, say, four factors each at two levels, the design is referred to as a $2\times2\times2\times2$, or 2^4, design, and in general for p factors each at two levels, the design is called 2^p. The analysis of 2^p designs can be simplified by direct calculation of each linear contrast. We shall illustrate the procedure for a 2^3 design.

Suppose there are n observations at each of the $8(=2^3)$ factor combinations. Since each factor is at two levels we can, by suitable conventions, regard each factor as being positive or negative—say by the presence or absence of some feature. Denoting the factors by A, B and C, we can identify each factor combination by writing in lower case letters those factors which are positive. Thus, (ab) indicates the combination with A and B positive and C negative, while (c) indicates the combination with only C positive; the combination with all factors negative will be written as (1). In formulae these symbols can be taken to mean the *totals* of the n observations at the different factor combinations.

The main effect of A may be estimated by the difference between the mean response at all combinations with A positive and that for A negative. This is a linear contrast,

$$\frac{(a)+(ab)+(ac)+(abc)}{4n}-\left\{\frac{(1)+(b)+(c)+(bc)}{4n}\right\}=[A]/4n, \tag{8.12}$$

where

$$[A]=-(1)+(a)-(b)+(ab)-(c)+(ac)-(bc)+(abc), \tag{8.13}$$

the terms being rearranged here so that the factors are introduced in order.

The main effects of B and C are defined in a similar way.

The two-factor interaction between A and B represents the difference between the estimated effect of A when B is positive, and that when B is negative. This is

$$\frac{(ab)+(abc)-(b)-(bc)}{2n}-\left\{\frac{(a)+(ac)-(1)-(c)}{2n}\right\}=[AB]/2n, \tag{8.14}$$

where

$$[AB]=(1)-(a)-(b)+(ab)+(c)-(ac)-(bc)+(abc). \tag{8.15}$$

To avoid the awkwardness of the divisor $2n$ in (8.14) when $4n$ appears in (8.12), it is useful to define the interaction as $[AB]/4n$, that is as *half* the difference referred to above. Note that the terms in (8.15) have a positive sign when A and B are either both positive or both negative, and a negative sign otherwise. Note also that $[AB]/4n$ can be written as

$$\frac{(ab)+(abc)-(a)-(ac)}{4n}-\left\{\frac{(b)+(bc)-(1)-(c)}{4n}\right\},$$

which is half the difference between the estimated effect of B when A is positive and that when A is negative. This emphasizes the symmetric nature of $[AB]$.

The three-factor interaction $[ABC]$ can similarly be interpreted in a number of equivalent ways. It represents, for instance, the difference between the estimated $[AB]$ interaction when C is positive and when C is negative. Apart from the divisor, this difference is measured by

$$\begin{aligned}[ABC] &= \{(c)-(ac)-(bc)+(abc)\}-\{(1)-(a)-(b)+(ab)\} \\ &= -(1)+(a)+(b)-(ab)+(c)-(ac)-(bc)+(abc), \qquad (8.16)\end{aligned}$$

and it is again convenient to define the interaction as $[ABC]/4n$.

TABLE 8.7 Calculation of main effects and interactions for 2^3 factorial design.

Effect		Multiplier for total (1)	(a)	(b)	(ab)	(c)	(ac)	(bc)	(abc)	Divisor for contrast	Contribution to SSq
Main effects	A	−1	1	−1	1	−1	1	−1	1	$4n$	$[A]^2/8n$
	B	−1	−1	1	1	−1	−1	1	1	$4n$	$[B]^2/8n$
	C	−1	−1	−1	−1	1	1	1	1	$4n$	$[C]^2/8n$
2-factor interactions	AB	1	−1	−1	1	1	−1	−1	1	$4n$	$[AB]^2/8n$
	AC	1	−1	1	−1	−1	1	−1	1	$4n$	$[AC]^2/8n$
	BC	1	1	−1	−1	−1	−1	1	1	$4n$	$[BC]^2/8n$
3-factor interaction	ABC	−1	1	1	−1	1	−1	−1	1	$4n$	$[ABC]^2/8n$

These results are summarized in Table 8.7. Note that the positive and negative signs for the two-factor interactions are easily obtained by multiplying together the coefficients for the corresponding main effects; and those for the three-factor interaction by multiplying the coefficients for $[A]$ and $[BC]$, $[B]$ and $[AC]$, or $[C]$ and $[AB]$.

The final column of Table 8.7 shows the formula for the SSq and (since each has 1 DF) for the MSq for each term in the analysis. Each term like $[A]$, $[AB]$, etc., has a variance $8n\sigma^2$ on the appropriate null hypothesis (since each of the totals (1), (a), etc., has a variance $n\sigma^2$). Hence $[A]^2/8n$ is an estimate of σ^2. In general, for a 2^p factorial, the divisors for the linear contrasts are $2^{p-1}n$, and those for the SSq are $2^p n$.

The significance of the main effects and of interactions may equivalently be tested by t tests. The residual mean square, s_R^2, has $8(n-1)$ DF, and the variance of each of the contrasts $[A]$, $[AB]$, etc., is estimated as $8ns_R^2$, to give a t test with $8(n-1)$ DF.

An alternative method of deriving the contrasts [A], [AB], etc., in a 2^p factorial, due to F.Yates, is described by Cochran and Cox (1957, section 5.24a).

Example 8.4

As an example of the analysis of a 2^3 design, consider a portion of the data of Table 8.6, corresponding to maternal strains 2 and 3, and paternal strains 2 and 3. Regard the main effects M and F as positive for strain 3, and main effect S as positive for males. There are $n=2$ replicates at each of the eight factor combinations. The sum and difference for each pair of readings and the linear contrasts obtained from the pair sums as in Table 8.7 are shown in Table 8.8. For (m), for example, the sum is $1{\cdot}96+2{\cdot}09=4{\cdot}05$, and the difference is $1{\cdot}96-2{\cdot}09=-0{\cdot}13$. The first linear contrast, [M], is

$$-3{\cdot}54+4{\cdot}05-4{\cdot}31+3{\cdot}25-1{\cdot}38+2{\cdot}00-1{\cdot}96+1{\cdot}39=-0{\cdot}50.$$

The SSq are obtained as in Table 8.7. For example, $S_M=[M]^2/16=0{\cdot}0156$. The Residual SSq is obtained either by subtraction after calculation of Total SSq, or directly from the differences, as $\{(0{\cdot}16)^2+\ldots+(0{\cdot}25)^2\}/2=0{\cdot}0588$.

TABLE 8.8 A 2^3 design derived from data in Table 8.6.

	(1)	(*m*)	(*f*)	(*mf*)	(*s*)	(*ms*)	(*fs*)	(*mfs*)
Subtotals	3·54	4·05	4·31	3·25	1·38	2·00	1·96	1·39
Differences	0·16	−0·13	−0·03	−0·01	0·06	0·08	0·04	0·25
Contrasts		[*M*]	[*F*]	[*MF*]	[*S*]	[*MS*]	[*FS*]	[*MFS*]
		−0·50	−0·06	−2·76	−8·42	0·60	0·00	0·38

Analysis of variance

	DF	SSq	MSq	VR
M	1	0·0156	0·0156	2·11
F	1	0·0002	0·0002	0·03
S	1	4·4310	4·4310	598·78*
MF	1	0·4761	0·4761	64·34*
MS	1	0·0225	0·0225	3·04
FS	1	0·0000	0·0000	0·00
MFS	1	0·0090	0·0090	1·22
Residual	8	0·0589	0·0074	1·00
Total	15	5·0133		

* $P<0{\cdot}005$

The variance ratios for sex and for the MF interactions are highly significant. The mean difference between responses for males and females is

$[S]/8 = -1{\cdot}05$; the variance of this quantity is estimated as $16s^2/8^2 = s^2/4 = 0{\cdot}00184$, and its standard error as $\sqrt{0{\cdot}00184} = 0{\cdot}043$. Ninety-five per cent confidence limits for the sex difference are therefore

$$-1{\cdot}05 \pm (2{\cdot}306)(0{\cdot}043)$$
$$= -0{\cdot}95 \quad \text{and} \quad -1{\cdot}15,$$

the factor 2·306 being the 5 per cent point of t on 8 DF.

The interaction can again be studied by tabulating totals for the four parental crosses.

		Father's strain	
		2	3
Mother's	2	4·92	6·27
strain	3	6·05	4·64

The difference between any two of these totals has a standard error $\sqrt{\{(2)(4)(0{\cdot}0074)\}} = 0{\cdot}243$. Clearly, for maternal strain 2, a significantly higher response is obtained from paternal strain 3 than paternal strain 2; for maternal strain 3 the difference is significant in the opposite direction.

INTERPRETATION OF FACTORIAL EXPERIMENTS WITH SIGNIFICANT INTERACTIONS

The analysis of a large-scale factorial experiment provides an opportunity to test simultaneously a number of main effects and interactions. The complexity of this situation sometimes gives rise to ambiguities of interpretation. The following points may be helpful.

(1) Whether or not two or more factors interact will depend on the scale of measurement of the variable under analysis. Sometimes a simpler interpretation of the data may be obtained by re-analysing the data after a logarithmic or other transformation (see Chapter 11). For instance, if we ignore random error the responses shown in (a) below present an interaction between A and B. Those shown in (b) present no interaction. The responses in (b) are the square roots of those in (a).

		(a) B Low	(a) B High	(b) B Low	(b) B High
A	Low	9	16	3	4
	High	16	25	4	5

The search for a scale of measurement on which interactions are small or non-significant is particularly worth trying if the main effects of one factor, as measured at different levels of the other(s), are related closely to the mean responses at these levels. If the estimated main effects of any one factor are in *opposite directions* for different levels of the other(s), transformations are not likely to be useful.

(2) In a multi-factor experiment many interactions are independently subjected to test; it will not be too surprising if one of these is mildly significant purely by chance. The use of a rather high significance level (say, 1 per cent) for interactions not regarded as inherently plausible is therefore quite reasonable. Another useful device is the 'half-normal plot' (section 12.7).

(3) If several high-order interactions are non-significant their SSq are often pooled with the Residual SSq to provide an increased number of DF and hence more sensitive tests of the main effects or low-order interactions.

There remain some further points of interpretation which are most usefully discussed separately according as the factors concerned are thought of as having fixed effects or random effects (section 7.2).

Fixed effects

If certain interactions are present they can often best be displayed by quoting the mean values of the variable at each of the factor combinations concerned. For instance, in an experiment with A, B and C at 2, 3 and 4 levels respectively, if the only significant interaction were BC, the mean values would be quoted at each of the 12 combinations of levels of B and C. These could be accompanied by a statement of the standard error of the difference between two of these means. The reader would then be able to see quickly the essential features of the interaction. Consider the following table of means:

		Level of C			
		1	2	3	4
Level	1	2·17	2·25	2·19	2·24
of	2	1·96	2·01	1·89	1·86
B	3	2·62	2·67	2·83	2·87

(Standard error of difference between two means = 0·05.)

Clearly the effect of C is not detectable at level 1 of B; at level 2 of B the two higher levels of C show a decrease in the mean; at level 3 of B the two higher levels of C show an increase.

In situations like this the main effects of B and C are of no great interest. If the effect of C varies with the level of B, the main effect increases the average effect of C over the levels of B; since it depends on the choice of levels of B it will usually be a rather artificial quantity and therefore hardly worth considering. Similarly, if a three-factor interaction is significant and deemed to exist, the interactions between any two of the factors concerned are rather artificial concepts.

Random effects

If, in the previous example, A and C were fixed-effect factors and B was a random-effect factor, the presence of an interaction between B and C would not preclude an interest in the main effect of C—regarded not as an average over the particular levels of B chosen in the experiment, but as an average over the whole population of potential B levels. Under certain conditions (discussed below) the null hypothesis for the main effect of C is tested by comparing the MSq for C against the MSq for the interaction BC. If C has more than two levels it may be more informative to concentrate on a particular contrast between the levels of B (say a comparison of level 1 with level 4), and obtain the interaction of *this contrast* with factor B.

If one of the factors in a multi-factor design is a blocking system it will usually be natural to regard this as a random-effect factor. Suppose the other factors are controlled treatments (say A, B and C). Then each of the main effects and interactions of A, B and C may be compared with the appropriate interaction with Blocks. Frequently the various interactions involving Blocks differ by no more than might be expected by random variation, and the SSq may be pooled to provide extra DF.

The situations referred to in the previous paragraphs are examples in which a *mixed model* is appropriate—some of the factors having fixed effects and some having random effects. If there is just one random factor (as with Blocks in the example in the last paragraph), any main effect or interaction of the other factors may be tested against the appropriate interaction with the random factor; for example, if D is the random factor, A could be tested against AD, AB against ABD. The justification for this follows by interpreting the interaction terms involving D in the model like (8.7) as independent observations on random variables with zero mean. The concept of a random interaction is reasonable; if, for example, D is a blocking system any linear contrast representing part of a main effect or interaction of the other factors can be regarded as varying randomly from block to block.

What is more arguable, though, is the assumption that all the components in (8.7) for a particular interaction, say AD, have the same distribution and are independent of each other. Hence the suggestion, made above, that attention should preferably be focussed on particular linear contrasts. Any such contrast, L, could be measured separately in each block and its mean value tested by a t test.

When there are more than two random factors further problems arise because there may be no valid tests for some of the main effects and interactions. For further discussion see Snedecor and Cochran (1967, section 12.11).

8.3 LATIN SQUARES

Suppose we wish to compare the effects of a treatments in an experiment in which there are two other known sources of variation, each at a levels. A complete factorial design, with only one observation at each factor combination, would require a^3 observations. Consider the following design, in which $a=4$. The principal treatments are denoted by A, B, C and D, and the two secondary factors are represented by the rows and columns of the table.

		Column			
		1	2	3	4
	1	*D*	*B*	*C*	*A*
Row	2	*C*	*D*	*A*	*B*
	3	*A*	*C*	*B*	*D*
	4	*B*	*A*	*D*	*C*

Only a^2 $(=16)$ observations are made, since at each combination of a row and a column only one of the four treatments is used. The design is cunningly balanced, however, in the sense that each treatment occurs precisely once in each row and precisely once in each column. If the effect of making an observation in row 1 rather than row 2 is to add a constant amount onto the measurement observed, the differences between the means for the four treatments are unaffected by the size of this constant. In this sense systematic variation between rows, or similarly between columns, does not affect the treatment comparisons and can be said to have been eliminated by the choice of design.

These designs, called Latin squares, were first used in agricultural experiments in which the rows and columns represented strips in two perpendicular directions across a field. Some analogous examples arise in medical research when treatments are to be applied to a two-dimensional array of experimental units. For instance, various substances may be inoculated subcutaneously over a two-dimensional grid of points on the skin of a human subject or an animal. In a plate diffusion assay various dilutions of an antibiotic preparation may be inserted in hollows in an agar plate which is seeded with bacteria and incubated, the inhibition zone formed by diffusion of antibiotic round each hollow being related to the dilution used.

In other experiments the rows and columns may represent two identifiable sources of variation which are, however, not geographically meaningful. The Latin square is being used here as a straightforward generalization of a randomized block design, the rows and columns representing two different systems of blocking. Examples are the following.

(1) An animal experiment in which rows represent litters and columns represent different days on which the experiment is performed. Individual animals receive different treatments.

(2) A clinical trial in which rows represent different subjects and columns represent the order of administration of treatments. Here each subject receives the various treatments on different occasions. In this type of application the investigator must satisfy himself that the response observed on any occasion is influenced only by the treatment currently given and not by any preceding treatments. It is easy to think of situations in which there is a carry-over, either of the pharmacological effect of a previously administered drug, or (in certain experiments) of the psychological effect of previous treatments. Some Latin squares are balanced for certain residual effects and may be used for their estimation. These are due mainly to E.J.Williams and are described by Cochran and Cox (1957, section 4.6a).

Latin squares are sometimes used in situations where either the rows or columns or both represent forms of treatment under the experimenter's control. They are then performing some of the functions of factorial designs, with the important proviso that some of the factor combinations are missing. This has important consequences which we shall note later.

In a randomized block design treatments are allocated at random within each block. How can randomization be applied in a Latin square, which is clearly a highly systematic arrangement? For any value of a many possible squares can be written down. The safeguards of randomization are introduced by making a random choice from these possible squares. Full details of the procedure are given in Fisher and Yates (1963) and in most books on experimental design. The reader will not go far wrong if he constructs a Latin square of the right size by shifting treatments cyclically by one place in successive rows—

$$\begin{array}{cccc} A & B & C & D \\ D & A & B & C \\ C & D & A & B \\ B & C & D & A \end{array}$$

and then permutes the rows and the columns randomly.

As an additive model for the analysis of the Latin square, suppose that the response, y_{ijk}, for the ith row, jth column and kth treatment is given by

$$y_{ijk} = \mu + \alpha_i + \beta_j + \gamma_k + \epsilon_{ijk}, \qquad (8.17)$$

where μ represents the general mean, α_i, β_j and γ_k are constants characteristic of the particular row, column and treatment concerned, and ϵ_{ijk} is a random observation from a normal distribution with zero mean and variance σ^2. The model is, in fact, that of a 3-factor experiment without interactions.

The notation for the observations is shown in Table 8.9. The analysis, shown at the foot of Table 8.9, follows familiar lines. The SSq for rows, columns and treatments are obtained by the usual formula in terms of the sub-totals, the Total SSq also as usual, and the residual term is obtained by subtraction:

$$\text{Residual SSq} = \text{Total SSq} - (\text{Rows SSq} + \text{Columns SSq} + \text{Treatments SSq}).$$

The degrees of freedom for the three factors are clearly $a-1$; the residual DF are found by subtraction to be $a^2-3a+2=(a-1)(a-2)$.

The basis of the division of the Total SSq is the following identity:

$$y_{ijk} - \bar{y} = (\bar{y}_{i..} - \bar{y}) + (\bar{y}_{.j.} - \bar{y}) + (\bar{y}_{..k} - \bar{y}) + (y_{ijk} - \bar{y}_{i..} - \bar{y}_{.j.} - \bar{y}_{..k} + 2\bar{y}). \qquad (8.18)$$

When each term is squared and a summation taken over all a^2 observations the four sums of squares are obtained. The product terms such as $\sum(\bar{y}_{.j.} - \bar{y})(\bar{y}_{..k} - \bar{y})$ are all zero as in the two-way analysis of section 8.1.

If the additive model (8.17) is correct the three null hypotheses about equality of the α's, β's and γ's can all be tested by the appropriate

TABLE 8.9 Notation for Latin square experiment.

		Column 1	2 ... j ... a	Total	Mean	Treatment	Total	Mean
	1			R_1	$\bar{y}_{1..}$	1	T_1	$\bar{y}_{..1}$
	2			R_2	$\bar{y}_{2..}$	2	T_2	$\bar{y}_{..2}$
	.			.	.	.	.	.
	.			.	.	.	.	.
	.			.	.	.	.	.
Row	i		y_{ijk}	R_i	$\bar{y}_{i..}$	k	T_k	$\bar{y}_{..k}$
	.			.	.	.	.	.
	.			.	.	.	.	.
	.			.	.	.	.	.
	a			R_a	$\bar{y}_{a..}$	a	T_a	$\bar{y}_{..a}$
Total		C_1	$C_2 \ldots C_j \ldots C_a$	T			T	
Mean		$\bar{y}_{.1.}$	$\bar{y}_{.2.}$ $\bar{y}_{.j.}$ $\bar{y}_{.a.}$		$\bar{y}$			

Analysis of variance

	SSq	DF	MSq	VR
Rows	$\sum R_i^2/a - T^2/a^2$	$a-1$	s_R^2	$F_R = s_R^2/s^2$
Columns	$\sum C_j^2/a - T^2/a^2$	$a-1$	s_C^2	$F_C = s_C^2/s^2$
Treatments	$\sum T_k^2/a - T^2/a^2$	$a-1$	s_T^2	$F_T = s_T^2/s^2$
Residual	by subtraction	$(a-1)(a-2)$	s^2	
Total	$y_{ijk}^2 - T^2/a^2$	a^2-1		

F tests. Confidence limits for differences between pairs of constants (say, between two rows) or for other linear contrasts can be formed in a straightforward way, the standard errors being estimated in terms of s^2. However, the additive model may be incorrect. If the rows and columns are blocking factors the effect of non-additivity will be to increase the estimate of residual variance. Tests for differences between rows or between columns are of no great interest in this case, and randomization ensures the validity of the tests and estimates for treatment differences; the extra imprecision is automatically accounted for in the increased value of s^2. If, on the other hand, the rows and columns are treatments, non-additivity means that some interactions exist. The trouble now is that the interactions cannot be measured independently of the main effects, and serious errors may result. In both sets of circumstances, therefore, additivity of responses is a desirable feature, although its absence is more regrettable in the second case than in the first.

Example 8.5

The experiment of Bacharach *et al.* (1940) discussed in Example 7.2 was designed as a Latin square. The design and the measurements are given in Table 8.10. The object of the experiment was to study the possible effects of

TABLE 8.10 Measurements of area of blister (cm²) following inoculation of diffusing factor into skin of rabbits in positions a–f on animals' backs, order of administration being denoted by i–vi (Bacharach *et al.*, 1940).

	Animals							
	1	2	3	4	5	6	Total	Mean
Positions								
	iii	v	iv	i	vi	ii		
a	7·9	8·7	7·4	7·4	7·1	8·2	46·7	7·783
	iv	ii	vi	v	iii	i		
b	6·1	8·2	7·7	7·1	8·1	5·9	43·1	7·183
	i	iii	v	vi	ii	iv		
c	7·5	8·1	6·0	6·4	6·2	7·5	41·7	6·950
	vi	i	iii	ii	iv	v		
d	6·9	8·5	6·8	7·7	8·5	8·5	46·9	7·817
	ii	iv	i	iii	v	vi		
e	6·7	9·9	7·3	6·4	6·4	7·3	44·0	7·333
	v	vi	ii	iv	i	iii		
f	7·3	8·3	7·3	5·8	6·4	7·7	42·8	7·133
Total	42·4	51·7	42·5	40·8	42·7	45·1	265·2	
Mean	7·067	8·617	7·083	6·800	7·117	7·517		7·367

Order	i	ii	iii	iv	v	vi
Total	43·0	44·3	45·0	45·2	44·0	43·7
Mean	7·167	7·383	7·500	7·533	7·333	7·283

$$\sum y_{ijk}^2 = 1{,}984 \cdot 0000$$
$$T^2/36 = 1{,}953 \cdot 6401$$

Analysis of variance

	SSq	DF	MSq	VR	
Rows (Positions)	3·8332	5	0·7667	1·17	
Columns (Animals)	12·8333	5	2·5667	3·91	($P<0·05$)
Treatments (Order)	0·5632	5	0·1106	<1	
Residual	13·1302	20	0·6565	1·00	
	30·3599	35			

order of administration in a series of inoculations on the same animal (the 'treatment' factor, represented here by Roman numerals) and the choice among six positions on the animal's skin (the row factor), and also to assess the variation between animals (the column factor) in comparison with that within animals.

The Total SSq is obtained as usual as

$$1{,}984{\cdot}0000 - 1{,}953{\cdot}6401 = 30{\cdot}3599.$$

The SSq for animal differences is calculated as

$$\{(42{\cdot}4)^2 + (51{\cdot}7)^2 + \ldots + (45{\cdot}1)^2\}/6 - 1{,}953{\cdot}6401 = 12{\cdot}8333,$$

the other two main effects follow similarly, and the Residual SSq is obtained by subtraction. The VR for order is less than 1 and need not be referred to the F table. That for positions is certainly not significant. The only significant effect is that for animal differences, and further examination of the between-animal component of variance has already been carried out in Example 7.2.

REPLICATION OF LATIN SQUARES

An important restriction of the Latin square is, of course, the requirement that the numbers of rows, columns and treatments must all be equal. The nature of the experimental material and the purpose of the experiment often demand that the size of the square should be small. On the other hand, treatment comparisons estimated from a single Latin square are likely to be rather imprecise. Some form of replication is therefore often desirable.

Simple replication with, say, r observations in each of the a^2 cells of the square will occasionally be possible. In this case the analysis of variance is amplified by the addition of $a^2(r-1)$ DF within cells, the total DF being ra^2-1. A comparison of the between-cell residual on $(a-1)(a-2)$ DF with the within-cell residual provides a validity test for the additive model. Note that, in calculating the main effect SSq, the squares of the sub-group totals must now be divided by ar instead of a; similarly the divisor for the correction term is a^2r instead of a^2.

More frequently replication will be possible only by extending the levels of the row or column classification or by introducing a further factor into the analysis. As illustrations, consider three different ways in which the experiment described in Example 8.5 could be replicated five-fold to give a total of 180 ($=5\times 36$) observations. The structures of the corresponding analyses of variance are given in Table 8.11.

TABLE 8.11 Structures of analyses of variance for three different forms of replication of a 6 × 6 Latin square (see text).

(a)	DF	(b)	DF	(c)	DF
				Occasions	4
Rows		Rows		Rows	
Position	5	Position	5	Position	5
P × Litters	20			P × Occ.	20
Columns		Columns		Columns	
Litters	4	Sub-groups	5	Animals	5
Animals within litters	25	Animals within sub-groups	24	A × Occ.	20
Treatments		Treatments		Treatments	
Order	5	Order	5	Order	5
O × Litters	20			Order × Occ.	20
Residual	100	Residual	140	Residual	100
	179		179		179

(a) If the animals in Table 8.10 were all from the same litter a total of five litters could be used. A separately randomized Latin square would be used for each of the five replicates. The analysis enables the interactions Litters × Positions and Litters × Orders to be isolated.

(b) If 30 animals were available, not separable into litters or other rational sub-groups, they could be divided randomly into six equal sub-groups each of which would be allotted to a column of the design used in Table 8.10 (or any other randomly chosen 6 × 6 Latin square). The interactions isolated in (a) have now no meaning and their DF are included in the Residual term.

(c) If the experiment described in Table 8.10 could be repeated *with the same animals* on five different occasions, a separate randomization could be performed on each occasion. The analysis is similar to that in (a) except that the new factor, Occasions, provides a main effect term and also interactions with the other three factors.

In general, the separate randomizations of (a) and (c) are desirable, but in similar situations with much smaller numbers of observations the extra residual DF afforded by (b) may be a useful asset and the extra precision gained in this way may compensate for the loss of information about the interactions.

8.4 OTHER INCOMPLETE DESIGNS

The Latin square may be regarded either as a design which allows simultaneously for two extraneous sources of variation—the rows and columns—or as an incomplete factorial design permitting the estimation of three main effects—rows, columns and treatments—from observations at only a fraction of the possible combinations of factor levels.

Many other types of incomplete design are known. This section contains a very brief survey of some of these designs, with details of construction and analysis omitted. Cox (1958, chapters 11 and 12) gives a much fuller account of the characteristics and purposes of the various designs, and Cochran and Cox (1957) should be consulted for details of statistical analysis. Most of the designs described in this section have found little use in medical research, examples of their application being drawn usually from industrial and agricultural research. This contrast is perhaps partly due to inadequate appreciation of the less familiar designs by medical research workers, but it is likely also that the organizational problems of experimentation are more severe in medical research than in many other fields, a feature which would tend to favour the use of simple designs.

GRAECO–LATIN SQUARES

The Latin square generalizes the randomized block design by controlling variation due to two blocking factors. The Graeco–Latin square extends this idea by superimposing on a Latin square a further system of classification which is balanced with respect to the rows, columns and treatments. This is conventionally represented by letters of the Greek alphabet. For example, the following design could be used for an experiment similar to that described in Example 8.5:

$$\begin{array}{ccccc} A\alpha & B\beta & C\gamma & D\delta & E\epsilon \\ B\delta & C\epsilon & D\alpha & E\beta & A\gamma \\ C\beta & D\gamma & E\delta & A\epsilon & B\alpha \\ D\epsilon & E\alpha & A\beta & B\gamma & C\delta \\ E\gamma & A\delta & B\epsilon & C\alpha & D\beta \end{array}$$

Note that both the Latin letters and the Greek letters form Latin squares with the rows and columns, and also that each Latin letter occurs precisely once with each Greek letter. Suppose that the experimenter wished to compare the effects of five different doses of diffusing factor, allowing simultaneously for the order of administration, differences between animals and differences between positions on the animals' backs. The design shown above could be used, with random allocation of columns to five different animals, rows to five positions, Greek letters to the five positions in the order of administration, and Latin letters to the five dilutions.

Graeco–Latin squares exist for all of the small sizes likely to be required, except for the 6×6 square. If the Greek letters are amalgamated in groups of two or more they may be used to represent a factor with a smaller number of levels than the size of the square. In the above example, order of administration could be chosen purely at random, thus releasing the Greek letters for some other use. Suppose there were three batches of diffusing factor: X, Y and Z. Two Greek letters (say α and γ) could be allotted to X, two (say β and ϵ) to Y, and one (δ) to Z. The resulting design is called an *orthogonal partition* of a Latin square. Some orthogonal partitions of Latin squares exist in addition to those derived from Graeco–Latin squares; for example, they exist for 6×6 squares.

A further development is in the use of more than two alphabets. With an $a \times a$ square not more than $a-1$ alphabets can be used, and this maximum cannot always be achieved.

A general point to remember with Graeco–Latin squares and those involving more than two alphabets is that the number of DF for the residual mean square is invariably low. Unless, therefore, an estimate of error variance can reliably be obtained from extraneous data, it will often be desirable to introduce sufficient replication to provide an adequately precise estimate of random variation.

INCOMPLETE BLOCK DESIGNS

In many situations in which a natural blocking system exists, a randomized block design may be ruled out because the number of treatments is greater than the number of experimental units which can conveniently be formed within a block. This limitation may be due to physical restrictions: in an experiment with intradermal inoculations into animals, with an individual animal forming a block, there may be a limit to the number of inoculation sites on an animal. The limitation may be one of convenience; if repeated clinical measurements are made on each of a number of patients, it may be undesirable to subject any one patient to more than a few such observations. There may be a time limit; for example if a block consists of observations made on a single day. Sometimes when an adequate number of units can be formed within each block this may be undesirable because it leads to an excessively high degree of within-block variation.

A possible solution to these difficulties lies in the use of an *incomplete block design*, in which only a selection of the treatments is used in any one block. In general this will lead to designs lacking the attractive symmetry of a randomized block design. However, certain designs, called *balanced incomplete block designs*, retain a considerable degree of symmetry. Consider the following design for comparing six treatments in 10 blocks, each containing three units; the allocation of treatments has been randomized within each block.

Block			
1	T_5	T_1	T_2
2	T_1	T_6	T_2
3	T_3	T_4	T_1
4	T_6	T_2	T_1
5	T_1	T_5	T_4
6	T_4	T_2	T_3
7	T_2	T_5	T_3
8	T_6	T_4	T_2
9	T_6	T_5	T_3
10	T_5	T_6	T_4

It is easily verified that in this design each treatment occurs the same number of times (five times) and each pair of treatments occurs together in a block the same number of times (twice). Denote the number of blocks by b, the number of treatments by t, the number of replicates (i.e., repetitions of each treatment) by r, and the number of units per block by k. Then the total number of units can be expressed either as bk or as tr; therefore $bk = tr$. In the example above, $b = 10$, $k = 3$, $t = 6$ and $r = 5$; $bk = tr = 30$.

There are various categories of balanced incomplete block designs, details of which may be found in books on experimental design. The incompleteness of the design introduces some complexity into the analysis. To compare mean effects of different treatments, for example, it is unsatisfactory merely to compare the observed means for all units receiving these treatments, for these means will be affected by differences between blocks. The observed means are therefore adjusted in a certain way to allow for systematic differences between blocks. This is equivalent to obtaining contrasts between treatments solely from within-block differences. For details see Cochran and Cox (1957, section 9.3).

A certain amount of extra information is available from between-block differences. If numbers are attached to blocks at random, and if one treatment (say T_1) has a large effect on the mean response, this should be exhibited not only in within-block differences, but also by the blocks which receive T_1 (in this case blocks 1, 2, 3, 4 and 5) tending to have higher observed means than the rest. However, this between-block information is relatively unimportant in most designs and is usually ignored in the analysis.

YOUDEN SQUARES

These designs are similar to balanced incomplete block designs, but have the further feature that a second source of extraneous variation is controlled by the introduction of a column classification. They bear the same relation to balanced incomplete block designs as do Latin squares to randomized block designs, and for this reason are sometimes called *incomplete Latin squares.* An example is shown below. This is a design for 7 treatments with 7 blocks and 3 columns.

	Column		
	1	2	3
Block			
1	T_1	T_2	T_4
2	T_2	T_3	T_5
3	T_3	T_4	T_6
4	T_4	T_5	T_7
5	T_5	T_6	T_1
6	T_6	T_7	T_2
7	T_7	T_1	T_3

The order in which the treatments are allotted to columns within a block is, of course, important. Columns, blocks and treatments are allocated at random to the relevant factors. Note that, in addition to the balancing features of the incomplete block design, in the Youden square each treatment occurs precisely once in each column. The number of treatments, t, equals the number of blocks, b, and the number of units in a block, k, equals the number of replicates, r. In the above example $t=b=7$ and $k=r=3$.

Youden squares are obtainable from some, but not all, balanced incomplete designs. Some, with $k=t-1$, may be obtained by writing down a Latin square and omitting the last column.

Youden square designs were used in an investigation into the carcinogenic action of mineral oils (Medical Research Council, 1968). In any one experiment on a group of rabbits a large number of treatments had to be compared. The columns of the design represented specific sites on the animals' skins (typically five sites) and the rows represented sub-groups of five rabbits. The variable analysed was the number of tumours (out of five) produced at each site in each sub-group.

In a Youden square the row and column classifications enter into the design in different ways. The number of rows (blocks) is equal to the number of treatments, so each column contains all the treatments; the number of columns is less than the number of treatments, so only a selection of treatments is used in each row. Sometimes designs are needed for two-way control of variability, in situations in which both classifications must be treated in an incomplete way. A type of design called a *set of balanced lattice squares* may be useful here. For a brief description see Cox (1958, section 11.3(iii)); for details see Cochran and Cox (1957, chapter 12).

PARTIALLY BALANCED INCOMPLETE BLOCK DESIGNS

In a balanced incomplete block design all treatments are handled in a symmetric way. All contrasts between pairs of treatments are, for example, estimated with equal precision. Some other incomplete block designs retain some, but not all, of the symmetry of the balanced designs. They may be adopted because of a deliberate wish to estimate some contrasts more precisely than others. Or it may be that physical restrictions on the size of the experiment do not permit any of the balanced designs to be used. *Lattice designs* (not to be confused with lattice squares), in particular, are useful when a large number of treatments is to be compared and where the smallest balanced design is likely to be too large for practical use.

Sometimes it may be necessary to use incomplete block designs which have no degree of symmetry. The analysis of unbalanced block designs is described by Yates (1934b); for some worked examples see Pearce (1965).

FRACTIONAL REPLICATION

If the rows and columns of a Latin square represent different treatment factors and the Latin letters represent a third treatment factor, we have an incomplete factorial design. As we have seen in discussing the analysis of the Latin square, one consequence is that the main effects of the factors can be studied if the interactions are assumed to be absent. There are many other incomplete or *fractional* factorial designs in which only a fraction of all the possible combinations of factor levels are used, with the consequence that not all the main effects or interactions can be separately investigated.

Such designs may be very useful for experiments with a large number of factors in which the number of observations required for a complete factorial experiment is greater than can conveniently be used, or where the main effects can be estimated sufficiently precisely with less than the complete number of observations. If by the use of a fractional factorial design we have to sacrifice the ability to estimate some of the main effects or interactions, it will usually be convenient if we can arrange to lose information about the higher order interactions rather than the main effects or lower order interactions, because the former are unlikely to be large without the latter also appearing large, whereas the converse is not true. A further point to remember is that SSq for high order interactions are often pooled in the analysis of variance to give an estimate of residual variance. The sacrifice of information about some of these will reduce the residual DF, and if this is done too drastically there will be an inadequately precise estimate of error unless an estimate is available from other data.

A simple fractional factorial design may be illustrated by referring to the 2^3 factorial described in section 8.2. The 8 factor combinations at which observations are made may be divided into two sets as follows:

(i)	(a)	(b)	(c)	(abc)
(ii)	(1)	(ab)	(ac)	(bc)

Comparison with (8.16) shows that (i) contains the factor combinations with a positive sign in $[ABC]$, and (ii) contains those with a negative sign. Since $[ABC]$ is a contrast between set (i) and set (ii), if we use only set (i) we cannot possibly estimate $[ABC]$. Can we estimate the main effects or first-order interactions? Consider the contrast

$$\tfrac{1}{2}\{(a)+(abc)-(b)-(c)\}. \qquad (8.19)$$

This estimates the main effect of factor A even if a main effect is present for B or C, or both B and C. (For a occurs in (8.19) with a positive sign only, whereas b and c occur once with a positive sign and once with a negative sign.) However, (8.19) can also be regarded as a method of estimating the interaction $[BC]$, for it can be written

$$\tfrac{1}{2}\{(abc)-(c)\}-\tfrac{1}{2}\{(b)-(a)\},$$

and *if A has no effect* this is the difference between the effect of B when C is present and the effect of B when C is absent, i.e. the interaction $[BC]$. So this design, called a $\frac{1}{2}$ replicate of a 2^3 factorial (or sometimes a 2^{3-1} fractional factorial) can estimate a main effect if any appropriate two-factor interaction is absent, or the two-factor interaction if the main effect is absent, but not both simultaneously. In this example $[ABC]$, which was used to select the half-replicate, is called the *defining contrast*, and $[A]$ and $[BC]$ are called *aliases*; similarly $[B]$ and $[AC]$ are aliases and so are $[C]$ and $[AB]$. Note the relation between the defining contrast and the pairs of aliases.

Fractional factorial designs have been much used in industrial and agricultural work where the simultaneous effects of large numbers of factors have to be studied and where attention very often focusses on the main effects and low order interactions.

CONFOUNDING

Suppose that in the 2^3 factorial, having divided our factor levels into sets (i) and (ii), we allocated set (i) to one block, (say, making the observations during one period of time) and set (ii) to another block. The main effects and two-factor interactions could now be estimated as in the ordinary 2^3 factorial, and would be based on contrasts made *within blocks*. The interaction $[ABC]$ would be based on a contrast between the two blocks, and if the random variation between blocks was large this would adversely affect the precision of estimation of $[ABC]$. However, we are usually less interested in the high-order interactions than those of low order, and may be willing to suffer this loss of precision for the advantages that blocking may bring.

The contrast $[ABC]$ is said to be *confounded* with blocks. There are many ways in which this can be done in factorial experiments. The aim should be to arrange that the contrasts which are of particular interest are estimated within blocks, while those of less interest are estimated between blocks. Exactly how this is done will depend upon the nature of the blocking system of which advantage is to be taken.

8.5 SPLIT-UNIT DESIGNS

In a factorial design in which confounding with blocks takes place, as outlined at the end of section 8.4, two types of random variation are important: the variation between experimental units within a block, and that between blocks. In some simple factorial designs it is convenient to recognize two such forms of experimental unit, one of whch is a subdivision of the other, and to arrange that the levels of some factors are spread across the larger units, while levels of other factors are spread across the smaller units within the larger ones.

This principle was first exploited in agricultural experiments where the designs are called *split-plot designs.* In some field experiments it is convenient to divide the field into 'main plots' and to compare the levels of one factor—say the addition of different soil organisms—by allocating them at random to the main plots. At the same time each main plot is divided into a number of 'sub-plots', and the levels of some other factor—say different fertilizers—are allocated at random to the sub-plots within a main plot, exactly as in a randomized block experiment. The comparison of fertilizers would be subject to the random variation between sub-plots which would be likely to be less than the variation between main plots which affects organism comparisons. The organisms are thus compared less precisely than the fertilizers. This inequality of precision is likely to be accepted because of the convenience of being able to spread organisms over relatively large areas of ground.

Similar situations arise in medical and other types of biological experimentation. In general the experimental units are not referred to as 'plots', and the design is therefore more appropriately called a *split-unit design.* Another term is *nested design.* Some examples of the distinction between main units and sub-units are as follows.

Main unit	Sub-unit
Individual human subject or animal	Different occasions with the same subject or animal
Litter	Animals within a litter
Day	Periods during a day

In the first of these instances a split-unit design might be employed to compare the long-term effects of drugs A_1, A_2 and A_3, and simultaneously the short-term effects of drugs B_1, B_2 and B_3. Suppose there are 12 subjects, each of whom must receive one of A_1, A_2 or A_3; and each subject is observed for three periods during which B_1, B_2 and B_3 are to be given in a random order. The design, determined by randomly allocating the A's to the different subjects and the B's to the periods within subjects, might be as follows.

Patient	*A* drug throughout	*B* drug during period 1	2	3
1	A_3	B_1	B_3	B_2
2	A_1	B_1	B_2	B_3
3	A_1	B_3	B_1	B_2
4	A_2	B_3	B_2	B_1
5	A_3	B_2	B_3	B_1
6	A_2	B_2	B_1	B_3
7	A_1	B_1	B_2	B_3
8	A_3	B_3	B_1	B_2
9	A_3	B_1	B_3	B_2
10	A_2	B_2	B_1	B_3
11	A_1	B_2	B_1	B_3
12	A_2	B_2	B_1	B_3

The analysis of such designs is illustrated in Example 8.6, using data from a survey rather than an experiment.

Example 8.6

The data in Table 8.12 are taken from a survey on the prevalence of upper respiratory tract infection. The variable to be analysed is the number of swabs positive for pneumococcus during a certain period. Observations were made on 18 families, each consisting of a father, a mother and three children, the youngest of whom was always a pre-school child. The children are numbered 1, 2 and 3 in descending order of age. Six families were a random selection of such families living in 'overcrowded' conditions, six were in 'crowded' conditions and six were in 'uncrowded' conditions.

The first point to notice is that two types of random variation are relevant: that between families (the main units in this example) and that between people within families (the sub-units). Comparisons between degrees of crowding must be made *between families*; comparisons of family status are made *within families*. With designs of any complexity it is a good idea to start the analysis by sub-dividing the degrees of freedom. The result is shown in the

TABLE 8.12 Numbers of swabs positive for pneumococcus during fixed periods.

Crowding category	Family serial number	Family status: Father	Mother	Child 1	Child 2	Child 3	Total
Overcrowded	1	5	7	6	25	19	62
	2	11	8	11	33	35	98
	3	3	12	19	6	21	61
	4	3	19	12	17	17	68
	5	10	9	15	11	17	62
	6	9	0	6	9	5	29
		41	55	69	101	114	380
Crowded	7	11	7	7	15	13	53
	8	10	5	8	13	17	53
	9	5	4	3	18	10	40
	10	1	9	4	16	8	38
	11	5	5	10	16	20	56
	12	7	3	13	17	18	58
		39	33	45	95	86	298
Uncrowded	13	6	3	5	7	3	24
	14	9	6	6	14	10	45
	15	2	2	6	15	8	33
	16	0	2	10	16	21	49
	17	3	2	0	3	14	22
	18	6	2	4	7	20	39
		26	17	31	62	76	212
Total		106	105	145	258	276	890

DF column of Table 8.13. The total DF are 89, since there are 90 observations. These are split (as in a one-way analysis of variance) into 17 $(=18-1)$ between families and 72 $(=18\times 4)$ within families. The between-families DF are split (again as in a one-way analysis) into 2 $(=3-1)$ between degrees of crowding and 15 $(=3\times 5)$ for residual variation within crowding categories. The within-families DF are split into 4 $(=5-1)$ between categories of family status, 8 $(=4\times 2)$ for the interaction between the two main effects, and 60 for within-family residual variation. The latter number can be obtained by subtraction $(60=72-4-8)$ or by regarding this source of variation as an interaction between the between-family residual and the status factor $(60=15\times 4)$.

TABLE 8.13 Analysis of variance for data in Table 8.12

	SSq		DF	MSq	VR against *a*	VR against *b*
Between families	1,146·09		17			
Crowding		470·49	2	235·24		5·22*
Residual		675·60	15	45·04[b]	1·78	1·00
Within families	3,122·80		72			
Status		1,533·67	4	383·42	15·17**	
Status × Crowding		72·40	8	9·05	0·36	
Residual		1,516·73	60	25·28[a]	1·00	
	4,268·89		89			

* $0{\cdot}01 < P < 0{\cdot}05$
** $P < 0{\cdot}01$

It may be wondered why the interaction between status and crowding is designated as within families when one main effect is between and the other is within families. The reason is that this interaction measures the extent to which the status differences, which are *within families*, vary from one degree of crowding to another; it is therefore based entirely on within-family contrasts.

The calculation of sums of squares follows familiar lines. Thus

$$\text{Correction term, C.T.} \doteq (890)^2/90 = 8{,}801{\cdot}11$$
$$\text{Total SSq} = 5^2 + 7^2 + \ldots + 20^2 - \text{C.T.} = 4{,}268{\cdot}89$$
$$\text{Between families SSq} = (62^2 + \ldots + 39^2)/5 - \text{C.T.} = 1{,}146{\cdot}09$$
$$\text{Within families SSq} = \text{Total SSq} - \text{Between families SSq} = 3{,}122{\cdot}80$$

Sub-dividing the between families SSq,

$$\text{Crowding SSq} = (380^2 + 298^2 + 212^2)/30 - \text{C.T.} = 470{\cdot}49$$
$$\text{Residual} = \text{Between families SSq} - \text{Crowding SSq} = 675{\cdot}60$$

Sub-dividing the within families SSq,

$$\text{Status SSq} = (106^2 + \ldots + 276^2)/18 - \text{C.T.} = 1{,}533{\cdot}67$$
$$S \times C \text{ SSq} = (41^2 + \ldots + 76^2)/6 - \text{C.T.} - \text{Status SSq} - \text{Crowding SSq} = 72{\cdot}40$$
$$\text{Residual} = \text{Within families SSq} - \text{Status SSq} - S \times C \text{ SSq} = 1{,}516{\cdot}73$$

The variance ratios against the within families residual MSq show that differences due to status are highly significant; we return to these below. The interaction is not significant; there is therefore no evidence that the relative effects of family status vary from one crowding group to another. The variance ratio of 1·78 between the two residuals is just on the borderline of significance at the 5 per cent level. But we should expect *a priori* that the between families residual variance would be greater than that within families, and we must certainly test the main effect for crowding against the between families residual. The variance ratio, 5·22, is significant.

The means for the different members of the family are:

		Child		
F	M	1	2	3
5·9	5·8	8·1	14·3	15·3

The standard error of the difference between two means is $\sqrt{\{2(25 \cdot 28)/18\}} = 1 \cdot 68$. There are clearly no significant differences between the father, mother and eldest child, but the two youngest children have significantly higher means than the other members of the family.

Split-unit designs more elaborate than the design described above may be useful. For example, the structure imposed on the main units (which in Example 8.6 was a simple one-way classification) could be a randomized block design or something more complex. The sub-unit section of the analysis would then be correspondingly enlarged by isolation of the appropriate interactions. Similarly, the sub-unit structure could be elaborated. Another direction of generalization is in the provision of more than two levels in the hierarchy of nested units. In a study similar to that of Example 8.6, for instance, there might have been several periods of observation for each individual, during which different treatments were administered. There would then be a third section in the analysis, within individuals, with its corresponding residual mean square. In none of these cases should the analysis cause any difficulty once the method illustrated above has been grasped.

The following example illustrates a case in which there are three levels of nested units, but in which the design is very simple. There are no structural factors, the purpose of the analysis being merely to estimate the components of random variation.

Example 8.7

Table 8.14 gives counts of particle emission during periods of 1,000 seconds, for 30 aliquots of equal size of certain radioactive material. Each aliquot is placed twice in the counter. There are three sources of random variation, each with its component of variance, as follows.

(a) Variation between aliquots, with a variance component σ_2^2. This may be due to slight variations in size or in radioactivity, or to differences in technique between the 30 occasions on which the different aliquots were examined.

TABLE 8.14 Radioactivity counts during periods of 1,000 seconds.

Aliquot	Counts		Aliquot	Counts	
1	281	291	16	325	267
2	309	347	17	284	296
3	316	356	18	255	281
4	289	277	19	347	285
5	322	292	20	326	302
6	287	321	21	347	307
7	338	320	22	292	344
8	333	275	23	322	308
9	319	311	24	294	272
10	258	302	25	307	303
11	338	294	26	281	331
12	319	281	27	284	322
13	307	247	28	287	305
14	279	259	29	318	352
15	326	272	30	307	301

(b) Systematic variation between replicate counts causing changes in the expected level of the count, with a variance component σ_1^2. This may be due to systematic biases in counting which affect different counts in different ways, or to inconsistency in the apparatus, due perhaps to variation in the way the material is placed in the counter.

(c) Random variation from one time period to another, all other conditions remaining constant; variance component σ_0^2. There is no replication of counts under *constant* conditions, but we know that this form of variation follows the Poisson distribution (section 2.6), in which the variance equals the mean. The mean will vary a little over the whole experiment, but to a close approximation we could estimate σ_0^2 by the observed mean for the whole data, 303·6.

The analysis of variance is that for a simple one-way classification and is as follows:

	SSq	DF	MSq	Expected value of MSq
Between aliquots	19,898	29	686·1	$\sigma_0^2+\sigma_1^2+2\sigma_2^2$
Within aliquots	20,196	30	673·2	$\sigma_0^2+\sigma_1^2$
	40,094	59		
Poisson			303·6	σ_0^2

The expected values of the mean squares follow from section 7.2, if we note that the within aliquots variance component is $\sigma_0^2+\sigma_1^2$ (since differences between replicate counts are affected by variation of both type (b) and type (c)), and that the between aliquots component is σ_2^2.

The estimates of the variance components are now obtained:

$$\sigma_2^2=(686{\cdot}1-673{\cdot}2)/2=\ \ 6{\cdot}4$$

$$\sigma_1^2=673{\cdot}2-303{\cdot}6\quad=369{\cdot}6$$

$$\sigma_0^2=303{\cdot}6.$$

These estimates are, of course, subject to sampling error, but there is clearly no evidence of any large component, σ_2^2, due to aliquot differences. Replicate counts vary, however, by substantially more than can be explained by the Poisson distribution.

8.6 MISSING READINGS

Many sets of data follow too unbalanced a design for any of the standard forms of the analysis of variance to be appropriate. The trouble here is that the various linear contrasts which together represent the sources of variation in which we are interested may not be orthogonal in the sense of section 7.3, and the corresponding sums of squares do not add to the total SSq. A general discussion of the analysis of non-orthogonal designs must be delayed until section 10.4. There are, however, one or two special situations which can conveniently be discussed at this stage. We have referred briefly in section 8.4 to the analysis of unbalanced block designs (Pearce, 1965). In this section we discuss some designs which are balanced except for a small number of missing readings. In section 8.7 we discuss two-way tables with disproportionate cell frequencies.

If an intended observation is missing for some reason or other, a general problem arises. The failure to make the observation may be related to its magnitude; for example, a measuring instrument may fail to record particularly high values. Essential information is then lost and no statistical manipulations can remove the bias caused by this failure. We shall assume in this section that the failure is unrelated to the magnitude of the observation which should have been made.

In a one-way classification no problem arises. The validity of the analysis of variance does not depend on equality of numbers in the various groups. The loss of one observation reduces by one the total frequency in the group concerned, and reduces also by one the degrees of freedom for the Residual SSq and for the Total SSq.

In more complex analyses the estimates of the constants in the linear model are those which minimize the residual sum of squares. Suppose the design has a simple form of replication with r observations at each of the factor combinations used in the design, and that one of the sub-groups has only $r-1$. The Residual SSq, being a SSq *within* sub-groups, does not depend on the estimated row and column effects, and can therefore be calculated directly from the data. The examination of row and column effects is, however, simplified if the missing reading is replaced by the observed mean value for that sub-group, and the analysis carried out as usual except that one degree of freedom is subtracted for the Residual and from the Total SSq.

In a two-way table without replication (as in a simple randomized block experiment), a similar procedure is followed, but the substituted observation now depends on the row and column effects estimated from the rest of the data. It can be shown that the inserted value should be such as to minimize the Residual SSq in the analysis of variance of the data including that value. This criterion leads to a simple use of differential calculus. An equivalent requirement is that the *residual* for the missing unit, calculated after the substitution, should be zero. In the notation of Table 8.1, suppose the observation y_{ij} is missing. This is replaced by the value

$$y'_{ij} = \frac{rR_i + cC_j - T}{(r-1)(c-1)}, \tag{8.20}$$

where R_i, C_j and T are the totals for the affected row, the affected column and the whole set, *ignoring the missing unit*. The usual analysis is then carried out. The Residual SSq and Total SSq have, respectively, $(r-1)(c-1)-1$ and $rc-2$ DF. The Residual MSq correctly estimates the residual variance. The Rows and Columns sums of squares are both rather too high. The correction for the test for columns, for example, is to subtract

$$\frac{\{R_i-(c-1)y'_{ij}\}^2}{c(c-1)^2} \tag{8.21}$$

from the Columns *mean square*. For a comparison between the mean of the affected column and that of another column, the means should be calculated *after* substitution of y'_{ij}. The standard error of the difference between the two means is then

$$\sqrt{\left[s^2\left\{\frac{2}{r}+\frac{c}{r(r-1)(c-1)}\right\}\right]} \tag{8.22}$$

For a Latin square design with the notation of Table 8.9, suppose the missing reading was y_{ijk} in row i, column j and on treatment k. The value to be substituted is

$$y'_{ijk}=\frac{a(R_i+C_j+T_k)-2T}{(a-1)(a-2)}, \tag{8.23}$$

totals being calculated ignoring the missing reading. Again, one DF is lost from the Residual and Total lines of the analysis. The Treatments MSq should be reduced by

$$\frac{\{T-R_i-C_j-(a-1)T_k\}^2}{(a-1)^3(a-2)^2}. \tag{8.24}$$

The standard error of the difference between two treatment means is

$$\sqrt{\left[s^2\left\{\frac{2}{a}+\frac{1}{(a-1)(a-2)}\right\}\right]}. \tag{8.25}$$

If there are two or more missing readings, the principle of minimizing the residual sum of squares, or that of making the residuals for the missing units zero, leads not to simple expressions like (8.20) and (8.23), but to a set of simultaneous linear equations: two equations for two missing readings, three equations for three missing readings, and so on. Alternatively formulae like (8.20) and (8.23) can be used iteratively. For example, if in a randomized block experiment there are two missing readings $y_{(1)}$ and $y_{(2)}$, a provisional value can be inserted for $y_{(1)}$, $y'_{(2)}$ is then calculated from (8.20), then $y'_{(1)}$ is recalculated from (8.20) using the previously calculated value $y'_{(2)}$ instead of $y_{(2)}$; and so on. The process rapidly converges to an equilibrium where further iterations produce no discernible change in the values of $y'_{(1)}$ and $y'_{(2)}$. A degree of freedom must be subtracted from the residual DF for each missing reading. The SSq and MSq for the relevant factors are again biased upwards. Formulae are available, but an alternative method of approach is perhaps more useful in general. Suppose we require the Column MSq in a randomized block design with a few missing readings. Calculate (a) the Residual SSq after substitution by the above rules; (b) the Residual SSq ignoring the column classification, i.e., in a one-way analysis of variance for data classified by rows. The difference (b) – (a) is the required Column SSq. The Column MSq is then obtained by dividing by the usual DF, $c-1$. In the analogous procedure for Latin squares, (b) would require a two-way analysis after substitution of missing readings.

8.7 NON-ORTHOGONAL TWO-WAY TABLES

It was stated in section 8.1 that two-way data with replication can be analysed by the standard method if the cell frequencies, n_{ij}, are proportionate, i.e., proportional to the row and column marginal frequencies. In many cases this is not so. An attempt to use the standard method of analysis may have misleading or even absurd consequences; for example, an interaction SSq may be calculated as a negative quantity!

In certain situations it is unnecessary to apply the relatively complex general solution to be discussed in section 10.4. Some of these situations are described in the present section.

The general approach in this section is as follows. (i) The Residual MSq, s^2, is always obtained from the pooled within-cell variation, for this depends on a one-way classification into Between and Within cells and for this purpose we can have arbitrary cell frequencies. (ii) We next attempt to get an exact or approximate test for interaction. If the interaction is not significant and there is no strong prior supposition that a substantial interaction is present, we proceed to examine main effects of rows and columns. If interaction is deemed to be present we shall not pursue the analysis in any formal way. For fixed-effect factors the interaction is best explored by examining cell means, calculating their standard errors from the Residual MSq. For random effects or a mixed model with interaction, the situation is very complex and is perhaps best tackled by studying simple contrasts between factor levels.

The methods outlined in the following sub-sections are different proposals for step (ii), appropriate in different circumstances.

NEARLY PROPORTIONATE CELL FREQUENCIES

If the n_{ij} are nearly proportionate they may be replaced by 'pseudo-frequencies'

$$n'_{ij}=n_{i.}n_{.j}/N,$$

which are exactly proportional to the marginal frequencies. The observed total, T_{ij}, of the values of y in the (i,j)th cell is now replaced by the pseudo-total

$$T'_{ij}=n'_{ij}\bar{y}_{ij},$$

where $\bar{y}_{ij}$ is the observed mean, T_{ij}/n_{ij}. The analysis of variance then proceeds as though the observed frequencies and totals had been T'_{ij} and n'_{ij}. The pseudo-frequency n'_{ij} may, of course, not be an integer, but this is of no importance from an algebraic point of view. The analysis assumes proportionate frequencies and therefore presents no difficulty. Tests for main effects and for the interaction follow as usual from the variance ratios in the analysis of variance table.

MAIN EFFECTS TESTED BY UNWEIGHTED MEANS

It may sometimes be obvious by inspection (aided, perhaps, by calculation of standard errors of some of the $\bar{y}_{ij}$'s using the Residual MSq), that there is no discernible interaction. If so, we could proceed immediately to test the main effects. This cannot be done solely from the observed row and column totals, for the corresponding means may give quite a false picture of the true row or column effects. Consider the following simple example, in which a glance at the $\bar{y}_{ij}$'s shows that there is no evidence of interaction.

			Column, j				
			1	2	3		
Row, i	1	$\bar{y}_{1j}$	10	12	15	$\bar{y}_{1.}$	13·6
		n_{1j}	*1*	*3*	*6*		
	2	$\bar{y}_{2j}$	12	14	17	$\bar{y}_{2.}$	13·1
		n_{2j}	*6*	*3*	*1*		
		$\bar{y}_{.j}$	11·71	13·00	15·29		

The row means, $\bar{y}_{1.}$ and $\bar{y}_{2.}$, are *weighted* means of the cell means with different weights along the two rows. From the row means, row 1 appears to give a higher response than row 2, whereas in each column row 2 gives the higher response. Similarly, the three column means do not exhibit as sharp a trend across the columns as is shown separately in each row.

To compare means for, say, columns, the rows ought to be weighted in the same way for each column. A simple method is to give equal weights. Thus, for column j, the unweighted mean of the cell means is

$$\bar{y}'_{.j}=(\bar{y}_{1j}+\bar{y}_{2j}+\ldots+\bar{y}_{rj})/r.$$

The variance of $\bar{y}'_{.j}$ is estimated as s^2/W_j, where

$$W_j = \frac{r^2}{\dfrac{1}{n_{1j}} + \dfrac{1}{n_{2j}} + \ldots + \dfrac{1}{n_{rj}}}.$$

The main effect for columns is then represented by the SSq

$$\sum_j W_j(\bar{y}'_{.j})^2 - \frac{(\sum W_j \bar{y}'_{.j})^2}{\sum W_j} \tag{8.26}$$

on $c-1$ DF, and the corresponding MSq can be tested against the Residual MSq (see the notes on 'Weighted analysis' in section 10.1 p. 319).

THE $2 \times c$ OR $r \times 2$ TABLE

If there are only two rows or two columns, an exact solution is available without undue complexity.

Suppose there are two rows: a $2 \times c$ table. With the usual notation for cell means we could estimate the row effect in column j by

$$d_j = \bar{y}_{1j} - \bar{y}_{2j}.$$

The variance of d_j is estimated as s^2/w_j, where

$$w_j = \frac{1}{\dfrac{1}{n_{1j}} + \dfrac{1}{n_{2j}}} = \frac{n_{1j}n_{2j}}{n_{1j}+n_{2j}}. \tag{8.27}$$

The best estimate of overall row effect is the weighted mean of the d_j's:

$$\bar{d} = \sum_j w_j d_j \Big/ \sum_j w_j, \tag{8.28}$$

and the interaction is represented by the weighted SSq of the d_j's about $\bar{d}$:

$$\sum_j w_j (d_j - \bar{d})^2,$$

which can also be written

$$\sum_j w_j d_j^2 - \frac{\left(\sum_j w_j d_j\right)^2}{\sum_j w_j}. \tag{8.29}$$

(8.29), then, is the Interaction SSq in the analysis of variance.

If the MSq from (8.29) is not significant, and we are willing to proceed on the assumption of no interaction, the Rows SSq is given by the second term of (8.29):

$$(\sum w_j d_j)^2 / \sum w_j. \tag{8.30}$$

An analysis of variance may now be formed from the following SSq terms:

Between cells	by the usual formula, using T_{ij}'s
Rows (adjusted for columns)	from (8.30)
Columns (unadjusted)	by the usual formula, using C_j's
Interaction	from (8.29)
Within cells	by the usual formula.

That the three components of the Between cells *SSq* add up correctly can be verified without too much algebraic difficulty. If the three components are calculated separately the Between cells term need not be calculated unless it is needed as an arithmetic check. Note that the Columns (unadjusted) term is of no great interest in its own right, since if a row effect is present the column means will vary partly because of the variable relative weighting given to the two rows.

For a valid test for columns, the column mean can be adjusted for row effects, as explained in Snedecor and Cochran (1957, section 16.6). Alternatively, the adjusted Column SSq can be calculated by subtraction in an alternative subdivision of the Between cells SSq:

(a) Between cells	by the usual formula, using T_{ij}'s
(b) Rows (unadjusted)	by the usual formula, using R_i's
(c) Columns (adjusted for rows)	by subtraction, (a) − (b) − (d)
(d) Interaction	from (8.29).

Example 8.8

Table 8.15 shows the numbers of cerebrovascular accidents experienced during a certain period by 41 men, each of whom had recovered from a previous cerebrovascular accident and was hypertensive. Sixteen of these men received treatment with hypotensive drugs and 25 formed a control group without such treatment. The data are shown in the form of frequency distributions as the variable to be analysed takes only the values 0, 1, 2 and 3. This was not a controlled trial with random allocation, but it was nevertheless useful to enquire whether the difference in the mean numbers of accidents for the two groups was significant, and since the age distributions of the two groups were markedly different it was thought that an allowance for age might

TABLE 8.15 Distributions of numbers of cerebrovascular accidents experienced by males in hypotensive-treated and control groups, subdivided by age.

		Age (years)		
		40–	50–	60–
	Number of accidents	Number of men	Number of men	Number of men
Control group	0	0	3	4
	1	1	3	8
	2	0	4	1
	3	0	1	0
		1	11	13
Treated group	0	4	7	1
	1	0	4	0
		4	11	1

be important. The two rows of Table 8.15 represent the two treatment groups and the three columns represent three age groups.

The preliminary steps of the analysis are shown in the body of Table 8.16. The sum T_{ij} and sum of squares S_{ij} for the n_{ij} observations in the ith row and jth column are obtained as usual for a frequency distribution (cf. Tables 1.8 and 1.13). The remaining entries are straightforward.

The next steps are to calculate the Total and Between cells SSq. The Total SSq is

$$S - \text{C.T.} = 45 - 20{\cdot}5122 = 24{\cdot}4878.$$

The Between cells SSq is

$$(1{\cdot}0000 + 17{\cdot}8182 + \ldots + 0{\cdot}0000) - \text{C.T.} = 7{\cdot}4528.$$

The Within cells SSq follows by subtraction.

The Interaction SSq is, from (8.29),

$$5{\cdot}8949 - 5{\cdot}8706 = 0{\cdot}0243,$$

and the Treatments SSq, adjusted for age, is 5·8706. The unadjusted SSq for age follows by subtraction as

$$7{\cdot}4528 - 5{\cdot}8706 - 0{\cdot}0243 = 1{\cdot}5579,$$

but could also have been obtained directly as

$$\sum_j (C_j^2/n_{\cdot j}) - \text{C.T.} = 22{\cdot}0702 - 20{\cdot}5122$$
$$= 1{\cdot}5580,$$

TABLE 8.16 Analysis of data from Table 8.15.

		Age	40–	50–	60–	All ages		
		j	1	2	3			
Group	i					R_i	n_i	
Control	1	T_{1j}	1	14	10	25		
		n_{1j}	1	11	13		25	
		$\bar{y}_{1j}$	1·0000	1·2727	0·7692			
		S_{1j}	1	28	12			41
		T_{1j}^2/n_{1j}	1·0000	17·8182	7·6923			
Treated	2	T_{2j}	0	4	0	4		
		n_{2j}	4	11	1		16	
		$\bar{y}_{2j}$	0·0000	0·3636	0·0000			
		S_{2j}	0	4	0			4
		T_{2j}^2/n_{2j}	0·0000	1·4545	0·0000			
		C_j	1	18	10	$T=29$		$S=45$
		$n_{.j}$	5	22	14		$N=41$	
		d_j	1·0000	0·9091	0·7692			
		w_j	0·8000	5·5000	0·9286			
		w_jd_j	0·8000	5·0000	0·7143			
		C_j^2/n_j	0·2000	14·7273	7·1429			

C.T., $T^2/N=20·5122$

Analysis of variance

	SSq	DF	MSq	VR
Between cells	7·4528	5		
Treatment (adjusted)	5·8706	1	5·8706	12·06*
Age (unadjusted)	1·5579	2		
T×A	0·0243	2	0·0122	<1
Within cells	17·0350	35	0·4867	1·00
Total	24·4878	40		

	SSq	DF	MSq	VR
Treatment (unadj.)	5·4878	1		
Age (adj.)	1·9407	2	0·9704	1·99

* $P<0·001$

the discrepancy from 1·5579 being due to rounding error. This analysis, shown on the left at the foot of Table 8.16, provides F tests for treatments and for the interaction $T\times A$. The treatment difference is highly significant; the interaction is very small and far from significant.

To test the age effect adjusted for treatments, calculate the Treatment SSq unadjusted:

$$\sum_i (R_i^2/n_{i.}) - \text{C.T.} = 26{\cdot}0000 - 20{\cdot}5122$$
$$= 5{\cdot}4878,$$

and the adjusted Age SSq follows by subtraction:

$$7{\cdot}4528 - 5{\cdot}4878 - 0{\cdot}0243 = 1{\cdot}9407.$$

The F test shows the age effect to be non-significant.

In the original publication (Marshall, 1964) a similar allowance was made for the possible effect of blood pressure, and data from female patients were also included.

For an alternative method of analysis, see Example 10.4, p. 331.

CHAPTER 9
FURTHER ANALYSIS OF STRAIGHT-LINE DATA

9.1 ANALYSIS OF VARIANCE APPLIED TO REGRESSION

In the last two chapters the analysis of variance has been used to study the effect, on the mean value of a random variable, of various types of classification of the data. We now return to the linear regression model of Chapter 5, in which the mean value of y is linearly related to a second variable x, and consider the analysis of variance for this situation.

Suppose, as in section 5.2, that there are n pairs of values, (x_1, y_1), ... (x_i, y_i), ... (x_n, y_n), and that the fitted regression line of y on x has the equation

$$Y = a + bx, \tag{9.1}$$

with a and b given by (5.2) and (5.3).

The deviation of y_i from the mean $\bar{y}$ can be divided into two parts:

$$y_i - \bar{y} = (y_i - Y_i) + (Y_i - \bar{y}), \tag{9.2}$$

where Y_i is the value of y calculated from the regression line (9.1) with $x = x_i$. See Fig. 9.1.

It can be shown that when both sides of (9.2) are squared, and the terms summed from $i = 1$ to n, the sum of the products of the terms on the right is zero, and the following relation holds:

$$\sum(y_i - \bar{y})^2 = \sum(y_i - Y_i)^2 + \sum(Y_i - \bar{y})^2. \tag{9.3}$$

The term on the left is the Total SSq; the first term on the right is the SSq of deviations of observed y's about the regression line, and the second is the SSq about the mean of the values Y_i predicted by the regression line. In short,

Total SSq = SSq about regression + SSq due to regression.

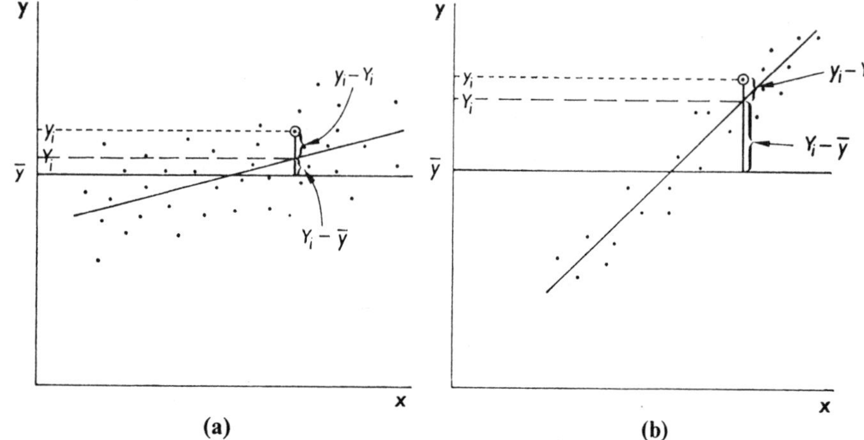

FIG. 9.1 Sub-division of a deviation about the mean into two parts: about regression and due to regression. In (a) the regression of y on x explains a much smaller fraction of the total variation of y than in (b).

In Fig. 9.1(a), most of the Total SSq is explained by the SSq about regression; in Fig. 9.1(b), by contrast, most of the Total SSq is due to regression.

An expression for $\sum(y_i - Y_i)^2$ has already been given in (5.7). From (1.3) and (5.9) the computing formulae shown in Table 9.1 immediately follow (the suffices i have now been dropped).

TABLE 9.1 Analysis of variance for linear regression.

	SSq	DF	MSq	VR
Due to regression	$\dfrac{\{(\sum xy - (\sum x)(\sum y)/n\}^2}{\sum x^2 - (\sum x)^2/n}$	1	s_1^2	s_1^2/s_0^2
About regression	by subtraction	$n-2$	s_0^2	
Total	$\sum y^2 - (\sum y)^2/n$	$n-1$		

Suppose, as in section 5.2, that the y's are distributed independently and normally, with variance σ^2, about expected values given by

$$E(y) = \alpha + \beta x. \tag{9.4}$$

The null hypothesis that $\beta = 0$ (that is, that the expectation of y is constant, irrespective of the value of x) may be tested by the analysis of variance in Table 9.1. If $\beta = 0$, s_1^2 and s_0^2 are independent unbiased estimates of σ^2. If $\beta \neq 0$, s_0^2 is an unbiased estimate of σ^2 (see (5.8)) but s_1^2 estimates a quantity *greater* than σ^2. The variance ratio $F = s_1^2/s_0^2$, on 1 and $n-2$ DF, may therefore be used to test whether $\beta = 0$.

The significance of the regression slope has previously been tested by

$$t = \frac{b}{\mathrm{SE}(b)} = \frac{b}{s_0/\sqrt{\sum(x-\bar{x})^2}}$$

on $n-2$ DF (as in (5.18) and (5.20)). Using the formula (5.3) for b, it is easy to see that $F = t^2$, and (as noted for example in sections 4.10 and 7.1) the tests are equivalent.

Example 9.1

The analysis of variance of y, from the data of Example 5.1 (sections 5.2 and 5.4) is as follows:

	SSq	DF	MSq	VR	
Due to regression	7,666·39	1	7,666·39	24·2	($P<0{\cdot}01$)
About regression	9,502·08	30	316·74	1·00	
	17,168·47	31			

The SSq have already been obtained in sections 5.2 and 5.4. The value of t obtained previously was $-4{\cdot}92$; note that $(4{\cdot}92)^2 = 24{\cdot}2$, the value of F.

TEST FOR LINEARITY

It is often important to know not only whether the slope of an assumed linear regression is significant, but also whether there is any reason to doubt the basic assumption of the linearity of the regression.

If the data provide a number of replicate readings of y for certain values of x, a test of linearity is easily obtained. Suppose that, at the value x_i of x, there are n_i observations on y, with a mean $\bar{y}_i$. Each such group of replicates is called an *array*. Fig. 9.2 illustrates three different situations. In (a) a linear regression seems to be consistent with the observed data in that the array means $\bar{y}_i$ are reasonably close to the regression line. In (b) and (c), however, the array means deviate from the line by more than can easily be explained by the within-array variation. In (b) the deviations seem to be systematic, suggesting that a curved regression line is required. In (c) the deviations seem to be patternless, suggesting perhaps an extra source of variation associated with each array; for example, if each array referred to observations on animals in a single cage the positioning of the cage in the laboratory might affect the whole array.

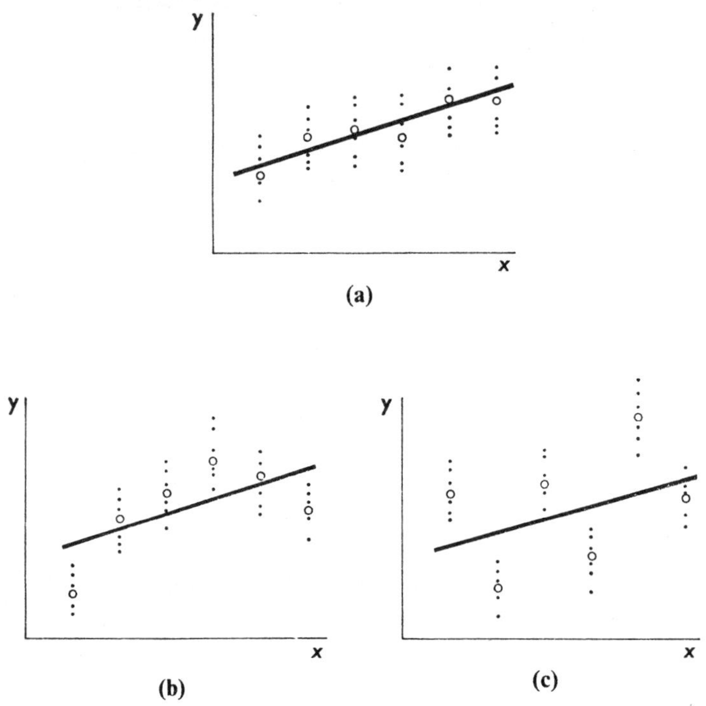

FIG. 9.2 Deviations of array means from linear regression. Those in (a) are explicable by within-array variation; those in (b) suggest a systematic departure from linearity; while those in (c) suggest a further source of variation.

In discussing Fig. 9.2 we made a rough comparison of the magnitude of deviations of array means from the regression line with the within-array variation. The comparison is made formally as follows. For any value y in the array corresponding to x_i, the residual $y-Y_i$ may be divided into two parts:

$$y-Y_i=(y-\bar{y}_i)+(\bar{y}_i-Y_i). \tag{9.5}$$

When both sides are squared and summed over all observations, the sum of products of the two terms on the right vanishes, and we have a partition of the Residual SSq:

$$\sum(y-Y_i)^2=\sum(y-\bar{y}_i)^2+\sum(\bar{y}_i-Y_i)^2, \tag{9.6}$$

the summations being taken over all n observations. The first term on the right is the SSq about array means; the second term is the SSq of deviations of array means from the regression line. The first of these is precisely what would be obtained as the Within arrays SSq in a one-way analysis of variance of the y's without reference to the x's.

TABLE 9.2 Analysis of variance with test for linearity.

	SSq	DF	MSq	VR
Due to regression	(as in Table 9.1)	1	s_1^2	$F_1 = s_1^2/s_3^2$
Deviation of array means from regression	by subtraction	$k-2$	s_2^2	$F_2 = s_2^2/s_3^2$
Within array residual	$\sum y^2 - \sum_i (T_i^2/n_i)$	$n-k$	s_3^2	
Total	$\sum y^2 - (\sum y)^2/n$	$n-1$		

The computing formulae are given in Table 9.2. Here k is the number of arrays, and T_i is the sum of values of y for the ith array. The variance ratio F_2 tests the deviation of the array means about linear regression, and F_1 tests the departure of β from zero assuming linear regression. If F_2 is not significant and $n-k$ is rather small it may be useful to combine the SSq in the second and third lines of the analysis, taking one back to Table 9.1. If F_2 is significant, thought should be given to the question whether the non-linearity is of type (b) or type (c). If it is of type (b), some form of non-linear regression should be fitted; see section 10.3. Type (c) may be handled approximately by testing s_1^2 against s_2^2 by a variance ratio $F_1' = s_1^2/s_2^2$ on 1 and $k-2$ DF.

Example 9.2

In one method of assaying vitamin D, rats are fed on a diet deficient in vitamin D for two weeks so as to develop rickets. The diet is then supplemented by one of a number of different doses of a standard vitamin D preparation or of a test preparation which is to be assayed against the standard. After a further two weeks the degree to which the rickets has been healed is assessed by radiographing the right knee of each animal. The photograph is matched against a standard set of photographs numbered from 0 to 12 (in increasing order of healing).

The results shown in Table 9.3 were obtained with three doses of vitamin D. Each score is the average of four assessments of a single photograph. General experience with this type of assay suggests a linear regression of the score, y, on the log dose, x.

TABLE 9.3 Radiographic assessments of bone healing for three doses of vitamin D.

Dose (i.u.)	3·5	7	14	
Log dose, x_i	0·544	0·845	1·146	
	0	1·50	2·00	
	0	2·50	2·50	
	1·00	5·00	5·00	
	2·75	6·00	4·00	
	2·75	4·25	5·00	
	1·75	2·75	4·00	
	2·75	1·50	2·50	
	2·25	3·00	3·50	
	2·25		3·00	
	2·50		2·00	
			3·00	
			4·00	
			4·00	
				Total
T_i	18·00	26·50	44·50	89·00
n_i	10	8	13	31
$\bar{y}_i$	1·8000	3·3125	3·4231	
$\sum y^2$	43·1250	106·3750	164·7500	314·2500
T_i^2/n_i	32·4000	87·7813	152·3269	

Analysis of variance

	SSq	DF	MSq	VR	
Due to regression	14·0880	1	14·0880	9·45	($P<0·01$)
Deviations of dose means	2·9041	1	2·9041	1·95	($P>0·05$)
Within dose residual	41·7418	28	1·4908	1·00	
Total	58·7339	30			

The Total SSq is

$$314{\cdot}2500-(89{\cdot}00)^2/31=58{\cdot}7339,$$

and the Within dose residual SSq is

$$314{\cdot}2500-(32{\cdot}4000+87{\cdot}7813+152{\cdot}3269)=41{\cdot}7418.$$

The calculation of the SSq due to regression makes use of the fact that only three values of x occur. Thus,

$$\sum x=10(0{\cdot}544)+8(0{\cdot}845)+13(1{\cdot}146)=27{\cdot}098$$

$$\sum(x-\bar{x})^2=10(0{\cdot}544)^2+8(0{\cdot}845)^2+13(1{\cdot}146)^2-(27{\cdot}098)^2/31=2{\cdot}0576$$

and

$$\Sigma(x-\bar{x})(y-\bar{y})=(0{\cdot}544)(18{\cdot}00)+(0{\cdot}845)(26{\cdot}50)+(1{\cdot}146)(44{\cdot}50)$$
$$-(27{\cdot}098)(89{\cdot}00)/31=5{\cdot}3840,$$

from which

$$\text{SSq due to regression}=(5{\cdot}3840)^2/2{\cdot}0576=14{\cdot}0880.$$

The variance ratio for deviations of dose means is not significant, and the conclusion that the regression is effectively linear is reinforced by general experience with this assay method. The regression slope is, of course, highly significant.

If the observations do not fall into arrays at fixed values of x, the testing of linearity is less simple. It is often adequate to form groups along the x-scale, and treat the data as though the arrays corresponded to the mid-points of the groups of x. Alternatively one can use the methods of section 10.3 to fit non-linear regression curves.

9.2 ERRORS IN BOTH VARIABLES

In studying the regression of y on x it has not been necessary to consider any form of random variation in the values of x. Clearly, in many sets of data, the values of x do vary randomly—either because the individual units on which the measurements are made are selected by an effectively random process, or because any observation on x is affected by measurement error or some other form of random perturbation. In the standard regression formulation these considerations are irrelevant. There are, however, some questions rather different from those answered by regression analysis in which random errors in x are relevant. These are, basically, questions involving the values of x which would have been observed had there been no random error.

Suppose that any pair of observed values (x, y) can be regarded as differing by random errors from a pair of 'true values' (X, Y) which are linearly related. Thus

$$Y=\alpha+\beta X, \tag{9.7}$$

where we observe

$$x=X+\delta$$

and

$$y=Y+\epsilon, \tag{9.8}$$

and δ and ϵ are distributed independently of each other and also independently of X and Y. Suppose that δ is distributed as $N(0, \sigma_\delta^2)$ and ϵ as $N(0, \sigma_\epsilon^2)$. See Fig. 9.3.

The first point to emphasize is that if the problem is to predict the behaviour of y or Y in terms of x (the *observed* value), ordinary regression analysis is appropriate. In many situations this is the case. If y is a measure of clinical change and x is a biochemical measurement, the purpose of an analysis may be to study the extent to which y can be predicted from x. Any value of x used in the analysis will be subject to random variation due to physiological fluctuations and measurement error, but this fact can be disregarded because predictions will be made from values of x which are equally subject to such variation.

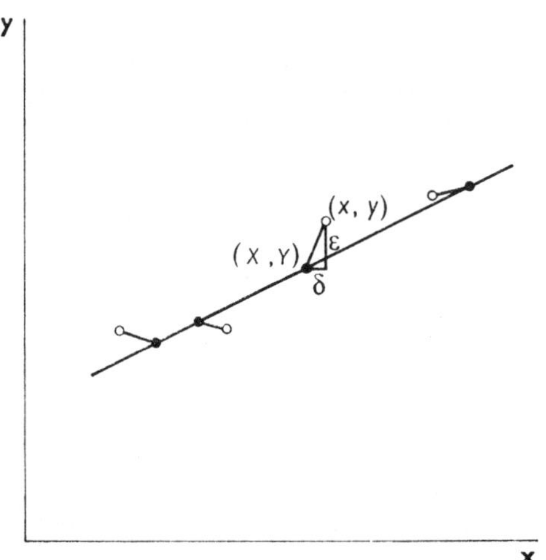

FIG. 9.3 Deviations of observed values from a linear functional relationship with errors in both variables.

Suppose, however, that the purpose is to estimate the value of β, the slope of the line relating Y to X (not to x). This problem is likely to arise in two different circumstances:

(a) The 'true' value X may be of much more interest than the 'observed' value, x, because future discussions will be in terms of X rather than x. For instance, in a geographic survey, x may be the mean household size of a certain town as estimated from the survey and y some measure of health in that town. The size of the random error component in x may be peculiar to this particular survey and of no relevance in future work. Any arguments should be based on the effect, on y, of changes in the true mean household size, X.

(b) The equation (9.7) may express a *functional relationship* between the true values X and Y, which is of particular scientific importance.

For instance, if X and Y are, respectively, the volume and mass of different specimens of a metal, equation (9.7) with $\alpha=0$ would clearly represent the relationship between X and Y with β measuring the density. The estimation of β would be a reasonable objective, but the complication arises that both X and Y are affected by random measurement errors, so that the investigator observes pairs of values (x, y).

The estimation of α and β from pairs of observed values (x, y) is a difficult problem (Kendall, 1951, 1952; Sprent, 1969). One general result is that b, the regression coefficient of y on x, *underestimates* β on the average. The expected value of b is approximately

$$\beta' = \beta\left\{1 - \frac{\sigma_\delta^2}{\text{var}(x)}\right\}. \tag{9.9}$$

If σ_δ^2 can be estimated (for example, by a special experimental study involving replicate observations of the same X), the correction term in brackets can be estimated, and a correction applied to the estimated slope b.

In many situations no direct estimate of σ_δ^2 will be possible because there is no way of selecting observations with different values of x but the same value of X. Usually the situation here is that a set of pairs (x, y) show some general linear trend which the investigator wishes to represent by a single straight line without making the distinction between x and y required in a regression analysis. He should make quite sure that any subsequent use of the line will not put either variable in the role of a predictor variable, and that a single line will perform a useful function in representing the general trend. If there is insufficient basis for any reasonable assumptions about σ_δ^2 and σ_ε^2 a simple visual approach is probably best: draw a freehand line through the cluster and refrain from any assertions of sampling error.

An interesting special situation is that in which x is a *controlled variable*. Suppose that x is known to differ from X by a random error, as in (9.8), but that the value of x is selected by the experimenter. For example, in drawing liquid into a pipette the experimenter may aim at a specified volume x, and would assume that he had carried out the experiment with a value x, although the true value X would differ from x by a random error. If there is no systematic bias, (9.8) will represent the situation, but the important difference between this problem and that considered earlier is that the random error δ is independent of x, whereas previously δ was independent of X. It follows, as Berkson (1950) pointed out, that the regression coefficient of y on x *does* in this case provide an unbiased estimate of β, and standard methods of regression analysis are appropriate.

9.3 STRAIGHT LINES THROUGH THE ORIGIN

Sometimes there may be good reason to suppose that a regression line must pass through the origin, in the sense that when $x=0$ the mean value of y must also be 0. For instance, in a psychological experiment the subject may be asked to guess how far a certain light falls to the left or to the right of a marker. If the guessed distance to the right is y (distances to the left corresponding to $y<0$) and the true distance is x, a subject whose responses showed no bias to left or right would have $E(y)=0$ when $x=0$.

The regression of y on x will then take the form

$$Y=\beta x, \tag{9.10}$$

and the least squares solution is similar to that of the ordinary regression formulae, except that sums of squares and products are not corrected for deviations about mean values. Thus, β is estimated by

$$b=\sum xy/\sum x^2, \tag{9.11}$$

and the SSq about regression is

$$\sum y^2-(\sum xy)^2/\sum x^2$$

on $n-1$ (*not* $n-2$) DF.

This result assumes, as usual, that the residual variance of y is independent of x. In many problems in which a line through the origin seems appropriate, particularly for variables which take *positive* values only, this is clearly not so. There is often a tendency for the variability of y to increase as x increases. Two other least squares solutions are useful here:

(a) If the residual var(y) increases in proportion to x, the best estimate of β is $b_1=\sum y/\sum x=\bar{y}/\bar{x}$, the ratio of the two means. An example of this situation would occur in a radioactivity counting experiment where the same material is observed for replicate periods of different lengths. If x_i is a time interval and y_i the corresponding count, Poisson theory shows that $\text{var}(y_i)=E(y_i\,|\,x_i)\propto x_i$. The estimate of the mean count per unit time is, as would be expected, $\sum y_i/\sum x_i$, the total count divided by the total time period.

(b) If the residual *standard deviation* of y increases in proportion to x, the best estimate of β is $b_2 = \sum(y/x)/n$, the mean of the individual ratios.

Care should be taken to enquire whether a regression line, rather than a functional relationship (section 9.2), is really needed in such problems. Suppose that x and y are estimates of a biochemical substance obtained by two different methods. If y is the estimate by the more reliable method, and x is obtained by a rapid but rather less reliable method, it may be reasonable to estimate y from x, and one of the above methods may be appropriate. If the question is rather 'How big are the discrepancies between x and y?' there is no reason to treat the problem as one of the regression of y on x rather than x on y. A useful device here is to rewrite (9.10) as

$$\log Y = \log \beta + \log x,$$

and to take the individual values of $z = \log y - \log x$ as estimates of $\log \beta$. If random variation in z is approximately independent of x or y (and this can be checked by simple scatter diagrams), the mean value of z will be the best estimate of $\log \beta$, confidence limits being obtained by the t distribution as is usual for a mean value. This situation is roughly equivalent to (b) above. If random variation in z depends heavily on x or y the observations could be grouped and some form of weighted average taken.

9.4 REGRESSION IN GROUPS

Frequently data are classified into groups, and within each group a linear regression of y on x may be postulated. For example, the regression of forced expiratory volume on age may be considered separately for men in different occupational groups. Possible differences between the regression lines are then often of interest.

In this section we consider comparisons of the slopes of the regression lines. If the slopes clearly differ, from one group to another, then so, of course, must the mean values of y—at least for some values of x. In Fig. 9.4(a), the slopes of the regression lines differ from group to group. The lines for groups (i) and (ii) cross. Those for (i) and (iii) and for (ii) and (iii) would also cross if extended sufficiently far, but here there is some doubt as to whether the linear regressions would remain valid outside the range of values of x observed.

If the slopes do not differ, the lines are parallel as in Fig. 9.4(b) and (c) and here it becomes interesting to ask whether, as in (b), the lines differ in their height above the x axis (which depends on the coefficient α in the equation $E(y)=\alpha+\beta x$), or whether, as in (c) the lines coincide. In practice the fitted regression lines would rarely have *precisely* the

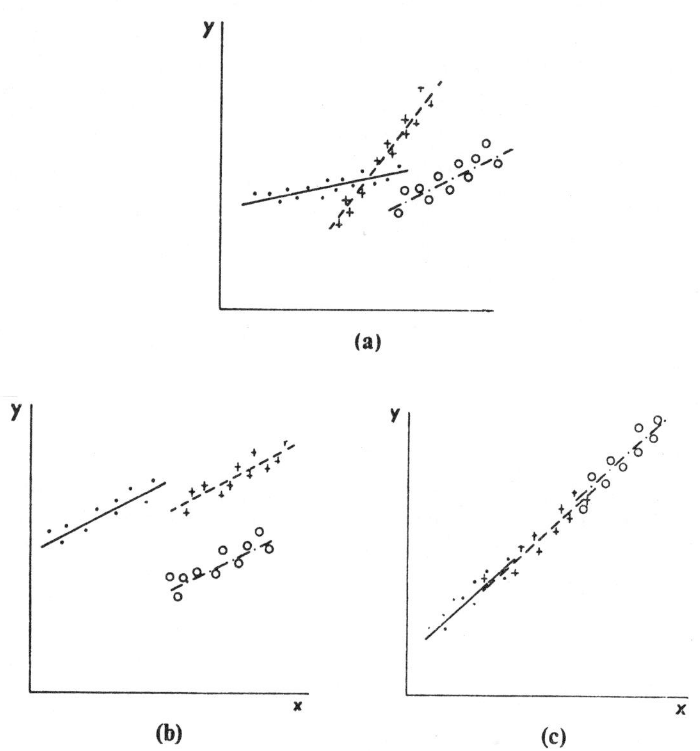

FIG. 9.4 Differences between regression lines fitted to three groups of observations. The lines differ in slope and position in (a), differ only in position in (b), and coincide in (c) (i)—— (ii) - - - (iii) —·— .

same slope or position, and the question is to what extent differences between the lines can be attributed to random variation. Differences in position between parallel lines are discussed in section 9.5. In this section we concentrate on the question of differences between slopes.

Suppose that there are k groups, with n_i pairs of observations in the ith group. Denote the mean values of x and y in the ith group by $\bar{x}_i$ and $\bar{y}_i$, and the regression line calculated as in section 5.2 by

$$Y_i=\bar{y}_i+b_i(x-\bar{x}_i). \tag{9.12}$$

If all the n_i are reasonably large a satisfactory approach is to estimate the variance of each b_i by (5.18) and to ignore the imprecision in these estimates of variance. Changing the notation of (5.18) somewhat, we shall denote the residual mean square for the ith group by s_i^2 and the sum of squares of x about $\bar{x}$ by $\sum_i(x-\bar{x}_i)^2$. Following a method similar to that used at (7.12) for comparing means, we write

$$w_i = \frac{1}{\text{var}(b_i)} = \frac{\sum_i(x-\bar{x}_i)^2}{s_i^2}, \qquad (9.13)$$

and calculate

$$G = \sum w_i b_i^2 - (\sum w_i b_i)^2 / \sum w_i. \qquad (9.14)$$

On the null hypothesis that the true slopes β_i are all equal, G follows approximately a $\chi^2_{(k-1)}$ distribution. High values of G indicate departures from the null hypothesis, i.e. real differences between the β_i. If G is nonsignificant, and the null hypothesis is tentatively accepted, the common value β of the β_i is best estimated by the weighted mean

$$\bar{b} = \sum w_i b_i / \sum w_i, \qquad (9.15)$$

with an estimated variance

$$\text{var}(\bar{b}) = 1/\sum w_i. \qquad (9.16)$$

The sampling variation of $\bar{b}$ is approximately normal.

It is difficult to say how large the n_i must be for this 'large-sample' approach to be used with safety. There would probably be little risk in adopting it if none of the n_i fell below 20.

A more exact treatment is available provided an extra assumption is made—that the residual variances σ_i^2 are all equal. Suppose the common value is σ^2. We consider first the situation where $k=2$, as a comparison of two slopes can be effected by use of the t distribution. For $k>2$ an analysis of variance is required.

TWO GROUPS

The residual variance σ^2 can be estimated either as

$$s_1^2 = \frac{\sum_1(y-Y_1)^2}{n_1-2} = \frac{\sum_1(y-\bar{y}_1)^2 - \{\sum_1(x-\bar{x}_1)(y-\bar{y}_1)\}^2/\sum_1(x-\bar{x}_1)^2}{n_1-2}$$

or by the corresponding mean square for the second group, s_2^2. (Note that the suffix 1 or 2 attached to the summation sign indicates summation only over the specified group.) A pooled estimate may be obtained (very much as in the two-sample t test for comparing means) as

$$s^2 = \frac{\sum_1(y-Y_1)^2+\sum_2(y-Y_2)^2}{n_1+n_2-4}. \qquad (9.17)$$

To compare b_1 and b_2 we estimate

$$\mathrm{var}(b_1-b_2)=s^2\left\{\frac{1}{\sum_1(x-\bar{x}_1)^2}+\frac{1}{\sum_2(x-\bar{x}_2)^2}\right\}. \qquad (9.18)$$

The difference is tested by

$$t=\frac{b_1-b_2}{\sqrt{\{\mathrm{var}(b_1-b_2)\}}} \text{ on } n_1+n_2-4 \text{ DF}. \qquad (9.19)$$

the DF being the divisor in (9.17).

If a common value is assumed for the regression slope in the two groups, its value β may be estimated by

$$b=\frac{\sum_1(x-\bar{x}_1)(y-\bar{y}_1)+\sum_2(x-\bar{x}_2)(y-\bar{y}_2)}{\sum_1(x-\bar{x}_1)^2+\sum_2(x-\bar{x}_2)^2}, \qquad (9.20)$$

with a variance estimated as

$$\mathrm{var}(b)=s^2/\{\textstyle\sum_1(x-\bar{x}_1)^2+\sum_2(x-\bar{x}_2)^2\}. \qquad (9.21)$$

Equations (9.20) and (9.21) can easily be seen to be equivalent to (9.15) and (9.16) if, in the calculation of w_i in (9.13) the separate estimates of residual variance s_i^2 are replaced by the common estimate s^2. For tests or the calculation of confidence limits for β using (9.21) the t distribution on n_1+n_2-4 may be used.

Example 9.3

In the assay described in Example 9.2, the other preparations were tested against the standard vitamin D preparation. Values of the score, y, representing degree of healing are shown for all three groups in Table 9.4. The mean values of y for the various doses of each preparation are plotted against the log dose, x, in Fig. 9.5.

The sums of squares and products of deviations about the mean, and the separate slopes b_i, are calculated as in Example 9.2. They are as follows:

Group	i	n_i	$\sum_i(x-\bar{x}_i)^2$	$\sum_i(x-\bar{x}_i)(y-\bar{y}_i)$	$\sum_i(y-\bar{y}_i)^2$	b_i
Standard	1	31	2·0576	5·3840	58·7339	2·6166
I	2	30	5·4361	15·2005	63·8417	2·7962
F	3	17	1·0872	5·3427	43·6176	4·9142
		78	8·5809	25·9272	166·1932	(3·0215)

TABLE 9.4 Radiographic assessment of bone healing for various doses of three preparations.

Standard preparation of vitamin D						
Dose (i.u.)	3·5	7	14			Total
Log dose, x	0·544	0·845	1·146			
	0	1·50	2·00			
	0	2·50	2·50			
	1·00	5·00	5·00			
	2·75	6·00	4·00			
	2·75	4·25	5·00			
	1·75	2·75	4·00			
	2·75	1·50	2·50			
	2·25	3·00	3·50			
	2·25		3·00			
	2·50		2·00			
			3·00			
			4·00			
			4·00			
Number	10	8	13			31
Mean	1·8000	3·3125	3·4231			
Preparation I						
Dose (mg)	2·5	5	10	20	40	
Log dose, x	0·398	0·699	1·000	1·301	1·602	
	0	1·00	1·50	3·00	3·50	
	1·00	1·50	1·00	3·00	3·50	
	0	1·50	2·00	5·50	4·50	
	0	1·00	3·50	2·50	3·50	
	0	1·00	2·00	1·00	3·50	
	0·50	0·50	0	2·00	3·00	
Number	6	6	6	6	6	30
Mean	0·2500	1·0833	1·6667	2·8333	3·5833	
Preparation F						
Dose (mg)	2·5	5	10			
Log dose, x	0·398	0·699	1·000			
	2·75	2·50	3·75			
	2·00	2·75	5·25			
	1·25	2·25	6·00			
	2·00	2·25	5·50			
	0	3·75	2·25			
	0·50		3·50			
Number	6	5	6			17
Mean	1·4167	2·7000	4·3750			

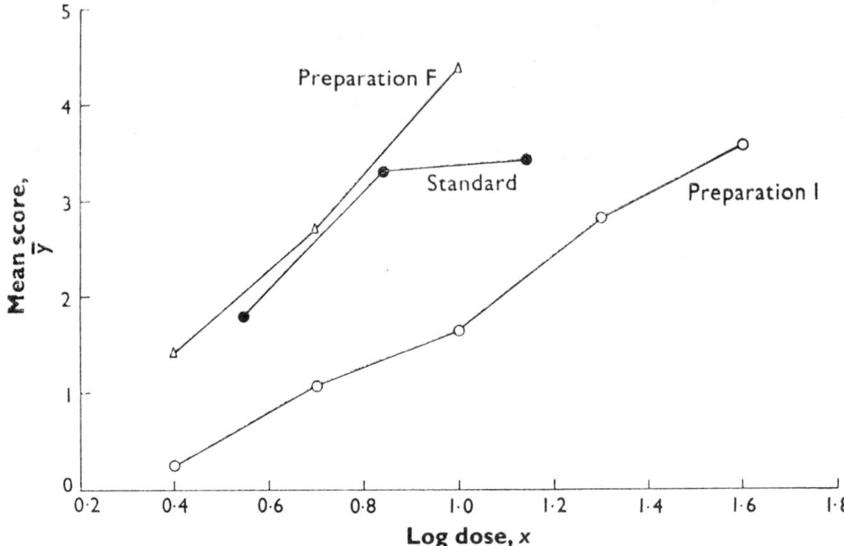

FIG. 9.5 Scores for bone healing in an assay of vitamin D (Table 9.4).

(Note that in Example 9.2, the suffix i distinguished the three doses of one preparation; here it distinguishes the preparation.) We shall test the differences between all three groups later in this section. For the moment, consider the vitamin D standard ($i=1$) and preparation I ($i=2$). The SSq about regression for the vitamin D group is obtained from Table 9.3 by pooling the second and third lines of the analysis. Or, directly,

$$\Sigma_1(y-Y_1)^2=58\cdot7339-(5\cdot3840)^2/2\cdot0576=44\cdot6458$$

and

$$\Sigma_2(y-Y_2)^2=63\cdot8417-(15\cdot2005)^2/5\cdot4361=21\cdot3379.$$

Thus,

$$s^2=(44\cdot6458+21\cdot3379)/(31+30-4)=1\cdot1576$$

and, for the difference between b_1 and b_2,

$$t=\frac{2\cdot6166-2\cdot7962}{\sqrt{\left\{(1\cdot1576)\left(\frac{1}{2\cdot0576}+\frac{1}{5\cdot4361}\right)\right\}}}$$

$$=-0\cdot1796/0\cdot8807$$

$$=-0\cdot20 \text{ on 57 DF.}$$

The difference is clearly not significant. This example is continued on p. 287.

MORE THAN TWO GROUPS

With any number of groups the pooled slope b is given by the generalization of (9.20):

$$b=\frac{\sum_i \sum_i (x-\bar{x}_i)(y-\bar{y}_i)}{\sum_i \sum_i (x-\bar{x}_i)^2}. \qquad (9.22)$$

To simplify the notation, denote the sum of squares about the mean of x in the ith group by

$$(Sx^2)_i \text{ instead of } \textstyle\sum_i (x-\bar{x}_i)^2, \qquad (9.23)$$

the sum of products of deviations $(Sxy)_i$, and so on. Then (9.22) may be written

$$b=\frac{\sum_i (Sxy)_i}{\sum_i (Sx^2)_i}. \qquad (9.24)$$

Parallel lines may now be drawn through the mean points $(\bar{x}_i, \bar{y}_i)$, each with the same slope b. That for the ith group will have this equation:

$$Y_{ci}=\bar{y}_i+b(x-\bar{x}_i). \qquad (9.25)$$

The suffix c is used to indicate that the predicted value Y_{ci} is obtained using the *common* slope, b.

The deviation of any observed value y from its group mean $\bar{y}_i$ may be divided as follows:

$$y-\bar{y}_i=(y-Y_i)+(Y_i-Y_{ci})+(Y_{ci}-\bar{y}_i). \qquad (9.26)$$

Again, it can be shown that the sums of squares of these components can be added in the same way. This means that

Within groups SSq = Residual SSq about separate lines

+ SSq due to differences between b_i's and b

+ SSq due to fitting common slope b. (9.27)

The middle term on the right is the one that particularly concerns us now. It can be obtained by noting that the SSq due to the common slope is

$$\left\{\sum_i (Sxy)_i\right\}^2 \Big/ \sum_i (Sx^2)_i; \qquad (9.28)$$

this follows directly from (5.7) and (9.24). From previous results,

$$\text{Within groups SSq} = \sum_i (Sy^2)_i \tag{9.29}$$

and Residual SSq about separate lines

$$= \sum_i \{(Sy^2)_i - (Sxy)_i^2/(Sx^2)_i\}. \tag{9.30}$$

From (9.27), (9.28), (9.29) and (9.30),

$$\text{SSq due to differences in slope} = \sum_i \frac{(Sxy)_i^2}{(Sx^2)_i} - \frac{\left\{\sum_i (Sxy)_i\right\}^2}{\sum_i (Sx^2)_i}. \tag{9.31}$$

It should be noted that (9.31) is equivalent to

$$\sum_i W_i b_i^2 - \frac{\left(\sum_i W_i b_i\right)^2}{\sum_i W_i} \tag{9.32}$$

where $W_i = (Sx^2)_i = \sigma^2/\text{var}(b_i)$, and that the pooled slope b equals $\sum W_i b_i / \sum W_i$, the weighted mean of the b_i's. The SSq due to differences in slope is thus essentially a weighted sum of squares of the b_i's about their weighted mean b, the weights being (as usual) inversely proportional to the sampling variances.

The analysis is summarized in Table 9.5. There is only one DF for the common slope, since the SSq is proportional to the square of one linear contrast, b. The $k-1$ DF for the second line follows because the

TABLE 9.5 Analysis of variance for differences between regression slopes.

	SSq	DF	MSq	VR
Due to common slope	$\dfrac{\left\{\sum_i (Sxy)_i\right\}^2}{\sum_i (Sx^2)_i}$	1		
Differences between slopes	$\sum_i \dfrac{(Sxy)_i^2}{(Sx^2)_i} - \dfrac{\left\{\sum_i (Sxy)_i\right\}^2}{\sum_i (Sx^2)_i}$	$k-1$	s_A^2	$F_A = s_A^2/s^2$
Residual about separate lines	$\sum_i (Sy^2)_i - \sum_i \dfrac{(Sxy)_i^2}{(Sx^2)_i}$	$n-2k$	s^2	
Within groups	$\sum_i (Sy^2)_i$	$n-k$		

SSq measures differences between k independent slopes, b_i. The residual DF follows because there are n_i-2 DF for the ith group and $\sum_i (n_i-2) = n-2k$. The total DF within groups is, correctly, $n-k$. The F test for differences between slopes follows immediately.

Example 9.3 (continued)

We now test the significance of differences between the three slopes, using the calculations summarized on p. 282.

The SSq due to the common slope is

$$(25{\cdot}9272)^2/8{\cdot}5809 = 78{\cdot}3391.$$

The Residual SSq about the separate lines has already been obtained for the Standard and Preparation I:

$$\Sigma_1(y-Y_1)^2 = 44{\cdot}6458;\ \Sigma_2(y-Y_2)^2 = 21{\cdot}3379.$$

Similarly, for preparation F, $\Sigma_3(y-Y_3)^2 = 17{\cdot}3626$. The Residual SSq about separate lines is therefore

$$44{\cdot}6458 + 21{\cdot}3379 + 17{\cdot}3626 = 83{\cdot}3463.$$

The Within groups SSq is, from p. 282, 166·1932. The SSq for differences between slopes may now be obtained by subtraction, as

$$166{\cdot}1932 - 78{\cdot}3391 - 83{\cdot}3463 = 4{\cdot}5078.$$

Alternatively, it may be calculated directly as

$$\frac{(5{\cdot}3840)^2}{2{\cdot}0576} + \frac{(15{\cdot}2005)^2}{5{\cdot}4361} + \frac{(5{\cdot}3427)^2}{1{\cdot}0872} - \frac{(25{\cdot}9272)^2}{8{\cdot}5809} = 4{\cdot}5078.$$

The analysis of variance can now be completed.

	SSq	DF	MSq	VR	
Common slope	78·3391	1	78·3391	67·67	
Between slopes	4·5078	2	2·2539	1·95	$(P>0{\cdot}05)$
Separate residuals	83·3463	72	1·1576	1·00	
Within groups	166·1932	75			

The common slope is highly significant. The introduction of the third group, Preparation F, for which the estimated slope is considerably higher than for the other two groups, has resulted in a rather large variance ratio between slopes, but the significance is not at all high.

Differences between slopes are important in biological assay, as will be seen in section 17.2. If the healing activity is due purely to vitamin D, the regression curves relating response to log dose should differ by a constant distance parallel to the log dose axis (i.e. horizontally in Fig. 9.5). If the regression curves are linear (as they are to a close approximation in this form of assay) this means that they should be parallel. Thus, a test for differences between slopes is effectively a check on the validity of the assumption that the assay response is specific to vitamin D.

The analysis of variance test can, of course, be applied even for $k=2$. The results will be entirely equivalent to the t test described at the beginning of this section, the value of F being, as usual, the square of the corresponding value of t.

9.5 THE ANALYSIS OF COVARIANCE

If, after an analysis of the type described in the last section, there is no strong reason for postulating differences between the slopes of the regression lines in the various groups, the following questions arise. What can be said about the relative position of parallel regression lines? Is there good reason to believe that the true lines differ in position, as in Fig. 9.4(b), or could they coincide, as in Fig. 9.4(c)? What sampling error is to be attached to an estimate of the difference in positions of lines for two particular groups?

The set of techniques associated with these questions is called the *analysis of covariance*. The relevance of the name will become apparent later in the section.

Before describing technical details it may be useful to note some important differences in the purposes of the analysis of covariance and in the circumstances in which it may be used:

1. *Main purpose*

(i) *To correct for bias.* If it is known that changes in x affect the mean value of y, and that the groups under comparison differ in their values of $\bar{x}$, it will follow that some of the differences between the values of $\bar{y}$ can be ascribed partly to differences between the $\bar{x}$'s. We may want to remove this effect as far as possible. For example, if y is FEV and x is age, a comparison of mean FEV's for men in different occupational groups may be affected by differences in their mean ages. A comparison would be desirable of the mean FEV's at the same age. If the regressions are linear and parallel, this means a comparison of the relative position of the regression lines.

(ii) *To reduce random variation.* Even if the groups have very similar values of $\bar{x}$, precision in the comparison of values of $\bar{y}$ can be increased by using the residual variation of y about regression on x rather than by analysing the y's alone.

2. *Type of investigation*

(i) *Uncontrolled study.* In many situations the observations will be made on units which fall naturally into the groups in question—with no element of controlled allocation. Indeed it will often be this lack of control which leads to the bias discussed in 1(i).

(ii) *Controlled study.* In a planned experiment, in which experimental units are allocated randomly to the different groups, the differences between values of $\bar{x}$ in the various groups will be no greater in the long run than would be expected by sampling theory. Of course, there will occasionally be large fortuitous differences in the x's; it may then be just as important to correct for their effect as it would be in an uncontrolled study. In any case, even with very similar values of x, the extra precision referred to in 1(ii) may well be worth acquiring.

TWO GROUPS

If the t test based on (9.19) reveals no significant difference in slopes, two parallel lines may be fitted with a common slope given by (9.20), which we rewrite as

$$b=\frac{(Sxy)_1+(Sxy)_2}{(Sx^2)_1+(Sx^2)_2}. \tag{9.33}$$

The equations of the two parallel lines are (as in (9.25)),

$$Y_{c1}=\bar{y}_1+b(x-\bar{x}_1)$$

and

$$Y_{c2}=\bar{y}_2+b(x-\bar{x}_2).$$

The difference between the values of Y at a given x is therefore

$$\begin{aligned} d &= Y_{c1}-Y_{c2} \\ &=\bar{y}_1-\bar{y}_2-b(\bar{x}_1-\bar{x}_2); \end{aligned} \tag{9.34}$$

(see Fig. 9.6).

The sampling error of d is due partly to that of $\bar{y}_1-\bar{y}_2$ and partly to that of b; (the term $\bar{x}_1-\bar{x}_2$ has no sampling error as we are considering

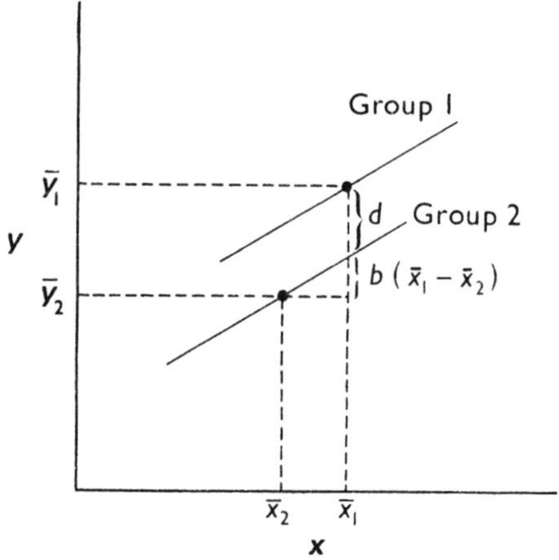

FIG. 9.6 Analysis of covariance for two groups, illustrating formula for vertical difference, d, between parallel lines.

x to be a non-random variable). The three variables, $\bar{y}_1$, $\bar{y}_2$ and b, are independent; consequently

$$\begin{aligned}\text{var}(d) &= \text{var}(\bar{y}_1) + \text{var}(\bar{y}_2) + (\bar{x}_1 - \bar{x}_2)^2 \,\text{var}(b) \\ &= \sigma^2\left\{\frac{1}{n_1} + \frac{1}{n_2} + \frac{(\bar{x}_1 - \bar{x}_2)^2}{(Sx^2)_1 + (Sx^2)_2}\right\},\end{aligned}$$

which is estimated as

$$s_c^2\left\{\frac{1}{n_1} + \frac{1}{n_2} + \frac{(\bar{x}_1 - \bar{x}_2)^2}{(Sx^2)_1 + (Sx^2)_2}\right\}, \tag{9.35}$$

where s_c^2 is the residual mean square about the parallel lines:

$$s_c^2 = \frac{(Sy^2)_1 + (Sy^2)_2 - \dfrac{\{(Sxy)_1 + (Sxy)_2\}^2}{(Sx^2)_1 + (Sx^2)_2}}{n_1 + n_2 - 3}. \tag{9.36}$$

Note that s_c^2 differs from the s^2 of (9.17). The latter is the residual mean square about separate lines, and is equivalent to the s^2 of Table 9.5. The residual mean square s_c^2 in (9.36) is taken about parallel lines (since parallelism is an initial assumption in the analysis of covariance), and would be obtained from Table 9.5 by pooling the second and third lines of the analysis. The resultant DF would be $(k-1) + (n-2k) = n-k-1$, which gives the $n_1 + n_2 - 3 (= n-3)$ of (9.36) when $k=2$.

The standard error of d, the square root of (9.35), may be used in a t test. On the null hypothesis that the regression lines coincide, $E(d) = 0$,

and

$$t = d/\text{SE}(d)$$

has $n_1 + n_2 - 3$ DF. Confidence limits for the true difference, E(d), are obtained in the usual way.

Example 9.4

Table 9.6 gives age and vital capacity (litres) for each of 84 men working in the cadmium industry. They are divided into three groups: A_1, exposed to cadmium fumes for at least 10 years; A_2, exposed to fumes for less than 10 years; B, not exposed to fumes. The main purpose of the study was to see whether exposure to fumes was associated with a change in respiratory function. However, those in group A_1 must be expected to be older on the average than those in Groups A_2 or B, and it is well known that respiratory test performance declines with age. A comparison is therefore needed which corrects for discrepancies between the mean ages of the different groups.

We shall first illustrate the calculations for two groups by amalgamating groups A_1 and A_2 (denoting the pooled group by A) and comparing groups A and B.

A preliminary test, as in Example 9.4, suggests that the two slopes may be different. The estimated slopes, and their standard errors calculated from the pooled variance estimate (9.17), are

$$b_A = -0{\cdot}0537 \pm 0{\cdot}0091, \; b_B = -0{\cdot}0306 \pm 0{\cdot}0075,$$

and $b_A - b_B = -0{\cdot}0231$ with a standard error calculated by (9.18) as 0·0118; $t = -1{\cdot}96$ on 80 DF, which is nearly significant at the 5 per cent level. We return to this point below. At present we ignore a possible difference in slopes and proceed to fit parallel lines.

The sums of squares and products within the two groups are:

$$(Sx^2)_A = 4{,}397{\cdot}3750 \qquad (Sx^2)_B = 6{,}197{\cdot}1591$$
$$(Sxy)_A = -236{\cdot}3850 \qquad (Sxy)_B = -189{\cdot}7116$$
$$(Sy^2)_A = 26{\cdot}5812 \qquad (Sy^2)_B = 20{\cdot}6067$$

Also

$$n_A = 40 \qquad n_B = 44$$
$$\bar{x}_A = 41{\cdot}3750 \qquad \bar{x}_B = 39{\cdot}7955$$
$$\bar{y}_A = 4{\cdot}3150 \qquad \bar{y}_B = 4{\cdot}4620$$

From (9.33), $b = -0{\cdot}04022$;
From (9.34), $d = -0{\cdot}0835$;
From (9.36) $s_C^2 = 0{\cdot}3710$;
From (9.35) var $(d) = 0{\cdot}01780$,
SE $(d) = 0{\cdot}1334$

TABLE 9.6 Ages and vital capacities for three groups of workers in the cadmium industry.

x: Age last birthday (yr)
y: Vital capacity (litres)

	Group A_1 Exposed > 10 yr		Group A_2 Exposed < 10 yr		Group B Not exposed			
	x	y	x	y	x	y	x	y
	39	4·62	29	5·21	27	5·29	43	4·02
	40	5·29	29	5·17	25	3·67	41	4·99
	41	5·52	33	4·88	24	5·82	48	3·86
	41	3·71	32	4·50	32	4·77	47	4·68
	45	4·02	31	4·47	23	5·71	53	4·74
	49	5·09	29	5·12	25	4·47	49	3·76
	52	2·70	29	4·51	32	4·55	54	3·98
	47	4·31	30	4·85	18	4·61	48	5·00
	61	2·70	21	5·22	19	5·86	49	3·31
	65	3·03	28	4·62	26	5·20	47	3·11
	58	2·73	23	5·07	33	4·44	52	4·76
	59	3·67	35	3·64	27	5·52	58	3·95
			38	3·64	33	4·97	62	4·60
			38	5·09	25	4·99	65	4·83
			43	4·61	42	4·89	62	3·18
			39	4·73	35	4·09	59	3·03
			38	4·58	35	4·24		
			42	5·12	41	3·88		
			43	3·89	38	4·85		
			43	4·62	41	4·79		
			37	4·30	36	4·36		
			50	2·70	36	4·02		
			50	3·50	41	3·77		
			45	5·06	41	4·22		
			48	4·06	37	4·94		
			51	4·51	42	4·04		
			46	4·66	39	4·51		
			58	2·88	41	4·06		
Sums	597	47·39	1,058	125·21			1,751	196·33
Number of observations		12		28				44
$\sum x^2$		30,613		42,260				75,879
$\sum xy$		2,280·01		4,624·93				7,623·33
$\sum y^2$		198·8903		572·4599				896·6401

and $t = -0{\cdot}0835/0{\cdot}1334 = -0{\cdot}63$ on 81 DF. The difference d is clearly not significant.

The scatter diagram in Fig. 9.7 shows the regression lines with slopes b_A and b_B fitted separately to the two groups, and also the two parallel lines with slope b. The steepness of the slope for group A may be partly or wholly due to a curvature in the regression: there is a suggestion that the mean value of y at high values of x is lower than is predicted by the linear regressions (see

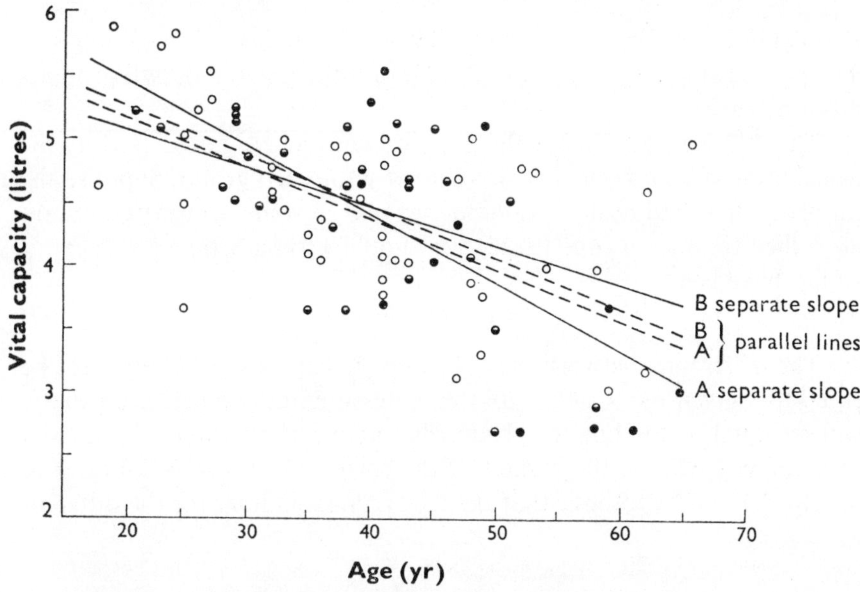

FIG. 9.7 Scatter diagram showing age and vital capacity of 84 men working in cadmium industry, divided into three groups (Table 9.6). Group A_1 ●, Group A_2 ◒, Group B ○.

p. 299). Alternatively it may be that a linear regression is appropriate for each group, but that for group A the vital capacity declines more rapidly with age than for group B. Suppose we abandon the assumption of parallelism and fit lines with separate slopes, b_A and b_B. The most pronounced difference between predicted values occurs at high ages. The difference at, say, age 60 is

$$\begin{aligned} d' &= \bar{y}_A - \bar{y}_B + b_A(60 - \bar{x}_A) - b_B(60 - \bar{x}_B) \\ &= -0{\cdot}5289, \end{aligned}$$

and

$$\begin{aligned} \text{var}(d') &= \text{var}(\bar{y}_A) + \text{var}(\bar{y}_B) + (60 - \bar{x}_A)^2 \,\text{var}(b_A) + (60 - \bar{x}_B)^2 \,\text{var}(b_B) \\ &= (0{\cdot}3588)\left\{\frac{1}{40} + \frac{1}{44} + \frac{(18{\cdot}6520)^2}{4{,}397{\cdot}3750} + \frac{(20{\cdot}2045)^2}{6{,}197{\cdot}1591}\right\} \\ &= 0{\cdot}06914. \end{aligned}$$

Thus $t = d'/\text{SE}(d') = -2{\cdot}01$ on 80 DF, $(P < 0{\cdot}05)$.

This test suggests, therefore, that in spite of the non-significant result in the main analysis of covariance test, there may nevertheless be a difference in mean vital capacity, at least at the higher ages.

MORE THAN TWO GROUPS

Parallel lines may be fitted to several groups as indicated in section 9.4. The pooled slope, b, is given by (9.24) and the line for the ith group is given by (9.25).

The relative positions of the lines are conveniently expressed by the calculation of a *corrected* mean value of y for each group. Suppose the ith group had had a mean value of x equal to some arbitrary constant x_0 rather than $\bar{x}_i$. From (9.25) we should estimate that the mean y would have been

$$\bar{y}' = \bar{y}_i + b(x_0 - \bar{x}_i). \tag{9.37}$$

The difference between, say, $\bar{y}_1'$ and $\bar{y}_2'$ can easily be seen to be equal to d given by (9.34). If all the regression lines coincide, all the $\bar{y}_i'$ will be equal. If the line for group i lies above all the others, at a fixed value of x, $\bar{y}_i'$ will be the highest of the corrected means. See Fig. 9.8.

On the null hypothesis that the true regression lines for the different

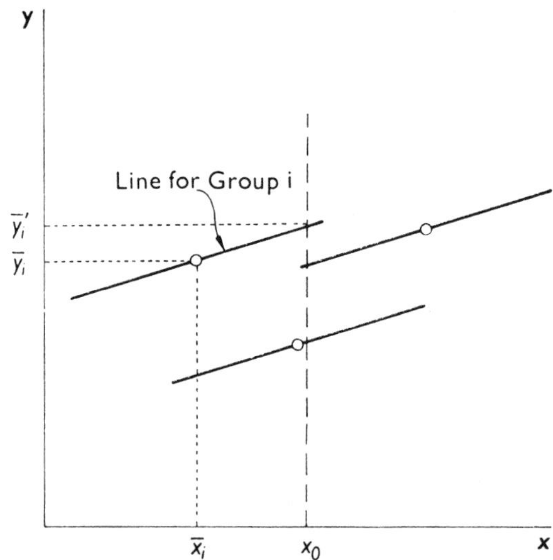

FIG. 9.8 Analysis of covariance with three groups, showing the corrected mean y_i' for the ith group.

groups coincide, the corrected means $\bar{y}'_i$ will differ purely by sampling error. The appropriate test is complicated by the fact that the sampling errors of the $\bar{y}'_i$ are not independent since the random variable b enters into each of the expressions (9.37). The procedure is indicated in Table 9.7.

TABLE 9.7 The analysis of covariance for k groups; regression of y on x.

Uncorrected sums of squares and products				Corrected SSq			
(1) y^2	(2) xy	(3) x^2	(4) DF	(5)	(6) DF	(7) MSq	(8) VR
Between groups							
$(Sy^2)_B$	$(Sxy)_B$	$(Sx^2)_B$	$k-1$	By subtraction	$k-1$	s_B^2	$F=s_B^2/s_C^2$
Within groups							
$(Sy^2)_W$	$(Sxy)_W$	$(Sx^2)_W$	$n-k$	$(Sy^2)_W-$ $-(Sxy)_W^2/(Sx^2)_W$	$n-k-1$	s_C^2	
Total							
$(Sy^2)_T$	$(Sxy)_T$	$(Sx^2)_T$	$n-1$	$(Sy^2)_T-$ $-(Sxy)_T^2/(Sx^2)_T$	$n-2$		

Columns (1) and (3) contain the SSq for straightforward one-way analyses of variance of y and x, respectively. The usual DF are shown in column (4). Column (2) contains a corresponding analysis of the *covariance* of x and y, the feature which provides the name for the whole procedure. This is a technique not previously encountered, but is closely analogous to the corresponding analysis of variance of, say, x, the difference being that any *square* of a quantity involving variable x in the analysis of variance is replaced in the analysis of covariance by the product of the corresponding terms in x and y. The various items in columns (2) and (3) are, therefore, as follows. The notation should be clear.

Between groups

Col (2) $$\frac{(\sum x)_1(\sum y)_1}{n_1}+\ldots+\frac{(\sum x)_k(\sum y)_k}{n_k}-\frac{(\sum x)_T(\sum y)_T}{n}$$

Col (3) $$\frac{(\sum x)_1^2}{n_1}+\ldots+\frac{(\sum x)_k^2}{n_k}-\frac{(\sum x)_T^2}{n}$$

Within groups

Col (2) $$\left(\sum xy\right)_T - \left\{\frac{(\sum x)_1(\sum y)_1}{n_1} + \ldots + \frac{(\sum x)_k(\sum y)_k}{n_k}\right\}$$

Col (3) $$\left(\sum x^2\right)_T - \left\{\frac{(\sum x)_1^2}{n_1} + \ldots + \frac{(\sum x)_k^2}{n_k}\right\}$$

Total

Col (2) $$\left(\sum xy\right)_T - \frac{(\sum x)_T(\sum y)_T}{n}$$

Col (3) $$\left(\sum x^2\right)_T - \frac{(\sum x)_T^2}{n}$$

The entries in column (5), on the 'Within groups' and 'Total' lines are each obtained by the usual formulae for a SSq about regression, using the entries in columns (1) to (3). These are called *Corrected SSq*. The Corrected Total SSq is, in fact, simply the SSq of residuals about a single regression line fitted to the whole data, and has the usual $n-2$ DF. The Corrected SSq within groups is the SSq of residuals about parallel regression lines; it is the sum of the SSq in the second and third lines of Table 9.5 and has $n-k-1$ DF. The Corrected SSq between groups is obtained by subtracting the Corrected SSq within groups from the Corrected Total SSq. The DF can be similarly subtracted, giving $n-2-(n-k-1)=k-1$. Mean squares follow as usual and lead to an F test.

Why is the Corrected SSq between groups obtained by subtraction and not formed in the same way as the other two corrected terms? We might have expected it to be given by

$$(Sy^2)_B - (Sxy)_B^2/(Sx^2)_B, \tag{9.38}$$

and to have $k-2$ DF. In fact (9.38) is a part, but not the whole, of the corrected SSq between groups. Let us write the result of the subtraction carried out in column (5) of Table 9.7. It is

$$\begin{aligned}
&\{(Sy^2)_T - (Sxy)_T^2/(Sx^2)_T\} - \{(Sy^2)_W - (Sxy)_W^2/(Sx^2)_W\}\\
&= \{(Sy^2)_T - (Sy^2)_W\} + (Sxy)_W^2/(Sx^2)_W - (Sxy)_T^2/(Sx^2)_T\\
&= \{(Sy^2)_B - (Sxy)_B^2/(Sx^2)_B\} + \{(Sxy)_B^2/(Sx^2)_B + (Sxy)_W^2/(Sx^2)_W\\
&\quad - (Sxy)_T^2/(Sx^2)_T\},
\end{aligned} \tag{9.39}$$

using the fact that $(Sy^2)_T - (Sy^2)_W = (Sy^2)_B$. Now the term in the first set of curly brackets in (9.39) is the same as (9.38); it represents deviations of group means about a regression line fitted to the between-group variation—that is, fitted to the group means. The term in the second set of curly brackets in (9.39) is of the same form as (9.31) and represents a difference between the slope of the parallel regression lines fitted *within* groups and that of the *between group* regression line fitted to the group means. This latter component has 1 DF because it is a contrast between two random variables, the within-group slope, $b=(Sxy)_W/S(x^2)_W$, and the between-group slope, $b_B=(Sxy)_B/(Sx^2)_B$. To summarize this point, then,

$$\underset{(k-1\text{ DF})}{\text{Corrected SSq between groups}}$$

$$=\underset{(k-2\text{ DF})}{\text{SSq of group means about between-group regression}}$$

$$+\underset{(1\text{ DF})}{\text{SSq for contrast of } b \text{ and } b_B} \tag{9.40}$$

Now, each of the components on the right of (9.40) reflects a type of departure from the null hypothesis of coincident regression lines.

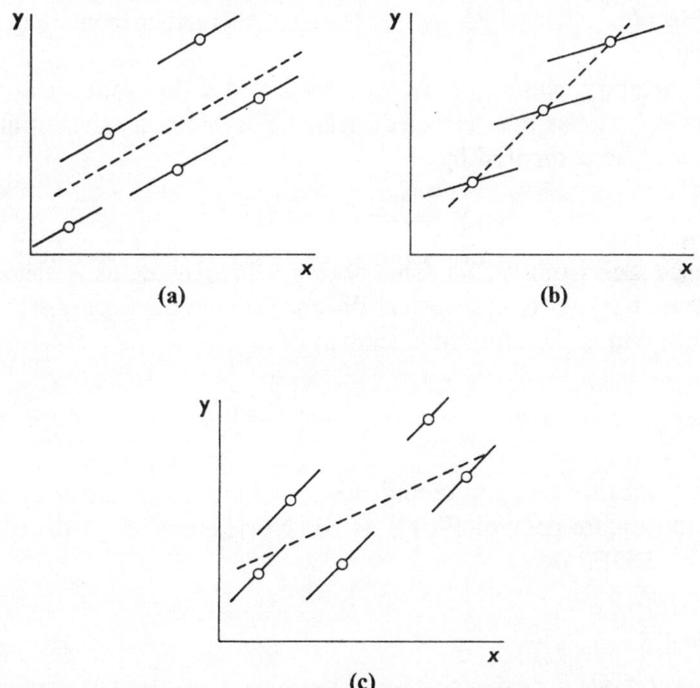

FIG. 9.9 Analysis of covariance: different forms of departure from the null hypothesis of coincident regression lines.

This is illustrated in Fig. 9.9. In (a) b and b_B are approximately equal, and the major component of (9.40) is the variation of group means about the between-group regression. In (b) the means fall on a line, but the between-group and within-group slopes differ; the major component of (9.40) is now the second term. In (c) both types of variation are important.

The Corrected SSq between groups in Table 9.7 thus provides a general test of departures from the null hypothesis of coincident lines. It could if necessary be subdivided as in (9.40).

The corrected means (9.37) provide a convenient summary of the relative positions of the parallel lines. The sampling variance of $\bar{y}'_i$ is estimated by

$$\begin{aligned} \text{var}(\bar{y}'_i) &= \text{var}(\bar{y}_i) + (x_0 - \bar{x}_i)^2 \text{ var}(b) \\ &= s_c^2\left\{\frac{1}{n_i} + \frac{(x_0 - \bar{x}_i)^2}{(Sx^2)_W}\right\}, \end{aligned} \tag{9.41}$$

which varies from group to group not only through n_i but also because of the term $(x_0 - \bar{x}_i)^2$ which increases as $\bar{x}_i$ gets further from x_0 in either direction.

The arbitary choice of x_0 can be avoided by concentrating on differences between the corrected means. For example, the ith and jth groups may be compared by

$$\bar{y}'_i - \bar{y}'_j = (\bar{y}_i - \bar{y}_j) - b(\bar{x}_i - \bar{x}_j), \tag{9.42}$$

as may be seen from (9.37). This does not involve x_0, as is clear from the fact that $\bar{y}'_i - \bar{y}'_j$ is the vertical distance between the parallel regression lines, and is therefore independent of x_0.

$$\text{var}(\bar{y}'_i - \bar{y}'_j) = s_c^2\left\{\frac{1}{n_i} + \frac{1}{n_j} + \frac{(\bar{x}_i - \bar{x}_j)^2}{(Sx^2)_W}\right\}, \tag{9.43}$$

and a significance test and confidence limits are immediately available, taking the square root of (9.43) as $\text{SE}(\bar{y}'_i - \bar{y}'_j)$ with the t distribution on $n-k-1$ DF.

Example 9.5

The data of Table 9.6, already used in Example 9.4, provide an example of an analysis of covariance with three groups, A_1, A_2 and B. The analysis of covariance table is as follows:

	Uncorrected				Corrected			
	y^2	xy	x^2	DF	SSq	DF	MSq	VR
Between groups	2·747	−57·390	1,254·7	2	0·161	2	0·080	0·22
Within groups	44·894	−373·573	9,392·1	81	30·035	80	0·375	
	47·641	−430·963	10,646·8	83	30·196	82		

The variance ratio is less than unity and thus provides no suggestion of a difference between the positions of the parallel lines. As in the two-group analysis of Example 9.5, however, there is some doubt about the validity of the assumption that the lines are parallel. An analysis of the slopes, as in Table 9.5, gives the following table:

	SSq	DF	MSq	VR	
Common slope	14·859	1	14·859	42·09	
Between slopes	2·500	2	1·250	3·54	($P<0·05$)
Residual	27·535	78	0·3530		
	44·894	81			

The differences between slopes are more significant than in the two-group analysis. The estimates of the separate slopes, with their standard errors, are:

$$b_{A1} = -0{\cdot}0851 \pm 0{\cdot}0237,\ b_{A2} = -0{\cdot}0465 \pm 0{\cdot}0113,\ b_B = -0{\cdot}0306 \pm 0{\cdot}0075.$$

The most highly exposed group, A_1, provides the steepest slope. Fig. 9.10 shows the separate regressions as well as the three parallel lines. As in the two-group analysis, a comparison of the positions of the non-parallel lines at, say, age 60 would be possible. This is left as an exercise for the reader.

The doubt about linearity suggests further that a curvilinear regression might be more suitable; however, analysis with a quadratic regression line (see section 10.3) shows the non-linearity to be quite non-significant. For an alternative approach to the analysis of these data see Example 10.2.

In considering the possible use of the analysis of covariance with a particular set of data, special care should be given to the identification of the dependent and independent variables. If, in the analysis of covariance of y on x, there are significant differences between groups, it does not follow that the same will be true of the regression of x on y. In many cases this is an academic point because the investigator is clearly interested in differences between groups in the mean value of y, after correction for x, and not in the reverse problem. Occasionally, when x and y have a symmetric type of relation to each other, as in section 9.2, *both* of the analyses of covariance (of y on x, and of x on y)

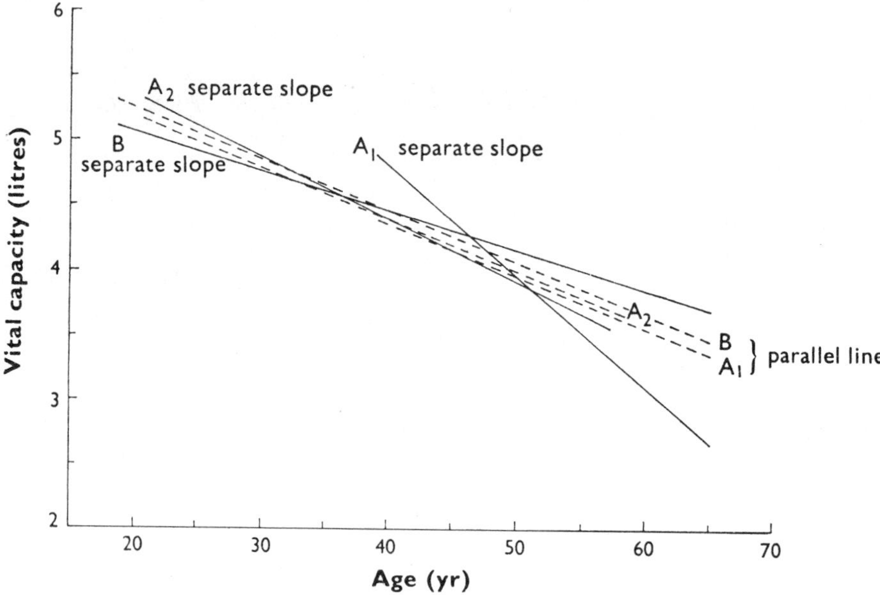

FIG. 9.10 Parallel regression lines and lines with separate slopes, for cadmium workers (Fig. 9.7).

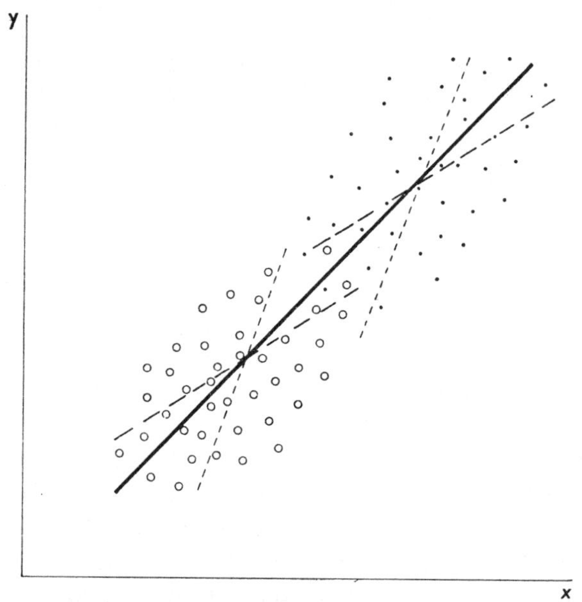

FIG. 9.11 Scatter diagram showing a common trend for two groups of observations but with non-coincident regression lines. Regression of y on x — — —; regression of x on y - - -.

will be misleading. Lines representing the general trend of a functional relationship may well be coincident (as in Fig. 9.11), yet both sets of regression lines are non-coincident. Here the difficulties of section 9.2 apply, and lines drawn by eye may provide the most satisfactory description of the data. For a fuller discussion see Ehrenberg (1968).

The analysis of covariance described in this section is appropriate for data forming a one-way classification into groups. Similar problems arise in the analysis of more complex data. For example in the analysis of a variable y in a Latin square one may wish to adjust the apparent treatment effects to correct for variation in another variable x. In particular, x may be some pre-treatment characteristic known to be associated with y; the covariance adjustment would then be expected to increase the precision with which the treatments can be compared. The general procedure is to isolate the two lines from the analysis of variance of y, corresponding to (a) the effect which is of particular interest (comparison of treatments in the previous example), and (b) the residual. For each of these lines the SSq for y and for x are calculated in the usual way, and the sum of products (SPr) is calculated by following the analogy used in the simpler case—replacing squares by products. The sums of the entries in these two lines are then formed, and the usual covariance correction is applied to the 'residual' and the 'sum' lines, that for the effect being obtained by subtraction. If the 'effect' and 'residual' have respectively n_1 and n_2 DF, the analysis is as follows:

		Uncorrected SSq and SPr			Corrected		
	DF	y^2	xy	x^2	SSq	DF	MSq VR
Effect	n_1	A_1	A_2	A_3	E_1-D_1	n_1	as usual
Residual	n_2	B_1	B_2	B_3	$D_1=B_1-B_2^2/B_3$	n_2-1	
Sum	n_1+n_2	C_1	C_2	C_3	$E_1=C_1-C_2^2/C_3$	n_1+n_2-1	

CHAPTER 10

MULTIPLE REGRESSION AND MULTIVARIATE ANALYSIS

10.1 MULTIPLE REGRESSION

In the earlier discussions of regression in Chapters 5 and 9 we have been concerned with the relationship between the mean value of one variable and the value of another variable, concentrating particularly on the situation in which this relationship can be represented by a straight line.

It is often useful to express the mean value of one variable in terms not of one other variable but of several others. Some examples will illustrate some slightly different purposes of this approach.

(a) The primary purpose may be to study the effect on variable y of changes in a particular single variable x_1, but it may be recognized that y may be affected by several other variables x_2, x_3, etc. The effect on y of simultaneous changes in x_1, x_2, x_3, etc., must therefore be studied. In the analysis of data on respiratory function of workers in a particular industry, such as those considered in Examples 9.4 and 9.5, the effect of duration of exposure to a hazard may be of primary interest. However, respiratory function is affected by age, and age is related to duration of exposure. The simultaneous effect on respiratory function of age and exposure must therefore be studied so that the effect of exposure on workers of a fixed age may be estimated.

(b) One may wish to derive insight into some causative mechanism by discovering which of a set of variables x_1, x_2, . . ., has apparently most influence on a dependent variable y. For example, the stillbirth rate varies considerably in different towns in Britain. By relating the stillbirth rate simultaneously to a large number of variables describing the towns—economic, social, meteorological or demographic variables, for instance—it may be possible to find which factors exert particular influence on the stillbirth rate. See Sutherland (1946). Another example is in the study of variations in the cost per patient in different hospitals.

This presumably depends markedly on the 'patient mix'—the proportions of different types of patient admitted—as well as on other factors. A study of the simultaneous effect of many such variables may explain much of the variation in hospital costs and, by drawing attention to particular hospitals whose high or low costs are out of line with the prediction, may suggest new factors of importance.

(c) To predict the value of the dependent variable in future individuals. After treatment of patients with advanced breast cancer by ablative procedures (Atkins *et al.*, 1960), prognosis is very uncertain. If future progress can be shown to depend on various variables available at the time of the operation, it may be possible to predict which patients have a poor prognosis and to consider alternative methods of treatment for them.

The appropriate technique is called *multiple regression.* In general, the approach is to express the mean value of the *dependent* variable in terms of the values of a set of other variables, usually called *independent* variables. The nomenclature is confusing, since some of the latter variables may be either closely related to each other logically (e.g., one might be age and another the square of the age), or highly correlated (e.g., height and arm length). It is preferable to use the terms *predictor* or *explanatory* variables, and we shall usually follow this practice.

The data to be analysed consist of observations on a set of n individuals, each individual providing a value of the dependent variable, y, and a value of each of the predictor variables, $x_1, x_2, \ldots, x_p$. The number of predictor variables, p, should preferably be considerably less than the number of observations, n, and the same p predictor variables must be available for each individual in any one analysis. As will be seen below, the complexity of the calculations increases rapidly with the value of p. Most computer installations can provide a standard program for multiple regression analysis, so the complexity of the calculations need not trouble the investigator. For $p=2$, 3 or perhaps 4, the calculations are perfectly feasible on a desk calculator, and it is instructive to learn the general method by following the details of some relatively simple examples.

Suppose that, for particular values of $x_1, x_2, \ldots, x_p$, an observed value of y is specified by the linear model:

$$y=\alpha+\beta_1x_1+\beta_2x_2+\ldots+\beta_px_p+\epsilon, \tag{10.1}$$

where ϵ is an error term. The various values of ϵ for different individuals are supposed to be independently distributed with zero mean and variance σ^2. The constants $\beta_1, \beta_2, \ldots, \beta_p$ are called *partial regression coefficients*; α is sometimes called the *intercept*. The coefficient β_1 is the amount by which y changes on the average when x_1 changes by one unit and all the other x_i's remain constant. In general, β_1 will be different from the ordinary regression coefficient of y on x_1 because the latter represents the effect of changes in x_1 on the average values of y with no attempt to keep the other variables constant.

The coefficients $\alpha, \beta_1, \beta_2, \ldots, \beta_p$ are idealized quantities, measurable only from an infinite number of observations. In practice, from n observations, we have to obtain estimates of the coefficients and thus an estimated regression equation:

$$Y = a + b_1x_1 + b_2x_2 + \ldots + b_px_p. \tag{10.2}$$

Statistical theory tells us that a satisfactory method of obtaining the estimated regression equation is to choose the coefficients such that the sums of squares of residuals, $\sum(y - Y)^2$, is minimized. Note that here y is an observed value and Y is the value predicted by (10.2) in terms of the predictor variables. A consequence of this approach is that the regression equation (10.2) is satisfied if all the variables are given their mean values. Thus

$$\bar{y} = a + b_1\bar{x}_1 + b_2\bar{x}_2 + \ldots + b_p\bar{x}_p,$$

and consequently a can be replaced in (10.2) by

$$\bar{y} - b_1\bar{x}_1 - b_2\bar{x}_2 - \ldots - b_p\bar{x}_p$$

to give the following form to the regression equation:

$$Y = \bar{y} + b_1(x_1 - \bar{x}_1) + b_2(x_2 - \bar{x}_2) + \ldots + b_p(x_p - \bar{x}_p). \tag{10.3}$$

The equivalent result for simple regression was proved at (5.5).

We now are left with the problem of finding the partial regression coefficients, b_i. We shall discuss the methods of obtaining these coefficients which satisfy the least squares criterion, illustrating the general method by considering in detail an example for which $p = 2$.

METHOD 1

Calculate the sum of squares about the mean of each x, the sums of products of deviations of each pair of x's, and those of each x with y.

With an obvious notation, for instance,

$$Sx_j^2 = \sum x_j^2 - (\sum x_j)^2/n,$$
$$Sx_jy = \sum x_jy - (\sum x_j)(\sum y)/n,$$

and so on.

Write down a set of simultaneous linear equations as follows:

$$\begin{aligned}
(Sx_1^2)b_1 + (Sx_1x_2)b_2 + \ldots + (Sx_1x_p)b_p &= Sx_1y \\
(Sx_2x_1)b_1 + (Sx_2^2)b_2 + \ldots + (Sx_2x_p)b_p &= Sx_2y \\
\cdot \qquad\qquad\qquad\qquad \cdot \quad & \quad \cdot \\
\cdot \qquad\qquad\qquad\qquad \cdot \quad & \quad \cdot \\
\cdot \qquad\qquad\qquad\qquad \cdot \quad & \quad \cdot \\
(Sx_px_1)b_1 + (Sx_px_2)b_2 + \ldots + (Sx_p^2)b_p &= Sx_py.
\end{aligned} \tag{10.4}$$

These are the so-called *normal equations*. There are p equations for p unknowns, $b_1, b_2, \ldots, b_p$, and in general there is a unique solution. The numerical coefficients on the left side of (10.4) form a *matrix* which is symmetric about the diagonal running from top left to bottom right; for example, $Sx_1x_2 = Sx_2x_1$. These coefficients involve only the x's. Those on the right involve also the y's.

There are various methods of solving (10.4) by successive elimination of the b_j's, one of which will be illustrated in Example 10.1. Those familiar with matrix algebra will recognize this problem as being soluble in terms of the *inverse matrix*, a fact which leads to Method 2.

METHOD 2

Corresponding to the matrix of coefficients on the left of (10.4):

$$\begin{pmatrix}
Sx_1^2 & Sx_1x_2 & \ldots & Sx_1x_p \\
Sx_2x_1 & Sx_2^2 & \ldots & Sx_2x_p \\
\cdot & & & \\
\cdot & & & \\
\cdot & & & \\
Sx_px_1 & Sx_px_2 & \ldots & Sx_p^2
\end{pmatrix} \tag{10.5}$$

there is an *inverse matrix*:

$$\begin{pmatrix}
c_{11} & c_{12} & \ldots & c_{1p} \\
c_{21} & c_{22} & \ldots & c_{2p} \\
\cdot & & & \\
\cdot & & & \\
\cdot & & & \\
c_{p1} & c_{p2} & \ldots & c_{pp}
\end{pmatrix}. \tag{10.6}$$

The inverse matrix can, if one wishes, be obtained by applying a standard computer program. Alternatively, it can be obtained by the following scheme of computation. Write down p sets of simultaneous linear equations for unknowns which we shall call $c_1, c_2, \ldots, c_p$.

$$\begin{array}{l|c|c|c|c}
 & \multicolumn{4}{c}{\text{Set of equations}} \\
 & 1 & 2 & \ldots & p \\
\hline
(Sx_1^2)c_1 + (Sx_1x_2)c_2 + \ldots + (Sx_1x_p)c_p = & 1 & 0 & \ldots & 0 \\
(Sx_2x_1)c_1 + (Sx_2^2)c_2 + \ldots + (Sx_2x_p)c_p = & 0 & 1 & & 0 \\
\cdot & \cdot & & & \\
\cdot & \cdot & & & \\
\cdot & \cdot & & & \\
(Sx_px_1)c_1 + (Sx_px_2)c_2 + \ldots + (Sx_p^2)c_p = & 0 & 0 & & 1
\end{array} \qquad (10.7)$$

Each set of equations has the same left side; indeed, the coefficients are the same as in (10.4). Each set differs, however, on the right side by taking a different column of figures. There are, therefore, p sets of solutions for the c's. Let us denote these as follows:

Unknown	Set of equations 1	2	...	p
c_1	c_{11}	c_{12}	...	c_{1p}
c_2	c_{21}	c_{22}		c_{2p}
.	.			
.	.			
.	.			
c_p	c_{p1}	c_{p2}		c_{pp}

This provides the inverse matrix. The solution of (10.7), if one wished to obtain it without a computer, would be less formidable than might be thought, since the same succession of operations can be carried out on the left side for each set of equations. This is the main purpose behind the rather compressed lay-out of (10.7). One method is illustrated in Example 10.1.

The symmetry of the matrix (10.5) of sums of squares and products of the x's, and the relationships between the entries (for example, that all variances are positive and all correlation coefficients are between 1 and -1) ensures two properties for the inverse matrix (10.6): (i) the terms in the diagonal $c_{11}, c_{22}, \ldots, c_{pp}$ are all positive; and (ii) the other entries are symmetric; e.g., $c_{12} = c_{21}$. These properties form a useful check on the arithmetic.

With the inverse matrix (10.6) obtained by solving (10.7), the b_i's are obtained as follows:

$$
\begin{aligned}
b_1 &= c_{11}(Sx_1y) + c_{12}(Sx_2y) + \ldots + c_{1p}(Sx_py)\\
b_2 &= c_{21}(Sx_1y) + c_{22}(Sx_2y) + \ldots + c_{2p}(Sx_py)\\
&\cdot\\
&\cdot\\
&\cdot\\
b_p &= c_{p1}(Sx_1y) + c_{p2}(Sx_2y) + \ldots + c_{pp}(Sx_py). \qquad (10.8)
\end{aligned}
$$

The resulting values will be the same as those obtained in Method 1 by solving (10.4).

Why go to all the trouble involved in Method 2 when Method 1 gives the same answer by an obviously quicker procedure? The answer is that all considerations of sampling variation—significance tests and confidence limits based on the b_j's for example—depend on the inverse matrix. These considerations can hardly be avoided in any multiple regression problem. If the inverse matrix is needed in any case for inferential procedures, it may as well be obtained at the outset and used for the subsequent calculation of the b_j's. Method 2 is therefore the method of choice. Most computer programs use this method, and it is therefore of some importance to understand the underlying method even though it may be rarely used in desk computation.

Example 10.1

The data shown in Table 10.1 are taken from a clinical trial to compare two hypotensive drugs used to lower the blood pressure during operations (Robertson and Armitage, 1959). The dependent variable, y, is the 'recovery time' (in minutes) elapsing between the time at which the drug was discontinued and the time at which the systolic blood pressure had returned to 100 mm.Hg. The data shown here relate to one of the two drugs used in the trial. The recovery time is very variable, and a question of interest is the extent to which it depends on the quantity of drug used and the level to which blood pressure was lowered during hypotension. The two predictor variables are:

x_1: log(quantity of drug used, mg.).

x_2: mean level of systolic blood pressure during hypotension (mm.Hg).

The table shows the values of x_1, x_2 and y for the 53 subjects. The columns headed Y and $y-Y$ will be referred to later. Below the data are shown the means and sums of squares and products about the means of the three

TABLE 10.1 Data on the use of a hypotensive drug.

x_1 = log (quantity of drug used, mg.)

x_2 = mean level of systolic blood pressure during hypotension (mm. Hg.)

y = recovery time (minutes)

x_1	x_2	y	Y	$y-Y$	x_1	x_2	y	Y	$y-Y$
2·26	66	7	29·3	−22·3	2·70	73	39	34·7	4·3
1·81	52	10	28·6	−18·6	1·90	56	28	27·9	0·1
1·78	72	18	13·6	4·4	2·78	83	12	29·4	−17·4
1·54	67	4	11·5	−7·5	2·27	67	60	28·8	31·2
2·06	69	10	22·4	−12·4	1·74	84	10	4·1	5·9
1·74	71	13	13·4	−0·4	2·62	68	60	36·3	23·7
2·56	88	21	20·6	0·4	1·80	64	22	19·8	2·2
2·29	68	12	28·5	−16·5	1·81	60	21	22·9	−1·9
1·80	59	9	23·4	−14·4	1·58	62	14	16·1	−2·1
2·32	73	65	25·7	39·3	2·41	76	4	25·7	−21·7
2·04	68	20	22·6	−2·6	1·65	60	27	19·1	7·9
1·88	58	31	26·0	5·0	2·24	60	26	33·1	−7·1
1·18	61	23	7·3	15·7	1·70	59	28	21·0	7·0
2·08	68	22	25·6	−1·6	2·45	84	15	20·9	−5·9
1·70	69	13	13·9	−0·9	1·72	66	8	16·5	−8·5
1·74	55	9	24·8	−15·8	2·37	68	46	30·4	15·6
1·90	67	50	20·0	30·0	2·23	65	24	29·3	−5·3
1·79	67	12	17·4	−5·4	1·92	69	12	19·1	−7·1
2·11	68	11	24·3	−13·3	1·99	72	25	18·6	6·4
1·72	59	8	21·5	−13·5	1·99	63	45	25·0	20·0
1·74	68	26	15·5	10·5	2·35	56	72	38·5	33·5
1·60	63	16	15·8	0·2	1·80	70	25	15·5	9·5
2·15	65	23	27·4	−4·4	2·36	69	28	29·5	−1·5
2·26	72	7	25·0	−18·0	1·59	60	10	17·7	−7·7
1·65	58	11	20·6	−9·6	2·10	51	25	36·2	−11·2
1·63	69	8	12·2	−4·2	1·80	61	44	22·0	22·0
2·40	70	14	29·7	−15·7					
					105·60	3516	1203		

$n = 53$ $\bar{x}_1 = 1\cdot9925$

$\bar{x}_2 = 66\cdot340$

$\bar{y} = 22\cdot698$

$Sx_1^2 = 6\cdot01758$ $Sx_1x_2 = 64\cdot0958$ $Sx_1y = 96\cdot4392$

$Sx_2^2 = 3105\cdot89$ $Sx_2y = -704\cdot566$

$Sy^2 = 13791\cdot2$

variables. *Method 1* proceeds as follows. Equations (10.4) are:

$$\left.\begin{aligned} 6{\cdot}01758\,b_1 + \;\; 64{\cdot}0958\,b_2 &= \;\;\; 96{\cdot}4392 \\ 64{\cdot}0958\,\; b_1 + 3105{\cdot}89\;\; b_2 &= -704{\cdot}566 \end{aligned}\right\} \qquad (10.9)$$

To solve these equations, divide the first line by 6·01758 and the second by 64·0958. This gives

$$b_1 + 10{\cdot}6514\, b_2 = \;\; 16{\cdot}0262 \qquad (10.10)$$

$$b_1 + 48{\cdot}4570\, b_2 = -10{\cdot}9924. \qquad (10.11)$$

Subtracting (10.10) from (10.11),

$$37{\cdot}8056\, b_2 = -27{\cdot}0186$$
$$b_2 = \;\; -0{\cdot}714672. \qquad (10.12)$$

From (10.10),

$$\begin{aligned} b_1 &= 16{\cdot}0262 - (10{\cdot}6514)(-0{\cdot}714672) \\ &= 11{\cdot}0262 + 7{\cdot}6123 \\ &\doteq 23{\cdot}6385. \end{aligned} \qquad (10.13)$$

As a check, the values of b_1 and b_2 may be substituted in the left sides of equations (10.9). The results are 96·4391 and −704·564, which agree well enough with the quantities on the right of (10.9).

Now to *Method 2*. Equations (10.7) are:

	Set 1	Set 2
$6{\cdot}01758\, c_1 + \;\; 64{\cdot}0958\, c_2 =$	1	0
$64{\cdot}0958\;\; c_1 + 3105{\cdot}89\;\; c_2 =$	0	1

Dividing through by the coefficient of c_1,

$c_1 + 10{\cdot}6514\, c_2 =$	0·166180	0	(10.14)
$c_1 + 48{\cdot}4570\, c_2 =$	0	0·0156016	(10.15)

Subtracting,

$37{\cdot}8056\, c_2 = -$	0·166180	0·0156016
$c_2 =$	−0·00439565	0·000412680

For c_1 it is simplest to use (10.15) for Set 1 and (10.14) for Set 2. This gives,

$c_1 =$	$-48{\cdot}4570\, c_2$	$-10{\cdot}6514\, c_2$
$=$	0·213000	−0·00439562

The inverse matrix is thus

$$\begin{pmatrix} c_{11} & c_{12} \\ c_{21} & c_{22} \end{pmatrix} = \begin{pmatrix} 0{\cdot}213000 & -0{\cdot}00439562 \\ -0{\cdot}00439565 & 0{\cdot}000412680 \end{pmatrix}$$

Note that c_{11} and c_{22} are positive, as expected, and $c_{21} = c_{12}$ apart from rounding errors.

Finally, from (10.8),

$$b_1=(0\cdot213000)(96\cdot4392)+(-0\cdot00439562)(-704\cdot566)$$
$$=23\cdot6386,$$

and

$$b_2=(-0\cdot00439565)(96\cdot4392)+(0\cdot000412680)(-704\cdot566)$$
$$=-0\cdot714670.$$

These values agree with those obtained by Method 1, apart from the rounding error.

From (10.3), the regression equation is

$$Y=22\cdot698+23\cdot6386(x_1-1\cdot9925)-0\cdot714670(x_2-66\cdot340)$$
$$=23\cdot009+23\cdot6386x_1-0\cdot714670x_2.$$

The recovery time increases on the average by about 24 min. for each increase of 1 in the log dose (i.e., each ten-fold increase in dose), and decreases by 0·71 min. for every increase of 1 mm.Hg in the mean blood pressure during hypotension. This example is continued on p. 312.

SAMPLING VARIATION

As in simple regression, the Total SSq of y may be divided into the SSq due to regression and the SSq about regression. For any one observation,

$$y-\bar{y}=(y-Y)+(Y-\bar{y}).$$

Squaring and summing,

$$\sum(y-\bar{y})^2=\sum(y-Y)^2+2\sum(y-Y)(Y-\bar{y})+\sum(Y-\bar{y})^2. \quad (10.16)$$

The middle term on the right of (10.16) is twice

$$\begin{aligned}&\sum\{(y-\bar{y})-b_1(x_1-\bar{x}_1)-\ldots-b_p(x_p-\bar{x}_p)\}\{b_1(x_1-\bar{x}_1)+\ldots+b_p(x_p-\bar{x}_p)\}\\&\quad=b_1\{Sx_1y-b_1(Sx_1^2)-\ldots-b_p(Sx_1x_p)\}\\&\qquad+b_2\{Sx_2y-b_1(Sx_1x_2)-\ldots-b_p(Sx_2x_p)\}\\&\qquad+\ldots\\&\qquad+b_p\{Sx_py-b_1(Sx_1x_p)-\ldots-b_p(Sx_p^2)\}\\&\quad=0+0+\ldots+0 \qquad (10.17)\end{aligned}$$

from (10.4). The third term on the right of (10.16) is

$$\begin{aligned}&\sum\{b_1(x_1-\bar{x}_1)+\ldots+b_p(x_p-\bar{x}_p)\}^2\\&\quad=b_1\{b_1(Sx_1^2)+\ldots+b_p(Sx_1x_p)\}\\&\qquad+\ldots+b_p\{b_1(Sx_1x_p)+\ldots+b_p(Sx_p^2)\}\\&\quad=b_1(Sx_1y)+b_2(Sx_2y)+\ldots+b_p(Sx_py). \qquad (10.18)\end{aligned}$$

From (10.16)–(10.18), then,

$$\text{Total SSq} = \text{SSq about regression} + \text{SSq due to regression},$$

the SSq due to regression being most easily calculated from (10.18), and the Residual SSq about regression being obtained by subtraction. This subdivision provides the opportunity for an analysis of variance. The subdivision of DF is as follows:

$$\begin{array}{cccc} \textit{Total} = & \textit{About regression} & + & \textit{Due to regression} \\ n-1 = & (n-p-1) & + & p \end{array}$$

The variance ratio

$$F = \frac{\text{MSq due to regression}}{\text{MSq about regression}} \tag{10.19}$$

provides a composite test of the null hypothesis that $\beta_1 = \beta_2 = \ldots = \beta_p = 0$, i.e., that all the predictor variables are irrelevant.

The ratio

$$\frac{\text{SSq due to regression}}{\text{Total SSq}} \tag{10.20}$$

is often denoted by R^2 (by analogy with the similar result (5.12) for r^2 in simple regression). The quantity R is called the *multiple correlation coefficient*. R^2 must be between 0 and 1, and so must its positive square root. In general no meaning can be attached to the direction of a multiple correlation with more than one predictor variable, and so R is always given a positive value. The appropriate test for the significance of the multiple correlation coefficient is the F test described above.

We have so far discussed the significance of the joint relationship of y with the predictor variables. It is usually interesting to study the sampling variation of each b_j separately. This not only provides information about the precision of the partial regression coefficients, but also enables each of them to be tested for a significant departure from zero. If a particular b_j is not significantly different from zero it may be thought sensible to call it zero (i.e., to drop it from the regression equation) to make the equation as simple as possible. It is important to realise, though, that if this is done the remaining b_j's would be changed; in general the new values would be obtained by doing a new analysis on the remaining x_j's.

The variance and standard error of b_j are

$$\left.\begin{aligned} \text{var}(b_j) &= s^2 c_{jj}, \\ \text{SE}(b_j) &= \sqrt{(s^2 c_{jj})}, \end{aligned}\right\} \tag{10.21}$$

where s^2 is the Residual MSq about regression. Tests and confidence limits are obtained in the usual way with the t distribution on $n-p-1$ DF. We note also, for future reference, that the *covariance* of b_j and b_h is

$$\text{cov}(b_j, b_h)=s^2c_{jh}. \tag{10.22}$$

Example 10.1 (continued)

Application of (10.18) gives the value 2783·22. The analysis of variance of y is

	SSq	DF	MSq	VR
Due to regression	2,783	2	1,392	6·32 ($P<0·01$)
About regression	11,008	50	220·2	
Total	13,791	52		

The variance ratio is highly significant and there is thus little doubt that either x_1 or x_2 is, or both are, associated with y. The squared multiple correlation coefficient, R^2, is $2{,}783/13{,}791=0·2018$; $R=\sqrt{0·2018}=0·45$. Of the total sum of squares of y, about 80 per cent ($0·80=1-R^2$) is still present after prediction of y from x_1 and x_2. The predictive value of x_1 and x_2 is, thus, rather low, even though it is highly significant.

From the analysis of variance, $s^2=220·2$. From (10.21),

$$\text{SE}(b_1)=\sqrt{46·89}=6·85$$

$$\text{SE}(b_2)=\sqrt{0·09086}=0·301.$$

To test the significance of b_1 and b_2 we have the following values of t on 50 DF:

$$\text{For } b_1\text{: } t=23·64/6·85=3·45 \ (P<0·001)$$

$$\text{For } b_2\text{: } t=-0·7147/0·301=2·37 \ (0·01<P<0·02).$$

Both partial regression coefficients are thus significant. Each predictor variable contributes separately to the effectiveness of the overall regression.

ANALYSIS OF VARIANCE TEST FOR DELETION OF VARIABLES

The t test for a particular regression coefficient, say b_j, tests whether the corresponding predictor variable x_j, can be dropped from the regression equation without any significant effect on the variation of y.

Sometimes we may wish to test whether variability is significantly affected by the deletion of a group of predictor variables. For example, in a clinical study there may be three variables concerned with bodily size: height (x_1), weight (x_2) and chest measurement (x_3). If all other variables represent quite different characteristics, it may be useful to know whether all three of the size variables can be dispensed with. Suppose that q variables are to be deleted, out of a total of p. If two multiple regressions are done, (a) with all p variables, and (b) with the reduced set of $p-q$ variables, the following analysis of variance is obtained:

	DF	
(i) Due to regression (a)	p	
(ii) Due to regression (b)		$p-q$
(iii) Due to deletion of q variables		q
(iv) Residual about regression (a)	$n-p-1$	
Total	$n-1$	

The SSq for (i) and (iv) are obtained from regression (a), that for (ii) from regression (b) and that for (iii) by subtraction: (iii) = (i) − (ii). The variance ratio from (iii) and (iv) provides the required F test.

When a computer is used for multiple regression, it is usually very simple to arrange for regressions to be done on several different subsets of predictor variables. Several tests of the form described above may therefore be done on the same data.

When only one variable is to be deleted the same procedure could in principle be followed instead of the t test. The analysis of variance would be as follows:

	DF		SSq
Due to regression on all variables	p		
Due to regression on all except x_j		$p-1$	
Due to deletion of x_j		1	A
Residual about regression on all variables	$n-p-1$		
Total	$n-1$		

If this were done it would be found that the SSq for deletion of x_j, denoted by A, was equal to b_j^2/c_{jj}. The variance ratio for deletion of x_j would be

$$F=(b_j^2/c_{jj})/s^2$$
$$=b_j^2/s^2c_{jj},$$

which is seen from (10.21) to be equal to t^2, thus giving the familiar equivalence between an F test on 1 and $n-p-1$ DF and a t test on $n-p-1$ DF. Since A can be obtained, as b_j^2/c_{jj}, from the regression on all variables, there is no need in this case to do the separate regression on the reduced number of variables. If one requires the new values of the regression coefficients, after deletion of x_j, it may be worth doing a separate regression if a computer is available. Even here, though, the new values can be obtained by fairly simple adjustment of the old values (Snedecor and Cochran, 1967, section 13.12).

It will sometimes happen that two or more predictor variables all give non-significant partial regression coefficients, yet the deletion of the whole group has a significant effect by the F test. This often happens when the variables within the group are highly correlated; any one of them can be dispensed with without appreciably affecting the prediction of y: the remaining variables in the group act as effective substitutes. If the whole group is omitted, though, there may be no other variables left to do the job. With a large number of inter-related predictor variables it often becomes quite difficult to sort out the meaning of the various partial regression coefficients.

AUTOMATIC ELIMINATION PROCEDURES

The difficulty referred to in the last sentence has led to the development of a number of procedures whereby the computer selects the 'best' subset of predictor variables, the criterion of optimality being somewhat arbitrary. There are three main approaches.

(a) *Step-up procedures*

The computer first tries all the p simple regressions with just one predictor variable, choosing that which provides the highest Regression SSq. Retaining this variable as the first choice, it now tries all the $p-1$ two-variable regressions obtained by the various possibilities for the second variable, choosing that which adds the largest increment to the Regression SSq. The process continues, all variables chosen at any stage being retained at subsequent stages. The process stops when the increments to the Regression SSq cease to be (in some sense) large in comparison with the Residual SSq.

(b) *Step-down procedures*

The computer first does the regression on *all* predictor variables. It then eliminates the least significant and does a regression on the remaining

$p-1$ variables. The process stops when all the retained regression coefficients are (in some sense) significant.

(c) *Optimal combination procedures*

Methods (a) and (b) do not necessarily reach the same final choice, even if they end with the same number of retained variables. Neither will necessarily choose the best possible regression (i.e. that with the largest Regression SSq) for any given number of predictor variables. To find the best possible regression with, say, p' retained variables is an immense task, even for a computer, but methods of doing this have recently been developed (Beale *et al.*, 1967).

None of these methods provides infallible tactics in the difficult problem of selecting predictor variables. Sometimes certain variables should be retained even though they have non-significant effects, because of their logical importance in the particular problem. Sometimes logical relationships between some of the variables suggest that a particular one should be retained in preference to another. Nevertheless, automatic elimination is often a useful exploratory device, even when the selected set of variables has to be modified on common sense grounds.

ADEQUACY OF MODEL

Sometimes, particularly in experimental work, data will be available in groups of replicates, each group corresponding to a particular combination of values of $x_1, x_2, \ldots, x_p$, but providing various values of y. The adequacy of the model can then be tested, as in section 9.1, by comparing the variation of the group mean values of y about the predicted values Y, with the variation within groups (obtained from a one-way analysis of variance). The method is a straightforward generalization of that of section 9.1. In general, with a total of n observations falling into k groups, the DF are partitioned as follows:

	DF	
(i) Between groups	$k-1$	
(ii) Due to regression		p
(iii) Deviations from regression		$k-p-1$
(iv) Within groups	$n-k$	
Total	$n-1$	

The SSq for (iii) is obtained by subtraction, (i)–(ii), and the adequacy of the model is tested by the variance ratio from lines (iii) and (iv).

In general, the above approach will not be feasible since the observations will not fall into groups of replicates. Much information may be gained by graphical study of the residuals, $y - Y$. These values, and the predicted values Y, are often printed in computer output. The values for the data in Example 10.1 are shown in Table 10.1. We now describe some potentially useful scatter diagrams involving the residuals, illustrating these by Fig. 10.1 which relates to Example 10.1.

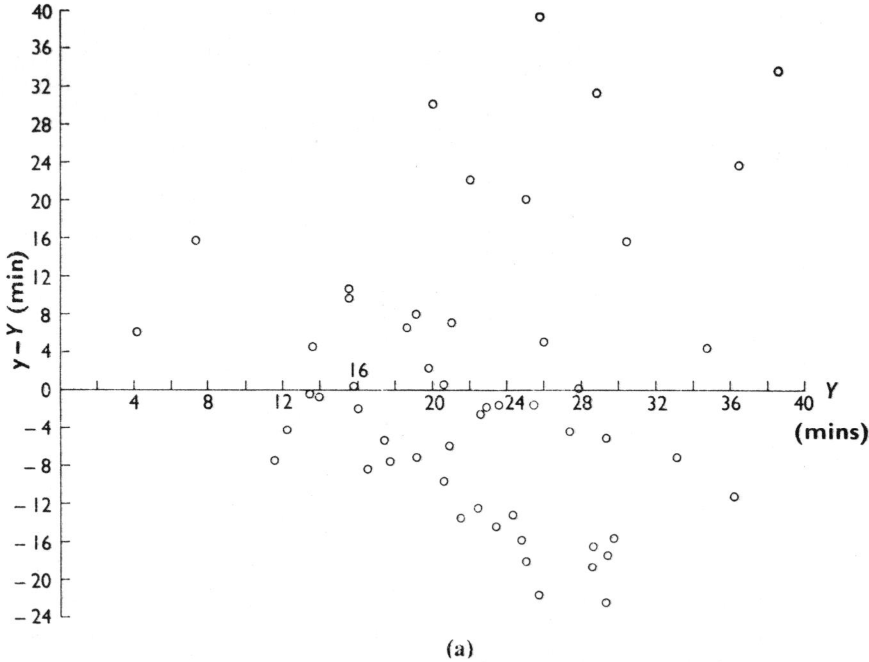

(a)

FIG. 10.1 Residuals of recovery time from multiple regression data of Table 10.1 plotted against (a) predicted value, (b) x_1, log quantity of drug, (c) x_2, mean systolic level during hypotension, (d) the product x_1x_2, (e) age.

(a) *Plot of* $y - Y$ *against* Y; (Fig. 10.1(a)). The residuals are always uncorrelated with the predicted value, as (10.17) shows. Nevertheless, the scatter diagram may provide some useful pointers. The distribution of the residuals may be markedly non-normal; in Fig. 10.1(a) there is some suggestion of positive skewness. The variability of the residuals may not be constant: in Fig. 10.1(a) it seems to increase as Y increases.

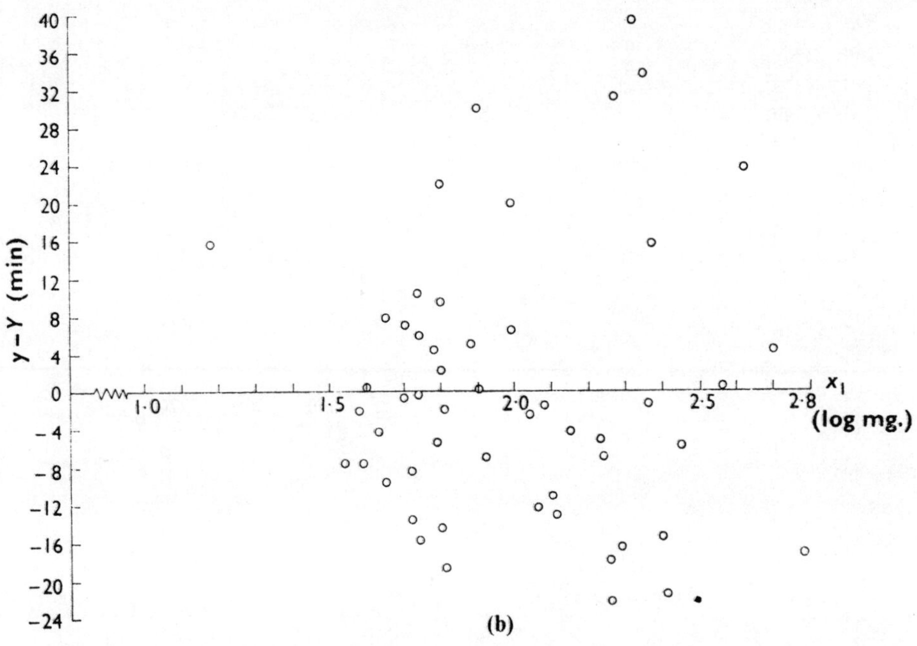
y−Y (min)
40
36
32
28
24
20
16
12
8
4
0
−4
−8
−12
−16
−20
−24
1·0
1·5
2·0
2·5
2·8
x_1
(log mg.)
(b)

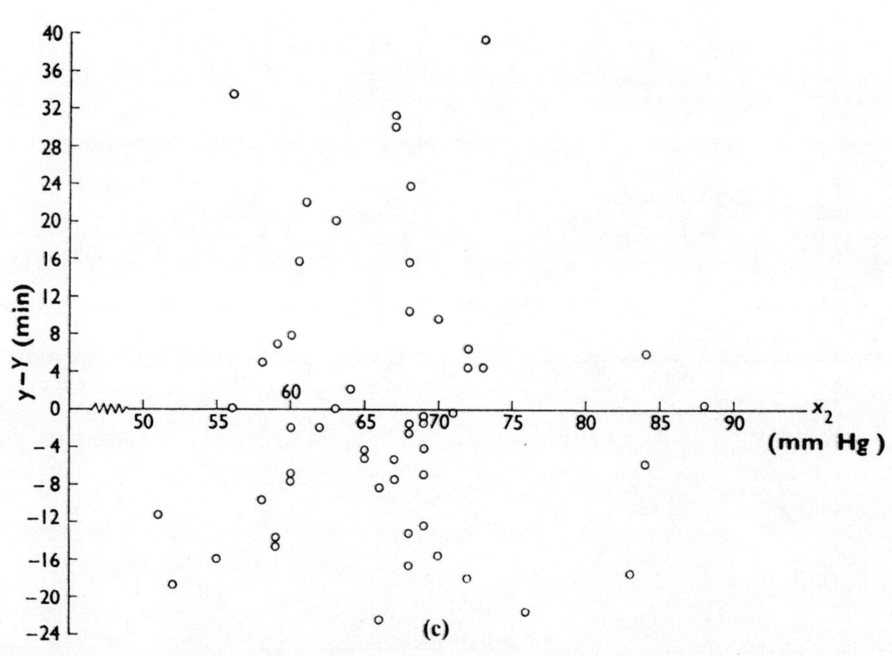
y−Y (min)
40
36
32
28
24
20
16
12
8
4
0
−4
−8
−12
−16
−20
−24
50
55
60
65
70
75
80
85
90
x_2
(mm Hg)
(c)

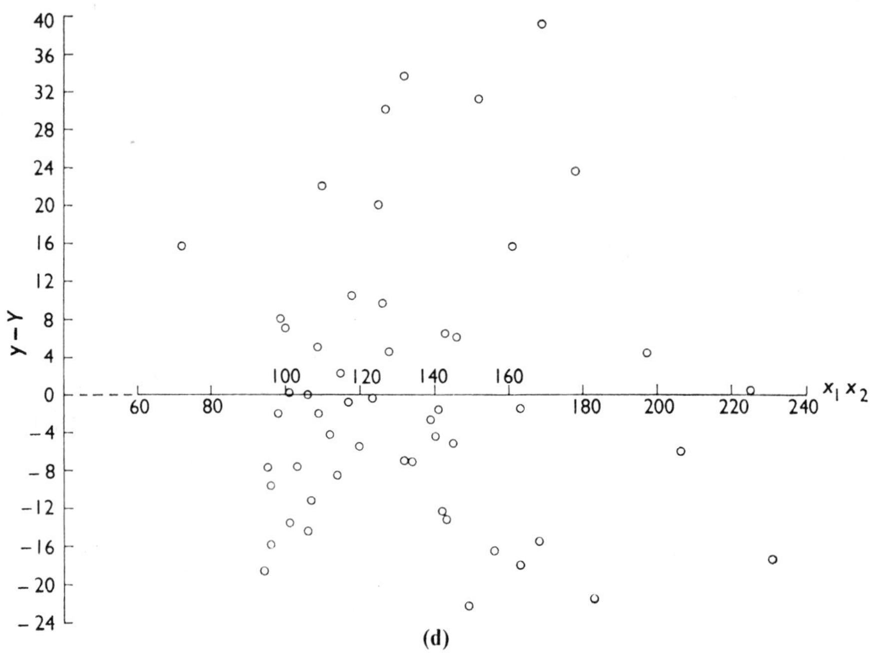

(d)

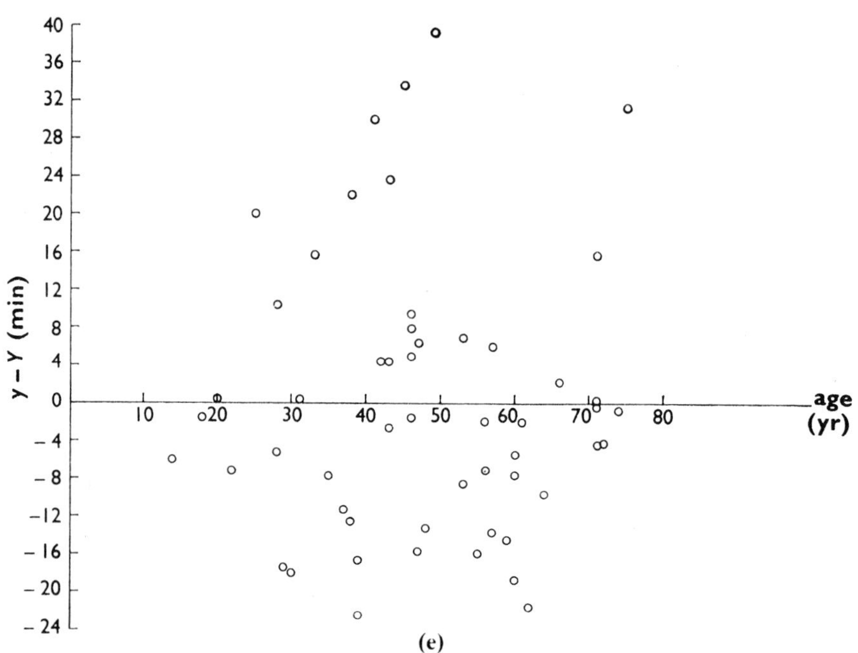

(e)

FIG. 10.1. (cont.)

Both these deficiencies may sometimes be remedied by transformation of the y variable and re-analysis (see Chapter 11). The trend in variability may call for a weighted analysis (see below). Even though the correlation is zero there may be a marked non-linear trend; if so, it is likely to appear also in the plots of type (b) below.

(b) *Plot of $y-Y$ against x_j*; (Fig. 10.1(b), (c)). The residuals may be plotted against the values of any or all of the predictor variables. Again, the correlation will always be zero. There may, however, be a non-linear trend, for example with the residuals tending to rise to a maximum somewhere near the mean, $\bar{x}_j$, and falling away on either side, as is perhaps suggested in Fig. 10.1(c); or showing a trend with a minimum value near $\bar{x}_j$. Such trends suggest that the effect of x_j is not adequately expressed by the linear term in the model. The simplest suggestion would be to add a term involving the square of x_j as an extra predictor variable. This so-called *quadratic* regression is described in section 10.3.

(c) *Plot of $y-Y$ against product x_jx_h*; (Fig. 10.1(d)). The model (10.1) postulates no interaction between the x's, in the sense of section 8.2. That is, the effect of changing one predictor variable is independent of the values taken by any other. This would not be so if a term x_jx_h were introduced into the model. If such a term is needed, but has been omitted, the residuals will tend to be correlated with the product x_jx_h. Fig. 10.1(d) provides no suggestion that interaction is important in our example.

(d) *Plot of $y-Y$ against a new variable x'*; (Fig. 10.1(e)). If x' is a variable not used in the regression, the presence of correlation in this plot will give a good visual indication that it should be included. In Fig. 10.1(e) we have introduced a variable not previously used in the calculations, i.e. the age of the patient. The diagram gives no suggestion of a correlation.

WEIGHTED ANALYSIS

Sometimes the various values of y are known to have different residual variances. Suppose the variance of y_i is known, or can be assumed to be σ^2/w_i, where the σ^2 is in general unknown, but the weights w_i are known. In other words, we know the *relative* precisions of the different observations. The correction procedure is to follow the general multiple regression method, replacing all sums like $\sum x_j$ and $\sum y$ by $\sum wx_j$ and $\sum wy$; (the subscript i, identifying the individual observation, has been dropped here to avoid confusion with j which identifies a particular explanatory variable). Similarly all sums of squares and products are weighted: $\sum y^2$ is replaced by $\sum wy^2$, $\sum x_j x_k$ by $\sum wx_j x_k$.

The standard t tests, F tests and confidence intervals are then valid. The Residual MSq is an estimate of σ^2, and may, in certain situations, be checked against an independent estimate of σ^2. For example, in the situation discussed above, where the observations fall into groups with particular combinations of values of predictor variables, y_i may be taken to be the mean of n_i observations at a specified combination of x's. The variance of y_i is then σ^2/n_i, and the analysis may be carried out by weighted regression, with $w_i = n_i$. The Residual MSq will be the same as that derived from line (iii) of the analysis on page 315, and may be compared (as indicated in the previous discussion) against the Within groups MSq in line (iv).

The book by Draper and Smith (1966) may be consulted for a full discussion of many of the practical aspects of multiple regression analysis.

10.2 MULTIPLE REGRESSION IN GROUPS

When the observations fall into k groups formed by a one-way classification, questions of the types discussed in sections 9.4 and 9.5 may arise. Can equations with the same b's (although perhaps different a's) be fitted to the different groups, or must each group have its own set of b's? (This is a generalization of the comparison of slopes in section 9.4.) If the same b's are appropriate for all groups, can the same a be used (thus leading to one equation for the whole data), or must each group have its own a? (This is a generalization of the analysis of covariance, section 9.5.)

The methods of approach are rather straightforward developments of those used previously and will be indicated only briefly. Suppose there are, in all, n observations falling into k groups, with p predictor variables observed throughout. To test whether the same b's are appropriate for all groups, an analysis of variance analogous to Table 9.5 may be derived, with the following subdivision of DF:

	DF
(i) Due to regression with common b's	p
(ii) Differences between b's	$p(k-1)$
(iii) Residual about separate regressions	$n-(p+1)k$
Within groups	$n-k$

The DF agree with those of Table 9.5 when $p=1$. The SSq within groups is exactly the same as in Table 9.5. The SSq for (iii) is obtained by fitting a separate regression equation to each of the k groups and adding the resulting Residual SSq. The residual for the ith group has $n_i-(p+1)$ DF, and these add to $n-(p+1)k$. The SSq for (i) is obtained by a simple multiple regression calculation using the pooled sums of squares and products *within groups* throughout; this is the appropriate generalization of the first line of Table 9.5. The SSq for (ii) is obtained by subtraction. The DF, obtained also by subtraction, are plausible as this SSq represents differences between k values of b_1, between k values of b_2, and so on; there are p predictor variables, each corresponding to $k-1$ DF.

It may be more useful to have a rather more specific comparison of some regression coefficients than is provided by the composite test described above. For a particular coefficient, b_j, for instance, the k separate multiple regressions will provide k values, each with its standard error. Straightforward comparisons of these will often suffice.

The analysis of covariance assumes common values for the b's and tests for differences betwee the a's. The corrected SSq and their DF are obtained by the following generalization of Table 9.7:

	Corrected SSq	DF
(iv) Between groups	by subtraction	$k-1$
(v) Within groups	Residual about Within groups regression	$n-k-p$
(vi) Total	Residual about Total regression	$n-p-1$

The correct Total SSq (vi) is obtained from a single multiple regression calculation for the whole data; the DF are $n-p-1$ as usual. That for (v) is obtained as the residual for the regression calculation using *within groups* sums of squares and products; it is in fact the residual corresponding to the regression term (i) in the previous table, and is the sum of the SSq for (ii) and (iii) in that table. That for (iv) is obtained by subtraction. Corrected means analogous to (9.37) are obtained as

$$\bar{y}_i'=\bar{y}_i+b_1(x_{01}-\bar{x}_{i1})+b_2(x_{02}-\bar{x}_{i2})+\ldots+b_p(x_{0p}-\bar{x}_{ip}) \quad (10.23)$$

where $b_1, b_2, \ldots, b_p$ are the coefficients in the Within groups regression and $\bar{x}_{ij}$ is the mean of x_j in the ith group. The corrected difference between two groups—say, groups 1 and 2—is

$$\bar{y}_1'-\bar{y}_2'=(\bar{y}_1-\bar{y}_2)-\sum_j b_j(\bar{x}_{1j}-\bar{x}_{2j}), \quad (10.24)$$

and its estimated variance is

$$\mathrm{var}(\bar{y}_1' - \bar{y}_2')$$
$$= s_c^2\left\{\frac{1}{n_1} + \frac{1}{n_2} + \sum_j c_{jj}(\bar{x}_{1j} - \bar{x}_{2j})^2 + 2\sum_{j\neq h} c_{jh}(\bar{x}_{1j} - \bar{x}_{2j})(\bar{x}_{1h} - \bar{x}_{2h})\right\}. \tag{10.25}$$

The second summation is taken over all *pairs* of predictor variables. The general form of (10.25) follows from (3.13) and (3.14), the variances and covariances of the b's being given by (10.21) and (10.22). The c's are the elements of the inverse matrix obtained in the Within groups regression, and s_c^2 is the Residual MSq from line (v) on page 321.

Multiple regression techniques offer an alternative approach to the analysis of covariance, enabling the whole analysis to be done by one application of multiple regression. Consider first the case of two groups. Let us introduce a new variable z, which is given the value 1 for all observations in Group 1 and 0 for all observations in Group 2. As a model for the data as a whole, suppose that

$$\mathrm{E}(y) = \alpha + \delta z + \beta_1 x_1 + \beta_2 x_2 + \ldots + \beta_p x_p. \tag{10.26}$$

Because of the definition of z, (10.26) is equivalent to assuming that

$$\mathrm{E}(y) = \begin{cases} \alpha + \delta + \beta_1 x_1 + \beta_2 x_2 + \ldots + \beta_p x_p & \text{for Group 1} \\ \alpha \qquad + \beta_1 x_1 + \beta_2 x_2 + \ldots + \beta_p x_p & \text{for Group 2.} \end{cases} \tag{10.27}$$

which is precisely the model required for the analysis of covariance. According to (10.27) the regression coefficients on the x's are the same for both groups, but there is a difference δ between the intercepts. The usual significance test in the analysis of covariance tests the hypothesis that $\delta = 0$. Since (10.26) and (10.27) are equivalent, it follows from (10.26) that the whole analysis can be performed by a single multiple regression of y on $z, x_1, x_2, \ldots, x_p$. The new variable, z, is called a *dummy variable*. The coefficient δ is the partial regression coefficient of y on z, and is estimated in the usual way by the multiple regression analysis, giving an estimate d, say. The variance of d is estimated as usual from (10.21), and the appropriate tests and confidence limits follow by use of the t distribution. Note that the residual mean square has $n-p-2$ DF (since the introduction of z increases the number of predictor variables from p to $p+1$), and that this agrees with (v) on page 321 (putting $k=2$).

When $k > 2$, the procedure described above is generalized by the introduction of $k-1$ dummy variables. These can be defined in many equivalent ways. One convenient method is as follows. The table shows the values taken by each of the dummy variables for all observations in each group.

Group	Dummy variables z_1	z_2	...	z_{k-1}
1	1	0	...	0
2	0	1	...	0
.	.	.		.
.	.	.		.
.	.	.		.
$k-1$	0	0		1
k	0	0		0

The model specifies that

$$E(y)=\alpha+\delta_1 z_1+\ldots+\delta_{k-1}z_{k-1}+\beta_1 x_1+\ldots+\beta_p x_p \qquad (10.28)$$

and the fitted multiple regression equation is

$$Y=a+d_1 z_1+\ldots+d_{k-1}z_{k-1}+b_1 x_1+\ldots+b_p x_p. \qquad (10.29)$$

The regression coefficients $d_1, d_2, \ldots, d_{k-1}$ represent contrasts between the mean values of y for Groups 1, 2, . . ., $k-1$ and that for Group k, after correction for differences in the x's. The overall significance test for the null hypothesis that $\delta_1=\delta_2=\ldots=\delta_{k-1}=0$ was previously done by the F test on $k+1$ and $n-k-p$ DF ((iv) and (v) on page 321). The equivalent procedure here is to test the composite significance of $d_1, d_2, \ldots, d_k$ by deleting the dummy variables from the analysis (page 313). This leads to exactly the same F test.

If the investigator is interested in a contrast between Group k and one of the other groups, the appropriate d_i, with its standard error given by the regression analysis, is immediately available; d_i is in fact the same as the difference between corrected means $\bar{y}'_i-\bar{y}'_k$. For a contrast between two groups other than Group k, say Groups 1 and 2, we use the fact that

$$\bar{y}'_1-\bar{y}'_2=d_1-d_2,$$

and

$$\text{var}(d_1-d_2)=\text{var}(d_1)+\text{var}(d_2)-2\,\text{cov}(d_1, d_2),$$

the variances and covariances being given as usual by (10.21) and (10.22).

Example 10.2

The three-group covariance analysis of Example 9.5 may be done by introducing two dummy variables: z_1, taking the value 1 in Group A_1 and 0 otherwise; and z_2, taking the value 1 in Group A_2 and 0 otherwise. As before, y represents vital capacity and x age. The multiple regression of y on z_1, z_2 and x, and the regression of y on x, give the following analysis of variance table:

	DF	SSq	MSq	VR
(1) Due to regression on x	1	17·444		
(2) Due to introduction of z_1 and z_2 (=(3)−(1))	2	0·162	0·081	0·22
(3) Due to regression on z_1, z_2 and x	3	17·606		
(4) Residual about regression on z_1, z_2 and x	80	30·033	0·3754	
Total	83	47·639		

Apart from rounding errors, the SSq from line (2) agrees with the Corrected SSq between groups in Example 9.5, and the Residual SSq from line (4) is the same as the Corrected SSq within groups.

The partial regression coefficients, with their standard errors

$$d_1 = -0{\cdot}1169 \pm 0{\cdot}2092$$
$$d_2 = -0{\cdot}0702 \pm 0{\cdot}1487$$
$$b_1 = -0{\cdot}0398 \pm 0{\cdot}0063 \ (t = -6{\cdot}29).$$

The coefficients d_1 and d_2 are estimates of the corrected differences between Groups A_1 and A_2, respectively, and Group B; neither is significant. The coefficient b_1, representing the age effect, is highly significant.

10.3 POLYNOMIAL AND OTHER CURVILINEAR REGRESSIONS

Reference was made in section 10.1 to the possibility of creating new predictor variables defined as the squares of existing variables, to cope with non-linear or *curvilinear* relationships. This is an important idea, and is most easily studied in situations in which there is originally only one predictor variable, x.

Instead of the linear regression equation

$$\mathrm{E}(y) = \alpha + \beta x \tag{10.30}$$

introduced in section 5.2, we consider the *polynomial* model

$$\mathrm{E}(y) = \alpha + \beta_1 x + \beta_2 x^2 + \ldots + \beta_p x^p. \tag{10.31}$$

The highest power of x, denoted here by p, is called the *degree* of the polynomial. Some typical shapes of low degree polynomial curves are shown in Fig. 10.2. The curve for $p = 2$, when the term in x^2 is added, is called *quadratic*; that for $p = 3$ *cubic*, and that for $p = 4$ *quartic*. Clearly,

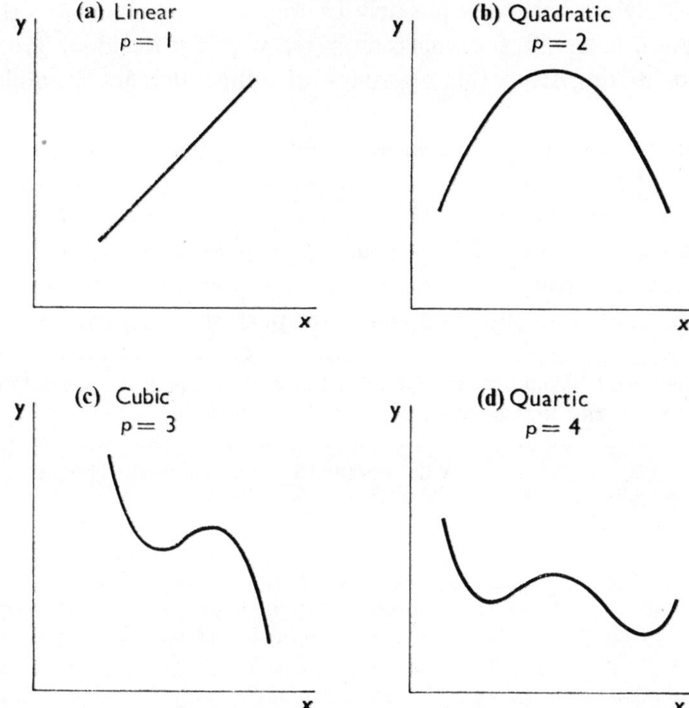

FIG. 10.2 Illustrations of polynomials of up to the 4th degree.

a wide variety of curves can be represented by polynomials. The quadratic curve has one peak or trough; the cubic has at most two peaks or troughs; and so on. A particular set of data may be fitted well by a portion of a low degree polynomial even though no peaks or troughs are present. In particular, data showing a moderate amount of curvature can often be fitted adequately by a quadratic curve.

The general principle of polynomial regression analysis is to regard the successive powers of x as separate predictor variables. Thus, to fit the p-degree polynomial (10.31), we could define $x_1=x$, $x_2=x^2$, . . ., $x_p=x^p$, and apply the standard methods of section 10.1. It will often be uncertain which degree of polynomial is required. Considerations of simplicity suggest that as low an order as possible should be used; for example, we should normally use linear regression unless there were any particular reason to use a higher degree polynomial. The usual approach is to use a slightly higher degree than one supposes to be necessary. The highest degree terms can then be dropped successively so long as they contribute, separately or together, increments to the SSq which are non-significant when compared with the Residual SSq. Some problems arising from this approach are illustrated in Example 10.3 below.

Note that, with n observations, all with different values of x, a polynomial of degree $p=n-1$ would leave $n-p-1=n-(n-1)-1=0$ DF. It is always possible to fit a polynomial of degree $n-1$, so as to pass through n points with different values of x, just as a straight line ($p=1$) can be drawn through any two points. The Residual SSq is, therefore, also zero, and no significance tests are possible. To provide a test of

TABLE 10.2 Trend in population of England and Wales between 1801 and 1951 fitted by polynomials up to sixth degree.

Year	Pop. E. & W. millions	Values predicted by polynomial of degree 1	2	3	4	5	6
1801	8·89	6·76	7·85	9·34	8·84	8·67	8·90
11	10·16	9·27	9·90	10·20	10·37	10·54	10·09
21	12·00	11·77	12·03	11·56	11·96	12·13	12·01
31	13·90	14·27	14·22	13·34	13·71	13·74	13·99
41	15·91	16·77	16·47	15·49	15·67	15·57	15·89
51	17·93	19·28	18·79	17·93	17·88	17·72	17·86
61	20·07	21·78	21·18	20·60	20·36	20·23	20·09
71	22·71	24·28	23·64	23·44	23·08	23·04	22·74
81	25·97	26·79	26·15	26·37	26·02	26·08	25·83
91	29·00	29·29	28·74	29·33	29·09	29·24	29·22
1901	32·53	31·79	31·39	32·25	32·22	32·37	32·62
11	36·07	34·29	34·11	35·07	35·27	35·35	35·69
21	37·89	36·80	36·89	37·72	38·12	38·04	38·14
31	39·95	39·30	39·74	40·13	40·58	40·35	39·89
41	—						
51	43·76	44·31	45·63	43·98	43·56	43·66	43·69
(61	46·10)	(46·81	48·68	45·28	43·61	44·75	49·13)
Multiple correlation coefficient		0·9947	0·9962	0·9992	0·9996	0·9996	0·9999
Residual MSq		1·526	1·185	0·287	0·160	0·152	0·041
DF		13	12	11	10	9	8
t for highest degree term		34·79**	2·18*	−6·21**	−3·11*	1·33	5·03**

* $0{\cdot}01<P<0{\cdot}05$
** $P<0{\cdot}01$

the adequacy of the model the degree of the polynomial should be considerably lower than the number of observations.

Example 10.3

Table 10.2 gives the population size of England and Wales (in millions) as recorded at decennial censuses between 1801 and 1951; there is a gap in the series at 1941, as no census was taken in that year. It is of some interest to fit a smooth curve to the trend in population size, first to provide estimates for intermediate years, and secondly, for projection beyond the end of the series (although demographers would in practice use more sophisticated methods of projection: P. R. Cox (1970)). The figure for 1961 is given at the foot of the main series to provide a comparison with estimates obtained by extrapolation from the main series.

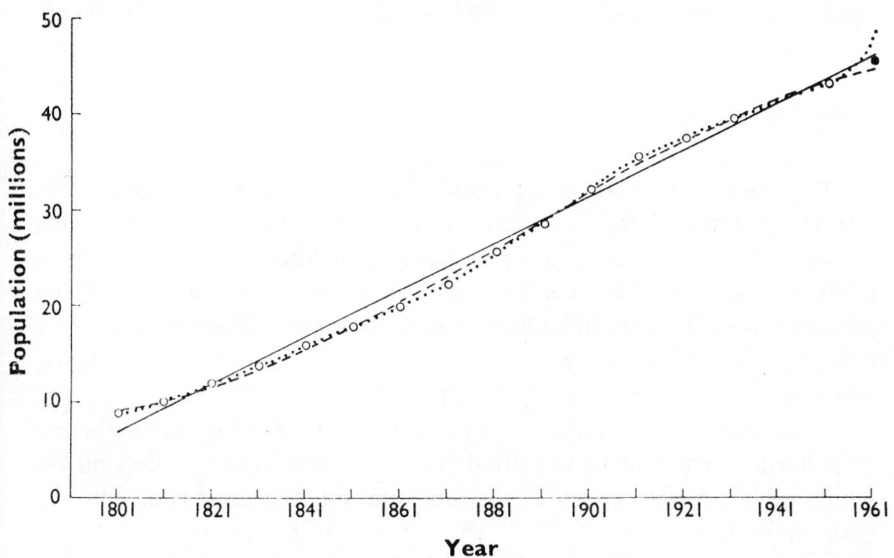

FIG. 10.3 Polynomial regressions fitted to population trend data (Table 10.2). $p=1$ ———; $p=3$ – – –; $p=6$ .....

The data are plotted in Fig. 10.3. The trend is not too far from linear, but there are obvious systematic deviations which suggest that a polynomial curve might fit quite well.

Table 10.2 shows the predicted values from polynomials of up to the sixth degree, and Fig. 10.3 illustrates the fits obtained by linear ($p=1$), cubic ($p=3$) and sixth-degree ($p=6$) curves. The entries at the foot of Table 10.2 show that the Residual MSq is reduced substantially by the introduction of the cubic term, and this curve seems from Fig. 10.3 to provide an excellent fit. However, there are slight systematic fluctuations of groups of adjacent points about the cubic, and Table 10.2 shows that the introduction of the fourth and sixth degree terms produces significant decreases in the Residual MSq (since the t values for these coefficients are significant).

The process could be continued beyond this stage, but it is doubtful whether any useful purpose would be achieved. We are left in a slight dilemma. There is no theoretical reason for expecting precisely a polynomial curve plus random error. The cubic is a close approximation to the best fitting smooth curve, but slight (yet significant) improvements can be made by introducing several higher degree terms. Note that the improvement is evident in the agreement between observed and predicted values within the range 1801–1951. Extrapolation, or prediction *outside* this range, is a different matter. The linear and cubic curves give adequate agreement between the predicted and observed values for 1961. Higher order curves are much less satisfactory. This is a rather common finding, and argues strongly for the use of a polynomial with as low a degree as possible for an acceptable fit, even though higher degree terms provide noticeable reductions in residual variation within the fitted range.

The various powers of x, which form the predictor variables in (10.31), are correlated with each other, often quite highly so. This occasionally causes some computational difficulties, as a computer is likely to lose accuracy due to rounding errors when calculating the inverse matrix. If such difficulties arise they can usually be overcome by redefining the powers of x as deviations from their own means (Healy, 1963).

These inter-correlations of the powers of x mean that the coefficient of a particular power in the fitted regression equation will depend on which other powers are present in the equation, as indeed is usually the case in multiple regression. If the powers were transformed to an equivalent set of predictor variables which were uncorrelated, we should be able to fit successively higher order polynomials by relatively simple methods, without re-calculating the coefficients previously obtained. This is particularly convenient when the x's are equally spaced, as often happens in controlled experiments (where the x's may represent quantities of some substance) or in time series (where the x's may be equally spaced points of time). The method uses what are called *orthogonal polynomials*. Full details and the necessary reference tables are given in Fisher and Yates (1963).

Orthogonal polynomials provide a useful way of incorporating curvilinear regression in the analysis of variance of balanced data. Suppose that a certain factor is represented by a variable x which is observed at k equally spaced values,

$$x_1, x_2 = x_1 + h, \ldots, x_k = x_1 + (k-1)h.$$

Suppose that there are n observations in each group, and that the observed totals of y are

$$T_1, T_2, \ldots, T_k.$$

If $k=2$, the regression coefficient, b, of y on x, is clearly estimated by

$$\frac{T_2 - T_1}{nh},$$

and the SSq due to regression on 1 DF coincides with the SSq Between groups, namely,

$$\frac{(T_2 - T_1)^2}{2n}$$

(as in (7.10)).

If $k=3$, we could consider a quadratic regression on x which would exactly fit the data, since a quadratic curve can always be found to go through three points. To obtain the regression equation, define two new variables (the orthogonal polynomials),

$$\begin{aligned} X_1 &= (x - \bar{x})/h \\ X_2 &= 3X_1^2 - 2, \end{aligned} \tag{10.32}$$

so that X_1 takes the values -1, 0 and 1, and X_2 takes the values 1, -2 and 1. The regression equation can be written

$$Y = \bar{y} + b_1 X_1 + b_2 X_2 \tag{10.33}$$

where

$$b_1 = (T_3 - T_1)/2n \quad \text{and} \quad b_2 = (T_3 - 2T_2 + T_1)/6n.$$

The equation may be written in terms of x and x^2 by substituting (10.32) in (10.33).

The SSq due to the linear and quadratic terms (which are independent, each on 1 DF, and add to the SSq between groups) are

$$S_1 = \frac{(T_3 - T_1)^2}{2n} \quad \text{and} \quad S_2 = \frac{(T_3 - 2T_2 + T_1)^2}{6n}.$$

The method can clearly be generalized for higher values of k. See Table 12.6.2 of Snedecor and Cochran (1967). The most useful features of the generalization are the SSq for the linear and quadratic terms.

These take the form $(\sum\lambda_i T_i)^2/\sum\lambda_i^2$, where for the linear term the λ_i's are integers centred about zero (e.g. $-1, 0, 1$ for $k=3$; $-3, -1, 1, 3$ for $k=4$). For the quadratic term each λ_i is obtained by squaring the corresponding λ_i for the linear term, subtracting the mean of the values thus obtained and multiplying by a convenient constant if this is necessary to give integer values. These SSq account for 2 DF out of the total $k-1$ DF between groups. The remaining $k-3$ DF represent deviations about the quadratic curve and can be tested against the appropriate residual in the analysis. If necessary the cubic and higher terms can be successively isolated until the MSq for deviations reaches a sufficiently low level.

Some forms of curvilinear trend, other than those represented by polynomials, are occasionally encountered. Two examples are illustrated in Fig. 10.4. The first is *asymptotic regression*, in which the regression line approaches an upper or lower limit exponentially. For methods of fitting the line, see Patterson (1956) or Finney (1958).

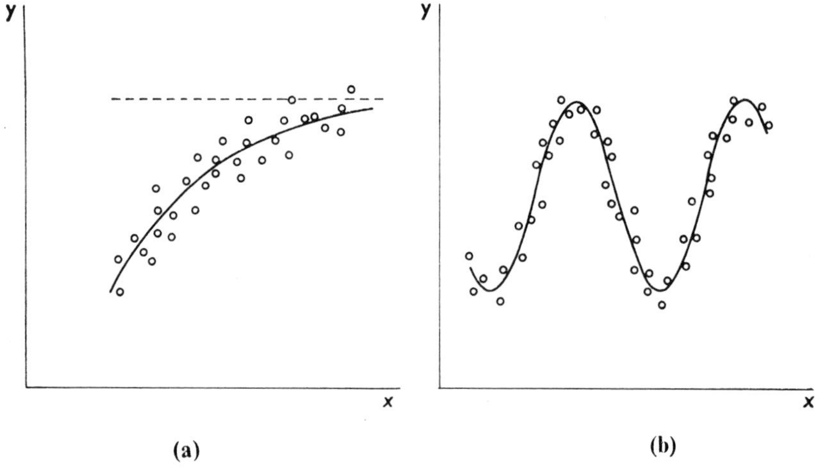

FIG. 10.4 Two forms of non-linear regression: (a) asymptotic, (b) periodic.

The second example in Fig. 10.4 is one of *periodic regression* in which the underlying regression equation has the sinusoidal form

$$Y=\alpha\sin(\beta x+\gamma). \tag{10.34}$$

This represents a cyclical curve which may be useful as a representation of certain cyclical time trends, for example in physiological processes (see also section 10.7). For details see Bliss (1958).

10.4 MULTIPLE REGRESSION IN THE ANALYSIS OF NON-ORTHOGONAL DATA

The analysis of variance was used in Chapter 8 to study the separate effects of various factors, for data classified in designs exhibiting some degree of balance. These so-called *orthogonal designs* enable sums of squares representing different sources of variation to be presented simultaneously in the same analysis. As was observed in section 8.6, non-orthogonality in a design often causes considerable complication in the analysis.

Multiple regression, introduced in section 10.1, is a powerful method of studying the simultaneous effect on a random variable of various predictor variables, and no special conditions of balance are imposed on their values. The effect of any variable, or any group of variables, can, as we have seen, be exhibited by an analysis of variance. We might, therefore, expect that the methods of multiple regression would be useful for the analysis of data classified in an unbalanced design. In section 10.2 the analysis of covariance was considered as a particular instance of multiple regression, the one-way classification into groups being represented by a system of dummy variables. This approach can be adopted for any factor with two or more levels. A significance test for any factor is obtained by performing two multiple regressions: first, including the dummy variables representing the factor; and second, without those variables. For a full analysis of any set of data many multiple regressions may be needed, and a computer with a flexible multiple regression program is almost essential.

Example 10.4

Consider the data in Table 8.15. These were analysed by special methods appropriate to two-way tables, but we could instead have adopted the general approach described above. We define the following dummy variables:

$$x_1=\begin{cases}1 & \text{for Control group}\\ 0 & \text{for Treated group}\end{cases}$$

$$x_2=\begin{cases}1 & \text{for Age group 40–}\\ 0 & \text{otherwise}\end{cases}$$

$$x_3=\begin{cases}1 & \text{for Age group 50–}\\ 0 & \text{otherwise}\end{cases}$$

These represent the main effects of the two factors, treatment and age, and to allow for possible interaction we need two other variables,

$$x_4 = x_1 x_2$$

and

$$x_5 = x_1 x_3.$$

The dependent variable, y, is the number of accidents; the frequency distributions of y are shown in Table 8.15. The total number of observations is 41. As an example of the specification of the variables, the single subject in the Control, 40– group, has the following values:

x_1	x_2	x_3	x_4	x_5	y
1	1	0	1	0	1

To obtain the necessary SSq for the analysis of variance shown in Table 8.16, we need the multiple regressions shown in Table 10.3. For many computer programs these can all be requested as part of the same job.

TABLE 10.3 Multiple regressions required for analysis of data in Table 8.15

Regression	Residual SSq		DF
y on x_1, x_2, x_3, x_4, x_5	17·0350	(a)	35
y on x_1, x_2, x_3	17·0593	(b)	37
y on x_2, x_3	22·9299	(c)	38
y on x_1	19·0000	(d)	39

The Residual SSq from (a) is 17·0350, the same as the Within cells Residual of Table 8.16, since the five dummy variables, x_1 to x_5, exactly account for the differences between the six cells. The difference between (b) and (a) is 0·0243 on 2 DF, the same as the SSq for the interaction $T \times A$ in Table 8.16. Having seen, by the F test given in Table 8.16, that the interaction is non-significant, we test Treatments by the difference (c)−(b), which is 5·8706 on 1 DF, essentially the same as the adjusted Treatments SSq in Table 8.16. As a test for Age, (d)−(b)=1·9407 on 2 DF, again agreeing with the adjusted Age SSq in Table 8.16.

For further examples of the use of dummy variables in the analysis of non-orthogonal data, see Hay (1967).

10.5 LINEAR DISCRIMINANT FUNCTIONS

In multiple regression each individual provides observations simultaneously on several variables. Yet only one of these, the dependent variable, is regarded as a *random* variable. Multiple regression is properly regarded, therefore, as a univariate technique, like all the other methods of analysis considered so far in this book. The function of the predictor variables in multiple regression is to classify the individual in a way which is rather similar to the qualitative classifications in an experimental design.

Multivariate analysis is a collection of techniques appropriate for situations in which the random variation in several variables has to be studied simultaneously. The subject is extensive and is treated fully in several textbooks. It cannot be explored in detail in the present book. The next section contains a brief survey of some methods which have been found useful in medical research. In the present section we concentrate on the most widely used multivariate method, that of the *linear discriminant function.*

Suppose there are k groups of individuals, with n_i individuals in the ith group, and that on each individual we measure p variables, x_1, x_2, ..., x_p. A rule is required for discriminating between the groups, so that for any new individual known to come from one of the groups (the particular group being unknown), the rule could be applied and the individual assigned to the most appropriate group. This situation might arise in taxonomic studies, the x's being physical measurements and the groups being species. The rule would then allocate a new individual to one or other of the species on the basis of its physical characteristics. Another example might arise in differential diagnosis. Observations would be made on patients known to fall into particular diagnostic groups. The object would be to obtain a rule for allotting a new patient to one of these groups by measuring the same variables. In each of these examples, and in all applications of discriminant functions, the original classification into groups must be made independently of the x variables. In the diagnostic situation, for example, the patients' diagnoses may be determined by authoritative but arduous procedures, and one may wish to see how reliably the same diagnoses can be reached by using variables (the x's) which are cheaper or less harrowing for the patient. Alternatively, the correct diagnoses may have become available only after the lapse of time, and one may wish to determine these as far as possible by variables measurable at a much earlier stage of the disease.

Consider first the situation with $k=2$, denoting the two groups by A and B. We shall approach this problem from three different points of view, all of which we shall find leading to the same solution.

(a) *Separation between groups*

Suppose we look for a linear function

$$z = b_1x_1 + b_2x_2 + \ldots + b_px_p. \tag{10.35}$$

If this is going to discriminate well between the groups we should expect the mean values of z in the two groups to be reasonably far apart in comparison with the variation of z within groups. We could therefore try to find values of the b's such that the ratio

$$\Delta^2 = \frac{(\bar{z}_A - \bar{z}_B)^2}{\text{variance of } z \text{ within groups}} \tag{10.36}$$

is as large as possible. The estimated variance of z will in general be different in the two groups, but a pooled estimate could be calculated as in the two-sample t test.

The solution of this problem is as follows:

(i) Calculate the pooled sums of squares and products of the x's within groups, and obtain the inverse matrix

$$\begin{pmatrix} c_{11} & c_{12} & \ldots & c_{1p} \\ c_{21} & c_{22} & \ldots & c_{2p} \\ \cdot & & & \\ \cdot & & & \\ \cdot & & & \\ c_{p1} & c_{p2} & \ldots & c_{pp} \end{pmatrix}$$

either by calculation as in (10.7) or by a computer program.

(ii) Calculate the b's as follows:

$$\left.\begin{aligned} b_1 &= c_{11}(\bar{x}_{A1} - \bar{x}_{B1}) + c_{12}(\bar{x}_{A2} - \bar{x}_{B2}) + \ldots + c_{1p}(\bar{x}_{Ap} - \bar{x}_{Bp}) \\ b_2 &= c_{21}(\bar{x}_{A1} - \bar{x}_{B1}) + c_{22}(\bar{x}_{A2} - \bar{x}_{B2}) + \ldots + c_{2p}(\bar{x}_{Ap} - \bar{x}_{Bp}) \\ &\cdot \\ &\cdot \\ &\cdot \\ b_p &= c_{p1}(\bar{x}_{A1} - \bar{x}_{B1}) + c_{p2}(\bar{x}_{A2} - \bar{x}_{B2}) + \ldots + c_{pp}(\bar{x}_{Ap} - \bar{x}_{Bp}) \end{aligned}\right\} \tag{10.37}$$

Here, $\bar{x}_{Ai}$ is the mean of x_i in group A, and so on.

Computer programs for the whole calculation are widely available.

To use z for allocating future individuals to one of the two groups we need an end-point to discriminate between A and B. A completely symmetrical rule would be to use as an end-point the mean, z_0, of

$\bar{z}_A$ and $\bar{z}_B$. From (10.35),

$$\left.\begin{aligned}\bar{z}_A &= b_1\bar{x}_{A1}+b_2\bar{x}_{A2}+\ldots+b_p\bar{x}_{Ap} \\ \text{and}\qquad \bar{z}_B &= b_1\bar{x}_{B1}+b_2\bar{x}_{B2}+\ldots+b_p\bar{x}_{Bp},\end{aligned}\right\} \quad (10.38)$$

whence

$$z_0 = b_1\left(\frac{\bar{x}_{A1}+\bar{x}_{B1}}{2}\right)+b_2\left(\frac{\bar{x}_{A2}+\bar{x}_{B2}}{2}\right)+\ldots+b_p\left(\frac{\bar{x}_{Ap}+\bar{x}_{Bp}}{2}\right). \quad (10.39)$$

If $\bar{z}_A > \bar{z}_B$ the allocation rule is: allocate an individual to A if $z > z_0$, and to B if $z < z_0$. Many computer programs calculate the value of z for each individual in the two original samples. It is thus possible to count how many individuals in the two groups would have been wrongly classified by the allocation rule. This unfortunately gives an over-optimistic picture, because the allocation rule has been determined to be the best (in a certain sense) for these two particular samples, and it is likely to perform rather less well on the average with subsequent observations from the two groups. See Hills (1966).

The allocation rule based on z_0 is intended to get near to minimizing the sum of two probabilities of misclassification—that of allocating an A individual to group B, and that of allocating a B individual to group A. If one group is *a priori* more likely than the other, or if the consequences of one type of misclassification are particularly severe, a different value of z_0 may be preferable. See section 16.3.

Another way of assessing the effectiveness of the discrimination is to calculate the ratio Δ^2 from (10.36). Its square root, Δ, is called the *generalized distance* between the two groups. If Δ is greater than about 4 the situation is like that in two univariate distributions whose means differ by more than 4 standard deviations: the overlap is quite small, and the probabilities of misclassification are correspondingly small. An alternative formula for Δ^2, equivalent to (10.36), is:

$$\Delta^2 = (n_1+n_2-2)\sum b_i(\bar{x}_{Ai}-\bar{x}_{Bi}). \quad (10.40)$$

(b) *Likelihood ratio*

If there were only one variable, x, following a continuous distribution in each group, it would be natural to allocate an individual to the group which gave the higher probability density for the observed value of x; another way of expressing this is to say that the allocation is to the group with the higher likelihood. If there are several x's we cannot easily depict the probability density, but given the mathematical form of the distribution of the x's this density, or likelihood, can be calculated. One particular form of distribution is called the *multivariate normal distribution*; it implies, among other things, that each x separately follows a normal distribution and that all regressions of one variable on any set of other variables are linear. If the x's followed multivariate normal distributions with the same variances and correlations for group A as for group B, but with different means, the ratio of the likelihoods of A and B would be found to depend on a linear function

$$Z = \beta_1 x_1 + \beta_2 x_2 + \ldots + \beta_p x_p,$$

and the β's would be estimated from the two initial samples precisely by the b's as calculated in (a). The rule described above, in which the allocation is to A or B according as $z > z_0$ or $z < z_0$, is equivalent to asking which of the two groups is estimated to have the higher likelihood.

In practice, of course, multivariate distributions are not normal, and are perhaps less likely to be nearly normal than are univariate distributions. Nevertheless, the discriminant function (10.35) is likely to be a good indication of the relative likelihoods of the two groups.

(c) *Regression with a dummy dependent variable*

Suppose we define a variable y which takes the value 1 in group B and 0 in group A. Putting all the observations into one group, we could do the multiple regression of y on $x_1, x_2, \ldots, x_p$. This would give a linear function of the x's which would predict the observed values of y as well as possible. If the multiple correlation coefficient is reasonably high, the predicted values of y for groups A and B should therefore be rather well separated (clustering near the observed values of 0 and 1). The estimated regression function can be shown to be (apart from a constant factor) the same as the linear discriminant function obtained by method (a). This is a useful identity since method (c) can be carried out on a computer with a multiple regression program, whereas method (a) requires a special program. The matrix inversion in step (i) of method (a) is similar to that required in the multiple regression, but there is an important difference: in (a) the sums of squares and products are calculated *within groups*, whereas for (c) the *total* sums of squares and products are required. A further advantage of the regression approach is that the usual variance ratio test for the significance of the multiple regression can be interpreted also as a valid test for the discriminant function. The null hypothesis is that in the two groups from which the samples are drawn the x's have exactly the same joint distribution; in that case, of course, no discrimination is possible. Furthermore, the usual t tests for the partial regression coefficients give a useful indication of the importance of particular variables in the discrimination.

Although multiple regression provides a useful way of calculating the discriminant function, it is important to realise that the usual model for multiple regression is no longer valid. Usually, in multiple regression, y is a random variable and the x's are arbitrary variables. In the present problem the x's are random variables and y is an arbitrary score characterizing the two groups. A related point is that the average value of y for a particular set of x's should not be interpreted as the probability that an individual with these x's falls in group B rather than in group A; if the regression equation were interpreted in this way it might lead to some predicted probabilities greater than 1 or less than 0. For further discussion of this point, see section 12.5.

The usual analysis of variance of y corresponding to the multiple regression analysis provides a useful method of estimating the generalized distance, Δ:

$$\Delta^2 = \frac{(n_1+n_2)(n_1+n_2-2)}{n_1 n_2} \cdot \frac{\text{SSq due to regression}}{\text{SSq about regression}}. \qquad (10.41)$$

Example 10.5

The data shown in Table 10.4 relate to 79 infants affected by haemolytic disease of the newborn, of whom 63 survived and 16 died. For each infant there is recorded the cord haemoglobin concentration, x (measured in g./100 ml.) and the bilirubin concentration, y (mg./100 ml.). It is required to predict by means of these two measurements whether any particular infant is more likely to die or to survive.

We follow method (a). The within groups SSqP matrix and its inverse are

$$\begin{pmatrix} 644{\cdot}0387 & -129{\cdot}7500 \\ -129{\cdot}7500 & 123{\cdot}6687 \end{pmatrix} \text{ and } \begin{pmatrix} 0{\cdot}00196886 & 0{\cdot}00206568 \\ 0{\cdot}00206568 & 0{\cdot}0102534 \end{pmatrix}.$$

The means, and their differences and means, are

	$\bar{x}$	$\bar{y}$
Survivals	13·897	3·090
Deaths	7·756	4·831
Difference, $S-D$	6·141	−1·741
Mean, $\frac{1}{2}(S+D)$	10·827	3·961

TABLE 10.4 Concentrations of haemoglobin and bilirubin for infants with haemolytic disease of the newborn

x: haemoglobin (g./100 ml.)

y: bilirubin (mg./100 ml.)

Survivals ($n = 63$)

x	y	x	y	x	y	x	y
18·7	2·2	15·8	3·7	14·3	3·3	11·8	4·5
17·8	2·7	15·8	3·0	14·1	3·7	11·6	3·7
17·8	2·5	15·8	1·7	14·0	5·8	10·9	3·5
17·6	4·1	15·6	1·4	13·9	2·9	10·9	4·1
17·6	3·2	15·6	2·0	13·8	3·7	10·9	1·5
17·6	1·0	15·6	1·6	13·6	2·3	10·8	3·3
17·5	1·6	15·4	4·1	13·5	2·1	10·6	3·4
17·4	1·8	15·4	2·2	13·4	2·3	10·5	6·3
17·4	2·4	15·3	2·0	13·3	1·8	10·2	3·3
17·0	0·4	15·1	3·2	12·5	4·5	9·9	4·0
17·0	1·6	14·8	1·8	12·3	5·0	9·8	4·2
16·6	3·6	14·7	3·7	12·2	3·5	9·7	4·9
16·3	4·1	14·7	3·0	12·2	2·4	8·7	5·5
16·1	2·0	14·6	5·0	12·0	2·8	7·4	3·0
16·0	2·6	14·3	3·8	12·0	3·5	5·7	4·6
16·0	0·8	14·3	4·2	11·8	2·3		
						875·5	194·7

Deaths ($n = 16$)

x	y	x	y
15·8	1·8	7·1	5·6
12·3	5·6	6·7	5·9
9·5	3·6	5·7	6·2
9·4	3·8	5·5	4·8
9·2	5·6	5·3	4·8
8·8	5·6	5·3	2·8
7·6	4·7	5·1	5·8
7·4	6·8	3·4	3·9
		124·1	77·3

Sums of squares and products within groups

	Sx^2	Sxy	Sy^2
Survivals	500·6593	−108·4219	96·6943
Deaths	143·3794	−21·3281	26·9744
Pooled	644·0387	−129·7500	123·6687

From (10.37),

$$b_1=(0{\cdot}00196886)(6{\cdot}141)+(0{\cdot}00206568)(-1{\cdot}741)=0{\cdot}008494$$

$$b_2=(0{\cdot}00206568)(6{\cdot}141)+(0{\cdot}0102534)(-1{\cdot}741)=-0{\cdot}005166.$$

The discriminant function is

$$z=0{\cdot}008494\,x-0{\cdot}005166\,y. \qquad (10.42)$$

The use of the discriminant function is unaffected by multiplication of all the b's by a constant factor. Dividing (10.42) by the first coefficient, we obtain

$$z=x-0{\cdot}608\,y.$$

From (10.39),

$$z_0=10{\cdot}827-(0{\cdot}608)(3{\cdot}961)=8{\cdot}419.$$

The usual allocation rule would predict survival if $z>8{\cdot}419$ and death if $z<8{\cdot}419$.

The position is shown in Fig. 10.5, where the diagonal line represents critical points for which $z=z_0$, i.e. for which $x-0{\cdot}608y=8{\cdot}419$. It is clear from Fig. 10.5 that discrimination by z is much better than by y alone, but hardly better than by x alone. This is confirmed by a count of the numbers of individuals misclassified by x alone (using a critical value of 10·83), by y alone (critical value 3·96) and by z:

	Group to which individual is allocated						
Actual	By x		By y		By z		Total
group	S	D	S	D	S	D	
S	53	10	47	16	54	9	63
D	2	14	5	11	2	14	16

It seems, therefore, that discrimination between deaths and survivals is improved little, if at all, by the use of bilirubin concentrations in addition to those of haemoglobin.

To calculate Δ, we find

$$\Sigma b_i(\bar{x}_{Ai}-\bar{x}_{Bi})=(0{\cdot}008494)(6{\cdot}141)+(-0{\cdot}005166)(-1{\cdot}741)$$
$$=0{\cdot}06116$$

and, from (10.40),

$$\Delta^2=77(0{\cdot}06116)$$
$$=4{\cdot}709,$$

and

$$\Delta=\sqrt{4{\cdot}709}=2{\cdot}17.$$

For two normal distributions with equal variance, separated by 2·17 standard deviations, the proportion of observations misclassified by the mid-point between the means would be the single tail-area beyond a normal deviate of

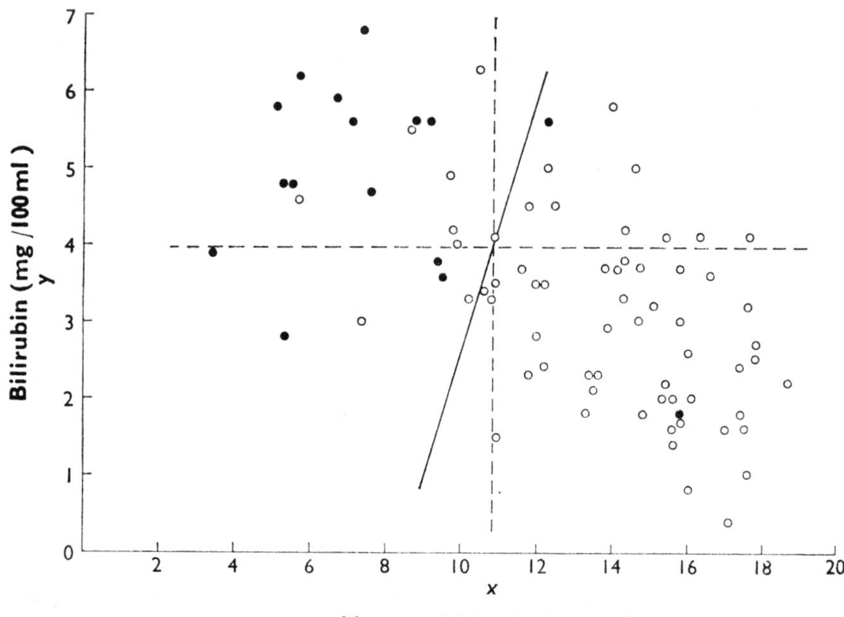

FIG. 10.5 Scatter diagram of haemoglobin and bilirubin values for infants with haemolytic disease (Table 10.4) showing a line of discrimination between deaths ● and survivals ○.

1·085, which is 0·139. As it happens the proportion of misclassifications by z is given above as $11/79=0{\cdot}139$, but the closeness of the agreement is fortuitous!

The reader with access to a multiple regression program is invited to analyse these data by method (c), using (10·41) as an alternative formula for Δ^2.

For references to a number of medical applications of discriminant function analysis see Radhakrishna (1964).

10.6 OTHER MULTIVARIATE METHODS

This section contains a very brief account of a few techniques of multivariate analysis. None of these methods is described in sufficient detail here to enable research workers to proceed without reference to other sources. Many standard techniques are not mentioned here. The present account may, however, give some indication of the sort of questions which multivariate methods are designed to answer. Computer programs have made generally accessible several methods of analysis which previously entailed heroic feats of arithmetic. There is a risk that multivariate methods may be applied blindly in circumstances different from those for which they were designed, and that incorrect conclusions may be drawn from them. This brief account may, therefore, help the computer user who is uncertain of the principles underlying the methods which he wishes to use. For much fuller details the reader should consult books like Kendall (1957), Seal (1964), Morrison (1967) or Hope (1968).

DISCRIMINATION WITH MORE THAN TWO GROUPS

The linear discriminant function was described in section 10.5 as a method of discrimination between *two* groups. The method can be generalized to the situation where there are $k(>2)$ groups in two different ways. The first approach leads to what are known as *canonical variates*. We saw from (10.36) that when $k=2$ the linear discriminant function maximizes the ratio of the difference in means *between* the groups to the standard deviation *within* groups. A natural generalization of this criterion is to maximize the ratio of the SSq between groups to the SSq within groups. This requirement is found to lead to a standard technique of matrix algebra—the calculation of *eigenvalues* or *latent roots* of a matrix. The appropriate equation, in fact, has several solutions. One solution, corresponding to the highest latent root, gives the coefficients in the linear function which maximizes the ratio of SSq. This is called the first *canonical variate*, W_1. If one wanted as good discrimination as possible from one linear function, this would be the one to choose. The second canonical variate, W_2, is the function with the highest ratio of SSq, subject to the condition that it is uncorrelated with W_1 both between and within groups. Similarly, W_3 gives the highest ratio subject to being uncorrelated with W_1 and W_2. The number of canonical variates is the smaller of p or $k-1$.

If most of the variation between groups is explained by W_1 and W_2, the ratios of SSq corresponding to the later canonical variates will be relatively small. It is then convenient to plot the data as a scatter diagram with W_1 and W_2 as the two axes. This will give a clear picture of any tendency of the groups to form clusters. It may also be interesting to see which of the original variables are strongly represented in each canonical variate. The magnitudes of the coefficients depend on the scales of measurement, so their relative sizes are of no great interest. Some computer programs print the correlations between each canonical variate and each x_i, a feature which helps to give some insight into the structure of the canonical variates.

For further discussion of this method, see the books referred to earlier; also Healy (1965) and Maxwell (1970).

A second generalization is to form the likelihood ratio of every pair of groups, following approach (b) of section 10.5. There are $\frac{1}{2}k(k-1)$ pairs of groups, but only $k-1$ likelihood ratios are needed. For example, if L_j is the log likelihood for the jth group, we could take

$$\begin{aligned} Z_1 &= L_1 - L_2 \\ Z_2 &= L_2 - L_3 \\ &\cdot \\ &\cdot \\ &\cdot \\ Z_{k-1} &= L_{k-1} - L_k, \end{aligned}$$

and any difference between pairs of L_j's (which is of course the log of the corresponding likelihood ratio) can be expressed in terms of the Z's. This could be done by calculating linear discriminant functions by the methods of section 10.5, for each of the $k-1$ pairs of groups. A modification which can conveniently be made is to calculate pooled Within groups SSq and SPr from all k groups, and to use the inverse of this pooled matrix in the calculation of each discriminant function. Computer programs exist for the whole procedure.

This likelihood ratio approach is more appropriate than that of canonical variates if the main purpose is to form an allocation rule. The simplest rule would be to allocate an individual to the group with the highest L_j, and this can be expressed in terms of the Z's. If the purpose is to gain insight into the way in which groups differ, using as few variables as possible, then canonical variates are the more appropriate method. There is a close relationship between the two methods. If, for example, $k=3$, and $p>1$, there will be $k-1=2$ canonical variates, W_1 and W_2, and 2 independent likelihood ratio discriminators, say $Z_1=L_1-L_2$ and $Z_2=L_2-L_3$. (Note that $L_3-L_1=-(Z_1+Z_2)$.) If the observations are plotted (a) with W_1 and W_2 as axes, and (b) with Z_1 and Z_2 as axes, it will be found that the scatter diagrams are essentially similar, differing only in the orientation and scaling of the axes. If

$k > 3$, of course, some loss is incurred by a 2-dimensional plot using W_1 and W_2; and the choice of two arbitrary Z's out of a possible three is even more wasteful.

SCORING SYSTEMS, USING CANONICAL VARIATES

Suppose that a variable is measured on a p-point scale from 1 to p. For example, a patient's response to treatment may be graded in categories ranging from 'much worse' (scored 1) to 'much better' (scored p). This sequence of equidistant integers may not be the best scale on which to analyse the data. The best method of scoring will depend on the criterion which we wish to optimize. Suppose, for example, that patients were classified into k treatment groups. It would be reasonable to choose a system of scoring which maximized differences between treatments as compared with those within treatments. For this purpose consider a set of p dummy variables, $x_1, x_2, \ldots, x_p$, such that if a patient is graded into category j, his value of x_j is 1 and that of all the other x_i's is 0. Now choose the first canonical variate of the x's, say

$$g = l_1 x_1 + l_2 x_2 + \ldots + l_p x_p.$$

Then g will take the value l_j in category j, and will define the system which maximizes the ratio of the Between groups SSq to that within groups. There is, however, no guarantee that the scores follow in magnitude the natural order of the categories. Bradley *et al.* (1962) have shown how the ratio of SSq can be maximized subject to there being no reversals of the natural order.

The investigator might want a scoring system which was as closely correlated as possible with some other variable. For instance, in dose-response experiments in serology, a reaction may be classified as $--$, $-$, 0, $+$ or $++$, and it may be useful to replace these categories by a score which forms a good linear regression on the log dose of some reagent. The approach is similar to that in the previous problem, the ratio of SSq to be maximized being that of the SSq due to regression to the Total SSq. (For an example see Ipsen, 1955.)

PRINCIPAL COMPONENTS

In the methods described above and in section 10.5, linear functions of variables have been chosen to satisfy some criterion related to further information about the data—for example, classification into groups or the values of a further variable. Suppose we merely have observations on p variables, $x_1, x_2, \ldots, x_p$, made on each of n individuals. We could ask whether it were possible to combine these variables into a small number of other variables which could provide almost all the information about the way in which one individual differed from another. One way of expressing this is to define new variables

$$y_1 = a_{11}x_1 + a_{12}x_2 + \ldots + a_{1p}x_p,$$

$$y_2 = a_{21}x_1 + a_{22}x_2 + \ldots + a_{2p}x_p,$$

etc., so that y_1 has the highest possible variance and so represents better than any other linear combination of the x's the general differences between individuals. (If no restrictions are placed on the a_{ij}'s this is a pointless requirement, since larger values of the coefficients will lead to a larger variance of y_1; we therefore standardize their general magnitude by requiring $\sum_{j=1}^{p} a_{ij}^2 = 1$). Then we could choose y_2 such that it is uncorrelated with y_1 and has the next largest variance; and so on. If $p = 3$, the individual observations can be visualized as a 3-dimensional scatter diagram with n points, perhaps clustered in the shape of an airship. The first *principal component*, y_1, will represent distances along the length of the airship. The second component, y_2, represents distances along the widest direction perpendicular to the length (say side-to-side); the third and last component, y_3, will then represent distances from top to bottom of the airship. There are in general p principal components, but the variation of all but a few may be quite small. If, in the previous example, the airship were very flat, almost like a disc, y_3 would have shown very little variation, and an individual's position in the whole diagram would be determined almost exactly by y_1 and y_2.

The method of analysis is very similar to that required for canonical variates, requiring the calculation of latent roots. Most computers have standard programs which can be used. An important point to note is that if the scale of measurement for any variable is changed, even by a multiplying factor, the whole results are changed. This fact has led some workers to standardize each variable initially by dividing by its standard deviation.

For examples of the use of principal component analysis in medicine and allied fields see Doll and Buckatzsch (1952; cancer mortality at various sites for different administrative areas), Drion (1961; nutrients and calories consumed by different families), and Jeffers (1962).

FACTOR ANALYSIS

This method has been used considerably by psychologists. It is closely related to principal component analysis, but differs in that it assumes a definite model for the way in which the observed variables, x_i, are influenced by certain hypothetical underlying factors. Suppose the x_i's are educational tests applied to children and that each test reflects to a differing extent certain factors; for example, general intelligence, verbal facility, arithmetical ability, speed of working, etc. Imagine that each individual has a certain value for each of these factors, $f_1, f_2, f_3, \ldots$, which are uncorrelated, but that these cannot be measured directly. All we can measure are

$$x_1 = b_{11}f_1 + b_{12}f_2 + b_{13}f_3 + \ldots + s_1 + \epsilon_1$$
$$x_2 = b_{21}f_1 + b_{22}f_2 + b_{23}f_3 + \ldots + s_2 + \epsilon_2,$$

etc. Here s_i is supposed to be a component specific to the ith test, over and above the factors, and ϵ_i is a random error. The factors f_1, f_2, $f_3, \ldots$ and the specific components s_i vary from one subject to another and are uncorrelated. The quantities b_{ij} are constants, like regression coefficients, indicating how much each test is affected by each factor. Unfortunately we cannot apply multiple regression methods because the values of the f's are unknown.

There are various methods of factor analysis which investigate how many factors need to be assumed and provide estimates of the b_{ij} (the *factor loadings*). A good general account is that Lawley and Maxwell (1963). If the basic model can be justified on psychological grounds, a factor analysis may be expected to throw some light on the number of factors apparently affecting the test scores and to show which tests are closely related to particular factors. The place of factor analysis in other scientific fields is very doubtful. It is often used in situations for which simpler multivariate methods would be more appropriate. For example, the interpretation placed on the factor loadings is usually very similar to that placed on the coefficients of the first few principal components. For an example of the use of factor analysis in the interpretation of body measurements see Burt and Banks (1947). Useful discussions by various authors are given in Vol. **12** of *The Statistician* (1962).

CLUSTER ANALYSIS

Component analysis and factor analysis are 'internal' methods of analysis, in that the individuals are not classified by any criteria other than the variables used in the analysis. In some problems no initial grouping is imposed on the data, but the object of the analysis is to see whether the individuals can be formed into any natural system of groups. The number of groups may not be specified in advance. The individuals could, of course, be grouped in an entirely arbitrary way, but the investigator seeks a system such that the individuals within a group resemble each other (in the values taken by the variables) more than do individuals in different groups. This specification is rather vague, and the best method of approach to the problem is correspondingly ill-determined.

Two broad approaches may be distinguished. The first is to do a principal component analysis of all the data. If most of the variation is explained by the first two or three components, the essential features of the multi-dimensional scatter can be seen by a two-dimensional scatter diagram, or perhaps a two-dimensional representation of a three-dimensional model. Any clustering of the individuals into groups would then become apparent—at least in its main features—although the precise definitions of the groups might be open to question. If the scatter is not largely represented by the first two or three components, the method will be very much less useful.

The second approach, that of *numerical taxonomy*, is discussed in detail by Sokal and Sneath (1963). The idea here is to calculate an index of similarity for each pair of individuals. The precise definition of this index will depend on the nature of the variables. If, as in some clinical applications, the variables are dichotomies (expressing the presence or absence of some feature), a suitable similarity index might be the proportion of variables for which the two individuals show the same response. Alternative measures are discussed fully by Sokal and Sneath. When the similarity indices have been calculated some form of sorting is carried out so that pairs of individuals with high values of the index are sorted into the same group. These procedures can be effected by a computer once the rules of the game have been laid down.

A medical application which suggests itself is the definition of a system of related diseases. Hayhoe *et al.* (1964), for instance, have studied the classification of the acute leukaemias from this point of view. Whether the methods are really useful will depend largely on whether the classifications subsequently perform any useful function. For example, in the definition of disease categories, one would hope that any system suggested might lead to suggestions about aetiology, recommendations about future treatment, or at the very least a useful system for tabulating vital statistics. It is perhaps too early to report success in these directions. One of the problems in medical applications is how to define generally any groups which may have been formed by a clustering procedure. Lists of particular individuals placed in the groups in any one study are, of course, of insufficient general interest, and some more general definitions are required. For some useful discussions see various papers in Vol. **17** of *The Statistician* (1967).

10.7 TIME SERIES

Some statistical investigations involve very long series of observations on a certain variable, made at successive points of time. Two medical examples are (i) a series of mortality rates from a certain cause of death, recorded in a particular community over a period of, say, 100 years; and (ii) a series of physiological measurements, such as pulse rates, observed at short intervals throughout a day. The investigator may wish to describe such time series by a relatively simple model embodying some element of random variation. Two possible reasons for wishing to do this may be to predict future readings from a historical series (as perhaps in a demographic study), and to gain insight into the mechanism underlying the variation (as perhaps in a physiological study).

This problem is essentially one of regression—the measurement in question being a dependent variable, with time playing the role of a predictor variable—but the methods outlined in Chapters 5 and 9 and in the earlier sections of this chapter are unlikely to be very useful. In the first place the general trends exhibited by long-term series are unlikely to be representable by the simple mathematical functions considered hitherto. Secondly, although individual observations are likely to show apparently random fluctuations about any long-term trend, these deviations are unlikely to be independently distributed. If one observation on a physiological variable is somewhat above a general trend, it is likely that neighbouring observations will also be somewhat higher than expected. This form of correlation between the random components of neighbouring observations is called *serial correlation.*

Sometimes the effect may be in the opposite direction. In a series of notifications of an infectious disease in successive years, a high value in one year may be associated with a low value in adjacent years, because a high proportion of the population acquires immunity during years of high incidence. Sometimes, also, the apparent effect of serial correlations may extend to observations separated by several time units, although it is usually found that the longer the 'lag' between paired observations, the lower in absolute magnitude is the serial correlation.

To overcome these problems a number of methods of time series analysis have been developed. They are based on rather more complicated models than those underlying the simpler regression methods, and the methods are too complex to be described adequately here. Two general approaches are (i) to postulate an *autoregressive* model; that is, one in which the predictor variables include not only functions of time, but also the values of the dependent variable itself at previous points of time; (ii) to suppose that the series is composed of a number of periodic terms like those in the periodic regression model of section 10.3, but with different wave frequencies. The second approach gives rise to *spectral analysis* which shows the contribution of waves in different frequency bands. The two approaches are interconnected. For a discussion of some ways of distinguishing between different models for time series, see Box and Jenkins (1968).

Time series analysis has not been used much in medical research, largely because it has been rare to find long series generated under sufficiently stable conditions to make it sensible to search for some model underlying the whole set of data. Recent developments in the automatic recording of biological signals and other physiological measurements are, however, likely to stimulate interest in these methods.

CHAPTER 11
DATA EDITING

11.1 PRELIMINARY REMARKS

The phase 'data editing' may conjure up a picture of the statistician as a skilful manipulator of evidence, able, by careful selection of data, to provide unassailable support for any stated hypothesis. Our purpose here is much less sinister. All statistical methods are founded on certain assumptions, for example about the forms of distributions or of relationships between variables. These assumptions are very rarely likely to be exactly true. It is not unreasonable to suppose, however, that in any particular instance they are sufficiently nearly true to make the relevant methods of analysis valid and useful. Frequently the data, as originally observed, will present some feature which is clearly incompatible with the theoretical model. One course of action might be try to develop a special theory for this situation; this is often the way in which new developments in statistical methodology come about. More usually it will be found possible to look at the data in a rather different way, for instance by using a different scale of measurement for one or more variables, and then to use standard methods of analysis.

The next three sections are concerned with various methods of transforming variables to different scales. In the final section we discuss the more contentious question of the detection of *outliers*—observations differing so widely from what the rest of the data would lead one to expect that a gross error may be suspected.

Most of the procedures described in this chapter are appropriate at a very early stage of examination of the data, before detailed analyses are carried out. It is useful to emphasize the great value, in this preliminary data screening, of simple descriptive tools—frequency distributions, mean values, scatter diagrams, etc. In particular the value of graphical methods such as scatter diagrams can hardly be overstated. A number of graphical devices are described in detail below.

11.2 TRANSFORMATIONS IN GENERAL

By a transformation we mean a change to a different scale of measurement for some variable. *Linear* transformations, which involve at most a change in origin and a scaling factor (such as the change from °F to °C in measuring temperature) may be useful in simplifying arithmetic (as we found in using working units in Chapter 1); or they may satisfy the investigator because the new scale is more readily understood than the old. However they rarely affect the essential features of a statistical analysis. More important are non-linear transformations in which equal increments on the original scale do not usually correspond to equal increments on the new scale. Examples are the logarithm and the square root.

There are five main purposes of transformations, the first three of which are the most important:

(i) to stabilize variances;
(ii) to linearize relationships;
(iii) to make distributions more normal;
(iv) to simplify the handling of data with other awkward features;
(v) to enable results to be presented in an acceptable scale of measurement.

VARIANCE-STABILIZING TRANSFORMATIONS

Many statistical methods require that the residual variance for different subgroups of data should be constant. If this is not so, an approximate solution may be available in which the subgroups are differentially weighted (as, for example, in (7.12)). A simpler solution would be to transform to a scale in which residual variances were approximately constant. Suppose the original variable is x and the transformed variable is y, this being some definite function of x. Then (3.16) shows that, for var(y) to be constant, the following relationship should be approximately true:

$$\frac{dy}{dx} = \frac{\text{constant}}{\sqrt{\{\text{var}(x)\}}}. \tag{11.1}$$

If var(x) is known as a function of x, (or, more strictly, of E(x)), (11.1) enables y to be found as a function of x, i.e. it defines the appropriate transformation. Some examples are discussed in the next section.

LINEARIZING TRANSFORMATIONS

If a regression line, say of v on u, is clearly non-linear a satisfactory solution may be to fit a curvilinear function as in section 10.3. Again, however, it may be simpler to transform one or both variables so as to give a nearly linear relationship. The problem is particularly acute when the dependent variable is a proportion, which necessarily lies between 0 and 1; regression curves similar to that shown in Fig. 11.2(a) below are often encountered. Transformations for proportions are discussed separately in section 11.4.

NORMALIZING TRANSFORMATIONS

A similar point arises here. Non-normal variation can be incorporated into a theoretical model, but the resulting methods of analysis are often very complex. Fortunately, many of the standard methods of analysis are *robust* (i.e. insensitive to non-normality), and this particular reason for transformation is less cogent than the other two. If the three principal criteria discussed here conflicted in the transformations required to satisfy them, the need for normality would present the weakest case. Fortunately, it often happens that the same transformation simultaneously stabilizes variance, produces linear relationships and provides more nearly normal distributions (see Fig. 11.1).

11.3 LOGARITHMIC AND POWER TRANSFORMATIONS

In the logarithmic transformation we change from one variable, x, to another variable, y, by the equation

$$y = \log x. \qquad (11.2)$$

Common logarithms, to base 10, are usually used except in purely mathematical work. The transformation can only be made for positive values of x, because $\log 0 = -\infty$ and logs of negative numbers do not exist. As x increases, larger and larger changes in x are needed to give equal changes in y, as shown by the following example:

x	2	20	200	2000
y	0·3	1·3	2·3	3·3

We should expect, therefore, that the logarithmic transformation would tend to stabilize variances when, in the original data, var(x) tended to increase markedly with x. In fact, (11.1) shows that var(y) will be approximately constant when var(x)$\propto\{\mathrm{E}(x)\}^2$. Equivalent statements are that the standard deviation of x is proportional to the mean, or that the coefficient of variation of x is constant.

Secondly, if x is related to a variable u by a trend with a consistently increasing slope, (11.2) will often result in a more nearly linear relationship between y and u, by 'compressing' the upper part of the scale of x.

Thirdly, if the distribution of a variable x, taking positive values, is positively skew, (11.2) will reduce this skewness and may result in a more nearly normal distribution for y.

Fig. 11.1, (a) and (b), illustrates a situation in which the logarithmic transformation from x to y simultaneously helps to stabilize variance, linearize the relationship with u and provide more normal distributions. This sort of situation is often found when a variable x is restricted to positive values and can vary over a wide range; examples are survival times and quantities or concentrations of some substance. Fig. 11.1(c) illustrates the use of a *logarithmic scale* for x. The quantities marked on the vertical axis are values of x, but the distances between them are proportional to the distances between the corresponding values of y. The effect is precisely the same as in (b), where the logarithms, y, were looked up in tables and then plotted on an ordinary arithmetic scale. Graph paper with scales marked as in (c) can be bought: it is called *semi-logarithmic* paper. Another variety, sometimes called *double-logarithmic* paper, has logarithmic scales along both axes.

The relation between the logarithmic transformation and the geometric mean has been described in section 1.5, where particular reference was made to the use of the transformation in microbiological and serological work. If confidence limits are required for a geometric mean they should be obtained in the usual way on the log scale, and then converted back to the original scale.

In reading logarithms from tables it is usually adequate to work to at most 2 decimal places.

Power transformations are defined by the equation

$$y=x^c. \tag{11.3}$$

Again, these are used mainly for a variable x taking positive values only. Equation (11.3) represents a family of transformations, distinguished by the value of c. Values of c less than 1 produce transforma-

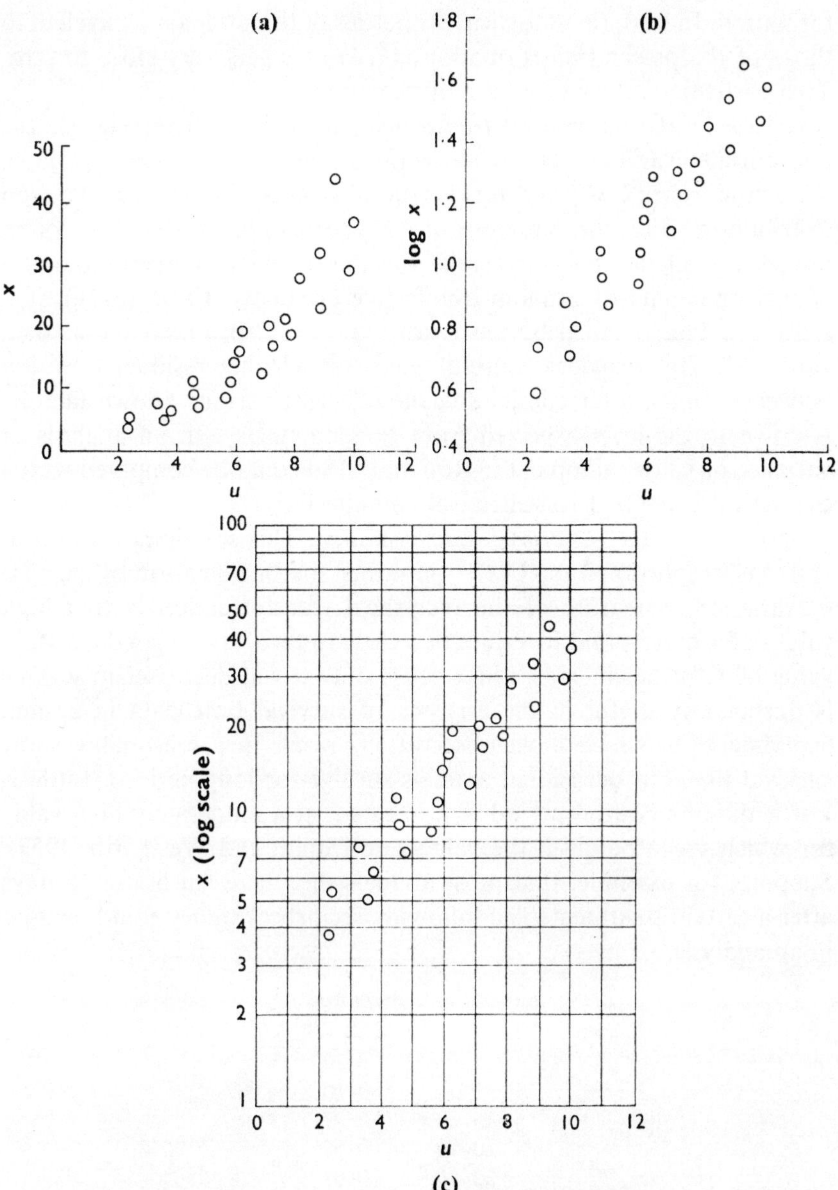

FIG. 11.1 Scatter diagram of hypothetical data plotted (a) with arithmetic scale for the ordinate, x, (b) with arithmetic scale for $\log x$, (c) with logarithmic scale for x (using semi-logarithmic paper).

tions with properties rather similar to those of the logarithmic transformation. Indeed, the statistical properties of the latter are equivalent to those of the power transformation (11.3) as c gets very close to zero. Two particular values of $c<1$ require comment.

(i) $c=\frac{1}{2}$: *the square-root transformation.* This is, from (11.1), the appropriate variance-stabilizing transformation when $\text{var}(x)\propto \text{E}(x)$. We know from (2.16) that this is true of counts following the Poisson distribution, and the square-root transformation is therefore often used for such data; for example, for the analysis of microbiological counts or counts of random events like accidents. From (3.16), if x follows a Poisson distribution (with $\text{var}(x)=\text{E}(x)$), and $y=\sqrt{x}$, then $\text{var}(y)=\frac{1}{4}$. This provides a useful check on whether residual variation between counts, after eliminating the effect of various known factors, is down to the level expected from Poisson theory. In an analysis of variance of y, for example, the Residual MSq could be compared with a theoretical value of $\frac{1}{4}$ (on effectively infinite DF).

(ii) $c=-1$: *the reciprocal transformation.* This stabilizes variance if $\text{var}(x)$ is proportional to $\{\text{E}(x)\}^4$—a rather spectacular form of increase in variance. A feature of the reciprocal transformation is that high values of x correspond to values of y close to zero, and beyond a certain value of x further increases in x cause only trivial decreases in y. This is particularly useful in the analysis of survival time data in animal experiments in which most observations result in a reasonably short survival time but occasional animals survive for long periods. Little is lost if the observation period is 'truncated' at a moderately high value for which y can be given the value zero (Smith and Westgarth, 1957). Suppose, for example, that most animals died between 5 and 15 days after a certain treatment. The following reciprocal values could be used in an analysis.

Survival time x (days)	Reciprocal y
5	0·20
10	0·10
15	0·07
20	0·05
30	0·03
>30	0

If a series of measurements is transformed to reciprocals, the arithmetic mean may be calculated on the transformed scale and converted back to the original scale by taking the reciprocal again. The resulting quantity is known as the *harmonic mean.* It bears the same relation to the reciprocal transformation as the geometric mean (section 1.5) bears to the logarithmic transformation.

Power transformations with $c>1$ are useful when the sorts of rectification required are the opposite of those for which the logarithmic transformation, and the power transformations with $c<1$, are appropriate. The *square transformation,* $y=x^2$ may, for example, be useful if var(x) tends to decrease with increasing x, if a curvilinear relationship bends downwards rather than upwards (as in Fig. 10.4(a)) and if the distribution of x is negatively skew.

In considering linearity requirements the possibility of transposing *other* variables should not be forgotten. For instance, if a scatter diagram of x on u shows the type of curvature referred to above (the trend in x curving downwards as u increases) it may be better to use a logarithmic or square root transformation of u rather than a square transformation of x.

11.4 TRANSFORMATIONS FOR PROPORTIONS

In some sets of data the context seems to require one of the standard methods of analysis—t test, analysis of variance, regression, etc.—but the problem is complicated because the basic observations are proportions for which the basic form of random variation might be expected to be binomial. In a study of insecticides applied under different controlled conditions, a known number of flies might be exposed under each set of conditions and a count made of the number killed. Such data give rise to many of the difficulties described in section 11.2. The variance of an observed proportion depends on the expected proportion, as well as on the denominator of the fraction; see (2.13). Regression curves are unlikely to be linear, because the scale of the proportion is limited by the values 0 and 1 and changes in any relevant explanatory variable (such as dose of an insecticide) at the extreme ends of its scale are unlikely to produce much change in the proportion. A *sigmoid* regression curve as in Fig. 11.2(a) is, in fact, likely to be found. Finally, the binomial distribution of random error is likely to be skew in opposite directions as the proportion approaches 0 or 1.

Three transformations are commonly used for proportions. They have very similar effects, and instances in which any one is clearly inferior to the others are rare.

(I) ANGULAR TRANSFORMATION

The motivation for this transformation is variance stabilization. Denoting the original variable by p instead of x and putting $\text{var}(p)=p(1-p)$ in (11.1), we obtain the *angular*, *inverse sine* or *arcsine transformation*

$$y=\sin^{-1}\sqrt{p}. \tag{11.4}$$

The right side of (11.4) is the angle whose sine is $\sqrt{p}$. If the angle is measured in degrees, y will range from 0° to 90° as p ranges from 0 to 1. A very brief table of the transformation is given in Table 11.1. For more extensive tables see Fisher and Yates (1963) or Snedecor and Cochran (1967). Equal changes in p correspond to greater changes in y towards the two ends of the scale than near the middle. From (3.16), $\text{var}(y)=820.7/n$, approximately; this may be used as a baseline in analyses to check whether residual variation is greater than binomial.

TABLE 11.1 Short table of transformations for proportions.

Proportion	Angle	Probit	Logit
0	0	$-\infty$	$-\infty$
0·05	13	3·36	−2·94
0·10	18	3·72	−2·20
0·15	23	3·96	−1·73
0·20	27	4·16	−1·39
0·25	30	4·33	−1·10
0·30	33	4·48	−0·85
0·35	36	4·61	−0·62
0·40	39	4·75	−0·41
0·45	42	4·87	−0·20
0·50	45	5·00	0·00
0·55	48	5·13	0·20
0·60	51	5·25	0·41
0·65	54	5·39	0·62
0·70	57	5·52	0·85
0·75	60	5·67	1·10
0·80	63	5·84	1·39
0·85	67	6·04	1·73
0·90	72	6·28	2·20
0·95	77	6·64	2·94
1·00	90	∞	∞

Note that the residual variance is independent of E(y), but depends on n. If all the exposed groups have equal values of n, the usual conditions of equality of variance will be satisfied and standard methods of analysis are approximately valid. If the n's differ, some form of weighted analysis is required.

If p is related to another variable u by a sigmoid curve as in Fig. 11.2(a), in which the upper and lower limits of 1 and 0 are only gradually approached, the corresponding curve with y against u will be straighter over most of the range, but must flatten out at the upper and lower limits. This limitation would be removed if y had infinite values corresponding to $p=0$ and 1; the two other transformations possess this feature.

(II) PROBIT TRANSFORMATION

For any proportion p, suppose y' is the *normal equivalent deviate* (NED) such that a proportion p of the standard normal distribution falls to the left of y'. The *probit* of p is defined as

$$y=5+y'. \tag{11.5}$$

The distinction between NED and probit is trivial, and it is perhaps regrettable that two such similar transformations have become established by usage. A short table of probits is given in Table 11.1. The entries may be checked immediately from Table A1, using (11.5). Any table of the normal distribution giving y' in terms of p may of course be used. Table IX of Fisher and Yates (1963) uses probits directly rather than NED's.

The probit transformation is similar to the angular transformation in that the ends of the scale of p are extended more than the middle. The range of the probit scale is infinite, however, and the two scales become less similar when p is very close to 0 or to 1. There is an obvious problem if the data contain some observations with $p=0$ or $p=1$, since the corresponding values of y, $-\infty$ and ∞, cannot conveniently be used in standard methods of analysis. In approximate solutions and graphical studies a useful device is to calculate y from an adjusted value of p derived by assuming that $\frac{1}{2}$ (rather than 0) positive or negative response occurred. That is, if $p=r/n$, calculate $p'=1/(2n)$ when $r=0$ and $p'=(2n-1)/2n$ when $r=n$, and obtain y from p'.

A further point is that, unlike the angular transformation, the probit transformation does not stabilize variances, even for observations with constant n. Some form of weighting is therefore desirable in any analysis. A rigorous approach is provided by the method called *probit analysis* (see sections 12.5(b), 17.4; also Finney (1952)).

The effect of the probit transformation in linearizing a relationship is shown in Fig. 11.2. Fig. 11.2(c) illustrates the use of *probability paper*, in which the distances between points on the vertical scale are

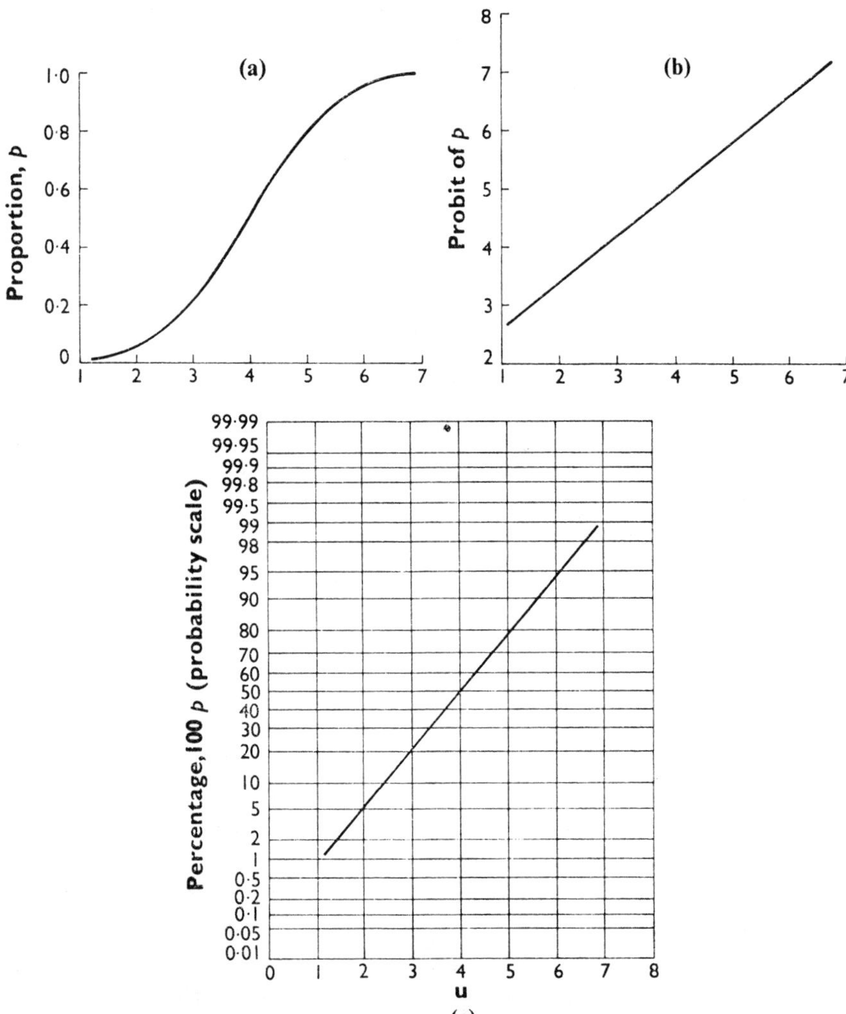

FIG. 11.2 Hypothetical response curve plotted (a) with arithmetic scale for the ordinate, p, (b) with an arithmetic scale for the probit of p, (c) with 'probability' scale for p (using probability paper).

proportional to the corresponding distances on the probit or NED scale. The use of probability paper is analogous to that of logarithmic paper. The shape of the curve (in this case, exactly a straight line) is the same as that in Fig. 11.2(b) in which the probit values are plotted on an arithmetic scale. Another variety, *log probability paper*, combines the same vertical scale as in Fig. 11.2(c) with a logarithmic scale for u.

(III) LOGIT TRANSFORMATION

The *logit* of p is defined as

$$y = \log_e \frac{p}{1-p}. \qquad (11.6)$$

Occasionally (Finney, 1964; Fisher and Yates, 1963) the definition incorporates a factor $\frac{1}{2}$, so that $y = \frac{1}{2}\log_e\{p/(1-p)\}$; this has the effect of making the values rather similar to those of the NED (i.e. probit -5). A short table is given in Table 11.1, and a more extensive one in Table A7. The effect of the logit (or *logistic*) transformation is very similar indeed to that of the probit transformation. Methods of analysis using logits are discussed more fully in section 12.5.

11.5 OUTLYING OBSERVATIONS

Occasionally a single observation is affected by a gross error, either of measurement or recording, or due to a sudden lapse from the general standards of investigation applying to the rest of the data. It is usually important to detect such errors if possible, partly because they are likely to invalidate the assumptions underlying standard methods of analysis and partly because they are usually irrelevant to the purpose of the investigation.

Recording errors can often be reduced by careful checking of all the steps at which results are copied onto paper. Frequently the original measurement will come under suspicion. The measurement may be repeatable (for example, the height of an individual if a short time has elapsed since the first measurement), or one may be able to check it by referring to an authoritative document (such as a birth certificate, if age is in doubt). A much more difficult situation arises when an observation is strongly suspected of being erroneous but no independent check is available. Possible courses of action are discussed at the foot of the page. First we discuss some methods of detecting gross errors.

(a) *Logical checks*

Certain values may be seen to be either impossible or extremely implausible by virtue of the meaning of the variable. Frequently the range of variation is known sufficiently well to enable upper and/or lower limits to be set; for example, an adult man's height below, say, 55 in. or above 80 in. would cause suspicion. Other results would be impossible because of relationships between variables; for example, a child aged 10 years cannot be married. Checks of this sort can be carried out routinely, once the rules of acceptability have been defined. They can readily be performed by computer; indeed, editing procedures of this sort should form a regular part of the analysis of large-scale bodies of data by computer.

(b) *Statistical checks*

Certain observations may be found to be unusual, not necessarily on *a priori* grounds, but at least by comparison with the rest of the data. Whether or not they are to be rejected or amended is a controversial matter to be discussed below; at any rate the investigator will probably wish to have his attention drawn to them.

A good deal of statistical checking can be done quite informally by graphical exploration and the formation of frequency distributions. If most of the observations follow an approximately normal distribution, with one or two aberrant values falling well away from the main distribution, the *normal plot* described in section 12.7 is a useful device. Sometimes observations are unusual only when considered in relation to other variables; for example, in an anthropometric survey of schoolchildren, a weight measurement may be seen to be unusually low or high in relation to the child's height; checking rules for weights in terms of heights will be much more effective than rules based on weights alone (Healy, 1952).

Should a statistically unusual reading be rejected or amended? If there is some external reason for suspicion, for example that an inexperienced technician made the observation in question, or that the air-conditioning plant failed at a certain point during an experiment, common sense would suggest the omission of the observation and (where appropriate) the use of missing reading techniques (section 8.6).

When there is no external reason for suspicion there are strong arguments for retaining the original observations. Clearly there are some observations which no reasonable person would retain: for example an adult height recorded as 10 in. However, the decision will usually have to be made as a subjective judgment on ill-defined criteria which depend on one's knowledge of the data under study, the purposes of the analysis and so on. For a good discussion, including references to some more formal methods of dealing with outliers, see Anscombe (1968).

CHAPTER 12

FURTHER ANALYSIS OF QUALITATIVE DATA

12.1 INTRODUCTION

The analysis of qualitative data has been discussed in several earlier sections of the book: particularly sections 2.5, 3.3, 4.4, 4.7, 7.4 and 7.5. In the present chapter we gather together a number of more advanced techniques for dealing with qualitative data, particularly those in which the variable to be analysed is a proportion. Some of these techniques make use of the χ^2 distributions which have been used extensively in the earlier sections. These χ^2 methods are, however, almost exclusively designed for significance testing. In many problems involving qualitative data the estimation of relevant parameters is much more important than the performance of significance tests. Throughout much of the chapter, therefore, methods going beyond the scope of χ^2 tests have to be introduced.

For a general introduction to the analysis of qualitative data, see Maxwell (1961). D. R. Cox's (1970) monograph provides a very comprehensive treatment of the subject.

12.2 COMPONENTS OF χ^2

Several of the χ^2 tests introduced earlier have involved test statistics distributed as χ^2 on several degrees of freedom. In each instance the test was sensitive to departures, from a null hypothesis, which could occur in various ways. In a $2 \times k$ contingency table, for instance, the null hypothesis postulates equality between the expected proportions of individuals in each column which fall into the first row. There are k of these proportions, and the null hypothesis can be falsified if any one of them differs from the others. These tests may be thought of as 'portmanteau' techniques, able to serve many different purposes. If, however, we were particularly interested in a certain form of departure from the null hypothesis it might be possible to formulate a test which was particularly sensitive to this situation, although perhaps less effective than the portmanteau χ^2 test in detecting other forms of departure. Sometimes these specially directed tests can be achieved by subdividing the total χ^2 statistic into portions which follow χ^2 distributions on reduced numbers of degrees of freedom.

The situation is very similar to that encountered in the analysis of variance, where a SSq can sometimes be subdivided into portions, on reduced numbers of DF, which represent specific contrasts between groups (section 7.3).

Three examples of the subdivision of χ^2 statistics are given below.

(a) TREND IN PROPORTIONS

Suppose that, in a $2 \times k$ contingency table of the type discussed in section 7.4, the k groups fall into a natural order. They may correspond to different values, or groups of values, of a quantitative variable like age; or they may correspond to qualitative categories, such as severity of a disease, which can be ordered but not readily assigned a numerical value. The usual $\chi^2_{(k-1)}$ test is designed to detect differences between the k proportions of observations falling into the first row. More specifically one might ask whether there is a significant trend in these proportions from Group 1 to Group k.

Let us assign a quantitative variable, x, to the k groups. If the definition of groups uses such a variable, this can be chosen to be x. If the definition is qualitative x can take integer values from 1 to k. The notation is as follows:

Group	1	2	...	i	...	k	All groups combined
Variable x	x_1	x_2	...	x_i	...	x_k	
Positive	r_1	r_2	...	r_i	...	r_k	R
Negative	n_1-r_1	n_2-r_2	...	n_i-r_i	...	n_k-r_k	$N-R$
Total	n_1	n_2	...	n_i	...	n_k	N
Proportion positive	p_1	p_2	...	p_i	...	p_k	$P=R/N$

The numerator of the χ^2 statistic, X^2, is from (7.25),

$$\sum n_i(p_i-P)^2,$$

a weighted sum of squares of the p_i about the (weighted) mean P; (see discussion below (7.28)). It also turns out to be a straightforward sum of squares, between groups, of a variable y taking the value 1 for each positive individual and 0 for each negative. This SSq can be divided (as in Section 9.1) into a SSq due to regression of y on x and a SSq due to departures from linear regression. If there is a trend of p_i with x_i we might find the first of these two portions to be greater than would be expected by chance. Dividing this portion by PQ, the denominator of (7.25), gives us a $\chi^2_{(1)}$ statistic, X_1^2, which forms part of X^2 and is particularly sensitive to trend.

A little algebraic manipulation (Armitage, 1955) provides the following formula for X_1^2:

$$X_1^2 = \frac{N(N\sum r_i x_i - R\sum n_i x_i)^2}{R(N-R)\{N\sum n_i x_i^2 - (\sum n_i x_i)^2\}}. \tag{12.1}$$

The difference between the two statistics,

$$X_2^2 = X^2 - X_1^2, \tag{12.2}$$

may be regarded as a $\chi^2_{(k-2)}$ statistic testing departures from linear regression of p_i on x_i. As usual, all these χ^2 tests are approximate, but the approximation is likely to be adequate if only a small proportion of the frequencies are less than about 5.

TABLE 12.1 Numbers of children who were nasal carriers or non-carriers of *Streptococcus pyogenes*, classified by size of tonsils (Holmes and Williams, 1954).

	Tonsils			
	Present but not enlarged	Enlarged	Greatly enlarged	Total
Carriers	19	29	24	72
Non-carriers	497	560	269	1,326
	516	589	293	1,398
Proportion of carriers	0·0368	0·0492	0·0819	
Score, x	−1	0	1	

Example 12.1

In the analysis of the data summarized in Table 12.1 it would be reasonable to ask whether the proportion of carriers tends to increase with the enlargement of the tonsils. In the absence of any accurate measure of size, scores of

-1, 0 and 1 seem appropriate. From (12.1),

$$X_1^2 = \frac{(1398)\{(1398)(5)-(72)(-223)\}^2}{(72)(1326)\{(1398)(809)-(-223)^2\}}$$
$$=(74{,}250\cdot 3\times 10^7)/(10{,}322\cdot 9\times 10^7)$$
$$=7\cdot 19,$$

which, as a $\chi^2_{(1)}$ variate, is highly significant ($P<0\cdot 01$).

The overall $\chi^2_{(2)}$ statistic, from (7.24) or (7.25), is calculated as

$$X^2=7\cdot 88.$$

The test for departures from a linear trend thus gives

$$X_2^2=X^2-X_1^2$$
$$=7\cdot 88-7\cdot 19$$
$$=0\cdot 69$$

as a $\chi^2_{(1)}$ variate, which is clearly non-significant. There is thus a definite trend which may well result in approximately equal increases in the proportion of carriers as we change successively to the more severe categories of tonsil enlargement.

See section 12.5 (particularly Example 12.8) for further discussion of this type of problem.

(b) HIERARCHICAL CLASSIFICATION

In (a), the numerator of the $\chi^2_{(k-1)}$ statistic (7.25) was regarded as the SSq between groups of a dummy variable y, taking the values 0 and 1. We proceeded to subdivide this in a standard way. Other types of subdivision encountered in Chapters 7 and 8 may equally be used if they are relevant to the data under study. For example, if the k groups form a factorial arrangement, and if the n_i are equal or are proportional to marginal totals for the separate factors, the usual techniques could be used to separate SSq and hence components of the $\chi^2_{(k-1)}$ statistic, representing main effects and interactions.

Another situation, in which no conditions need be imposed on the n_i, is that in which the groups form a hierarchical arrangement.

Example 12.2

Table 12.2 shows proportions of houseflies killed by two different insecticides. There are two batches of each insecticide, and each of the four batches is

TABLE 12.2 Proportions of houseflies killed in experiments with two insecticides.

	Insecticide A					Insecticide B					
	Batch $A1$		Batch $A2$			Batch $B1$		Batch $B2$			
	Test 1	Test 2	Test 1	Test 2	Total A	Test 1	Test 2	Test 1	Test 2	Total B	Total $A+B$
Flies											
killed	49	43	43	48	183	41	44	39	39	163	346
surviving	2	5	4	1	12	5	8	11	9	33	45
Total	51	48	47	49	195	46	52	50	48	196	391
Proportion killed					0·9385					0·8316	0·8849

subjected to two tests. The overall $\chi^2_{(7)}$ test gives

$$X_7^2=(2^2/51+\ldots+9^2/48-45^2/391)/(0{\cdot}8849)(0{\cdot}1151)$$
$$=1{\cdot}6628/0{\cdot}1019=16{\cdot}32 \text{ on 7 DF,}$$

which is significant ($0{\cdot}01<P<0{\cdot}025$). This can be subdivided as follows:

Between tests (4 DF):

$$X_4^2=\frac{(2^2/51+5^2/48-7^2/99)+\ldots+(11^2/50+9^2/48-20^2/98)}{0{\cdot}1019}$$
$$=2{\cdot}75 \quad (\mathrm{P}>0{\cdot}5);$$

Between batches (2 DF):

$$X_2^2=\frac{(7^2/99+5^2/96-12^2/195)+(13^2/98+20^2/98-33^2/196)}{0{\cdot}1019}$$
$$=2{\cdot}62 \quad (P>0{\cdot}25);$$

Between insecticides (1DF):

$$X_1^2=\frac{(12^2/195+33^2/196-45^2/391)}{0{\cdot}1019}$$
$$=10{\cdot}95 \quad (P<0{\cdot}001).$$

As a check, $X_1^2+X_2^2+X_4^2=16{\cdot}32$, agreeing with X_7^2. There is thus clear evidence of a difference in toxicity of the two insecticides, but no evidence of differences between batches or between tests.

A few remarks about this analysis:

(a) Since a difference between A and B has been established it would be logical, in calculating X_2^2 and X_4^2, to use separate denominators for the contributions from the two insecticides. Thus, in calculating X_2^2, the first term in the numerator would have a denominator (0·9385)(0·0615)=0·0577, and the second term would have a denominator (0·8316)(0·1684)=0·1400. The effect of this correction is usually small. If it is made the various χ^2 indices no longer add exactly to the total.

(b) In entomological experiments it is common to find significant differences between replicate tests, perhaps because the response is sensitive to small changes in the environment and all the flies used in one test share the same environment (for example, being often kept in the same box). In such cases comparisons between treatments must take account of the random variation between tests. It is useful, therefore, to have adequate replication. The analysis can often be done satisfactorily by measuring the proportion of deaths at each test and analysing these proportions with or without one of the standard transformations.

(c) An experiment of the size of that shown in Table 12·2 is not really big enough to detect variation between batches and tests. Although the numbers of flies are quite large, more replication both of tests and of batches is desirable.

(c) LARGER CONTINGENCY TABLES

The hierarchical principle can be applied to larger contingency tables (section 7.5). In an $r \times c$ table, the total χ^2 statistic, X^2, can be calculated from (7.24). It has $(r-1)(c-1)$ DF, and represents departures of the cell frequencies from those expected by proportionality to row and column totals. It may be relevant to ask whether proportionality holds in some segment of the whole table; then in a second segment chosen after collapsing either rows or columns in the first segment; then in a third segment; and so on. If, in performing these successive χ^2 calculations one uses expected frequencies derived from the whole table, the various χ^2 statistics can be added in a natural way. If, however, the expected frequencies are derived separately for each sub-table the various components of χ^2 will not add exactly to the total. The discrepancy is unlikely to be important in practice.

Example 12.3

Table 12.3, taken from Example 9.13.2 of Snedecor and Cochran (1967), shows data from a study of the relationship between blood groups and disease. The small number of AB patients have been omitted from the analysis. The overall $\chi^2_{(4)}$ test for the whole table gives X^2=40·54, a value which is highly significant. A study of the proportions in the three blood groups, for each group of subjects, suggests that there is little difference between the

TABLE 12.3 Frequencies of *ABO* Blood groups in patients with peptic ulcer, patients with gastric cancer and controls (Snedecor and Cochran, 1967, Ex. 9.13.2).

Blood group	Peptic ulcer	Gastric cancer	Controls	Total
O	983	383	2892	4528
A	679	416	2625	3720
B	134	84	570	788
Total	1796	883	6087	8766

controls and the patients with gastric cancer, but that patients with peptic ulcer show an excess in group *O*. These comparisons correspond to a breakdown of the whole table as follows.

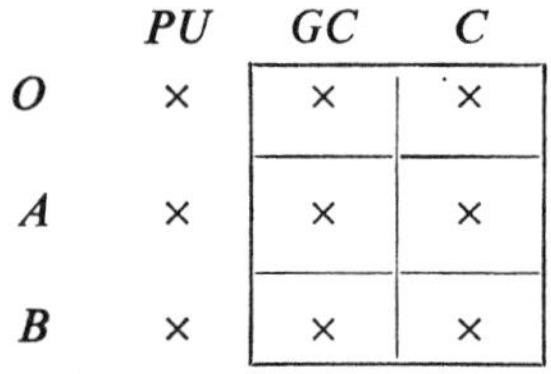

	PU	*GC*	*C*
O	×	×	×
A	×	×	×
B	×	×	×

(a)

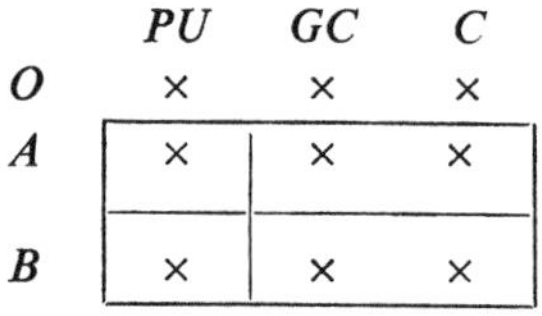

	PU	*GC*	*C*
O	×	×	×
A	×	×	×
B	×	×	×

(b)

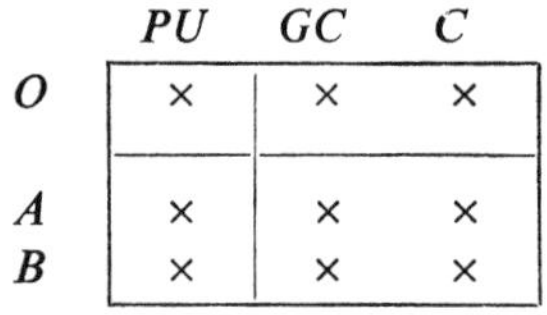

	PU	*GC*	*C*
O	×	×	×
A	×	×	×
B	×	×	×

(c)

The corresponding values of X^2 are as follows:

	Row comparison	Column comparison	X^2	DF
(a)	*O* v. *A* v. *B*	*GC* v. *C*	5·64	2
(b)	*A* v. *B*	*PU* v. (*GC*, *C*)	0·68	1
(c)	*O* v. (*A*, *B*)	*PU* v. (*GC*, *C*)	34·29	1
			40·61	4

As noted earlier the total of the X^2 statistics is a little different from the X^2 value of 40·54 for the whole table, but the difference is slight. The value of X^2 for (a) does not quite reach the 5 per cent level. The outstanding contrast is that between the proportions of group *O* amongst the patients with peptic ulcer and amongst the other subjects.

12.3 COMBINATION OF 2 × 2 TABLES

Sometimes a number of 2 × 2 tables, all bearing on the same question, are available, and it seems natural to combine the evidence for an association between the row and column factors. For example, there may be a number of retrospective studies, each providing evidence about a possible association between a certain disease and a certain environmental factor. Or, in a multi-centre clinical trial, each centre may provide evidence about a possible difference between the proportions of patients whose condition is improved with treatment *A* and treatment *B*. How should such data be combined?

The first point to make is that it may be quite misleading to pool the frequencies in the various tables, and examine the association suggested by the table of pooled frequencies. An extreme illustration is provided by the following hypothetical data.

Example 12.4

The frequencies in the lower left hand corner of Table 12.4 are supposed to have been obtained in a retrospective survey in which 1,000 patients with a certain disease are compared with 1,000 control subjects. The proportion with a certain characteristic *A* is very slightly higher in the control group than

TABLE 12.4 Retrospective survey to study the association between a disease and an aetiologic factor; data subdivided by sex.

		Observed frequencies			Expected frequencies	
		Disease	Control	Total	Disease	Control
Male	*A*	160	80	240	144	96
	not *A*	440	320	760	456	304
		600	400	1000	600	400
Female	*A*	240	330	570	228	342
	not *A*	160	270	430	172	258
		400	600	1000	400	600
Male	*A*	400	410	810	(372)	(438)
+ female	not *A*	600	590	1190	(628)	(562)
		1000	1000	2000		

in the disease group. If anything, therefore, the data suggest a negative association between the disease and factor A, although of course the difference would be far from significant. However, suppose the two groups had not been matched for sex, and that the data for the two sexes separately are as shown in the upper left part of the table. For each sex there is a *positive* association between the disease and factor A, as may be seen by comparing the observed frequencies on the left with the expected frequencies on the right. The latter are calculated in the usual way, separately for each sex; for example $144=(240)(600)/1{,}000$. What has happened here is that the control group contains a higher proportion of females than the disease group, and females have a higher prevalence of factor A than do males. The association suggested by the pooled frequencies is in the opposite direction from that suggested in each of the component tables.

How should the evidence from separate tables be pooled? There is no unique answer. The procedure to be adopted will depend on whether the object is primarily to test the significance of a tendency for rows and columns to be associated in one direction throughout the data, or whether the association is to be measured, and if so in what way.

In some situations it is natural or convenient to study the association in each table by looking at the difference between two proportions. Suppose that, in the ith table, we are interested in a comparison between the proportion of individuals classified as 'positive', in each of two categories A and B, and that the frequencies in this table are as follows:

	A	B	Total $A+B$
Positive	r_{Ai}	r_{Bi}	$r_{.i}$
Negative	$n_{Ai}-r_{Ai}$	$n_{Bi}-r_{Bi}$	$n_{.i}-r_{.i}$
Total	n_{Ai}	n_{Bi}	$n_{.i}$
Proportion +ve	$p_{Ai}=r_{Ai}/n_{Ai}$	$p_{Bi}=r_{Bi}/n_{Bi}$	$p_{0i}=r_{.i}/n_{.i}$ $q_{0i}=1-p_{0i}$

The difference which interests us is

$$d_i=p_{Ai}-p_{Bi}. \tag{12.3}$$

These differences could be pooled in the form of a weighted mean

$$\bar{d}=\sum_i w_i d_i \Big/ \sum_i w_i. \tag{12.4}$$

Cochran (1954) suggested the use of the weights defined as follows:

$$w_i=\frac{n_{Ai}n_{Bi}}{n_{Ai}+n_{Bi}}. \tag{12.5}$$

These have the property that in general more weight is given to tables with larger numbers. It can be shown that this system of weights is the best for detecting small systematic differences between p_{Ai} and p_{Bi} of such a magnitude that the difference between their logits is constant. This is a plausible requirement because a differential effect between A and B is likely to produce a larger d_i when the p's are near $\frac{1}{2}$ than when they are near 0 or 1.

Using the usual formula, appropriate to the null hypothesis:

$$\text{var}(d_i) = p_{0i}q_{0i}(n_{Ai}+n_{Bi})/n_{Ai}n_{Bi}, \tag{12.6}$$

we find

$$\text{var}(\bar{d}) = \sum_i w_i p_{0i} q_{0i} / (\sum w_i)^2,$$

$$\text{SE}(\bar{d}) = \sqrt{\text{var}(\bar{d})},$$

and, on the null hypothesis, $\bar{d}/\text{SE}(\bar{d})$ can be taken as approximately a standardized normal deviate; or its square, $\bar{d}^2/\text{var}(\bar{d})$ as a $\chi^2_{(1)}$ variate. An equivalent formula for the normal deviate is

$$\sum w_i d_i / \sqrt{(\sum w_i p_{0i} q_{0i})}.$$

Example 12.5

Table 12.5 shows some results taken from a trial to compare the mortality from tetanus in patients receiving antitoxin and in those not receiving antitoxin. The treatments were allocated at random, but by chance a higher proportion of patients in the 'No antitoxin' group had a more severe category of disease (as defined in terms of incubation period and period of onset of spasms). The third category (unknown severity) is clearly numerically unimportant, but may as well be included in the calculations. The overall results favour the use of antitoxin, but this may be due partly to the more favourable distribution of cases.

TABLE 12.5 Mortality from tetanus in a clinical trial to compare the effects of using and not using antitoxin, with classification of patients by severity of disease (Brown *et al.*, 1960).

	No antitoxin		Antitoxin	
Severity group	Deaths/Total	Proportion deaths	Deaths/Total	Proportion deaths
I (most severe)	22/26	0·8462	15/21	0·7143
II (least severe)	6/11	0·5455	4/18	0·2222
III (unknown)	1/1	1·0000	1/2	0·5000

Cochran's test proceeds as follows.

Group	p_{0i}	d_i	$p_{0i}q_{0i}$	w_i
I	37/47 = 0·7872	0·1319	0·1675	11·62
II	10/29 = 0·3448	0·3233	0·2259	6·83
III	2/3 = 0·6667	0·5000	0·2222	0·67
				19·12

$$\bar{d} = 4{\cdot}0758/19{\cdot}12 = 0{\cdot}2132$$

$$\text{SE}(\bar{d}) = (\sqrt{3{\cdot}6381})/19{\cdot}12 = 0{\cdot}0997$$

$$\bar{d}/\text{SE}(\bar{d}) = 2{\cdot}14,$$

beyond the 5 per cent level of significance.

SOME OTHER TESTS

(i) *Comparison of observed and expected frequencies*

Cochran's test could have been applied in Table 12.4, by calling the disease and control groups A and B, and regarding p_i as the proportion of individuals with factor A in the ith table ($i=1$ for males, 2 for females). Another approach would be to calculate the expected frequencies for each sex, as in the right half of Table 12.4, and to add these over the two sexes to give the expected totals in the lower-right-hand corner. A comparison of the observed and expected totals shows an excess of factor A in the disease group (400 observed, 372 expected). One is tempted to do an ordinary χ^2 test on these observed and expected frequencies. This would not be correct, however, since the expected frequencies have not been obtained simply from the observed margins; their calculation requires a knowledge of the results for the two component tables. A theoretical study (Radhakrishna, 1965) shows that the correct test for this situation is almost exactly the same as Cochran's test, which may therefore be used in the form given above.

(ii) *Addition of χ^2 statistics*

Each component tables gives a value of X^2, the usual $\chi^2_{(1)}$ statistic; say X_i^2 for the ith table. If each X_i^2 is calculated without continuity correction, they may be added, and the total,

$$X_0^2 = \sum_i X_i^2,$$

taken as a $\chi^2_{(k)}$ statistic (k being the number of tables). This is a perfectly valid test, but it is rarely advisable because the individual values X_i^2 take no account of the direction of the association. If there is a systematic tendency towards an association in the same direction, in each table, Cochran's test will be much more effective in detecting it.

(iii) *Addition of* χ *statistics*

To overcome the difficulty just mentioned, one could use the square-root of the $\chi^2_{(1)}$ statistic, X_i, again uncorrected for continuity, taking care that the sign of X_i correctly reflects the direction of the association. Then the sum

$$X'_0 = \sum_i X_i$$

has, on the null hypothesis, mean zero and standard deviation $\sqrt{k}$; therefore $X'_0/\sqrt{k}$ can be taken as a standardized normal deviate. This method is likely to give similar results to Cochran's test if the separate tables have similar numbers of observations. In general, though, it suffers from two defects: it gives equal weight to all values of X_i, even though there may be great disparities in the sizes of the tables (as there are in Table 12.5); and secondly it is not associated with any estimate comparable to the $\bar{d}$ of Cochran's test.

This remark is a useful reminder that the methods considered in this section are predominantly significance tests. Even Cochran's method in the form given above is not quite appropriate for *estimating* a non-zero difference, since the variance formula assumes the null hypothesis to be true. More general methods are discussed in section 12.5, and, in relation to epidemiological surveys, in section 16.2.

12.4 COMBINATION OF $r \times c$ TABLES

The sort of problem considered in the last section can clearly arise with larger contingency tables. The investigator may be interested in the association between two qualitative factors, with r and c categories respectively, and data may be available for k subgroups or strata, these thus forming k separate tables. An exact treatment is difficult. A natural approach is to generalize method (i) of p. 372. Expected frequencies are calculated from the margin of each table by (7.23), these are added over the k tables, and a comparison is made of the total observed and the total expected frequencies. A convenient test statistic is the usual χ^2

quantity (7.24), calculated from these pooled frequencies. However, as in the corresponding problem with 2×2 tables, this statistic, X^2, does not follow the χ^2 distribution with $(r-1)$ $(c-1)$ DF. The correct DF should be somewhat lower, making high values of X^2 more significant than would at first be thought, but a convenient correction is not known. The effect is likely to be quite small. The usual χ^2 test may, therefore, be regarded as conservative, making one somewhat too cautious in claiming a significant association.

TABLE 12.6 Most recent amount smoked by all patients other than those with cancer of the lung, from a retrospective survey. (Expected numbers shown in brackets, are obtained within age-sex groups and added).

Disease group	Cigarettes daily 0	1–	5–	15–	25–	Total
Cancer, other than lung	236 (220·0)	78 (85·3)	237 (236·9)	110 (122·8)	57 (53·0)	718 (718·0)
Respiratory disease, not cancer	42 (47·0)	33 (29·7)	128 (136·1)	98 (84·1)	34 (38·1)	335 (335·0)
Cardiovascular disease	22 (17·7)	19 (16·7)	64 (73·8)	38 (39·5)	23 (18·3)	166 (166·0)
Gastro-intestinal disease	39 (55·7)	31 (32·3)	143 (130·2)	81 (75·8)	34 (34·5)	328 (328·5)
Other categories	38 (36·6)	24 (21·1)	91 (86·0)	44 (48·9)	18 (22·1)	215 (214·7)
Total	377 (377·0)	185 (185·1)	663 (663·0)	371 (371·1)	166 (166·0)	1762 (1762·2)

Example 12.6

Doll and Hill (1950) reported the results summarized in Table 12.6. These relate to the cigarette consumption of patients in various diagnostic groups. These patients all formed part of the control series in a retrospective study in which patients with lung cancer were matched, for age and sex, with patients suffering from other diseases. Different sub-groups of the control series may therefore differ in their age and sex composition; indeed they would be expected to do so because of the different age and sex patterns of different diseases. Any associaton between disease group and cigarette consumption shown in the observed frequencies of Table 12.6 may therefore be caused by age and sex disparities, since smoking habits are known to vary with age and sex. The patients were therefore subdivided into age and sex groups, within each of which expected frequencies were calculated in the usual way, and these were then added to give the total expected frequencies shown in brackets in Table 12.6.

The usual calculation gives $X^2 = 20{\cdot}14$. Without stratification this would be a $\chi^2_{(16)}$ variable, with P between 0·1 and 0·25. The fact that adjustment has been made for age and sex stratification means that X^2 is really slightly more significant than this test suggests, but it is unlikely that a correction would affect the result sufficiently to make it significant at, say, the 0·05 level.

A correction formula for $2 \times c$ tables has been given by Armitage (1966). In practice it seems to have relatively little effect.

12.5 LINEAR MODELS FOR TRANSFORMED PROPORTIONS

The emphasis so far in this chapter has been on significance testing. We now need to consider some problems of estimation and also to consider the analysis of proportions when the data fall into more complex structures than those studied earlier.

In the study of continuous variables, considerable progress was made by postulating a linear model, either in the analysis of variance for data classified in various ways or in simple or multiple regression. A similar approach seems indicated for binomial variables, but the arguments of section 11.4 suggest that changes in the dependent variable, corresponding to a certain change in an explanatory variable, would be more nearly constant on a transformed scale than on the original scale of a proportion.

Any of the transformations described in section 11.4 could be considered. Experience suggests that for most sets of data arising in practice no transformation gives an appreciably better fit than any other (Naylor 1964). In the following discussion we shall rely primarily on the logit transformation. One reason is that for linear models with the logit transformation several familiar methods turn out to be theoretically appropriate; one such method is the Fisher-Irwin-Yates exact test for the 2×2 table (section 4.8); another is the $X^2_{(1)}$ test for trend in proportions (equation (12.1)). Another reason is that approximate solutions are algebraically somewhat simpler than for the probit transformation (requiring, for instance, log tables rather than tables of the normal distribution).

We shall discuss two approaches: first an approximate method of analysis using *empirical weights*, and secondly (and rather briefly) the theoretically more satisfactory maximum likelihood solution. For a fuller treatment see D. R. Cox (1970).

(a) APPROXIMATE SOLUTION WITH EMPIRICAL WEIGHTS

Suppose that in a sample of n individuals there are r positives and $n-r$ negatives, with $p=r/n$, and that the expected proportion of positives is π. Define $q=1-p$. The logit of p is defined as

$$y=\log_e \frac{p}{q}; \tag{12.7}$$

(see (11.6)). A difficulty arises if $r=0$ or n, for then $p=0$ or 1 and $y=-\infty$ or ∞, respectively. A modified definition

$$y=\log_e \frac{r+\frac{1}{2}}{n-r+\frac{1}{2}} \tag{12.8}$$

is useful. If a high proportion of the values of p in any set of data are 0 or 1, it is probably wise to use (12.8) throughout; otherwise (12.8) can be used merely for the occasional 0 or 1 values.

From (3.16), an approximate formula for var(y) is

$$\mathrm{var}(y) \simeq \frac{1}{n\pi(1-\pi)}, \tag{12.9}$$

which may be estimated by

$$\frac{1}{npq}. \tag{12.10}$$

Defining a weighting coefficient

$$w=pq, \tag{12.11}$$

we could attach a weight nw to the logit, y, and thereby weight each value of y in inverse proportion to its variance. This is the general approach adopted in weighted multiple regression (p. 319), and we may expect the general method of weighted regression to provide an approximate solution. Values of w are given in Table A7.

The model here would be of the form

$$Y=\alpha+\beta_1 x_1+\beta_2 x_2+\ldots+\beta_m x_m, \tag{12.12}$$

where Y is the population logit:

$$Y = \log_e \frac{\pi}{1-\pi}. \tag{12.13}$$

The proposed method is *not* exact; first because the y's are not normally distributed about the Y's; and secondly because the weight now used for any y is not exactly in inverse proportion to var(y), being expressed in terms of the estimated proportion p. For this reason the weights are often called *empirical.*

In problems requiring an analysis of variance approach, the empirical weight now takes the place of the number of observations in a particular sub-group. Since the various values of nw will in general be different, the situation is analogous to an unbalanced experimental design, and the methods of non-orthogonal analysis described in section 8.6 may often be used.

TABLE 12.7 A 2^4 factorial set of proportions (Lombard and Doering, 1947).

Factor combination	(1) Number of individuals n	(2) Number with good score r	(3) Proportion (2)/(1) p	(4) Logit (p) y	(5) Weighting coefficient $w=pq$	(6) Weight (1)×(5) nw	(7) Variance 1/(6) $1/nw$
(1)	477	84	0·176	−1·54	0·1450	69·16	0·014
(*a*)	231	75	0·325	−0·73	0·2194	50·68	0·020
(*b*)	63	13	0·206	−1·35	0·1636	10·31	0·097
(*ab*)	94	35	0·372	−0·52	0·2336	21·96	0·046
(*c*)	150	67	0·447	−0·21	0·2472	37·08	0·027
(*ac*)	378	201	0·532	0·13	0·2490	94·12	0·011
(*bc*)	32	16	0·500	0·00	0·2500	8·00	0·125
(*abc*)	169	102	0·604	0·42	0·2392	40·42	0·025
(*d*)	12	2	0·167	−1·61	0·1391	1·67	0·600
(*ad*)	13	7	0·538	0·15	0·2486	3·23	0·310
(*bd*)	7	4	0·571	0·29	0·2450	1·72	0·581
(*abd*)	12	8	0·667	0·69	0·2222	2·67	0·375
(*cd*)	11	3	0·273	−0·98	0·1985	2·18	0·459
(*acd*)	45	27	0·600	0·41	0·2400	10·80	0·093
(*bcd*)	4	1	0·250	−1·10	0·1875	0·75	1·333
(*abcd*)	31	23	0·742	1·06	0·1914	5·93	0·169
							4·285

Example 12.7

Table 12.7 shows some data reported by Lombard and Doering (1947) from a survey of knowledge about cancer. These data have been used by several other authors (Dyke and Patterson, 1952; Yates, 1960; Naylor, 1964). Each line of the table corresponds to a particular combination of factors in a 2^4 factorial arrangement, n being the number of individuals in this category and r the number who gave a good score in response to questions about cancer knowledge. The four factors are: A, newspaper reading; B, listening to radio; C, solid reading; D, attendance at lectures.

Although the data are obtained from a survey rather than from a randomized experiment, we can usefully study the effect on cancer knowledge of the four main effects and their interactions. In a 2^p factorial design with disproportionate numbers the usual analysis of variance is inappropriate, but the main effects and interactions, although no longer orthogonal, can be estimated by simple linear contrasts of the type shown in Table 8.7. The same approach can be followed here. Columns (3) and (4) of Table 12.7 show the proportion of good scorers and its logit. For the main effect of A, following Table 8.7, we form a linear contrast by multiplying the entries in column (4) by

$$-1 \quad +1 \quad -1 \quad +1 \ldots -1 \quad +1,$$

and dividing by 8 (see p. 234, where the n referred to there is taken as unity since there is only one value of y at each factor combination). Proceeding similarly for the other main effects we find:

	Contrast (1)	Effect (2) $=(1)/8$
A	8·11	1·014
B	3·87	0·484
C	4·35	0·544
D	2·71	0·339

Interactions could be estimated similarly, but details are omitted here.

The variance of each of the estimates of factor effects in column (2) above is the same, namely

$$\sum \text{var}(y_i)/8^2,$$

the summation being taken over the 16 values of y. The estimated var(y_i), from (12.10), is obtained in columns (5)–(7) of Table 12.7. These values sum to 4·285, so the estimated variance of each factor effect is

$$4{\cdot}285/64,$$

and the standard error is

$$(\sqrt{4{\cdot}285})/8 = 0{\cdot}259.$$

On a large sample normal-theory test, factor A is highly significant, C is moderately significant ($P<0{\cdot}05$), while B and D fail to reach the 5 per cent level. Interactions, if estimated in the same way, all fail to reach significance.

Although the procedure described above provides estimates of main effects and (if required) interactions, it is not fully efficient, for in each of the linear contrasts all values of y are given equal weight. Several of the entries in Table 12.7 are based on much larger values of n than others, and should if possible be given more weight in the calculations. An alternative procedure, essentially the same as used in (8.28) for the estimation of row effect in a non-orthogonal $2\times c$ table, will be illustrated by estimation of the main effect of A. This may be estimated separately from each of 8 pairs of values of y: (a) and (1), (ab) and (b), and so on. Each pair provides a difference

$$d=y_1-y_2,$$

an estimated var(d), obtained from the sum of the two entries in column (7) of Table 12.7, and a weight w equal to the reciprocal of var(d). These are as follows:

	d	var(d)	w
$(a)-(1)$	0·81	0·034	29·2
$(ab)-(b)$	0·83	0·143	7·0
$(ac)-(c)$	0·34	0·038	26·6
$(abc)-(bc)$	0·42	0·150	6·7
$(ad)-(d)$	1·76	0·910	1·1
$(abd)-(bd)$	0·40	0·956	1·0
$(acd)-(cd)$	1·39	0·552	1·8
$(abcd)-(bcd)$	2·16	1·502	0·7
			74·1

(The values of var(d) vary so widely that it would have been preferable to calculate to a constant number of significant digits, in order to achieve adequate accuracy in the values of w; this would have required the use of more decimal places for some of the smaller entries in column (7) of Table 12.7). These values of d may be combined in a weighted mean, as in (8·28), giving

$$\bar{d}=47{\cdot}67/74{\cdot}1=0{\cdot}643$$

$$\text{var}(\bar{d})=1/\textstyle\sum w=0{\cdot}0135$$

and

$$\text{SE}(\bar{d})=0{\cdot}116.$$

The estimated main effect has been reduced from 1·014 to 0·643 by weighting, but its standard error has also been substantially reduced. The effect is still highly significant. See Yates (1960) for further details of this method of analysis (remembering that his logit is half that used here). The revised estimates of the four main effects, with standard errors, are:

A	$0{\cdot}643 \pm 0{\cdot}116$
B	$0{\cdot}292 \pm 0{\cdot}124$
C	$0{\cdot}997 \pm 0{\cdot}111$
D	$0{\cdot}441 \pm 0{\cdot}196$

(b) MAXIMUM LIKELIHOOD

A general method of estimation, that of *maximum likelihood*, has certain desirable theoretical properties. It consists in estimating the values of parameters to be such that they maximize the likelihood calculated from the observed data (see section 4.11). For the linear model with the probit transformation the maximum likelihood solution is called *probit analysis*; see section 17.4 and Finney (1952). When applied to the linear logit model (12.12) the method results in the following procedure:

(i) Guess values of the parameters and evaluate each predicted Y from (12.12), and hence the corresponding π from (12.13).

(ii) For each observation, calculate a *working logit*,

$$y = Y + \frac{p - \pi}{\pi(1-\pi)} \tag{12.14}$$

in terms of the predicted Y and π. (Table XI of Fisher and Yates (1963) is useful here, but entries must be multiplied by two to conform to the present definition of logit). Also calculate a weight nw, where now

$$w = \pi(1-\pi); \tag{12.15}$$

The weighting coefficient, w, is expressed in (12.15) in terms of the predicted π, rather than (as in (12.11)) in terms of the observed p.

(iii) Do a weighted multiple regression of y on the x's, using weights nw, and obtain revised estimates of Y.

(iv) Repeat (ii)—(iii) until the process 'converges', i.e. until successive cycles produce little change in the Y's.

The initial guess is not important, except in its effect on the speed of convergence. A simple start would be to set each of the parameter values to zero.

This process is obviously rather tedious and a general computer program is a great help. Dyke and Patterson (1952) analyse the factorial experiment described in Example 12.7 by formulating the model as a regression equation like (12.12), and applying the method given above (in a slightly different form). Estimates of the main effects with standard errors are as follows; (these values have been recalculated and are slightly different from those given by the authors).

$$\begin{array}{ll} A & 0{\cdot}650 \pm 0{\cdot}115 \\ B & 0{\cdot}310 \pm 0{\cdot}122 \\ C & 0{\cdot}981 \pm 0{\cdot}111 \\ D & 0{\cdot}420 \pm 0{\cdot}191. \end{array}$$

These values are much closer to the second set of estimates given in Example 12.7 (i.e. closer to the weighted than to the unweighted estimates). Note that if interactions are estimated, by introducing predictor variables which are products of the dummy variables representing main effects, the estimates of the main effects will change (see Dyke and Patterson, 1952).

If the observed proportions p are based on $n=1$ observation only, their values will be either 0 or 1, and the empirical method cannot be used. The maximum likelihood method is, however, perfectly valid. This is a useful tool in the analysis of prognostic data, where an individual patient is classified as 'success' or 'failure', several explanatory variables x_j are observed, and the object is to predict the probability of success in terms of the x's.

Example 10.5 could be treated in this way. As a model we could suppose that the logit of the probability of survival was related to haemoglobin, x_i, and bilirubin, x_2, by the formula

$$Y=\alpha+\beta_1x_1+\beta_2x_2.$$

Application of the maximum likelihood method (using a computer program) gave the following estimates of α, β_1 and β_2 with their standard errors:

$$\begin{aligned} \hat{a} &= -2{\cdot}354 \pm 2{\cdot}416 \\ \hat{\beta}_1 &= 0{\cdot}5324 \pm 0{\cdot}1487 \\ \hat{\beta}_2 &= -0{\cdot}4892 \pm 0{\cdot}3448. \end{aligned} \qquad (12.16)$$

The picture is similar to that presented by the discriminant analysis of Example 10.5. Haemoglobin is an important predictor; bilirubin is not. An interesting point is that if the distributions of the x's are multivariate normal, with the same variances and covariances for both successes and failures (the basic model for discriminant analysis), the discriminant function (10.35) can also be used to predict Y. The formula is:

$$Y = \alpha' + \beta_1' x_1 + \beta_2' x_2 + \ldots + \beta_m' x_m,$$

where

$$\beta_j' = (n_1 + n_2 - 2) b_j$$

and

$$\alpha' = -\tfrac{1}{2}\{\beta_1'(\bar{x}_{A1} + \bar{x}_{B1}) + \ldots + \beta_m'(\bar{x}_{Am} + \bar{x}_{Bm})\} + \log_e(n_A/n_B). \qquad (12.17)$$

In Example 10.5, using the discriminant function coefficients b_1 and b_2 given there, we find

$$\left.\begin{aligned} \alpha' &= -4{\cdot}134 \\ \beta_1' &= 0{\cdot}6540 \\ \beta_2' &= -0{\cdot}3978 \end{aligned}\right\}$$

which lead to values of Y not differing greatly from those obtained from (12.16), except for extreme values of x_1 and x_2.

An example of the use of the linear discriminant function to predict the probability of coronary heart disease is given by Truett *et al.* (1967). The point should be emphasized that in situations in which the distributions of x's are far from multivariate normal this method may be unreliable, and the maximum likelihood solution will be preferable.

To test the adequacy of the linear logit model (12.12), after fitting by maximum likelihood, an approximate χ^2 test statistic may be calculated by either of two equivalent methods:

(i) in the last cycle of the iterative procedure, take X^2 as the weighted sum of squares about regression; or

(ii) calculate predicted logits, Y, from the maximum likelihood estimates of the coefficients in (12.12), obtain the corresponding proportions, $\hat{\pi}$, and calculate the usual χ^2 index,

$$X^2 = \sum n(p - \hat{\pi})^2 \left(\frac{1}{\hat{\pi}} + \frac{1}{1 - \hat{\pi}}\right) = \sum \frac{n(p - \hat{\pi})^2}{\hat{\pi}(1 - \hat{\pi})}.$$

X^2 follows approximately the $\chi^2_{(N-m-1)}$ distribution, where N is the number of observations (i.e. the number of separate values of p) and m is the number of predictor variables. This approximation is unreliable if a high proportion of the observations are based on small values of n, and is particularly useless in the case discussed above, where all values of n are 1. In the maximum likelihood fit to the data of Example 12.7, $X^2 = 13{\cdot}6$ with $16 - 5 = 11$ DF (since four main effects were estimated, requiring four dummy predictor variables). The fit is clearly adequate, suggesting that for these data there is no need to postulate interactions.

A more detailed discussion of the fitting of linear models for transformed proportions is given by D. R. Cox (1970). To summarize some of the points that have been raised in this section and in earlier sections we consider in Example 12.8 a number of alternative solutions to the problem of fitting a trend to a series of proportions.

Example 12.8

Table 12.8 shows the number of strains of *Staphylococcus aureus*, isolated from patients of a certain hospital between 1947 and 1950, which were resistant or sensitive to 1 unit per c.c. of penicillin.

TABLE 12.8 Number of strains of *Staphylococcus aureus* resistant or sensitive to 1 unit per c.c of penicillin.

	1947	1948	1949	1950	Total
Resistant	45	41	113	53	252
Sensitive	194	145	185	107	631
	239	186	298	160	883
Proportion resistant, p_i	0·19	0·22	0·38	0·33	
SE (p_i)	0·025	0·030	0·028	0·037	

The proportion of resistant strains increases during the 4 year period and it would be useful to know whether this trend is clearly significant, and if so, whether the trend is gradual throughout the period or whether a sudden change seems to have occurred.

The standard errors of the proportions, calculated separately from each p_i as $\sqrt{(p_i q_i/n_i)}$, are shown at the foot of the table. Clearly the proportions for 1947 and 1948 do not differ significantly from each other, nor do those for 1949 and 1950, whereas there is a significant change between 1948 and 1949. The data could, nevertheless, be consistent with a smooth trend, and this possibility must be investigated.

One method would be the test for trend given in section 12.2(a). For this purpose we define a working unit, x, taking values -3, -1, 1 and 3 for the four years 1947–1950. The overall $\chi^2_{(3)}$ test gives $X^2=29{\cdot}4$ ($P<0{\cdot}001$), and the $\chi^2_{(1)}$ test (12.1) for linear trend on x gives $X^2_1=21{\cdot}0$ ($P<0{\cdot}001$). The difference

$$X^2-X^2_1=8{\cdot}5,$$

which as a $\chi^2_{(2)}$ variable is significant ($P<0{\cdot}025$). This suggests that a linear trend of the proportions is not tenable.

There might, however, be a linear trend on x for some transformed scale of proportions. Regressions have been carried out for each of the transformations: logit, angle and probit; in each case both the empirical and maximum likelihood methods have been used. The weighted sums of squares due to and about regression can be regarded as approximately $\chi^2_{(1)}$ and $\chi^2_{(2)}$ variables, respectively. The results are as follows:

	Trend $\chi^2_{(1)}$	Residual $\chi^2_{(2)}$
Logit, empirical	20·2	8·8
ML	21·2	8·7
Angle, empirical	22·0	8·2
ML	21·6	8·2
Probit, empirical	20·8	8·4
ML	21·4	8·5

The results for all three transformations are very similar, and are close to those for the simple test for linear trend (12.1). All methods of analysis suggest a sharp change in the proportion of resistant organisms between 1948 and 1949.

For another method of analysis of these data see p. 402.

12.6 STANDARDIZATION

Problems similar to those discussed in sections 12.3–12.5 arise frequently in vital statistics and have given rise to a group of methods called standardization. We shall describe briefly one or two of the most well-known methods, and discuss their relationship to the methods described above.

Mortality in a population is usually measured by an annual death rate; for example, the number of individuals dying during a certain calendar year divided by the estimated population size mid-way through the year. Frequently this ratio is multiplied by a convenient base such as 1,000, to avoid small decimal fractions; it is then called the annual death rate per 1,000 population. If the death rate is calculated for a population covering a wide age-range it is called a *crude death rate*.

In a comparison of the mortality of two populations, say those of two different countries, the crude rates may be misleading. Mortality depends strongly on age. If the two countries have different age structures this contrast alone may explain a difference in crude rates (just as, in Table 12.4, the contrast between the 'crude' proportions with factor A

was strongly affected by the different sex distributions in the disease and control groups). An example is given in Table 12.9, which shows the numbers of individuals and numbers of deaths separately in different groups, for two countries: *A*, typical of highly industrialized countries, with a rather high proportion of individuals at the older ages; and *B*, a developing country with a smaller proportion of old people. The death rates at each age (which are called *age-specific death rates*) are substantially higher for *B* than for *A* yet the crude death-rate is higher for *A* than for *B*.

The situation here is precisely the same as that discussed at the beginning of section 12.3, in connection with Example 12.4. Sometimes, however, mortality has to be compared for a large number of different populations, and some form of adjustment for age differences is required. For example, the mortality in one country may have to be compared over several different years; different regions of the same country may be under study; or one may wish to compare the mortality for a large number of different occupations. Two obvious generalizations are (a) in standardizing for factors other than, or in addition to, age—for example, sex, as in Table 12.4; and (b) in morbidity studies where the criterion studied is the occurrence of a certain illness rather than of a death. We shall discuss the usual situation—the standardization of mortality rates for age.

The basic idea in standardization is that we introduce a *standard population* with a fixed age structure. The mortality for any *special population* is then adjusted to allow for discrepancies in age structure between the standard and special populations. There are two main approaches: *direct* and *indirect* methods of standardization. The following brief account may be supplemented by reference to Bradford Hill (1966), Liddell (1960) or Kalton (1968).

The following notation will be used.

	Standard			Special		
	(1)	(2)	(3)	(4)	(5)	(6)
Age group	Population	Deaths	D. rate (2)/(1)	Population	Deaths	D. rate (5)/(4)
1	N_1	R_1	P_1	n_1	r_1	p_1
.						
.						
.						
i	N_i	R_i	P_i	n_i	r_i	p_i
.						
.						
.						
k	N_k	R_k	P_k	n_k	r_k	p_k

TABLE 12.9 Death rates for two populations, *A* and *B*, with direct standardization using *A*, *B* and a mid-way population *C*.

	A				*B*				*C*	
Age, yrs.	Population 1,000's	%	Deaths	Age-specific D.R. per 1,000	Population 1,000's	%	Deaths	Age-specific D.R. per 1,000	Population 1,000's	%
0–	2,100	*8·97*	10,000	4·67	185	*14·51*	4,100	22·16	1,174	*11·74*
5–	1,900	*8·12*	800	0·42	170	*13·33*	100	0·59	1,072	*10·72*
10–	1,700	*7·26*	700	0·41	160	*12·55*	100	0·62	990	*9·90*
15–	1,900	*8·12*	2,000	1·05	120	*9·41*	180	1·50	876	*8·76*
20–	1,700	*7·26*	1,700	1·00	100	*7·84*	190	1·90	755	*7·55*
25–	1,500	*6·41*	1,400	0·93	80	*6·27*	160	2·00	634	*6·34*
30–	1,500	*6·41*	1,700	1·13	70	*5·49*	170	2·43	595	*5·95*
35–	1,500	*6·41*	2,700	1·80	65	*5·10*	200	3·08	576	*5·76*
40–	1,600	*6·84*	4,800	3·00	65	*5·10*	270	4·15	597	*5·97*
45–	1,500	*6·41*	7,800	5·20	60	*4·71*	370	6·17	556	*5·56*
50–	1,500	*6·41*	14,200	9·47	55	*4·31*	530	9·64	536	*5·36*
55–	1,500	*6·41*	23,800	15·87	40	*3·14*	690	17·25	478	*4·78*
60–	1,300	*5·56*	34,900	26·85	30	*2·35*	880	29·33	396	*3·96*
65–	900	*3·85*	40,700	45·22	30	*2·35*	1,500	50·00	310	*3·10*
70–	600	*2·56*	42,000	70·00	20	*1·57*	1,520	76·00	207	*2·07*
75–	700	*2·99*	98,100	140·14	25	*1·96*	4,100	164·00	248	*2·48*
	23,400	*99·99*	287,300		1,275	*99·99*	15,060		10,000	*100·00*
Crude rate				**12·28**				**11·81**		
(a) *Standardization by population A*										
Expected deaths			287,300				365,815			
Standardized rate				**12·28**				**15·63**		
(b) *Standardization by population B*										
Expected deaths			10,781				15,060			
Standardized rate				**8·03**				**11·81**		
(c) *Standardization by population C*										
Expected deaths			105,074				137,338			
Standardized rate				**10·17**				**13·73**		

DIRECT METHOD

The standardized death rate for the special population, by the direct method, is

$$p' = \frac{\sum N_i p_i}{\sum N_i}. \tag{12.18}$$

It is obtained by applying the special death rates, p_i, to the standard population sizes, N_i. Alternatively, p' can be regarded as a weighted mean of the p_i, using the N_i as weights. The variance of p' may be estimated as

$$\text{var}(p') = \frac{\sum(N_i^2 p_i q_i/n_i)}{(\sum N_i)^2}, \tag{12.19}$$

where $q_i = 1 - p_i$; if, as is often the case, the p_i are all small, the binomial variance of p_i, $p_i q_i/n_i$, may be replaced by the Poisson term p_i/n_i $(=r_i/n_i^2)$, giving

$$\text{var}(p') \simeq \frac{\sum(N_i^2 p_i/n_i)}{(\sum N_i)^2}. \tag{12.20}$$

To compare two special populations, A and B, we could calculate a standardized rate for each (p'_A and p'_B), and consider

$$\bar{d} = p'_A - p'_B.$$

From (12.18),

$$\bar{d} = \frac{\sum N_i(p_{Ai} - p_{Bi})}{\sum N_i},$$

which has exactly the same form as (12.4), with $w_i = N_i$, and $d_i = p_{Ai} - p_{Bi}$ as in (12.3). The method differs from that of Cochran's test only in using a different system of weights. The variance of $\bar{d}$ is given by

$$\text{var}(\bar{d}) = \frac{\sum N_i^2 \, \text{var}(d_i)}{(\sum N_i)^2}, \tag{12.21}$$

with var(d_i) given by (12.6). Again, when the p_{oi}'s are small, q_{oi} can be put approximately equal to 1 in (12.6).

Example 12.9

In Table 12.9 a standardized rate p' could be calculated for each population. What should be taken as the standard population? There is no unique answer to this question. The choice may not greatly affect the comparison of two populations, although it will certainly affect the absolute values of the standardized rates. If the contrast between the age-specific rates is very different at different age-groups we may have to consider whether we wish the standardized rates to reflect particularly the position at certain parts of the age-scale; for example, it might be desirable to give less weight to the higher age-groups because the purpose of the study is mainly to compare mortality at younger ages, or because the information at higher ages is less reliable, or because the death rates at high ages are more affected by sampling error.

At the foot of Table 12.9 we give standardized rates with three choices of standard population: (a) population A, (b) population B, and (c) a hypothetical population, C, whose *proportionate* distribution is mid-way between A and B, i.e.

$$N_{0i} \propto \frac{1}{2}\left(\frac{n_{Ai}}{\sum n_{Ai}} + \frac{n_{Bi}}{\sum n_{Bi}}\right).$$

Note that for method (a) the standardized rate for A is the same as the crude rate; similarly for (b) the standardized rate for B is the same as the crude rate. Although the absolute values of the standardized rates are different for the three choices of standard population, the contrast is broadly the same in each case.

INDIRECT METHOD

This method is more easily thought of as a comparison of observed and expected deaths than in terms of standardized rates. In the special population the total number of deaths observed is $\sum r_i$. The number of deaths expected if the age-specific death rates were the same as in the standard population is $\sum n_i P_i$. The overall mortality experience of the special population may be expressed in terms of that of the standard population by the ratio of observed to expected deaths:

$$M = \frac{\sum r_i}{\sum n_i P_i}. \qquad (12.22)$$

When multiplied by 100 and expressed as a percentage, (12.22) is known as the *Standardized Mortality Ratio* (SMR).

To obtain the variance of M we can use the result $\text{var}(r_i) = n_i p_i q_i$, and regard the P_i as constants without any sampling fluctuation (since we shall often want to compare one SMR with another using the same standard population; in any case the standard population will often be much larger than the special population, and $\text{var}(P_i)$ will be much smaller than $\mathrm{var}(p_i)$). This gives

$$\mathrm{var}(M)=\frac{\sum n_i p_i q_i}{(\sum n_i P_i)^2}. \quad (12.23)$$

As usual, if the p_i are small, $q_i \simeq 1$ and

$$\mathrm{var}(M)\simeq\frac{\sum r_i}{(\sum n_i P_i)^2}. \quad (12.24)$$

If the purpose of calculating $\mathrm{var}(M)$ is to see whether M differs significantly from unity, $\mathrm{var}(r_i)$ could be taken as $n_i P_i Q_i$, on the assumption that p_i differs from a population value P_i by sampling fluctuations. If again the P_i are small, and $Q_i \simeq 1$, we have

$$\mathrm{var}(M)=\frac{\sum n_i P_i}{(\sum n_i P_i)^2}=\frac{1}{\sum n_i P_i}, \quad (12.25)$$

the reciprocal of the total expected deaths. Denoting the numerator and denominator of (12.22) by O and E (for 'observed' and 'expected'), an approximate significance test would be to regard O as following a Poisson distribution with mean E. If E is not too small, the normal approximation to the Poisson leads to the use of $(O-E)/\sqrt{E}$ as a standardized normal deviate, or, equivalently, $(O-E)^2/E$ as a $\chi^2_{(1)}$ variate. This is, of course, the familiar formula for a $\chi^2_{(1)}$ variate.

Example 12.10

Table 12.10 shows some occupational mortality data, a field in which the SMR is traditionally used. The special population is that of farmers in 1951, aged 20 to 65 years. The standard population is that of all males in these age groups, whether occupied or retired. Deaths of farmers over a 5 year period are used to help reduce the sampling errors, and the observed and expected numbers are expressed on a 5 year basis.

The SMR is

$$100M=\frac{(100)(7{,}678)}{11{,}005}=69{\cdot}8 \text{ per cent,}$$

and

$$\begin{aligned}\mathrm{var}(\mathrm{SMR}) &= 10^4\,\mathrm{var}(M)\\ &= \frac{(10^4)(7{,}678)}{(11{,}005)^2} \qquad \text{from (12.24)}\\ &= 0{\cdot}634,\end{aligned}$$

and

$$\mathrm{SE}(\mathrm{SMR})=0{\cdot}80 \text{ per cent.}$$

TABLE 12.10 Mortality of farmers in England and Wales, 1949–53, in comparison with that of the male population.

Age i	(i) Annual death rate per 100,000, all males (1949–53) $\frac{1}{5}P_i \times 10^5$	(ii) Farmers, 1951 census population n_i	(iii) Deaths of farmers 1949–53 r_i	(iv) Deaths expected in five years $5 \times$ (i) $\times$ (ii) $\times 10^{-5}$ n_iP_i
20–	129·8	8,481	87	55
25–	152·5	39,729	289	303
35–	280·4	65,700	733	921
45–	816·2	73,376	1,998	2,994
55–64	2,312·4	58,226	4,571	6,732
			7,678	11,005

Source: Registrar General's Decennial Supplement, England and Wales 1951, Occupational Mortality, Part II, Vol. 2 (1958).

The smallness of the standard error of the SMR in Example 12.10 is typical of much vital statistical data, and is the reason why sampling errors are often ignored in this type of work. Indeed there are problems in the interpretation of occupational mortality statistics which often overshadow sampling errors. For example, occupations may be less reliably stated in censuses than in the registration of deaths, and this may lead to biases in the estimated death rates for certain occupations. Even if the data are wholly reliable, it is not clear whether a particularly high or low SMR for a certain occupation reflects a health risk in that occupation or a tendency for selective groups of people to enter it. In Example 12.10, for example, the SMR for farmers may be low because farming is healthy, or because unhealthy people are unlikely to enter farming or are more likely to leave it. Note also that in the lowest age group there is an *excess* of deaths among farmers (87 observed, 55 expected). Any method of standardization carries the risk of over-simplification, and the investigator should always compare age-specific rates to see whether the contrasts between populations vary greatly with age.

The method of indirect standardization is very similar to that described as the comparison of observed and expected frequencies on p. 372. Indeed if, in the comparison of two groups, A and B, the standard population were defined as the pooled population $A+B$, the methods would be precisely the same. It was stated on p. 372 that the appropriate significance test for the comparison of observed and expected frequencies was Cochran's test (p. 371), and we have seen (p. 387) that Cochran's test is equivalent to a comparison of two *direct*-standardized rates. There is thus a very close relationship between the direct and indirect methods when the standard population is chosen to be the sum of the two special populations.

12.7 GOODNESS OF FIT OF FREQUENCY DISTRIBUTIONS

It is often useful to regard a random variable as following a standard distributional form; common examples are the normal, binomial and Poisson distributions. The observed frequencies at different values, or in different grouping intervals, of the variables will not be precisely those expected by theory, and the question arises whether the discrepancy between observed and expected frequencies can easily be explained by sampling fluctuation.

In the examples mentioned above, a theoretical probability distribution can be fitted by using certain simple statistics calculated from the data. For a normal distribution, for instance, we need to estimate the mean μ and variance σ^2 by the sample mean $\bar{x}$ and estimate of variance s^2 (after application of Sheppard's correction if necessary). For the binomial the parameter π is estimated by the sample mean $\bar{r}$ divided by n (using the notation of section 2.5). For the Poisson the parameter μ is estimated by $\bar{x}$ (see section 2.6). Expected values of the frequencies can now be calculated, from exact formulae in the case of the binomial and Poisson distributions and from tables in the case of the normal distribution.

Suppose the frequency for any value or grouping interval is denoted by O_i, and the expected value by E_i. Then if E_i is a small fraction of the total frequency, the random variation of O_i about E_i is approximately represented by a Poisson distribution. Unless E_i is quite small, $(O_i - E_i)/\sqrt{E_i}$ can be taken as approximately a standardized normal deviate, and $(O_i - E_i)^2/E_i$ as a $\chi^2_{(1)}$ variate. If there were k such frequencies, and if all the deviations $O_i - E_i$ were independent, we should expect from the general theory of section 3.4 that the familiar statistic

$$X^2 = \sum \frac{(O_i - E_i)^2}{E_i} \qquad (12.26)$$

would follow the $\chi^2_{(k)}$ distribution. In fact, the deviations are not independent, if only because the values of E_i will have been chosen to add to the same total, n, as the values of O_i. Furthermore, the expected frequencies E_i have been calculated in terms of parameter estimates which closely fit the data. It turns out that, with efficient methods of estimating parameters, the degrees of freedom for (12.26) are $k-k_0$, where k_0 is

(1 + the number of parameters independently estimated from the data).

The term 1 accounts for the equality of observed and expected totals. Like most methods this is an approximation, and it is wise not to use more than a small proportion of values of E_i less than about 5; values smaller than about 2 are best avoided. This can be done by pooling adjacent cells with small values of E_i.

Example 12.11

Table 2.3 on p. 71 shows certain observed frequencies of bacterial counts, with expected frequencies calculated from the Poisson distribution with the same mean as that observed. No cells have very small frequencies, although if the original table had shown frequencies for $x=7$ and >7 separately they would probably have had to be pooled for the χ^2 test. The value of X^2 is 6·02, and the degrees of freedom are 6, since there are 8 groups, and one parameter and the total frequency have been estimated from the data. From Table A2 $0{\cdot}25<P<0{\cdot}5$. The discrepancies are not significant. As mentioned on p. 71 this suggests that the anti-clumping treatment has been effective.

The χ^2 test using (12.26) is a 'portmanteau' test, sensitive to a variety of types of departure from the assumed distributional form. The fact that individual frequencies follow approximately a Poisson distribution is cleverly exploited in Tukey's 'hanging rootogram' illustrated in Fig. 12.1, taken from Healy (1968). The frequencies are plotted on a square-root scale, with the observed frequencies 'hanging' down from the expected values. From p. 354 the variance of the square-root transform is $\frac{1}{4}$; the standard deviation is $\frac{1}{2}$; and approximately 95 per cent of the discrepancies should be within the range -1 to $+1$. The two parallel lines above and below the horizontal axis represent these percentiles. Aberrant discrepancies can easily be picked out by eye.

If interest centres round a particular form of divergence from the postulated model, the χ^2 test of goodness-of-fit is likely to be too insensitive. In studying the departures of microbiological counts from a

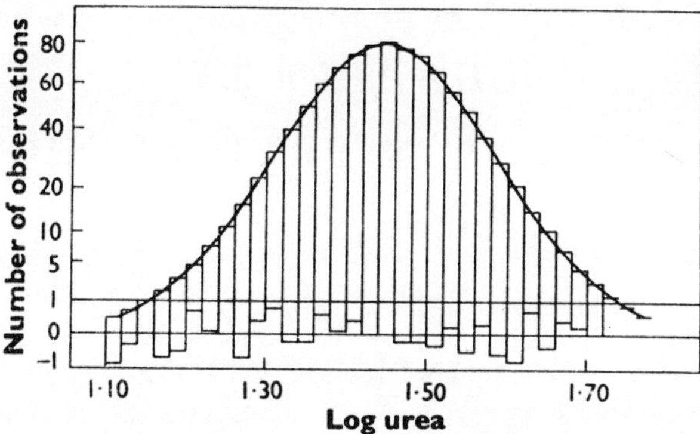

FIG. 12.1 A hanging rootogram for a frequency distribution of log serum urea (mg./100 ml.) fitted by a normal distribution. (Reprinted from Healy (1968) by permission of the author and publishers.)

Poisson distribution, for example, it will often be important to test for increased variability, and this can best be done by the Poisson heterogeneity test of section 7.7.

A useful visual device for checking the approximate normality of an observed distribution is to plot the cumulative distribution on probability paper (see section 11.4). If the observations are grouped, the boundary points between the groups may be plotted horizontally and the cumulative frequencies below each boundary point are plotted on the transformed probability scale. Any systematic departure from a normal distribution will produce a systematic deviation from a straight line in this graph. If the observations are not grouped, one can either (a) introduce a convenient system of group intervals; (b) arrange the individual observations in order of magnitude and plot on probability paper, the ordinate for the ith observation out of n being the proportion $p'=(2i-1)/2n$; or (c) plot the individual observations *on ordinary graph paper* against the so-called *normal scores* (see section 13.3).

In a 2^p factorial experiment it is often useful to test the joint significance of a large set of main effects and interactions. On the null hypothesis that none of the relevant effects are present, the observed contrasts should follow approximately a normal distribution. The signs of the contrasts are, however, arbitrary, and it is useful to have a visual test which ignores these signs. In the *half-normal plot* (Daniel, 1959) the observed contrasts are put into order of absolute magnitude (ignoring sign) and plotted on the upper half of a sheet of probability paper. The value $\frac{1}{2}(1+p')$, which lies between $\frac{1}{2}$ and 1, is used for the ordinate.

CHAPTER 13

DISTRIBUTION-FREE METHODS

13.1 INTRODUCTION

Some of the statistical methods described earlier in connection with qualitative data have involved rather simple assumptions: for example, χ^2 methods often test simple hypotheses about the probabilities for various categories—that they are equal, or that they are proportional to certain marginal probabilities. The methods used for quantitative data, by contrast, have relied on relatively complex assumptions about distributional forms—that the random variation is normal, Poisson, etc. These assumptions are often likely to be clearly untrue; to overcome this problem we sometimes argue that methods are *robust*—that is, not very sensitive to non-normality. At other times we may use transformations to make the assumptions more plausible.

Clearly, there would be something to be said for methods which avoided unnecessary distributional assumptions. Such methods, called *distribution-free methods*, exist and are widely used by some statisticians. The elementary book by Lehmann and Hodges (1964), for example, leans so heavily in this direction that it carries no description of a t test except for a disparaging reference in the preface. Standard statistical methods frequently use statistics which in a fairly obvious way estimate certain population parameters; the sample estimate of variance s^2, for example, estimates the population parameter σ^2. In distribution-free methods there is little emphasis on population parameters, since the whole object is to avoid a particular functional form for a population distribution. The hypotheses to be tested usually relate to the nature of the distribution as a whole rather than to the values assumed by some of its parameters. For this reason they are often called *non-parametric hypotheses* and the appropriate techniques are often called *non-parametric tests* or *methods*.

The justification for the use of distribution-free methods will usually be along one of the following lines.

(a) There may be obvious non-normality.

(b) There may be possible non-normality, perhaps to a very marked extent, but the sample sizes may be too small to establish whether or not this is so.

(c) One may seek a rapid statistical technique, perhaps involving little or simple calculation. Many distribution-free methods have this property: J.W.Tukey's epithet 'quick and dirty methods' is often used to describe them.

(d) A measurement to be analysed may consist of a number of ordered categories, such as $--$, $-$, 0, $+$ and $++$ for degrees of clinical improvement; or a number of observations may form a rank order—for example, patients may be asked to classify six pharmaceutical formulations in order of palatability. In such cases the investigator may be unwilling to allot a numerical scale, but would wish to use methods which took account of the rank order of the observations. Many distribution-free methods are of this type.

The methods described in the following sections are merely a few of the most useful distribution-free techniques. They are mainly significance tests. Some problems of estimation are discussed in section 13.5, where we return to some of the general issues about these methods.

13.2 ONE-SAMPLE TESTS FOR LOCATION

In this section we consider tests of the null hypothesis that the distribution of a random variable x is symmetric about zero. If, in some problem, the natural hypothesis to test is that of symmetry about some other value, μ, all that need be done is to subtract μ from each observation; the test for symmetry about zero can then be used.

The normal-theory test for this hypothesis is, of course, the one-sample t test, and we shall illustrate the present methods by reference to Table 4.1, the data of which were analysed by a paired t test in Example 4.5.

THE SIGN TEST

Suppose the observations in a sample of size n are $x_1, x_2, \ldots, x_n$, and that of these r are positive and s negative. Some values of x may be exactly zero, and these would not be counted with either the positives or the negatives. The sum $r+s$ may therefore be less than n, and will be denoted by n'.

On the null hypothesis positive and negative values of x are equally likely. Both r and s therefore follow a binomial distribution with parameters n' (instead of the n of section 2.5) and $\frac{1}{2}$ (for the parameter π of section 2.5). Excessively high or low values of r (or, equivalently, of s) can be tested exactly from tables of the binomial distribution. For large enough samples, any of the normal approximations given in section 4.8 may be used (with r and s replacing x_1 and x_2 in the formulae given there).

Example 13.1

Consider the differences in the final column of Table 4.1. Here $n'=n=10$ (since there are no zero values), $r=4$ and $s=6$. For a two-sided significance test the probability level is twice the probability of $r \leq 4$, which from tables of the binomial distribution is 0·75. The normal approximation, with continuity correction, would give, for a $\chi^2_{(1)}$ test,

$$X^2 = \frac{(5\frac{1}{2}-4\frac{1}{2})^2}{6+4} = 0{\cdot}10 \ (P=0{\cdot}75).$$

The verdict agrees with that of the t test in Example 4·5: there is no evidence that differences in anxiety score tend to be positive more (or less) often than they are negative.

THE SIGNED RANK SUM TEST

The sign test clearly loses something by ignoring all information about the numerical magnitudes of the observations other than their sign. If a high proportion of the numerically large observations were positive this would strengthen the evidence that the distribution was asymmetric about zero, and it seems reasonable to try to take this evidence into account. Wilcoxon's (1945) signed rank sum test works as follows. The observations are put in ascending order of magnitude, ignoring the sign, and given the ranks 1 to n' (zero values being ignored as in the sign test). Let T_+ be the sum of the ranks of the positive values and T_- that of the negative. On the null hypothesis T_+ and T_- would not be expected to differ greatly; their sum $T_+ + T_-$ is $\frac{1}{2}n'(n'+1)$, so an appropriate test would consist in evaluating the probability of a value of, say, T_+ equal to or more extreme than that observed. A table on page 128 of the Documenta Geigy Scientific Tables, 6th edition, gives various percentiles for different sample sizes (our n' being the n of that table). For large values of n', T_+ and T_- are approximately normally distributed with variance $n'(n'+1)(2n'+1)/24$, and a standardized normal deviate, with continuity correction, is given by

$$\frac{|T_+-\frac{1}{4}n'(n'+1)|-\frac{1}{2}}{\sqrt{\{n'(n'+1)(2n'+1)/24\}}}. \qquad (13.1)$$

If some of the observations are numerically equal they are given tied ranks equal to the mean of the ranks which would otherwise have been used. This feature reduces the variance of T_+ by $(t^3-t)/48$ for each group of t tied ranks.

Example 13.2

The 10 differences in Table 4.1 may be ranked numerically as follows:

	1	2	3	4		6	7		9	10
Rank	Equal $2\frac{1}{2}$				5	$6\frac{1}{2}$		8	$9\frac{1}{2}$	
Numerical value	1	1	1	1	2	3	3	7	8	8
Sign	+	+	+	−	−	−	−	−	+	−

$$T_+=2\tfrac{1}{2}+2\tfrac{1}{2}+2\tfrac{1}{2}+9\tfrac{1}{2}=17$$

$$T_-=2\tfrac{1}{2}+5+6\tfrac{1}{2}+6\tfrac{1}{2}+8+9\tfrac{1}{2}=38$$

$$\mathrm{E}(T_+)=\tfrac{1}{4}(10)(11)=27{\cdot}5,$$

$$\begin{aligned}\mathrm{var}(T_+)&=\frac{10(11)(21)}{24}-\frac{1}{48}\{(4^3-4)+(2^3-2)+(2^3-2)\}\\&=96{\cdot}25-1{\cdot}50\\&=94{\cdot}75,\end{aligned}$$

$$\mathrm{SE}(T_+)=\sqrt{94{\cdot}75}=9{\cdot}73,$$

and the standardized normal deviate is $(10{\cdot}5-0{\cdot}5)/9{\cdot}73=1{\cdot}03$, clearly non-significant.

13.3 TWO-SAMPLE TESTS FOR LOCATION

Suppose we have two groups of observations: a random sample of n_1 observations, x_i, from population X and a random sample of n_2 observations, y_i, from population Y. The null hypothesis to be tested is that the distribution of x in population X is exactly the same as that of y in population Y. We should like the test to be sensitive to situations in which the two distributions differ primarily in location, so that x tends to be greater (or less) than y.

The normal-theory test is the two-sample (unpaired) t test described in section 4.6. Three distribution-free tests in common usage are all essentially equivalent to each other. They are described briefly here.

THE MANN-WHITNEY U TEST

The observations are ranked together in order of increasing magnitude. There are n_1n_2 pairs (x_i, y_j); of these,

U_{XY} is the number of pairs for which $x_i < y_j$,

and U_{YX} is the number of pairs for which $x_i > y_j$.

Any pairs for which $x_i = y_j$ count $\frac{1}{2}$ a unit towards both U_{XY} and U_{YX}.

Either of these statistics may be used for a test, with exactly equivalent results. Using U_{YX}, for instance, the statistic must lie between 0 and n_1n_2. On the null hypothesis its expectation is $\frac{1}{2}n_1n_2$. High values will suggest a difference between the distributions, with x tending to take higher values than y. Conversely, low values of U_{YX} suggest that x tends to be less than y.

WILCOXON'S RANK SUM TEST

Again there are two equivalent statistics:

T_1 is the sum of the ranks of the x_i's;

T_2 is the sum of the ranks of the y_i's.

Low values assume low ranks (i.e. rank 1 is allotted to the smallest value). Any group of tied ranks is allotted the mid-rank of the group.

The smallest value which T_1 can take arises when all the x's are less than all the y's; then $T_1 = \frac{1}{2}n_1(n_1+1)$. The maximum value possible for T_1 arises when all x's are greater than all y's; then $T_1 = n_1n_2 + \frac{1}{2}n_1(n_1+1)$. The null expectation of T_1 is $\frac{1}{2}n_1(n_1+n_2+1)$.

KENDALL'S S

This is defined in terms of the two Mann-Whitney statistics:

$$S = U_{XY} - U_{YX}. \tag{13.2}$$

Its minimum value (when all y's are less than all x's) is $-n_1n_2$; its maximum value (when all x's are less than all y's) is n_1n_2. The null expectation is 0.

INTER-RELATIONSHIPS BETWEEN TESTS

There are, first, two relationships between the two Mann-Whitney statistics and between the two Wilcoxon statistics:

$$U_{XY}+U_{YX}=n_1n_2, \qquad (13.3)$$

$$T_1+T_2=\tfrac{1}{2}(n_1+n_2)(n_1+n_2+1). \qquad (13.4)$$

These show that tests based on either of two statistics in each pair are equivalent; given T_1 and the two sample sizes, for example, T_2 can immediately be calculated from (13.4).

Secondly, the three tests are inter-related by the following formulae:

$$U_{YX}=n_1n_2+\tfrac{1}{2}n_2(n_2+1)-T_2, \qquad (13.5)$$

$$U_{XY}=n_1n_2+\tfrac{1}{2}n_1(n_1+1)-T_1, \qquad (13.6)$$

and

$S=U_{XY}-U_{YX}$, as already given in (13.2).

The three tests are exactly equivalent. From (13.5) for instance, the probability of observing a value of T_2 less than or equal to that observed is exactly equal to the probability of a value of U_{YX} greater than or equal to that observed. Significance tests based on T_2 and U_{YX} will therefore yield exactly the same significance level. The choice between these tests depends purely on familiarity with a particular form of computation and accessibility of tables.

The probability distributions of the various statistics are independent of the distributions of x and y. They have been tabulated for small and moderate sample sizes, for situations in which there are no ties. A useful table of critical values of U_{YX} for $n_1 \leq 40$ and $n_2 \leq 20$ is given by Milton (1964). A table of similar extent for T_1 (for $n_1 \leq 25$ and $n_2 \leq 50$) is in Documenta Geigy Scientific Tables, 6th edition, pp. 124–127. Tabulated entries for some of the higher values of n in the Geigy tables are obtained by a normal approximation. This is based on the variance formulae given in Table 13.1, and the fact that the distributions of all these statistics approach normality as n_1 and n_2 get larger.

TABLE 13.1 Some properties of three equivalent two-sample distribution-free tests.

	Bounds		Sampling distribution		
	All $x_i <$ all y_j	All $y_j <$ all x_i	Mean	Variance (no ties)	Variance (ties)
Mann-Whitney U test					
U_{XY} = No. of pairs with $x_i < y_j$	$n_1 n_2$	0	$\frac{1}{2}n_1 n_2$	$\frac{n_1 n_2(n+1)}{12}$	$\frac{n_1 n_2}{12n(n-1)}\left\{n^3 - n - \sum_t (t^3 - t)\right\}$
U_{YX} = No. of pairs with $y_j < x_i$	0	$n_1 n_2$			
Wilcoxon rank sum test					
T_1 = Sum of ranks for x_i's	$\frac{1}{2}n_1(n_1+1)$	$n_1 n_2 + \frac{1}{2}n_1(n_1+1)$	$\frac{1}{2}n_1(n_1+n_2+1)$	as above	
T_2 = Sum of ranks for y_j's	$n_1 n_2 + \frac{1}{2}n_2(n_2+1)$	$\frac{1}{2}n_2(n_2+1)$	$\frac{1}{2}n_2(n_1+n_2+1)$		
Kendall's S test					
$S = U_{XY} - U_{YX}$	$n_1 n_2$	$-n_1 n_2$	0	$\frac{n_1 n_2(n+1)}{3}$	$\frac{n_1 n_2}{3n(n-1)}\left\{n^3 - n - \sum_t (t^3 - t)\right\}$

Notation: n_1 = Sample size of x_i's.
n_2 = Sample size of y_j's.
$n = n_1 + n_2$.

When there are ties the variance formulae are modified as shown in Table 13.1. The summations in the formulae are taken over all groups of tied observations, t being the number of observations in a particular group.

Example 13.3

It will be unnecessary to illustrate the calculations for each of these equivalent tests. We illustrate the use of S in a set of data shown in Table 13.2. The observations are measurements of the percentage change in area of gastric ulcers after three months' treatment, the comparison being between 32 in-patients and 32 out-patients. A percentage change is an awkward measurement; its minimum value is -100 (when the ulcer has disappeared); each group contains several readings bunched at or near this lower limit. In the other direction very large values may be recorded (when the ulcer was initially very small and increased greatly during the period of observation).

TABLE 13.2 Percentage change in area of gastric ulcer after three months' treatment (Doll and Pygott, 1952).

	Number	
X: In-patients	32	$-100^{(12)}$, -93, -92, $-91^{(2)}$, -90, -85, -83, -81, -80, -78, -46, -40, -34, 0, 29, 62, 75, 106, 147, 1,321
Y: Out-patients	32	$-100^{(5)}$, -93, -89, -80, -78, -75, -74, -72, -71, -66, -59, -41, -30, -29, -26, -20, -15, 20, 25, 37, 55, 68, 73, 75, 145, 146, 220, 1,044

Notation: $-100^{(5)}$ indicates 5 observations at -100, etc.

A point which may be noted in the calculation of S when there are ties is that there is no need to count $\frac{1}{2}$ for each (x, y) tie, for these contributions form part of both U_{XY} and U_{YX} and therefore cancel out in S because of (13.2). We can therefore calculate S as $P-Q$, where P and Q are calculated like U_{XY} and U_{YX} except that nothing is added for (x, y) ties.

In this example, denote the in-patients by X and the out-patients by Y. To calculate P, take each member of the X sample in turn and count the number of members of the Y sample greater than this value. For the first few values of X, we find:

x_i	$-100^{(12)}$	-93	-92	$-91^{(2)}$	-90	-85	...
Number of $y_j > x_i$	27	26	26	26	26	25	...

Thus,

$$P = 12(27) + 5(26) + 3(25) + 24 + 23 + 17 + 2(16) + 11 + 9 + 7 + 2(4) + 2 + 0$$
$$= 662,$$
$$Q = 5(20) + 19 + 15 + 11 + 7(10) + 9 + 5(7) + 2(6) + 2(5) + 2(4) + 3 + 2(2) + 2(1)$$
$$= 298,$$

and

$$S = 662 - 298 = 364.$$

From Table 13.1,

$$\mathrm{var}(S) = \frac{(32)(32)}{3(64)(63)}\{64^3 - 64 - (17^3 - 17) - \ldots\},$$

where the terms arising from the small groups of ties (like the 2 observations at -93) have been omitted as they can easily be seen to be very much smaller than the other terms.

$$\mathrm{var}(S) = (0{\cdot}084656)(257{,}184)$$
$$= 21{,}772.$$
$$\mathrm{SE}(S) = \sqrt{21{,}772} = 147{\cdot}5.$$

Using the normal approximation, the standardized normal deviate is $364/147{\cdot}5 = 2{\cdot}47 (0{\cdot}01 < P < 0{\cdot}02)$.

This is an example in which the difference between the X and Y samples would not have been detected by a t test. The distributions are exceedingly non-normal, and the 2-sample t test gives $t = 0{\cdot}51$—clearly non-significant.

The ability to handle ties by these two-sample tests provides an interesting link with some tests already described for contingency tables. In Example 12.8 (see Table 12.8), for instance, we could ask whether the resistant strains could be distributed over the four years in the same way as the sensitive strains. A tendency for the proportion of resistant strains to increase during the four-year period would mean that the resistant strains were concentrated in the later years in comparison with the sensitive strains. Taking the four years as the values of a heavily grouped variable, the distribution-free tests just described could be applied. It can be shown (Armitage, 1955) that the resulting normal deviate is (apart from a factor $\sqrt{\{n/(n-1)\}}$ which is near unity except for very small samples) exactly equivalent to the test for trend of section 12.2 (equation 12.1), provided that in the latter test the x-scores are given values equal to the mid-ranks of the different groups. In Example 12.8, this method gives a $\chi^2_{(1)}$ value of 21·0, very similar to that of the other tests described there.

A 2×2 contingency table is an extreme case of this situation, and here the normal deviate from the distribution-free test (making due allowance for the ties) is the same as that for the usual normal approximation of sections 4.7 and 4.8, apart from the same factor of $\sqrt{\{n/(n-1)\}}$.

NORMAL SCORES

An alternative approach to the two-sample distribution-free problem is provided by the Fisher-Yates *normal scores.* Instead of using ranks, the observations are transformed to a different set of scores which depend purely on the ranks in the combined sample of size n. The score for the observation of rank number r is, in fact, numerically equal to the mean value of the rth smallest observation in a sample of n from a standardized normal distribution, $N(0, 1)$. The scores are tabulated for various sample sizes by Fisher and Yates (1963, Table XX).

Now these scores can be regarded as a method of transforming to normality as a preliminary step to the use of standard normal methods, and this is usually a perfectly adequate use of the method. However, normal methods inevitably introduce an approximation, the validity of which will depend to some extent on the original distributions; in other words, this would not be a distribution-free approach. If one wished to have a distribution-free test, one could calculate the difference between the means of the two sets of scores and use the fact that its sampling distribution does not depend on the distribution of the original observations. Tables are given by Klotz (1964).

An incidental use of normal scores is to provide a graphical test of normality (see section 12.7). Given sample observations $z_1, z_2, \ldots, z_n$, ranked in order, z_i can be plotted against the ith normal score for a sample of n. If the sample is from a normal distribution the points should lie fairly close to a straight line (the closeness being better for large samples than for small ones). Systematic departures from normality will tend to produce non-linearity in very much the same way as in the use of the probit transformation or probability paper (section 11.4).

Some further general comments about the value of two-sample distribution-free tests are made in section 13.5.

13.4 RANK CORRELATION

Suppose, in a group of n individuals, each individual provides observations on two variables, x and y. The closeness of the association between

x and y is usually measured by the ordinary correlation coefficient r (section 5.3). The use of this statistic might be thought objectionable on one of the following grounds: (a) it is based on the concept of closeness to linear regression, and its value may be affected drastically by a non-linear transformation; (b) the measurements to be analysed may be qualitative, although ordered, and the investigator may not wish to assume any particular numerical scale; (c) the sampling variation of r depends on the distribution of the variables, normality being usually assumed—a distribution-free approach may be desired.

These objections would be overcome by a correlation coefficient dependent only on the ranks of the observations. To preserve comparability with r (which is often called the *product-moment* correlation coefficient), a rank correlation coefficient should have at least the following properties.

(1) It should lie between -1 and $+1$, taking the value $+1$ when the individuals are ranked in exactly the same order by x as by y, and -1 when the order is reversed.

(2) For large samples in which the distribution of x is independent of y (and conversely), the value should be zero.

A satisfactory rank correlation coefficient can be obtained from Kendall's S statistic described in the last section, with a generalization of the definition used there. The total number of pairs of individuals is $\frac{1}{2}n(n-1)$. Let P be the number of pairs which are ranked in the *same* order by x and by y, and Q the number of pairs in which the rankings are in the opposite order. Then

$$S = P - Q.$$

(The previous definition is a particular case of this in which one variable represents a dichotomy into the two groups, with group X being ranked before group Y; and the other variable represents the measurement under test, both x_i and y_i as previously defined being values of this second variable).

The rank correlation coefficient, τ, is now defined by

$$\tau = \frac{S}{\frac{1}{2}n(n-1)}. \tag{13.7}$$

It is fairly easy to see that for complete agreement of rankings $\tau = 1$, and for complete reversal $\tau = -1$. A significance test of the null hypothesis that the x ranking is independent of the y ranking can conveniently be done on S. The null expectation of S (as of τ) is zero, and, in the absence of ties,

$$\text{var}(S) = n(n-1)(2n+5)/18. \tag{13.8}$$

If there are ties, (13.8) is modified to give

$$\text{var}(S) = \frac{1}{18}\left\{n(n-1)(2n+5) - \sum_t t(t-1)(2t+5) - \sum_u u(u-1)(2u+5)\right\}$$
$$+ \frac{1}{9n(n-1)(n-2)}\left\{\sum_t t(t-1)(t-2)\right\}\left\{\sum_u u(u-1)(u-2)\right\}$$
$$+ \frac{1}{2n(n-1)}\left\{\sum_t t(t-1)\right\}\left\{\sum_u u(u-1)\right\},$$

where the summations are over groups of ties, t being the number o tied individuals in a group of x values and u the number of a group tied y values.

For further discussion of rank correlation, including tables fo significance of S, see Kendall (1955). The reader is referred to Ken book for a description of an earlier method of rank correlation, due to Spearman.

Example 13.4

A sample of 10 students training as clinical psychologists are ranked by a tutor at the end of the course according to (a) suitability for their career, and (b) knowledge of psychology.

Student	*A*	*B*	*C*	*D*	*E*	*F*	*G*	*H*	*I*	*J*
Rank on (a)	4	10	3	1	9	2	6	7	8	5
Rank on (b)	5	8	6	2	10	3	9	4	7	1

Re-arranging according to the (a) ranking, we have:

(a)	1	2	3	4	5	6	7	8	9	10
(b)	2	3	6	5	1	9	4	7	10	8

To calculate P take each of the (b) rankings in turn and count how many individuals to the right of this position have a higher ranking. These counts are then added. Thus, starting with the first individual, with rank 2, there are 8 ranks greater than 2 to the right of this; for the next individual with rank 3 there are 7 ranks greater than 3 to the right of this; and so on. Similarly, Q is defined by counting lower rather than higher ranks.

$$P = 8+7+4+4+5+1+3+2+0+0 = 34$$
$$Q = 1+1+3+2+0+3+0+0+1+0 = 11.$$

As a check, $P+Q=\frac{1}{2}n(n-1)$ in the absence of ties; here $P+Q=45=\frac{1}{2}(10)(9)$.

$$S=P-Q=23.$$

From Appendix Table 1 of Kendall (1955), the null probability of a value of S equal to 23 or more is 0·023. A one-sided test is perhaps appropriate here. For a two-sided test, the significance probability would be $2\times 0{\cdot}023=0{\cdot}046$, still rather low. There is therefore a definite suggestion of an association between the two rankings.

The rank correlation coefficient is, by (13.7)

$$\tau=\frac{23}{\frac{1}{2}(10)(9)}=\frac{23}{45}=0{\cdot}51.$$

For the normal approximation to the significance test, from (13.8)

$$\text{var}(S)=10(9)(25)/18=125$$

$$\text{SE}(S)=11{\cdot}18.$$

It is useful to apply a continuity correction of 1 unit, since the possible values of S turn out to be separated by an interval of 2 units. The standardized normal deviate is $22/11{\cdot}18=1{\cdot}97$, for which $P=0{\cdot}049$, rather close to the exact value.

13.5 ESTIMATION AND GENERAL COMMENTS

Distribution-free *tests* are supported by remarkably strong theoretical arguments. Suppose that, in the two-sample problem of section 13.3, one wished to test the null hypothesis that the two samples were drawn from the same distribution, and that one wished the test to have high power against alternative hypotheses specifying that the distributions differed only in their location, i.e., one distribution could be changed into the other by a simple shift along the scale of the measurement.

If the distributions are normal with the same variance, the t test is the most efficient test, but the rank test (Wilcoxon, Mann-Whitney, or Kendall) has a relative efficiency* of 0·96. If the distributions are not normal, the relative efficiency of the rank test is never less than 0·86 and may be infinitely high. For detecting a shift in location, therefore, the rank test is never much worse than the t test, and can be very much better.

* This measure of efficiency can be interpreted as the ratio of sample sizes needed to provide a certain power of detecting a given small shift in location.

Furthermore the distribution-free test based on normal scores has a relative efficiency against the t test which is never less than unity and may be infinite. Why, then, should one not always use either the rank test or the normal score test in preference to the t test? The first point to make is that significance tests form only a part of the apparatus of statistical analysis. The main purpose of an analysis is usually to provide as much information as possible about the nature of the random variation affecting a set of observations. This can usually be done only by specifying a model for that variation, estimating the parameters of the model in a reasonably efficient way and informing oneself about the precision of these estimates.

Distribution-free methods are basically tests and are not easily adapted for purposes of estimation. It is true that the statistics used can often be said to estimate something, but the parameter estimated may be of limited interest. In the two-sample rank test, for instance, U_{XY}/n_1n_2 is clearly an estimate of the probability that a randomly chosen value of x is less than a randomly chosen value of y. Suppose, though, that one assumed a possible difference, δ, in the location of the two distributions (i.e., a displacement along the scale of the measurement), and wished to estimate this difference. One would proceed by trial and error, adding possible values of δ to the observations in one group until $S=0$; this gives a single estimate of δ. Confidence limits are obtained by finding the values of δ which make S just significantly positive and just significantly negative. The procedure is somewhat laborious.

A second point about the theoretical results on power is that they refer to one particular form of difference between two distributions, namely a displacement or difference in location. In other situations the position is less clear.

In general, then, distribution-free methods are perhaps best regarded as a set of techniques to fall back on when standard assumptions have particularly doubtful validity; it is often useful to be able to confirm the results of a normal-theory significance test by performing an appropriate distribution-free test.

CHAPTER 14

SURVIVORSHIP TABLES

14.1 LIFE TABLES

The *life table*, first developed adequately by the astronomer E. Halley (1656–1742), is one of the basic tools of vital statistics and actuarial science. Standardization was introduced in section 12.6 as a method of summarizing a set of age-specific death rates, thus providing a composite measure of the mortality experience of a community at all ages and permitting useful comparison with the experience of other groups of people. The life table is an alternative summarizing procedure with rather similar attributes. Its purpose is to exhibit the pattern of survival of a group of individuals subject, throughout life, to the age-specific rates in question.

There are two distinct ways in which a life table may be constructed from mortality data for a large community; the two forms are usually called the *current life table* and the *cohort* or *generation life table*. The current life table describes the survival pattern of a group of individuals subject throughout life to the age-specific death rates currently observed in a particular community. This group is necessarily hypothetical. A group of individuals now aged 60 years will next year experience approximately the current mortality rate specific to ages 60–61; but those who survive another 10 years will, in the 11th year, experience not the *current* rate for ages 70–71 but the rate prevailing 10 years hence. The current life table, then, is a convenient summary of current mortality rather than a description of the actual mortality experience of any group.

The method of constructing the current life tables published in national sources of vital statistics or in those used in life assurance offices is rather complex (Benjamin, 1968). A simplified approach is described by Hill (1966). The main features of the life table can be seen from Table 14.1, the left side of which summarizes the English Life Table No. 10 based on the mortality of males in England and Wales in 1930–32. The second column gives q_x, the probability that an individual, alive at age x years exactly, will die before his next birthday. The third column shows l_x, the number of individuals out of an arbitrary 1,000 born alive who would survive to their xth birthday. To survive for this period an individual must survive the first year, then the second, and so on. Consequently,

$$l_x = l_0 p_0 p_1 \ldots p_{x-1}, \tag{14.1}$$

where $p_x = 1 - q_x$. This formula can be checked from Table 14.1 for $x = 1$, but not subsequently because values of q_x are given here only for selected values of x; such a table is called an *abridged life table*.

The fourth column shows $\mathring{e}_x$, the expectation of life at age x. This is the mean length of additional life beyond age x of all the l_x people alive at age x. In a complete table $\mathring{e}_x$ can be calculated approximately as

$$\mathring{e}_x = (l_{x+1} + l_{x+2} + \ldots)/l_x \quad + \tfrac{1}{2}, \tag{14.2}$$

since the term in brackets is the total number of years lived beyond age x by the l_x individuals if those dying between age y and age $y+1$ did so immediately after the yth birthday, and the $\frac{1}{2}$ is a correction to allow for the fact that deaths take place throughout each year of age which very roughly adds half a year to the mean survival time.

TABLE 14.1 Current and cohort life tables for men in England and Wales born around 1931.

	Current life tables 1930–1932			Cohort life table 1931 cohort
Age, years x	Probability of death between age x and $x+1$ q_x	Life table survivors l_x	Expectation of life $\mathring{e}_x$	Life table survivors l_x
0	0·0719	1,000	58·7	1,000
1	0·0153	928·1	62·2	927·8
5	0·0034	900·7	60·1	903·6
10	0·0015	890·2	55·8	894·8
20	0·0032	872·4	46·8	884·2
30	0·0034	844·2	38·2	874·1
40	0·0056	809·4	29·6	—
50	0·0113	747·9	21·6	—
60	0·0242	636·2	14·4	—
70	0·0604	433·6	8·6	—
80	0·1450	162·0	4·7	—

The cohort life table describes the actual survival experience of a group, or 'cohort', of individuals born at about the same time. Those born in 1900, for instance, are subject during their first year to the mortality under 1 year of age prevailing in 1900–01; if they survive to 10 years of age they are subject to the mortality at that age in 1910–11; and so on. Cohort life tables summarize the mortality at different ages at the times when the cohort would have been at these ages. Cohort life tables for England and Wales have been given by Case *et al.* (1962). The right side of Table 14.1 summarizes the l_x column from the cohort life table for men in England and Wales born in the five years centred around 1931. As would be expected, the values of l_1 in the two life tables are very similar, being dependent on infant mortality in about the same calendar years. At higher ages the values of l_x are greater for the cohort table because this is based on mortality rates at the higher ages which were experienced *since* 1931 and which are lower than the 1931 rates.

Both forms of life table are useful for vital statistical and epidemiological studies. Current life tables summarize current mortality and may be used as an alternative to methods of standardization for comparisons between the mortality patterns of different communities. Cohort life tables are particularly useful in studies of occupational mortality. Men employed in an industrial organization during a particular period will vary in the duration of their employment and in their ages. The expected numbers of deaths of employed men can be calculated by sub-dividing the men into cohorts according to date of birth, counting the total number of years worked in each age group, and then referring to published cohort life tables based on national mortality. The number of deaths observed may then be compared with those expected at national rates. For a fuller discussion see Case and Lea (1955).

14.2 FOLLOW-UP STUDIES

Many medical investigations are concerned with the survival pattern of special groups of patients—for example, those suffering from a particular form of malignant disease. Survival may be on average much shorter than for members of the general population. Since age is likely to be a less important factor than the progress of the disease, it is natural to measure survival from a particular stage in the history of the disease, such as the date when symptoms were first reported or the date on which a particular operation took place.

The application of life table methods to data from follow-up studies of this kind will now be considered in some detail. In principle the methods are applicable to situations in which the critical endpoint is not death, but some non-fatal event such as the appearance of symptoms after a remission. Indeed, the event may be favourable rather than unfavourable; the disappearance of symptoms after the start of treatment is an example. The discussion below is in terms of survival after an operation.

At the time of analysis of such a follow-up study patients are likely to have been observed for varying lengths of time, some having had the operation a long time before, others having been operated on recently. Some patients will have died, at times which can usually be ascertained relatively accurately*; others are known to be alive at the time of analysis; others may have been lost to follow-up for various reasons between one examination and the next; others may have had to be withdrawn from the study for medical reasons—perhaps by the intervention of some other disease or an accidental death.

If there were no complications like those just referred to, and if every patient was followed until the time of death, the construction of a life table in terms of time after operation would be a simple matter. The life table survival rate, l_x, is l_0 times the proportion of survival times greater than x. The problem would be merely that of obtaining the distribution of survival time—a very elementary task. To overcome the complications of incomplete data, a table like Table 14.2 is constructed.

This table is adapted from that given by Berkson and Gage (1950) in one of the first papers describing the method.† The columns (1)–(8) are formed as follows.

(1) The choice of time intervals will depend on the nature of the data. In the present study estimates were needed of survival rates for integral numbers of years, to 10, after operation. If survival after 10 years had been of particular interest, the intervals could easily have been extended beyond 10 years. In that case, to avoid the table becoming too cumbersome it might have been useful to use two-year intervals for at least some of the groups. Unequal intervals cause no problem; for an example see Merrell and Shulman (1955).

* With end-points other than death, such as the recurrence of symptoms or signs it may not be possible to determine the precise time of recurrence.

† The time intervals in the original data were measured from the time of hospital dismissal. For purposes of exposition we have changed these to intervals following operation.

TABLE 14.2 Life table calculations for patients with a particular form of malignant disease, adapted from Berkson and Gage (1950).

(1) Interval since operation, years x to $x+1$	(2) Last reported during this interval: Died d_x	(3) Withdrawn w_x	(4) Living at start of interval n_x	(5) Adjusted number at risk n'_x	(6) Estimated probability of death q_x	(7) Estimated probability of survival p_x	(8) Percentage of survivors after x years l_x
0–1	90	0	374	374·0	0·2406	0·7594	100
1–2	76	0	284	284·0	0·2676	0·7324	75·9
2–3	51	0	208	208·0	0·2452	0·7548	55·6
3–4	25	12	157	151·0	0·1656	0·8344	42·0
4–5	20	5	120	117·5	0·1702	0·8298	35·0
5–6	7	9	95	90·5	0·0773	0·9227	29·1
6–7	4	9	79	74·5	0·0537	0·9463	26·8
7–8	1	3	66	64·5	0·0155	0·9845	25·4
8–9	3	5	62	59·5	0·0504	0·9496	25·0
9–10	2	5	54	51·5	0·0388	0·9612	23·7
10–	21	26	47	—	—	—	22·8

(2) and (3) The patients in the study are now classified according to the time interval during which their condition was last reported. If the report was of a death, the patient is counted in column (2); if the patient was alive at the last report he is counted in column (3). The term 'withdrawn' thus includes patients recently reported as alive, who would continue to be observed at future follow-up examinations, and those who have been lost to follow-up for some reason.

(4) The numbers of patients living at the start of the intervals are obtained by cumulating columns (2) and (3) from the foot. Thus, the number alive at 10 years is $21+26=47$. The number alive at 9 years includes these 47 and also the $2+5=7$ died or withdrawn in the interval 9–10 years; the entry is therefore $47+7=54$.

(5) The adjusted number at risk during the interval x to $x+1$ is

$$n'_x = n_x - \tfrac{1}{2} w_x. \qquad (14.3)$$

The purpose of this formula is to provide a denominator for the next column. The rationale is discussed below.

(6) The estimated probability of death during the interval x to $x+1$ is

$$q_x = d_x / n'_x. \qquad (14.4)$$

For example, in the first line,

$$q_0 = 90/374\cdot0 = 0\cdot2406.$$

The adjustment from n_x to n'_x is needed because the w_x withdrawals are necessarily at risk for only part of the interval. It is possible to make rather more sophisticated allowance for the withdrawals, particularly if the point of withdrawal during the interval is known. However, it is usually quite adequate to assume that the withdrawals have the same effect as if half of them were at risk for the whole period; hence the adjustment (14.3). An alternative argument is that if the w_x patients had *not* withdrawn, we might have expected about $\frac{1}{2}q_x w_x$ extra deaths. The total number of deaths would then have been $d_x + \frac{1}{2}q_x w_x$, and we should have an estimated death rate

$$q_x = \frac{d_x + \frac{1}{2}q_x w_x}{n_x}. \tag{14.5}$$

(14.5) can easily be seen to be equivalent to (14.3) and (14.4).

(7) $p_x = 1 - q_x$.

(8) The estimated probability of survival to, say, three years after the operation is $p_0 p_1 p_2$. The entries in the last column, often called the *life table survival rates*, are thus obtained by successive multiplication of those in column (7), with an arbitrary multiplier $l_0 = 100$. Formally,

$$l_x = l_0 p_0 p_1 \ldots p_{x-1}, \tag{14.6}$$

as in (14.1).

Two important assumptions underlie these calculations. First, it is assumed that the withdrawals are subject to the same probabilities of death as the non-withdrawals. This is a reasonable assumption for withdrawals who are still in the study and will be available for future follow-up. It may be a dangerous assumption for patients who were lost to follow-up, since failure to examine a patient for any reason may be related to the patient's health. Secondly, the various values of p_x are obtained from patients who entered the study at different points of time. It must be assumed that these probabilities remain reasonably constant over time; otherwise the life table calculations represent quantities with no simple interpretation.

In Table 14.2 the calculations could have been continued beyond 10 years. Suppose, however, that d_{10} and w_{10} had both been zero, as they would have been if no patients had been observed for more than 10 years. Then n_{10} would have been zero, no values of q_{10} and p_{10} could have been calculated and in general no value of l_{11} would have been available.* This point can be put more obviously by saying that no survival information is available for periods of follow-up longer than the maximum observed in the study. This means that the expectation of life (which implies an indefinitely long follow-up) cannot be calculated from follow-up studies unless the period of follow-up, at least for some patients, is sufficiently long to cover virtually the complete span of survival. For this reason the life table survival rate (column (8) of Table 14.2) is a more generally useful measure of survival. Note that the value of x for which $l_x = 50$ per cent is the *median* survival time; for a symmetric distribution this would be equal to the expectation of life.

For further discussion of life table methods in follow-up studies, see Berkson and Gage (1950), Merrell and Shulman (1955), Cutler and Ederer (1958) and Newell *et al.* (1961).

14.3 SAMPLING VARIATION

Each of the values of p_x in a life table calculation is subject to sampling variation. Were it not for the withdrawals the variation could be regarded as binomial, with a sample size n_x. The effect of withdrawals is approximately the same as that of reducing the sample size to n'_x. The variance of l_x is given approximately by the following formula due to Greenwood (1926), which can be obtained by taking logarithms in (14.6) and using an extension of (3.17).

$$\text{var}(l_x) = l_x^2 \sum_{i=0}^{x-1} \frac{d_i}{n'_i(n'_i - d_i)}. \tag{14.7}$$

In Table 14.2, for instance, where $l_4 = 35{\cdot}0$ per cent,

$$\text{var}(l_4) = (35{\cdot}0)^2 \left\{ \frac{90}{(374)(284)} + \frac{76}{(284)(208)} + \frac{51}{(208)(157)} + \frac{25}{(151{\cdot}0)(126{\cdot}0)} \right\}$$

$$= 6{\cdot}14$$

and

$$\text{SE}(l_4) = \sqrt{6{\cdot}14} = 2{\cdot}48.$$

Approximate 95 per cent confidence limits for l_4 are

$$35{\cdot}0 \pm (1{\cdot}96)(2{\cdot}48) = 30{\cdot}1 \text{ and } 39{\cdot}9.$$

For further discussion of sampling variation see Ederer (1961).

* An exception to this statement would occur if l_{10} were zero (as it would be if any one of $p_0, p_1, \ldots, p_9$ were zero); in that case l_{11} would also be zero.

CHAPTER 15
SEQUENTIAL METHODS

15.1 GENERAL

In most of the examples described in earlier chapters the number of observations could reasonably be assumed to be determined quite independently of the numerical values of the observations. In controlled laboratory experiments the number of observations will usually be decided in advance. In many other medical studies, such as clinical trials or epidemiological surveys, the ultimate sample size may depend on the ease with which observations can be made or on the rate at which suitable patients become available. Even here, though, the sample size is not necessarily affected by the observed values of the random variables on which the analysis is performed.

In these circumstances it seems reasonable to regard the sample size as a variable whose main importance lies in its effect on precision, giving in itself no information about the contrasts which are under study. In assessing the effect of random variation it is usual to imagine the sample size to be fixed; that is, one enquires about the random variation which would be observed in hypothetical repetitions of the investigation with the same sample size.

Some other types of investigation are rather different in that the ultimate size of the study may not only be unpredictable before its start but may depend on the numerical values of the observations. Certain classes of observation may, for instance, lead to a relatively early closure of the study; others may lead to a long investigation. A study of this type is called *sequential*. If the sequential aspect of the design is sufficiently formal, it will be described by a *stopping rule*, which defines the way in which the decision to stop the investigation at some stage depends on the results obtained. The stopping rule is thus a special feature of sequential design, supplementing the more familiar features of randomization and blocking (in experiments) and random selection (in surveys).

The methods of analysis of data collected sequentially form a subject called *sequential analysis*, the classical work on which is due to Wald (1947).

Before even a brief consideration of detailed methods of sequential design and analysis it may be useful to note a few of the possible reasons for using sequential methods.

(a) *Economy*

In industrial sampling inspection there may be a large number of materials to be classified as being of good or bad quality on the basis of tests the outcome of which are subject to random variation. In the pharmaceutical industry, for example, drugs may be screened for specific activity by their performance in a particular biological test. Instead of a constant amount of experimentation with each drug it may be more efficient to experiment sequentially so that most drugs are quickly rejected but a minority of drugs with initially promising results are allowed more observations before a decision is reached (Armitage and Schneiderman, 1958; King, 1963). Such sequential procedures usually reduce the total amount of experimentation, and perhaps the cost of the whole operation, whilst achieving a given level of discrimination between good and bad quality.

(b) *To achieve specified precision*

In section 6.5 it was noted that the size of a random sample required to reduce the standard error of a mean to some specified level depends on the residual standard deviation, σ. If σ is initially unknown it can be estimated from a pilot study. Alternatively one could merge the pilot study into the definitive sampling by maintaining a sequence of estimates of σ, using all observations made so far, and stopping the survey when the estimated standard error reaches its required level. This procedure is discussed in section 15.2.

(c) *Clinical trials*

Ethical considerations usually preclude random allocation in a clinical trial if there is strong prior evidence that one of the rival treatments is better than another. In the same way it will often be undesirable to continue a trial beyond a point at which one treatment is clearly seen to be better than a rival treatment. To find when such a situation is reached the investigator must proceed sequentially: the observations will be analysed continuously and the decision when to stop the trial will depend in some way on the results obtained. Such a sequential design is often possible in clinical trials since patients are usually entered into a trial serially, over a period of time, rather than all at the same time.

In all these different situations, one condition in particular is necessary for a sequential approach to be worth considering. Any observation must be recorded and made available for analysis relatively soon after it is planned; otherwise, it may not contribute to the decision when to stop the collection of data until much too late a stage. In a clinical trial of analgesics, for instance, observations on a particular patient may become available within a few days after the patient is treated; if the period of intake of patients into the trial is measured in months there will be ample opportunity for a feedback of information. If, on the other hand, a trial is concerned with the effect of a two-year period of treatment for patients with rheumatic conditions feedback will be negligible and the trial must be designed on a non-sequential basis.

15.2 SEQUENTIAL ESTIMATION

A typical situation is described briefly at (b) in section 15.1. Suppose that, in a random sample of size n from a distribution with mean μ and variance σ^2, the estimated mean is $\bar{x}_n$ and the estimated standard deviation is s_n. The subscripts here emphasize the fact that both these statistics will change randomly as n increases. The estimated standard error of $\bar{x}_n$ is

$$\mathrm{SE}(\bar{x}_n) = s_n/\sqrt{n}, \tag{15.1}$$

and, although s_n will fluctuate randomly, this standard error will tend to decrease as n increases.

Suppose the purpose of the investigation is to estimate μ with specified precision, as in section 6.5 (a); specifically, suppose we require $\mathrm{SE}(\bar{x}_n) < \epsilon$. Then an appropriate stopping rule will be: continue sampling until $s_n/\sqrt{n}$ first falls below ϵ.

The question arises whether the formula (15.1) for the standard error is valid with this form of sequential sampling; its original interpretation was in terms of repeated sampling with a fixed sample size. The answer is, broadly, that the method *is* valid. First, if we choose to interpret the standard error as measuring the dispersion of the likelihood function, or as the standard deviation of the posterior distribution with dispersed prior knowledge (section 4.11), we have an important result: *likelihood functions and posterior distributions are unaffected by the choice of stopping rule*. The sequential design is, from this point of view, irrelevant. Secondly, on the more traditional frequency view, the usual confidence limits are approximately valid, particularly in reasonably large samples. That is, if the sequential sampling procedure is repeated many times, the usual 95 per cent confidence limits will include the true value μ approximately 95 per cent of the time.

15.3 SEQUENTIAL TESTS

Wald's original work was primarily concerned with sequential significance tests, which give rise to rather more difficult problems than does the estimation procedure described in section 15.2.

It is useful to illustrate some of these by referring to a hypothetical, yet typical, clinical trial like that described in Example 4.3. Each patient receives two analgesic drugs, X and Y, in adjacent weeks. The order of administration is random and the drugs are made to be indistinguishable by the patients. At the end of the two-week period each patient gives a preference for the drug received in the first week or that received in the second week, on the basis of alleviation of pain. These are then decoded to form a series of preferences for X or Y.

A typical set of results might be that shown in Table 15.1. It seems reasonable to test the cumulative results at any stage to see whether there is a significant preponderance of preferences in favour of X or Y. The appropriate conventional test, at the nth stage, would be that based on the binomial distribution with parameter n and with $\pi=\frac{1}{2}$; the normal approximation is illustrated in Example 4.3. The critical values for significance at the 5 per cent level are shown in Table 15.1. No result is significant until $n=25$, when the number of preferences in favour of X reaches the critical level. The investigator, proceeding sequentially, might be inclined to stop the trial at this stage and publish his results claiming a significant difference at the 5 per cent level. Indeed this is a correct assessment of the evidence *at this particular stage*. The principle enunciated in the last section shows that the relative likelihoods of different parameters (in this example, different values of the probability π of obtaining a preference for X) are unaffected by the stopping rule. However, some selection of evidence has taken place.

TABLE 15.1 Example illustrating the repeated use of significance tests on a series of preferences for one of two analgesic drugs.

Patient number	Preference	(1) Cumulative number of preferences for X	Critical values for (1) at 2-sided 5 per cent level
1	Y	0	—
2	X	1	—
3	X	2	—
4	X	3	—
5	X	4	—
6	X	5	0, 6
7	X	6	0, 7
8	Y	6	0, 8
9	Y	6	1, 8
10	X	7	1, 9
11	X	8	1, 10
12	Y	8	2, 10
13	Y	8	2, 11
14	X	9	2, 12
15	X	10	3, 12
16	X	11	3, 13
17	X	12	4, 13
18	X	13	4, 14
19	X	14	4, 15
20	Y	14	5, 15
21	X	15	5, 16
22	Y	15	5, 17
23	X	16	6, 17
24	X	17	6, 18
25	X	18	7, 18

The investigator has given himself a large number of opportunities to stop at the 5 per cent level. Even if the null hypothesis is true there is a substantial probability that a 'significant' result will be found in due course, and this probability will clearly increase the longer the trial continues.

The position is very similar to that discussed in section 7.3 in connection with multiple comparisons. The probability, on the null hypothesis, that a sequential trial will stop with a verdict in favour of one or the other treatment may be termed the *overall* significance level;

(a more formal term is the probability of an error of the first kind). To control the overall significance level at a low value such as 5 per cent, a much higher significance level (that is, a *lower* probability) is required to assess the results at any one stage. This condition by itself is insufficient to determine the stopping rule: many different rules can be constructed to satisfy a specified overall significance level. Wald's (1947) theory provides one important general method. Some rather different sequential plans, designed specially for medical trials, are described in detail by Armitage (1960). An alternative approach is outlined below.

Suppose the stopping rule is to stop the trial if the cumulative results at any stage show a significant difference at the two-sided $2\alpha'$ level, or to stop after N stages if the trial has not stopped earlier. To achieve an overall two-sided significance level, 2α, of 5 per cent, what value should be chosen for $2\alpha'$, the significance level at any one stage? The answer clearly depends on N; the larger N, the smaller $2\alpha'$ must be. Some results are given in Table 15.2.

TABLE 15.2 Repeated significance tests on cumulative binomial and normal observations; significance level to be used for individual tests for overall level $2\alpha=0\cdot05$.

Number of stages, N	Significance level (two-sided), $2\alpha'$, for individual tests: Binomial	Normal
1	—	0·050
5	—	0·015
10	0·031	0·010
15	0·023	0·008
20	0·022	0·007
50	0·013	0·005
100	0·008	0·004
150	0·007	0·003

The left side of Table 15.2 refers to repeated significance tests based on the binomial distribution, as in the example at the beginning of this section. The right side refers to repeated tests on cumulative series of observations on normally distributed random variables when the variance is known. This situation rarely occurs in practice; the residual variance cannot usually be assumed in advance, and the t test is the standard technique. It is likely, though, that the results shown in Table 15.2 for the normal distribution will provide a good approximation in other situations where tests are based on continuous random variables. The distinction between the two sets of results in Table 15.2 arises primarily from the discreteness of the binomial distribution.

The choice of N, the maximum sample size in a sequential test, will depend on much the same considerations as those outlined in section 6.5. In particular, as in criterion (c) of that section, one may wish to select a sequential plan which not only controls the overall significance level, 2α, but has a specified power, say $1-\beta$, of providing a significant result when a certain alternative to the null hypothesis is true. In the binomial test described earlier, a particular alternative hypothesis might specify that the probability of a preference for drug X, which we denote by π, is some value π_1 different from $\frac{1}{2}$. If the sequential plan is symmetrical it will automatically provide the same power for $\pi=\pi_0$ $(=1-\pi_1)$ as for $\pi=\pi_1$. For example, if $\pi_1=0{\cdot}8$ and $\pi_0=0{\cdot}2$, the hypothesis $\pi=\pi_1$ indicates a benefit from using drug X, and the hypothesis $\pi=\pi_0$ indicates an equal benefit from using drug Y; each of these alternatives would have an equal chance of detection by a symmetrical sequential plan.

TABLE 15.3 Maximum sample size, N, and significance levels for individual tests, $2\alpha'$, for binomial sequential plans with overall level $2\alpha=0{\cdot}05$ and power $1-\beta=0{\cdot}95$ against various values of π differing from the null value of 0·5.

π_1	$2\alpha'$	N
0·95	0·0313	10
0·90	0·0225	16
0·85	0·0193	25
0·80	0·0147	38
0·75	0·0116	61
0·70	0·0081	100

Table 15.3 shows the maximum sample sizes, and the significance levels for individual tests, for binomial sequential plans with the overall significance level $2\alpha=0{\cdot}05$ and a power $1-\beta=0{\cdot}95$ against various alternative values of π.

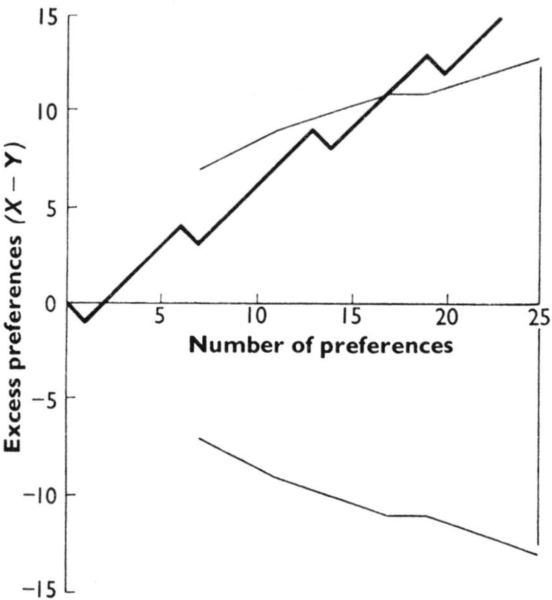

FIG. 15.1 A sequential plan for repeated binomial tests on a series of preferences. The overall significance level is 0·05, individual tests are performed at the 0·0193 level, and the plan has a power of 0·95 against a situation in which the probability of a preference for X is 0·85 or 0·15. The data are taken from a trial of cough suppressants (Table 15.4).

Any of these sequential plans can be represented graphically by a diagram like that in Fig. 15.1 (which depicts the plan for Table 15.3 with $\pi_1 = 0{\cdot}85$). In this diagram the horizontal axis represents the number of preferences recorded at any stage. The vertical axis represents the difference between the numbers of preferences for X and Y. The boundary points are obtained from tables of the binomial distribution; the usual normal approximation of section 2.7 could be used if desired. The course of any trial is charted by starting a zig-zag line at the origin and moving the unit to the right and upwards (i.e. in a 'north-easterly' direction) for each X preference, and one unit to the right and downwards (a 'south-easterly' direction) for each Y preference. The data plotted in Fig. 15.1 are taken from a trial to assess some cough suppressants (Snell and Armitage, 1957; see also Armitage 1960, Example 3.3); X is an active drug, Y is a placebo. The results are summarized in Table 15.4. The superiority of the active drug is demonstrated by the 17th preference.

TABLE 15.4 Preferences expressed by patients between an active drug *X*, and a placebo *Y*, as cough suppressants.

Patient number	Preference	Patient number	Preference
1	—	24	*X*
2	*Y*	25	*X*
3	—	26	*X*
4	*X*	27	—
5	*X*	28	—
6	—	29	—
7	—	30	*X*
8	—	31	*X*
9	*X*	32	—
10	*X*	33	*Y*
11	—	34	*X*
12	—	35	*X*
13	—	36	—
14	*X*	37	*Y*
15	*Y*	38	—
16	—	39	*X*
17	*X*	40	*X*
18	*X*	41	*X*
19	*X*	42	*X*
20	*X*	43	—
21	*X*	44	—
22	*X*	45	*Y*
23	*Y*		

A dash indicates that the patient stated no preference.

The data in Table 15.4 were originally analysed by the slightly different methods of sequential analysis described in Armitage (1960). A comparison of Fig. 15.1 with Fig. 3.7 of that book or the chart in the original paper shows that the two plans are extremely similar; the essential difference is that the earlier plans had approximately linear boundaries whereas the present boundaries are rather more curved.*

In any trial using a series of preferences, it is likely that some comparisons will fail to yield a definite preference in either direction. In the

* A further difference is that in the earlier plans the vertical part of the boundary was modified by stopping the trial as soon as it became clear that neither of the outer boundaries could be reached; the resulting boundary was shaped thus: $<$. The same device could be used here.

data of Table 15.4, for instance, some patients were unwilling to state a preference for either preparation. For the purposes of a significance test only the definite preferences are used; the others may be ignored. However, in estimating the relative merits of the treatments it will be extremely important to know whether many patients were unable to make a preference, and any summary of the data must certainly contain a clear statement on this point.

In many clinical trials the crucial assessment is made by comparing two proportions—for example the proportion of patients who show a certain degree of improvement with drug X and the corresponding proportion of improvements with drug Y. The standard non-sequential methods of analysis are described in sections 4.7 and 4.8. Sequential tests can be facilitated by a useful device which reduces the problem to that of analysing a *single* binomial series, which has been discussed above. Observations from the two series are paired, either in order of treatment (the first patient on X being paired with the first on Y, and so on), or in order within some defined subgroups or 'blocks' (a severely affected patient, for instance, being paired with a patient of similar severity). The results for any pair will be of one of the four following types:

		Patient treated with		Preference
	Type	X	Y	
	1	improved	improved	—
Untied pairs	2	improved	not improved	X
Untied pairs	3	not improved	improved	Y
	4	not improved	not improved	—

The second and third types are often called *untied pairs*, because for the other two types the comparison between X and Y results in a 'tie'. On the null hypothesis that X and Y are equally effective, preferences for X and Y occur in the long run with equal frequency amongst the untied pairs. If X causes more improvements than Y, X preferences will occur more frequently than Y preferences, and vice versa. A reasonable sequential test for the comparison of the two proportions of improvement is, therefore, to treat the preferences as a single binomial series and to apply exactly the same form of stopping rule as in the more direct case discussed earlier.

This approach is precisely that used for the comparison of proportions in two *paired* series, in section 4.7. If the observations in the two series are paired within subgroups the sequential method is therefore a direct development from the appropriate non-sequential method. The rather unexpected point is that the method can be used also for trials in which observations are paired effectively at random; except when the number of observations is small very little efficiency is lost by this procedure.

If the pairing is entirely at random, the probability of a preference for drug X can be related to the probabilities of improvement for the two drugs. Suppose the probability of improvement is π_1 for drug X and π_2 for drug Y. The probability of an untied pair of type 2 is, by the multiplication rule, $\pi_1(1-\pi_2)$, and that for an untied pair of type 3 is $(1-\pi_1)\pi_2$. The probability of an X preference is the same as the probability that an untied pair is of type 2, namely

$$\theta = \frac{\pi_1(1-\pi_2)}{\pi_1(1-\pi_2)+(1-\pi_1)\pi_2}. \qquad (15.2)$$

If $\pi_1 = \pi_2$ (the null hypothesis), $\theta = \frac{1}{2}$; if $\pi_1 > \pi_2$, $\theta > \frac{1}{2}$; and if $\pi_1 < \pi_2$, $\theta < \frac{1}{2}$. Alternative hypotheses against which high power is required may be formulated in terms of π_1 and π_2. From (15.2), the corresponding value of θ can be calculated and an appropriate sequential plan selected. It must be remembered that the maximum sample sizes given in Table 15.3 refer to the number of preferences; that is, the number of *untied* pairs. The corresponding *total* number of pairs is clearly greater. The proportion of pairs which are untied is

$$\phi = \pi_1(1-\pi_2)+(1-\pi_1)\pi_2. \qquad (15.3)$$

A table of θ and ϕ in terms of π_1 and π_2 is given by Armitage (1960, Table 4.1); this book may be consulted for further details and for references to examples of sequential trials.

CHAPTER 16
STATISTICAL METHODS IN EPIDEMIOLOGY

16.1 INTRODUCTION

Precise definitions of the branch of medical science called *epidemiology* are elusive. In broad terms epidemiology is concerned with the distribution of disease, and it is now customary to include within its orbit the study of chronic diseases as well as the communicable diseases which give rise to epidemics of the classical sort. The subject overlaps to some extent with *social medicine* or *community medicine*. These terms also are difficult to define precisely, but they would usually be understood to include social and administrative topics, such as the organization of health services, which might not be regarded as part of epidemiology.

Epidemiology is by definition concerned with certain problems affecting groups of individuals rather than single subjects, and inevitably gives rise to statistical problems. Many of these are conceptually similar to statistical problems arising in other branches of medical science and indeed in the non-medical sciences, and can be approached by the methods of analysis described earlier in this book; several examples in earlier chapters have been drawn from epidemiological studies. Other methodological problems in epidemiology, although of statistical interest, are bound up with considerations of a non-statistical nature and cannot be discussed here. Examples are the interpretation of vital and health statistical data, which requires a close knowledge of administrative procedures for the recording of such data and of the classification of diseases and causes of death (Benjamin, 1968; Swaroop, 1960; World Health Organization, 1967); and the proper use and potential developments of medical records of various sorts (Acheson, 1967). There is also a considerable body of literature concerned with the mathematical theory of epidemic diseases; the monograph by Bailey (1957) provides a useful summary of this work. For general accounts of epidemiological methods the reader may consult MacMahon *et al.* (1960) and Taylor and Knowelden (1964).

In the next three sections we consider briefly certain problems arising in epidemiological research for which special statistical methods have been developed.

16.2 RELATIVE RISK

Case-control and cohort methods for studying the aetiology of disease have been discussed in section 6.3. In such studies it is often useful to measure the increased risk (if any) of incurring a particular disease if a certain factor is present. In cohort studies such estimation can be done directly, by observing the experience of groups of subjects with and without the factor. In a case-control study the data do not present an immediate answer to this type of question, and we now consider how to obtain a useful solution.

Suppose that each subject in a large population has been classified as positive or negative according to some aetiological factor, and positive or negative according to some disease state. The factor might be based on a current classification or (more usually in a retrospective study) on the subject's past history. The disease state may refer to the presence or absence of a certain category of disease at a particular instant, or to a certain occurrence (such as diagnosis or death) during a stated period. (These two forms of disease classification relate to *prevalence* and *incidence*, respectively.)

For any such categorization the population may be enumerated in a 2×2 table, as follows. The entries in the table are *proportions* of the total population.

		Disease +	Disease −	
Factor	+	P_1	P_3	P_1+P_3
	−	P_2	P_4	P_2+P_4
		P_1+P_2	P_3+P_4	1

(16.1)

If these proportions were known, the association (if any) between the factor and the disease could be measured by the ratio of the risks of being disease positive for those with and those without the factor.

$$\text{Ratio of risks} = \frac{P_1}{(P_1+P_3)} \div \frac{P_2}{(P_2+P_4)}$$

$$= \frac{P_1(P_2+P_4)}{P_2(P_1+P_3)}. \qquad (16.2)$$

Now, in many (although not all) situations in which aetiological studies are done, the proportion of subjects classified as disease positive will be small. That is, P_1 will be small in comparison with P_3, and P_2 will be small in comparison with P_4. In such a case, (16.2) will be very nearly equal to

$$\frac{P_1P_4}{P_2P_3} \ (=\psi, \text{ say}). \qquad (16.3)$$

The ratio (16.3) is properly called an *approximate relative risk* (because of the approximation referred to above), but it is often referred to simply as *relative risk*. Other terms are *odds ratio* (because it is the ratio of P_1/P_3 to P_2/P_4, and these two quantities can be thought of as odds in favour of having the disease), and *cross-ratio* (because the two products P_1P_4 and P_2P_3 which appear in (16.3) are obtained by multiplying diagonally across the table).

The relative risk (16.3) could be estimated from a random sample of the population, or from a sample stratified by the two levels of the factor (such as a prospective cohort study started some time before the disease assessments are made). It could also be estimated from a sample stratified by the two disease states (i.e. from a case-control study), and it is this fact which makes it such a useful measure of relative risk. Suppose a case-control study is carried out by selecting a random sample of non-diseased individuals, and that the *frequencies* (not proportions) are as follows:

		Disease +	Disease −	
Factor	+	a	c	$a+c$
	−	b	d	$b+d$
		$a+b$	$c+d$	n

(16.4)

Frequently, of course, the sampling plan will lead to equal numbers of cases and controls; then $a+b=c+d=\frac{1}{2}n$. Now, a/b can be regarded as a reasonable estimate of P_1/P_2, and c/d similarly estimates P_3/P_4. The observed relative risk

$$\hat{\psi}=\frac{ad}{bc} \tag{16.5}$$

is the ratio of a/b to c/d, and therefore can be taken as an estimate of

$$\frac{P_1}{P_2}\div\frac{P_3}{P_4}=\frac{P_1P_4}{P_2P_3}\,(=\psi),$$

the population relative risk defined by (16.3).

The assumption that the case and control groups are random samples of relevant population groups is rarely, if ever, satisfied in case-control studies. Nevertheless, the estimates of relative risk derived from case-control studies often agree quite well with those obtained from corroborative cohort studies, and the theory seems likely to be useful as a rough guide. In retrospective studies cases are often matched with control individuals for various factors; the effect of this matching is discussed below.

The sampling variation of a relative risk estimated by (16.5) is best considered by using a logarithmic scale. Approximately,

$$\text{var}\,(\log_e\hat{\psi})=\frac{1}{a}+\frac{1}{b}+\frac{1}{c}+\frac{1}{d}. \tag{16.6}$$

Here, $\log_e$ denotes the natural or Naperian logarithm. (If tables of natural logarithms are not available, the natural logarithm of any number can be obtained by taking the logarithm to base 10 (i.e. the common logarithm) and multiplying this by 2·3026.) Approximate confidence limits can be obtained by using the square root of (16.6) as the standard error of $\log_e\hat{\psi}$, applying normal theory, and transforming the limits back to the original ψ scale.

Frequently an estimate of relative risk is made from each of a number of sub-sets of the data, and there is some interest in the comparison and combination of these different estimates. There may, for example, be several studies of the same aetiological problem done at different times and places; or in any one study, the data may have been subdivided into one or more categories such as age groups, which affect the relative proportions in the rows of the 2×2 table or in the columns or in both rows and columns. One approach, illustrated in Example 16.1 below, is to take the separate estimates of $\log_e\hat{\psi}$ and weight them by the reciprocal of the sampling variance (16.6). The estimates can then be combined by taking a weighted mean, and they can be tested for heterogeneity by a χ^2 index like (7.28) (Woolf, 1955). A rather simpler method of combination, due to Mantel and Haenszel (1959) leads in practice to a very similar result for the pooled estimate. Denote the frequencies in the 2×2 table for the ith subdivision by:

		Disease +	Disease −	
Factor	+	a_i	c_i	
	−	b_i	d_i	
				n_i

The pooled estimate of ψ is then

$$R = \frac{\sum(a_i d_i / n_i)}{\sum(b_i c_i / n_i)}. \tag{16.7}$$

The calculation is illustrated in Example 16.1.

A special case of subdivision occurs in case-control studies in which each case is matched with a control subject for certain important factors, such as age, sex, residence etc. Strictly, each pair of matched subjects should form a subdivision for the calculation of relative risk, although of course the individual estimates from such pairs would be valueless. The Mantel-Haenszel pooled estimate (16.7) can, however, be calculated, and takes a particularly simple form. Suppose there are altogether $\frac{1}{2}n$ matched pairs. These can be entered into a 2×2 table according as the two individuals are factor-positive or -negative, with frequencies as follows:

		Control: Factor +	Control: Factor −	
Case	Factor +	t	r	a
	Factor −	s	u	b
		c	d	$\frac{1}{2}n$

(16.8)

The marginal totals in (16.8) are the cell frequencies in the earlier table (16.4). The Mantel-Haenszel estimate is then

$$R = \frac{r}{s}. \tag{16.9}$$

This can be shown to be a particularly satisfactory estimate if the true relative risk, as measured by the cross-ratio of the probabilities in (16.1), is the same for every pair.

A final general point is that the logarithm of ψ is, from (16.3),

$$\log_e(P_1/P_3) - \log_e(P_2/P_4)$$
$$= \text{logit (probability of disease when factor+)}$$
$$- \text{logit (probability of disease when factor}-\text{)}.$$

The methods of analysis suggested in this section can thus be seen to be particularly appropriate if the effect of changing from factor+ to factor− is to change the probability of being in the diseased state by a constant amount *on the logit scale*. It has been indicated in section 12.5 that this is a reasonable general approach to a wide range of problems, but in any particular instance it may be far from true. The investigator should therefore guard against too ready an assumption that a relative risk calculated in one study is necessarily applicable under somewhat different circumstances.

Example 16.1

Table 16.1 summarizes results from 10 retrospective surveys in which patients with lung cancer and control subjects were classified as smokers or non-smokers. In most or all of these surveys cases and controls would have been matched, but the original data are usually not presented in sufficient detail to enable relative risks to be estimated from (16.9) and matching is ignored in the present analysis. (The effect of ignoring matching when it is present is, if anything, to underestimate the departure of the relative risk from unity.) The data were compiled by Cornfield (1956) and have been referred to also by Gart (1962).

In the calculations using log $\hat{\psi}$ it is convenient to take logs to base 10 and to do any necessary correction later. Thus, the weighted mean is

$$\frac{\Sigma w_i \log \hat{\psi}_i}{\Sigma w_i} = \frac{70{\cdot}07}{105{\cdot}4} = 0{\cdot}665,$$

and the pooled estimate of ψ is antilog $(0{\cdot}665) = 4{\cdot}62$. No correction for the base of the logs is needed at this stage.

For the heterogeneity test, the $\chi^2_{(9)}$ statistic is

$$(2{\cdot}3026)^2\left\{\Sigma w_i(\log \hat{\psi}_i)^2 - \frac{(\Sigma w_i \log \hat{\psi}_i)^2}{\Sigma w_i}\right\}$$

$$= (2{\cdot}3026)^2(47{\cdot}827 - 46{\cdot}583) = 6{\cdot}60 \; (0{\cdot}5 < P < 0{\cdot}75).$$

There is evidently no strong evidence of heterogeneity between separate estimates. It is, of course, likely that the relative risk varies to some extent

TABLE 16.1 Combination of relative risks from ten retrospective surveys on smoking and lung cancer. (Cornfield, 1956; Gart, 1962.)

Study number	Lung cancer patients: Smokers a_i	Lung cancer patients: Non-smokers b_i	Control patients: Smokers c_i	Control patients: Non-smokers d_i	$a_i d_i$	$b_i c_i$	$\hat{\psi}_i$	$\log \hat{\psi}_i$	(1) $1/a_i + 1/b_i + 1/c_i + 1/d_i$	$w_i = \frac{1}{(1)}$	$w_i \log \hat{\psi}_i$	n_i	$a_i d_i / n_i$	$b_i c_i / n_i$
1	83	3	72	14	1162	216	5·38	0·731	0·4307	2·3	1·68	172	6·756	1·256
2	90	3	227	43	3870	681	5·68	0·754	0·3721	2·7	2·04	363	10·661	1·876
3	129	7	81	19	2451	567	4·32	0·636	0·2156	4·6	2·93	236	10·386	2·403
4	412	32	299	131	53972	9568	5·64	0·751	0·0447	22·4	16·82	874	61·753	10·947
5	1350	7	1296	61	82350	9072	9·08	0·958	0·1608	6·2	5·94	2714	30·343	3·343
6	60	3	106	27	1620	318	5·09	0·707	0·3965	2·5	1·77	196	8·265	1·622
7	459	18	534	81	37179	9612	3·87	0·588	0·0720	13·9	8·17	1092	34·047	8·802
8	499	19	462	56	27944	8778	3·18	0·502	0·0747	13·4	6·73	1036	26·973	8·473
9	451	39	1729	636	286836	67431	4·25	0·628	0·0300	33·3	20·91	2855	100·468	23·619
10	260	5	259	28	7280	1295	5·62	0·750	0·2434	4·1	3·08	522	13·188	2·346
Total	3793	136	5065	1096						105·4	70·07		302·840	64·687

from study to study, particularly as the factor 'smoking' covers such a wide range of activity. However, the sampling variation of the separate estimates is evidently too large to enable such real variation to emerge. If we assume that all the variation is due to sampling error, the variance of the weighted mean of log $\hat{\psi}_i$ can be obtained as

$$\frac{1}{(2{\cdot}3026)^2 \sum w_i} = 0{\cdot}00179.$$

Approximate 95 per cent confidence limits for log ψ are

$$\begin{aligned} &0{\cdot}665 \pm (1{\cdot}96)\sqrt{0{\cdot}00179} \\ &= 0{\cdot}582 \quad \text{and} \quad 0{\cdot}748. \end{aligned}$$

The corresponding limits for ψ are obtained by antilogs as 3·82 and 5·60.

The Mantel-Haenszel estimate of ψ is

$$R = \frac{302{\cdot}840}{64{\cdot}687} = 4{\cdot}68,$$

very similar indeed to the pooled estimate derived above by the more complicated method.

16.3 DIAGNOSTIC TESTS

In epidemiological studies much use is made of diagnostic tests, based either on clinical observations or on laboratory techniques, by means of which individuals are classified as healthy or as falling into one of a number of disease categories. Such tests are, of course, important throughout the whole of medicine, and in particular form the basis of screening programmes for the early diagnosis of disease. Most such tests are imperfect instruments, in the sense that healthy individuals will occasionally be classified wrongly as being ill, while some individuals who are really ill may fail to be detected. How should we measure the ability of a particular diagnostic test to give the correct diagnosis both for healthy and for ill subjects?

Suppose that each individual in a large population can be classified as truly positive or negative for a particular diagnosis. This true diagnosis may be based on more refined methods than are used in the test; or it may be based on evidence which emerges after the passage of time, for instance at autopsy. For each class of individual, true positive and true negative, we can consider the probabilities that the test gives a positive or negative verdict; as in the table below.

		Test +	Test −	Total	
True	+	$1-\beta$	β	1	(16.10)
	−	α	$1-\alpha$	1	

An individual in the top right corner of this 2×2 table is called a *false negative*; β is the probability of a false negative, and $1-\beta$ is called the *sensitivity* of the test. Those in the lower left corner are called *false positives*; α is the probability of a false positive, and $1-\alpha$ is the *specificity* of the test. There is an analogy here with significance tests. If the null hypothesis is that an individual is a true negative, and a positive test result is regarded as 'significant', then α is analogous to the significance level and $1-\beta$ is analogous to the power of detecting the alternative hypothesis that the individual is a true positive (section 6.5(c)).

Clearly it is desirable that a test should have small values of α and β, although other considerations such as cost and ease of application are highly relevant. Other things being equal, if test A has smaller values of both α and β than test B it can be regarded as a better test. Suppose, though, that A has a smaller value of α but a larger value of β. Unless some relative weight can be attached to the two forms of error—false positives and false negatives—no clear judgement is possible. If the two errors are judged to be of approximately equal importance a natural method of combination is by the sum of two error probabilities, $\alpha+\beta$. Youden (1950) proposed an essentially equivalent index,

$$J=1-(\alpha+\beta). \qquad (16.11)$$

If the test has no diagnostic value, $\alpha=1-\beta$ and $J=0$. If the test is invariably correct, $\alpha=\beta=0$ and $J=1$. Values of J between -1 and 0 could arise if the test result were negatively associated with the true diagnosis, but this situation is unlikely to arise in practice.

The discussion above has been in terms of probabilities. In practice these could be estimated from surveys. Suppose a special survey of a random sample of the population gave the following frequencies:

		Test +	Test −	
True	+	a	b	(16.12)
	−	c	d	

The probability of a false negative would be estimated by $\hat{\beta}=b/(a+b)$; the probability of a false positive by $\hat{\alpha}=c/(c+d)$. Youden's index J would be estimated by $\hat{J}=1-(\hat{\alpha}+\hat{\beta})$. The sampling errors of these estimates follow from standard binomial expressions.

An important point to note is that the expected proportions of misdiagnoses amongst the *apparent* positives and negatives depend not only on α and β but on the true prevalence of the disease. This may be seen from the following two sets of frequencies. In each case the estimated probabilities of mis-diagnosis, $\hat{\alpha}$ and $\hat{\beta}$, are 0·1.

Case (a)

		Test +	Test −	
True	+	450	50	500
	−	50	450	500
		500	500	1000
Proportion of true +ves		0·90	0·10	

Case (b)

		Test +	Test −	
True	+	90	10	100
	−	90	810	900
		180	820	1000
Proportion of true +ves		0·50	0·01.	

(16.13)

In case (a), the true prevalence is 500/1,000 = 0·5; the proportion of true positives amongst the apparent positives is high (0·9), and amongst the apparent negatives it is low (0·1). In case (b), however, where the true prevalence is 100/1,000 = 0·1, the proportion of true positives amongst the apparent positives is only 0·5. Case (b) illustrates the position in many pre-symptomatic screening procedures where the true prevalence is very low. Of the subjects found positive by the screening test a rather high proportion may be false positives. To avoid this situation the test may sometimes be modified to reduce α, but such a step often results in an increased value of β and hence a reduced value of $1-\beta$; the number of false positives amongst the apparent positives will have reduced, but so will the number of true positives detected.

The sort of modification referred to in the last sentence is particularly relevant when the test, although dichotomous, is based on a continuous measurement. Examples are the diagnosis of diabetes by blood sugar level, or of glaucoma by intra-ocular pressure. Any change in the critical level of the measurement will affect α and β. One very simple model for this situation would be to assume that the variable, x, on which the test is based is normally distributed with the same variance σ^2 for the normal and diseased populations, but with different means, μ_N and μ_D (Fig.

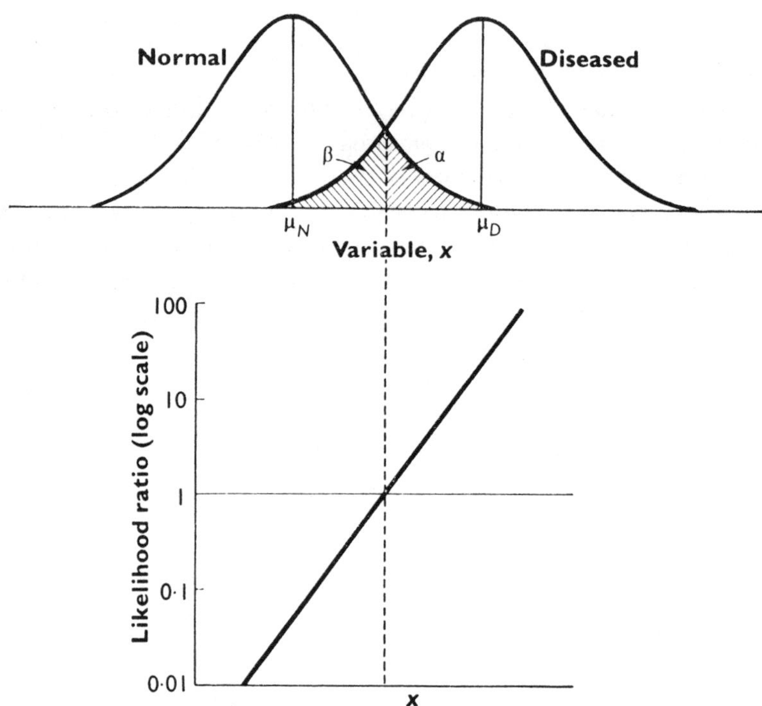

FIG. 16.1 The performance of a diagnostic test based on a normally distributed variable when the normal and diseased groups differ in the mean but have the same variance. The lower diagram shows on a log scale the ratio of the likelihood that an observation comes from the diseased group to that of its coming from the normal group.

16.1). For any given α, the value of β depends solely on the standardized distance between the means,

$$\Delta = \frac{\mu_D - \mu_N}{\sigma}. \tag{16.14}$$

If the critical value for the test is the mid-point between the means, $\frac{1}{2}(\mu_N + \mu_D)$, α and β will both be equal to the single-tail area of the normal distribution beyond a standardized deviate of $\frac{1}{2}\Delta$. To compare the merits of different tests one could, therefore, compare their values of Δ; tests with high values of Δ will differentiate between normal and diseased groups better than those with low values. There is a clear analogy here with the generalized distance as a measure of the effectiveness of a discriminant function (section 10.5); the discrimination is performed here by the single variable x.

Instead of an all-or-none classification as healthy or diseased it may sometimes be useful to express the strength of the evidence for any individual falling into each of the two groups. For the model described above, the logarithm of the likelihood ratio is linearly related to x, as shown in the lower part of Fig. 16.1. (This is a particular case of the more general result for discriminant functions referred to in section 10.5). The likelihood ratio may, from Bayes's theorem (section 2.8), be combined with the ratio of prior probabilities to give the ratio of posterior probabilities. Suppose, for example, that a particular value of x corresponded to a likelihood ratio of 10, and that the prior probability of a diseased individual (i.e. the population prevalence) was 0·01. The posterior odds that the individual is diseased are then

$$\frac{10}{1}\times\frac{0\cdot01}{0\cdot99}=0\cdot10 \text{ to } 1.$$

It is thus much more likely that the individual is healthy than that he is diseased; as in case (b) of (16.13) where the prevalence was low, a high proportion of apparent positives are in fact false positives.

The assumptions underlying the above discussion are unlikely to be closely fulfilled in practice. Distributions may be non-normal and have different variances; there may be various categories of disease, each with a different distribution of x. Nevertheless the concepts introduced here usually provide a good basis for discussing the performance of a diagnostic test. For further discussion see Greenhouse and Mantel (1950).

Misclassification errors are not restricted to the classification of disease. In a retrospective case-control study, for example, the disease classification is likely to be based on highly accurate diagnostic methods, but the factor classification often depends on personal recollection and may therefore be imperfectly accurate. False positives and false negatives can be defined in terms of the factor classification in an obvious way. If the probabilities of false positives and false negatives are the same for the disease group as for the control group the effect is to reduce any measures of association between factor and disease; for instance the relative risk is, on average, brought nearer to unity than it would be if the errors were not present, and the difference between the two proportions of positives is reduced numerically. Under other less plausible assumptions about the error probabilities this need not be so (Newell, 1962; Diamond and Lilienfeld, 1962a, b).

Our discussion of diagnostic tests has been restricted to a comparison of the result of a single test with the true diagnosis. In many situations the true diagnosis cannot conveniently be established in a large survey population but there may be an opportunity to compare a new test against a reference test. Buck and Gart (1966; also Gart and Buck, 1966) discuss the rather complicated analysis of data of this type. Under certain assumptions about the reference test it may be possible to infer something about the sensitivity and specificity of the new test.

16.4 DISEASE CLUSTERING

Many epidemiological investigations are concerned with the detection of some form of clustering of cases of a certain disease—clustering in time, in space, or in both time and space. For example, one might enquire whether cases of a certain congenital malformation (which might normally occur at a fairly constant rate in a community) appear with unduly high frequency in certain years. Such a tendency towards clustering in time might indicate aetiological factors, such as maternal virus infections, which were particularly severe in certain years. Again, one might suspect that certain forms of illness are more common amongst people who work or live in certain areas, perhaps because of environmental factors peculiar to these places. The groups in which cases tend to be clustered may be families or households; such familial aggregation might again be caused by environmental factors, but it might be due also to intra-familial infection or to genetic predisposition to disease. In the study of the possible infectious aetiology of rare diseases such as leukaemia or certain congenital malformations, clustering in either space or time will be less interesting than a space-time association. By this term we mean a tendency for those cases which are relatively close together in space also to be relatively close together in time.

Many of these problems give rise to quite complicated considerations and it will not be possible to explore the subject fully here. This section contains a brief account of some of these considerations. Further details may be obtained from the references given here.

CLUSTERING IN TIME

A rather simple approach to many problems of this sort is to divide the time period into equal intervals, to express the incidence rate in each interval as a proportion and to test the significance of differences between these proportions by standard $2 \times k$ contingency table methods. If the population at risk is almost constant and the incidence rate is low, the number of cases appearing in the different intervals will, on the null hypothesis of constant risk, follow a Poisson distribution; the usual heterogeneity test (section 7.7) may be used.

It may be sensible to concentrate attention on the maximum of the various numbers of cases, on the grounds that occasional clustering may affect only one or two of the time intervals. Ederer *et al.* (1964) describe some methods for doing this.

CLUSTERING IN SPACE

Rather similar methods can be applied to detect clustering in space which may result in differences in incidence between different groups of people. It will usually be convenient to subdivide the total population into administrative areas containing quite different numbers of individuals; the Poisson distribution is not then applicable, but contingency table methods can be used.

CLUSTERING IN FAMILIES

Clustering of disease in families may be due to an infective agent or to a genetic cause. These are the main reasons for studying familial aggregation, but other possible causes often complicate the issue. Members of the same family or household share the same natural environment and social conditions, all of which may affect the incidence of a particular disease. Age is a further complication, particularly in sibling studies, since siblings tend to be more similar in age than do members of different sibships.

If we ignore these complications, the testing of heterogeneity of disease incidence between families seems a similar problem to that of testing heterogeneity between any other groups of individuals. There is, however, a special problem of *ascertainment*. Family data may be collected by several different methods.

(a) *Complete ascertainment*

This is obtained by random sampling from a complete list of families or perhaps by inclusion of the whole population of families.

(b) *Single ascertainment*

In this method families are obtained through affected individuals. (This is a natural method if one wishes to estimate the proportion of affected individuals amongst close relatives of affected individuals; the original cases are then called '*probands*' or '*propositi*'). An immediate consequence is that families with no affected individuals are not included; the frequency of these is therefore not observed directly. There are two important sub-divisions of (b):

(i) *Complete selection,* in which all the relevant families are detected and multiply ascertained families are counted only once; or where they are obtained from a register of probands in which each family would appear only once (e.g. from a register of births during a period of 6 months).

(ii) *Single selection,* in which the sampling fraction is so small that only a small fraction of families are included and the chance of a family being ascertained more than once is ignored; or where no attempt is made to avoid duplication caused by multiple ascertainment.

The importance of these distinctions is the following. Suppose we are studying families of size n. In (a) and (b) (i) the expected frequencies of families with r affected individuals, on the null hypothesis of a constant risk for each person, will be given by a binomial distribution, the term for $r=0$ being missing in (b) (i). In (b) (ii), however, the probability of a family with r affected individuals being ascertained is proportional to r; the expected frequencies will therefore be proportional to the binomial probabilities multiplied by r.

These distinctions have been much considered in genetic research (Bailey, 1951) and have given rise to a number of methods of estimating the mean risk per individual and of testing for heterogeneity. A useful simple method for case (b) (i) has, for instance, been published by Gart (1968). Haenszel (1959) discusses the problem particularly in relation to chronic disease studies.

CLUSTERING IN TIME AND SPACE

Knox (1964) pointed out that if a relatively rare condition was in part caused by an infectious agent one would expect to find a space-time interaction in the sense that cases which occurred close together in space would tend also to be close in time. In a study of childhood leukaemia in North-east England he obtained information about 96 cases occurring in a certain area during a particular period of time, and tabulated each pair of cases in a 2 × 2 table according to certain 'closeness' criteria. A pair of cases was called 'adjacent' in time if the interval between times of onset was less than 60 days, and 'adjacent' in space if the distance was less than 1 kilometre. The results are shown in Table 16.2. The total frequency, 4560, is the number of pairs formed from 96 cases, 96 × 95/2.

TABLE 16.2 Pairs of cases of childhood leukaemia tabulated according to adjacency in time and space (Knox, 1964).

		Space		
		Adjacent	Not adjacent	Total
Time	Adjacent	5	147	152
	Not adjacent	20	4388	4408
		25	4535	4560

If there were no relationship between the time at which a case occurred and the spatial position the cell frequencies in Table 16.2 would have been expected to be proportional to the marginal totals. In particular the expected value for the smallest frequency, is (152)(25)/4560 = 0·83. The deviations of observed from expected frequencies cannot be tested by the usual methods for 2 × 2 tables since the entries are not independent; (if cases *A* and *B* form an adjacent pair, and so do *B* and *C*, it is rather likely that *A* and *C* will also do so). However, it can be shown that a good approximation to the correct significance test is to test the observed frequency as a possible observation from a Poisson distribution with mean equal to the expected frequency. In a Poisson distribution with mean 0.83 the probability of observing 5 or more events is 0·0017, so the excess must be judged highly significant.

A number of developments of the theory have been made recently; for a review see Mantel (1967).

CHAPTER 17
BIOLOGICAL ASSAY

17.1 INTRODUCTION

Biological assay, or *bioassay*, is an important, although specialized, area of application of statistical methods. The general principles were established mainly during the 1930s and 1940s, and were rapidly developed in detail to an extent which cannot be adequately covered here. The interested reader will find a good survey of the principal methods in Chapter 3 (by D.J.Finney) of Burn *et al.* (1952) and a really comprehensive account in Finney (1964).

A biological assay is an experiment to determine the concentration of a key substance $\mathscr{S}$ in a preparation $\mathscr{P}$ by measuring the activity of $\mathscr{P}$ in a biological system $\mathscr{B}$. There are three important items in this definition.

$\mathscr{S}$, the substance under investigation, may be a pharmaceutical preparation like digitalis or penicillin, a steroid like gonadotrophin, or an ill-defined material like the protective antigen in a certain vaccine.

$\mathscr{P}$, the preparation, is usually some quantity of a naturally occurring diluent or of a product of a manufacturing process, containing an unknown concentration of $\mathscr{S}$.

$\mathscr{B}$, the biological system, usually is a response in experimental animals which should as far as possible be specific to $\mathscr{S}$. For example, vitamin D can be assayed by its anti-rachitic activity in rats. The biological material may, however, be humans, plants or micro-organisms. The important point is that the system is purely a measuring device; the response of $\mathscr{S}$ in $\mathscr{B}$ is of interest only in so far as it permits one to measure the concentration of $\mathscr{S}$ in $\mathscr{P}$.

The strength of $\mathscr{S}$ in $\mathscr{P}$ cannot usually be measured directly as a function of the specific response, since this is likely to vary according to experimental conditions and the nature of the biological material $\mathscr{B}$. This difficulty is overcome by the use of a standard preparation which contains $\mathscr{S}$ at constant concentration in an inert diluent and is maintained under conditions which as far as possible preserve its activity. The institution of a standard preparation usually leads to the definition of the *standard unit* as the activity of a certain amount of the standard. Any test preparation, T, can now be assayed against the standard, S, by simultaneous experimentation. If, say, S is defined to contain 1,000 units per g. and T happens to contain 100 units per g., a dose $10X$ g. of T should give the same response as Xg. of S. The *potency* or *potency-ratio* of T in terms of S is then said to be 1/10, or equivalently T may be said to have a potency of 100 units per g.

In the ideal situation described above we have assumed that S and T both contain different concentrations of exactly the same substance $\mathscr{S}$ in inert diluents, and any assay with a response specific to $\mathscr{S}$ will measure the unique potency-ratio. Such an assay is called an *analytical dilution assay*; it perhaps rarely exists in the real world. In practice most biological responses are specific to a range of substances, perhaps closely related chemically like the various penicillins. In such cases the potency may depend to some extent on the assay system, because the different varieties of the active substances may have differential effects in different biological systems. An assay which for a particular biological system behaves *as though* the ideal situation were true is called a *comparative dilution assay*.

The simplest form of assay is the *direct assay*, in which increasing doses of S and T can be administered to an experimental unit until a certain critical event takes place. This situation is rare; an example is the assay of prepared digitalis in the guinea pig, in which the critical event is arrest of heart beat. The dose given to any one animal is a measure of the individual tolerance of that animal, which can be expected to vary between animals through biological and environmental causes. On any one occasion for a particular animal, suppose that the tolerance dose of S would be X_S and that of T would be X_T; (in practice, of course, only one of these can be observed). Then the potency, ρ, of T in terms of S is given by X_S/X_T. If S and T were each administered to large random samples from a population of animals the tolerance doses X_S and X_T would form two distributions related to each other as in Fig. 17.1(a); the distribution of X_S would differ from that of X_T by a multiplying factor ρ, exactly as if the scale were extended or contracted by this factor. From random samples on T and S, ρ could be estimated from the distributions of X_T and X_S. The estimation problem becomes much simpler, though, if the doses are recorded logarithmically, as in Fig. 17.1(b). If $x_S = \log X_S$ and $x_T = \log X_T$, we can estimate log ρ from two sample means $\bar{x}_S$ and $\bar{x}_T$ by

$$M = \bar{x}_S - \bar{x}_T.$$

The distributions of x_S and x_T are automatically guaranteed to be the same shape, and in practice they are likely to be reasonably normal. The standard theory of the t distribution in the two-sample case thus provides confidence limits for log ρ, centred about M, and (by taking antilogs) the corresponding limits for ρ. Unfortunately, the continuous

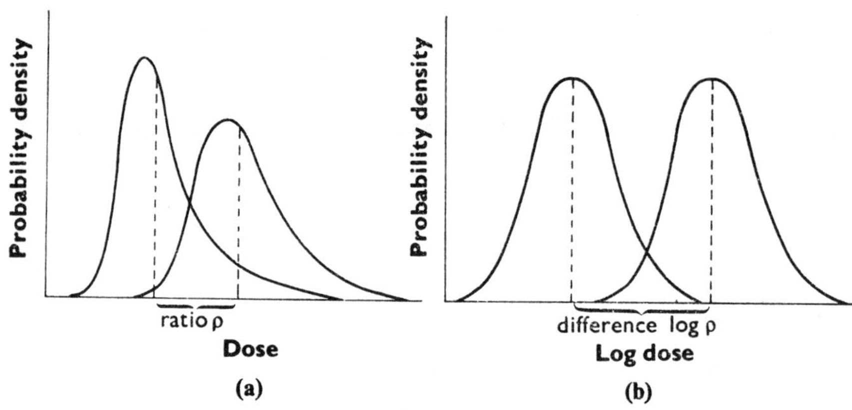

FIG. 17.1 Direct assay. Distributions of tolerance doses and their logarithms for standard and test preparations.

administration of doses and the immediate response needed for direct assays are rarely feasible. Instead, the assayer has to rely on *indirect assays*, in which predetermined doses of T and S are given to groups of experimental units and the resulting responses are observed. Two different models for this situation are considered in the next two sections.

17.2 PARALLEL-LINE ASSAYS

Suppose that, for a particular assay system, the mean response, y, is linearly related to log dose, x. That is, for a log dose x_S of S, the expected response is

$$E(y) = \alpha + \beta x_S. \quad (17.1)$$

Now, the same expected response would be obtained by a log dose x_T of T, where $x_S - x_T$ = log ρ, the log potency-ratio of T in terms of S.

Consequently the equation of the regression line for T is

$$\left.\begin{aligned} E(y) &= \alpha + \beta(x_T + \log \rho) \\ &= (\alpha + \beta \log \rho) + \beta x_T. \end{aligned}\right\} \quad (17.2)$$

The regression lines (17.1) and (17.2) for S and T respectively are parallel, but differ in position if $\log \rho$ is different from zero (i.e. if ρ is different from 1). The horizontal distance between the two lines is $\log \rho$.

In any one assay, values of y will be observed at various values of x_S for S and at values of x_T for T. The regression relationships (17.1) and (17.2) are estimated by fitting two parallel lines exactly as in section 9.5 (equation (9.33)), giving equations:

$$Y_S = \bar{y}_S + b(x_S - \bar{x}_S) \quad (17.3)$$

and

$$Y_T = \bar{y}_T + b(x_T - \bar{x}_T). \quad (17.4)$$

The estimate, M, of the log potency ratio is the difference $x_S - x_T$ when $Y_S = Y_T$; from (17.3) and (17.4), this gives

$$M = \bar{x}_S - \bar{x}_T - \frac{\bar{y}_S - \bar{y}_T}{b}. \quad (17.5)$$

The position is indicated in Fig. 17.2. The only difference in emphasis from the treatment of the problem in section 9.5 is that in the earlier discussion we were interested in estimating the vertical distance between the parallel lines, whereas now we estimate, from (17.5), the horizontal distance.

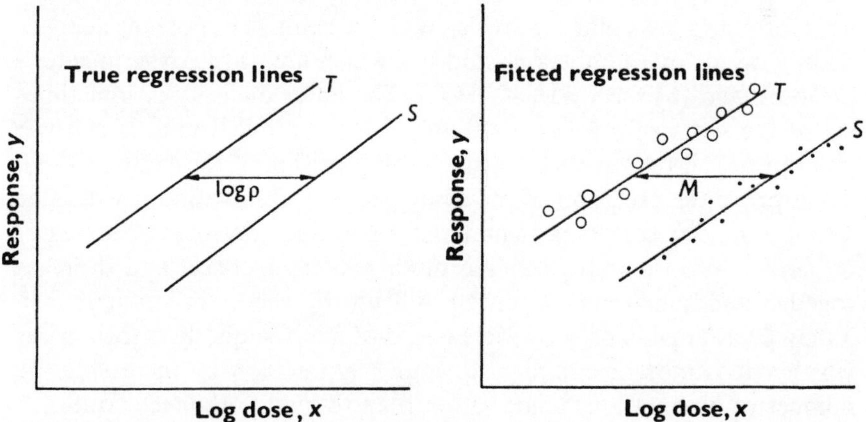

FIG. 17.2 Parallel-line assay. True and fitted regression lines for standard and test preparations.

Note that if the regression is not linear, the two regression curves will still be 'parallel' in the sense that their *horizontal* distance on the log-dose scale will be constant. In general, though, the *vertical* distance will not be constant unless the regression is linear. To achieve linear regression some transformation of the response variable may be necessary. For the analysis described below we assume also that the residual variance about the line is normal and has constant variance. These conditions may be difficult to fulfil simultaneously.

Suppose that there are n_S and n_T observations on S and T respectively, and that the residual MSq about parallel lines (the s_c^2 of (9.36)) is s^2. An approximate formula for var(M) is, from (3.17),

$$\mathrm{var}(M) \simeq \frac{s^2}{b^2}\left\{\frac{1}{n_S}+\frac{1}{n_T}+\frac{(M-\bar{x}_S+\bar{x}_T)^2}{\sum(Sx^2)}\right\}, \tag{17.6}$$

where $\sum(Sx^2)$ is the pooled Within preparations SSq of x. The last term in the curly brackets can also be written, from (17.5), as

$$\frac{(\bar{y}_S-\bar{y}_T)^2}{b^2\sum(Sx^2)},$$

and will be relatively small if the doses of T and S are so chosen that the mean responses $\bar{y}_S$ and $\bar{y}_T$ are nearly equal. (To achieve this one needs either luck or some preliminary estimate of the potency.) To a further degree of approximation, then,

$$\mathrm{var}(M) \simeq \frac{s^2}{b^2}\left(\frac{1}{n_S}+\frac{1}{n_T}\right). \tag{17.7}$$

This formula shows that the precision of the estimate of potency depends mainly on (a) the numbers n_S and n_T, which are at the experimenter's disposal, and (b) the value of $\lambda = s/b$. The latter quantity is sometimes called the *index of precision* (although 'imprecision' would be a better description); it represents the inherent imprecision of the assay method. To improve the precision of the assay per unit observation it would be useful to modify the experimental method so that s decreases, b increases or both. Unfortunately, s and b often tend to increase and decrease together and improvement may be difficult. Furthermore, reductions in λ may be attainable only by increased cost and the question then arises whether it is more economical to improve precision by increasing the number of observations made rather than to modify the technique.

Approximate confidence limits for log ρ may be obtained by setting limits around M, using the t distribution on the DF appropriate for

s^2, n_1+n_2-3. Corresponding limits for ρ are then obtained by taking antilogs. A more exact expression for confidence limits uses a result known as Fieller's theorem. Suppose $100\times(1-2\alpha)$ per cent limits are required. Let $t_{\nu,\,2\alpha}$ be the percentage point of the distribution on $\nu=n_1+n_2-3$ DF and corresponding to a two-sided probability of 2α. The limits are then

$$\bar{x}_S-\bar{x}_T+\frac{M-\bar{x}_S+\bar{x}_T\pm\dfrac{t_{\nu,\,2\alpha}s}{b}\left\{(1-g)\left(\dfrac{1}{n_S}+\dfrac{1}{n_T}\right)+\dfrac{(M-\bar{x}_S+\bar{x}_T)^2}{\sum(Sx^2)}\right\}^{\frac{1}{2}}}{1-g}, \quad (17.8)$$

where

$$g=\frac{t^2_{\nu,\,2\alpha}s^2}{b^2\sum(Sx^2)} \quad (17.9)$$

and $\{\quad\}^{\frac{1}{2}}$ indicates a square root.

The quantity g depends on the significance level of the departure of b from zero. If b is just significant at the 2α level, $g=1$; more highly significant values of b give values of $g<1$. If g is very small, (17.8) becomes close to the limits given by (17.7) using $t_{\nu,\,2\alpha}$ times the standard error of M. A safe rule is to use (17.7) whenever $g<0{\cdot}1$, otherwise to check the adequacy of the approximation by calculating (17.8). If $g>1$, the quantity in curly brackets may be negative and therefore have no real square root; or the limits may not include the estimate M. The method is therefore useful only when the slope of the parallel lines is significant at the level required for the confidence limits.

Example 17.1

Table 9.4 gave the results of a parallel line assay of vitamin D in which two test preparations were compared with the standard. We could generalize the method described above by obtaining a pooled slope from all three preparations. The latter part of Example 9.3 (pp. 287–288) has already shown that differences between slopes are non-significant. However, we restrict attention here to the two preparations, Standard and I. The relevant basic statistics are as follows.

Group	n	$\bar{x}$	y	Sx^2	Sxy	Sy^2	Within dose groups Sy^2
Standard	31	0·8741	2·8710	2·0576	5·3840	58·7339	41·7418
I	30	1·0000	1·8833	5·4361	15·2005	63·8417	20·9583
				7·4937	20·5845	122·5756	62·7001

The Within dose groups Sy^2 was obtained for the Standard in Example 9.2; that for I is obtained likewise. The other SSq and SPr are as in Example 9.3.

TABLE 17.1 Analysis of variance for vitamin D assay, using Standard preparation and Preparation I (data from Table 9.4).

	DF	SSq		MSq	VR
(1) Between dose groups	7	74·7467			
(2) Between preparations	1		14·8712	14·8712	
(3) Common slope	1		56·5437	56·5437	47·80 ($P<0·01$)
(4) Between slopes	1		0·0481	0·0481	<1
(5) Non-linearity	4		3·2837	0·8209	<1
(6) Within dose groups	53	62·7001		1·1830	1·00
(7) Total	60	137·4468			

Before making any potency estimation it is useful to check the validity of the model by the analysis of variance shown in Table 17.1. The SSq for items (1), (2), (6) and (7) are all straightforward. Those for (3) and (4) are obtained as in the latter part of Example 9.3, and that for (5) follows by subtraction. There is clearly no evidence to contradict the assumption of parallel linear regression.

Proceeding with the analysis, the common slope is estimated as

$$b=\frac{20·5845}{7·4937}=2·7469.$$

From (17.5),

$$\begin{aligned}M&=0·8741-1·0000-\frac{2·8710-1·8833}{2·7469}\\&=-0·1259-0·3596\\&=-0·4855.\end{aligned}$$

Writing M as $\bar{1}·5145$, the estimate of potency is

$$\text{antilog } M=0·327,$$

measured in international units per mg. (these being the scales on which doses of S and I are measured). As a rough check we note from Table 9.4 that the doses of 3·5, 7 and 10 i.u. of S give about the same mean responses as 10, 20 and 40 mg. of I, which suggests that I has a potency of about 0·35 i.u. per mg.

In considering the sampling variation of M we need the residual MSq about parallel lines. This is obtained from Table 17.1 as

$$\begin{aligned} s^2 &= \frac{62{\cdot}7001+3{\cdot}2837+0{\cdot}0481}{53+4+1} \\ &= 66{\cdot}0319/58 \\ &= 1{\cdot}1385, \end{aligned}$$

very little different from the Within dose groups MSq in Table 17.1. From (17.9), noting that $t_{58,\cdot05}=2{\cdot}002$,

$$\begin{aligned} g &= \frac{(2{\cdot}002)^2(1{\cdot}1385)}{(2{\cdot}7469)^2(7{\cdot}4937)} \\ &= 0{\cdot}081. \end{aligned}$$

This is sufficiently small to permit the use of the approximate formula (17.6).

$$\begin{aligned} \text{var}(M) &= \frac{1{\cdot}1385}{(2{\cdot}7469)^2}\left\{\frac{1}{31}+\frac{1}{30}+\frac{(0{\cdot}3596)^2}{7{\cdot}4937}\right\} \\ &= (0{\cdot}15089)(0{\cdot}03226+0{\cdot}03333+0{\cdot}01726) \\ &= (0{\cdot}15089)(0{\cdot}08285) \\ &= 0{\cdot}012501, \\ \text{SE}(M) &= \sqrt{0{\cdot}012501} = 0{\cdot}1118. \end{aligned}$$

Approximate 95 per cent confidence limits for log ρ are

$$\begin{aligned} &-0{\cdot}4855 \pm (2{\cdot}002)(0{\cdot}1118) \\ &= -0{\cdot}7093 \quad \text{and} \quad -0{\cdot}2617. \end{aligned}$$

Taking antilogs, the limits for ρ are 0·195 and 0·548 i.u. per mg.

The design used for the assay analysed in Example 17.1, which may be called a 3+5 design since there were 3 doses of the standard and 5 doses of the test preparation, allowed the possibility of testing for departures from parallelism and linearity. Non-linearity can often be corrected by a transformation of the response scale. Non-parallelism when the regressions are apparently linear is more troublesome, and may indicate a basically invalid assay system. Both these types of departure from the model can be tested provided there are sufficient dose levels; a 2+2 design is too small for this purpose, since non-parallelism and non-linearity both affect the same SSq in the analysis. A 2+3 design or a 3+3 design allows the effects to be separated. There is considerable advantage in the use of a completely symmetric design, with the same number of doses in each preparation, the same number of observations at each dose level, and a constant log dose interval throughout. The component parts of the SSq between dose groups, and many of the quantities entering into the calculation of M and its confidence limits, can then be expressed in terms of simple linear contrasts. Examples will be found in Finney (1964), where there is a very detailed account of experimental design in biological assays.

17.3 SLOPE-RATIO ASSAYS

In some assay systems the response, y, can conveniently be related linearly to the dose, rather than to the log dose, the residual variation being approximately normal and having approximately constant variance. This situation arises particularly in microbiological assays where the response is a turbidometric measure of growth of micro-organisms. If the potency of T in terms of S is ρ, the same expected response will be given by doses X_T of T and X_S of S, where $X_S = \rho X_T$. If, therefore, the regression equation of S is

$$E(y) = \alpha + \beta_S X_S, \tag{17.10}$$

that for T will be

$$\begin{aligned} E(y) &= \alpha + \beta_S(\rho X_T) \\ &= \alpha + \beta_T X_T, \end{aligned} \tag{17.11}$$

where $\beta_T = \rho\beta_S$. Equations (17.10) and (17.11) represent two straight lines with the same intercept, α, on the vertical axis and with slopes in the ratio $1 : \rho$. Hence the term *slope-ratio*. The intercept α is the expected response at zero dose, whether of T or of S. The position is shown in Fig. 17.3.

In the analysis of results from a slope ratio assay the observed responses at various doses X_S of S and at doses X_T of T must be fitted by two lines of the form

$$Y = a + b_S X_S \tag{17.12}$$

and

$$Y = a + b_T X_T, \tag{17.13}$$

which are, like the true regression lines, constrained to pass through the same intercept on the vertical axis (Fig. 17.3). This is a form of regression analysis not previously considered in this book. The problem can be conveniently regarded as one of multiple regression. For each observation we consider the values of three variables, y, X_S and X_T, of

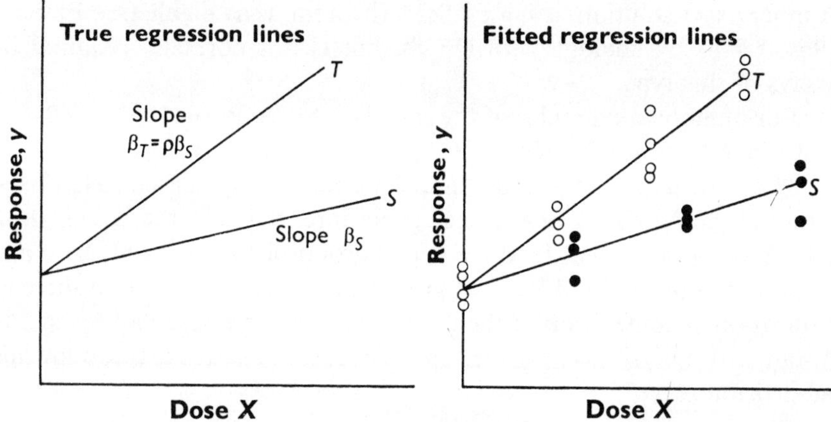

FIG. 17.3 Slope-ratio assay. True and fitted regression lines for standard and test preparations.

which y is the dependent variable and X_S and X_T are predictor variables. For any observation on S, X_S is non-zero and $X_T=0$; for an observation on T, $X_S=0$ and X_T is non-zero. The assay may include control observations (so-called *blanks*) without either S or T; for these, $X_S=X_T=0$. The true regression equations (17.10) and (17.11) can now be combined into one multiple regression equation

$$E(y)=\alpha+\beta_S X_S+\beta_T X_T, \tag{17.14}$$

and the estimated regressions (17.12) and (17.13) are combined in the estimated multiple regression:

$$Y=a+b_S X_S+b_T X_T. \tag{17.15}$$

This relationship can be fitted by standard multiple regression methods, and the potency $\rho(=\beta_T/\beta_S)$ estimated by

$$R=b_T/b_S. \tag{17.16}$$

The residual variance of y is estimated by the usual residual MSq, s^2, and the variances and covariances of b_S and b_T are obtained from (10.21) and (10.22). Write v_{jh} instead of the c_{jh} of (10.21) and (10.22), so that

$$\text{var}(b_S)=v_{11}s^2,\ \text{var}(b_T)=v_{22}s^2,\ \text{covar}(b_S, b_T)=v_{12}s^2.$$

Approximate confidence limits for ρ are obtained by the following formula derived from (3.17):

$$\text{var}(R)=\frac{s^2}{b_S^2}(v_{22}-2Rv_{12}+R^2v_{11}). \tag{17.17}$$

A more exact solution, using Fieller's theorem, is available (see Finney, 1964, § 7.6) by analogy with (17.8), but is not normally required in assays of this type.

For numerical examples of the calculations see Burn (1952, §§ 60–67) and Finney (1964, Chapter 7).

The adequacy of the model in a slope-ratio assay can be tested by a rather elegant analysis of variance procedure. Suppose the design is of a $1+k_S+k_T$ type; that is, there is one group of 'blanks' and there are k_S dose groups of S and k_T dose groups of T. Suppose also that there is replication at some or all of the dose levels, giving n observations in all. A standard analysis (as described on pages 315–316) leads to the following subdivision of DF:

Between dose groups	k_S+k_T	
Regression		2
Deviations from model		k_S+k_T-2
Within dose groups	$n-k_S-k_T-1$	
Total	$n-1$	

The SSq for deviations from the model can be subdivided into the following parts:

Blanks	1
Intersection	1
Non-linearity for non-zero doses	k_S+k_T-4
	k_S+k_T-2

The SSq for 'blanks' indicates whether the 'blanks' observations are sufficiently consistent with the remainder. It can be obtained by re-fitting the multiple regression with an extra dummy variable (1 for 'blanks', 0 otherwise), and noting the reduction in the Deviations SSq. A significant variance-ratio test for 'blanks' might indicate non-linearity for very low doses; if the remaining tests were satisfactory the assay could still be analysed adequately by omitting the 'blanks'.

The SSq for 'intersection' shows whether the data can justifiably be fitted by two lines intersecting on the vertical axis. Significance here is more serious and usually indicates invalidity of the assay system. It can be obtained by fitting two separate lines to the observations at non-zero doses of S and to those at non-zero doses of T. The difference in residual between this analysis and that referred to above (for the 'blanks' test) gives the required SSq.

The third component, due to non-linearity at non-zero doses, can be obtained either by subtraction or directly from the two separate regressions (k_S-2 DF for S and k_T-2 for T add to the required k_S+k_T-4).

Further details, with examples, will be found in Finney (1964, Chapter 7) which also discusses the use of symmetric designs which permit simplification of the analysis by the use of linear contrasts.

17.4 QUANTAL RESPONSE ASSAYS

Frequently the response is quantal, as in direct assays, yet the assay has to be done indirectly by selection of doses and observation of the responses elicited. If a particular dose of one preparation is applied to n_i experimental units, the investigator observes that a certain number of responses, say r_i, are positive and n_i-r_i are negative. Examples of assays yielding this type of response are as follows:

Pyrethrin, the response being death in house flies;

Insulin, the response being presence of convulsions in mice;

Virus preparations, the response being presence of viral growth in egg membranes.

For any one preparation the response curve relating the expected response (expressed as the probability of a positive response) to the dose or to the log dose is likely to be sigmoid in shape, as described in section 11.4. Indeed, the fitting of the response curve for one preparation presents precisely the problem considered in section 12.5 and, as we shall see, the methods described there are immediately applicable.

A further point is worth noting. The response curve, rising from 0 to 1 on the vertical scale, may be regarded as the cumulative distribution function of a random variable which can be called the *tolerance* of experimental units to the agent under test. The tolerances are precisely the critical doses which would be observed in a direct assay. If, for example, a dose X corresponds to a response P, we can interpret this as showing that a proportion P of the animals have a tolerance less than X (and therefore succumb to X), and $1-P$ have a tolerance greater than X. The response function P is thus the distribution function of tolerance; the corresponding density function is called the *tolerance distribution*; see Fig. 17.4. A very similar situation holds in psychological tests of the stimulus-response type. An individual given a stimulus X will respond if his threshold (corresponding to the tolerance in biological assay) is less than X. Neither in the psychological example nor in biological

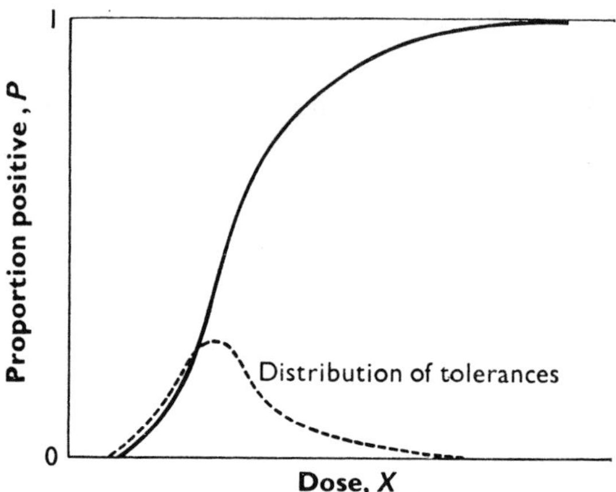

FIG. 17.4 Quantal response curve with the corresponding tolerance distribution.

assay is there any need to suppose that X is a constant quantity for any individual; it may vary considerably from occasion to occasion in the same individual.

In an assay of T and S, the response curves, plotted against $x = \log X$, will be parallel in the sense that they differ by a constant horizontal distance, $\log \rho$, and a full analysis requires that the data be fitted by two parallel curves of this sort (Fig. 17.5). A natural approach is to linearize the response curves by applying to the response one of the transformations described in sections 11.4 and 12.5. Using the logit transformation,

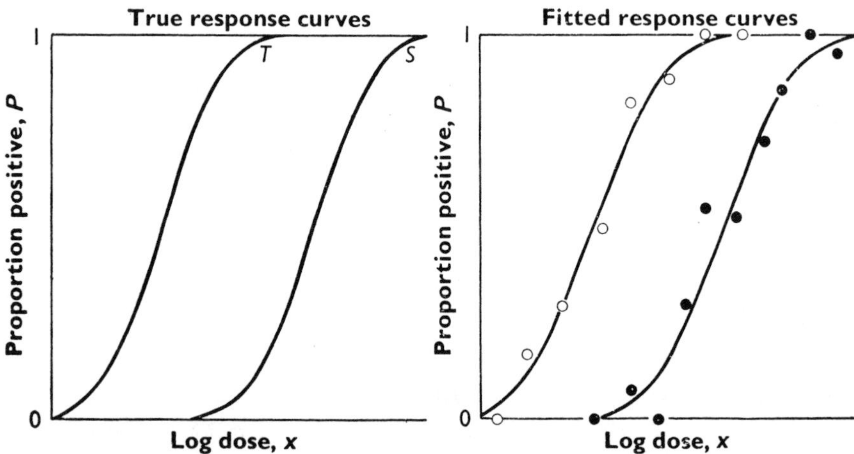

FIG. 17.5 Quantal response assay. True and fitted response curves for standard and test preparations.

for example, one could suppose that Y, the logit of P, is linearly related to the log dose, x, by the equations

$$\left.\begin{aligned} Y &= \alpha_S + \beta x \quad \text{for } S \\ \text{and} \qquad & \\ Y &= \alpha_T + \beta x \quad \text{for } T. \end{aligned}\right\} \tag{17.18}$$

The relationships (17.18) could be fitted iteratively by the maximum likelihood procedure described in section 12.5, using a dummy variable to distinguish between S and T, as in section 10.4. Alternatively, and more simply, they can be treated as simple regression relationships; an iterative procedure like that of section 12.5 is followed, but in the regression-like calculations at each stage of the iteration the standard method of fitting parallel lines (section 9.4) is used.

The use of the logistic transformation in biological assay has been strongly advocated by J.Berkson who favours non-iterative curve-fitting by the use of empirical weights (Berkson, 1944). The maximum likelihood calculations for the *probit* transformation are fully described, with examples, by Finney (1952), and this method, called *probit analysis*, is perhaps more widely used in biological assay than the corresponding logit method. There is no evidence to suggest that either model is more consistent with real data than the other, and curves fitted by the two methods are invariably very similar indeed.

Another group of short-cut methods for the analysis of quantal response assays relies effectively on attempts to measure the horizontal distance between the two log-dose response curves without estimating the entire curves. The position of either of the curves in the first diagram of Fig. 17.5 can be summarized by the dose at which $P = 0{\cdot}5$. This is called the ED50 (ED standing for 'effective dose') or median effective dose; it is clearly the median of the underlying tolerance distribution. Now the ED50's for T and S are in the ratio $1 : \rho$. If they were estimated by X_{0T} and X_{0S}, the ratio X_{0S}/X_{0T} would provide an estimate of ρ; equivalently, the quantity

$$M = \log X_{0S} - \log X_{0T}$$

would estimate $\log \rho$.

The ED50 is sometimes given slightly different names according to the type of response: LD50 or median lethal dose if the response is lethal; ImD50 if the response is the proportion of animals protected by an immunizing agent from a challenge dose of virulent organisms, and so on. It can often be estimated roughly by eye from a plot of the observed responses, but a subjective estimation of this sort suffers from its lack of reproducibility, even on the same data, and has the further disadvantage that an adequate estimate of sampling error is virtually unobtainable. Several simple objective methods of estimating the ED50 have become widely used, the best of which are probably the Spearman-Kärber method and Thompson's moving average method. For a detailed description of these and other short-cut methods, with a discussion of their merits, see Finney (1964, chapter 20). It is an interesting illustration of the interconnections between statistical methods that one of the last techniques to receive mention in this book, the Spearman-Kärber method, is closely related to one of the most elementary techniques—the calculation of a mean from a frequency distribution. Equally, it is indicative of the persistence and ubiquity of statistical problems that this method, which was described by C.Spearman, a psychologist, in 1908 (and attributed by him to the German psychologist, G.E.Müller), was rediscovered by G.Kärber, a pharmacologist, in 1931 (and no doubt by many others since then), and is still the object of attention by theoretical statisticians.

APPENDIX TABLES

TABLE A1 AREAS IN TAIL OF THE NORMAL DISTRIBUTION

Single-tail areas in terms of standardized deviates

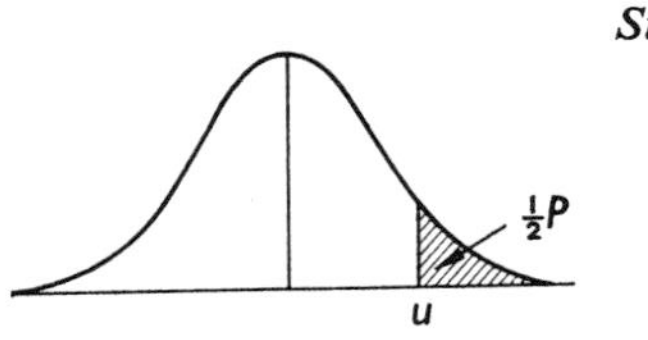

The function tabulated is $\frac{1}{2}P$, the probability of obtaining a standardized normal deviate greater than u, *in one direction*. The two-tail probability, P, is twice the tabulated value.

u	0·00	0·01	0·02	0·03	0·04	0·05	0·06	0·07	0·08	0·09
0·0	0·5000	0·4960	0·4920	0·4880	0·4840	0·4801	0·4761	0·4721	0·4681	0·4641
0·1	0·4602	0·4562	0·4522	0·4483	0·4443	0·4404	0·4364	0·4325	0·4286	0·4247
0·2	0·4207	0·4168	0·4129	0·4090	0·4052	0·4013	0·3974	0·3936	0·3897	0·3859
0·3	0·3821	0·3783	0·3745	0·3707	0·3669	0·3632	0·3594	0·3557	0·3520	0·3483
0·4	0·3446	0·3409	0·3372	0·3336	0·3300	0·3264	0·3228	0·3192	0·3156	0·3121
0·5	0·3085	0·3050	0·3015	0·2981	0·2946	0·2912	0·2877	0·2843	0·2810	0·2776
0·6	0·2743	0·2709	0·2676	0·2643	0·2611	0·2578	0·2546	0·2514	0·2483	0·2451
0·7	0·2420	0·2389	0·2358	0·2327	0·2296	0·2266	0·2236	0·2206	0·2177	0·2148
0·8	0·2119	0·2090	0·2061	0·2033	0·2005	0·1977	0·1949	0·1922	0·1894	0·1867
0·9	0·1841	0·1814	0·1788	0·1762	0·1736	0·1711	0·1685	0·1660	0·1635	0·1611
1·0	0·1587	0·1562	0·1539	0·1515	0·1492	0·1469	0·1446	0·1423	0·1401	0·1379
1·1	0·1357	0·1335	0·1314	0·1292	0·1271	0·1251	0·1230	0·1210	0·1190	0·1170
1·2	0·1151	0·1131	0·1112	0·1093	0·1075	0·1056	0·1038	0·1020	0·1003	0·0985
1·3	0·0968	0·0951	0·0934	0·0918	0·0901	0·0885	0·0869	0·0853	0·0838	0·0823
1·4	0·0808	0·0793	0·0778	0·0764	0·0749	0·0735	0·0721	0·0708	0·0694	0·0681

1·5	0·0668	0·0655	0·0643	0·0630	0·0618	0·0606	0·0594	0·0582	0·0571	0·0559
1·6	0·0548	0·0537	0·0526	0·0516	0·0505	0·0495	0·0485	0·0475	0·0465	0·0455
1·7	0·0446	0·0436	0·0427	0·0418	0·0409	0·0401	0·0392	0·0384	0·0375	0·0367
1·8	0·0359	0·0351	0·0344	0·0336	0·0329	0·0322	0·0314	0·0307	0·0301	0·0294
1·9	0·0287	0·0281	0·0274	0·0268	0·0262	0·0256	0·0250	0·0244	0·0239	0·0233
2·0	0·02275	0·02222	0·02169	0·02118	0·02068	0·02018	0·01970	0·01923	0·01876	0·01831
2·1	0·01786	0·01743	0·01700	0·01659	0·01618	0·01578	0·01539	0·01500	0·01463	0·01426
2·2	0·01390	0·01355	0·01321	0·01287	0·01255	0·01222	0·01191	0·01160	0·01130	0·01101
2·3	0·01072	0·01044	0·01017	0·00990	0·00964	0·00939	0·00914	0·00889	0·00866	0·00842
2·4	0·00820	0·00798	0·00776	0·00755	0·00734	0·00714	0·00695	0·00676	0·00657	0·00639
2·5	0·00621	0·00604	0·00587	0·00570	0·00554	0·00539	0·00523	0·00508	0·00494	0·00480
2·6	0·00466	0·00453	0·00440	0·00427	0·00415	0·00402	0·00391	0·00379	0·00368	0·00357
2·7	0·00347	0·00336	0·00326	0·00317	0·00307	0·00298	0·00289	0·00280	0·00272	0·00264
2·8	0·00256	0·00248	0·00240	0·00233	0·00226	0·00219	0·00212	0·00205	0·00199	0·00193
2·9	0·00187	0·00181	0·00175	0·00169	0·00164	0·00159	0·00154	0·00149	0·00144	0·00139
3·0	0·00135									
3·1	0·00097									
3·2	0·00069									
3·3	0·00048									
3·4	0·00034									
3·5	0·00023									
3·6	0·00016									
3·7	0·00011									
3·8	0·00007									
3·9	0·00005									
4·0	0·00003									

Standardized deviates in terms of two-tail areas

P	1·0	0·9	0·8	0·7	0·6	0·5	0·4
u	0	0·126	0·253	0·385	0·524	0·674	0·842
P	0·3	0·2	0·1	0·05	0·02	0·01	0·001
u	1·036	1·282	1·645	1·960	2·326	2·576	3·291

Reproduced in part from Table 3 of Murdoch and Barnes (1968) by permission of the authors and publishers.

TABLE A2 PERCENTAGE POINTS OF THE χ^2 DISTRIBUTION

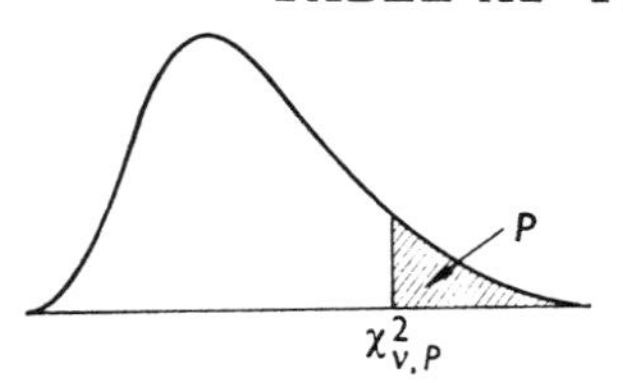

The function tabulated is $\chi^2_{\nu,\,P}$, the value exceeded with probability P in a χ^2 distribution with ν degrees of freedom (the $100P$ percentage point).

Degrees of freedom, ν	Probability of a greater value, P 0·975	0·900	0·750	0·500	0·250	0·100	0·050	0·025	0·010	0·001
1	—	0·02	0·10	0·45	1·32	2·71	3·84	5·02	6·63	10·83
2	0·05	0·21	0·58	1·39	2·77	4·61	5·99	7·38	9·21	13·82
3	0·22	0·58	1·21	2·37	4·11	6·25	7·81	9·35	11·34	16·27
4	0·48	1·06	1·92	3·36	5·39	7·78	9·49	11·14	13·28	18·47
5	0·83	1·61	2·67	4·35	6·63	9·24	11·07	12·83	15·09	20·52
6	1·24	2·20	3·45	5·35	7·84	10·64	12·59	14·45	16·81	22·46
7	1·69	2·83	4·25	6·35	9·04	12·02	14·07	16·01	18·48	24·32
8	2·18	3·49	5·07	7·34	10·22	13·36	15·51	17·53	20·09	26·12
9	2·70	4·17	5·90	8·34	11·39	14·68	16·92	19·02	21·67	27·88
10	3·25	4·87	6·74	9·34	12·55	15·99	18·31	20·48	23·21	29·59
11	3·82	5·58	7·58	10·34	13·70	17·28	19·68	21·92	24·72	31·26
12	4·40	6·30	8·44	11·34	14·85	18·55	21·03	23·34	26·22	32·91
13	5·01	7·04	9·30	12·34	15·98	19·81	22·36	24·74	27·69	34·53
14	5·63	7·79	10·17	13·34	17·12	21·06	23·68	26·12	29·14	36·12
15	6·27	8·55	11·04	14·34	18·25	22·31	25·00	27·49	30·58	37·70

16	6·91	9·31	11·91	15·34	19·37	23·54	26·30	28·85	32·00	39·25
17	7·56	10·09	12·79	16·34	20·49	24·77	27·59	30·19	33·41	40·79
18	8·23	10·86	13·68	17·34	21·60	25·99	28·87	31·53	34·81	42·31
19	8·91	11·65	14·56	18·34	22·72	27·20	30·14	32·85	36·19	43·82
20	9·59	12·44	15·45	19·34	23·83	28·41	31·41	34·17	37·57	45·32
21	10·28	13·24	16·34	20·34	24·93	29·62	32·67	35·48	38·93	46·80
22	10·98	14·04	17·24	21·34	26·04	30·81	33·92	36·78	40·29	48·27
23	11·69	14·85	18·14	22·34	27·14	32·01	35·17	38·08	41·64	49·73
24	12·40	15·66	19·04	23·34	28·24	33·20	36·42	39·36	42·98	51·18
25	13·12	16·47	19·94	24·34	29·34	34·38	37·65	40·65	44·31	52·62
26	13·84	17·29	20·84	25·34	30·43	35·56	38·89	41·92	45·64	54·05
27	14·57	18·11	21·75	26·34	31·53	36·74	40·11	43·19	46·96	55·48
28	15·31	18·94	22·66	27·34	32·62	37·92	41·34	44·46	48·28	56·89
29	16·05	19·77	23·57	28·34	33·71	39·09	42·56	45·72	49·59	58·30
30	16·79	20·60	24·48	29·34	34·80	40·26	43·77	46·98	50·89	59·70
40	24·43	29·05	33·66	39·34	45·62	51·80	55·76	59·34	63·69	73·40
50	32·36	37·69	42·94	49·33	56·33	63·17	67·50	71·42	76·15	86·66
60	40·48	46·46	52·29	59·33	66·98	74·40	79·08	83·30	88·38	99·61
70	48·76	55·33	61·70	69·33	77·58	85·53	90·53	95·02	100·42	112·32
80	57·15	64·28	71·14	79·33	88·13	96·58	101·88	106·63	112·33	124·84
90	65·65	73·29	80·62	89·33	98·64	107·56	113·14	118·14	124·12	137·21
100	74·22	82·36	90·13	99·33	109·14	118·50	124·34	129·56	135·81	149·45

Condensed from Table 8 of Pearson and Hartley (1966) by permission of the authors and publishers.

TABLE A3 PERCENTAGE POINTS OF THE *t* DISTRIBUTION

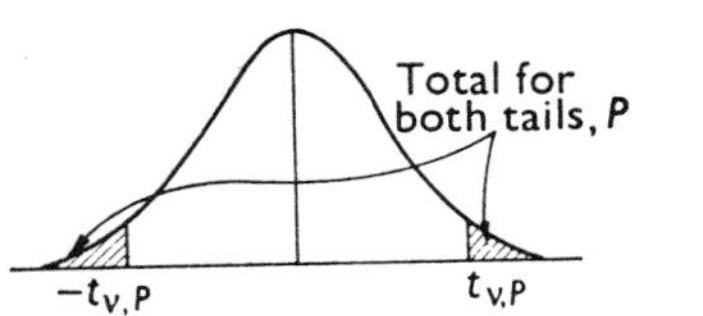

The function tabulated is $t_{\nu,P}$, the value exceeded in both directions with probability P in a t distribution with ν degrees of freedom (the $100P$ percentage point).

Degrees of freedom, ν	Probability of greater value, P												
	0·9	0·8	0·7	0·6	0·5	0·4	0·3	0·2	0·1	0·05	0·02	0·01	0·001
1	0·158	0·325	0·510	0·727	1·000	1·376	1·963	3·078	6·314	12·706	31·821	63·657	636·619
2	0·142	0·289	0·445	0·617	0·816	1·061	1·386	1·886	2·920	4·303	6·965	9·925	31·598
3	0·137	0·277	0·424	0·584	0·765	0·978	1·250	1·638	2·353	3·182	4·541	5·841	12·924
4	0·134	0·271	0·414	0·569	0·741	0·941	1·190	1·533	2·132	2·776	3·747	4·604	8·610
5	0·132	0·267	0·408	0·559	0·727	0·920	1·156	1·476	2·015	2·571	3·365	4·032	6·869
6	0·131	0·265	0·404	0·553	0·718	0·906	1·134	1·440	1·943	2·447	3·143	3·707	5·959
7	0·130	0·263	0·402	0·549	0·711	0·896	1·119	1·415	1·895	2·365	2·998	3·499	5·408
8	0·130	0·262	0·399	0·546	0·706	0·889	1·108	1·397	1·860	2·306	2·896	3·355	5·041
9	0·129	0·261	0·398	0·543	0·703	0·883	1·100	1·383	1·833	2·262	2·821	3·250	4·781
10	0·129	0·260	0·397	0·542	0·700	0·879	1·093	1·372	1·812	2·228	2·764	3·169	4·587
11	0·129	0·260	0·396	0·540	0·697	0·876	1·088	1·363	1·796	2·201	2·718	3·106	4·437
12	0·128	0·259	0·395	0·539	0·695	0·873	1·083	1·356	1·782	2·179	2·681	3·055	4·318
13	0·128	0·259	0·394	0·538	0·694	0·870	1·079	1·350	1·771	2·160	2·650	3·012	4·221
14	0·128	0·258	0·393	0·537	0·692	0·868	1·076	1·345	1·761	2·145	2·624	2·977	4·140
15	0·128	0·258	0·393	0·536	0·691	0·866	1·074	1·341	1·753	2·131	2·602	2·947	4·073

16	0·128	0·258	0·392	0·535	0·690	0·865	1·071	1·337	1·746	2·120	2·583	2·921	4·015
17	0·128	0·257	0·392	0·534	0·689	0·863	1·069	1·333	1·740	2·110	2·567	2·898	3·965
18	0·127	0·257	0·392	0·534	0·688	0·862	1·067	1·330	1·734	2·101	2·552	2·878	3·922
19	0·127	0·257	0·391	0·533	0·688	0·861	1·066	1·328	1·729	2·093	2·539	2·861	3·883
20	0·127	0·257	0·391	0·533	0·687	0·860	1·064	1·325	1·725	2·086	2·528	2·845	3·850
21	0·127	0·257	0·391	0·532	0·686	0·859	1·063	1·323	1·721	2·080	2·518	2·831	3·819
22	0·127	0·256	0·390	0·532	0·686	0·858	1·061	1·321	1·717	2·074	2·508	2·819	3·792
23	0·127	0·256	0·390	0·532	0·685	0·858	1·060	1·319	1·714	2·069	2·500	2·807	3·767
24	0·127	0·256	0·390	0·531	0·685	0·857	1·059	1·318	1·711	2·064	2·492	2·797	3·745
25	0·127	0·256	0·390	0·531	0·684	0·856	1·058	1·316	1·708	2·060	2·485	2·787	3·725
26	0·127	0·256	0·390	0·531	0·684	0·856	1·058	1·315	1·706	2·056	2·479	2·779	3·707
27	0·127	0·256	0·389	0·531	0·684	0·855	1·057	1·314	1·703	2·052	2·473	2·771	3·690
28	0·127	0·256	0·389	0·530	0·683	0·855	1·056	1·313	1·701	2·048	2·467	2·763	3·674
29	0·127	0·256	0·389	0·530	0·683	0·854	1·055	1·311	1·699	2·045	2·462	2·756	3·659
30	0·127	0·256	0·389	0·530	0·683	0·854	1·055	1·310	1·697	2·042	2·457	2·750	3·646
40	0·126	0·255	0·388	0·529	0·681	0·851	1·050	1·303	1·684	2·021	2·423	2·704	3·551
60	0·126	0·254	0·387	0·527	0·679	0·848	1·046	1·296	1·671	2·000	2·390	2·660	3·460
120	0·126	0·254	0·386	0·526	0·677	0·845	1·041	1·289	1·658	1·980	2·358	2·617	3·373
∞	0·126	0·253	0·385	0·524	0·674	0·842	1·036	1·282	1·645	1·960	2·326	2·576	3·291

Reproduced from Table III of Fisher and Yates (1963) by permission of the authors and publishers.

TABLE A4 PERCENTAGE POINTS OF THE F DISTRIBUTION: $P = 0\cdot05,\ 0\cdot025,\ 0\cdot01,\ 0\cdot005$

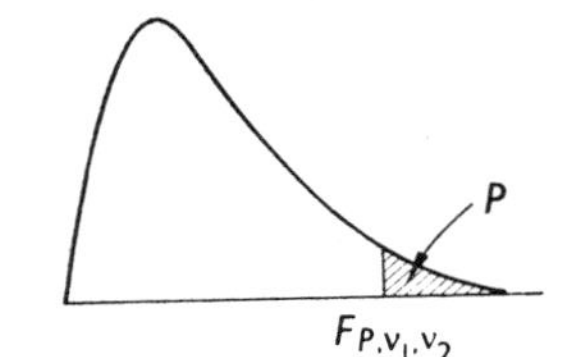

The function tabulated is F_{P,ν_1,ν_2}, the value exceeded with probability P in the F distribution with ν_1 degrees of freedom for the numerator and ν_2 degrees of freedom for the denominator (the 100P percentage point). The values for $P=0\cdot05$ and $0\cdot01$ are shown in bold type.

DF for denominator, ν_2	P	DF for numerator, ν_1: 1	2	3	4	5	6	7	8	12	24	∞
1	*0·05*	**161·4**	**199·5**	**215·7**	**224·6**	**230·2**	**234·0**	**236·8**	**238·9**	**243·9**	**249·1**	**254·3**
	0·025	647·8	799·5	864·2	899·6	921·8	937·1	948·2	956·7	976·7	997·2	1018
	0·01	**4052**	**5000**	**5403**	**5625**	**5764**	**5859**	**5928**	**5981**	**6106**	**6235**	**6366**
	0·005	16211	20000	21615	22500	23056	23437	23715	23925	24426	24940	25465
2		**18·51**	**19·00**	**19·16**	**19·25**	**19·30**	**19·33**	**19·35**	**19·37**	**19·41**	**19·45**	**19·50**
		38·51	39·00	39·17	39·25	39·30	39·33	39·36	39·37	39·41	39·46	39·50
		98·50	**99·00**	**99·17**	**99·25**	**99·30**	**99·33**	**99·36**	**99·37**	**99·42**	**99·46**	**99·50**
		198·5	199·0	199·2	199·2	199·3	199·3	199·4	199·4	199·4	199·5	199·5
3		**10·13**	**9·55**	**9·28**	**9·12**	**9·01**	**8·94**	**8·89**	**8·85**	**8·74**	**8·64**	**8·53**
		17·44	16·04	15·44	15·10	14·88	14·73	14·62	14·54	14·34	14·12	13·90
		34·12	**30·82**	**29·46**	**28·71**	**28·24**	**27·91**	**27·67**	**27·49**	**27·05**	**26·60**	**26·13**
		55·55	49·80	47·47	46·19	45·39	44·84	44·43	44·13	43·39	42·62	41·83
4		**7·71**	**6·94**	**6·59**	**6·39**	**6·26**	**6·16**	**6·09**	**6·04**	**5·91**	**5·77**	**5·63**
		12·22	10·65	9·98	9·60	9·36	9·20	9·07	8·98	8·75	8·51	8·26
		21·20	**18·00**	**16·69**	**15·98**	**15·52**	**15·21**	**14·98**	**14·80**	**14·37**	**13·93**	**13·46**
		31·33	26·28	24·26	23·15	22·46	21·97	21·62	21·35	20·70	20·03	19·32

5	**6·61**	**5·79**	**5·41**	**5·19**	**5·05**	**4·95**	**4·88**	**4·82**	**4·68**	**4·53**	**4·36**
	10·01	8·43	7·76	7·39	7·15	6·98	6·85	6·76	6·52	6·28	6·02
	16·26	**13·27**	**12·06**	**11·39**	**10·97**	**10·67**	**10·46**	**10·29**	**9·89**	**9·47**	**9·02**
	22·78	18·31	16·53	15·56	14·94	14·51	14·20	13·96	13·38	12·78	12·14
6	**5·99**	**5·14**	**4·76**	**4·53**	**4·39**	**4·28**	**4·21**	**4·15**	**4·00**	**3·84**	**3·67**
	8·81	7·26	6·60	6·23	5·99	5·82	5·70	5·60	5·37	5·12	4·85
	13·75	**10·92**	**9·78**	**9·15**	**8·75**	**8·47**	**8·26**	**8·10**	**7·72**	**7·31**	**6·88**
	18·63	14·54	12·92	12·03	11·46	11·07	10·79	10·57	10·03	9·47	8·88
7	**5·59**	**4·74**	**4·35**	**4·12**	**3·97**	**3·87**	**3·79**	**3·73**	**3·57**	**3·41**	**3·23**
	8·07	6·54	5·89	5·52	5·29	5·12	4·99	4·90	4·67	4·42	4·14
	12·25	**9·55**	**8·45**	**7·85**	**7·46**	**7·19**	**6·99**	**6·84**	**6·47**	**6·07**	**5·65**
	16·24	12·40	10·88	10·05	9·52	9·16	8·89	8·68	8·18	7·65	7·08
8	**5·32**	**4·46**	**4·07**	**3·84**	**3·69**	**3·58**	**3·50**	**3·44**	**3·28**	**3·12**	**2·93**
	7·57	6·06	5·42	5·05	4·82	4·65	4·53	4·43	4·20	3·95	3·67
	11·26	**8·65**	**7·59**	**7·01**	**6·63**	**6·37**	**6·18**	**6·03**	**5·67**	**5·28**	**4·86**
	14·69	11·04	9·60	8·81	8·30	7·95	7·69	7·50	7·01	6·50	5·95
9	**5·12**	**4·26**	**3·86**	**3·63**	**3·48**	**3·37**	**3·29**	**3·23**	**3·07**	**2·90**	**2·71**
	7·21	5·71	5·08	4·72	4·48	4·32	4·20	4·10	3·87	3·61	3·33
	10·56	**8·02**	**6·99**	**6·42**	**6·06**	**5·80**	**5·61**	**5·47**	**5·11**	**4·73**	**4·31**
	13·61	10·11	8·72	7·96	7·47	7·13	6·88	6·69	6·23	5·73	5·19
10	**4·96**	**4·10**	**3·71**	**3·48**	**3·33**	**3·22**	**3·14**	**3·07**	**2·91**	**2·74**	**2·54**
	6·94	5·46	4·83	4·47	4·24	4·07	3·95	3·85	3·62	3·37	3·08
	10·04	**7·56**	**6·55**	**5·99**	**5·64**	**5·39**	**5·20**	**5·06**	**4·71**	**4·33**	**3·91**
	12·83	9·43	8·08	7·34	6·87	6·54	6·30	6·12	5·66	5·17	4·64

TABLE A4 (*contd.*)

DF for denominator, ν_2	*P*	DF for numerator, ν_1										
		1	2	3	4	5	6	7	8	12	24	∞
12	*0·05*	**4·75**	**3·89**	**3·49**	**3·26**	**3·11**	**3·00**	**2·91**	**2·85**	**2·69**	**2·51**	**2·30**
	0·025	6·55	5·10	4·47	4·12	3·89	3·73	3·61	3·51	3·28	3·02	2·72
	0·01	**9·33**	**6·93**	**5·95**	**5·41**	**5·06**	**4·82**	**4·64**	**4·50**	**4·16**	**3·78**	**3·36**
	0·005	11·75	8·51	7·23	6·52	6·07	5·76	5·52	5·35	4·91	4·43	3·90
14		**4·60**	**3·74**	**3·34**	**3·11**	**2·96**	**2·85**	**2·76**	**2·70**	**2·53**	**2·35**	**2·13**
		6·30	4·86	4·24	3·89	3·66	3·50	3·38	3·29	3·05	2·79	2·49
		8·86	**6·51**	**5·56**	**5·04**	**4·69**	**4·46**	**4·28**	**4·14**	**3·80**	**3·43**	**3·00**
		11·06	7·92	6·68	6·00	5·56	5·26	5·03	4·86	4·43	3·96	3·44
16		**4·49**	**3·63**	**3·24**	**3·01**	**2·85**	**2·74**	**2·66**	**2·59**	**2·42**	**2·24**	**2·01**
		6·12	4·69	4·08	3·73	3·50	3·34	3·22	3·12	2·89	2·63	2·32
		8·53	**6·23**	**5·29**	**4·77**	**4·44**	**4·20**	**4·03**	**3·89**	**3·55**	**3·18**	**2·75**
		10·58	7·51	6·30	5·64	5·21	4·91	4·69	4·52	4·10	3·64	3·11
18		**4·41**	**3·55**	**3·16**	**2·93**	**2·77**	**2·66**	**2·58**	**2·51**	**2·34**	**2·15**	**1·92**
		5·98	4·56	3·95	3·61	3·38	3·22	3·10	3·01	2·77	2·50	2·19
		8·29	**6·01**	**5·09**	**4·58**	**4·25**	**4·01**	**3·84**	**3·71**	**3·37**	**3·00**	**2·57**
		10·22	7·21	6·03	5·37	4·96	4·66	4·44	4·28	3·86	3·40	2·87
20		**4·35**	**3·49**	**3·10**	**2·87**	**2·71**	**2·60**	**2·51**	**2·45**	**2·28**	**2·08**	**1·84**
		5·87	4·46	3·86	3·51	3·29	3·13	3·01	2·91	2·68	2·41	2·09
		8·10	**5·85**	**4·94**	**4·43**	**4·10**	**3·87**	**3·70**	**3·56**	**3·23**	**2·86**	**2·42**
		9·94	6·99	5·82	5·17	4·76	4·47	4·26	4·09	3·68	3·22	2·69

30	**4·17**	**3·32**	**2·92**	**2·69**	**2·53**	**2·42**	**2·33**	**2·27**	**2·09**	**1·89**	**1·62**
	5·57	4·18	3·59	3·25	3·03	2·87	2·75	2·65	2·41	2·14	1·79
	7·56	**5·39**	**4·51**	**4·02**	**3·70**	**3·47**	**3·30**	**3·17**	**2·84**	**2·47**	**2·01**
	9·18	6·35	5·24	4·62	4·23	3·95	3·74	3·58	3·18	2·73	2·18
40	**4·08**	**3·23**	**2·84**	**2·61**	**2·45**	**2·34**	**2·25**	**2·18**	**2·00**	**1·79**	**1·51**
	5·42	4·05	3·46	3·13	2·90	2·74	2·62	2·53	2·29	2·01	1·64
	7·31	**5·18**	**4·31**	**3·83**	**3·51**	**3·29**	**3·12**	**2·99**	**2·66**	**2·29**	**1·80**
	8·83	6·07	4·98	4·37	3·99	3·71	3·51	3·35	2·95	2·50	1·93
60	**4·00**	**3·15**	**2·76**	**2·53**	**2·37**	**2·25**	**2·17**	**2·10**	**1·92**	**1·70**	**1·39**
	5·29	3·93	3·34	3·01	2·79	2·63	2·51	2·41	2·17	1·88	1·48
	7·08	**4·98**	**4·13**	**3·65**	**3·34**	**3·12**	**2·95**	**2·82**	**2·50**	**2·12**	**1·60**
	8·49	5·79	4·73	4·14	3·76	3·49	3·29	3·13	2·74	2·29	1·69
120	**3·92**	**3·07**	**2·68**	**2·45**	**2·29**	**2·17**	**2·09**	**2·02**	**1·83**	**1·61**	**1·25**
	5·15	3·80	3·23	2·89	2·67	2·52	2·39	2·30	2·05	1·76	1·31
	6·85	**4·79**	**3·95**	**3·48**	**3·17**	**2·96**	**2·79**	**2·66**	**2·34**	**1·95**	**1·38**
	8·18	5·54	4·50	3·92	3·55	3·28	3·09	2·93	2·54	2·09	1·43
∞	**3·84**	**3·00**	**2·60**	**2·37**	**2·21**	**2·10**	**2·01**	**1·94**	**1·75**	**1·52**	**1·00**
	5·02	3·69	3·12	2·79	2·57	2·41	2·29	2·19	1·94	1·64	1·00
	6·63	**4·61**	**3·78**	**3·32**	**3·02**	**2·80**	**2·64**	**2·51**	**2·18**	**1·79**	**1·00**
	7·88	5·30	4·28	3·72	3·35	3·09	2·90	2·74	2·36	1·90	1·00

Condensed from Table 18 of Pearson and Hartley (1966) by permission of the authors and publishers.

TABLE A5 PERCENTAGE POINTS OF THE DISTRIBUTION OF STUDENTIZED RANGE: $\alpha = 0\cdot05,\ 0\cdot01$

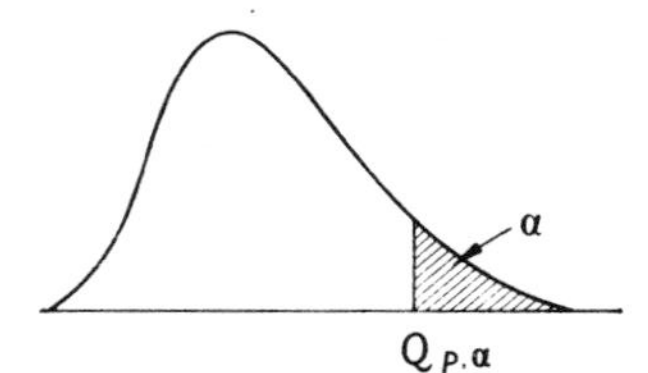

The function tabulated is $Q_{p,\,\alpha}$, the value exceeded with probability α in the distribution of studentized range, for p groups and f_2 DF within groups (the 100α percentage point). The values for $\alpha = 0\cdot05$ are shown in bold type.

	Number of groups, p								
f_2	2	3	4	5	6	7	8	9	10
5	**3·64** 5·70	**4·60** 6·98	**5·22** 7·80	**5·67** 8·42	**6·03** 8·91	**6·33** 9·32	**6·58** 9·67	**6·80** 9·97	**6·99** 10·24
6	**3·46** 5·24	**4·34** 6·33	**4·90** 7·03	**5·30** 7·56	**5·63** 7·97	**5·90** 8·32	**6·12** 8·61	**6·32** 8·87	**6·49** 9·10
7	**3·34** 4·95	**4·16** 5·92	**4·68** 6·54	**5·06** 7·01	**5·36** 7·37	**5·61** 7·68	**5·82** 7·94	**6·00** 8·17	**6·16** 8·37
8	**3·26** 4·75	**4·04** 5·64	**4·53** 6·20	**4·89** 6·62	**5·17** 6·96	**5·40** 7·24	**5·60** 7·47	**5·77** 7·68	**5·92** 7·86
9	**3·20** 4·60	**3·95** 5·43	**4·41** 5·96	**4·76** 6·35	**5·02** 6·66	**5·24** 6·91	**5·43** 7·13	**5·59** 7·33	**5·74** 7·49
10	**3·15** 4·48	**3·88** 5·27	**4·33** 5·77	**4·65** 6·14	**4·91** 6·43	**5·12** 6·67	**5·30** 6·87	**5·46** 7·05	**5·60** 7·21

12	**3·08**	**3·77**	**4·20**	**4·51**	**4·75**	**4·95**	**5·12**	**5·27**	**5·39**
	4·32	5·05	5·50	5·84	6·10	6·32	6·51	6·67	6·81
14	**3·03**	**3·70**	**4·11**	**4·41**	**4·64**	**4·83**	**4·99**	**5·13**	**5·25**
	4·21	4·89	5·32	5·63	5·88	6·08	6·26	6·41	6·54
16	**3·00**	**3·65**	**4·05**	**4·33**	**4·56**	**4·74**	**4·90**	**5·03**	**5·15**
	4·13	4·79	5·19	5·49	5·72	5·92	6·08	6·22	6·35
18	**2·97**	**3·61**	**4·00**	**4·28**	**4·49**	**4·67**	**4·82**	**4·96**	**5·07**
	4·07	4·70	5·09	5·38	5·60	5·79	5·94	6·08	6·20
20	**2·95**	**3·58**	**3·96**	**4·23**	**4·45**	**4·62**	**4·77**	**4·90**	**5·01**
	4·02	4·64	5·02	5·29	5·51	5·69	5·84	5·97	6·09
30	**2·89**	**3·49**	**3·85**	**4·10**	**4·30**	**4·46**	**4·60**	**4·72**	**4·82**
	3·89	4·45	4·80	5·05	5·24	5·40	5·54	5·65	5·76
40	**2·86**	**3·44**	**3·79**	**4·04**	**4·23**	**4·39**	**4·52**	**4·63**	**4·73**
	3·82	4·37	4·70	4·93	5·11	5·26	5·39	5·50	5·60
60	**2·83**	**3·40**	**3·74**	**3·98**	**4·16**	**4·31**	**4·44**	**4·55**	**4·65**
	3·76	4·28	4·59	4·82	4·99	5·13	5·25	5·36	5·45
120	**2·80**	**3·36**	**3·68**	**3·92**	**4·10**	**4·24**	**4·36**	**4·47**	**4·56**
	3·70	4·20	4·50	4·71	4·87	5·01	5·12	5·21	5·30
∞	**2·77**	**3·31**	**3·63**	**3·86**	**4·03**	**4·17**	**4·29**	**4·39**	**4·47**
	3·64	4·12	4·40	4·60	4·76	4·88	4·99	5·08	5·16

Condensed from Table 29 of Pearson and Hartley (1966) by permission of the authors and publishers.

TABLE A6 RANDOM SAMPLING NUMBERS

I

03	47	43	73	86	36	96	47	36	61	46	98	63	71	62	33	26	16	80	45	60	11	14	10	95
97	74	24	67	62	42	81	14	57	20	42	53	32	37	32	27	07	36	07	51	24	51	79	89	73
16	76	62	27	66	56	50	26	71	07	32	90	79	78	53	13	55	38	58	59	88	97	54	14	10
12	56	85	99	26	96	96	68	27	31	05	03	72	93	15	57	12	10	14	21	88	26	49	81	76
55	59	56	35	64	38	54	82	46	22	31	62	43	09	90	06	18	44	32	53	23	83	01	30	30
16	22	77	94	39	49	54	43	54	82	17	37	93	23	78	87	35	20	96	43	84	26	34	91	64
84	42	17	53	31	57	24	55	06	88	77	04	74	47	67	21	76	33	50	25	83	92	12	06	76
63	01	63	78	59	16	95	55	67	19	98	10	50	71	75	12	86	73	58	07	44	39	52	38	79
33	21	12	34	29	78	64	56	07	82	52	42	07	44	38	15	51	00	13	42	99	66	02	79	54
57	60	86	32	44	09	47	27	96	54	49	17	46	09	62	90	52	84	77	27	08	02	73	43	28
18	18	07	92	46	44	17	16	58	09	79	83	86	19	62	06	76	50	03	10	55	23	64	05	05
26	62	38	97	75	84	16	07	44	99	83	11	46	32	24	20	14	85	88	45	10	93	72	88	71
23	42	40	64	74	82	97	77	77	81	07	45	32	14	08	32	98	94	07	72	93	85	79	10	75
52	36	28	19	95	50	92	26	11	97	00	56	76	31	38	80	22	02	53	53	86	60	42	04	53
37	85	94	35	12	83	39	50	08	30	42	34	07	96	88	54	42	06	87	98	35	85	29	48	39
70	29	17	12	13	40	33	20	38	26	13	89	51	03	74	17	76	37	13	04	07	74	21	19	30
56	62	18	37	35	96	83	50	87	75	97	12	25	93	47	70	33	24	03	54	97	77	46	44	80
99	49	57	22	77	88	42	95	45	72	16	64	36	16	00	04	43	18	66	79	94	77	24	21	90
16	08	15	04	72	33	27	14	34	09	45	59	34	68	49	12	72	07	34	45	99	27	72	95	14
31	16	93	32	43	50	27	89	87	19	20	15	37	00	49	52	85	66	60	44	38	68	88	11	80
68	34	30	13	70	55	74	30	77	40	44	22	78	84	26	04	33	46	09	52	68	07	97	06	57
74	57	25	65	76	59	29	97	68	60	71	91	38	67	54	13	58	18	24	76	15	54	55	95	52
27	42	37	86	53	48	55	90	65	72	96	57	69	36	10	96	46	92	42	45	97	60	49	04	91
00	39	68	29	61	66	37	32	20	30	77	84	57	03	29	10	45	65	04	26	11	04	96	67	24
29	94	98	94	24	68	49	69	10	82	53	75	91	93	30	34	25	20	57	27	40	48	73	51	92

16	90	82	66	59	83	62	64	11	12	67	19	00	71	74	60	47	21	29	68	02	02	37	03	31
11	27	94	75	06	06	09	19	74	66	02	94	37	34	02	76	70	90	30	86	38	45	94	30	38
35	24	10	16	20	33	32	51	26	38	79	78	45	04	91	16	92	53	56	16	02	75	50	95	98
38	23	16	86	38	42	38	97	01	50	87	75	66	81	41	40	01	74	91	62	48	51	84	08	32
31	96	25	91	47	96	44	33	49	13	34	86	82	53	91	00	52	43	48	85	27	55	26	89	62
66	67	40	67	14	64	05	71	95	86	11	05	65	09	68	76	83	20	37	90	57	16	00	11	66
14	90	84	45	11	75	73	88	05	90	52	27	41	14	86	22	98	12	22	08	07	52	74	95	80
68	05	51	18	00	33	96	02	75	19	07	60	62	93	55	59	33	82	43	90	49	37	38	44	59
20	46	78	73	90	97	51	40	14	02	04	02	33	31	08	39	54	16	49	36	47	95	93	13	30
64	19	58	97	79	15	06	15	93	20	01	90	10	75	06	40	78	78	89	62	02	67	74	17	33
05	26	93	70	60	22	35	85	15	13	92	03	51	59	77	59	56	78	06	83	52	91	05	70	74
07	97	10	88	23	09	98	42	99	64	61	71	62	99	15	06	51	29	16	93	58	05	77	09	51
68	71	86	85	85	54	87	66	47	54	73	32	08	11	12	44	95	92	63	16	29	56	24	29	48
26	99	61	65	53	58	37	78	80	70	42	10	50	67	42	32	17	55	85	74	94	44	67	16	94
14	65	52	68	75	87	59	36	22	41	26	78	63	06	55	13	08	27	01	50	15	29	39	39	43
17	53	77	58	71	71	41	61	50	72	12	41	94	96	26	44	95	27	36	99	02	96	74	30	83
90	26	59	21	19	23	52	23	33	12	96	93	02	18	39	07	02	18	36	07	25	99	32	70	23
41	23	52	55	99	31	04	49	69	96	10	47	48	45	88	13	41	43	89	20	97	17	14	49	17
60	20	50	81	69	31	99	73	68	68	35	81	33	03	76	24	30	12	48	60	18	99	10	72	34
91	25	38	05	90	94	58	28	41	36	45	37	59	03	09	90	35	57	29	12	82	62	54	65	60
34	50	57	74	37	98	80	33	00	91	09	77	93	19	82	74	94	80	04	04	45	07	31	66	49
85	22	04	39	43	73	81	53	94	79	33	62	46	86	28	08	31	54	46	31	53	94	13	38	47
09	79	13	77	48	73	82	97	22	21	05	03	27	24	83	72	89	44	05	60	35	80	39	94	88
88	75	80	18	14	22	95	75	42	49	39	32	82	22	49	02	48	07	70	37	16	04	61	67	87
90	96	23	70	00	39	00	03	06	90	55	85	78	38	36	94	37	30	69	32	90	89	00	76	33

TABLE A6 (*continued*)

II

53	74	23	99	67	61	32	28	69	84	94	62	67	86	24	98	33	41	19	95	47	53	53	38	09
63	38	06	86	54	99	00	65	26	94	02	82	90	23	07	79	62	67	80	60	75	91	12	81	19
35	30	58	21	46	06	72	17	10	94	25	21	31	75	96	49	28	24	00	49	55	65	79	78	07
63	43	36	82	69	65	51	18	37	88	61	38	44	12	45	32	92	85	88	65	54	34	81	85	35
98	25	37	55	26	01	91	82	81	46	74	71	12	94	97	24	02	71	37	07	03	92	18	66	75
02	63	21	17	69	71	50	80	89	56	38	15	70	11	48	43	40	45	86	98	00	83	26	91	03
64	55	22	21	82	48	22	28	06	00	61	54	13	43	91	82	78	12	23	29	06	66	24	12	27
85	07	26	13	89	01	10	07	82	04	59	63	69	36	03	69	11	15	83	80	13	29	54	19	28
58	54	16	24	15	51	54	44	82	00	62	61	65	04	69	38	18	65	18	97	85	72	13	49	21
34	85	27	84	87	61	48	64	56	26	90	18	48	13	26	37	70	15	42	57	65	65	80	39	07
03	92	18	27	46	57	99	16	96	56	30	33	72	85	22	84	64	38	56	98	99	01	30	98	64
62	95	30	27	59	37	75	41	66	48	86	97	80	61	45	23	53	04	01	63	45	76	08	64	27
08	45	93	15	22	60	21	75	46	91	98	77	27	85	42	28	88	61	08	84	69	62	03	42	73
07	08	55	18	40	45	44	75	13	90	24	94	96	61	02	57	55	66	83	15	73	42	37	11	61
01	85	89	95	66	51	10	19	34	88	15	84	97	19	75	12	76	39	43	78	64	63	91	08	25
72	84	71	14	35	19	11	58	49	26	50	11	17	17	76	86	31	57	20	18	95	60	78	46	75
88	78	28	16	84	13	52	53	94	53	75	45	69	30	96	73	89	65	70	31	99	17	43	48	76
45	17	75	65	57	28	40	19	72	12	25	12	74	75	67	60	40	60	81	19	24	62	01	61	16
96	76	28	12	54	22	01	11	94	25	71	96	16	16	88	68	64	36	74	45	19	59	50	88	92
43	31	67	72	30	24	02	94	08	63	38	32	36	66	02	69	36	38	25	39	48	03	45	15	22
50	44	66	44	21	66	06	58	05	62	68	15	54	35	02	42	35	48	96	32	14	52	41	52	48
22	66	22	15	86	26	63	75	41	99	58	42	36	72	24	58	37	52	18	51	03	37	18	39	11
96	24	40	14	51	23	22	30	88	57	95	67	47	29	83	94	69	40	06	07	18	16	36	78	86
31	73	91	61	19	60	20	72	93	48	98	57	07	23	69	65	95	39	69	58	56	80	30	19	44
78	60	73	99	84	43	89	94	36	45	56	69	47	07	41	90	22	91	07	12	78	35	34	08	72

84	37	90	61	56	70	10	23	98	05	85	11	34	76	60	76	48	45	34	60	01	64	18	39	96
36	67	10	08	23	98	93	35	08	86	99	29	76	29	81	33	34	91	58	93	63	14	52	32	52
07	28	59	07	48	89	64	58	89	75	83	85	62	27	89	30	14	78	56	27	86	63	59	80	02
10	15	83	87	60	79	24	31	66	56	21	48	24	06	93	91	98	94	05	49	01	47	59	38	00
55	19	68	97	65	03	73	52	16	56	00	53	55	90	27	33	42	29	38	87	22	13	88	83	34
53	81	29	13	39	35	01	20	71	34	62	33	74	82	14	53	73	19	09	03	56	54	29	56	93
51	86	32	68	92	33	98	74	66	99	40	14	71	94	58	45	94	19	38	81	14	44	99	81	07
35	91	70	29	13	80	03	54	07	27	96	94	78	32	66	50	95	52	74	33	13	80	55	62	54
37	71	67	95	13	20	02	44	95	94	64	85	04	05	72	01	32	90	76	14	53	89	74	60	41
93	66	13	83	27	92	79	64	64	72	28	54	96	53	84	48	14	52	98	94	56	07	93	89	30
02	96	08	45	65	13	05	00	41	84	93	07	54	72	59	21	45	57	09	77	19	48	56	27	44
49	83	43	48	35	82	88	33	69	96	72	36	04	19	76	47	45	15	18	60	82	11	08	95	97
84	60	71	62	46	40	80	81	30	37	34	39	23	05	38	25	15	35	71	30	88	12	57	21	77
18	17	30	88	71	44	91	14	88	47	89	23	30	63	15	56	34	20	47	89	99	82	93	24	98
79	69	10	61	78	71	32	76	95	62	87	00	22	58	40	92	54	01	75	25	43	11	71	99	31
75	93	36	57	83	56	20	14	82	11	74	21	97	90	65	96	42	68	63	86	74	54	13	26	94
38	30	92	29	03	06	28	81	39	38	62	25	06	84	63	61	29	08	93	67	04	32	92	08	09
51	29	50	10	34	31	57	75	95	80	51	97	02	74	77	76	15	48	49	44	18	55	63	77	09
21	31	38	86	24	37	79	81	53	74	73	24	16	10	33	52	83	90	94	76	70	47	14	54	36
29	01	23	87	88	58	02	39	37	67	42	10	14	20	92	16	55	23	42	45	54	96	09	11	06
95	33	95	22	00	18	74	72	00	18	38	79	58	69	32	81	76	80	26	92	82	80	84	25	39
90	84	60	79	80	24	36	59	87	38	82	07	53	89	35	96	35	23	79	18	05	98	90	07	35
46	40	62	98	82	54	97	20	56	95	15	74	80	08	32	16	46	70	50	80	67	72	16	42	79
20	31	89	03	43	38	46	82	68	72	32	14	82	99	70	80	60	47	18	97	63	49	30	21	30
71	59	73	05	50	08	22	23	71	77	91	01	93	20	49	82	96	59	26	94	66	39	67	98	60

Reproduced from Table XXXIII of Fisher and Yates (1963) by permission of the authors and publishers.

NOTES ON THE USE OF RANDOM SAMPLING NUMBERS (TABLE A6)

1 Random permutation

This is a rearrangement of the integers from 1 to n, each order being equally likely to be chosen.

Method 1. Start at an arbitrary point in the table. Use as many columns in the table as there are digits in n (e.g. if $n=16$ use two columns). Go down the columns and continue to the next group of columns, writing down the numbers from 1 to n as they occur. Count 03 as 3, etc. Ignore 00 . . . 0. Ignore repetitions.

Method 2. This makes more effective use of the table. Start as in Method 1, but divide each entry by a convenient round number $\geq n$ (e.g. for $n=16$, divide by 20) and use the *remainders*. Ignore remainders of 0 or greater than n. (If dividing by n exactly, count a remainder of 0 as if it were n.) Ignore repetitions. Ignore entries above the highest possible multiple of the divisor. Thus, if $n=27$ and the divisor is 30, ignore entries 00, 28, 29, 30, 58, 59, 60, 88, 89, 90, 91, 92, . . ., 99.

Tables of random permutations. Direct tables are published, e.g. in Fisher and Yates (1963), Cochran and Cox (1957) and Cox (1958). For $n>20$ see Moses and Oakford (1963).

2 Random selection of sample of size n from population of size N

Number the members of the population from 1 to N, start to make a random permutation of N and stop as soon as n numbers have been selected. These form the required sample.

3 Random allocation

To allocate n individuals randomly to k groups (e.g. in experimental design), form a random permutation of n and divide these from left to right into groups of the appropriate size. The permutation need not be continued beyond the stage at which $k-1$ groups have been formed, since the remaining individuals must fall into the kth group.

4 Random allocation with serial entry

Here n may be unknown. If allocation is to two treatments with equal probability, use odd and even numbers. For three treatments use 1–3, 4–6, 7–9, ignoring 0; and so on.

5 Restricted randomization with serial entry

It may be desirable to ensure that numbers allocated to different treatments are equal at various stages; e.g. two treatments may have to be balanced after each set of 10 individuals. In this case select 5 individuals out of each set of 10 to be allocated to one treatment (as in §2); the other 5 are allocated to the other treatment.

6 Extended use of tables

The tables can be used by reading entries in different directions, e.g. along the rows. If several random selections are needed in any investigation, different parts of the table should be used. More extensive tables are given in various books, e.g. Fisher and Yates (1963).

The table gives values of the empirical logit*, $y = \log_e \{p/(1-p)\}$, and the weighting coefficient, $w = p(1-p)$, for various values of a proportion p. Values of y are shown in bold type.

p		0·00	0·01	0·02	0·03	0·04	0·05	0·06	0·07	0·08	0·09
0·0	y	**−∞**	**−4·60**	**−3·89**	**−3·48**	**−3·18**	**−2·94**	**−2·75**	**−2·59**	**−2·44**	**−2·31**
	w	0·0000	0·0099	0·0196	0·0291	0·0384	0·0475	0·0564	0·0651	0·0736	0·0819
0·1		**−2·20**	**−2·09**	**−1·99**	**−1·90**	**−1·82**	**−1·73**	**−1·66**	**−1·59**	**−1·52**	**−1·45**
		0·0900	0·0979	0·1056	0·1131	0·1204	0·1275	0·1344	0·1411	0·1476	0·1539
0·2		**−1·39**	**−1·32**	**−1·27**	**−1·21**	**−1·15**	**−1·10**	**−1·05**	**−0·99**	**−0·94**	**−0·90**
		0·1600	0·1659	0·1716	0·1771	0·1824	0·1875	0·1924	0·1971	0·2016	0·2059
0·3		**−0·85**	**−0·80**	**−0·75**	**−0·71**	**−0·66**	**−0·62**	**−0·58**	**−0·53**	**−0·49**	**−0·45**
		0·2100	0·2139	0·2176	0·2211	0·2244	0·2275	0·2304	0·2331	0·2356	0·2379
0·4		**−0·41**	**−0·36**	**−0·32**	**−0·28**	**−0·24**	**−0·20**	**−0·16**	**−0·12**	**−0·08**	**−0·04**
		0·2400	0·2419	0·2436	0·2451	0·2464	0·2475	0·2484	0·2491	0·2496	0·2499
0·5		**0·00**	**0·04**	**0·08**	**0·12**	**0·16**	**0·20**	**0·24**	**0·28**	**0·32**	**0·36**
		0·2500	0·2499	0·2496	0·2491	0·2484	0·2475	0·2464	0·2451	0·2436	0·2419
0·6		**0·41**	**0·45**	**0·49**	**0·53**	**0·58**	**0·62**	**0·66**	**0·71**	**0·75**	**0·80**
		0·2400	0·2379	0·2356	0·2331	0·2304	0·2275	0·2244	0·2211	0·2176	0·2139
0·7		**0·85**	**0·90**	**0·94**	**0·99**	**1·05**	**1·10**	**1·15**	**1·21**	**1·27**	**1·32**
		0·2100	0·2059	0·2016	0·1971	0·1924	0·1875	0·1824	0·1771	0·1716	0·1659
0·8		**1·39**	**1·45**	**1·52**	**1·59**	**1·66**	**1·73**	**1·82**	**1·90**	**1·99**	**2·09**
		0·1600	0·1539	0·1476	0·1411	0·1344	0·1275	0·1204	0·1131	0·1056	0·0979
0·9		**2·20**	**2·31**	**2·44**	**2·59**	**2·75**	**2·94**	**3·18**	**3·48**	**3·89**	**4·60**
		0·0900	0·0819	0·0736	0·0651	0·0564	0·0475	0·0384	0·0291	0·0196	0·0099

* *Note*. Many authors define the logit as half the value tabulated above, in which case the weighting coefficient is four times that shown.

SOME BOOKS FOR FURTHER READING

A number of books dealing with special topics have been referred to in various chapters and are not listed again here. The reader should, for example, refer to the sections indicated for references on the following topics: sample surveys (6.2), multivariate analysis (10.6), sequential analysis (15.1–15.3), epidemiology (16.1), biological assay (17.1).

Introductory medical statistics

1. HILL A. BRADFORD (1966). *Principles of Medical Statistics.* 8th ed. London: Lancet.
2. BOURKE G.J. and MCGILVRAY J. (1969). *Interpretation and Uses of Medical Statistics.* Oxford: Blackwell Scientific Publications.
3. DUNN O.J. (1964). *Basic Statistics: a Primer for the Biomedical Sciences.* New York: Wiley.
4. MAINLAND D. (1963). *Elementary Medical Statistics.* Philadelphia: Saunders.
5. GOLDSTEIN A. (1964). *Biostatistics: an Introductory Text.* New York: Macmillan.
6. BAILEY N.T.J. (1959). *Statistical Methods in Biology.* London: English Universities Press.

1 should certainly be read by anyone interested in the subject and includes an introduction to vital statistics; 2 is a very simple introduction; 3 to 6 are more advanced, 4 being useful particularly for clinical applications and 5 for pharmacological research. All these books have a less detailed coverage of general methodology than the present book.

General statistical methods

7. SNEDECOR G.W. and COCHRAN W.G. (1967). *Statistical Methods.* 6th ed. Ames: Iowa State University Press.
8. WETHERILL G.B. (1967). *Elementary Statistical Methods.* London: Methuen.
9. BLISS C.I. (1967). *Statistics in Biology,* Vol. I. New York: McGraw-Hill.

These are at about the same mathematical level as the present book. 7 has a particularly wide coverage. 9 is very detailed, but covers only part of the field.

Mathematical Theory

10. HOEL P.G. (1962). *Introduction to Mathematical Statistics.* 3rd ed. New York: Wiley.
11. FRASER D.A.S. (1958). *Statistics: an Introduction.* New York: Wiley.
12. MOOD A.M. and GRAYBILL F.A. (1963). *Introduction to the Theory of Statistics.* 2nd ed. New York: McGraw-Hill.
13. BROWNLEE K.A. (1965). *Statistical Theory and Methodology in Science and Engineering.* 2nd ed. New York: Wiley.

This is an almost arbitrary selection from a very large number of books of varying difficulty. 11 and 12 are similar in difficulty and coverage, 10 is slightly simpler and 13 is more comprehensive.

Experimental Design

14. Cox D.R. (1958). *Planning of Experiments*. New York: Wiley.
15. Finney D.J. (1955). *Experimental Design and its Statistical Basis*. London: Cambridge University Press.
16. Cochran W.G. and Cox G.M. (1957). *Experimental Designs*. 2nd ed. New York: Wiley.

14 and 15 provide non-mathematical accounts of the basic principles. 16 is a comprehensive handbook.

Vital Statistics and Medical Research Investigations

17. Benjamin B. (1968). *Health and Vital Statistics*. London: Allen and Unwin.
18. Witts L.J. (ed.) (1964). *Medical Surveys and Clinical Trials*. 2nd ed. London: Oxford University Press.
19. Hill A. Bradford (1962). *Statistical Methods in Clinical and Preventive Medicine*. Edinburgh: Livingstone.

19 is a set of selected papers and includes reports of several trials organized by the (British) Medical Research Council.

Computing

20. Taylor T.R. (1967). *The Principles of Medical Computing*. Oxford: Blackwell Scientific Publications.
21. Dixon W.J. (ed.) (1967). *BMD Biomedical Computer Programs*. Berkeley and Los Angeles: University of California Press.

The use of a computer requires some familiarity with the arrangements at the relevant computer centre and perhaps instruction in a programming language like FORTRAN. Good manuals are easily obtainable. 21 is a very well documented description of a collection of statistical programs written in FORTRAN and implemented on many large computers.

Tables

22. Murdoch J. and Barnes J.A. (1968). *Statistical Tables for Science, Engineering and Management*. London: Macmillan.
23. Fisher R.A. and Yates F. (1963). *Statistical Tables for Biological, Agricultural and Medical Research*. 6th ed. Edinburgh: Oliver and Boyd.
24. Pearson E.S. and Hartley H.O. (1966). *Biometrika Tables for Statisticians*, Vol. 1. 3rd ed. Cambridge: University Press.
25. Documenta Geigy (1962). *Scientific Tables*. 6th ed. Manchester: Geigy.

22 is an inexpensive short collection of some of the most useful tables. 23 and 24 are the two standard collections. 25 includes a large collection of statistical tables and a useful account of statistical methods.

REFERENCES

ACHESON E.D. (1967). *Medical Record Linkage*. London: Oxford University Press.

ANSCOMBE F.J. (1968). Outliers. In 'Statistical analysis, special problems of', *International Encyclopedia of the Social Sciences*, **15,** 178–182.

ARMITAGE P. (1955). Tests for linear trends in proportions and frequencies. *Biometrics*, **11,** 375–386.

ARMITAGE P. (1957). Studies in the variability of pock counts. *J. Hyg., Camb.*, **55,** 564–581.

ARMITAGE P. (1960). *Sequential Medical Trials*. Oxford: Blackwell Scientific Publications.

ARMITAGE P. (1966). The chi-square test for heterogeneity of proportions, after adjustment for stratification. *Jl R. statist. Soc.*, B, **28,** 150–163 (see also **29,** 197).

ARMITAGE P. and SCHNEIDERMAN M.A. (1958). Statistical problems in a mass screening program. *Ann. N.Y. Acad. Sci.*, **76,** 896–908.

ATKINS H.J.B., FALCONER M.A., HAYWARD J.L., MACLEAN K.S., SCHURR P.H. and ARMITAGE P. (1960). Adrenalectomy and hypophysectomy for advanced cancer of the breast. *Lancet*, i, 1148–1157.

BACHARACH A.L., CHANCE M.R.A. and MIDDLETON T.R. (1940). The biological assay of testicular diffusing factor. *Biochem. J.*, **34,** 1464–1471.

BAILEY N.T.J. (1951). A classification of methods of ascertainment and analysis in estimating the frequencies of recessives in man. *Ann. Eugen.*, **16,** 223–225.

BAILEY N.T.J. (1957). *The Mathematical Theory of Epidemics*. London: Griffin.

BAILEY N.T.J. (1967). *The Mathematical Approach to Biology and Medicine*. New York: Wiley.

BARTLETT M.S. (1937). Properties of sufficiency and statistical tests. *Proc. R. Soc.*, A, **160,** 268–282.

BEALE E.M.L., KENDALL M.G. and MANN D.W. (1967). The discarding of variables in multivariate analysis. *Biometrika*, **54,** 357–366.

BENJAMIN B. (1968). *Health and Vital Statistics*. London: Allen and Unwin.

BERKSON J. (1944). Application of the logistic function to bio-assay. *J. Am. statist. Ass.*, **39,** 357–365.

BERKSON J. (1950). Are there two regressions? *J. Am. statist. Ass.*, **45,** 164–180.

BERKSON J. and GAGE R.P. (1950). Calculation of survival rates for cancer. *Proc. Staff Meet. Mayo Clinic*, **25,** 270–286.

BLISS C.I. (1958). *Periodic regression in biology and climatology*. Bull. no. 615. New Haven: Connecticut Agric. Exp. Station.

BOX G.E.P. and JENKINS G.M. (1968). Some recent advances in forecasting and control. Part I. *Appl. Statist.*, **17,** 91–109.

BRADLEY R.A., KATTI S.K. and COONS I.J. (1962). Optimal scaling for ordered categories. *Psychometrika*, **27,** 355–374.

BRINKLEY D. and HAYBITTLE J.L. (1959). Results of treatment of carcinoma of the breast. *Lancet*, i, 86–90.

BRINKLEY D. and HAYBITTLE J.L. (1966). Treatment of stage-II carcinoma of the female breast. *Lancet*, ii, 291–295.

BROWN A., MOHAMED S.D., MONTGOMERY R.D., ARMITAGE P. and LAURENCE D.R. (1960). Value of a large dose of antitoxin in clinical tetanus. *Lancet*, ii, 227–230.

BUCK A.A. and GART J.J. (1966). Comparison of a screening test and a reference test in epidemiologic studies. I. Indices of agreement and their relation to prevalence. *Am. J. Epidem.*, **83,** 586–592.

BURN J.H., FINNEY D.J. and GOODWIN L.G. (1952). *Biological Standardization.* 2nd ed. London: Oxford University Press.

BURT C. and BANKS C. (1947). A factor analysis of body measurements for British adult males. *Ann. Eugen.*, **13,** 238–256.

BUTLER N.R. and BONHAM D.G. (1963). *Perinatal Mortality.* Edinburgh: Livingstone.

BUXBAUM C. and COLTON T. (1966). Relationship of motor vehicle inspection to accident mortality. *J. Am. med. Ass.*, **197,** 31–36.

CASE, R.A.M., COGHILL C., HARLEY J.L. and PEARSON J.T. (1962). *The Chester Beatty Institute Serial Abridged Life Tables. England and Wales 1841–1960. Part 1.* London: Institute of Cancer Research.

CASE R.A.M. and LEA A.J. (1955). Mustard gas poisoning, chronic bronchitis, and lung cancer. *Br. J. prev. soc. Med.*, **9,** 62–72.

COCHRAN W.G. (1954). Some methods for strengthening the common χ^2 tests. *Biometrics*, **10,** 417–451.

COCHRAN W.G. (1963). *Sampling Techniques.* 2nd ed. New York: Wiley.

COCHRAN W.G. and COX G.M. (1957). *Experimental Designs.* 2nd ed. New York: Wiley.

CORNFIELD J. (1956). A statistical property arising from retrospective studies. *Proc. Third Berkeley Symp. math. Stat. Prob.*, **4,** 135–148.

COX D.R. (1958). *Planning of Experiments.* New York: Wiley.

COX D.R. (1970). *The Analysis of Binary Data.* London: Methuen.

COX P.R. (1970). *Demography.* 4th ed. Cambridge: University Press.

CRAMÉR H. (1946). *Mathematical Methods of Statistics.* Princeton: University Press.

CUTLER S.J. and EDERER F. (1958). Maximum utilization of the life table method in analysing survival. *J. chron. Dis.*, **8,** 699–712.

DANIEL C. (1959). Use of half-normal plots in interpreting factorial two-level experiments. *Technometrics*, **1,** 311–341.

DIAMOND E.L. and LILIENFELD A.M. (1962a). Effects of errors in classification and diagnosis in various types of epidemiological studies. *Am. J. publ. Hlth.*, **52,** 1137–1144.

DIAMOND E.L. and LILIENFELD A.M. (1962b). Misclassification errors in 2×2 tables with one margin fixed: some further comments. *Am. J. publ. Hlth.*, **52,** 2106–2110.

DOCUMENTA GEIGY (1962). *Scientific Tables.* 6th ed. Manchester: Geigy.

DOLL R. and BUCKATZSCH J. (1952). An experimental factor analysis of cancer mortality in England and Wales 1921–30. *J. Hyg., Camb.*, **50,** 384–393.

DOLL R. and HILL A.BRADFORD (1950). Smoking and carcinoma of the lung. Preliminary report. *Br. med. J.*, ii, 739–748.

DOLL R. and HILL A.BRADFORD (1954). The mortality of doctors in relation to their smoking habits. A preliminary report. *Br. med. J.*, i, 1451–1455.

DOLL R. and HILL A.BRADFORD (1956). Lung cancer and other causes of death in relation to smoking. A second report on the mortality of British doctors. *Br. med. J.*, ii, 1071–1081.

DOLL R. and HILL A.BRADFORD (1964). Mortality in relation to smoking: ten years' observations of British doctors. *Br. med. J.*, i, 1399–1410 and 1460–1467.

DOLL R. and PYGOTT F. (1952). Factors influencing the rate of healing of gastric ulcers: admission to hospital, phenobarbitone, and ascorbic acid. *Lancet*, i, 171–175.

DRAPER N.R. and SMITH H. (1966). *Applied Regression Analysis*. New York: Wiley.

DRION E.F. (1961). The intercorrelations between the nutrients consumed by a group of families in the Netherlands. *Jl R. statist. Soc.*, A, **124,** 314–335.

DYKE G.V. and PATTERSON H.D. (1952). Analysis of factorial arrangements when the data are proportions. *Biometrics*, **8,** 1–12.

EDERER F. (1961). A parametric estimate of the standard error of the survival rate. *J. Am. statist. Ass.*, **56,** 111–118.

EDERER F., MYERS M.H. and MANTEL N. (1964). A statistical problem in space and time: do leukemia cases come in clusters? *Biometrics*, **20,** 626–638.

EHRENBERG A.S.C. (1968). The elements of lawlike relationships. *Jl R. statist. Soc.*, A, **131,** 280–302.

FINNEY D.J. (1952). *Probit Analysis: a Statistical Treatment of the Sigmoid Response Curve*. 2nd ed. Cambridge: University Press.

FINNEY D.J. (1958). The efficiencies of alternative estimators for an asymptotic regression equation. *Biometrika*, **45,** 370–388.

FINNEY D.J. (1964). *Statistical Method in Biological Assay*. 2nd ed. London: Griffin.

FINNEY D.J., LATSCHA R., BENNETT B.M. and HSU P. (1963). *Tables for Testing Significance in a* 2×2 *Contingency Table*. Cambridge: University Press.

FISHER R.A. (1950, 1964). The significance of deviations from expectation in a Poisson series. *Biometrics*, **6,** 17–24; reprinted in **20,** 265–272.

FISHER R.A. and YATES F. (1963). *Statistical Tables for Biological, Agricultural and Medical Research*. 6th ed. Edinburgh: Oliver and Boyd.

GART J.J. (1962). On the combination of relative risks. *Biometrics*, **18,** 601–610.

GART J.J. (1968). A simple nearly efficient alternative to the simple sib method in the complete ascertainment case. *Ann. hum. Genet.*, **31,** 283–291.

GART J.J. and BUCK A.A. (1966). Comparison of a screening test and a reference test in epidemiologic studies. II. A probabilistic model for the comparison of diagnostic tests. *Am. J. Epidem.*, **83,** 593–602.

GOOD I.J. (1950). *Probability and the Weighing of Evidence*. London: Griffin.

GREENHOUSE S.W. and MANTEL N. (1950). The evaluation of diagnostic tests. *Biometrics*, **6,** 399–412.

GREENWOOD M. (1926). *The Natural Duration of Cancer*. Rep. Publ. Hlth Med. Subj., No. 33. London: H.M. Stationery Office.

HAENSZEL W. (1959). Some problems in the estimation of familial risks of disease. *J. natn. Cancer Inst.*, **23,** 487–505.

HAY W.A. (1967). Non-standard designs. *Statistician*, **17,** 371–384.

HAYHOE F.G.J., QUAGLINO D. and DOLL R. (1964). *The Cytology and Cyto-chemistry of Acute Leukaemias*. Med. Res. Coun. Spec. Rep. Ser. No. 304. London: H.M. Stationery Office.

HEALY M.J.R. (1952). Some statistical aspects of anthropometry. *Jl R. statist. Soc.*, B, **14,** 164–177.

HEALY M.J.R. (1963). Fitting a quadratic. *Biometrics*, **19,** 362–363.

HEALY M.J.R. (1965). Descriptive uses of discriminant functions. In: *Mathematics and Computer Science in Biology and Medicine*, 93–102. London: H.M. Stationery Office.

HEALY M.J.R. (1968). The disciplining of medical data. *Br. med. Bull.*, **24,** 210–214.

HILL A.BRADFORD (1962). *Statistical Methods in Clinical and Preventive Medicine.* Edinburgh: Livingstone.

HILL A.BRADFORD (1966). *Principles of Medical Statistics.* 8th ed. London: Lancet.

HILLS M. (1966). Allocation rules and their error rates. *Jl R. statist. Soc.*, B, **28,** 1–20.

HOGBEN L. and CROSS K.W. (1960). *Design of Documents: a Study of Mechanical Aids to Field Enquiries.* London: Macdonald and Evans.

HOLMES M.C. and WILLIAMS R.E.O. (1954). The distribution of carriers of *Streptococcus pyogenes* among 2,413 healthy children. *J. Hyg., Camb.*, **52,** 165–179.

HOPE K. (1968). *Methods of Multivariate Analysis.* London: University of London Press.

HUFF D. (1954). *How to Lie with Statistics.* New York: Norton.

IPSEN J. (1955). Appropriate scores in bio-assays using death-times and survivor symptoms. *Biometrics*, **11,** 465–480.

JAMES G.S. (1951). The comparison of several groups of observations when the ratios of the population variances are unknown. *Biometrika*, **38,** 324–329.

JEFFERS J.N.R. (1962). Principal component analysis of designed experiment. *Statistician*, **12,** 230–242.

JEFFREYS H. (1961). *Theory of Probability.* 3rd ed. Oxford: Clarendon Press.

KALTON G. (1968). Standardization: a technique to control for extraneous variables. *Appl. Statist.*, **17,** 118–136.

KENDALL M.G. (1951, 1952). Regression, structure and functional relationship. Part I. *Biometrika*, **38,** 11–25; Part II. *Biometrika*, **39,** 96–108.

KENDALL M.G. (1955). *Rank Correlation Methods.* 2nd ed. London: Griffin.

KENDALL M.G. (1957). *A Course in Multivariate Analysis.* London: Griffin.

KENDALL M.G. and STUART A. (1966). *The Advanced Theory of Statistics*, Vol. 3. London: Griffin.

KEULS M. (1952). The use of 'Studentized range' in connection with an analysis of variance. *Euphytica*, **1,** 112–122.

KING E.P. (1963). A statistical design for drug screening. *Biometrics*, **19,** 429–440.

KLOTZ, J.H. (1964). On the normal scores two-sample rank test. *J. Am. statist. Ass.*, **59,** 652–664.

KNOX E.G. (1964). Epidemiology of childhood leukaemia in Northumberland and Durham. *Br. J. prev. soc. Med.*, **18,** 17–24.

KRAMER M. and GREENHOUSE S.W. (1959). Determination of sample size and selection of cases. In *Psychopharmacology: Problems in Evaluation*, ed. J.O. Cole and R.W.Gerard, 356–371. Washington: National Academy of Sciences, National Research Council.

LANCASTER H.O. (1950). Statistical control in haematology. *J. Hyg., Camb.*, **48,** 402–417.

LANCASTER H.O. (1965). Symmetry in multivariate distributions. *Aust. J. Statist.*, **7,** 115–126.

LAWLEY D.N. and MAXWELL A.E. (1963). *Factor Analysis as a Statistical Method.* London: Butterworth.

LEHMANN E.L. and HODGES J.L., Jr. (1964). *Basic Concepts of Probability and Statistics.* San Francisco: Holden-Day.

LIDDELL F.D.K. (1960). The measurement of occupational mortality. *Br. J. ind. Med.*, **17,** 228–233.

LINDLEY D.V. (1965). *Introduction to Probability and Statistics from a Bayesian Viewpoint. Part* 1, *Probability. Part* 2, *Inference.* Cambridge: University Press.

LOMBARD H.L. and DOERING C.R. (1947). Treatment of the four-fold table by partial correlation as it relates to public health problems. *Biometrics*, **3,** 123–128.

MACMAHON B., PUGH T.F. and IPSEN J. (1960). *Epidemiologic Methods.* Boston: Little, Brown.

MAINLAND D., HERRERA L. and SUTCLIFFE M.I. (1956). *Statistical Tables for Use with Binomial Samples—Contingency Tests, Confidence Limits and Sample Size Estimates.* New York: University College of Medicine.

MAINLAND D. (1960). The clinical trial—some difficulties and suggestions. *J. chron. Dis.*, **11,** 484–496.

MAINLAND D. (1963). *Elementary Medical Statistics.* 2nd ed. Philadelphia: Saunders.

MANTEL N. (1967). The detection of disease clustering and a generalized regression approach. *Cancer Res.*, **27,** 209–220.

MANTEL N. and HAENSZEL W. (1959). Statistical aspects of the analysis of data from retrospective studies of disease. *J. natn. Cancer Inst.*, **22,** 719–748.

MARSHALL J. (1964). A trial of long-term hypotensive therapy in cerebrovascular disease. *Lancet*, i, 10–12.

MARTIN W.J. (1949). *The Physique of Young Adult Males.* Med. Res. Coun. Mem. No. 20. London: H.M. Stationery Office.

MAXWELL A.E. (1961). *Analysing Qualitative Data.* London: Methuen.

MAXWELL A.E. (1970). Multivariate analysis. Chap. 12 in *Data Handling in Epidemiology*, ed. W.W.Holland. London: Oxford University Press.

MEDICAL RESEARCH COUNCIL (1950). Treatment of pulmonary tuberculosis with streptomycin and para-amino-salicylic acid. *Br. med. J.*, ii, 1073–1085.

MEDICAL RESEARCH COUNCIL (1968). *The Carcinogenic Action of Mineral Oils: A Chemical and Biological Study.* Med. Res. Coun. Spec. Rep. Ser. No. 306. London: H.M. Stationery Office.

MERRELL M. and SHULMAN L.E. (1955). Determination of prognosis in chronic disease, illustrated by systemic lupus erythematosus. *J. chron. Dis.*, **1,** 12–32.

MILLER R.G., Jr. (1966). *Simultaneous Statistical Inference.* New York: McGraw-Hill.

MILTON R.C. (1964). An extended table of critical values for the Mann-Whitney (Wilcoxon) two-sample statistic. *J. Am. statist. Ass.*, **59,** 925–934.

MORIGUTI S. (1954). Confidence limits for a variance component. *Rep. statist. Appl. Res., Jap. Union Sci. Engns.*, **3** (2), 29–41.

MORRISON D.F. (1967). *Multivariate Statistical Methods.* New York and London: McGraw-Hill.

MOSER C.A. (1958). *Survey Methods in Social Investigation.* London: Heinemann.

Moses L.E. and Oakford R.V. (1963). *Tables of Random Permutations.* London: Allen and Unwin.

Murdoch J. and Barnes J.A. (1968) *Statistical Tables for Science, Engineering and Management.* London: Macmillan.

National Bureau of Standards (1950). *Tables of the Binomial Probability Distribution.* Applied Mathematics Series No. 7. Washington: U.S. Dept. of Commerce.

Naylor A.F. (1964). Comparisons of regression constants fitted by maximum likelihood to four common transformations of binomial data. *Ann. hum. Genet.*, **27,** 241–246.

Newell D.J. (1962). Errors in the interpretation of errors in epidemiology. *Am. J. publ. Hlth.*, **52,** 1925–1928.

Newell D.J., Greenberg B.G., Williams T.F. and Veazey P.B. (1961). Use of cohort life tables in family studies of disease. *J. chron. Dis.*, **13,** 439–452.

Newman D. (1939). The distribution of range in samples from a normal population, expressed in terms of an independent estimate of standard deviation. *Biometrika,* **31,** 20–30.

Oldham P.D. (1968). *Measurement in Medicine: the Interpretation of Numerical Data.* London: English Universities Press.

Owen D.B. (1962). *Handbook of Statistical Tables.* London: Pergamon.

Patterson H.D. (1956). A simple method for fitting an asymptotic regression curve. *Biometrics,* **12,** 323–329.

Pearce S.C. (1965). *Biological Statistics: an Introduction.* New York: McGraw-Hill.

Pearson E.S. and Hartley H.O. (1966). *Biometrika Tables for Statisticians,* Vol. 1, 3rd ed. Cambridge: University Press.

Radhakrishna S. (1964). Discrimination analysis in medicine. *Statistician,* **14,** 147–167.

Radhakrishna S. (1965). Combination of results from several 2 × 2 contingency tables. *Biometrics,* **21,** 86–98.

Registrar General of England and Wales (1958). *Decennial Supplement. Occupational Mortality.* Part II, Vol. 2. Tables. London: H.M. Stationery Office.

Roberts E., Dawson W.M. and Madden M. (1939). Observed and theoretical ratios in Mendelian inheritance. *Biometrika,* **31,** 56–66.

Robertson A. (1962). Weighting in the estimation of variance components in the unbalanced single classification. *Biometrics,* **18,** 413–417.

Robertson J.D. and Armitage P. (1959). Comparison of two hypotensive agents. *Anaesthesia,* **14,** 53–64.

Romig H.G. (1947). *50–100 Binomial Tables.* New York: Wiley.

Rose G.A. (1962). A study of blood pressure among Negro schoolchildren. *J. chron. Dis.*, **15,** 373–380.

Savage L.J. (1954). *The Foundations of Statistics.* New York: Wiley.

Scheffé H. (1959). *The Analysis of Variance.* New York: Wiley.

Seal H.L. (1964). *Multivariate Statistical Analysis for Biologists.* London: Methuen.

Smith C.E.Gordon, Turner L.H. and Armitage P. (1962). Yellow fever vaccination in Malaya by subcutaneous injection and multiple puncture. *Bull. Wld Hlth Org.*, **27,** 717–727.

SMITH C.E.GORDON and WESTGARTH D.R. (1957). The use of survival time in the analysis of neutralization tests for serum antibody surveys. *J. Hyg. Camb.*, **55**, 224–238.

SNEDECOR G.W. and COCHRAN W.G. (1967). *Statistical Methods.* 6th ed. Ames: Iowa State University Press.

SNELL E.S. and ARMITAGE P. (1957). Clinical comparison of diamorphine and pholcodine as cough suppressants, by a new method of sequential analysis. *Lancet*, i, 860–862.

SOKAL R.R. and SNEATH P.H.A. (1963). *Principles of Numerical Taxonomy.* San Francisco and London: Freeman.

SPEIZER F.E., DOLL R. and HEAF P. (1968). Observations on recent increase in mortality from asthma. *Br. med. J.*, i, 335–339.

SPRENT P. (1969). *Models in Regression and Related Topics.* London: Methuen.

'STUDENT' (W.S.GOSSETT) (1907). On the error of counting with a haemocytometer. *Biometrika*, **5**, 351–360.

SUTHERLAND I. (1946). The stillbirth-rate in England and Wales in relation to social influences. *Lancet* ii, 953–956.

SWAROOP S. (1960). *Introduction to Health Statistics.* Edinburgh and London: Livingstone.

TANNER J.M. (1951). Some notes on the reporting of growth data. *Hum. Biol.*, **23**, 93–159.

TAYLOR I. and KNOWELDEN J. (1964). *Principles of Epidemiology.* 2nd ed. London: Churchill.

TRUETT J., CORNFIELD J. and KANNEL W. (1967). A multivariate analysis of the risk of coronary heart disease in Framingham. *J. chron. Dis.*, **20**, 511–524.

UNITED NATIONS and FOOD AND AGRICULTURE ORGANIZATION OF THE UNITED NATIONS (1959, 1962). *Handbook of Data Processing Methods.* Parts 1 and 2. Rome.

WALD A. (1947). *Sequential Analysis.* New York: Wiley.

WARNER H.R., TORONTO A.F., VEASEY L.G. and STEPHENSON R. (1961). A mathematical approach to medical diagnosis. *J. Am. med. Ass.*, **177**, 177–183.

WELCH B.L. (1951). On the comparison of several mean values: an alternative approach. *Biometrika*, **38**, 330–336.

WILCOXON F. (1945). Individual comparisons by ranking methods. *Biometrics Bull.*, **1**, 80–83.

WILSON P.W. and KULLMAN E.D. (1931). A statistical inquiry into methods for estimating numbers of rhizobia. *J. Bact.*, **22**, 71–90.

WOOLF B. (1955). On estimating the relation between blood group and disease. *Ann. hum. Genet.*, **19**, 251–253.

WORLD HEALTH ORGANIZATION (1966). *Sampling Methods in Morbidity Surveys and Public Health Investigations.* Technical Report Series No. 336. Geneva.

WORLD HEALTH ORGANIZATION (1967). *Manual of the International Statistical Classification of Diseases, Injuries and Causes of Death.* Vols. 1 and 2. Geneva.

YATES F. (1934a). Contingency tables involving small numbers and the χ^2 test. *Jl R. statist. Soc. Suppl.*, **1**, 217–235.

YATES F. (1934b). The analysis of multiple classifications with unequal numbers in the different classes. *J. Am. statist. Ass.*, **29**, 51–66.

YATES F. (1960). *Sampling Methods for Censuses and Surveys.* 3rd ed. London: Griffin.

YOUDEN W.J. (1950). Index for rating diagnostic tests. *Cancer*, **3**, 32–35.

YULE G.U. and KENDALL M.G. (1950). *An Introduction to the Theory of Statistics.* 14th ed. London: Griffin.

AUTHOR INDEX

SUBJECT INDEX